GW00726753

MEASURING DAMAGES IN THE LAW OF OBLIGATIONS

This book challenges certain differences between contract, tort and equity in relation to the measure (in a broad sense) of damages. Damages are defined as the monetary award made by a court in consequence of a breach of contract, a tort or an equitable wrong. In all these causes of action, damages usually aim to put the claimant into the position the claimant would be in without the wrong. Even though the main objective of damages is thus the same for each cause of action, their measure is not.

While some aspects of the measure of damages are more or less harmonised between contract, tort and equity (for example causation in fact and mitigation), significant differences exist in relation to:

(1) remoteness of damage, which is the question of whether, when and to what degree damage needs to be foreseeable to be recoverable;

(2) the compensability of non-pecuniary loss such as pain and suffering, distress and loss of reputation;

(3) the effect of contributory negligence, which is the victim's contribution to the occurrence of the wrong or the ensuing loss through unreasonable conduct prior to the wrong;

(4) the circumstances under which victims of wrongs can claim the gain the wrongdoer has made from the wrong; and

(5) the availability and scope of exemplary (or punitive) damages.

For each of the five topics, this book examines the present position in contract, tort and equity and establishes the differences between the three areas. It goes on to scrutinise the arguments in defence of existing differences. The conclusion on each topic is that the present differences between contract, tort and equity cannot be justified on merits and should be removed through a harmonisation of the relevant principles.

Measuring Damages in the Law of Obligations

The Search for Harmonised Principles

Sirko Harder

Senior Lecturer, Monash Law School

·HART·
PUBLISHING

OXFORD AND PORTLAND, OREGON
2010

Published in the United Kingdom by Hart Publishing Ltd
16C Worcester Place, Oxford, OX1 2JW
Telephone: +44 (0)1865 517530
Fax: +44 (0)1865 510710
E-mail: mail@hartpub.co.uk
Website: http://www.hartpub.co.uk

Published in North America (US and Canada) by
Hart Publishing
c/o International Specialized Book Services
920 NE 58th Avenue, Suite 300
Portland, OR 97213–3786
USA
Tel: +1 503 287 3093 or toll-free: (1) 800 944 6190
Fax: +1 503 280 8832
E-mail: orders@isbs.com
Website: http://www.isbs.com

© Sirko Harder 2010

Sirko Harder has asserted his right under the Copyright, Designs and Patents Act 1988, to be
identified as the author of this work.

All rights reserved. No part of this publication may be reproduced, stored in a retrieval system, or
transmitted, in any form or by any means, without the prior permission of Hart Publishing, or as
expressly permitted by law or under the terms agreed with the appropriate reprographic rights
organisation. Enquiries concerning reproduction which may not be covered by the above should be
addressed to Hart Publishing Ltd at the address above.

British Library Cataloguing in Publication Data

Data Available

ISBN: 978-1-84113-863-3

Typeset by Columns Design Ltd, Reading
Printed and bound in Great Britain by
TJ International Ltd, Padstow, Cornwall

For Huan and Oliver

Foreword

Coming from a background in German law where the measure of damages is generally the same for all civil wrongs, I am struck by the fact that the measure of damages in common law jurisdictions differs to a large extent between contract, tort and equity. The diversity seems problematic, not least because concurrent liability in two or even all three of those areas is by no means uncommon. This raises important questions: What exactly are the differences between contract, tort and equity with regard to the measure of damages? Are the differences mere accidents of legal history or can they be justified on merits? This book attempts to address those questions.

The book covers five aspects of the measure of damages: remoteness of damage, which is the question of whether, when and to what degree damage needs to be foreseeable to be recoverable; the compensability of non-pecuniary loss such as pain and suffering, distress and loss of reputation; the effect of contributory negligence, which is the victim's contribution to the occurrence of the wrong or the ensuing loss through unreasonable conduct prior to the wrong; the circumstances under which victims of wrongs can claim the gain the wrongdoer has made from the wrong; and the availability and scope of exemplary (or punitive) damages.

For each of the five topics, this book examines the present position in contract, tort and equity and establishes the differences between the three areas. It goes on to scrutinise the arguments in defence of existing differences. The conclusion on each topic is that the present differences between contract, tort and equity cannot be justified on merits and should be removed through a harmonisation of the relevant principles. The arguments in support of that conclusion relate specifically to the relevant aspect of the measure of damages. They are consistent with, but not dependent on, the idea of a fusion of common law and equity.

Parts of this book have grown out of a PhD thesis which I wrote at the University of Aberdeen. I am very grateful for many helpful comments and challenging questions from my PhD supervisors Professor Angelo Forte and James Chalmers and from my PhD examiners Professor Hector MacQueen and Professor Roger Brownsword.

I have discussed aspects of this book with my colleague Normann Witzleb and, while working at the University of Leicester, with my then colleagues Christopher Bisping and Edward Goodwin. I would like to thank all of them for their patience and insightful comments. I am grateful to the University of Leicester for granting me study leave for this project.

Finally, I would like to thank the team at Hart Publishing for their diligence and support.

The book focuses on the law of England and Wales, although there are numerous references to material from all major common law jurisdictions and from Scotland. I have considered material available to me before 1 January 2010.

Melbourne, April 2010
Sirko Harder

Contents

Contents

Table of Cases

England and Wales

Table of Cases

Table of Cases

Table of Cases

Australia

Table of Cases

European Union

Guyana

Hong Kong

Ireland

Israel

Jamaica

Table of Cases

Scotland

Trinidad and Tobago

United States

Table of Cases

West Indies

Table of Statutes

England and Wales

Australia

Ireland

United States

Table of Statutory Instruments

(all England and Wales)

1

Introduction

I The Law of Obligations

In common law systems, there is no monolith law of obligations that has developed as a coherent whole. What may be called the law of obligations is made up of several areas of law that have developed more or less independently of each other: contract, tort, unjust enrichment (or restitution) and that part of equity that concerns obligations. These four areas are usually dealt with in separate university courses and separate textbooks.[1] There are two main reasons for the disparity within the law of obligations: the old writ system and the development of equity alongside the common law.[2]

Prior to the mid-nineteenth century, the royal courts could be accessed only by buying a writ from the chancery. Each writ prescribed a particular manner of proceedings or form of action. Contracts made under seal could be enforced through the actions of debt, concerning promises to pay a definite sum of money, or covenant, concerning promises to do something else. Wrongs or torts were addressed through the action of trespass, which involved a jury trial and the remedy of damages. Trespass was initially confined to wrongs committed 'with force and arms' (*vi et armis*) but the relevant writ form was flexible and could be adapted to the special circumstances of the case. These writs 'on the case' gave rise, for instance, to the actions of conversion, defamation, nuisance and what we now call negligence. They also gave rise to the action of *assumpsit*, concerning the careless performance of an obligation voluntarily undertaken. *Assumpsit* became the action to enforce agreements not made under seal. It was also used in instances of unjust enrichment, based on an implied or even fictitious contract.

---

[1] Some books do cover contract, tort and unjust enrichment together: J Cooke and D Oughton, *The Common Law of Obligations*, 3rd edn (London, 2000); G Samuel, *Law of Obligations and Legal Remedies*, 2nd edn (London, 2001).

[2] For the historical development of contract, tort and unjust enrichment see, eg, D Ibbetson, *A Historical Introduction to the Law of Obligations* (Oxford, 1999). For the historical development of equity see, eg, RP Meagher, JD Heydon and MJ Leeming, *Meagher, Gummow and Lehane's Equity: Doctrines and Remedies*, 4th edn (Australia, 2002) [1–015]–[1–075].

The formalistic writ system of the royal courts led to harsh and rigid rules of common law. An oft-cited example is that of a 'debtor who gave his creditor a sealed bond, but did not ensure that it was cancelled when he paid up. The law regarded the bond as incontrovertible evidence of the debt, and so payment was no defence'.[3] Some aggrieved parties sought redress from the king, who was regarded as the ultimate fount of justice. The kings delegated the task to their chancellors, who requested the parties to act according to good conscience irrespective of their rights. Decisions by the chancellors were initially made ad hoc, but over time a system of rules crystallised. This system became known as equity, and the Chancery became a court of constant resort. In the 1870s, the court system in England and Wales was restructured with the effect that every court would henceforth administer the rules of both common law and equity.[4] This was a complete fusion of administration but not of the substantive rules. Common law and equity persist as two distinct, albeit heavily interacting, areas of law.

Since the 1980s, if not before, there has been an ongoing debate on how to reclassify and restructure the areas of law that make up the law of obligations, in order to create a coherent and logical whole. This debate has featured several not mutually exclusive streams. One stream is the call for a substantive fusion of common law and equity, subjecting every obligation to the considerations of both areas.[5]

Another stream is to put all obligations into a logical system irrespective of their provenance. Birks has suggested a classification of obligations according to the causative events from which they arise: 'every obligation arises from a contract, from a wrong, from an unjust enrichment, or from some other kind of event' such as 'salvage, judgments, taxable events, and becoming a parent'.[6] Stapleton has suggested a classification of obligations according to the measure of damages.[7] For instance, the ambit of contract should be confined to obligations the breach of which entitles the claimant to be put into the position as if a specific end state of affairs had existed or been achieved ('entitled result measure'). Tort should encompass all obligations the breach of which entitles the

---

[3] JH Baker, An *Introduction to English Legal History*, 4th edn (London, 2002) 102.

[4] Re-enacted in the Supreme Court Act 1981 s 49(1): 'every court exercising jurisdiction in England or Wales in any civil cause or matter shall continue to administer law and equity'.

[5] eg A Burrows, *Fusing Common Law and Equity: Remedies, Restitution and Reform* (Hong Kong, 2002); J Stapleton, 'A New "Seascape" for Obligations: Reclassification on the Basis of Measure of Damages' in P Birks (ed), *The Classification of Obligations* (Oxford, 1997) 222–26, 229. A fusion is opposed, eg, by RP Meagher, JD Heydon and MJ Leeming, *Meagher, Gummow and Lehane's Equity: Doctrines and Remedies*, 4th edn (Australia, 2002) [2–270]–[2–320].

[6] P Birks, 'Definition and Division: A Meditation on *Institutes* 3.13' in P Birks (ed), *The Classification of Obligations* (Oxford, 1997) 19. A classification of obligations according to causative events is criticised by C Webb, 'What is Unjust Enrichment?' (2009) 29 *Oxford Journal of Legal Studies* 215, 216–36.

[7] J Stapleton, 'A New "Seascape" for Obligations: Reclassification on the Basis of Measure of Damages' in P Birks (ed), *The Classification of Obligations* (Oxford, 1997) 193–231.

claimant to be put into the position as if the relevant conduct of the defendant had not occurred ('normal expectancies measure'). A promise to take care would thus give rise to a tortious rather than contractual obligation even where no duty of care would exist absent the promise.

A third stream is to structure the law of obligations from the vantage point of a single concept. Weinrib uses the concept of corrective justice, which treats the claimant as the sufferer and the defendant as the performer of the same injustice.[8] Liability unravels the injustice by replicating its correlative structure while reversing its active and passive poles, so that the performer of injustice becomes the sufferer of liability. Remedies are merely the reflexes of the rights and their correlative duties. There is no room for discretion on the part of the courts as to the remedy granted.[9]

Independent of Weinrib's theory, there are calls for coherence in the law of remedies, especially with regard to the nomenclature and/or substantive principles in the law of damages. It is this stream in the law-of-obligations 'movement' in which the present book participates.

II The Law of Damages

Damages are usually defined as the pecuniary recompense given by process of law for an actionable wrong.[10] Used without any epithet, the term 'damages' denotes a monetary award which compensates the victim of a wrong for the loss suffered. Other categories of damages are also recognised, including the following ones.[11] Aggravated damages reflect the aggravation of the claimant's injury by the manner in which the defendant has committed the wrong; they should be assimilated into the category of compensatory damages.[12] Exemplary (or punitive) damages aim to punish a wrongdoer and deter him and others from committing such wrong.[13] Nominal damages may be awarded to mark wrongful conduct where a claimant has failed to prove any (compensable) loss but has established a wrong actionable per se, ie irrespective of the proof of loss.[14]

[8] EJ Weinrib, 'The Juridical Classification of Obligations' in P Birks (ed), *The Classification of Obligations* (Oxford, 1997) 37–55.

[9] The courts' remedial discretion is defended by M Tilbury, 'Remedies and the Classification of Obligations' in A Robertson (ed), *The Law of Obligations: Connections and Boundaries* (London, 2004) 19–22.

[10] *F & K Jabbour v Custodian of Israeli Absentee Property* [1954] 1 WLR 139, 143–44; *Broome v Cassell & Co* [1972] AC 1027 (HL) 1070 (Lord Hailsham LC); H McGregor, *McGregor on Damages*, 18th edn (London, 2009) [1–001].

[11] eg J Edelman, 'The Meaning of "Damages": Common Law and Equity' in A Robertson (ed), *The Law of Obligations: Connections and Boundaries* (London, 2004) 35–44; H McGregor, ibid [1–002].

[12] Below ch 14, I.

[13] Below ch 15.

[14] eg *Stone & Rolls Ltd (in liq) v Moore Stephens (a firm)* [2009] UKHL 39, [2009] 3 WLR 455 [99].

Restitutionary (or gain-based) damages strip a wrongdoer of (some of) the gain he has made from the wrong.[15] At least in cases of serious police misconduct, there is an emerging concept of vindicatory damages aimed at vindicating the right infringed.[16]

The law of damages concerns the availability and measure of the various forms of damages, but not the establishment of a wrong as such. In other words, it concerns the extent rather than the existence of liability.[17] The two issues overlap though in the case of torts actionable only on proof of damage, such as negligence, nuisance and deceit.[18]

Since 'damages' is an expression of the common law, the term 'wrong' in the foregoing paragraph includes only torts and breaches of contract.[19] The main monetary remedies for equitable wrongs such as breach of fiduciary duty are an account of profits and equitable compensation.[20] One stream in the law-of-obligations 'movement' is the call for a uniform nomenclature of monetary remedies for civil wrongs, using the term 'damages' both at common law and in equity.[21] For convenience, the present book follows that suggestion in that it uses the term 'law of damages' to denote the law of monetary remedies for all civil wrongs. Individual remedies such as equitable compensation will be called by their traditional name, however.

The law of damages as just defined may conceivably contain general principles common to contract, tort and equity. Some general principles may exist already. Causation doctrine, in the narrow sense of dealing with the 'but for' test and intervening events,[22] is virtually uniform within the common law[23] and conquers

---

[15] The appropriateness of both the term 'damages' and the term 'restitutionary' is controversial: below ch 12, I.

[16] *Attorney-General of Trinidad and Tobago v Ramanoop* [2005] UKPC 15, [2006] 1 AC 328 [19]; *Merson v Cartwright* [2005] UKPC 38, 67 WIR 17 [18]; *Ashley v Chief Constable of Sussex Police* [2008] UKHL 25, [2008] 1 AC 962 [22]–[23], [28]–[29]. A role of vindicatory damages for civil wrongs in general is seen by Lord Scott, 'Damages' [2007] *Lloyd's Maritime and Commercial Law Quarterly* 465, 468–71 (who argues that the only legitimate purposes of damages awards are compensation and vindication); D Pearce and R Halson, 'Damages for Breach of Contract: Compensation, Restitution and Vindication' (2008) 28 *OJLS* 73, 86–98; N Witzleb and R Carroll, 'The role of vindication in torts damages' (2009) 17 *Tort Law Review* 16. But a right to award vindicatory damages at common law is not (yet) established: H McGregor, *McGregor on Damages*, 18th edn (London, 2009) [42–009].

[17] H McGregor, ibid [1–019]–[1–020].

[18] A Burrows, *Remedies for Torts and Breach of Contract*, 3rd edn (Oxford, 2004) 4–5.

[19] Under the theory of efficient breach, a breach of contract is not always a 'wrong'. This theory is considered and rejected below ch 16, I A and B.

[20] eg *Murad v Al-Saraj* [2005] EWCA Civ 959, [2005] WTLR 1573 [136].

[21] R Chambers, 'Liability' in P Birks and A Pretto (eds), *Breach of Trust* (Oxford, 2002) 21; J Edelman, 'The Meaning of "Damages": Common Law and Equity' in A Robertson (ed), *The Law of Obligations: Connections and Boundaries* (London, 2004) 46–56.

[22] Below ch 2, I.

[23] *East Suffolk Rivers Catchment Board v Kent* [1941] AC 74 (HL) 93 (Lord Atkin); *Galoo Ltd v Bright Grahame Murray* [1994] 1 WLR 1360 (CA) 1369; *Beoco Ltd v Alfa Laval Co Ltd* [1995] QB 137 (CA) 151; H McGregor, *McGregor on Damages*, 18th edn (London, 2009) [6–140], [19–006]; HG Beale, 'Damages' in HG Beale (gen ed), *Chitty on Contracts, Vol 1: General Principles*, 30th edn (London, 2008) [26–032] fn 182.

equity too.[24] Mitigation doctrine, which bars recovery for loss that the claimant could have avoided by taking reasonable steps subsequent to the wrong, applies uniformly at common law.[25] Since it is 'intuitively just',[26] the mitigation principle may also apply in equity,[27] at least under the doctrines of laches or acquiescence,[28] or as a matter of causation[29] or of the court's discretion.[30] Contract and tort have a lot in common with regard to the date as at which damages are assessed,[31] the awardability of interest,[32] certainty of loss and recovery for past and prospective loss.[33]

Uniformity further exists in a jurisdictional aspect. Section 2 of the Chancery Amendment Act 1858, commonly known as Lord Cairns' Act, empowered the Court of Chancery, in cases where it had jurisdiction to entertain an application for an injunction or specific performance, to award damages in addition to, or in substitution for, an injunction or specific performance. Despite the repeal of that Act it is commonly accepted that the jurisdiction thereby conferred has survived and is now exercised by the fused courts of common law and equity.[34] Even though this power to award equitable damages for common law wrongs does not

---

[24] Below ch 5.

[25] eg *The Maersk Colombo* [2001] EWCA Civ 717, [2001] 2 Lloyd's Rep 275 [25] (Clarke LJ: 'Common to the law of tort and contract are the principles that a loss is only recoverable if … it could not have been mitigated.'); *Freemans plc v Park Street Properties (Lincoln) Ltd* [2002] EWHC 477, [2002] 2 P & CR 30 [79] (Seymour J: 'On general principle a person who has been the victim of a tort or a breach of contract must seek to mitigate the loss caused by such tort or breach of contract.').

[26] J Glover, *Commercial Equity: Fiduciary Relationships* (Sydney, 1995) [6.128].

[27] Mitigation doctrine was held applicable to breach of fiduciary duty in *Burke v Cory* (1959) 19 DLR (2d) 252 (*ONCA*) 263–64; *Laskin v Bache & Co* (1971) 23 DLR (3d) 385 (ONCA) 393; *Permanent Building Society v Wheeler* (1994) 14 ACSR 109 (WASC) 168. For a rejection of its application to breach of trust see *Target Holdings Ltd v Redferns* [1994] 1 WLR 1089 (CA) 1098 (Ralph Gibson LJ); V Vann, *Equitable Compensation in Australia: Principles and Problems* (Saarbrücken, 2009) 340.

[28] WMC Gummow, 'Compensation for Breach of Fiduciary Duty' in TG Youdan (ed), *Equity, Fiduciaries and Trusts* (Toronto, 1989) 75. Significant differences between laches and acquiescence on the one hand and mitigation on the other are seen by V Vann, ibid 343–44.

[29] *Canson Enterprises Ltd v Boughton & Co* [1991] 3 SCR 534 (SCC) 556 (McLachlin J, dissenting); L Ho, 'Attributing losses to a breach of fiduciary duty' (1998) 12 *Trust L Int* 66, 75–76; C Rickett, 'Compensating for Loss in Equity—Choosing the Right Horse for Each Course' in P Birks and F Rose (eds), *Restitution and Equity, Vol 1: Resulting Trusts and Equitable Compensation* (London, 2000) 183. See also *Commonwealth Bank of Australia v Smith* (1991) 102 ALR 453 (FCA) 479–81.

[30] V Vann, *Equitable Compensation in Australia: Principles and Problems* (Saarbrücken, 2009) 344 (for breach of fiduciary duty).

[31] eg *Miliangos v George Frank (Textiles) Ltd* [1976] AC 443 (HL) 468 (Lord Wilberforce: 'as a general rule in English law damages for tort or for breach of contract are assessed as at the date of the breach'); *County Personnel (Employment Agency) Ltd v Alan R Pulver & Co* [1987] 1 WLR 916 (CA) 925 (Bingham LJ: 'the general rule undoubtedly is that damages for tort or breach of contract are assessed as at the date of the breach').

[32] Supreme Court Act 1981 s 35A; County Courts Act 1984 s 69. These provisions distinguish between personal injuries and other cases, but not between contract and tort.

[33] H McGregor, *McGregor on Damages*, 18th edn (London, 2009), [19–004].

[34] eg *Attorney-General v Blake (Jonathan Cape Ltd Third Party)* [2001] 1 AC 268 (HL) 281 (Lord Nicholls). See Supreme Court Act 1981 s 50 for the High Court and the Court of Appeal.

presuppose an entitlement to legal damages for the wrong in question,[35] the House of Lords has held that equity follows the law in the measure of the damages.[36]

Uniformity within the law of damages is the exception though. Contract, tort and equity have different principles on important aspects of the measure of damages. Diversity exists in particular with regard to the question of whether, when and to which degree damage needs to be foreseeable to be recoverable; the compensability of non-pecuniary loss; the effect of the claimant's contribution to her loss through unreasonable behaviour prior to the wrong; and the availability of gain-based and exemplary (punitive) awards. Both judges and commentators have called for a harmonisation of the measure of damages within the law of obligations and the creation of general principles common to contract, tort and equity.[37] It is this stream in the law-of-obligations 'movement' in which the present book participates.

It should be noted at the outset that the general principles suggested in this book provide a default regime only, in two respects. First, they are rules to which exceptions can be made for certain types of wrong (but not for contract, tort or equity as a whole, for then the rule would no longer be 'general' in the sense used here). Intentional torts, for instance, are said to require special treatment in relation to remoteness of damage[38] and contributory negligence.[39] Even if that is accepted, remoteness of damage and contributory negligence may still be governed by principles spanning tort *in general,* contract and equity. Secondly, subject to the unfair-terms legislation and other control devices, the parties to a wrong can regulate the measure (in a broad sense) of damages through a contract entered into either before or after the wrong. This is obvious where the contract expressly addresses issues such as remoteness of damage or contributory negligence. But even in the absence of an express term, the nature and scope of the contractual obligations as well as the allocation of risks in the contract may still contain an implied regulation of those issues.

---

[35] *Johnson v Agnew* [1980] AC 367 (HL) 400.

[36] ibid; *Attorney-General v Blake (Jonathan Cape Ltd Third Party)* [2001] 1 AC 268 (HL) 281 (Lord Nicholls). Some commentators insist that the usual discretion in granting equitable relief applies: C Rickett and T Gardner, 'Compensating for loss in equity: The evolution of a remedy' (1994) 24 *Victoria University of Wellington Law Review* 19, 23–24; ICF Spry, *The Principles of Equitable Remedies,* 8th edn (Sydney, 2010) 646–49.

[37] eg *Mouat v Clark Boyce* [1992] 2 NZLR 559 (NZCA) 574575 (Gault J); A Burrows, 'We Do This At Common Law But That In Equity' (2002) 22 *OJLS* 1.

[38] Below ch 2, VII.

[39] Below ch 9, II.

III   Desirability of a Harmonised Measure of Damages

Why should we strive for a harmonised measure of damages and not accept the present diversity between contract, tort and equity? Uniformity has four advantages. First, the differences between contract, tort and equity with regard to the measure of damages create problems where the wrong in question is actionable in more than one of those three areas. Concurrent liability is by no means rare, particularly since it has been established that professionals can be concurrently liable in both contract and tort[40] and that liability in negligence can, under certain conditions, extend to pure economic loss,[41] which has significantly increased the potential for an overlap with liability in contract or equity. A professional whose carelessness causes loss to the client may be liable in both contract and tort, and also in equity where there is a fiduciary relationship, as in the case of a solicitor.[42]

In cases of concurrent liability, the claimant enjoys 'the right to assert the cause of action that appears to be the most advantageous to him in respect of any particular legal consequence'.[43] This may prove complicated where the measure of damages differs between the causes of action open to the claimant. Suppose that a solicitor acts in such a way that there exists a conflict of interest, and becomes liable to his client in contract, tort and equity. The client claims compensation not only for her financial loss but also for the distress suffered while the solicitor seeks a reduction in the damages on the ground that the client has contributed to her loss through unreasonable behaviour prior to the wrong. If the claimant has the right to choose each of the three concurrent causes of action separately for each of the two issues, nine different outcomes are possible. The question then is: When does the claimant have to make her choice? At the beginning of the trial she may not know which of the nine alternatives is best for her, but to require the court to present nine alternative judgments to the claimant to choose from would be preposterous.

The New Zealand Court of Appeal, when facing this very situation in *Mouat v Clark Boyce*[44] (with the slight difference that the majority denied liability in contract), took the most sensible approach and held that the outcome in either issue does *not* depend on the cause of action chosen. With regard to the

---

[40]   *Midland Bank Trust Co Ltd v Hett, Stubbs & Kemp* [1979] Ch 384, 415; *Henderson v Merrett Syndicates Ltd* [1995] 2 AC 145 (HL).

[41]   The breakthrough came in *Hedley Byrne & Co v Heller & Partners Ltd* [1964] AC 465.

[42]   C Rickett and T Gardner, 'Compensating for loss in equity: The evolution of a remedy' (1994) 24 *VUWLR* 19, 29.

[43]   *Henderson v Merrett Syndicates Ltd* [1995] 2 AC 145 (HL) 191 (Lord Goff), quoting *Central Trust Co v Rafuse* (1986) 31 DLR (4th) 481 (SCC) 522 (Le Dain J). A hierarchy of obligations in cases of concurrent liability is called for by M Tilbury and JW Carter, 'Converging Liabilities and Security of Contract: Contributory Negligence in Australian Law' (2000) 16 *Journal of Contract Law* 78, 89–93.

[44]   [1992] 2 NZLR 559 (NZCA); reversed on the question of liability in principle in [1994] 1 AC 428 (PC). Discussed below ch 8, III and ch 11

compensability of non-pecuniary loss and the effect of contributory negligence, the Court aligned the position in both contract and equity with the one in tort (the same approach is taken in this book). Gault J observed:

> Where, as here, findings in negligence are made on pleadings and evidence that are advanced in the same terms in both contract and tort and the same failure amounts to breach of fiduciary duty it would be formalistic in the extreme to draw distinctions as to remedy.[45]

Secondly, controversies on the correct classification of certain wrongs or the availability of certain monetary remedies would be much less significant or even obsolete were the measure of damages essentially the same in contract, tort and equity. One example is the controversy on whether breach of confidence, in particular its new branch called breach of privacy, is a tort or an equitable wrong.[46] The classification is currently crucial for issues on which equity and tort differ, such as the effect of contributory negligence or the availability of exemplary (punitive) awards. But the treatment of those issues should not depend upon the technicality of whether the wrong is a tort or an equitable wrong.[47] Another example is the controversy on whether a purely equitable wrong may be remedied not only by equitable compensation under equity's inherent jurisdiction but also, alternatively, by equitable damages under Lord Cairns' Act.[48] Since the measure of equitable damages follows common law principles, the controversy would become obsolete if equitable compensation and common law damages were measured in the same way.[49]

Thirdly, a harmonised measure of damages would foster the refinement of the principles in their application to particular fact patterns. Where a court refines a principle that differs between the three areas of law—for instance decides on the foreseeability of certain loss in certain circumstances, or the value of certain non-pecuniary loss, or the distribution of blame between the parties in a certain contributory negligence situation—the decision forms a true precedent only for the cause of action concerned. A subsequent court deciding the same issue in a different cause of action cannot simply rely upon the previous case but must basically start from scratch. If the principles were uniform, all decisions on them would serve as precedent irrespective of the cause of action. Refining the

---

[45] [1992] 2 NZLR 559 (NZCA) 574–75.

[46] See L Clarke, 'Remedial Responses to Breach of Confidence: The Question of Damages' (2005) 24 *Civil Justice Quarterly* 316, 324–27; below ch 8, I and II.

[47] N Witzleb, 'Monetary remedies for breach of confidence in privacy cases' (2007) 27 *Legal Studies* 430, 450.

[48] The availability of equitable damages is denied by RP Meagher, JD Heydon and MJ Leeming, *Meagher, Gummow and Lehane's Equity: Doctrines and Remedies*, 4th edn (Australia, 2002) [23–105]. For the opposite view, see *Attorney-General v Observer Ltd, sub nom Attorney-General v Guardian Newspapers Ltd (No 2)* [1990] 1 AC 109 (HL) 286 (Lord Goff) (with regard to breach of confidence); A Burrows, *Remedies for Torts and Breach of Contract*, 3rd edn (Oxford, 2004) 606; C Rickett and T Gardner, 'Compensating for loss in equity: The evolution of a remedy' (1994) 24 *VUWLR* 19, 21–22. For Lord Cairns' Act see above II in this chapter.

[49] C Rickett and T Gardner, ibid 25.

principles would become much easier. It might be no coincidence that the strongest judicial support for a harmonised measure of damages comes from New Zealand, which has a small population and hence little litigation.

Finally, a harmonised measure of damages would be of great assistance in the case of fresh statutory wrongs. At present, a statute introducing a new wrong must define the measure of monetary remedies by either regulating all details itself or referring to the measure established in contract, tort or equity. If neither is done, the measure will be uncertain. Harmonised principles would naturally apply to every new wrong unless statute provides otherwise. The legislator would be absolved from addressing the measure in every case, and the law would be more certain.

IV Possibility of a Harmonised Measure of Damages

Is the quest for a harmonised measure of damages not futile from the beginning on the ground that the overall purpose of the remedies differs between contract, tort and equity? No fundamental difference can be seen. Since gain-based and exemplary (punitive) awards are specifically addressed in Parts 4 and 5 respectively, the following discussion is confined to compensatory relief, the subject matter of Parts 1 to 3.

Damages for breach of contract normally compensate the claimant for her 'expectation loss', that is the loss that results from not obtaining the performance the defendant promised.[50] A buyer of goods, for instance, may have sold them on for a higher price and loses that profit if the seller fails to deliver. A party aggrieved by a breach of contract may, alternatively, claim compensation for her 'reliance loss', that is the loss that results from relying on the defendant performing.[51] A purchaser of land, for instance, may have incurred expenses in investigating the vendor's title. However, where the claimant would not have recouped her expenses had the defendant performed properly, damages for the reliance loss are capped at the amount of the expectation loss.[52] 'Ultimately, then, the reliance interest bows to the expectation interest',[53] and the reliance measure of contractual damages has little practical significance.

It is therefore appropriate to focus on the expectation measure of contractual damages and to say, as Parke B did in *Robinson v Harman*, that 'where a party

[50] The terms 'expectation interest' and 'reliance interest' were introduced by LL Fuller and WR Perdue, 'The Reliance Interest in Contract Damages: 1' (1936) 46 *Yale LJ* 52, 54.

[51] *CCC Films (London) Ltd v Impact Quadrant Films Ltd* [1985] QB 16.

[52] It is for the defendant to prove that the expenses would not have been recouped, at least where his breach prevented the claimant from exploiting the subject matter of the contract: ibid 40.

[53] A Burrows, *Remedies for Torts and Breach of Contract*, 3rd edn (Oxford, 2004) 68. See also J Cartwright, 'Compensatory Damages: Some Central Issues of Assessment' in A Burrows and E Peel (eds), *Commercial Remedies: Current Issues and Problems* (Oxford, 2003) 8.

sustains a loss by reason of a breach of contract, he is, so far as money can do it, to be placed in the same situation, with respect to damages, as if the contract had been performed'.[54] Tortious damages were described by Lord Blackburn in *Livingstone v Rawyards Coal Company* as 'that sum of money which will put the party who has been injured, or who has suffered, in the same position as he would have been in if he had not sustained the wrong'.[55] Merging both formulae, Lord Diplock said in *Albacruz (Cargo Owners) v Albazero (Owners) (The Albazero)*:

> The general rule in English law today as to the measure of damages recoverable for the invasion of a legal right, whether by breach of a contract or by commission of a tort, is that damages are compensatory. Their function is to put the person whose right has been invaded in the same position as if it had been respected so far as the award of a sum of money can do so.[56]

In the decision by the High Court of Australia in *Gates v City Mutual Life Assurance Society Ltd*, Mason J, Wilson J and Dawson J still insisted on a different purpose of damages in contract and tort:

> The differences and the similarities between the two approaches are best illustrated by contrasting the damages recoverable for breach of contractual warranty on a purchase of goods with those recoverable for a fraudulent misrepresentation inducing entry into a contract for the purchase of goods on the assumption that the contracts are identical except that in one case the representation amounts to a warranty and in the other it is merely a noncontractual representation. For breach of warranty the plaintiff is prima facie entitled to recover the difference between the real value of the goods and the value of the goods as warranted. In deceit the measure of damages is the difference at the time of purchase between the real value of the goods, and the price paid[.][57]

True, the amount of damages in the two examples is different. But this is simply the result of a different nature of the rights or interests protected, not of a different purpose of relief.[58] The warranty example involves the violation of the claimant's entitlement to goods of a certain quality. It follows that the claimant

---

[54] (1848) 1 Exch 850, 855; 154 ER 363, 365.

[55] (1880) LR 5 App Cas 25 (HL) 39. Lord Blackburn's statement has been quoted in numerous subsequent cases, eg *Devenish Nutrition Ltd v Sanofi-Aventis SA (France)* [2008] EWCA Civ 1086 [42] (Arden LJ).

[56] [1977] AC 774 (HL) 841. See also A Burrows, *Fusing Common Law and Equity: Remedies, Restitution and Reform* (Hong Kong, 2002) 6; D Friedmann, 'The Performance Interest in Contract Damages' (1995) *Law Quarterly Review* 628, 639; NJ McBride, 'A Case for Awarding Punitive Damages in Response to Deliberate Breaches of Contract' (1995) 24 *Anglo-American Law Review* 369, 383. A fused formula is rejected by J Stapleton, 'The Normal Expectancies Measure in Tort Damages' (1997) 113 *LQR* 257, 260 ff.

[57] (1986) 160 CLR 1 (HCA) 12. Similar examples are given by A Burrows, *Remedies for Torts and Breach of Contract*, 3rd edn (Oxford, 2004) 6–7, 33–34; J Cartwright, 'Compensatory Damages: Some Central Issues of Assessment' in A Burrows and E Peel (eds), *Commercial Remedies: Current Issues and Problems* (Oxford, 2003) 4–5; H McGregor, *McGregor on Damages*, 18th edn (London, 2009) [19–003].

[58] D Friedmann, 'The Performance Interest in Contract Damages' (1995) *LQR* 628, 642.

will be put into the position as if goods of such quality had been delivered. By contrast, the deceit example involves the violation of the right not to be induced to enter a contract by deception. It follows that the claimant will be put into the position as if she had never entered the contract. In both examples, the claimant will be put into the position as if the wrong in question had not been committed.

It remains true that: 'Tort obligations are imposed on the parties; contractual obligations are voluntarily assumed'.[59] It also remains true that, in general, contract protects expectations engendered by a binding promise whereas tort protects the status quo.[60] But why should this compel a different treatment of, say, non-pecuniary loss flowing from the wrong or of the claimant's contribution to the loss? Suppose that a car driver suffers an accident and is injured because the brakes fail. Should a decision on the compensability of pain and suffering or the effect of speeding on the part of the driver be fundamentally different depending on whether the defendant sold the car to the claimant with defective breaks (expectation measure) or maliciously damaged the brakes (status quo measure)?

Compensation of loss is also the aim of equitable compensation. There have been suggestions that equitable compensation may be measured not only by reference to the principal's loss but also, alternatively, by reference to the fiduciary's gain.[61] But since both an account of profits, which may always be ordered as an alternative to equitable compensation, and a constructive trust strip the fiduciary of (some of) the gain made from his breach, equitable compensation should be reserved for what its name indicates: the compensation of the principal's loss.[62] The aim of equitable compensation used to be described as the restoration of the principal to her position prior to the equitable wrong.[63] Taken literally, this would allow the principal to recover all losses suffered since the wrong even if not caused by it. But to order the fiduciary to compensate loss not caused by his wrong can hardly be justified, and the causation requirement is now established.[64] The aim of equitable compensation may therefore be described as the restoration of the principal to the position as if the wrong in

---

[59] *Astley v Austrust Ltd* (1999) 197 CLR 1 (HCA) [84] (Gleeson CJ, McHugh J, Gummow J and Hayne J).

[60] A Burrows, *Understanding the Law of Obligations: Essays on Contract, Tort and Restitution* (Oxford, 1998) 9.

[61] *Hill v Rose* [1990] VR 129 (VSC) 143; K Mason, JW Carter and GJ Tolhurst, *Mason and Carter's Restitution Law in Australia*, 2nd edn (Chatswood, 2008) [1726].

[62] C Rickett and T Gardner, 'Compensating for loss in equity: The evolution of a remedy' (1994) 24 *VUWLR* 19, 30; V Vann, *Equitable Compensation in Australia: Principles and Problems* (Saarbrücken, 2009) 18–25.

[63] *Nocton v Lord Ashburton* [1914] AC 932 (HL) 952 (Viscount Haldane LC); below ch 5, III.

[64] *Target Holdings Ltd v Redferns* [1996] AC 421 (HL) 432, 434; *Swindle v Harrison* [1997] 4 All ER 705 (CA); *Bristol and West Building Society v Mothew* [1998] Ch 1 (CA) 17 (Millett LJ); below ch 5.

question had not been committed,[65] which is identical to the aim of common law damages. As Cooke P in the New Zealand Court of Appeal said in *Day v Mead*:

> Compensation or damages in equity were traditionally said to aim at restoration or restitution, whereas common law tort damages are intended to compensate for harm done; but in many cases, the present being one, that is a difference without a distinction.[66]

In conclusion, the differences between contract, tort and equity with regard to the measure of damages are not necessitated by a different overall purpose of compensatory relief. It follows that a justification of those differences can only come from considerations specifically relating to the particular aspect of measure (remoteness of damage and so on). Whether different considerations in fact apply, will be investigated in this book.

V The Methodology Adopted in This Book

This book suggests general principles in the law of damages by challenging the present differences between contract, tort and equity in five areas: remoteness of damage (Part1), non-pecuniary loss (Part 2), contributory negligence (Part 3), gain-based relief (Part 4) and exemplary damages (Part 5). Since equity already follows the common law in the measure of equitable damages for common law wrongs under Lord Cairns' Act,[67] the examination of equitable principles is confined to those under equity's inherent or exclusive jurisdiction. The five parts of this book are more or less independent studies. Only one overall theme runs through the whole book: the idea that a harmonised measure of damages is possible and in general desirable. Of course, harmonisation is not an end in itself. Present differences may be retained if there are cogent reasons for it. But historical accidents alone provide no good reason. As Michalik has observed:

> Where substantive differences in rights call for different or restricted remedies, the differences between remedies available can and should persist. Where purely historical factors have led to different restrictions on the shape or availability of remedies, the restrictions, in place for no good reason, should be abolished.[68]

---

[65] *Day v Cook* [2000] PNLR 178, 193; *Canson Enterprises Ltd v Boughton & Co* [1991] 3 SCR 534 (SCC) 577; A Burrows, *Remedies for Torts and Breach of Contract*, 3rd edn (Oxford, 2004) 600; IE Davidson, 'The Equitable Remedy of Compensation' (1982) 13 *Melbourne University Law Review* 349, 354; MJ Tilbury, *Civil Remedies, Vol 1: Principles of Civil Remedies* (Sydney, 1990) [3248]; V Vann, *Equitable Compensation in Australia: Principles and Problems* (Saarbrücken, 2009) 23.

[66] [1987] 2 NZLR 443 (NZCA) 451. Approvingly quoted in *Canson Enterprises Ltd v Boughton & Co* [1991] 3 SCR 534 (SCC) 585 (La Forest J). See also A Burrows, ibid; MJ Tilbury, ibid.

[67] Above II in this chapter.

[68] PW Michalik, 'The availability of compensatory and exemplary damages in equity: A note on the *Aquaculture* decision' (1991) 21 *VUWLR* 391, 413.

Michalik opposes the idea of a fusion of common law and equity. His statement thus demonstrates that the pro-harmonisation arguments advanced in this book are consistent not only with the idea of such fusion but also with a continued separation of common law and equity. When it is suggested, for instance, that the claimant's contribution to her loss through unreasonable conduct prior to the wrong should lead to a proportionate reduction of equitable compensation, this can be achieved in two ways: by fusing common law and equity so that all common law concepts, including contributory negligence, apply to equitable wrongs too, or by equity independently developing an apportionment regime out of established equitable doctrines such as 'he who seeks equity must do equity'. 'Whether the courts refine the equitable tools such as the remedy of compensation, or follow the common law on its own terms, seems not particularly important where the same policy objective is sought.'[69]

An investigation into the merits of particular differences between contract, tort and equity cannot start before it is clear what exactly those differences are. This book therefore endeavours to set out the present principles in the five areas covered as well as to analyse them. It is sometimes difficult to make a crystal-clear distinction between an analysis and a pure description of the law, in particular where the law is uncertain. In general, however, this book attempts to clearly separate analysis and description, sometimes through an allocation to separate chapters. In Part 4, for instance, chapter twelve describes the present law of 'restitution for wrongs' whereas chapter thirteen discusses the desirable regime.

While this book compares contract, tort and equity, it does not compare the law of different jurisdictions. The focus is on the law of England and Wales. It will not be ignored, however, that all or most of the legal principles examined in this book exist also in other common law and in mixed jurisdictions where they are often discussed with no less intensity than in England and Wales. Indeed, economic arguments come in the main from scholars in the United States. This book therefore refers frequently to cases, scholarly writings and law commission reports from other common law jurisdictions and from Scotland. But nothing in this book is meant to set out the present law, or to propose a change in the law, for any jurisdiction other than England and Wales.

---

[69]   *Canson Enterprises Ltd v Boughton & Co* (1991) 85 DLR (4th) 129 (SCC) 153 (La Forest J, with whom Sopinka J, Gonthier J and Cory J concurred). See also C Rickett and T Gardner, 'Compensating for loss in equity: The evolution of a remedy' (1994) 24 *VUWLR* 19, 48: 'in situations where both law and equity have the same policy objectives, the only distinction which *must* still exist between equitable compensation and damages is that equitable remedies are hedged about by discretions'.

Part 1

Remoteness of Damage

2

The Present Remoteness Test in Tort

I Terminology

The term 'remoteness of damage' is ambiguous. Some regard it as an aspect of causation,[1] McGregor sees it just the other way round,[2] yet others regard causation and remoteness as separate, though related, issues.[3] Adopting the last-mentioned view, this book understands 'causation' to deal only with factual causation in the 'but for' sense (loss is irrecoverable unless it would not have arisen but for the wrong) and intervening events breaking the causal chain, and understands 'remoteness of damage' to deal only with the scope of protection afforded by the law once causation as just defined has been established. Since causation doctrine (in the narrow sense) is already uniform at least within the common law,[4] the following study focuses on remoteness of damage (in the narrow sense), although it will sometimes be necessary to stray into the area of causation. The study starts with tort and will there focus on negligence, the most important tort. Other torts will be glanced at afterwards.

II The Foreseeability Criterion in Negligence

From the mid-nineteenth century until 1961 the courts vacillated between two different concepts of remoteness of damage in negligence. Under one concept, damage is too remote if a reasonable man in the defendant's position would not

---

[1] S Deakin, A Johnston and B Markesinis, *Markesinis and Deakin's Tort Law*, 6th edn (Oxford, 2008) 244–45; G Samuel, *Law of Obligations and Legal Remedies*, 2nd edn (London, 2001) 211, 227.

[2] H McGregor, *McGregor on Damages*, 18th edn (London, 2009) [1–024], [4–023], [6–002].

[3] A Burrows, *Remedies for Torts and Breach of Contract*, 3rd edn (Oxford, 2004) 74–75; R Halson, 'Remedies for Breach of Contract' in M Furmston (ed), *The Law of Contract*, 2nd edn (London, 2003) [8.84], [8.88]; D Harris, D Campbell and R Halson, *Remedies in Contract and Tort*, 2nd edn (London, 2002) 84, 296; J Murphy, *Street on Torts*, 12th edn (Oxford, 2007) 135; MJ Tilbury, *Civil Remedies, Vol 1: Principles of Civil Remedies* (Sydney, 1990) [3060].

[4] Above ch 1, II.

have foreseen it.[5] Under the second concept, liability extends to all direct consequences of the careless act.[6] Of course, an act can be qualified as careless only if some damage to the claimant was foreseeable. But once this has been established, the second concept regards the question of foreseeability as no longer relevant; this question 'goes to culpability, not to compensation'.[7]

The most prominent decision in favour of the second concept was made by the Court of Appeal in *Re Polemis v Furness, Withy & Co Ltd*.[8] In that case, the owners of a ship claimed from the charterers damages for the destruction of the ship. The charterers' stevedores carelessly allowed a plank to fall into the hold of the ship. When hitting the cargo-deck, the plank caused a spark, which ignited petrol vapour and produced a fire destroying the ship. The arbitrators found that some (unspecified) damage could have reasonably been anticipated from the falling of the plank, but not the causing of a spark. Nevertheless the Court of Appeal held the charterers liable: allowing the plank to fall was negligent since some damage to the ship was foreseeable, and the fire was a direct consequence of the negligent act.

In 1961, however, the foreseeability test made its breakthrough with the Privy Council's advice in the New South Wales case *Overseas Tankship (UK) Ltd v Morts Dock & Engineering Co Ltd (The Wagon Mound [No 1])*,[9] which was immediately regarded as authority for English law too.[10] An employee on the ship *Wagon Mound*, chartered by the appellants, carelessly discharged furnace oil into Sydney harbour. The oil spread to the respondents' wharf, where welding work on two ships was being undertaken. The workmen on the wharf halted their work but, after being advised that the oil could not be ignited, they resumed work. Two days later the oil ignited because molten metal had fallen from the wharf and set fire to cotton waste or rags floating in the oil. The wharf and the two ships caught fire and were damaged.

The trial judge found that the appellants did not know, and could not reasonably be expected to have known, that the oil was capable of being set on fire when spread on water.[11] Nevertheless, applying *Re Polemis*, he held them liable in negligence: The fire was a direct consequence of spilling the oil into the water, which was negligent because pollution damage could have been foreseen.[12]

---

[5] eg *Rigby v Hewitt* (1850) 5 Ex 240, 243 (Pollock CB); *Greenland v Chaplin* (1850) 5 Ex 243, 248. See also *Sharp v Powell* (1872) LR 7 CP 253.

[6] *Smith v London and South Western Railway Co* (1870) LR 6 CP 14; *Weld-Blundell v Stephens* [1920] AC 956 (HL) 983–84 (Lord Sumner); *Thurogood v Van Den Berghs & Jurgens Ltd* [1951] 2 KB 537 (CA).

[7] *Weld-Blundell v Stephens* [1920] AC 956 (HL) 984 (Lord Sumner).

[8] [1921] 3 KB 560 (CA).

[9] [1961] AC 388 (PC).

[10] *Smith v Leech Brain & Co Ltd* [1962] 2 QB 405, 415–16; *Doughty v Turner Manufacturing Co Ltd* [1964] 1 QB 518 (CA). See also *Hughes v Lord Advocate* 1963 SC (HL) 31. *Doughty* and *Hughes* are considered in detail below III in this chapter.

[11] *The Wagon Mound (No 1)* [1958] 1 Lloyd's Rep 575, 582.

[12] ibid 584–85; confirmed in [1959] 2 Lloyd's Rep 697 (NSWCA).

The Privy Council reversed the decision. Viscount Simonds, speaking for the board, disapproved *Re Polemis* by saying that:

> [I]t does not seem consonant with current ideas of justice or morality that for an act of negligence, however slight or venial, which results in some trivial foreseeable damage the actor should be liable for all consequences however unforeseeable and however grave, so long as they can be said to be 'direct'.[13]

His Lordship went on to point out that 'there can be no liability until the damage has been done. It is not the act but the consequences on which tortious liability is founded'.[14] Accordingly, he said, one cannot first establish liability in negligence as such and then ask to which damage it extends.[15] His Lordship gave the following example: B causes similar unforeseeable damage to A and C, and other, foreseeable damage to A only. 'A system of law which would hold B liable to A but not to C for the similar damage suffered by each of them could not easily be defended.'[16]

Re Polemis has been defended with the argument that where loss must fall on either of two parties, one of them at fault in causing the loss and the other faultless, the party at fault ought to bear the loss.[17] At first sight, this concept, which may be described as one of localised distributive justice,[18] is appealing. Innocence must be protected, and fault is generally an appropriate trigger of liability. And the consequences of this concept are all but outrageous where, like in *Re Polemis*, the damage that was foreseeable and the unforeseeable damage in suit are both damage to the same thing.

However, if the concept of localised distributive justice were accepted, its scope could not be confined to the situation just described. In order to be consistent, the concept would have to apply to other situations too.[19] Kidner gives the following example.[20] Due to B's fault, A and B collide on a country road, and, unforeseeably, the fields on both sides of the road catch fire. One field is owned by A and the other by C. Under the approach taken in *Re Polemis*, A could sue for the damage to his field on the grounds that he was a foreseeable victim (as road

---

[13] [1961] AC 388 (PC) 422.

[14] ibid 425.

[15] ibid.

[16] ibid.

[17] WL Prosser, 'Palsgraf Revisited' (1953) 52 *Michigan Law Review* 1, 17; JA Weir, 'Compensability of Unforeseeable Damage Resulting Directly from Negligent Acts' (1961) *Tulane Law Review* 619, 626; D Payne, 'Foresight and Remoteness of Damage in Negligence' (1962) 25 *Modern Law Review* 1, 23; HLA Hart and T Honoré, *Causation in the Law*, 2nd edn (Oxford, 1985) 259, 267–68; WVH Rogers, *Winfield and Jolowicz on Tort*, 17th edn (London, 2006) [6–25]. See also JG Fleming, 'The Passing of Polemis' (1961) 39 *Canadian Bar Rev* 489, 501–502.

[18] SR Perry, 'Responsibility for Outcomes, Risk, and the Law of Torts' in GJ Postema (ed), *Philosophy and the Law of Torts* (Cambridge, 2001) 72–130, 116–17.

[19] ibid 117.

[20] R Kidner, 'Remoteness of damage: the duty-interest theory and the re-interpretation of the Wagon Mound' (1989) 9 *Legal Studies* 1, 3.

user) and that the damage to his field was a direct consequence of the accident. Kidner considers this result odd since C, being an unforeseeable victim, cannot recover.

This last conclusion is wrong, however, if the concept of localised distributive justice is truly applied: C was innocent, whereas B was at fault in driving carelessly, and this carelessness caused the damage to C's field. Hence, B should bear C's loss. This result is, of course, even stranger than allowing only A to sue for the field damage. Moreover, if B's liability for the fire is triggered by mere carelessness on his part, it must all the more be triggered by criminal behaviour. To combine Kidner's example with one given by Seavey,[21] A and C could still sue for the damage to their fields if B drove with perfect care but had a kidnapped person in his car: The fire would not have occurred but for B's violation of the criminal law.

Results as in the last example are plainly absurd, and nobody has ever defended them, but they would be the logical consequence if no relationship between fault and damage above a purely causal connection were necessary. The instrument of avoiding these absurdities is to require, as *The Wagon Mound (No 1)* effectively did, that the defendant's fault consisted in creating a foreseeable risk of such damage as suffered by the claimant.[22]

Notwithstanding the doctrinal change of paradigm, *The Wagon Mound (No 1)* 'has made little difference to the law in terms of practical result'.[23] Indeed, Viscount Simonds himself doubted that the decision would alter the result in many cases.[24] This paradox can be explained on the ground that the notion of foreseeability is flexible enough to take account of policy considerations and value judgments.[25] Nevertheless, although the courts may still be able to produce the same outcomes as under the *Re Polemis* concept, they are now compelled to argue along the correct conceptual lines, and to explain that and why the loss in suit was foreseeable.

III Damage Versus Risk

Confining liability in negligence to foreseeable damage cannot mean that the course of events leading to the damage and the extent of the damage need to be foreseeable in all details. Such precise foreseeability is hardly ever present, and requiring it would virtually abolish the tort of negligence. The Privy Council, in *The Wagon Mound (No 1)*, made allowance for this fact and said that only the

---

[21] WA Seavey, 'Mr. Justice Cardozo and the Law of Torts' (1939) 39 *Columbia Law Review* 20, 34.
[22] EJ Weinrib, 'Restitutionary Damages as Corrective Justice' (2000) 1 *Theoretical Inquiries in Law* 1, 9–10.
[23] WVH Rogers, *Winfield and Jolowicz on Tort*, 17th edn (London, 2006) [6–23].
[24] [1961] AC 388 (PC) 422.
[25] JC Smith, *Liability in Negligence* (London, 1984) 100, 111.

kind of damage needs to be foreseeable.[26] Accordingly, the foreseeability requirement does not extend to the exact nature and the extent of the damage.[27] But the
courts have gone further, at least they did so in the first time after *The Wagon
Mound (No 1)*, and effectively extended the exemption from the foreseeability
requirement to the course of events leading to the damage. Under this concept,
an unusual and unforeseeable causal sequence does not bar recovery as long as
the damage is of a foreseeable kind.[28]

In consequence, the issue of how broad or narrow the kind of damage is to be
defined became crucial. But should liability really depend on such a technicality?
Negligence involves the creation of a foreseeable and unreasonable hazard or,
used synonymously, risk.[29] Liability should therefore be determined by the
question of whether the damage in suit resulted from the foreseeable risk that the
defendant created.[30] Of course, a risk can only be described in relation to a
certain kind of damage. The risk of smoking, for instance, can only be described
by reference to the damage that smoking might produce, such as lung cancer. But
a risk is more than potential damage. It also includes the general manner in
which this damage is likely to occur. Risk of lung cancer, for instance, would be
too vague a term in the context of negligence, for it makes a big difference
whether lung cancer is caused by smoking or by genetic disposition.

Revealingly, the superiority of considering the risk created by the defendant is
demonstrated by the very case that most prominently excluded the causal
sequence from the foreseeability requirement: *Hughes v Lord Advocate*.[31] Post
Office workers temporarily left a manhole in the road, covered only with an
unclosed tent and surrounded by burning paraffin lights. Two boys, aged eight
and ten, took one of the lamps and entered the tent. The lamp fell into the
manhole and broke. Paraffin vaporised, exploded and burnt one of the boys
badly. It could have been foreseen that children might play with a lamp and get
burnt by contact with the flame or with burning paraffin, but the explosion was
not foreseeable. Nevertheless, the House of Lords held the Post Office liable on
the ground that, as long as the type of damage (here burning) was foreseeable,
the precise chain of events is immaterial.

---

[26] [1961] AC 388 (PC) 426.

[27] eg *Vacwell Engineering Co Ltd v BDH Chemicals Ltd* [1971] 1 QB 88, 110 (Rees J): 'the
explosion and the type of damage being foreseeable, it matters not in the law that the magnitude of
the former and the extent of the latter were not'.

[28] *Hughes v Lord Advocate* 1963 SC (HL) 31 (considered in detail in the text below); MJ Tilbury,
Civil Remedies, Vol 1: Principles of Civil Remedies (Sydney, 1990) [3092].

[29] JC Smith, *Liability in Negligence* (London, 1984) 5 *passim*.

[30] M Weaver, 'The Fragile Glassware Rule or How to Take a Risk' (1970) 33 *MLR* 446, 449–50.
Risk considerations find much support in the US, see WA Seavey, 'Mr. Justice Cardozo and the Law of
Torts' (1939) 39 *Colum LRev* 20, 29–39; critically WP Keeton (gen ed), *Prosser and Keeton on the Law
of Torts*, 5th edn (St Paul, 1984) 283–84; J Stapleton, 'Legal Cause: Cause-In-Fact and the Scope of
Liability for Consequences' (2001) 54 *Vanderbilt Law Review* 941, 992–94.

[31] 1963 SC (HL) 31. Even though the appeal came from Scotland, the decision by the House of
Lords is regarded as authority for English law too: *Tomlinson v Congleton BC* [2003] UKHL 47, [2004]
1 AC 46 [44] (Lord Hoffmann).

The House of Lords thus compared the injured boy with a child that is burnt through contact to the naked flame, and regarded the difference in the causal sequence as immaterial. The desire to award compensation in that case is understandable, but the House of Lords chose the wrong way to this end. This becomes clear if one compares the victim in *Hughes* not to a child burnt through contact with the flame but to a child to whom the explosion caused an injury other than burning. Since it was crucial for their Lordships that the victim in *Hughes* was burnt, they would apparently have denied compensation for any other injury. But surely, where the same explosion causes burning to one child and, say, a broken leg to another, the question of liability must be decided identically for both children.

This demonstrates that solely focusing on the type of damage cannot produce consistent results. Also considered must be the general course of events leading to the damage, in other words, the risk involved. Lord Romer acknowledged this *obiter* in the Scottish case *Muir v Glasgow Corp*,[32] where children were injured in a shop by having an urn of hot tea spilt over them as it was being carried past them. The House of Lords denied liability on the ground that the accident had been unforeseeable. Lord Romer observed that even if it had been foreseeable that tea might be spilt due to the urn-carrier tripping or being jostled by children, there would still have been no liability had spilling been caused by an unforeseeable fall of the ceiling on the urn-carrier.

Glanville Williams has emphasised the significance of the causal chain with the following example.[33] The owner of a horse lets the horse stray on the highway. It is assumed (contrary to existing law) that this is negligent because a collision of the horse and a car can be foreseen. What then happens is that the horse unforeseeably kicks a person who goes past. Even if the same injury could have been caused through a collision, the owner of the horse is not liable because the injury resulted from a different type of causal sequence.

The crucial question in the *Hughes* situation is thus: is the risk of getting injured through contact with the flame or burning paraffin distinct from the risk of getting injured through an explosion of escaping paraffin vapour, or are these simply two forms of the same risk, namely getting injured through the improper use of paraffin lamps?[34] Whatever the answer, the outcome is the same for all children affected by the same explosion regardless of the type of injury suffered. The imposition of liability in *Hughes* can only be explained on the basis of a single, generalised risk which is by no means inconceivable. The key factor in either causal sequence is the naked flame, and the naked flame is what makes paraffin lamps so dangerous.

---

[32] 1943 SC (HL) 3, 18–19.

[33] G Williams, 'The Risk Principle' (1961) 77 *Law Quarterly Review* 179, 181–83.

[34] This question was in effect considered decisive by the Court of Session which, by majority, distinguished two separate risks and denied liability: 1961 SC 310.

Within a year of *Hughes*, the Court of Appeal, in *Doughty v Turner Manufac-turing Co Ltd*,[35] acknowledged that the manner in which damage of foreseeable kind occurred cannot be ignored. A worker in the defendant's foundry inadvert-ently knocked the loose asbestos cement cover of a cauldron into the molten metal in the cauldron. Due to an unforeseeable chemical reaction between the cover and the metal, the molten liquid erupted and injured the plaintiff. Since it was foreseeable that the cover may fall into the cauldron and cause the hot liquid to splash onto persons nearby, the type of injury suffered, namely burning by molten metal, was foreseeable. Nevertheless, the Court of Appeal denied liability, distinguishing *Hughes* (though the basis remains unclear). Diplock LJ based his judgment expressly on the consideration of risks: causing the liquid to splash was a different risk from causing a chemical explosion.[36] Similarly, Lord Pearce held that the chemical explosion was not a variant of splashing but a new and unexpected factor.[37] Harman LJ said that 'the damage here was of an entirely different kind from the foreseeable splash'.[38] Even though he used the notion 'kind of damage', it is clear from his judgment that he too distinguished between two different risks.

The risk concept can also reconcile the seemingly conflicting categorisations of damage by the courts. In *Page v Smith*,[39] the House of Lords held, by majority, that the foreseeability of bodily injury triggers liability for an unforeseeable psychiatric illness even if bodily injury was not in fact suffered. Even though the House of Lords has meanwhile restricted this principle to psychiatric harm resulting from a fear of instant physical harm, as opposed to a fear of developing a long-term illness in future,[40] *Page v Smith* might still be taken as authority for the proposition that all personal injuries, physical or psychiatric, are of the same kind. In *Tremain v Pike*,[41] by contrast, Payne J had refused to regard even all human illnesses caused by rats as the same kind of damage. He distinguished between diseases spread by rats' urine on the one hand, and rat-bites and the effects of consuming food contaminated by rats on the other. Under an approach that solely focuses on the kind of damage, these two cases are irreconcilable and *Page v Smith* must be taken to have impliedly overruled *Tremain v Pike*.

A consideration of the risks involved can perfectly harmonise these two cases. It is possible to regard the risk of contracting a disease through contact with rats'

---

[35] [1964] 1 QB 518 (CA).
[36] ibid 529–30.
[37] ibid 527.
[38] ibid 529.
[39] [1996] AC 155 (HL) especially 197 (Lord Lloyd). Followed, eg, in *Donachie v Chief Constable of Greater Manchester* [2004] EWCA Civ 405 [11]; *Simmons v British Steel plc* [2004] UKHL 20, 2004 SC (HL) 94 [21], [67].
[40] *Rothwell v Chemical & Insulating Co Ltd, sub nom Grieves v FT Everard & Sons Ltd* [2007] UKHL 39, [2008] 1 AC 281 especially [55], [95].
[41] [1969] 1 WLR 1556, 1561.

urine as distinct from the risk of getting bitten by rats or consuming contaminated food. There is a significant difference in the way human health is affected and accordingly in the kind of precautions necessary.[42] What happened in *Page v Smith* was that the defendant suddenly drove his car onto the wrong side of the road into the plaintiff's path, making a frontal collision at a speed of 30 mph inevitable. Such action creates the risk of numerous physical illnesses. Given the frightening experience of facing a frontal collision and the correlation between physical health and mental well-being, it also creates the risk of various psychological illnesses, including, what in fact happened, the recurrence of the chronic fatigue syndrome. It is therefore justified to say that causing a frontal car collision creates the risk of any personal injury.[43]

The concept of considering the risk rather than the type of damage alone seems to be on the advance, as indicated by *Jolley v Sutton LBC*.[44] The defendant council left an abandoned and rotten cabin cruiser lying in the grounds of a block of council flats. It was foreseeable that children might climb onto the boat and get injured by the rotten planks giving way. What in fact happened was that two young teenage boys jacked the boat up in order to repair it. When one of them was working underneath the boat, it fell on him and he suffered spinal injuries. Under the *Hughes* concept it would have been decisive whether these injuries were of the same kind as injuries sustained by falling through rotten planks. Instead, the courts asked whether the type of accident could have been foreseen or, synonymously, whether the accident fell within the foreseeable risk created by the council (with the House of Lords giving an affirmative answer).

In conclusion, what needs to be foreseeable is not only the type of damage but also the type of risk leading to the damage. However, since the foreseeability of the risk becomes relevant only in the rare case of an unusual causal sequence, the foreseeability of the type of damage is a shorthand test sufficient to resolve the vast majority of cases. For the purpose of comparing tort with contract and equity, where unusual causal sequences are rarer still, it is unnecessary to depart from the parlance of referring to the type of damage.

---

[42] This was pointed out by Payne J in *Tremain v Pike* [1969] 1 WLR 1556, 1561, which proves that, although he spoke of 'kinds of damage', he in truth distinguished kinds of risk. Since he regarded as relevant the general foreseeability of the causal sequence leading to the damage, *Tremain v Pike* is irreconcilable with *Hughes v Lord Advocate*. M Weaver, 'The Fragile Glassware Rule or How to Take a Risk' (1970) 33 *MLR* 446, 450.

[43] See also *Bradford v Robinson Rentals Ltd* [1967] 1 WLR 337. The plaintiff was told by his employer to drive 500 miles in freezing weather conditions in a van without heater. During the journey a window had to be kept open to prevent ice forming on the windscreen. The plaintiff suffered permanent injury to his hands and feet through frostbite. Frostbite was not foreseeable, but common cold, chilblains and pneumonia were. Rees J considered whether frostbite belonged to the type of injury that could have been foreseen. He answered this question in the affirmative by saying (at 346) that the plaintiff had been exposed 'to a reasonably foreseeable risk of injury arising from exposure to severe cold and fatigue'.

[44] [2000] 1 WLR 1082 (HL).

IV Degree of Foresight Required

What degree of probability does the tort of negligence require for damage to be reasonably foreseeable?[45] Two cases deliver the answer, one being *Bolton v Stone*.[46] A cricket ball was driven out of the ground onto an adjacent street where it struck and severely injured a woman. On that side of the cricket ground, the top of the fence stood seventeen feet above the level of the pitch. In previous years balls had been struck over the fence on rare occasions, but damage had never been caused. The House of Lords denied liability on the ground that although the possibility of balls being hit onto the street might have been foreseen, the risk of injury to anyone was so remote that a reasonable person would not have anticipated it.

The second case is *Overseas Tankship (UK) Ltd v Miller Steamship Co Pty Ltd (The Wagon Mound [No 2])*,[47] which arose out of the same facts as *The Wagon Mound (No 1)*.[48] The defendant was again the charterer of the ship *Wagon Mound*, who this time was sued by the owners of the two ships damaged in the fire. The findings of fact in this case differed slightly, but significantly, from those in the first *Wagon Mound* litigation. With regard to the risk of fire created by the spillage of furnace oil into the harbour, the trial judge concluded that reasonable people in the defendant's position would have regarded this risk as 'a possibility, but one which could become an actuality only in very exceptional circumstances'.[49]

The Privy Council found this sufficient to hold the defendant liable in negligence. Lord Reid, speaking for the board, saw no conflict with *Bolton v Stone* (where he had also sat on the bench). That case, he said, did not completely rule out liability for creating risks of small magnitude. It merely recognised that a reasonable person may disregard a small risk because, for instance, 'it would involve considerable expense to eliminate the risk'.[50] But where, as in the instant case, the elimination of the risk 'presented no difficulty, involved no disadvantage, and required no expense', it was a risk that a reasonable person 'would not brush aside as far-fetched'.[51]

---

[45] The present study deals with this question in the context of breach of duty and remoteness only. At a more abstract level, the foreseeability of damage influences the imposition of a duty of care. For the different stages see D Harris, 'Remoteness' in D Harris, D Campbell and R Halson, *Remedies in Contract and Tort*, 2nd edn (London, 2002) 315–16.

[46] [1951] AC 850 (HL).

[47] [1967] 1 AC 617 (PC).

[48] [1961] AC 388 (PC); above II in this chapter. *The Wagon Mound (No 1)* gave no guidance as to the degree of foresight required. Viscount Simonds said (at 422–23) that probable consequences are foreseeable, but it is not clear whether he intended to say that *only* probable consequences are foreseeable: JG Fleming, 'The Passing Of Polemis' (1961) 39 *Can Bar Rev* 489, 515–16.

[49] [1963] 1 Lloyd's Rep 402, 426 (Walsh J).

[50] [1967] 1 AC 617 (PC) 642.

[51] ibid 643–44.

As the two cases demonstrate, the qualification of an act as negligent is not solely dependent on the degree of probability with which damage can be foreseen. Also important are the gravity of the foreseeable damage, the cost of preventing the risk, and the utility of the act in question.[52] *Bolton v Stone* concerned the socially desirable activity of playing cricket, and the extremely small risk of injury to passers-by could only have been eliminated by raising the fence or quitting the game altogether.[53] In *The Wagon Mound (No 2)*, by contrast, the spilling of the oil into the harbour did not save great expenses and was even an offence. The difference between the two cases lies not in the degree of probability with which damage could be foreseen, but in the reasonableness of the conduct creating the risk.

The Wagon Mound (No 2) further laid down that a low degree of probability with which damage could be foreseen suffices for liability in negligence. Considering that liability also requires the unreasonableness of the risk created, it is indeed neither necessary nor desirable to erect a 'probability threshold'. It is not necessary because the reasonableness of the risk may exclude liability where the probability of damage was low, as in *Bolton v Stone*. It is not desirable because there should be liability, even if the probability of damage was low, where the magnitude of the damage was great and the cost of avoiding it minimal, as in *The Wagon Mound (No 2)*.

Picking up Lord Reid's phrase in *The Wagon Mound (No 2)*, Lord Upjohn stated in *The Heron II* that a negligent actor 'is liable for any damage which he can reasonably foresee may happen as a result of the breach however unlikely it may be, unless it can be brushed aside as far fetched'.[54] This test, still used by the House of Lords and the Privy Council,[55] solely determines liability where the unreasonableness of the defendant's conduct is in no doubt, in particular where liability for the initial injury has been established and ulterior harm remains to be considered.[56]

---

[52] eg *Walker v Northumberland CC* [1995] 1 All ER 737, 750.

[53] Where injury is frequent, the club will be liable: *Miller v Jackson* [1977] QB 966 (CA).

[54] *Koufos v C Czarnikow Ltd (The Heron II)* [1969] 1 AC 350 (HL) 422. To the same effect, Lord Reid said (at 385–86): 'The defendant will be liable for any type of damage which is reasonably foreseeable as liable to happen even in the most unusual case, unless the risk is so small that a reasonable man would in the whole circumstances feel justified in neglecting it'. See also below ch 3, III.

[55] *Attorney-General of the British Virgin Islands v Hartwell* [2004] UKPC 12, [2004] 1 WLR 1273 [21]; *Rothwell v Chemical & Insulating Co Ltd, sub nom Grieves v FT Everard & Sons Ltd* [2007] UKHL 39, [2008] 1 AC 281 [29] (Lord Hoffmann).

[56] JG Fleming, 'The Passing Of Polemis' (1961) 39 *Can Bar Rev* 489, 511–12.

V The 'Thin Skull' Rule

It has long been established that a tortfeasor is still liable for the whole of the victim's damage even if the amount of the damage has been increased by an extraordinary susceptibility on the victim's part,[57] the leading example being an unusually thin skull.[58] This principle, it should be noted, is only concerned with the extent of liability, not with the question of culpability. Liability in negligence requires the foreseeability of either damage to people of normal condition[59] or of the individual victim's extraordinary susceptibility.[60] In *Bourhill v Young*, Lord Wright coined the phrase that 'if the wrong is established, the wrongdoer must take the victim as he finds him'.[61]

Since *The Wagon Mound (No 1)*[62] laid down that the foreseeability test governs not only the question of culpability but also the extent of liability in negligence, the 'thin skull' rule has still been applied in negligence cases. It was applied, for instance, where a small burn of the lower lip turned to cancer due to a pre-malignant condition of the tissue,[63] where the pricking of a finger by poisoned wire resulted in the worsening of the sight of one eye which was already in an ulcerated condition,[64] and where a minor graze led to encephalitis because the injured suffered an allergic reaction to an anti-tetanus serum.[65] In these cases, the further injuries resulting from the victim's special susceptibility were seen as part of the initial injury so that the foreseeability of the latter founded liability for the whole damage.[66] While this is a possible explanation for why the 'thin skull' rule has survived *The Wagon Mound (No 1)*, it actually renders the rule redundant,[67] for within the same type of foreseeable damage liability extends to all direct consequences anyway.

---

[57] *Dulieu v White & Sons* [1901] 2 KB 669, 679; *Owens v Liverpool Corp* [1939] 1 KB 394 (CA) 400–401; *Bourhill v Young* [1943] AC 92 (HL) 109; *Love v Port of London Authority* [1959] 2 Lloyd's Rep 541.

[58] 'If a man is negligently run over or otherwise negligently injured in his body it is no answer to the sufferer's claim for damages that he would have suffered less injury ... if he had not had an unusually thin skull or an unusually weak heart': *Dulieu v White & Sons* [1901] 2 KB 669, 679 (Kennedy J). Ironically, cases actually involving thin skulls are hard to find: AM Linden, 'Down With Foreseeability! Of Thin Skulls and Rescuers' (1969) 47 *Can Bar Rev* 545, 550–51.

[59] *Bourhill v Young* [1943] AC 92 (HL) 110; *McLaughlin v Trimmer* (1946) 79 Ll L Rep 649–50; *Cook v Swinfen* [1967] 1 WLR 457 (CA) 461–62 (Lord Denning MR).

[60] *Haley v London Electricity Board* [1965] AC 778 (HL); *Cook v Swinfen* [1967] 1 WLR 457 (CA) 461–62 (Lord Denning MR).

[61] [1943] AC 92 (HL) 109–10.

[62] [1961] AC 388 (PC). Above II in this chapter.

[63] *Smith v Leech Brain & Co Ltd* [1962] 2 QB 405.

[64] *Warren v Scruttons Ltd* [1962] 1 Lloyd's Rep 497.

[65] *Robinson v Post Office* [1974] 1 WLR 1176 (CA). Further examples are *Lines v Harland & Wolff Ltd* [1966] 2 Lloyd's Rep 400; *Bradford v Robinson Rentals Ltd* [1967] 1 WLR 337, 346; *Wieland v Cyril Lord Carpets Ltd* [1969] 3 All ER 1006, 1010.

[66] This view is shared by H McGregor, *McGregor on Damages*, 18th edn (London, 2009) [6–091], [6–095]; MJ Tilbury, *Civil Remedies, Vol 1: Principles of Civil Remedies* (Sydney, 1990) [3094].

[67] PJ Rowe, 'The Demise of the Thin Skull Rule?' (1977) 40 *MLR* 377, 387–88.

Some commentators suggest that the foreseeability requirement and the 'thin skull' rule collide, and that the latter should be seen as an exception to the former.[68] As a matter of precedent, this solution would be possible[69] since the Privy Council in *The Wagon Mound (No 1)* did not mention the 'thin skull' rule and thus had apparently no intention of making an inroad into it.[70] However, since the foreseeability requirement is of fundamental importance,[71] any real exception to it needs compelling reasons.

Glanville Williams sees such a reason in the fragility of human bodies and the precariousness of human life.[72] But these factors relate to the prevention of injuries in the first place, not to the extent of liability once an injury has been inflicted; injuries can never be repaired by an award of damages.[73] The fragility of human bodies and the precariousness of human life could only be used to establish a general duty of care towards hypersensitive persons. But nobody goes that far. All are agreed that it would be too great a restraint on human conduct if the effect of one's actions upon hypersensitive persons had to be considered.[74]

Others reconcile the 'thin skull' rule with the foreseeability requirement by suggesting that abnormalities can always be foreseen as possible (although not probable): 'We all know that the average man is not necessarily the average man.'[75] This argument too faces the objection that it must equally apply to the initial injury and thus to the question of culpability. This is true but foreseeability of the risk created does not alone establish liability. Another requirement is the unreasonableness of creating that risk.[76] Since it is commonplace that the general possibility of meeting hypersensitive persons may be left out of account, a risk is reasonable unless an injury to people of normal condition or to a particular hypersensitive individual can be foreseen.

The problem with explaining the 'thin skull' rule as a simple application of the foreseeability test is that although the degree of foresight required in negligence is very low, it still excludes liability for consequences that could 'be brushed aside as far fetched'.[77] Abnormal conditions addressed by the 'thin skull' rule may be so rare that they can indeed be brushed aside as far fetched. On balance, therefore,

---

[68] A Burrows, *Remedies for Torts and Breach of Contract*, 3rd edn (Oxford, 2004) 80; HLA Hart and T Honoré, *Causation in the Law*, 2nd edn (Oxford, 1985) 274.

[69] *Stephenson v Waite Tileman Ltd* [1973] 1 NZLR 152 (NZCA) 165 (Richmond J).

[70] This was considered crucial in *Smith v Leech Brain & Co Ltd* [1962] 2 QB 405, 414–15.

[71] Above II in this chapter.

[72] G Williams, 'The Risk Principle' (1961) 77 *LQR* 179, 196.

[73] RWM Dias, 'Remoteness of Liability and Legal Policy' [1962] *Cambridge LJ* 178, 186.

[74] G Williams, 'The Risk Principle' (1961) 77 *LQR* 179, 195.

[75] AL Goodhart, *Essays in Jurisprudence and the Common Law* (Cambridge, 1937) 127. See also WVH Rogers, *Winfield and Jolowicz on Tort*, 17th edn (London, 2006) [6–32]; AM Linden, 'Down With Foreseeability! Of Thin Skulls and Rescuers' (1969) 47 *Can Bar Rev* 545, 557, who adds that the 'thin skull' rule is mainly based on policy grounds which may be obscured by solely focusing on foreseeability.

[76] Above IV in this chapter.

[77] ibid; *Koufos v C Czarnikow Ltd (The Heron II)* [1969] 1 AC 350 (HL) 422 (Lord Upjohn).

the best way to reconcile the 'thin skull' rule with the foreseeability requirement is an incorporation of the rule into the distinction between the type of damage and its extent, as done by the courts.

What is the scope of the 'thin skull' rule? From bodily susceptibility the rule has spread to mental susceptibility.[78] It should also apply to property damage where clear authority is absent.[79] A distinction between abnormally vulnerable persons and abnormally vulnerable things would be inexplicable.[80] It has been objected that an application of the 'thin skull' rule to property damage would re-introduce the *Re Polemis*[81] principle through the backdoor since the existence of petrol vapour in the hold of a ship could be regarded as a special susceptibility of the ship.[82] But the 'thin skull' rule applies only to characteristics of things, not to their areal position. Finally, financial weakness cannot be treated differently from the weakness of human bodies or things. Loss due to the victim's impecuniosity must be recoverable.[83] The House of Lords acknowledged this in *Lagden v O'Connor*,[84] overruling *The Liesbosch*.[85]

Closely related to the 'thin skull' rule is the 'true value' rule according to which liability in tort extends to the whole damage where property destroyed has an unusually high value or where the victim's loss of income is unusually high due to the victim's unusually high earning-capacity.[86] Since in these situations damage and risk are foreseeable in kind,[87] the 'true value' rule has survived *The Wagon Mound (No 1)*. It relates to the calculation of damage rather than remoteness.[88]

---

[78] *Owens v Liverpool Corp* [1939] 1 KB 394 (CA) 400–401; *Malcolm v Broadhurst* [1970] 3 All ER 508, 511, where Geoffrey Lane J saw 'no difference in principle between an egg-shell skull and an egg-shell personality'; *Page v Smith* [1996] AC 155 (HL).

[79] PJ Rowe, 'The Demise of the Thin Skull Rule?' (1977) 40 *MLR* 377, 381.

[80] JG Fleming, *The Law of Torts*, 9th edn (Sydney, 1998) 236; H McGregor, *McGregor on Damages*, 18th edn (London, 2009) [6–090]; MA Jones, 'Causation in Tort: General Principles' in AM Dugdale and MA Jones, *Clerk & Lindsell on Torts*, 19th edn (London, 2006) [2–138].

[81] [1921] 3 KB 560 (CA); above II in this chapter.

[82] G Williams, 'The Risk Principle' (1961) 77 *LQR* 179, 194–95; R Kidner, 'Remoteness of damage: the duty-interest theory and the re-interpretation of the Wagon Mound' (1989) 9 *LS* 1, 12.

[83] B Coote, 'Damages, The Liesbosch, and Impecuniosity' [2001] *Camb LJ* 511, 534–35; H McGregor, *McGregor on Damages*, 18th edn (London, 2009) [6–111].

[84] [2003] UKHL 64, [2004] 1 AC 1067.

[85] *Owners of Dredger Liesbosch v Owners of Steamship Edison (The Liesbosch)* [1933] AC 449 (HL). *The Liesbosch* had already been doubted in *Dodd Properties Ltd v Canterbury City Council* [1980] 1 WLR 433 (CA); *Perry v Sidney Phillips & Son* [1982] 1 WLR 1297 (CA).

[86] *Locus classicus* is *Smith v London and South Western Railway Co* (1870) LR 6 CP 14, 22–23 (Blackburn J): 'if a person fires across a road when it is dangerous to do so and kills a man who is in the receipt of a large income, he will be liable for the whole damage'. In *The Arpad (No 2)* [1934] P 189 (CA) 202–203, Scrutton LJ gave the example of injuring the favourite for the Derby.

[87] G Williams, 'The Risk Principle' (1961) 77 *LQR* 179, 197.

[88] PJ Rowe, 'The Demise of the Thin Skull Rule?' (1977) 40 *MLR* 377, 378.

VI   The 'Scope Of The Duty' Concept

While damage of an unforeseeable type cannot be recovered in negligence,[89] the reverse is not true. Damage of a foreseeable type may still be irrecoverable on the ground that it lies outside the scope of the duty breached. This was highlighted by the House of Lords in *South Australia Asset Management Corp v York Montague Ltd (SAAMCO)*, *sub nom Banque Bruxelles Lambert SA v Eagle Star Insurance Co Ltd*.[90]

SAAMCO consolidated several cases with the same factual setting. A lender instructed a valuer to value property on the security of which the lender was considering to advance money on mortgage. Due to carelessness, the valuer considerably overvalued the property. The loan was made, which it would not have been had the lender known the true value of the property. Subsequently the borrower defaulted. The property was sold but it brought much less than its value at the time of the valuation because in the meantime the property market had fallen substantially. The lender sued the valuer for negligence and breach of contract, and claimed as damages the outstanding loan less net recovery from the realisation of the security. The valuer was only prepared to pay the difference between the value indicated in the valuation report and the property's true value at that time, but not the extra loss attributable to market fall.

The Court of Appeal held that where the lender would not have entered into the transaction with the borrower but for the overvaluation, the valuer's liability extends to the loss attributable to a fall in the property market because such fall is foreseeable and is no intervening cause.[91] Reversing that decision, the House of Lords confined liability to the difference between the valuation and the true value of the property at the date of valuation.[92] Lord Hoffmann, speaking for the House, said that in an action for breach of a duty imposed by law (contract, tort or statute) it must be shown that the duty was owed to the claimant and that it was a duty in respect of the kind of loss occurred.[93] The scope of the duty is determined by the purpose of the rule (statute, tort or contractual term) imposing the duty.[94] The valuer had the duty, identical in contract and tort, to make a correct valuation of the property, and is only liable for the (foreseeable) loss attributable to the inaccuracy of the valuation.[95]

---

[89]   Subject to the 'thin skull' rule if this rule is seen as an exception to the foreseeability criterion: above V in this chapter.

[90]   [1995] QB 375 (CA); [1997] AC 191 (HL). The name of the case was *Banque Bruxelles* before the Court of Appeal and *South Australia* before the House of Lords. Widely used is the acronym *SAAMCO*.

[91]   [1995] QB 375 (CA).

[92]   [1997] AC 191 (HL).

[93]   ibid 211.

[94]   ibid 212.

[95]   ibid 212–15.

Lord Hoffmann illustrated the role played by the purpose of the breached rule with the following example.[96] A mountaineer about to undertake a difficult climb consults his doctor as to the fitness of his knee. The doctor negligently pronounces the knee fit. The climber goes on the expedition, which he would not have undertaken had he known the true state of his knee. He suffers an injury that is an entirely foreseeable consequence of mountaineering but has nothing to do with his knee. On the Court of Appeal's principle, the doctor is liable for the injury, for if he had given correct information, the mountaineer would not have undertaken the expedition and would have suffered no injury. But this result is wrong because the injury would have occurred even if the doctor's advice had been correct, and because the doctor was asked for information on the knee only and not on other safety factors.

SAAMCO was not the first case, not even the first concerning misstatements, to tie liability in negligence to the scope of the duty breached.[97] But it moved the 'scope of the duty' concept into the limelight, triggering both its hypertrophic application in actions for negligent misstatements or negligent failures to give correct information[98] and fierce scholarly criticism.[99] The main thrust of the criticism is directed, however, not against the 'scope of the duty' concept as such but against Lord Hoffmann's approach of restoring the lender to the position it would have been in had the valuation been correct, that is, had the property actually been of the value stated.[100] This is not the place to scrutinise Lord Hoffmann's calculation in detail. The present interest lies in the general validity of the 'scope of the duty' concept. As a demonstration of how the concept may work in the *SAAMCO* scenario, the following sketchy remarks must suffice.

The key question in the *SAAMCO* situation is the following: did the valuer's duty to give a correct valuation aim to assist the lender solely in its decision on *how much* to loan, or also on its decision on *whether* to loan at all?[101] If the duty is considered confined to the question of 'how much', and this is what the House of Lords effectively said, then the lender made its decision on the question of 'whether' at its own risk and has to bear the consequences of the market decline. For the purpose of calculating the loss recoverable, it must therefore be assumed that the lender, if told the true value of the property, would still have advanced a

---

[96] ibid 213–14.

[97] 'It is never sufficient to ask simply whether A owes B a duty of care. It is always necessary to determine the scope of the duty by reference to the kind of damage from which A must take care to save B harmless': *Caparo Industries v Dickman* [1990] 2 AC 605 (HL) 627 (Lord Bridge). In that case, the liability of auditors for inaccurate reports was limited by carefully examining the scope of their duty of care.

[98] eg the cases cited in A Burrows, *Remedies for Torts and Breach of Contract*, 3rd edn (Oxford, 2004) 117 fns 7–11.

[99] eg A Burrows, ibid 112–22; J Stapleton, 'Negligent Valuers and Falls in the Property Market' (1997) 113 *LQR* 1–7.

[100] [1997] AC 191 (HL) 213 ff.

[101] E Peel, 'SAAMCO Revisited' in A Burrows and E Peel (eds), *Commercial Remedies: Current Issues and Problems* (Oxford, 2003) 58.

loan, although, of course, of a lesser amount. Since the hypothetical loan would, in a stable market, have been covered by the proceeds of the sale of the property, the loss recoverable by the lender is the difference in amount between the hypothetical loan and the actual loan. The amount of the hypothetical loan should be determined by considering which percentage of the property's stated value was given as a loan, and appling this percentage to the property's true value.

An attack on the 'scope of the duty' concept that goes beyond the valuation scenario while perhaps still being confined to misstatements is launched by Burrows who argues on the basis of Lord Hoffmann's mountaineer example that the concept is neither necessary nor sufficient to achieve correct results.[102] It is not necessary because an exoneration of the doctor from liability can also be achieved by regarding the event injuring the mountaineer (for instance rock-fall or avalanche) as an intervening event breaking the chain of causation. The 'scope of the duty' concept is not sufficient because, since Lord Hoffmann exonerated the doctor on the ground that the same injury would have happened even if the advice 'the knee is fine' had been correct,[103] his approach alone renders the doctor liable where the mountaineer's knee swells up and a rock-fall injures him while being carried down on a stretcher. Here causation doctrine is needed to achieve the still correct exoneration of the doctor.

Burrows' assertion that Lord Hoffmann's pointing to the mountaineer's knee being fit would render the doctor liable where the knee swells up, is not necessarily correct as Lord Hoffmann's other justification for exonerating the doctor, namely that the doctor was asked for information on the knee only and not on other safety factors, still applies. In any event, the doctor must be exonerated if the 'scope of the duty' concept is applied properly. The injuries that the doctor's duty to give proper advice on the knee aims to prevent are only those resulting from the knee being swollen, not those resulting from the fact that the patient, because of the swollen knee, is at a particular place at a particular time.

Burrows' assertion that all results achieved under the scope of the duty concept can also be achieved under causation doctrine might be true. But the latter leads back to the former: What, other than the scope of the duty breached, can determine whether or not a particular event breaks the chain of causation? Indeed, as Burrows himself demonstrates,[104] a break in the chain of causation has often been denied on the ground that it was the purpose of the duty broken to guard against the event in question.[105] Conversely, cases recognising a break in the chain of causation have effectively said that it was *not* the purpose of the duty

---

[102] A Burrows, *Remedies for Torts and Breach of Contract*, 3rd edn (Oxford, 2004) 114. He accepts (at 116) the concept with regard to breach of statutory duty, considered below VII in this chapter.

[103] [1997] AC 191 (HL) 213.

[104] A Burrows, *Remedies for Torts and Breach of Contract*, 3rd edn (Oxford, 2004) 99–101.

[105] 'Of course, if a duty of care is imposed to guard against deliberate wrongdoing by others, it can hardly be said that the harmful effects of such wrongdoing are not caused by such breach of duty': *Smith v Littlewoods Organisation Ltd* [1987] AC 241 (HL) 272 (Lord Goff).

breached to guard against the event in question. In *Aneco Reinsurance Underwriting Ltd v Johnson & Higgins Ltd*, Evans LJ observed with regard to *SAAMCO* and subsequent cases applying it: 'These authorities mean that the former search for an effective cause has been replaced by an inquiry into the scope of the duty of care which was owed by the defendant to the claimant in the particular case'.[106]

Some commentators regard the 'scope of the duty' concept as a novel liability-limiting device that is additional to, and separate from, causation and remoteness doctrine.[107] It is submitted, however, that the 'scope of the duty' concept constitutes the 'mother' of those other doctrines. The law imposes duties in order to prevent certain loss from occurring. Once a breach of duty has otherwise been established, the key question is whether the duty in question aims at preventing the type of loss in question.[108] Whether this question is asked before the basic measure formula—the claimant is to be put in as good a position as if the wrong had not occurred[109]—is applied[110] or vice versa,[111] should be immaterial. Causation, mitigation and remoteness doctrine may be regarded as refined devices assisting in determining the scope of the duty. A tortious (or contractual) duty does not generally aim to prevent loss that has not been caused by the (alleged) breach of duty,[112] or loss that could have been avoided by the claimant, or loss that was unforeseeable.[113] But the scope of the duty remains the overriding criterion to which the refined doctrines must yield.

---

[106] [1999] CLC 1918 (CA) [20]. Furthermore, causation doctrine has been invoked to hold that auditors who negligently fail to reveal the insolvency of a company are not liable for any loss the company incurs in continuing to trade: *Galoo Ltd v Bright Grahame Murray* [1994] 1 WLR 1360 (CA); *Alexander v Cambridge Credit Co* (1987) 9 NSWLR 310 (NSWCA). With regard to these cases, Langley J said in *Equitable Life Assurance Society v Ernst & Young* [2003] EWHC 112 (Comm), [2003] PNLR 23 [85]: 'The decisions were based on want of causation but as Lord Hoffmann himself has pointed out (lecture to the Chancery Bar Association June 15, 1999) the same result might (even might better) have been reached by application of the "scope of duty" concept'. See also H McGregor, *McGregor on Damages*, 18th edn (London, 2009) [6–135].

[107] A Burrows, *Remedies for Torts and Breach of Contract*, 3rd edn (Oxford, 2004) 109–10, 113; D Harris, 'Remoteness' in D Harris, D Campbell and R Halson, *Remedies in Contract and Tort*, 2nd edn (London, 2002) 321.

[108] E Peel, 'SAAMCO Revisited' in A Burrows and E Peel (eds), *Commercial Remedies: Current Issues and Problems* (Oxford, 2003) 66–67.

[109] Above ch 1, IV.

[110] 'Before one can consider the principle on which one should calculate the damages to which a plaintiff is entitled as compensation for loss, it is necessary to decide for what kind of loss he is entitled to compensation. A correct description of the loss for which the valuer is liable must precede any consideration of the measure of damages': *SAAMCO* [1997] AC 191 (HL) 211 (Lord Hoffmann).

[111] H McGregor, *McGregor on Damages*, 18th edn (London, 2009) [1–022], [4–010]; A Burrows, *Remedies for Torts and Breach of Contract*, 3rd edn (Oxford, 2004) 110 fn 9.

[112] *Calvert v William Hill Credit Ltd* [2008] EWCA Civ 1427, [2009] Ch 330 [45]; A Kramer, 'Proximity as principles: Directness, community norms and the tort of negligence' (2003) 11 *Tort Law Review* 70,100–103. A clear separation between the causal inquiry and the scope inquiry is favoured by HLA Hart and T Honoré, *Causation in the Law*, 2nd edn (Oxford, 1985) lii.

[113] 'Loss which is not the reasonably foreseeable consequence of the breach of duty is, as a matter of policy, outwith the scope of the defendant's liability': *Bank of Tokyo-Mitsubishi UFJ Ltd v Başkan Gida Sanayi Ve Pazarlama AS* [2009] EWHC 1276 (Ch) [1010] (Briggs J).

Turning to remoteness of damage in negligence, the foreseeability test is a device of determining the scope of a duty of care in the usual case. The tort of negligence exists in order to prevent the creation of foreseeable risks. Where an act creates a foreseeable and an unforeseeable risk at the same time, the actor will not be liable for the consequences of the unforeseeable risk because the actor had no duty to guard against those consequences. It is but a semantic difference whether unforeseeable damage is described as being too remote or as falling outside the scope of the duty breached.[114] But the scope of the duty remains the overriding criterion and may bar recovery even for foreseeable damage, as Lord Hoffmann's mountaineer example illustrates. This may have been recognised in cases in which it was asked whether the damage in suit had resulted from the foreseeable risk against which it had been the defendant's duty to guard.[115]

VII   Torts Other Than Negligence

It has long been recognised that loss caused by a breach of statutory duty cannot be recovered unless it is loss of a type that the duty aims to prevent.[116] *SAAMCO*[117] highlighted that the same applies to duties at common law. Liability in tort therefore depends on the following question: 'In respect of what risks or damage does the law seek to afford protection by means of the particular tort?'[118] This is not the place to discuss the purpose of every single tort. What should be noted though is that the ambit of protection afforded by a tort may go beyond the primarily protected interest and include consequential injury to other interests.[119] For instance, the torts of defamation and trespass to the person aim to

---

[114]   J Cartwright, 'Remoteness of Damage in Contract and Tort: A Reconsideration' [1996] *Camb LJ* 488, 499; R Oppenheim, 'The "Mosaic" Of Tort Law: The Duty Of Care Question' [2003] *Journal of Personal Injury Law* 151, 158; J Stapleton, 'Negligent Valuers and Falls in the Property Market' (1997) 113 *LQR* 1, 7. The conceptual separation between duty of care and remoteness was already doubted in *Spartan Steel & Alloys Ltd v Martin & Co (Contractors) Ltd* [1973] QB 27 (CA) 37 (Lord Denning MR).

[115]   *Jebson v Ministry of Defence* [2000] 1 WLR 2055 (CA) [26]; *Darby v National Trust* [2001] EWCA Civ 189, [2001] PIQR P27 [22]–[25].

[116]   *Gorris v Scott* (1874) LR 9 Ex 125; *Nicholls v F Austin (Leyton) Ltd* [1946] AC 493 (HL); *Close v Steel Co of Wales Ltd* [1962] AC 367 (HL); *Sparrow v Fairey Aviation Co Ltd* [1964] AC 1019 (HL); *Blue Circle Industries plc v Ministry of Defence* [1999] Ch 289 (CA) 313.

[117]   *South Australia Asset Management Corp v York Montague Ltd* [1997] AC 191 (HL); above VI in this chapter.

[118]   *Kuwait Airways Corp v Iraqi Airways Co (Nos 4 and 5)* [2002] UKHL 19, [2002] 2 AC 883, 1066 [71] (Lord Nicholls). Some old dicta suggested an extension of liability beyond the protected interests; eg in *Horton v Colwyn Bay* [1908] 1 KB 327 (CA) 341 (Buckley LJ). These dicta were already rejected in *Spartan Steel & Alloys Ltd v Martin & Co (Contractors) Ltd* [1973] QB 27 (CA) 35 (Lord Denning MR), 49 (Lawton LJ).

[119]   H McGregor, *McGregor on Damages*, 18th edn (London, 2009) [6–120]–[6–129].

protect, respectively, reputation and bodily integrity, but they also guard against loss, pecuniary and otherwise, that flows from an injury to the primarily protected interest.[120]

The purpose of the particular tort must also decide whether liability requires foreseeability of the damage. Again, here is not the place to examine every single tort, and some general remarks must suffice. Prior to *The Wagon Mound (No 1)*,[121] which confined liability in negligence to foreseeable damage, the Court of Appeal had already held that a victim of conversion who has entered into an unusually profitable contract on the goods may recover more than their market value only if the defendant could have anticipated the extra loss.[122] Since *The Wagon Mound (No 1)* the foreseeability requirement has been confirmed for (innocent[123]) conversion[124] and has spread to nuisance,[125] to the rule in *Rylands v Fletcher*,[126] and to the liability of the originator of a defamatory statement for repetitions.[127] These developments seem to indicate that the foreseeablity requirement is advancing through the law of torts.[128] Indeed, Cartwright calls it the default rule.[129] It further shows that the strict nature of liability does not necessarily entail liability for unforeseeable damage.[130] Strict liability merely means that there can be liability even though the actor takes all reasonable precautions. An expansion of the foreseeability requirement to statutory strict liability is thus possible but always subject to the purpose of the particular statute.[131]

Damage intended by a tortfeasor will rarely qualify as unforeseeable. Even where intended damage was, exceptionally, unforeseeable, the tortfeasor will still

---

[120]   eg *The Gleaner Co Ltd v Abrahams* [2003] UKPC 55, [2004] 1 AC 628 [56] (for defamation); *Boodoosingh v Ramnarace* [2005] UKPC 9 [4] (for trespass to the person); R Stevens, *Torts and Rights* (Oxford, 2007) 25.

[121]   [1961] AC 388 (PC); above II in this chapter.

[122]   *The Arpad (No 2)* [1934] P 189 (CA).

[123]   In *Kuwait Airways Corp v Iraqi Airways Co (Nos 4 and 5)* [2002] UKHL 19, [2002] 2 AC 883, 1066 [104], Lord Nicholls said *obiter* that liability for dishonest conversion should extend to all direct and natural consequences.

[124]   *Saleslease Ltd v Davis* [1999] 1 WLR 1664 (CA); *Sandeman Coprimar SA v Transitos y Transportes Integrales SL* [2003] EWCA Civ 113, [2003] QB 1270 [28], [31].

[125]   *The Wagon Mound (No 2)* [1967] 1 AC 617 (PC); above IV in this chapter.

[126]   (1868) LR 3 HL 330 (HL): *Cambridge Water Co Ltd v Eastern Counties Leather plc* [1994] 2 AC 264 (HL).

[127]   *Slipper v BBC* [1991] 1 QB 283 (CA) 296, 300, 301; *McManus v Beckham* [2002] EWCA Civ 939, [2002] 1 WLR 2982 [43]; E Descheemaeker, 'Protecting Reputation: Defamation and Negligence' (2009) 29 Oxford Journal of Legal Studies 603, 632–34.

[128]   Descheemaeker, ibid 603, 605, 624, 633, describes the tort of negligence as a 'magnet'.

[129]   J Cartwright, 'Remoteness of Damage in Contract and Tort: A Reconsideration' [1996] *Camb LJ* 488, 507.

[130]   *Kuwait Airways Corp v Iraqi Airways Co (Nos 4 and 5)* [2002] UKHL 19, [2002] 2 AC 883, 1066 [103] (Lord Nicholls); MJ Tilbury, *Civil Remedies, Vol 1: Principles of Civil Remedies* (Sydney, 1990) [3083].

[131]   D Harris, 'Remoteness' in D Harris, D Campbell and R Halson, *Remedies in Contract and Tort*, 2nd edn (London, 2002) 329–30.

be liable,[132] for the intentional torts guard against the deliberate infliction of any damage (within their scope). Moreover, liability for deceit[133] and trespass to the person[134] extends to all losses directly attributable to the tort, irrespective of their foreseeability. The idea of extending this principle to all intentional torts enjoys great popularity.[135] It should be considered though that the intentional torts protect primarily the deliberately injured interest. Unintended consequences will often concern other, only secondarily protected interests. Imposing a harsh liability for consequences outside the primary focus of a tort is a concept with little appeal.

---

[132] 'The intention to injure the plaintiff ... disposes of any question of remoteness of damage': *Quinn v Leathem* [1901] AC 495 (HL[Ir]) 537 (Lord Lindley). See also GL Williams, *Joint Torts and Contributory Negligence* (London, 1951) 201.

[133] *Doyle v Olby (Ironmongers) Ltd* [1969] 2 QB 158 (CA); *Royscot Trust Ltd v Rogerson* [1991] 2 QB 297 (CA); *Smith New Court Securities Ltd v Citibank NA* [1997] AC 254 (HL).

[134] '[I]f damage is caused by a trespass it is recoverable simply on the basis of causation, and does not additionally require foreseeability to be established': *Wainwright v Home Office* [2001] EWCA Civ 2081, [2002] QB 1334 [69] (Buxton LJ).

[135] 'I can see no good reason why the remoteness test of "directly and naturally" applied in cases of deceit should not apply in cases of conversion where the defendant acted dishonestly': *Kuwait Airways Corp v Iraqi Airways Co (Nos 4 and 5)* [2002] UKHL 19, [2002] 2 AC 883, 1066, [104] (Lord Nicholls). See also A Burrows, *Remedies for Torts and Breach of Contract*, 3rd edn (Oxford, 2004) 81–82; SB Elliott, 'Remoteness Criteria in Equity' (2002) 65 *MLR* 588, 589; D Harris, 'Remoteness' in D Harris, D Campbell and R Halson, *Remedies in Contract and Tort*, 2nd edn (London, 2002) 330–31; MA Jones, 'Causation in Tort: General Principles' in AM Dugdale and MA Jones, *Clerk & Lindsell on Torts*, 19th edn (London, 2006) [2–113]; MJ Tilbury, *Civil Remedies, Vol 1: Principles of Civil Remedies* (Sydney, 1990) [3083].

3

The Present Remoteness Test in Contract

I *Hadley v Baxendale*

Locus classicus for the remoteness test in contract is the 1854 case of *Hadley v Baxendale*. Alderson B, speaking for the Court of Exchequer, laid down two rules.[1] First, the victim of a breach of contract is entitled to recover damages for loss that 'may fairly and reasonably be considered [as] arising naturally, i.e., according to the usual course of things, from such breach of contract'. Secondly, the victim is further entitled to recover damages for loss that 'may reasonably be supposed to have been in the contemplation of both parties, at the time they made the contract, as the probable result of breach of it'.

In that case, owners of a flour mill engaged common carriers to convey a broken crankshaft to engineers, who needed it for manufacturing a new shaft. The delivery of the broken shaft was delayed, in consequence of which the mill could not work for five days longer than it should have been. The mill owners' claim for damages for lost profit was denied. Alderson B denied liability under the first rule mentioned above on the ground that the lost profits were not something that flowed in the usual course of things from the carriers' breach of contract.[2] The mill might have had a spare shaft, or there might have been other defects in the machinery of the mill, causing a standstill in any event. Hence, in the great multitude of cases where a carrier conveys the broken shaft of a mill to a third person, a delay in delivery does not result in the loss of profit on the miller's part. The carriers could only have been liable, under the second rule mentioned above, if they had known that the running of the mill depended on the delivery of a new shaft. But there was no evidence of such knowledge.[3]

---

[1] (1854) 9 Ex 341, 354; 156 ER 145, 151. For the law prior to 1854 see GT Washington, 'Damages in Contract at Common Law, II, The Period Transitional to the Modern Law' (1932) 48 *Law Quarterly Review* 90–102.

[2] (1854) 9 Ex 341, 355–56.

[3] This conclusion seems to conflict with the headnote of the case, according to which the defendants were told that the mill had been stopped. It was said in *Victoria Laundry (Windsor) Ltd v*

II *Victoria Laundry*

Almost 100 years later *Hadley* v *Baxendale* was reviewed in *Victoria Laundry (Windsor) Ltd* v *Newman Industries Ltd*.[4] A laundry ordered a boiler from engineers. The boiler was delivered some five months later than promised as a result of which the laundry lost business with new customers. In particular it did not obtain some especially lucrative dyeing and laundering contracts from the Ministry of Supply.

Asquith LJ, delivering the judgment of the Court of Appeal, reviewed *Hadley* and other authorities on the extent of contractual liability, and derived the following principles.[5] A contract-breaker is liable for such part of the other party's loss as was at the time of the contract reasonably foreseeable as liable to result from the breach. What was reasonably foreseeable depends on the knowledge of the parties. Knowledge is of two kinds, one imputed, the other actual. Everybody is deemed to know the ordinary course of things, which is the subject matter of the first rule in *Hadley*. In addition, the contract-breaker may have actual knowledge of unusual circumstances, which must be proved. This is the subject matter of the second rule in *Hadley*. It is not necessary under either rule that the contract-breaker actually contemplated what loss was liable to result from the breach. It suffices that, *had* he contemplated the question, he would have concluded that the loss in suit was liable to result from a breach. The notion 'liable to result' was meant to express that the loss was a 'serious possibility' or 'real danger',[6] or was 'on the cards'.[7]

Applying these principles to the facts at hand, the Court made the following distinction.[8] Since the engineers knew that the boiler was to be used in a laundry, they could foresee *some* loss of business as a result of delay. On the other hand, they had no knowledge of how the boiler was to be used or which contracts had been made. Accordingly, the laundry was awarded a general sum for lost profit but could not recover all lost profit, in particular not the profit on contracts with the Ministry.

Since the ultimate aim of the present study is to compare contract with tort, it is noteworthy that *Victoria Laundry* brought the remoteness tests in both areas

---

Newman Industries Ltd [1949] 2 KB 528 (CA) 537 (below II in this chapter) that the court in *Hadley* had regarded this fact as not established. Another explanation is that although the defendants knew of the stoppage they were not told that this was for want of a new shaft: E Peel, *Treitel on the Law of Contract*, 12th edn (London, 2007) [20–083] fn 473.

  [4] [1949] 2 KB 528 (CA).

  [5] ibid 539–40.

  [6] The phrases 'serious possibility' and 'real danger' were first used in *A/B Karlshamns Oljefabriker* v *Monarch Steamship Co* 1949 SC (HL) 1, 29–30 (Lord du Parcq).

  [7] The phrase 'on the cards' was adopted in *East Ham Corp* v *Bernard Sunley & Sons Ltd* [1966] AC 406 (HL) 445 (Lord Upjohn), 451 (Lord Pearson).

  [8] [1949] 2 KB 528 (CA) 540–44.

closer together, if only semantically.[9] Previously, it had not been uncommon for the courts to express the contractual remoteness test by requiring that the 'loss was within the contemplation of the defaulting party'.[10] This formula gives the impression that a contract-breaker, unlike a tortfeasor, must have actually reflected about the possibility of such loss as occurred. *Victoria Laundry* made clear that in contract too the possibility of reflection suffices.

Victoria Laundry further transformed the two rules of *Hadley* into two types of knowledge and integrated them into a single test of reasonable foreseeability, thereby using the notion subsequently used in *The Wagon Mound (No 1)*[11] to express the remoteness test in negligence. This enabled Lord Denning MR, in *Cook v Swinfen*, decided after *Victoria Laundry* and *The Wagon Mound (No 1)*, to make the following statement: 'So both in tort and in contract the measure of damages depends on what may be reasonably foreseen'.[12]

III   *The Heron II*

The actual or seeming harmony between the remoteness tests in contract and negligence came to an end in *Koufos v C Czarnikow Ltd (The Heron II)*.[13] The case involved a charter to carry a cargo of sugar to Basrah where the charterers intended to sell it immediately after unloading. The shipowner knew that the charterers were sugar merchants and that there was a sugar market in Basrah, but he did not know that the charterers intended to sell the sugar promptly after its arrival. In breach of contract the shipowner deviated from the contract route with the result that the cargo arrived in Basrah nine or ten days later. Just within this period the market price for sugar in Basrah dropped. The charterers recovered damages in respect of this fall.

The House of Lords took the opportunity to lay down that liability in contract, compared with tort, requires a higher degree of probability with which the loss occurred could have been foreseen, although a probability of less than 50 per cent may suffice. This higher degree is not conveyed by the phrase 'on the cards' used in *Victoria Laundry*. Unfortunately, their Lordships' unanimity ended there. Different formulae were used to express the degree of foresight required in

---

[9] A substantial identity has been made out by M Whincup, 'Remoteness reconsidered' (1992) 142 *New Law Journal* 389.

[10] *Foaminol Laboratories Ltd v British Artid Plastics Ltd* [1941] 2 All ER 393, 400 (Hallett J). In *The Arpad (No 2)* [1934] P 189 (CA) 205, Scrutton LJ distinguished 'between a tort, the damages for which do not require notice to the wrongdoer of their probability, and contract, where *Hadley* v *Baxendale* requires the consequences to be in the contemplation of the parties'.

[11] [1961] AC 388 (PC); above ch 2, II.

[12] [1967] 1 WLR 457 (CA) 461.

[13] [1969] 1 AC 350 (HL).

contract. Lord Upjohn favoured 'real danger' or 'serious possibility'.[14] So did Lord Pearce,[15] who regarded both phrases as synonymous with 'liable to result'. Lord Hodson considered the latter phrase colourless but impossible to improve on.[16] Interestingly, all three phrases had been regarded in *Victoria Laundry* as being equivalent to 'on the cards'. For this reason, Lord Reid disapproved of these phrases and preferred 'not unlikely' or 'very substantial degree of probability'.[17] Lord Morris, finally, refused to commit to any phrase and said that the question must be decided on the facts of each case.[18]

IV Parsons

The Heron II failed to settle the remoteness test in contract. A further clarification, or modification, of the test was made in *Parsons (Livestock) Ltd v Uttley Ingham & Co Ltd*,[19] which involved concurrent liability in contract and negligence. The defendants sold a pig-food hopper to the plaintiff pig farmers. When installing the hopper the defendants forgot to unseal the ventilator. This caused the nuts in the hopper to become mouldy and 254 pigs died of E. coli, a rare intestinal infection. The trial judge found that at the time of the contract the parties could not have reasonably contemplated that there was a real danger or serious possibility that the feeding of mouldy pignuts would cause illness in the pigs that ate them. Notwithstanding this finding, the Court of Appeal held the defendants liable in contract. The decision was unanimous but the explanations differed.

Lord Denning MR, having listed the various formulae offered in *The Heron II* to describe the remoteness tests in contract and negligence, found it difficult to apply any formula universally to all cases of contract or to all cases of tort, and to draw a line between what a man 'contemplates' and what he 'foresees'.[20] 'I cannot swim in this sea of semantic exercises', he complained, 'I am swept under by the conflicting currents'.[21] He therefore adopted a concept developed by Hart and Honoré,[22] and distinguished two classes of case.[23]

---

[14] [1969] 1 AC 350 (HL) 425.
[15] ibid 415.
[16] ibid 410–11.
[17] ibid 388–90.
[18] ibid 396–99.
[19] [1978] QB 791 (CA).
[20] ibid 802. Any real difference was also denied in *Kienzle v Stringer* (1981) 130 DLR (3d) 272 (ONCA) 276 (Zuber JA).
[21] [1978] QB 791 (CA) 802.
[22] See now HLA Hart and T Honoré, *Causation in the Law*, 2nd edn (Oxford, 1985) 313–21.
[23] [1978] QB 791 (CA) 802–804.

First, there are those cases where the aggrieved party suffers no damage to person or property, but only economic loss such as loss of profit. This was the situation in *Hadley v Baxendale, Victoria Laundry* and *The Heron II*. According to these authorities liability is confined to consequences that the defaulting party, at the time of the contract, ought reasonably to have contemplated as a serious possibility or real danger. Secondly, there are those cases where the aggrieved party claims compensation for damage to person or property or for ensuing expense (*damnum emergens*). Here liability should extend to all loss that the defaulting party ought reasonably to have foreseen at the time of the breach as a possible consequence even if it was only a slight possibility. This is the test established for negligence in the two *Wagon Mound* decisions. The case at hand fell into the second category. Illness of the pigs could have been foreseen as a slight possibility. Since the type of damage had been foreseeable, it was irrelevant that the illness had been far worse than could be foreseen.

Rejecting this approach, Orr LJ[24] and Scarman LJ[25] held that *The Heron II* test applies to all types of loss. However, they stressed that it is only the type of loss and not its extent that must have been contemplated as a serious possibility. If the defendants had asked themselves, at the time of the contract, what was likely to happen to the pigs if the hopper were unfit for storing nuts suitable to be fed to them, they would have contemplated the serious possibility of illness and even death among the pigs. It was irrelevant that an outbreak of E. coli had not been foreseeable. A comparison to the remoteness test in tort was not undertaken by Orr LJ, and Scarman LJ made conflicting statements.[26]

V SAAMCO

The remoteness regimes in contract and tort continued to converge in *SAAMCO* discussed earlier.[27] Speaking for the Court of Appeal, Sir Thomas Bingham MR saw no great difference between contract and tort:

---

[24] ibid 804–805.

[25] ibid 806, 811–13.

[26] First (at 806) he considered it 'absurd that the test for remoteness of damage should, in principle, differ according to the legal classification of the cause of action'. Then (at 806) he said that the 'formulation of the remoteness test is not the same in tort and in contract because the relationship of the parties in a contract situation differs from that in tort'. Still later (at 807) he said that 'in a factual situation where all have the same actual or imputed knowledge and the contract contains no term limiting the damages recoverable for breach, the amount of damages recoverable does not depend upon whether, as a matter of legal classification, the plaintiff's cause of action is breach of contract or tort. A reconciliation of those passages is attempted by R Halson, 'Remedies for Breach of Contract' in M Furmston (ed), *The Law of Contract*, 2nd edn (London, 2003) [8.91].

[27] *South Australia Asset Management Corp v York Montague Ltd, sub nom Banque Bruxelles Lambert SA v Eagle Star Insurance Co Ltd* [1995] QB 375 (CA); [1997] AC 191 (HL); above ch 2, VI.

The test is whether, at the date of the contract or tort, damage of the kind for which the plaintiff claims compensation was a reasonably foreseeable consequence of the breach of contract or tortious conduct of which the plaintiff complains. If the kind of damage was reasonably foreseeable it is immaterial that the extent of the damage was not.[28]

While the House of Lords said nothing about remoteness of damage in its traditional meaning, Lord Hoffmann's leading speech harmonised contract and tort on a different route. After explaining that liability for breach of a duty is limited by the scope of that duty he determined the scope of the duty owed by a valuer of property.[29] Nowhere in this discussion did he differentiate according to the cause of action (the action was for negligence and breach of contract).[30]

VI *Brown v KMR Services Ltd*

The distinction between the type of damage and its extent resurfaced in *Brown v KMR Services Ltd*.[31] An underwriting Name at Lloyd's suffered substantial loss as a result of his involvement in 'excess of loss' syndicates. His members' agent was held liable in contract and negligence for failing to warn the Name of the dangers of such syndicates. Now the loss suffered by the Name was exceptionally high due to an unprecedented series of catastrophes occurring between 1987 and 1990 (including the *Exxon Valdez* oil spill and the San Francisco earthquake). Nevertheless, the Court of Appeal held the agent liable for the whole loss. Since 'excess of loss' syndicates make losses to an excessive extent, said the Court, the type of losses suffered was foreseeable even though their scale was not.[32] The Court approved the approach taken by the majority in *Parsons*.[33] Hobhouse LJ,[34] with whom Peter Gibson LJ agreed, referred also to Sir Thomas Bingham's dictum in *SAAMCO*.[35]

The defendant had objected to a categorisation of all financial loss as being of the same type. He referred to *Victoria Laundry* where ordinary loss of business profit had been held recoverable while the loss of unusually lucrative contracts had not.[36] Only Stuart Smith LJ addressed this argument. He tried to reconcile

---

[28]   [1995] QB 375 (CA) 405.

[29]   [1997] AC 191 (HL) 211–15.

[30]   He only distinguished between a duty to take care to provide accurate information and a (necessarily contractual) warranty that information provided is correct: [1997] AC 191 (HL) 216.

[31]   [1995] 4 All ER 598 (CA).

[32]   ibid 620–21, 642–43.

[33]   *Parsons (Livestock) Ltd v Uttley Ingham & Co Ltd* [1978] QB 791 (CA) 804–805, 806, 811–13; above IV in this chapter.

[34]   [1995] 4 All ER 598 (CA) 643.

[35]   [1995] QB 375 (CA) 405; above V in this chapter.

[36]   *Victoria Laundry (Windsor) Ltd v Newman Industries Ltd* [1949] 2 KB 528 (CA) 540–44; above II in this chapter.

Victoria Laundry and *Parsons* in the following way: 'I do not see any difficulty in holding that loss of ordinary business profit are different in kind from those flowing from a particular contract which gives rise to very high profits'.[37]

VII *Jackson v Royal Bank of Scotland plc*

The distinction between the type of damage and its extent was probably also crucial in *Jackson v Royal Bank of Scotland plc*.[38] A business partnership called Samson Lancastrian imported dog chews from Thailand and sold them to a business partnership called Economy Bag, which used Samson as a middleman because it did not want to handle the import formalities. Economy Bag knew the identity and contact details of Samson's Thai supplier but not the price the supplier charged from Samson. Economy Bag paid Samson by way of a letter of credit issued by the Royal Bank of Scotland (RBS), which coincidentally was the bank of both Economy Bag and Samson.

Economy Bag placed a substantial number of orders with Samson between September 1990 and March 1993. In March 1993, RBS erroneously sent to Economy Bag documents meant for Samson. These documents revealed to Economy Bag the size of Samson's profit margin, which was higher than Economy Bag's own margin. Economy Bag placed no further orders with Samson and thenceforth bought the dog chews directly from the Thai supplier. Since Economy Bag had been Samson's principal customer, Samson had to cease trading.

Samson sued RBS for breach of contract and claimed damages for the lost opportunity to earn profit through trading with Economy Bag. The judge held that RBS had breached its contract with Samson (which was not challenged on appeal) and that there was a significant chance that Samson's trading relationship with Economy Bag would have continued for a further four years had Economy Bag not learnt of Samson's profit margin. He awarded damages in the amount of four years' loss of profit, less a deduction to reflect the vicissitudes of any business relationship. The Court of Appeal reduced the damages to one year's loss of profit on the ground that further loss had not been in RBS's contemplation at the time of breach due to its limited insight into Samson's relationship with Economy Bag.[39] The House of Lords restored the judge's damages award.

---

[37] [1995] 4 All ER 598 (CA) 621. Adopted in *North Sea Energy Holdings NV v Petroleum Authority of Thailand* [1997] 2 Lloyd's Rep 418, 438 (Thomas J): 'In my judgment, loss of profits claimed by reference to an extravagant or unusual bargain are not of the same type as damages referable to bargains that are usual'. This distinction is criticised by D McLauchlan, 'Remoteness Re-Invented?' (2009) 9 *Oxford University Commonwealth Law Journal* 109, 113, 139.

[38] [2005] UKHL 3, [2005] 1 WLR 377.

[39] [2000] CLC 1457 (CA) [31]–[33].

Lord Hope, with whom all the other Law Lords agreed, identified two errors in the Court of Appeal's approach. First, he said, it is the date of the making of the contract, not the date of the breach, that is relevant to what was in the contract-breaker's contemplation.[40] This error was of no consequence, however, as RBS's knowledge of Samson's circumstances had not changed in the two months between the making of the relevant contract and the breach. Secondly, he said, there is no 'cut-off point' once the remoteness test according to *Hadley v Baxendale* has been satisfied.[41] Surprisingly, Lord Hope did not clarify why he considered that test satisfied *in casu*. Nor did Lord Walker, who gave the only other reasoned speech. It seems though that their Lordships' judgments were based on the foreseeability of the *type* of loss suffered by Samson. That had been Samson's key argument in favour of RBS's liability,[42] and Lord Walker quoted the judge's conclusion that 'loss of the type which [Samson] claims arises in the normal course of things'.[43]

VIII *The Achilleas*

The latest case on the contractual remoteness test, and one that may mark the beginning of a new development, is *Transfield Shipping Inc v Mercator Shipping Inc (The Achilleas)*.[44] The vessel *Achilleas* was chartered with redelivery due on 2 May 2004. In April 2004, the vessel's owner fixed a follow-on charter with another company for four to six months at a daily rate of US$39,500. The latest date for the vessels' delivery to the new charterer was 8 May 2004. It then became clear that the existing charterer, who was not aware of the new charter, would not be able to return the vessel before 11 May, and the owner negotiated with the new charterer for an extension of the delivery date to 11 May. Due to a sudden and sharp fall of the market rate, the owner was forced to reduce the daily rate for the new charter to US$31,500. There was no suggestion that the owner had breached its 'duty' to mitigate its loss.

The owner claimed damages for breach of contract in the amount of the difference between the original rate for the new charter and the reduced rate over the period of the new charter. That was a loss of US$8,000 per day over 191 days. Giving credit for the additional sum earned under the old charter by reason of the late redelivery, the owner's total claim was for US$1,364,584.37. The charterer took the view that the owner could not claim more than the difference between the market rate and the charter rate for the nine days during which the owner

---

[40] [2005] UKHL 3, [2005] 1 WLR 377 [36].
[41] ibid [37].
[42] As noted by Lord Hope, ibid [51].
[43] ibid [37].
[44] [2008] UKHL 48, [2009] 1 AC 61.

was deprived of the vessel's use. That came to US$158,301.17. The owner was held entitled to damages in the amount of US$1,364,584.37 by the majority of an arbitration panel, the trial judge[45] and the Court of Appeal.[46] This decision was based on the view that the *type* of the loss had been foreseeable as not unlikely, even though its extent might not, since charterers know that owners fix follow-on charters and that the charter market is volatile. The House of Lords allowed the charterer's appeal.

While the House of Lords was in effect unanimous as to the outcome (although Baroness Hale expressed doubts), there was disagreement as to its correct basis. Lord Hoffmann and Lord Hope took the view that even if it was assumed that the loss of the higher rate for the new charter had been foreseeable as not unlikely, the charterer was still not liable for it because the charterer had not assumed responsibility for that loss, considering that it was entirely the owner's decision whether and when to fix a new charter and on what terms.[47] Lord Hoffmann[48] derived the requirement of an assumption of responsibility from the 'scope of the duty' concept which he himself had highlighted in *SAAMCO*.[49]

Both Lord Hoffmann and Lord Hope regarded an 'assumption of responsibility' as the ultimate criterion for contractual liability, qualifying the rule that a party aggrieved by a breach of contract may recover loss of a type that was foreseeable as not unlikely.[50] That rule, said Lord Hoffmann, is 'a prima facie assumption about what the parties may be taken to have intended, no doubt applicable in the great majority of cases but capable of rebuttal' where the context, surrounding circumstances or general understanding in the relevant market shows that the contract-breaker assumed no responsibility for the loss in question.[51] Lord Hope said in similar vein:

> The fact that the loss was foreseeable ... is not the test. Greater precision is needed than that. The question is whether the loss was a type of loss for which the party can reasonably be assumed to have assumed responsibility.[52]

[45] [2006] EWHC 3030 (Comm), [2007] 1 Lloyd's Rep 19.

[46] [2007] EWCA Civ 901, [2007] 2 Lloyd's Rep 555.

[47] [2008] UKHL 48, [2009] 1 AC 61 [11]–[26] (Lord Hoffmann), [30]–[36] (Lord Hope). McLauchlan criticises the outcome of the case while supporting the concept of an assumption of responsibility: D McLauchlan, 'Remoteness Re-Invented?' (2009) 9 *OUCLJ* 109, 112–16, 135–38.

[48] [2008] UKHL 48, [2009] 1 AC 61 [14]–[16].

[49] *South Australia Asset Management Corp v York Montague Ltd* [1997] AC 191 (HL) 211–15; above ch 2, VI.

[50] This view had already been expressed *obiter* in *Mulvenna v Royal Bank of Scotland plc* [2003] EWCA Civ 1112, [2004] CP Rep 8 [24]–[26].

[51] [2008] UKHL 48, [2009] 1 AC 61 [9].

[52] ibid [32].

Lord Rodger expressly refrained from taking a stand on the 'assumption of responsibility' concept.[53] He rejected the charterer's liability for the loss of the higher charter rate simply on the ground that loss of such kind had been unforeseeable. That loss, he said, was not the ordinary consequence of the breach but occurred only because of the extreme market volatility which produced both the initial (particularly lucrative) rate for the new charter and the subsequent pressure on the owner to accept a lower rate.[54] He mentioned the distinction, made in *Victoria Laundry*, between ordinary loss of business and the loss of a particularly lucrative contract,[55] and seems to have drawn an analogy to that distinction.

Lord Walker's speech is rather unclear. On the one hand, he advanced arguments similar to those advanced by Lord Rodger.[56] On the other hand, he described as 'very helpful' works by certain scholars who 'demonstrate that foreseeability by itself is not a satisfactory test' and who 'emphasise the importance of what I have rather imprecisely referred to as the nature and object of the contract entered into by the parties'.[57] Moreover, Lord Walker expressed agreement with the reasons given by Lord Hoffmann, Lord Hope and Lord Rodger.

Finally, Baroness Hale voiced doubts as to whether the appeal should be allowed at all but added that if it was to be allowed, she would prefer Lord Rodger's reasons. She left the 'assumption of responsibility' concept 'to be fully explored in another case and another context' as she thought that this concept was novel, it could cause injustice in some future case, and it could 'introduce much room for argument in other contractual contexts'.[58]

'It is not easy to formulate a precise majority ratio from the diverse judgments in *The Achilleas*'.[59] Lord Hoffmann and Lord Hope firmly supported an assimilation of the traditional foreseeability test into an overarching requirement of an 'assumption of responsibility'. Lord Rodger and Baroness Hale made clear that they did not want to be taken as supporting that idea. Lord Walker failed to clarify his position. Judicial and scholarly opinion on the *ratio* of *The Achilleas* is divided. Some High Court decisions[60] and

---

[53] ibid [63].

[54] ibid [60]. Lord Rodger's view is considered 'unconvincing' by A Kramer, 'The New Test of Remoteness in Contract' (2009) 125 *LQR* 408, 409; D McLauchlan, 'Remoteness Re-Invented?' (2009) 9 *OUCLJ* 109, 123.

[55] [2008] UKHL 48, [2009] 1 AC 61 [58].

[56] ibid [82]–[83], [86].

[57] ibid [79]. He was referring to A Kramer, 'An Agreement-Centred Approach to Remoteness and Contract Damages' in N Cohen and E McKendrick (eds), *Comparative Remedies for Breach of Contract* (Oxford, 2005) 249–86; A Robertson, 'The basis of the remoteness rule in contract' (2008) 28 *Legal Studies* 172; A Tettenborn, 'Hadley v Baxendale Foreseeability: a Principle Beyond Its Sell-by Date?' (2007) 23 *Journal of Contract Law* 120.

[58] [2008] UKHL 48, [2009] 1 AC 61 [93].

[59] D McLauchlan, 'Remoteness Re-Invented?' (2009) 9 *OUCLJ* 109, 127.

[60] *ENE Kos v Petroleo Brasileiro SA (Petrobas)* [2009] EWHC 1843 (Comm) [35], [38]; *Oceanbulk Shipping & Trading SA v TMT Asia Ltd* [2009] EWHC 1946 (Comm) [12]. See also *Ryan v Islington*

commentators[61] have taken the view that a majority in the House of Lords endorsed the concept of an assumption of responsibility. Other High Court decisions[62] and McGregor[63] have taken the opposite view. But even the latter interpretation must recognise that neither Lord Rodger nor Lord Walker displayed hostility towards the concept of assumption of responsibility, and that Baroness Hale did not firmly reject that concept either. *The Achilleas* may be the starting shot for a reshaping of the contractual remoteness test.

IX Conclusion

Over the past 150 years, the courts have used quite different formulae to describe when damage caused by a breach of contract is too remote to attract liability. These differences cannot be merely semantic. While the millers in *Hadley v Baxendale* were denied compensation for lost profit although the carriers had known that they transported a part of the machinery of a mill at standstill, the Name in *Brown* recovered damages for its whole loss even though nobody could have foreseen the magnitude of the financial disaster. And yet, in none of the cases following *Hadley v Baxendale* did the court intend, or admit to intend, to depart substantially from precedents. Exceptions are the speeches made by Lord Hoffmann and Lord Hope in *The Achilleas*, which is the latest case on the subject and has no clear *ratio*. All this makes it difficult to determine what the contractual remoteness test is today.

In the centre of the remoteness test stands the notion of 'contemplation'. Four things are relatively certain. First, even though the courts have often referred to the contemplation of 'the parties'[64] or 'both parties',[65] the foreseeability of the aggrieved party's loss depends on what the contract-breaker, not the aggrieved party, could have contemplated. 'No case has been found in which recovery was

---

LBC [2009] EWCA Civ 578 [72]; *Mayhaven Healthcare Ltd v Bothma (t/a DAB Builders)* [2009] EWHC 2634 (TCC) [46]; *Donoghue v Greater Glasgow Health Board* [2009] CSOH 115 [12], [14].

[61] HG Beale, 'Damages' in HG Beale (gen ed), *Chitty on Contracts, Vol 1: General Principles*, 30th edn (London, 2008) [26–100A]–[26–100G]; A Kramer, 'The New Test of Remoteness in Contract' (2009) 125 *LQR* 408; D McLauchlan, 'Remoteness Re-Invented?' (2009) 9 *OUCLJ* 109, 127.

[62] *ASM Shipping Ltd of India v TTMI Ltd of England (The Amer Energy)* [2009] 1 Lloyd's Rep 293 [17]–[18]; *Classic Maritime Inc v Lion Diversified Holdings Bhd* [2009] EWHC 1142 (Comm) [71].

[63] H McGregor, *McGregor on Damages*, 18th edn (London, 2009) [6–173].

[64] eg *Koufos v C Czarnikow Ltd (The Heron II)* [1969] 1 AC 350 (HL) 384, 385 ff; *Transfield Shipping Inc v Mercator Shipping Inc (The Achilleas)* [2008] UKHL 48, [2009] 1 AC 61 [30], [61], [91].

[65] eg *Hadley v Baxendale* (1854) 9 Ex 341, 354; 156 ER 145, 151; *Hawkins v Woodhall* [2008] EWCA Civ 932 [44].

denied because the injured party did not foresee the loss.'[66] What the aggrieved party could have contemplated may, however, influence the scope of the duty breached.[67]

Secondly, the courts' preference for the notion of 'contemplation' above 'foreseeability', which is used in tort, does not require the contract-breaker to have actually reflected about the possibility and consequences of a breach. 'The court has to assume, though it be contrary to the fact, that the parties had in mind the breach that has occurred.'[68] What matters is whether the contract-breaker, in the course of this assumed reflection about breach, *could* have contemplated the loss suffered.[69] Thirdly, what could have been contemplated is not judged by the contract-breaker's personal abilities but by the standard of a reasonable person in his position.[70] Finally, the time at which the loss suffered must have been able to be contemplated is the time of the contract's conclusion, not the time of the breach. Lord Denning thought otherwise in his minority judgment in *Parsons*, but the House of Lords reaffirmed the established position in *Jackson v Royal Bank of Scotland plc*.

A slight uncertainty lies in the degree of probability with which the loss in suit must have been able to be contemplated. In *SAAMCO* the Court of Appeal saw no great difference between contract and tort in that respect. But the law is still fixed by the House of Lords' statement in *The Heron II* that contract requires a higher probability than does negligence although it may be less than 50 per cent. In describing the degree of foresight required in contract, the phrases 'not unlikely'[71] and, without substantial difference,[72] 'serious possibility'[73] have proved most popular.

---

[66] AG Murphey, 'Consequential Damages in Contracts for the International Sale of Goods and the Legacy of Hadley' (1989) 23 *George Washington Journal of International Law and Economics* 415, 435.

[67] A Tettenborn, 'Hadley v Baxendale Foreseeability: a Principle Beyond Its Sell-by Date?' (2007) 23 *JCL* 120, 146.

[68] *Parsons (Livestock) Ltd v Uttley Ingham & Co Ltd* [1978] QB 791 (CA) 807 (Scarman LJ). See also *Christopher Hill Ltd v Ashington Piggeries Ltd* [1969] 3 All ER 1496 (CA) 1524; J Beatson, *Anson's Law of Contract*, 28th edn (Oxford, 2002) 608; A Robertson, 'The basis of the remoteness rule in contract' (2008) 28 *LS* 172, 176–78.

[69] eg *Victoria Laundry (Windsor) Ltd v Newman Industries Ltd* [1949] 2 KB 528 (CA) 540; above II in this chapter.

[70] eg *Koufos v C Czarnikow Ltd (The Heron II)* [1969] 1 AC 350 (HL) 385 (Lord Reid), 424 (Lord Upjohn); *Christopher Hill Ltd v Ashington Piggeries Ltd* [1969] 3 All ER 1496 (CA) 1524.

[71] eg *Berryman v Hounslow LBC* [1997] PIQR P83 (CA) P87–P88; *Silvey v Pendragon plc* [2001] EWCA Civ 784 [31]; *Transfield Shipping Inc v Mercator Shipping Inc (The Achilleas)* [2008] UKHL 48, [2009] 1 AC 61 [9], [17], [34], [83], [91].

[72] In *Christopher Hill Ltd v Ashington Piggeries Ltd* [1969] 3 All ER 1496 (CA) 1524, Davies LJ considered synonymous the expressions 'liable to', 'not unlikely', 'real danger' and 'serious possibility'.

[73] eg *North Sea Energy Holdings NV v Petroleum Authority of Thailand* [1997] 2 Lloyd's Rep 418, 437; *Malik v BCCI SA* [1998] AC 20 (HL) 37; *Giles v Rhind* [2002] EWCA Civ 1428, [2003] Ch 618 [54].

But it is only the type of loss and not its extent that needs to be contemplatable.[74] The Court of Appeal has applied this distinction in *Parsons*, *SAAMCO* and *Brown*, and lower courts have followed suit.[75] While the House of Lords left the correctness of that approach open in a Scottish case,[76] it then tacitly approved the type/extent distinction in *Jackson v Royal Bank of Scotland plc*, and Lord Hoffmann expressly approved the distinction in *The Achilleas*.[77] A 'rollback' is very unlikely.[78] *Parsons* did not really introduce the type/extent distinction but only highlighted it for the first time. Prior to *Parsons* the courts had already excluded the precise nature and extent of the damage from the ambit of the contemplation requirement,[79] and some dicta had already referred to the 'type' or 'kind' of damage as the object of contemplation.[80] Indeed, the shipowner in *The Heron II* would have escaped liability had the House of Lords required that he could have contemplated by *how much* the sugar price in Basrah would drop. Since the type/extent distinction in tort carries 'pick-a-back' the 'thin skull' rule,[81] the rule must now[82] also apply in contract,[83] provided the initial injury meets the contractual foreseeability test. But the 'thin skull' rule has little importance in contract.

Another slight uncertainty in determining the present remoteness test lies in the question of whether the test should be expressed as a single rule or as a set of two rules. *Hadley v Baxendale* distinguished between ordinary and unusual loss. A single test with two subcategories was expressed in *Victoria Laundry* and in *The Heron II*.[84] An undivided single test (for contract and tort) was stated *obiter* by

---

[74] More correctly, one should speak of the type of *risk* created by the breach, as done in H Street, *Principles of the Law of Damages* (London, 1962) 237 fn 3. But the difference is of little practical significance. For the same issue in tort see above ch 2, III.

[75] eg *The Kriti Rex* [1996] 2 Lloyd's Rep 171, 203; *North Sea Energy Holdings NV v Petroleum Authority of Thailand* [1997] 2 Lloyd's Rep 418, 437.

[76] *Balfour Beatty Construction (Scotland) Ltd v Scottish Power plc* 1994 SC (HL) 20, 32.

[77] [2008] UKHL 48, [2009] 1 AC 61 [21].

[78] A Burrows, *Understanding the Law of Obligations: Essays on Contract, Tort and Restitution* (Oxford, 1998) 162.

[79] 'If grounding [of a ship] takes place in breach of contract, the precise nature of the damage incurred by grounding is immaterial': *Great Lakes SS Co v Maple Leaf Milling Co Ltd* (1924) 41 TLR 21 (PC) 23 (Lord Carson). See also *Vacwell Engineering Co Ltd v BDH Chemicals Ltd* [1971] 1 QB 88, 110; H Street, *Principles of the Law of Damages* (London, 1962) 237 fn 3.

[80] eg *Wroth v Tyler* [1974] Ch 30, 61, where Megarry J said that a claimant invoking the second rule in *Hadley v Baxendale* 'need show only a contemplation of circumstances which embrace the head or type of damage in question, and need not demonstrate a contemplation of the quantum of damages under that head or type'; *Koufos v C Czarnikow Ltd (The Heron II)* [1969] 1 AC 350 (HL) 382–83 (Lord Reid), 417 (Lord Pearce); *Christopher Hill Ltd v Ashington Piggeries Ltd* [1969] 3 All ER 1496 (CA) 1524.

[81] Above ch 2, V.

[82] It used to be rejected: H Street, *Principles of the Law of Damages* (London, 1962) 250.

[83] H McGregor, *McGregor on Damages*, 18th edn (London, 2009) [6–179]. A seller's warranty does not, however, necessarily imply the fitness of the goods for people with abnormal susceptibilities: *Griffiths v Peter Conway Ltd* [1939] 1 All ER 685 (CA), where a coat caused dermatitis to a buyer with abnormal skin; *Ingham v Emes* [1955] 2 QB 366 (CA), where a hair dye caused dermatitis to a customer who knew that she had previously had an allergic reaction to the dye.

[84] [1969] 1 AC 350 (HL) 385 (Lord Reid), 424 (Lord Upjohn).

the Court of Appeal in *SAAMCO*. In *The Achilleas*,[85] the House of Lords spoke of the two limbs of *Hadley v Baxendale*, which is still common practice among the courts.[86] In the end, the difference between a single test and a test consisting of two rules is purely semantic.[87] The second limb of the *Hadley* test concerns loss that the contract-breaker could have contemplated at the time of the contract, based on the knowledge then possessed by him.[88] The first limb, dealing with ordinary loss, is but a special case of the second limb,[89] for a reasonable person entering a contract contemplates the loss arising in the usual course of things from a breach of contract.[90] It may simplify things if the two limbs of the *Hadley* test are integrated into a single test of reasonable contemplation.

The principles outlined so far are neatly summarised in *Chitty on Contracts*:

> A type or kind of loss is not too remote a consequence of a breach of contract if, at the time of contracting (and on the assumption that the parties actually foresaw the breach in question), it was within their reasonable contemplation as a not unlikely result of that breach.[91]

That is not the end of the matter though. *SAAMCO* highlighted that liability for breach of a contractual (or tortious) duty of care requires the type of loss to be not only foreseeable but also within the protective ambit of the duty breached. *SAAMCO* concerned fault-based liability and is no direct authority for an application of the 'scope of the duty' concept to strict contractual liability. However, Lord Hoffmann said in *The Achilleas*: 'What is true of an implied

---

[85]   [2008] UKHL 48, [2009] 1 AC 61 [58], [59], 67], [68], [69], [93].

[86]   eg *Mayhaven Healthcare Ltd v Bothma (t/a DAB Builders)* [2009] EWHC 2634 (TCC) [36]–[49].

[87]   *Koufos v C Czarnikow Ltd (The Heron II)* [1969] 1 AC 350 (HL) 421 (Lord Upjohn): 'for my part I care not whether it is regarded as stating two rules or two branches of one rule'; A Burrows, 'Limitations on Compensation' in A Burrows and E Peel (eds), *Commercial Remedies: Current Issues and Problems* (Oxford, 2003) 30.

[88]   The relevant information must come from the other party and not 'casually from a stranger': *British Columbia and Vancouver's Island Spar, Lumber and Saw-Mill Co Ltd v Nettleship* (1868) LR 3 CP 499, 509 (Willes J). In that case it was further held (at 506, 509) that unusual loss is only recoverable if the contract expressly or impliedly provides to that effect. This requirement has since been eroded: H McGregor, *McGregor on Damages*, 18th edn (London, 2009) [6–198]; MJ Tilbury, *Civil Remedies, Vol 1: Principles of Civil Remedies* (Sydney, 1990) [3080]; J Wightman, 'Negligent Valuations and a Drop in the Property Market: the Limits of the Expectation Loss Principle' (1998) 61 *Modern Law Review* 68, 75–76 (who opines though that the requirement resembles the 'scope of the duty' concept).

[89]   *Jackson v Royal Bank of Scotland plc* [2005] UKHL 3, [2005] 1 WLR 377 [25], [47]–[49].

[90]   MA Eisenberg, 'The Principle of Hadley v Baxendale' (1992) 80 *California Law Review* 563, 565–66.

[91]   HG Beale, 'Damages' in HG Beale (gen ed), *Chitty on Contracts, Vol 1: General Principles*, 30th edn (London, 2008) [26–054]. Approvingly quoted in, eg, *Deadman v Bristol City Council* [2007] EWCA Civ 822, [2007] IRLR 888 [45].

contractual duty (to take reasonable care in the valuation) is equally true of an express contractual duty (to redeliver the ship on the appointed day)'.[92] In that case, which involved strict contractual liability, both Lord Hoffmann and Lord Hope opined that the traditional foreseeability test in contract is just a prima facie indicator of liability and yields to the ultimate requirement of an assumption of responsibility, which Lord Hoffmann derived from the 'scope of the duty' concept highlighted in *SAAMCO*. It is unclear though whether the 'assumption of responsibility' requirement forms the ratio of *The Achilleas*.

It is respectfully submitted that Lord Hoffmann and Lord Hope were correct. Foreseeability of the loss in question cannot be the sole criterion for the extent of contractual liability, whether strict or fault-based.[93] It is a useful prima facie indicator, but the extent of contractual liability must ultimately depend on the parties' assumption of responsibility[94] or, what should amount to the same, the scope of the duty breached.[95] As Wightman observes:

> [I]t would surely be extraordinary if a taxi firm, booked by someone who mentions they need to get to Heathrow to fly to an important business appointment in New York, were to be liable for the lost business caused by the person missing the flight.[96]

It seems widely accepted that in such a situation the taxi firm is not liable for the passenger's exorbitant loss[97] unless they responded to the passenger's information by drastically increasing the fare.[98] But how can the absence of liability be explained? It cannot be said that the passenger's loss was unforeseeable, for the taxi firm did know the magnitude of the potential loss. What can be said is that the taxi firm assumed no responsibility for the passenger's exorbitant loss simply by accepting the passenger.[99] The loss, in other words, falls outside the scope of the duty breached.[100]

---

[92] [2008] UKHL 48, [2009] 1 AC 61 [16]. The opposite view seems to have been taken without explanation in *Sentinel International Ltd v Cordes* [2008] UKPC 60 [50] (Lord Walker): 'a contractual claim for damages for loss of bargain is not of course subject to the *SAAMCO* principle'.

[93] A Robertson, 'The basis of the remoteness rule in contract' (2008) 28 *LS* 172, 188–95; he emphasises the importance of fairness considerations.

[94] A Kramer, 'An Agreement-Centred Approach to Remoteness and Contract Damages' in N Cohen and E McKendrick (eds), *Comparative Remedies for Breach of Contract* (Oxford, 2005) 249–83; A Tettenborn, 'Hadley v Baxendale Foreseeability: a Principle Beyond Its Sell-by Date?' (2007) 23 *JCL* 120, 134–47; D McLauchlan, 'Remoteness Re-Invented?' (2009) 9 *OUCLJ* 109, 112–16.

[95] H Street, *Principles of the Law of Damages* (London, 1962) 236: 'the harm claimed must be within the scope of the protection afforded by the particular contract'; J Wightman, 'Negligent Valuations and a Drop in the Property Market: the Limits of the Expectation Loss Principle' (1998) 61 *MLR* 68, 75–76.

[96] J Wightman, 'Negligent Valuations and a Drop in the Property Market: the Limits of the Expectation Loss Principle' (1998) 61 *MLR* 68, 76.

[97] *British Columbia and Vancouver's Island Spar, Lumber and Saw-Mill Co Ltd v Nettleship* (1868) LR 3 CP 499, 510 (Willes J).

[98] A Kramer, 'An Agreement-Centred Approach to Remoteness and Contract Damages' in N Cohen and E McKendrick (eds), *Comparative Remedies for Breach of Contract* (Oxford, 2005) 269–70.

[99] R Halson, 'Remoteness' in D Harris, D Campbell and R Halson, *Remedies in Contract and Tort*, 2nd edn (London, 2002) 97; A Kramer, 'An Agreement-Centred Approach to Remoteness and

The Achilleas demonstrates that the 'scope of the duty' concept is useful in cases of strict contractual liability as well as fault-based liability.[101] It is much more convincing to say that the owner's loss in that case fell outside the scope of the duty breached by the charterer, than that the owner's loss was not foreseeable to the degree required. Furthermore, the 'scope of the duty' concept may assimilate not only the foreseeability test but also the principles of legal causation.[102] Suppose that a seller of goods fails to deliver and the buyer then views an alternative supply in a warehouse where he is injured by a falling barrel. It is probably uncontroversial that the seller should not be liable for that injury even though his breach of contract was a factual ('but for') cause of it. But how can the absence of liability be explained? Discussing this example, Paterson, Robertson and Duke suggest that a causal link between the seller's breach and the buyer's injury be denied 'as a matter of common sense'.[103] It may be more straightforward to say that the seller's duty to deliver the goods did not aim to protect the buyer from the general risk of getting injured while shopping.

Contract Damages' in N Cohen and E McKendrick (eds), *Comparative Remedies for Breach of Contract* (Oxford, 2005) 269–70; D McLauchlan, 'Remoteness Re-Invented?' (2009) 9 *OUCLJ* 109, 113; A Tettenborn, 'Hadley v Baxendale Foreseeability: a Principle Beyond Its Sell-by Date?' (2007) 23 *JCL* 120, 144–45.

[100] J Wightman, 'Negligent Valuations and a Drop in the Property Market: the Limits of the Expectation Loss Principle' (1998) 61 *MLR* 68, 76.

[101] A Kramer, 'The New Test of Remoteness in Contract' (2009) 125 *LQR* 408, 410, who prefers the term 'extent of liability' to 'scope of the duty'.

[102] A Kramer, 'An Agreement-Centred Approach to Remoteness and Contract Damages' in N Cohen and E McKendrick (eds), *Comparative Remedies for Breach of Contract* (Oxford, 2005) 281 fn 148.

[103] J Paterson, A Robertson and A Duke, *Principles of Contract Law*, 3rd edn (Sydney, 2009) [27.10].

4

A Uniform Remoteness Test
throughout the Common Law

I Contract and Tort Compared

What are the commonalities and differences between the remoteness regimes in
contract (the '*Hadley* test') and tort, specifically negligence (the '*Wagon Mound*
test')? Something that the two regimes (should) have in common is the limitation
of liability by the scope of the duty breached. 'The fundamental proposition that
a defendant is only liable for losses he may have caused if it was also part of his
duty to prevent or avoid them is one of universal application.'[1] This is demonstrated by *SAAMCO*,[2] where the House of Lords made no difference between
contract and tort in defining the scope of the duty owed by a valuer to the lender.
It should also be noted that the 'scope of the duty' concept may be used to
explain results traditionally reached through causation doctrine,[3] which is uniform within the common law.[4]

There remains the question of how courts determine the general scope of
duties in contract and negligence, that is, the usual extent of liability absent
special considerations relating to the purpose of the particular duty. At this stage,
the remoteness test in its traditional understanding comes into play. Again,
contract and negligence have much in common. Both areas focus on the
anticipation of the wrongdoer but neither area requires an actual reflection about
the loss in suit. It suffices that the loss *could* have been 'contemplated' (contract)
or 'foreseen' (negligence), the different usage being purely semantic and not
substantial.[5] What could have been contemplated or foreseen is judged by the

---

[1] E Peel, 'SAAMCO Revisited' in A Burrows and E Peel (eds), *Commercial Remedies: Current
Issues and Problems* (Oxford, 2003) 65. See also above ch 2, VI and ch 3, IX.

[2] *South Australia Asset Management Corp v York Montague Ltd* [1997] AC 191 (HL); above ch 2
VI.

[3] *Equitable Life Assurance Society v Ernst & Young* [2003] EWHC 112 (Comm), [2003] PNLR 23
[85]; H McGregor, *McGregor on Damages*, 18th edn (London, 2009), [6–135]. Causation is defined
above ch 2, I.

[4] Above ch 1, II.

[5] A Burrows, *Remedies for Torts and Breach of Contract*, 3rd edn (Oxford, 2004) 91.

standard of a reasonable person in the wrongdoer's position, taking into account knowledge actually possessed by the wrongdoer. In defining the reasonable person, there seems to be no difference, and no reason for a difference, between contract and tort. It is only the type of damage and not its extent that needs to be foreseeable. This principle has probably assimilated the 'thin skull' rule.[6]

The remoteness regimes in contract and negligence do, however, differ in two respects,[7] which renders liability potentially wider in negligence than in contract.[8] One difference is the degree of probability required. Contractual liability is confined to loss that can be contemplated as 'not unlikely' or as a 'serious possibility'.[9] Such a threshold is absent in negligence where loss qualifies as foreseeable if it is possible 'unless it can be brushed aside as far fetched'.[10] The other difference lies in the time at which the necessary anticipation is judged. In negligence it is the time of the wrong, that is the careless conduct. In contract it is not the time of the wrong, that is the breach of contract, but the earlier time of the contract's conclusion. The extent of contractual liability is not widened by knowledge that the contract-breaker acquires in the time between the conclusion of the contract and the breach. As explained by Harry Street:

> [I]f D agreed to manufacture some plant and later became aware of its special pecuniary importance to P this additional loss consequent on a breach of contract would be irrecoverable, but if D negligently manufactured the product he would be accountable in tort for that extra loss.[11]

II   Reforming Both Contract and Tort

Is it desirable and possible to have a remoteness regime no longer dependent on the cause of action (contract or tort)? Lord Cooke has suggested, first extrajudicially[12] and then in his former capacity as President of the New Zealand Court of Appeal,[13] that both the *Hadley* test and the *Wagon Mound* test be replaced with the following regime. Any damage caused by the defendant's tort or breach of contract is prima facie recoverable, but it may be just, on the facts of

---

    6   Above ch 2, V and ch 3, IX.
    7   MG Bridge, 'Contractual Damages for Intangible Loss: A Comparative Analysis' (1984) 62 *Canadian Bar Review* 323, 344; A Burrows, *Remedies for Torts and Breach of Contract*, 3rd edn (Oxford, 2004), 91; J Cartwright, 'Compensatory Damages: Some Central Issues of Assessment' in A Burrows and E Peel (eds), *Commercial Remedies: Current Issues and Problems* (Oxford, 2003) 6–7.
    8   J Cartwright, ibid.
    9   Above ch 3, III and IX.
    10   *Koufos v C Czarnikow Ltd (The Heron II)* [1969] 1 AC 350 (HL) 422 (Lord Upjohn); above ch 2, IV.
    11   H Street, *Principles of the Law of Damages* (London, 1962) 249.
    12   R Cooke, 'Remoteness of Damages and Judicial Discretion' [1978] *Cambridge LJ* 288, 298.
    13   *McElroy Milne v Commercial Electronics Ltd* [1993] 1 NZLR 39 (NZCA) 43; *Thomson v Rankin* [1993] 1 NZLR 408 (NZCA) 410.

the case, to limit liability. When deciding on such limitation, the court should have regard to a range of considerations, the main ones being the degree of foreseeability of the damage in suit, the directness of causation, the nature of the damage, the degree of the defendant's culpability, and the defendant's opportunity to limit liability by agreement. Even though such a regime might be considered the most just in an individual case, it cannot be supported. A virtually unlimited discretion of the courts in deciding on remoteness would render the outcome of actions unpredictable, and this unpredictability would be the greatest injustice of all. Of course, the remoteness test, whatever its content, must and will always be flexible enough to accommodate different circumstances. In order to avoid unnecessary litigation, however, prospective litigants must be able to determine remoteness at least by a rule of thumb.[14]

Whincup, who recognises the need for clear principles, steers a middle course between the 'unduly restrictive' *Hadley* test and the 'excessively liberal' *Wagon Mound* test by merging the degrees of foresight required under the two tests to a test of 'realistic possibility'.[15] He says nothing about the time at which foreseeability is judged, which is the more important difference between the two tests. In any event, Whincup's test is not the golden mean it might seem to be. In both contract and tort it has taken the courts considerable efforts to find the best formula for expressing the degree of foresight required. This process seems to have been completed with the phrases 'not unlikely' or 'serious possibility' in contract[16] and 'possible unless it can be brushed aside as far fetched' in negligence.[17] The courts should not now be required to go back to square one and establish the meaning of yet another degree of foresight located in the gap between the existing two, a gap that is rather small anyway (as Whincup himself points out).

A uniform remoteness regime that uses the established degrees of foresight could be developed out of Lord Denning's approach in *Parsons (Livestock) Ltd v Uttley Ingham & Co Ltd.*[18] He suggested an application of the *Wagon Mound* test to contractual actions for personal injury, property damage and ensuing expense while leaving the *Hadley* test in place for loss of profit. This could be developed into a regime that requires, in contract and tort alike, a *Hadley* degree of foresight for pure economic loss and a *Wagon Mound* degree of foresight for all other types of loss, with the time of the wrong (tort or breach of contract) being relevant for

---

[14] The need for clear principles was emphasised, with respect to causation in *Alexander v Cambridge Credit Co Ltd* (1987) 9 NSWLR 310 (NSWCA) 332 (Mahoney JA), and with respect to causation and remoteness of damage in equity, in *Bank of New Zealand v New Zealand Guardian Trust Co Ltd* [1999] 1 NZLR 213, 239–40.

[15] M Whincup, 'Remoteness reconsidered' (1992) 142 *New LJ* 433, 434.

[16] Above ch 3, III and IX.

[17] Above ch 2, IV.

[18] [1978] QB 791 (CA) 802–804; above ch 3, IV. This is not the present law: J Cartwright, 'Remoteness of Damage in Contract and Tort: A Reconsideration' [1996] *Camb LJ* 488, 505–506.

the judgment of foresight in all cases, including—contrary to Lord Denning's view—in contractual actions for loss of profit. However, such a regime would be problematic.

It is true that liability in negligence is more restricted for pure economic loss than for consequential or derivative economic loss. But this is achieved by requiring a higher degree of proximity between the parties rather than a higher degree of foresight. Moreover, it would not always be easy to draw the line between the different types of loss. Suppose that X drives carelessly and collides with Y. A traffic jam emerges, in which Z is caught. Both Y and Z miss a business opportunity and lose profit. Z's loss of profit is pure economic loss whereas Y's loss of profit is consequential or derivative economic loss as it results from property damage. It is hardly defensible to apply different remoteness tests to Y's loss of profit and Z's loss of profit.

III Reforming Tort Only

Burrows suggests that 'where the parties are in a contractual relationship, the [*Hadley*] test applies even where the claim is being brought in tort because of the equal opportunity that the claimant has had to inform the other party of unusual risks'.[19] Since under this approach the remoteness test would no longer depend upon the cause of action but upon the existence of a contract between the parties, it would unify the remoteness test throughout the common law. But the underlying assumption that only the *Hadley* test provides a fair allocation of risks between contracting parties[20] is dubious, as will be shown later.[21] In addition, if concurrent liability in contract reduced liability in tort, a defendant sued in tort would be keen on demonstrating that he is also liable in contract while the claimant would be keen on relieving the defendant from contractual liability. Burrows himself denounces a similar 'odd reversal of roles' in the context of contributory negligence.[22] The reversal of roles might be avoided by following Burrows' further suggestion of applying the *Hadley* test in tort wherever there is a 'pre-existing relationship', even if non-contractual, between the parties.[23] But

---

[19] A Burrows, 'Limitations on Compensation' in A Burrows and E Peel (eds), *Commercial Remedies: Current Issues and Problems* (Oxford, 2003) 36; A Burrows, *Remedies for Torts and Breach of Contract*, 3rd edn (Oxford, 2004) 94. Citation omitted.

[20] A Burrows, 'Limitations on Compensation' ibid, 35; A Burrows, *Remedies for Torts and Breach of Contract*, ibid 92.

[21] Below IV A in this chapter.

[22] A Burrows, *Remedies for Torts and Breach of Contract*, 3rd edn (Oxford, 2004) 141; below ch 10, IV.

[23] A Burrows, ibid 94 fn 3; A Burrows, 'Limitations on Compensation' in A Burrows and E Peel (eds), *Commercial Remedies: Current Issues and Problems* (Oxford, 2003) 36 fn 31.

Kramer convincingly objects that 'the mere opportunity to give notice of a special risk does not necessarily imply an agreement as to the allocation of that risk'.[24]

Cartwright offers a concept similar to Burrows'. Arguing that the *Hadley* test confines contractual liability to loss for which the contract-breaker accepted responsibility when concluding the agreement, he suggests an application of the *Hadley* test to those tort cases where liability arises only because the defendant assumed responsibility on the model of contract, while leaving the *Wagon Mound* test in place for tortious liability tied to an activity.[25] Semantically, this concept unifies the remoteness regime within the common law as the dividing line runs not between contract and tort as such but between assumed and imposed liability. However, the latter distinction leads inevitably back to the former, for liability in tort is always imposed and never truly assumed. Where a defendant is held to have 'assumed' responsibility in tort, an inference is made from his actions.[26] Moreover, if we did distinguish between assumed and imposed liability, it would not be clear why the latter should be wider than the former.[27] An assumption of responsibility by a potential tortfeasor may in fact lessen his need of a limitation of liability by the general law, for he can limit his liability by way of a contract or disclaimer.

IV Aligning Contract with Tort

A The Fairness Argument

By far the most discussed way of unifying the remoteness regime within the common law is an extension of the *Wagon Mound* test to contract. Are there

---

[24] A Kramer, 'Remoteness: New Problems with the Old Test' in D Saidov and R Cunnington (eds), *Contract Damages: Domestic and International Perspectives* (Oxford, 2008) 284.

[25] J Cartwright, 'Remoteness of Damage in Contract and Tort: A Reconsideration' [1996] *Camb LJ* 488, 505. Similar concepts are offered by A Kramer, ibid 290–94; R Stevens, *Torts and Rights* (Oxford, 2007) 207–208.

[26] 'It is sometimes said that there has to be an assumption of responsibility by the person concerned. That phrase can be misleading in that it can suggest that the professional person must knowingly and deliberately accept responsibility. It is, however, clear that the test is an objective one … The phrase means simply that the law recognises a duty of care. It is not so much that responsibility is assumed as that it is recognised or imposed by the law': *Phelps v Hillingdon LBC* [2001] 2 AC 619 (HL) 654 (Lord Slynn). See also A Kramer, 'Proximity as principles: Directness, community norms and the tort of negligence' (2003) 11 *Tort Law Review* 70, 87.

[27] 'No reason is apparent why a party who has undertaken by contract a duty of care to another should ipso facto be less at risk as to damages than one on whom a duty is imposed by the general law': *McElroy Milne v Commercial Electronics Ltd* [1993] 1 NZLR 39 (NZCA) 43 (Cooke P).

cogent reasons for retaining the *Hadley* test in contract?[28] Traditionally the *Hadley* test has been said to provide a fair allocation of risks. The argument runs as follows.

Parties entering a contract can only negotiate an adequate liability clause and calculate a price that correctly reflects the risk undertaken if they are able to assess the extent of their liability in the event of breach. Without specific information from the other side, parties can only assess the extent of their liability in the usual course of things. By denying recovery for unusual loss unless the possibility of such loss was brought to the attention of the contract-breaker prior to the contract, the *Hadley* test forces contracting parties to reveal an extraordinary vulnerability to their partner, which enables the latter to react accordingly, whether by refusing to contract, or by negotiating a clause limiting liability, or by charging a higher price that reflects the extra cost for insurance or precaution.[29] An explanation to this effect has featured in scholarly works[30] as well as cases,[31] including *Hadley v Baxendale* itself[32] and *The Heron II* where the fairness argument was crucial for three of their Lordships in narrowing the extent of liability in contract compared to tort.[33]

Some commentators have pointed out that the fairness argument sits ill with the rule that only the type of loss, not its extent, needs to be foreseeable.[34] If contracting parties need to know the extent of potential liability in order to be able to assess the risk they undertake, contractual liability for any item of unforeseeable loss must be excluded, whether or not the type of loss was foreseeable. What matters to contracting parties is the likely amount of liability they face in the event of breach, not the technicalities of classifying types of loss.

---

[28] Since juries no longer decide contract cases, it is a moot point whether the *Hadley* test is needed to prevent juries from being too harsh on contract-breakers. This has been described as the initial purpose of the *Hadley* test: *A/B Karlshamns Oljefabriker v Monarch Steamship Co* 1949 SC (HL) 1, 28 (Lord du Parcq); *Koufos v C Czarnikow Ltd (The Heron II)* [1969] 1 AC 350 (HL) 397 (Lord Morris).

[29] It lies in the consequence of this argument to exempt from any liability for unusual loss persons required by law to charge a fixed price (such as taxi drivers): I Ramsay, Note (1977) 55 *Can Bar Rev* 169, 176.

[30] DW Barnes, 'The Anatomy of Contract Damages and Efficient Breach Theory' (1998) 6 *Southern California Interdisciplinary Law Journal* 397, 475; A Burrows, *Remedies for Torts and Breach of Contract*, 3rd edn (Oxford, 2004) 92–94; J Cartwright, 'Remoteness of Damage in Contract and Tort: A Reconsideration' [1996] *Camb LJ* 488, 491–92; A Robertson, 'The basis of the remoteness rule in contract' (2008) 28 *Legal Studies* 172, 181, 195.

[31] *British Columbia and Vancouver's Island Spar, Lumber, and Saw-Mill Co Ltd v Nettleship* (1868) LR 3 CP 499, 508 (Willes J): 'one of two contracting parties ought not to be allowed to obtain an advantage which he has not paid for'; *Seven Seas Properties Ltd v Al-Essa (No 2)* [1993] 1 WLR 1083, 1088; *Jackson v Royal Bank of Scotland plc* [2005] UKHL 3, [2005] 1 WLR 377 [36] (Lord Hope).

[32] (1854) 9 Ex 341, 355 (Alderson B): 'For, had the special circumstances been known, the parties might have specially provided for the breach of contract by special terms as to the damages in that case; and of this advantage it would be very unjust to deprive them.'

[33] [1969] 1 AC 350 (HL) 385–86 (Lord Reid), 395 (Lord Morris), 422 (Lord Upjohn).

[34] R Danzig, 'Hadley v. Baxendale: A Study in the Industrialization of the Law' (1975) 4 *Journal of Legal Studies* 249, 283; A Tettenborn, 'Hadley v Baxendale Foreseeability: a Principle Beyond Its Sell-by Date?' (2007) 23 *Journal of Contract Law* 120, 128.

Furthermore, the fairness argument rests on three tacit assumptions: that parties entering a contract envisage the possibility of the other party breaking the contract, that they know the *Hadley* test, and that they can correctly categorise their circumstances as usual or unusual. Where all these assumptions are true, a *Wagon Mound* default would not necessarily produce unfair outcomes. A supplier of goods or services would then be cautious and initially charge the higher price that reflects the risk of liability for unusual loss. Customers with usual circumstances could identify themselves and bargain for a lower price in exchange for a contractual limitation of liability. Although it may be easier to calculate usual loss than unusual loss, there appears to be no major difference between the two tests in terms of fairness.[35] A *Hadley* default compels high-risk partners to identify themselves in order to get full insurance from the other party (in exchange for a higher price) whereas a *Wagon Mound* default compels low-risk partners to identify themselves in order to get a lower price (in exchange for lower insurance).

Moreover, the three tacit assumptions upon which the fairness argument rests are usually false for the consumer in a consumer contract. A consumer contract is a contract where one party deals in the course of a business (the seller or supplier) and the other party does not (the consumer).[36] Where a consumer buys goods from a retailer, employs a plumber, goes on a trip and so on, she will think about whether or not to enter into the contract, and she may also compare the prices of different suppliers, but it will normally not cross her mind that the supplier might breach the contract.[37] Even where the consumer does envisage the possibility of the supplier breaking the contract, she will seldom know that the law requires her to communicate the possibility of unusual loss to the supplier in order to get compensation for that loss. And even where the consumer envisages the possibility of a breach by the supplier and knows the law, she is not necessarily able to categorise herself as a low-risk or high-risk party. She may not be able to anticipate the circumstances that influence her loss in the event of breach, or she may not be able to put them into the correct legal category of usual or unusual. It follows that a consumer expecting unusual loss will rarely communicate this fact to the supplier and will thus rarely obtain full compensation.

Compare this to the situation under a *Wagon Mound* default. Here the consumer needs to do nothing to get full compensation even for unusual loss. The supplier, who is usually aware of the possibility of breach and, at least over time, knows the law, is not disadvantaged, for he may limit his liability through a clause in the contract. Where the supplier offers the consumer a contract with a liability limitation clause, the consumer becomes aware of both the possibility of

---

[35] Arguments based on economic efficiency are considered below IV B–D in this chapter.

[36] Unfair Contract Terms Act 1977 s 12; Unfair Terms in Consumer Contracts Regulations 1999 Reg 3(1).

[37] See A Kramer, 'An Agreement-Centred Approach to Remoteness and Contract Damages' in N Cohen and E McKendrick (eds), *Comparative Remedies for Breach of Contract* (Oxford, 2005) 261.

the supplier breaking the contract and the extent of the supplier's liability in that event. Admittedly, many consumers pay no attention to the small print, but the unfair-terms legislation affords sufficient protection. A *Wagon Mound* default thus nicely balances the interests of consumer and supplier whereas under a *Hadley* default the consumer loses out simply because her knowledge and experience is inferior to that of the supplier. Therefore, with regard to consumer contracts, which form a large group among all contracts, fairness considerations may even point to a *Wagon Mound* default.

B   The Efficiency Argument

Economic efficiency has superseded fairness as the key rationale said to stand behind the *Hadley* principle.[38] This principle, it is argued, gives contracting parties an incentive to inform their partner about the risk of unusually high loss in the event of breach, thus enabling the latter to take optimal precautions against breach.[39] In other words, the *Hadley* principle penalises, through the denial of recovery, the withholding of information where revelation would increase efficiency. Because of this punitive effect, the *Hadley* principle has been described as a 'penalty default'.[40]

The efficiency argument, it should be noted at the outset, is highly controversial. Law-and-economics scholars have taken the debate to a very detailed level, which cannot be pursued in this book. An outline of the main arguments for and against[41] should sufficiently demonstrate that the efficiency argument is too weak to play a major part in deciding the fate of the *Hadley* principle.

Particularly detailed studies in support of the efficiency argument have been presented by Ayres and Gertner[42] (who speak of 'carrier' and 'shipper' to denote the potential contract-breaker and the potential victim) and by Bebchuk and

---

[38]   I Ayres and R Gertner, 'Filling Gaps in Incomplete Contracts: An Economic Theory of Default Rules' (1989) 99 *Yale LJ* 87, 101–104; LA Bebchuk and S Shavell, 'Information and the Scope of Liability for Breach of Contract: The Rule of *Hadley v. Baxendale*' (1991) 7 *Journal of Law, Economics and Organization* 284, 285 ff; RA Posner, *Economic Analysis of Law*, 7th edn (Austin, 2007) 126–127; P Cane, *Tort Law and Economic Interests*, 2nd edn (Oxford, 1996) 145; R Halson, 'Remoteness' in D Harris, D Campbell and R Halson, *Remedies in Contract and Tort*, 2nd edn (London, 2002) 91–93; HG Beale, 'Damages' in HG Beale (gen ed), *Chitty on Contracts, Vol 1: General Principles*, 30th edn (London, 2008) [26–061] fn 306.

[39]   And to accurately assess the efficiency of a breach contemplated: DW Barnes, 'The Anatomy of Contract Damages and Efficient Breach Theory' (1998) 6 *SCILJ* 397, 474–75. See also R Danzig, 'Hadley v. Baxendale: A Study in the Industrialization of the Law' (1975) 4 *JLS* 249, 282–83. The theory of efficient breach is discussed below ch 16, I, A and B.

[40]   I Ayres and R Gertner, 'Filling Gaps in Incomplete Contracts: An Economic Theory of Default Rules' (1989) 99 *Yale LJ* 87, 91 ff.

[41]   For the objections to the efficiency argument, see below IV C in this chapter.

[42]   I Ayres and R Gertner, 'Filling Gaps in Incomplete Contracts: An Economic Theory of Default Rules' (1989) 99 *Yale LJ* 87, 101–104.

Shavell[43] (who speak of 'seller' and 'buyer'). Both studies argue as follows (in the terminology used by Ayres and Gertner). Under a *Hadley* default, a carrier who is uninformed about the shipper's expected loss will take an average level of precautions against breach. These precautions are insufficient for shippers who expect unusually large losses in the event of breach, and the precautions are unnecessarily high for shippers who expect unusually low losses. Both parties can benefit if the carrier learns about the magnitude of the shipper's expected loss. If the shipper expects low loss, the carrier can lower the level of precautions and, consequently, charge a lower price. If the shipper expects high loss, the carrier can take higher precautions, but will, of course, also charge a higher price. The shipper will then compare the increase in price with the cost of buying insurance from a third party and will choose the cheaper, more efficient option.

Under a *Wagon Mound* default, by comparison, high-loss shippers have no incentive to reveal their identity to the carrier, for such revelation would lead to a higher price. It would, of course, also lead to a higher level of precautions taken. But there is no reason for high-loss shippers to care about the precautions since they are fully covered against their loss. The carrier will then become liable to some high-loss shippers and will cover the cost of this liability through raising the price charged. If all shippers pay the same price, the low-loss shippers will cross-subsidise the high-loss shippers, which is inefficient.[44]

A possible objection is that a *Wagon Mound* default gives low-loss shippers an incentive to identify themselves. If the carrier learns that a particular shipper expects below-average loss in the event of breach, the carrier can lower the precautions and the price charged. A division between low-loss shippers and high-loss shippers would emerge, preventing cross-subsidisation. In the same way in which a *Hadley* default forces high-loss shippers to identify themselves (in order to get full insurance), a *Wagon Mound* default would force low-loss shippers to identify themselves (in order to get a lower price).[45]

The pro-*Hadley* studies acknowledge the incentive that low-loss shippers have to bargain around a *Wagon Mound* default, but they bring the effect of transaction costs into play. Bebchuck and Shavell argue that if low-loss shippers outnumber high-loss shippers, the total transaction costs will be lower under a *Hadley* default because then only the minority of high-loss shippers are forced to bargain around the default rule whereas a *Wagon Mound* default forces the majority of low-loss shippers to bargain around the default.[46]

---

[43] LA Bebchuk and S Shavell, 'Information and the Scope of Liability for Breach of Contract: The Rule of *Hadley v. Baxendale*' (1991) 7 *J.L.Econ. & Org.* 284, 285 ff.

[44] For the problem of cross-subsidisation see ibid 307; GD Quillen, 'Contract Damages and Cross-subsidization' (1988) 61 *Southern California Law Review* 1125, 1129–32.

[45] JS Johnston, 'Strategic Bargaining and the Economic Theory of Contract Default Rules' (1990) 100 *Yale LJ* 615, 623.

[46] LA Bebchuk and S Shavell, 'Information and the Scope of Liability for Breach of Contract: The Rule of *Hadley v. Baxendale*' (1991) 7 *J.L.Econ & Org* 284, 285 ff.

Ayres and Gertner go further and argue that transactions costs may even inhibit low-loss shippers from bargaining around a *Wagon Mound* default.[47] Their argument rests on the assumption that the number of high-loss shippers is infinitesimal. In that case, the average level of precautions, that is the level taken by an uninformed carrier, comes very close to the level of precautions sufficient for low-loss shippers. Accordingly, there is only a small difference between the price charged from an unidentified shipper and the lower price charged from an identified low-loss shipper. Low-loss shippers have therefore little to gain from bargaining around a *Wagon Mound* default, so that this bargaining will be prohibited by its costs. By comparison, transaction costs will not prevent high-loss shippers from bargaining around a *Hadley* default. If the number of high-loss shippers is infinitesimal, the level of precautions optimal for those shippers will be much higher than the level taken by an uninformed carrier. As a result, the gain high-loss shippers make from bargaining around a *Hadley* default will be large enough to exceed the cost of this bargaining.

The arguments made by Bebchuk and Shavell and by Ayres and Gertner are based on the assumption that the number of high-loss shippers is (much) smaller than the number of low-loss shippers. This assumption seems to be justified. If low-loss shippers are those shippers who get full compensation under the *Hadley* principle, and high-loss shippers are those shippers who get full compensation only under the *Wagon Mound* principle, then the difference between the two types is that all or a part of the loss suffered by high-loss shippers arose out of unusual circumstances. By definition, unusual circumstances are present only in a small number of cases.

Ayres and Gertner, it should be noted, have undertaken a second study, in which they qualify their initially unreserved praise of the *Hadley* test. They now suggest that the optimal default rule depends on a number of underlying variables, such as the transaction cost, the carrier's market power, the shipper's knowledge of the default rule, and the question of whether the carrier pools all shippers or separates between high-loss shippers and low-loss shippers.[48] Ayres and Gertner still maintain an overall superiority of the *Hadley* test but they acknowledge that there are circumstances where a *Wagon Mound* default is more efficient or where the default rule has no effect. This is a major concession towards the *Wagon Mound* test.

---

[47] I Ayres and R Gertner, 'Filling Gaps in Incomplete Contracts: An Economic Theory of Default Rules' (1989) 99 *Yale LJ* 87, 101–102.

[48] I Ayres and R Gertner 'Strategic Contractual Inefficiency and the Optimal Choice of Legal Rules' (1992) 101 *Yale LJ* 729, 735–62.

C   Objections to the Efficiency Argument

i   Prohibitive Costs

Eisenberg impugns the efficiency argument in defence of the *Hadley* test on the ground that a revelation of unusual circumstances and an adjustment of the level of precaution against breach will often be prohibited by the costs involved.[49] He itemises the following costs. First, there is the shipper's cost of assembling the relevant information and communicating it to the carrier. This cost can be significant considering the uncertainty of what information will be relevant. Secondly, there is the carrier's cost of collecting and processing the information, which includes, for instance, the cost of instructing the carrier's employees in recognising and handling the information. Thirdly, there is the carrier's cost of adjusting the precautions to the needs of the individual shipper. That this cost must not be underestimated is shown by the fact that in practice many carriers who know the value of the goods transported abstain from varying the level of precautions according to the value. Moreover, all these costs are only relevant in the case of breach, and since in practice the breach probability is generally low, it pays even less to incur these costs.

ii   Monopoly Situations

The *Hadley* test is said to produce inefficient outcomes where the carrier enjoys a monopoly or is otherwise strong enough to determine prices without the constraints of competition.[50] The argument runs as follows. A carrier under competition who learns that he is dealing with a high-loss shipper will raise the initially offered price by exactly his extra cost for precautions or insurance; a greater increase is prohibited by competition. A monopolist carrier, by contrast, will raise the initially offered price by at least the shipper's cost to buy insurance from a third party, for it makes no difference to the shipper whether she pays the extra amount to the carrier or to a third party. High-loss shippers have thus nothing to gain from a disclosure of their identity to a monopolist carrier. They might even lose. Knowledge of the shipper's circumstances may allow the carrier to determine the maximum price the shipper will accept, which is the price that makes it just profitable for the shipper to contract rather than not to contract. The carrier will then no longer accept a price lower than this maximum price. Facing this risk, high-loss shippers will choose to keep silent. They will pay the default price and buy insurance from a third party. This is inefficient where, as is

---

[49]   MA Eisenberg, 'The Principle of Hadley v Baxendale' (1992) 80 *California Law Review* 563, 592–96. The argument is supported by A Tettenborn, 'Hadley v Baxendale Foreseeability: a Principle Beyond Its Sell-by Date?' (2007) 23 *JCL* 120, 132–33.

[50]   JS Johnston, 'Strategic Bargaining and the Economic Theory of Contract Default Rules' (1990) 100 *Yale LJ* 615, 627–31; LE Wolcher, 'Price Discrimination and Inefficient Risk Allocation under the Rule of *Hadley v Baxendale*' (1989) 12 *Research in Law and Economics* 9, 19–20.

usual,[51] the carrier's cost for precautions or insurance is lower than the shipper's cost for insurance, in other words, where the carrier is the least-cost avoider.

No such dilemma exists under a *Wagon Mound* default. Here high-loss shippers will accept the default contract offered by the carrier. Low-loss shippers will seek a contract with lower insurance and lower price. They will therefore reveal their identity, and they will do so even if the carrier enjoys a monopoly, for they have nothing to lose. The worst that can happen is that the carrier refuses to alter the default contract; the default contract itself stays open for acceptance.

iii   Strategic Dilemma for Reliable Carriers

Johnston argues that the supporters of the *Hadley* test consider only the carrier's wish to learn about the shipper's expected loss and neglect the shipper's wish to learn about the carrier's probability of breaching the contract.[52] In order to bring the latter issue into play, he assumes that there are two types of carrier. One is the reliable carrier who works with a low probability of breach; the other is the unreliable carrier who works with a high probability of breach. All carriers vary their precautions according to the extent of their liability, which is the assumption made by the defenders of the *Hadley* principle. Johnston now argues that in such a situation a *Hadley* default fails to produce efficient outcomes in the case of high-loss shippers. His argument runs as follows.

Under a *Hadley* default reliable carriers are at a natural cost disadvantage, for their precautions are unnecessarily high given the limited carrier liability. As a result, they have to charge a higher price than unreliable carriers for contracts with limited liability. They are more efficient though where the shipper expects high loss and carrier liability is increased, for under these circumstances the precautions taken by unreliable carriers are insufficient. In order to stay in the market, reliable carriers will therefore try to win contracts with high-loss shippers who, according to the *Hadley* defenders, have an incentive to bargain for increased liability. Consequently, reliable carriers seek to signal their reliability to potential customers. Since high quality is usually reflected through a high price, reliable carriers signal their reliability already through the higher price charged for contracts with limited liability. They have no need to offer contracts with increased liability in order to signal their reliability. And such an offer would even be dangerous, for the following reason.

A shipper who believes the carrier is reliable will perceive little benefit from increasing the carrier's liability. An increased carrier liability pays off only in the case of breach, and if the carrier works with a low probability of breach, the shipper might not consider it worth buying higher insurance from the carrier. If the carrier now offers a contract with increased carrier liability and accordingly

---

[51]   For the opposite view see *Photo Production Ltd v Securicor Transport Ltd* [1980] AC 827 (HL) 851 (Lord Diplock); SM Waddams, *The Law of Damages*, 3rd edn (Toronto, 1997) [14.330]–[14.340].

[52]   JS Johnston, 'Strategic Bargaining and the Economic Theory of Contract Default Rules' (1990) 100 *Yale LJ* 615, 632–36.

higher price, the shipper might get suspicious that the higher price is merely an attempt to extract additional profit and that this carrier is not a good contract-partner. This shows a strategic dilemma for reliable carriers: If they want to convince a high-loss shipper of entering into a contract with high liability and high price, they may eventually scare off the shipper and get no contract at all. Consequently, they will only offer contracts with limited liability, signalling their reliability through the higher price charged for those contracts, and high-loss shippers will not bargain for increased carrier liability. The outcome is inefficient as the carrier will not take the precautions optimal for high-loss shippers.

Such a dilemma does not exist under a *Wagon Mound* default. Here unreliable carriers are at a natural cost disadvantage, for their precautions are insufficient given the high level of liability. They have to charge a higher price than reliable carriers for contracts with high liability. They might hope that shippers misread the higher price as an indicator of higher quality, but this would not work for long. In order to stay in the market, they must distinguish themselves by offering contracts with limited liability, for which they have a cost advantage. They then attract low-loss shippers, who do not need increased liability. As a result, there will be contracts between low-loss shippers and unreliable carriers with limited liability, and contracts between high-loss shippers and reliable carriers with high liability. This is exactly the efficient outcome.

iv Possibility of Menu

So far it has been assumed that the carrier initially offers only one liability-price-package. But the carrier may also design a menu of several different packages, between which the shipper then may choose. The *Hadley* defenders Ayres and Gertner attribute little practical importance to this situation on the ground that devising the appropriate menu requires significant effort and will thus often be prohibited by the cost involved.[53] Some carriers, however, do offer a menu of different liability-price-packages (the Royal Mail for instance). Where this is the case, Johnston argues, every shipper will choose the package optimal for her, irrespective of whether the default rule is *Hadley* or *Wagon Mound*. High-loss shippers will choose the package with high liability and a high price, low-loss shippers will choose the package with low liability and a low price.[54]

D Preventing Unreasonable Reliance upon Performance

The efficiency of the *Hadley* principle has been asserted with an emphasis on the prevention of unreasonable reliance upon performance. Posner provides the

---

[53] I Ayres and R Gertner, 'Filling Gaps in Incomplete Contracts: An Economic Theory of Default Rules' (1989) 99 *Yale LJ* 87, 103.

[54] JS Johnston, 'Strategic Bargaining and the Economic Theory of Contract Default Rules' (1990) 100 *Yale LJ* 615, 636–38, who observes, however, that the carrier cannot extract all profit out of high-loss shippers as he must give them an incentive to opt for the high price.

following example.[55] A commercial photographer takes pictures of the Himalayas, thereby incurring heavy expenses (including the hire of an airplane). He mails the film to a developer but it is mislaid and never found. An expensive re-take of the pictures is necessary. The photographer could have cheaply avoided the huge loss by using two rolls of film or requesting special handling from the developer. In such scenarios, it is argued, a denial of recovery through the *Hadley* test gives the promisee an incentive to take cost-effective precautions.

Inefficient over-reliance must indeed be prevented. But the *Hadley* principle is neither sufficient nor necessary to achieve this objective. It is not sufficient because a promisor will still be fully liable where the promisee's over-reliance can be contemplated at the time of the contract as not unlikely.[56] It is not necessary, for three not mutually exclusive reasons. First, the promisor may expressly disclaim liability for loss resulting from over-reliance.[57] Secondly, even in the absence of such express disclaimer it may be argued that loss resulting from over-reliance is outside the protective scope of the promisor's duty to perform or, what amounts to the same, the promisor did not accept responsibility for such loss.[58]

Finally, where liability cannot be denied per se on either of those grounds, the promisee's inefficient over-reliance should at least lead to a reduction in the promisor's liability on the ground of contributory negligence.[59] At present, contributory negligence affects a contractual claim only where a duty of care co-extensive in contract and tort is broken.[60] Chapter ten argues that an apportionment of liability by virtue of contributory negligence should be available in all contractual actions. Epstein objects that the *Hadley* principle obviates the

---

[55] RA Posner, *Economic Analysis of Law*, 7th edn (Austin, 2007) 126; *Evra Corp v Swiss Bank Corp* (1982) 673 F.2d 951 (US CA for 7th Circuit) 957–958 (Posner J). See also R Cooter and T Ulen, *Law and Economics*, 5th edn (Boston, 2008) 274–75.

[56] See *Willard Van Dyke Productions Inc v Eastman Kodak Co* (1963) 12 N.Y.2d 301 (NY CA). A commercial photographer had to retake photos in Alaska after the film developer in New York had negligently damaged the only roll initially made. Remoteness was no issue, perhaps because the necessity of retaking the photos had been foreseeable.

[57] R Danzig, 'Hadley v. Baxendale: A Study in the Industrialization of the Law' (1975) 4 *JLS* 249, 281. In *Willard Van Dyke Productions Inc v Eastman Kodak Co*, ibid, the film developer was liable for the cost of retaking the photos only because its disclaimer had not been sufficiently clear and unequivocal.

[58] See A Kramer, 'An Agreement-Centred Approach to Remoteness and Contract Damages' in N Cohen and E McKendrick (eds), *Comparative Remedies for Breach of Contract* (Oxford, 2005) 264–65; A Tettenborn, 'Hadley v Baxendale Foreseeability: a Principle Beyond Its Sell-by Date?' (2007) 23 *JCL* 120, 141–43.

[59] A Porat, 'Contributory Negligence in Contract Law: Toward a Principled Approach' (1994) 28 *University of British Columbia Law Review* 141, 151–53. Similarly, mitigation doctrine (if still separated from contributory negligence: below ch 10, VI C) is a better instrument than remoteness doctrine to deal with imprudent promisee behaviour after the breach: MA Eisenberg, 'The Principle of Hadley v Baxendale' (1992) 80 *CLR* 563, 583–84.

[60] Below ch 10, III.

inquiry into contributory negligence.[61] But the inquiry into what the promisor knew, and could contemplate as not unlikely, at the time of the contract seems not much easier.

E   Contractual Liability is Generally Strict

Leaving aside contracts for service where the service provider cannot generally be in breach of contract without being at fault,[62] contractual liability is strict, that is the exercise of reasonable care and skill does not relieve the contract-breaker from liability.[63] The *Hadley* test might be defended on the ground that a combination of strict liability with a *Wagon Mound* remoteness test would be too harsh on contract-breakers.[64]

Accepting this argument for a moment, there are, theoretically, still two ways of challenging the general application of the *Hadley* test in contract. First, the need for a restrictive remoteness test could be obviated by introducing a general fault requirement for contractual liability, as it exists in many civil law countries.[65] Such a fundamental change in contract law is, however, extremely unlikely to occur.

Secondly, the scope of the *Hadley* test could be confined to innocent breaches, leaving deliberate and negligent breaches to the wider *Wagon Mound* test. Such a regime, which comes close to the one adopted in Article 9:503 of the Principles of European Contract Law and Article III-3:703 of the European Union's Draft Common Frame of Reference,[66] would not fit well into the contract law of common law jurisdictions. It could be regarded as an introduction of the fault principle through the back door, and it would load many proceedings with an inquiry into the circumstances of the breach only to make the choice between two remoteness tests that are not so different anyway. The law should remain straightforward and should not make remoteness dependent on culpability. If innocent contract-breakers need the protection afforded by the *Hadley* test, the same benefit must be granted to careless and deliberate contract-breakers.

---

[61]   RA Epstein, 'Beyond Foreseeability: Consequential Damages in the Law of Contract' (1989) 18 *JLS* 105, 133–34.

[62]   *Greaves & Co (Contractors) Ltd v Baynham Meikle & Partners* [1975] 1 WLR 1095 (CA) 1100; *Thake v Maurice* [1986] QB 644 (CA) 685–87 (for medical treatment); *Barclays Bank plc v Weeks Legg & Dean* [1999] QB 309 (CA) 327–28 (for solicitors).

[63]   *Raineri v Miles* [1981] AC 1050 (HL) 1086; *Parsons (Livestock) Ltd v Uttley Ingham & Co Ltd* [1978] QB 791 (CA) 800 (for the warranty implied by the Sale of Goods Act 1979 ss 12 and 14); *Barclays Bank plc v Fairclough Building Ltd (No 1)* [1995] QB 214 (CA) 223 (for a building firm's obligation to execute the work in accordance with the contractual specifications; below ch 10, V).

[64]   The argument is raised by M Whincup, 'Remoteness reconsidered' (1992) 142 *New LJ* 389, 390, who, however, considers the present law unsatisfactory.

[65]   GH Treitel, *Remedies for Breach of Contract: A Comparative Account* (Oxford, 1988) [8]–[16].

[66]   These instruments require no foreseeability for intentional and grossly negligent breaches, and require foreseeability 'as a likely result' for other breaches.

But do innocent contract-breakers actually need that protection? They do not need it where the loss in question was foreseeable, if only as a slight possibility, at the time of the contract. In this case the contract-breaker had the opportunity to refuse to contract, to limit liability, or to charge a higher price and take extra precautions against breach. It should not matter whether the loss in question was foreseeable as a slight or serious possibility. Parties negotiating a contract can be required to take account of a slight possibility of their potential contract-partner suffering certain loss, considering that, in order to avoid tortious liability, people are expected to take account in their conduct of the slight possibility of another person suffering loss.

Innocent contract-breakers can do without the protection afforded by the *Hadley* test even where the loss in question was foreseeable as possible at the time of the breach but not at the time of the contract. In such a situation of post-contractual changes rendering the aggrieved party more vulnerable in the event of breach, the *Hadley* test excludes liability whereas the *Wagon Mound* test would impose liability. It is increasingly recognised, however, that the extent of contractual liability depends ultimately on the parties' assumption of responsibility or, synonymously, the scope of the duty breached.[67] In the present situation, therefore, liability must ultimately depend on which party undertook to bear the risk of post-contractual changes. Even if the *Wagon Mound* test were to be used in general, the unforeseeability of the loss in question at the time of the contract may indicate that the contract-breaker did not bear the risk of post-contractual changes and thus escapes liability.

F Conclusion

Even though the arguments in defence of the *Hadley* test cannot be brushed aside as far fetched, they are weaker than they may look at first sight. The argument of economic efficiency is highly controversial, and the other arguments have been challenged. Since a remoteness regime uniform in contract and tort is desirable particularly with regard to concurrent liability,[68] an extension of the *Wagon Mound* test to contract stands to reason. What would be the effects of taking this step?

---

[67] eg *Transfield Shipping Inc v Mercator Shipping Inc (The Achilleas)* [2008] UKHL 48, [2009] 1 AC 61 [11]–[26] (Lord Hoffmann), [30]–[36] (Lord Hope); A Kramer, 'An Agreement-Centred Approach to Remoteness and Contract Damages' in N Cohen and E McKendrick (eds), *Comparative Remedies for Breach of Contract* (Oxford, 2005) 249–73; D McLauchlan, 'Remoteness Re-Invented?' (2009) 9 *OUCLJ* 109, 112–16; A Tettenborn, 'Hadley v Baxendale Foreseeability: a Principle Beyond Its Sell-by Date?' (2007) 23 *JCL* 120, 134–47. Similarly A Robertson, 'The basis of the remoteness rule in contract' (2008) 28 *LS* 172, 188–95, who speaks of a 'fair' allocation of risk whether or not this is implicit in the contract.

[68] 'It would be surprising if the breach of duty is the same ... but a different result was obtained depending on whether the cause of action was framed in contract or in tort': *Berryman v Hounslow LBC* [1997] PIQR P83 (CA) P90–P91 (Stuart-Smith LJ). See also above ch 1, III.

First, the degree of foresight required for loss to be recoverable in contract would drop from 'serious possibility' to 'slight possibility'.[69] The difference between the two degrees has never been huge and has further shrunk since it was recognised that in contract, just as in tort, it is only the type of loss and not its extent that needs to be foreseeable. Take for instance *Parsons*. Even though the fatal disease the pigs fell victim to was unlikely to occur, the Court of Appeal held the defendant liable, with the majority basing this decision on the serious possibility of *any* illness. Or take *Brown* where the serious possibility of *some* loss from the investment founded liability for all loss even though nobody could foresee the actual magnitude of the loss. It may be doubted whether a lowering of the degree of foresight required for contractual liability would have any significant impact at all.

The real effect of extending the *Wagon Mound* test to contract is the change of the time at which foreseeability is judged. The contract-breaker would be liable for loss unforeseeable at the time of the contract if it was foreseeable at the time of the breach. Suppose that a promisor, at the time of the contract, foresees that a breach of contract by him will inflict loss X on the other party. After the contract has been made the circumstances change and the promisor now foresees that a breach by him will inflict on the other party not only loss X but also loss Y. While the *Hadley* test confines liability to X, the *Wagon Mound* test imposes liability for X and Y.

Liability for Y might be considered too harsh as the prevention of Y may require significantly higher efforts than the prevention of X. But where this is the case, it must first be asked whether the promisor actually undertook to make these higher efforts, in other words, whether the promisor undertook to bear the risk of the post-contractual event occurring. There is increasing support for the proposition that liability depends ultimately on the implicit allocation of risks in the contract and that the foreseeability test is just a (useful) default rule defining such allocation in the absence of contrary indicators. Where the promisor's liability for Y appears inappropriate in the circumstances of the case, it should be carefully examined whether the other party impliedly undertook to bear the risk in question. Where the promisor does bear the risk and has a real choice between performance and breach, it is even desirable that the promisor must take Y into account.

In conclusion, an extension of the *Wagon Mound* test to contract is not too harsh on contract-breakers. It is the appropriate way of unifying the remoteness regime within the common law.

---

[69] The latter is sufficient under Art 74(2) of the United Nations Convention on Contracts for the International Sale of Goods: M Bridge, *The International Sale of Goods: Law and Practice*, 2nd edn (Oxford, 2007) [12.55]–[12.56]; F Ferrari, 'Comparative Ruminations on the Foreseeability of Damages in Contract Law' (1993) 53 *Louisiana Law Review* 1257, 1268; AG Murphey, 'Consequential Damages in Contracts for the International Sale of Goods and the Legacy of Hadley' (1989) 23 *George Washington Journal of International Law and Economics* 415, 439–43.

5

Remoteness of Damage in Equity

I Misapplication of Trust Property

Following judicial suggestion,[1] the issue of remoteness of damage in equity will be discussed separately for three important equitable wrongs: misapplication of trust property, breach of an equitable duty of care and skill, and breach of fiduciary duty.[2] The investigation starts with the mother of all equitable wrongs, the misapplication of trust property by a trustee. This wrong manifests itself where a trustee disposes of trust funds without being authorised by the trust deed to do so. In that case, the trustee has traditionally been said to be under an obligation to effect 'restitution' to the trust by restoring the assets concerned *in specie* or, if that is unfeasible, by handing over their money value. The notion of remoteness of damage is foreign to that concept. In the New South Wales case *Re Dawson*, for instance, Street J pronounced that 'the trustee is liable to place the trust estate in the same position as it would have been in if no breach had been committed. Considerations of causation, foreseeability and remoteness do not readily enter into the matter.'[3]

This concept is now under threat due to the decision by the House of Lords in *Target Holdings Ltd v Redferns*.[4] Redferns, a firm of solicitors, acted for a prospective purchaser of land (Crowngate) and also for the prospective mortgagee (Target). Target gave Redferns over £1.5 million to be held on bare trust and be transferred to Crowngate once the property had been purchased and charged to Target. In breach of trust Redferns paid away the money before Crowngate

---

[1] *Bank of New Zealand v New Zealand Guardian Trust Co Ltd* [1999] 1 NZLR 664 (NZCA), 687–88 (Tipping J).

[2] In cases of breach of confidence, 'issues of foreseeability and remoteness will rarely arise': V Vann, *Equitable Compensation in Australia: Principles and Problems* (Saarbrücken, 2009) 257. In cases of dishonest assistance in an equitable wrong, remoteness of damage should be decided identically for primary wrongdoer and assistant: SB Elliott and C Mitchell, 'Remedies for Dishonest Assistance' (2004) 67 *Modern Law Review* 16–23, 37–38.

[3] [1966] 2 NSWR 211, 214.

[4] [1996] AC 421 (HL). The decision is embraced by A Burrows, *Remedies for Torts and Breach of Contract*, 3rd edn (Oxford, 2004) 604–606; CEF Rickett, 'Where are We Going with Equitable Compensation' in AJ Oakley (ed), *Trends in Contemporary Trust Law* (Oxford, 1996) 183–89.

purchased the property. One month later, the property was charged to Target. Subsequently, Crowngate became insolvent and Target sold the property for £500,000. (There were signs of fraud on Crowngate's part but this issue was left for further trial.)

Target sued Redferns for 'restitution' of the entire sum (£1.5 million), reduced by the sum realised on the sale of the property. Target argued as follows. When wrongfully paying out the money, Redferns immediately became obliged to restore it. This obligation was not affected by Target eventually receiving exactly the security it had intended to obtain, as the common law principles of causation have no application to a claim for breach of trust. The House of Lords rejected that argument.

Lord Browne-Wilkinson, speaking for the House, pointed to the fact that the trust in suit was a bare trust, where the beneficiary is absolutely entitled to the trust fund, as opposed to a traditional trust, where the fund is held in trust for several beneficiaries having different, usually successive, interests (such as a trust for A for life with the remainder to B).[5] The remedies for breach of trust have largely been developed in relation to traditional trusts, and the rationale of each rule determines whether it is equally applicable to bare trusts. The obligation of a defaulting trustee to reconstitute the trust fund is not applicable to bare trusts, for this obligation is rooted in the fact that it is the only way to protect the rights of all beneficiaries of a traditional trust. In the case of bare trusts it would be entirely artificial to order a defaulting trustee to reconstitute the trust fund as opposed to paying compensation directly to the beneficiary. The beneficiary of a bare trust can therefore only claim compensation for the loss resulting from the breach of trust. In assessing this claim foreseeability is no concern, but a common sense view of causation applies.[6] On this basis, Redferns' breach of trust had caused no loss to Target.

Lord Browne-Wilkinson's reasoning is obscure, as Lord Millett, extrajudicially, points out.[7] First, it was seen as crucial in *Target* that the trust in suit was a bare trust, but it is hardly conceivable that a different outcome would have been reached in the case of a traditional trust. Where, for instance, the trustees of a traditional family trust with the power to invest in a mortgage, negligently part with the trust money a few days before the mortgage is executed, should they really be liable for more than a few days' loss of interest? Secondly, Lord Browne-Wilkinson failed to explain why, in the case of bare trusts, the trustee's liability is only limited by a common sense view of causation and not by the common law doctrines of causation and remoteness of damage.

---

[5] [1996] AC 421 (HL) 434–39.

[6] With regard to causation and remoteness, Lord Browne-Wilkinson adopted McLachlin J's minority judgment in *Canson Enterprises Ltd v Boughton & Co* [1991] 3 SCR 534 (SCC) 551, 556.

[7] PJ Millett, 'Equity's Place in the Law of Commerce' (1998) 114 *Law Quarterly Review* 214, 224–25.

The critics of *Target* defend the traditional strict liability for the misapplication of trust funds with the following compelling analysis.[8] Where a trustee misapplies trust funds, the beneficiary may falsify the account and ask for the disbursement to be disallowed. The unauthorised investment will then be treated as having been bought with the trustee's own money and on his own behalf. Consequently, the trustee is entitled to the proceeds of the investment, if any, but he must pay into the trust fund, out of his own pocket, the full amount of the disbursement. Since it is irrelevant what has happened to the assets taken out, questions of causation, remoteness of damage, mitigation or contributory negligence cannot arise. This does not mean that the actual outcome in *Target* was wrong. Although Redferns, when paying out the trust money, immediately came under an obligation to reconstitute the trust fund, they discharged this obligation by providing the mortgage. The trustee's obligation to restore misapplied trust property is not an obligation to restore it in the very form in which he disbursed it but an obligation to restore it in any form authorised by the trust, and Redferns were authorised to part with the money in exchange for the mortgage.

Elliott and Mitchell explain that two meanings of 'compensation' and 'loss' must be distinguished.[9] Predominantly these terms are used where the defendant's misconduct has caused injury to the claimant's interests. The claimant suffers 'reparable loss' by being worse off than without the wrong, and can claim 'reparative compensation'. This is the meaning of compensation and loss in the context of common law compensatory damages. 'Substitutive compensation', by contrast, consists in the money equivalent to property of which a person has been deprived or denied. Here 'loss' consists in the objective value of the property denied or of the deterioration in the property. Whether the claimant's overall financial position has been diminished is immaterial to that valuation. The second meaning of compensation and loss is used in the context of expropriation and the misapplication of trust property.

In *Bairstow v Queens Moat Houses plc*,[10] the Court of Appeal seemed to side with the critics of *Target*. Directors of a company were held liable to replace capital improperly paid out as dividends even though there may have been no loss to the company as lawful dividends of the same amount could have been

---

[8] ibid 226–27; S Elliott and J Edelman, '*Target Holdings* Considered in Australia' (2003) 119 *LQR* 545, 548; SB Elliott and C Mitchell, 'Remedies for Dishonest Assistance' (2004) 67 *MLR* 16, 26–28; V Vann, *Equitable Compensation in Australia: Principles and Problems* (Saarbrücken, 2009) 98–105. See also P Birks, 'Equity in the Modern Law: An Exercise in Taxonomy' (1996) 26 *University of Western Australia Law Review* 1, 47. *Target* is re-interpreted in the light of the critics' analysis by D Hayton, P Matthews and C Mitchell, *Underhill and Hayton: Law Relating to Trusts and Trustees*, 17th edn (London, 2007) [89.21].

[9] SB Elliott and C Mitchell, ibid 24–28. See also S Elliott and J Edelman, ibid; D Hayton, P Matthews and C Mitchell, ibid [89.7].

[10] [2001] EWCA Civ 712, [2002] BCC 91.

paid out. Robert Walker LJ, speaking for the Court, distinguished *Target* on the ground that the directors had acted fraudulently, but he also indicated that *Target* may have to be reconsidered:

> It may be that a more satisfactory dividing line is not that between the traditional trust and the commercial trust, but between a breach of fiduciary duty in the wrongful disbursement of funds of which the fiduciary has this sort of trustee-like stewardship and a breach of fiduciary duty of a different character.[11]

In conclusion, the obligation to restore trust assets wrongfully given away is not subject to remoteness doctrine the reasons for which, however, also bring the case outside the scope of the present study. A trustee has to account for disbursements, and unauthorised disbursements will simply be disallowed. The obligation to restore the assets is akin to the specific performance of a contract[12] whereas the present study concerns what Elliott and Mitchell call 'reparative compensation', the compensation for an injury inflicted upon the claimant's interests by the defendant's conduct.

II Breach of an Equitable Duty of Care and Skill

Fiduciaries, like trustees, agents, directors and so on must act in the interest of the principal, and they must do so with due care and skill.[13] But not every breach of duty by a fiduciary is a breach of fiduciary duty, as explained in *Bristol and West Building Society v Mothew*.[14] A solicitor acted for both the purchasers of a house and the mortgagee. The mortgagee offered the money on the condition that the purchasers pay the balance of the purchase price without resort to further borrowing, and instructed the solicitor to report, prior to completion, any arrangements by the purchasers for a second mortgage or other loans. The solicitor knew that the purchasers were arranging a second mortgage but, due to an oversight, reported to the mortgagee that the condition was met. The mortgagee advanced the money. When the purchasers defaulted, the mortgagee sought to recover its loss from the solicitor.

The Court of Appeal held that the solicitor's misstatement did not amount to a breach of fiduciary duty as he was merely careless and not deliberately disloyal to the mortgagee. Breach of fiduciary duty, said Millett LJ, connotes disloyalty or infidelity, so that a servant who loyally does his incompetent best for his master is

---

[11] ibid [53].
[12] SB Elliott and C Mitchell, 'Remedies for Dishonest Assistance' (2004) 67 *MLR* 16, 28.
[13] *White v Jones* [1995] 2 AC 207 (HL) 271 (Lord Browne-Wilkinson).
[14] [1998] Ch 1 (CA).

not guilty of a breach of fiduciary duty.[15] It follows that a trustee who merely fails to make a lucrative investment will not incur the absolute liability described earlier.[16]

A loyal but careless fiduciary remains liable for breach of an equitable duty of care and skill.[17] An equitable duty of care goes usually hand in hand with a duty of care in tort, and they were even regarded as the same duty by Lord Browne-Wilkinson in *Henderson v Merrett Syndicates Ltd*:

> The liability of a fiduciary for the negligent transaction of his duties is not a separate head of liability but the paradigm of the general duty to act with care imposed by law on those who take it upon themselves to act for or advise others.[18]

Under the concept of a fusion of common law and equity, the breach of an equitable duty of care is but an instance of tortious negligence.[19] In the light of the closeness, or even identity, of equitable and tortious duty of care, it would be strange if the extent of liability for breach of that duty differed between equity and tort,[20] as is recognised in two dicta. In *Bristol and West Building Society v Mothew* Millett LJ observed that equitable compensation for breach of the duty of care and skill resembles common law damages in that it is to compensate the claimant's loss: 'There is no reason in principle why the common law rules of causation, remoteness of damage and measure of damages should not be applied by analogy in such a case'.[21]

Referring to that case, Evans LJ, in *Swindle v Harrison*, said about equitable duties: 'The consequent need to identify the scope of the particular duty which has been breached is entirely consistent, in my view, with the approach to

---

[15]   ibid 18. See also *Permanent Building Society v Wheeler* (1994) 14 ACSR 109 (WASC) 157 (Ipp J); *Bank of New Zealand v New Zealand Guardian Trust Co Ltd* [1999] 1 NZLR 213, 240, 246; [1999] 1 NZLR 664 (NZCA) 680, 687–88. A separation of diligence and loyalty is opposed by J Getzler, 'Equitable Compensation and the Regulation of Fiduciary Relationships' in P Birks and F Rose (eds), *Restitution and Equity, Vol 1: Resulting Trusts and Equitable Compensation* (London, 2000) 254–57.

[16]   Above I in this chapter: SB Elliott and C Mitchell, 'Remedies for Dishonest Assistance' (2004) 67 *MLR* 16, 30; PJ Millett, 'Equity's Place in the Law of Commerce' (1998) 114 *LQR* 214, 225–26.

[17]   *White v Jones* [1995] 2 AC 207 (HL) 271; *Swindle v Harrison* [1997] 4 All ER 705 (CA) 716; *Bristol and West Building Society v Mothew* [1998] Ch 1 (CA) 16–17. An equitable liability for mere carelessness (without disloyalty) separate from liability in negligence is opposed by PD Finn, 'The Fiduciary Principle' in TG Youdan (ed), *Equity, Fiduciaries and Trusts* (Toronto, 1989) 28–31, and in the case of careless advice also by IE Davidson, 'The Equitable Remedy of Compensation' (1982) 13 *Melbourne University Law Review* 349, 372–76.

[18]   [1995] 2 AC 145 (HL) 205.

[19]   A Burrows, 'We Do This At Common Law But That In Equity' (2002) 22 *Oxford Journal of Legal Studies* 1, 9; A Burrows, *Fusing Common Law and Equity: Remedies, Restitution and Reform* (Hong Kong, 2002) 6. The present book takes no stand in the fusion debate: above ch 1, V.

[20]   A Burrows, 'We Do This At Common Law But That In Equity' (2002) 22 *OJLS* 1, 11–12; SB Elliott, 'Remoteness Criteria in Equity' (2002) 65 *MLR* 588, 594–95; C Rickett, 'Compensating for Loss in Equity—Choosing the Right Horse for Each Course' in P Birks and F Rose (eds), *Restitution and Equity, Vol 1: Resulting Trusts and Equitable Compensation* (London, 2000) 188.

[21]   [1998] Ch 1 (CA) 17. See also *Permanent Building Society v Wheeler* (1994) 14 ACSR 109 (SCWA) 166 (Ipp J); *Bank of New Zealand v New Zealand Guardian Trust Co Ltd* [1999] 1 NZLR 213, 247; [1999] 1 NZLR 664 (NZCA) 681, 688.

common law damages set out in Lord Hoffmann's *South Australia* speech'.[22] The remoteness regime governing the tort of negligence seems, therefore, to be conquering the terrain of the breach of an equitable duty of care.

III Breach of Fiduciary Duty

A breach of fiduciary duty occurs where a fiduciary acts disloyally towards the principal by, for instance, making a secret unauthorised profit from his position.[23] Extending the remedy against defaulting trustees to other fiduciaries, equity originally developed a 'restitutionary'[24] response to a breach of fiduciary duty, under which the aim of compensation was described as the restoration of the principal to the position she was in when the fiduciary acted disloyally.[25] This is not identical to the aim of putting the principal into the position she would be in without the breach, for under the first formula the principal will be put into her position at the time of the breach even if her present situation would be exactly the same without the breach, in other words, even if the fiduciary's disloyal behaviour was not the cause of the loss the principal has suffered since.[26]

An expression of the traditional approach may be the principle, pronounced by the Privy Council in the Ontario case *Brickenden v London Loan & Savings Co*, that a fiduciary who failed to inform the principal about facts relevant to a transaction 'cannot be heard to maintain that disclosure would not have altered the decision to proceed with the transaction'.[27] If this passage is understood as rendering irrelevant what the principal would have done on disclosure,[28] the

---

[22] [1997] 4 All ER 705 (CA) 717. He was referring to *South Australia Asset Management Corp v York Montague Ltd* [1997] AC 191 (HL); above ch 2, VI. The 'scope of the duty' concept was applied to an equitable duty of care in *Bank of New Zealand v New Zealand Guardian Trust Co Ltd* [1999] 1 NZLR 664 (NZCA) 682–86.

[23] The main types of a breach of fiduciary duty for which equitable compensation is, or ought to be, available are discussed by IE Davidson, 'The Equitable Remedy of Compensation' (1982) 13 *MULR* 349, 372–96.

[24] In equity, the term 'restitution' has confusingly been used for both compensation of loss and disgorgement of gain: R Chambers, 'Liability' in P Birks and A Pretto (eds), *Breach of Trust* (Oxford, 2002) 13–16; V Vann, *Equitable Compensation in Australia: Principles and Problems* (Saarbrücken, 2009) 18–25.

[25] *Nocton v Lord Ashburton* [1914] AC 932 (HL) 952 (Viscount Haldane LC). See JD Davies, 'Equitable Compensation: "Causation, Foreseeability and Remoteness"' in DWM Waters (ed), *Equity, Fiduciaries and Trusts 1993* (Toronto, 1993) 301–302. The formula is still used by J Glover, *Commercial Equity: Fiduciary Relationships* (Sydney, 1995) [6.122], [6.125].

[26] *Swindle v Harrison* [1997] 4 All ER 705 (CA) 713–14 (Evans LJ).

[27] [1934] 3 DLR 465 (PC) 469 (Lord Thankerton).

[28] It was so understood in *Bristol and West Building Society v May May & Merrimans* [1996] 2 All ER 801, 826–27. The courts in Canada and New Zealand regard *Brickenden* as a merely evidential rule; see the cases cited in S Harder, 'Is a Defaulting Fiduciary Exculpated by the Principal's Hypothetical Consent?' (2008) 8 *Oxford University Commonwealth Law Journal* 25, 33–34. This view may rely on the fact that Lord Thankerton in *Brickenden*, ibid, went on to say that 'speculation as to what course

fiduciary will be liable even where a disclosure of the facts in question would not have altered the fiduciary's decision to proceed with the transaction.[29] In other words, the fiduciary may be liable for loss that the principal has suffered since the fiduciary's breach of duty even though the principal would have suffered the same loss without that breach. If neither the establishment of a breach of fiduciary duty nor the availability of equitable compensation requires even a causal link between the fiduciary's breach and the principal's loss, the foreseeability of the loss will not be expected to be a requirement either.

In several cases decided since 1997, however, the Court of Appeal has laid down that the availability of equitable compensation for breach of fiduciary duty does require a causal link between the fiduciary's breach and the principal's loss. The 'breakthrough' came in *Swindle v Harrison*.[30] Mrs Harrison intended to acquire a hotel and start a restaurant business. When she desperately needed a bridging loan in order to go ahead with the purchase, the solicitors advising her on the transaction offered to lend her the money through their bank. In breach of fiduciary duty, the solicitors concealed the fact that they were entitled to half of the arrangement fee to be paid by Mrs Harrison. She took the loan and acquired the hotel, but the restaurant business proved unsuccessful. Based on the solicitors' breach of fiduciary duty, Mrs Harrison sought equitable compensation for the loss suffered through the business failure. The Court of Appeal denied her claim.

Mummery LJ based this decision on the 'scope of the duty' concept which *SAAMCO* had highlighted for common law duties and which, in his opinion, also applies to equity.[31] The solicitors, he said, had no duty to abstain from lending money to Mrs Harrison in all circumstances or to prevent her from buying the hotel. They had a duty to disclose all material facts relevant to the bridging loan, but the breach of that duty was not the cause of Mrs Harrison's loss because, as the judge had found, she would have bought the hotel in any event. Similarly, Hobhouse LJ opined that Mrs Harrison 'cannot use a breach of fiduciary duty to obtain a remedy in respect of a transaction other than that in relation to which the fiduciary was dealing with his client'.[32] In his view, the specifically equitable remedies for breach of fiduciary duty are rescission and account of profits, but where a principal seeks compensation for loss suffered she must discharge the same burden of proof as at common law.[33]

---

the [principal], on disclosure, would have taken is not relevant'. No speculation takes place where the fiduciary produces conclusive evidence: J Berryman, 'Equitable Compensation for Breach by Fact-Based Fiduciaries: Tentative Thoughts on Clarifying Remedial Goals' (1999) 37 *Alberta Law Review* 95, 106; JD Heydon, 'Causal Relationships Between a Fiduciary's Default and the Principal's Loss' (1994) 110 *LQR* 328, 332.

[29] What the principal would have done on disclosure is indeed irrelevant to the remedies of rescission, account of profits and, if recognised in principle, constructive trust: S Harder, ibid 28–32.

[30] [1997] 4 All ER 705 (CA).

[31] ibid 734–35. For *SAAMCO* and the 'scope of the duty' concept see above ch 2, VI.

[32] [1997] 4 All ER 705 (CA) 726.

[33] ibid.

On a different route, Evans LJ opined that the stringent measure of damages expressed in *Brickenden* applies only to breaches of equitable duties equivalent to fraud whereas in other cases, like the present one, the principal will be placed into as good a position as without the breach, which requires proof of causation.[34] While this distinction between fraud-like and other breaches of fiduciary duty found support (again *obiter*) by Blackburne J in *Nationwide Building Society v Balmer Radmore*,[35] it does not seem to have been shared by the other members of the Court in *Swindle v Harrison*.[36]

The Court of Appeal has since confirmed the requirement of factual causation for the availability of equitable compensation. In *Gwembe Valley Development Co Ltd v Koshy*, for instance, Mummery LJ said on behalf of the Court that:

> [W]hen determining whether any compensation, and, if so, how much compensation, should be paid for loss claimed to have been caused by actionable non-disclosure, the court is not precluded by authority or by principle from considering what would have happened if the material facts had been disclosed ... In our judgment, a director is not legally responsible for loss, which the company would probably have suffered, even if the director had complied with the fiduciary-dealing rules on disclosure of interests.[37]

Since it is now established that equitable compensation is unavailable unless the fiduciary's breach was the factual cause of the principal's loss, the aim of equitable compensation for breach of fiduciary duty can no longer be described as the restoration of the principal to the position prior to the wrong. Rather, it is the restoration of the principal to the same position as if no wrong had occurred. This is the same aim as that of (compensatory) damages at common law.[38]

Swindle v Harrison may have harmonised equitable compensation with common law damages not only with regard to factual causation but also with regard to remoteness of damage. In that case, Mummery and Hobhouse LJJ held that the solicitor's duty of loyalty did not aim to protect Mrs Harrison against the usual risk of business failure. Evans LJ, although not basing his decision on this issue, also acknowledged that in cases where the traditional measure has no application, the scope of the duty breached needs to be identified.[39] *Swindle v Harrison* may thus have laid down that the 'scope of the duty' concept, as highlighted in

---

[34] ibid 717–18. The distinction is criticised in C Rickett, 'Compensating for Loss in Equity—Choosing the Right Horse for Each Course' in P Birks and F Rose (eds), *Restitution and Equity, Vol 1: Resulting Trusts and Equitable Compensation* (London, 2000), 184–86.

[35] [1999] PNLR 606, 671.

[36] As pointed out in *Collins v Brebner* [2000] Lloyd's Rep PN 587 (CA) [57].

[37] [2003] EWCA Civ 1048 [147]. See also *Satnam Investments Ltd v Dunlop Heywood & Co Ltd* [1999] 3 All ER 652 (CA) 668; *Murad v Al-Saraj* [2005] EWCA Civ 959, [2005] WTLR 1573 [110], [120], [136].

[38] Above ch 1, IV.

[39] [1997] 4 All ER 705 (CA) 717. The relevant passage is quoted above II in this chapter. See also *Canson Enterprises Ltd v Boughton & Co* [1991] 3 SCR 534 (SCC): an intervening event may break the causal chain between the breach of fiduciary duty and the principal's loss; approved in *Target Holdings Ltd v Redferns* [1996] AC 421 (HL) 438–39.

SAAMCO for common law duties, should be extended to the equitable duty of loyalty, with the effect that a disloyal fiduciary will only be liable for loss that his duty of loyalty aimed to prevent.[40]

There is no authority, however, for the principle that liability for breach of fiduciary duty is confined to loss that the fiduciary, at the time of the breach, could have foreseen as possible.[41] On the contrary, Mummery LJ said in *Swindle v Harrison* that foreseeability and remoteness of damage are in general irrelevant to liability.[42] Nevertheless, once it is accepted that certain losses may fall outside the scope of a fiduciary duty, the general scope of fiduciary duties moves into the limelight. Is the duty of loyalty imposed to protect the principal against *all* loss caused by the fiduciary's infidelity, or only against foreseeable loss?

Holding disloyal fiduciaries liable for unforeseeable loss is said to be necessary to deter them from exploiting the principal's vulnerability.[43] But what renders the principal more vulnerable than the party to a non-fiduciary contractual or tortious relationship is that the fiduciary, due to his intimate knowledge of the principal's circumstances and the trust the principal places in him, may be tempted to abuse his position and make a secret profit. Making a secret profit is already deterred by the availability of an account of profits.[44] Further deterrence could be provided by exemplary damages[45] (if accepted in principle[46]) or even criminal sanctions, but a principal will hardly refrain from being disloyal just because he faces liability for unforeseeable loss.

Another argument in support of wide liability is that a breach of fiduciary duty involves the conscience of the wrongdoer and is thus akin to fraud,[47] where

---

[40] An application of the 'scope of the duty' concept to breach of fiduciary duty is supported by V Vann, *Equitable Compensation in Australia: Principles and Problems* (Saarbrücken, 2009) 205–10; for honest breaches also L Ho, 'Attributing losses to a breach of fiduciary duty' (1998) 12 *Trust Law International* 66, 70–71. See further JD Davies, 'Equitable Compensation: "Causation, Foreseeability and Remoteness"' in DWM Waters (ed), *Equity, Fiduciaries and Trusts 1993* (Toronto, 1993) 310–12; C Rickett and T Gardner, 'Compensating for loss in equity: The evolution of a remedy' (1994) 24 *Victoria University of Wellington Law Review* 19, 39–40.

[41] This principle is favoured by C Rickett and T Gardner, ibid 37–38.

[42] [1997] 4 All ER 705 (CA) 733. See also *Day v Mead* [1987] 2 NZLR 443 (NZCA) 661 (Somers J): 'Equitable compensation is not fettered by the requirements of foresight and remoteness which control awards of damages at law'.

[43] *Hodgkinson v Simms* [1994] 3 SCR 377 (SCC) 452–54; *Maguire v Makaronis* (1997) 188 CLR 449 (HCA) 492 (Kirby J); *Bank of New Zealand v New Zealand Guardian Trust Co Ltd* [1999] 1 NZLR 213, 243; [1999] 1 NZLR 664 (NZCA) 681; SB Elliott, 'Remoteness Criteria in Equity' (2002) 65 *MLR* 588, 595.

[44] CEF Rickett, 'Where are We Going with Equitable Compensation' in AJ Oakley (ed), *Trends in Contemporary Trust Law* (Oxford, 1996) 177, 190, who even questions the necessity of an alternative compensatory remedy in that case.

[45] See J Berryman, 'Equitable Compensation for Breach by Fact-Based Fiduciaries: Tentative Thoughts on Clarifying Remedial Goals' (1999) 37 *Alta L Rev* 95, 112.

[46] Below ch 17.

[47] *Bank of New Zealand v New Zealand Guardian Trust Co Ltd* [1999] 1 NZLR 664 (NZCA) 688 (Tipping J); SB Elliott, 'Remoteness Criteria in Equity' (2002) 65 *MLR* 588, 595–96; C Rickett, 'Compensating for Loss in Equity—Choosing the Right Horse for Each Course' in P Birks and F Rose (eds), *Restitution and Equity, Vol 1: Resulting Trusts and Equitable Compensation* (London, 2000) 186.

liability extends to unforeseeable loss caused directly by the fraud.[48] This argument cannot convince either. First, some wrongs that do not attract as harsh a liability as fraud can be said to be unconscionable, for instance an intensive and persistent nuisance committed out of malice. Secondly, not all instances of a breach of fiduciary duty resemble fraud.[49] Some do, namely where the fiduciary actually commits a fraud or where he, in order to benefit himself, puts the principal's assets into an investment completely disadvantageous to the principal. But there are other cases too. Where a fiduciary makes a secret profit from an investment of the principal's assets, the investment may otherwise be proper.[50] Why should the fiduciary in that case face liability for unforeseeable detrimental consequences of the investment and not only for the loss that reflects the improper gain? The dissimilarity to fraud becomes even more striking where the fiduciary, without seeking a profit for himself, makes an unauthorised investment in the genuine belief that this would be in the principal's best interest.[51]

Following a suggestion made by Evans LJ in *Swindle v Harrison*,[52] an imposition of extensive liability where the breach of fiduciary duty is the equivalent of fraud, and a limitation of liability where it is not, might be considered. This would be problematic, however. First, it would be difficult to place each individual case on the right side of the line. Secondly, it would be inexpedient if the extent of liability for breach of fiduciary duty were dependent on the fiduciary's reasons for the breach. Equity protects the weaker party in certain relationships by imposing a duty of loyalty upon the stronger party. Once a breach of that duty has been established, it should not matter *why* the fiduciary was disloyal, just as the extent of liability for breach of contract is not influenced by the reason of the breach.

While there are thus no cogent reasons for ordering disloyal fiduciaries to compensate unforeseeable loss, there is a good reason for limiting their liability to foreseeable loss: Liability for breach of fiduciary duty often concurs with liability at common law, which is restricted to foreseeable loss.[53] Where the same facts give rise to concurrent claims in equity and at common law, a difference between the causes of action in determining the extent of liability could not be defended. As Hoyano observes: 'In situations of true concurrent liability in tort, contract and equity, such as *bona fide* non-disclosure, it would be anomalous to make a greater monetary award in equity than at law'.[54] If this is accepted, equitable

---

[48] Above ch 2, VII.

[49] JD Davies, 'Equitable Compensation: "Causation, Foreseeability and Remoteness"' in DWM Waters (ed), *Equity, Fiduciaries and Trusts 1993* (Toronto, 1993) 308–309.

[50] As in *Hodgkinson v Simms* [1994] 3 SCR 377 (SCC): the principal paid the fair market value for the investments out of which the fiduciary made a secret profit.

[51] Conceded in SB Elliott, 'Remoteness Criteria in Equity' (2002) 65 *MLR* 588, 595.

[52] [1997] 4 All ER 705 (CA) 717.

[53] Above chs 2 – 4.

[54] L Hoyano, 'The Flight to the Fiduciary Haven' in P Birks (ed), *Privacy and Loyalty* (Oxford, 1997) 222–23.

liability must equally be limited where it does not concur with liability at common law. Otherwise there would be the strange situation that a fiduciary is keen on demonstrating that he is also liable at common law while the principal is keen on exonerating the fiduciary from common law liability.

The need for an identical treatment of concurrent claims was seen, albeit in a different context, in *Cia de Seguros Imperio v Heath (REBX) Ltd*,[55] where the defendant's breach of fiduciary duty rendered him liable in contract, tort and equity. However, the claimant's actions in contract and tort were time-barred pursuant to sections 2 and 5 of the Limitation Act 1980. Using the power granted by section 36 of that Act, the Court of Appeal applied the same time limit by analogy to the claimant's action in equity.[56] The following remark by Clarke LJ is striking:

> If the claims for damages for breach of contract and duty are time barred, as it is agreed that they are, no rational system of law should permit the plaintiff to proceed with a claim for damages which is essentially based on the same facts, merely because it is strictly a claim for compensation in equity.[57]

Exactly the same can be said about remoteness of damage: If the claims for damages for breach of contract and tort fail because the claimant's loss was unforeseeable, no rational system of law should permit the claimant to proceed with a claim for damages which is essentially based on the same facts, merely because it is strictly a claim for compensation in equity.

In conclusion, equitable compensation for breach of fiduciary duty and for breach of an equitable duty of care should be subject to the same remoteness regime which this book[58] suggests as the uniform regime at common law.[59] The following principles should therefore govern remoteness of damage in contract, tort and equity. Liability is restricted by the scope of the duty breached. Absent special considerations relating to the particular duty at issue, loss is recoverable if a reasonable person in the position of the wrongdoer could, at the time of the wrong, foresee the type of loss as possible unless it could be brushed aside as far fetched.

---

[55] [2001] 1 WLR 112 (CA).

[56] A similar analogy was drawn, based on the maxim 'He who seeks equity must do equity', in *Matai Industries Ltd v Jensen* [1989] 1 NZLR 525, 544.

[57] [2001] 1 WLR 112 (CA) 126.

[58] Above ch 4, IV F.

[59] 'Interestingly, remoteness is one aspect of the New Zealand law of civil obligations where there may well be convergence in respect of the entirety of tort, contract and equity in the not too distant future': C Rickett and T Gardner, 'Compensating for loss in equity: The evolution of a remedy' (1994) 24 *VUWLR* 19, 38.

Part 2

Non-Pecuniary Loss

6

Non-Pecuniary Loss in Tort

Civil wrongs may inflict upon the victim harm of a non-pecuniary nature, such as 'injury to comfort and well-being, mental and emotional distress, harm to mental concern and solicitude, annoyance and inconvenience, and the "shattering of dreams"'.[1] It is common to speak not only of non-pecuniary *harm* but also of non-pecuniary *loss*.[2] Its compensability is more settled in tort than in contract or equity. This part will therefore start with an examination of tort. Since the interest of the following study lies in the extent rather than the establishment of liability, it will not investigate under which circumstances the infliction of non-pecuniary loss alone may amount to a tort. It will be assumed that there is an actionable tort whether or not the claimant's non-pecuniary loss is compensable.

It has been shown that the purpose of the particular tort determines the extent of liability.[3] Non-pecuniary loss is no exception in that respect.[4] This is not the place to examine every tort in detail. It can safely be said that the compensation of non-pecuniary loss is the rule.[5] All non-pecuniary harm could be regarded as some sort of distress or loss of happiness.[6] Nevertheless, five different types of non-pecuniary loss are recognised in tort: loss resulting from personal injury,

---

[1] JP Tomain, 'Contract Compensation in Nonmarket Transactions' (1985) 46 *University of Pittsburgh Law Review* 867, 889; citations omitted.

[2] The term 'non-pecuniary damages' should be avoided. It is sometimes used as a synonym for non-pecuniary loss: D Harris, D Campbell and R Halson, *Remedies in Contract and Tort*, 2nd edn (London, 2002) 371. This parlance blurs the established distinction between damage and damages. The term 'non-pecuniary damages' is further used as a short form for damages for non-pecuniary loss: *Farley v Skinner* [2001] UKHL 49, [2002] 2 AC 732 [16] (Lord Steyn); D Harris, D Campbell and R Halson, above, 376, 596 fn 14; J Murphy, *Street on Torts*, 12th edn (Oxford, 2007) 675; JA Sebert, 'Punitive and Nonpecuniary Damages in Actions Based Upon Contract: Toward Achieving the Objective of Full Compensation' (1986) 33 *University of California at Los Angeles Law Review* 1565, 1570 *passim*. This parlance too is misleading as an award of damages is an order to pay money and thus a pecuniary remedy.

[3] Above ch 2, VII.

[4] MG Bridge, 'Contractual Damages for Intangible Loss: A Comparative Analysis' (1984) 62 *Canadian Bar Review* 323, 328–29; M Tilbury, 'Factors Inflating Damages Awards' in PD Finn (ed), *Essays on Damages* (Sydney, 1992) 93–94.

[5] H McGregor, *McGregor on Damages*, 18th edn (London, 2009) [3–001]–[3–002].

[6] A Burrows, *Remedies for Torts and Breach of Contract*, 3rd edn (Oxford, 2004) 31.

physical inconvenience and discomfort, loss of reputation, mental distress, and bereavement.[7] These types will now be briefly examined.

I Loss Resulting From Personal Injury

Non-pecuniary loss resulting from bodily or psychiatric injury[8] can be recovered in negligence[9] and probably all other torts.[10] Although usually compensated in a single sum, it is divided into two heads. One is the pain and suffering—both actual and prospective[11]—attributable to the injury[12] or its consequences.[13] 'Pain and suffering' has become a term of art without a clear distinction between pain on the one hand and suffering on the other.[14] It includes fright on impact;[15] pain caused by medical malpractice;[16] and suffering due to disability,[17] disfigurement[18] or awareness that expectation of life has been shortened.[19] The other head is loss of amenity (or faculty),[20] such as loss of taste and smell,[21] deprivation of sexual pleasures,[22] inability to fish,[23] and loss of a holiday,[24] of an enjoyable job[25] or the comfort of marriage.[26] A permanently unconscious victim is still entitled to damages for loss of amenity but not for pain and suffering.[27]

---

[7] H McGregor, *McGregor on Damages*, 18th edn (London, 2009) [3–003]–[3–012].

[8] It is assumed that the defendant's conduct is actionable. 'Secondary victims' can bring an action in negligence for psychiatric harm only in certain circumstances: *Alcock v Chief Constable of South Yorkshire Police* [1992] 1 AC 310 (HL).

[9] eg *Darg v Metropolitan Police Commissioner* [2009] EWHC 684 (QB) (bodily injury); *Page v Smith* [1996] AC 155 (HL) (psychiatric injury).

[10] H McGregor, *McGregor on Damages*, 18th edn (London, 2009) [3–006]–[3–008].

[11] *Heaps v Perrite Ltd* [1937] 2 All ER 60 (CA) 60–61.

[12] *Cutler v Vauxhall Motors Ltd* [1971] 1 QB 418 (CA).

[13] *James v Woodall Duckham Construction Co* [1969] 1 WLR 903 (CA) (compensation neurosis); *Lucy v Mariehamns Rederi* [1971] 2 Lloyd's Rep 314 (anxiety neurosis).

[14] For definitions see H McGregor, *McGregor on Damages*, 18th edn (London, 2009) [3–003].

[15] *Thompson v Royal Mail Lines Ltd* [1957] 1 Lloyd's Rep 99.

[16] *Kralj v McGrath* [1986] 1 All ER 54.

[17] *H West & Son Ltd v Shephard* [1964] AC 326 (HL) 340; *Cutts v Chumley* [1967] 1 WLR 742.

[18] *Taylor v RV Chuck (Transport) Ltd* (1963) 107 Sol Jo 910.

[19] Administration of Justice Act 1982 s 1(1)(b). Section 1(1)(a) of that Act abolished damages for loss of expectation of life as a separate head of damage.

[20] The various concepts that may underlay this head of damage are discussed by AI Ogus, 'Damages for Lost Amenities: For a Foot, a Feeling or a Function?' (1972) 35 *Modern Law Review* 1–17.

[21] *Cook v JL Kier & Co Ltd* [1970] 1 WLR 774.

[22] ibid; *Povey v Governors of Rydal School* [1970] 1 All ER 841, 845.

[23] *Moeliker v A Reyrolle & Co Ltd* [1977] 1 WLR 132 (CA).

[24] *Ichard v Frangoulis* [1977] 1 WLR 556.

[25] *Hearnshaw v English Steel Co* (1971) 11 KIR 306 (CA) 309.

[26] *Harris v Harris* [1973] 1 Lloyd's Rep 445 (CA).

[27] *Wise v Kaye* [1962] 1 QB 638 (CA) 654, 659–60; *H West & Son Ltd v Shephard* [1964] AC 326 (HL); *Andrews v Freeborough* [1967] 1 QB 1 (CA) 10–11; *Cutts v Chumley* [1967] 1 WLR 742, 748; *Lim Poh Choo v Camden and Islington Area Health Authority* [1980] AC 174 (HL) 188.

II Physical Inconvenience or Discomfort

Physical inconvenience or discomfort short of injury has been compensated in nuisance,[28] deceit[29] and negligence.[30] Furthermore, where the victim of false imprisonment suffers neither injury nor pecuniary loss, she may still claim damages for the deprivation of liberty.[31] In assessing these damages, the court may consider the impact of the imprisonment on the victim[32] and thus the inconvenience and discomfort suffered.[33]

III Loss of Reputation

It goes without saying that the tort of defamation, whose *raison d'être* is the protection of reputation, allows recovery for non-pecuniary loss consequent on an injury to reputation, called social discredit or (mere) loss of reputation.[34] It has been held that the tort of defamation is in general the *only* cause of action in which damages for such loss may be claimed: 'a claim for mere loss of reputation is the proper subject of an action for defamation, and cannot ordinarily be sustained by means of any other form of action, subject to certain recognised exceptions'.[35] In tort, these exceptions are false imprisonment,[36] malicious prosecution[37] and, where it causes indignity in public, assault.[38] Recovery for loss of

---

[28] *Halsey v Esso Petroleum Co Ltd* [1961] 1 WLR 683; *Bone v Seale* [1975] 1 WLR 797 (CA); *Bunclark v Hertfordshire CC* (1977) 243 EG 455.

[29] *Mafo v Adams* [1970] 1 QB 548 (CA); *Archer v Brown* [1985] QB 401, 421; *Saunders v Edwards* [1987] 1 WLR 1116 (CA).

[30] *Ward v Cannock Chase DC* [1986] Ch 546, 579 (for living in unsuitable property). See also *Perry v Sidney Phillips & Son* [1982] 1 WLR 1297 (CA) 1307 (Kerr LJ).

[31] *Kuchenmeister v Home Office* [1958] 1 QB 496, 513.

[32] *R v Governor of Brockhill Prison, ex parte Evans (No 2)* [1999] QB 1043 (CA) 1060.

[33] AS Burrows, 'Mental distress damages in contract—a decade of change' [1984] *Lloyd's Maritime Commercial Law Quarterly* 119, 129 fn 54.

[34] *McCarey v Associated Newspapers Ltd (No 2)* [1965] 2 QB 86 (CA) 104–105; *Fielding v Variety Inc* [1967] 2 QB 841 (CA); *John v MGN Ltd* [1997] QB 586 (CA) 607.

[35] *Foaminol Laboratories Ltd v British Artid Plastics Ltd* [1941] 2 All ER 393, 399 (Hallett J). See also *Spring v Guardian Assurance plc* [1995] 2 AC 296 (HL) 310–11, 323, 330, 347–48, 350; *Kpohraror v Woolwich Building Society* [1996] 4 All ER 119 (CA) 125 (quoted below ch 7, VI).

[36] *Walter v Alltools Ltd* (1944) 61 TLR 39 (CA) 40; *Hook v Cunard Steamship Co* [1953] 1 WLR 682, 686; *Lonrho plc v Fayed (No 5)* [1993] 1 WLR 1489 (CA) 1504.

[37] *Lonrho plc v Fayed (No 5)* [1993] 1 WLR 1489 (CA) 1504; *Clark v Chief Constable of Cleveland Police* [2000] CP Rep 22 (CA). See also *Gregory v Portsmouth City Council* [2000] 1 AC 419 (HL) 426–32.

[38] *Hurst v Picture Theatres Ltd* [1915] 1 KB 1 (CA), where the plaintiff, without justification, was forcibly removed from a cinema seat for which he had paid 6d. A jury awarded him £150 for assault and false imprisonment. Buckley LJ (at 11) regarded this as compensation 'for the serious indignity to a gentleman of being seized and treated in this way in a place of public resort'.

reputation has been denied in conspiracy,[39] malicious falsehood[40] and, at least where a statement is involved,[41] in torts affecting goods.[42] Compensating loss of reputation in causes of action other than defamation would, it is argued, side-step the defences available in defamation and thus endanger free speech.[43]

On the other hand, it is established that torts other than defamation allow recovery for *financial* loss consequent on an injury to reputation.[44] In *Spring v Guardian Assurance plc*,[45] the House of Lords (Lord Keith dissenting) held that that employers who carelessly give a defamatory reference for a (former) employee can be liable in negligence and contract for the employee's financial loss. The majority had no fear of thereby inhibiting the giving of full and frank references, and rejected an exclusive status of the tort of defamation. Lord Woolf observed:

> I can see no justification for erecting a fence around the whole of the field to which defamation can apply and treating any other tort, which can beneficially from the point of justice enter into part of that field, as a trespasser if it does so.[46]

Since the general exclusivity of the tort of defamation has been abandoned in relation to pecuniary consequences of an injury to reputation, it can hardly be upheld in relation to non-pecuniary consequences. If the compensation of pecuniary loss in torts other than defamation does not endanger free speech, how can the compensation of non-pecuniary loss have such an effect? Moreover, the aim of maintaining the defences available in an action for defamation cannot justify an exclusion of loss of reputation per se from the ambit of other actions even where the requirements of those defences are not fulfilled. Where the requirements are fulfilled, a circumvention of the defences can be prevented by allowing them in all actions based on defamatory statements. It is hard to see why such an extension should be 'objectionable and embarrassing' as Lord Atkinson asserted in *Addis v Gramophone Co Ltd*,[47] or 'impractical' and 'unfair' as Gallen J asserted in the New Zealand case *Whelan v Waitaki Meats Ltd*.[48] Indeed, the

---

[39] *Lonrho plc v Fayed (No 5)* [1993] 1 WLR 1489 (CA); *Gregory v Portsmouth City Council* [2000] 1 AC 419 (HL) 431–32.

[40] *Joyce v Sengupta* [1993] 1 WLR 337 (CA) 348, 351. See also *Gregory v Portsmouth City Council* [2000] 1 AC 419 (HL) 431. Aggravated damages (below ch 14, I) can be awarded, however, in order to take account of the injury to the victim's feelings: *Khodaparast v Shad* [2000] 1 WLR 618 (CA).

[41] H McGregor, *McGregor on Damages*, 18th edn (London, 2009) [6–126]–[6–128].

[42] *Lonrho plc v Fayed (No 5)* [1993] 1 WLR 1489 (CA) 1495–96, 1504.

[43] ibid 1496, 1502–504, 1509.

[44] ibid 1496, 1501, 1508 (for conspiracy); *Spring v Guardian Assurance plc* [1995] 2 AC 296 (HL) (for negligence). See also *Bella v Young* [2006] SCC 3, [2006] 1 SCR 108 [56], and the cases cited by A Burrows, *Remedies for Torts and Breach of Contract*, 3rd edn (Oxford, 2004) 318.

[45] [1995] 2 AC 296 (HL).

[46] ibid 351. See also E Descheemaeker, 'Protecting Reputation: Defamation and Negligence' (2009) 29 *Oxford Journal of Legal Studies* 603, 641: 'there is no reason why reputation should be treated differently from all other interests, and the tort of negligence uniquely be prevented from taking an interest in the redress of its injuries'.

[47] [1909] AC 488 (HL) 496.

[48] [1991] 2 NZLR 74, 89.

Supreme Court of Canada has pointed out that: 'Freedom of expression and the policies underlying qualified privilege can be taken into account in determining the appropriate standard of care in negligence'.[49]

IV Mental Distress

Non-pecuniary loss resulting from psychiatric injury has already been considered. The focus now is on mental distress (or anxiety or injured feelings) short of psychiatric injury. Such distress attracts compensatory damages[50] in actions for battery,[51] defamation,[52] deceit,[53] false imprisonment,[54] malicious prosecution,[55] and wrongful eviction, framed as nuisance or trespass to land.[56] Distress is also compensable where the statutory duty not to infringe exclusive burial rights has been breached,[57] and under the anti-discrimination legislation,[58] the Human Rights Act 1998,[59] and section 3(2) of the Protection from Harassment Act 1997. Mental distress is not compensable in actions for conspiracy[60] nor probably in actions for malicious falsehood.[61]

The compensability of distress in negligence is somewhat unclear. In *Hunter v Canary Wharf Ltd*, Lord Hoffmann observed that 'the law of negligence gives no remedy for discomfort or distress which does not result in bodily or psychiatric illness'.[62] However, that statement concerned the question of whether distress *alone* can ground an action in negligence.[63] Lord Hoffmann was not necessarily

---

[49] *Bella v Young* [2006] SCC 3, [2006] 1 SCR 108 [56] (McLachlin CJC and Binnie J).

[50] As opposed to aggravated and exemplary damages considered in Part 5 below.

[51] *Wainwright v Home Office* [2002] QB 1334 (CA).

[52] *McCarey v Associated Newspapers Ltd (No 2)* [1965] 2 QB 86 (CA) 104–105; *Fielding v Variety Inc* [1967] 2 QB 841 (CA); *John v MGN Ltd* [1997] QB 586 (CA) 607.

[53] *Archer v Brown* [1985] QB 401, 405; *Saunders v Edwards* [1987] 1 WLR 1116 (CA); *East v Maurer* [1991] 1 WLR 461 (CA) 464.

[54] *Holden v Chief Constable of Lancashire* [1987] QB 380 (CA) 384.

[55] *Clark v Chief Constable of Cleveland Police* [2000] CP Rep 22 (CA).

[56] *Millington v Duffy* (1985) 17 HLR 232 (CA); *Branchett v Beaney* [1992] 3 All ER 910 (CA) 914; *Mehta v Royal Bank of Scotland* (1999) 32 HLR 45.

[57] *Reed v Madon* [1989] Ch 408.

[58] Sex Discrimination Act 1975 s 66(4); Race Relations Act 1976 s 57(4); Disability Discrimination Act 1995 ss 17A(4), 25(2); Employment Equality (Religion or Belief) Regulations 2003/1660 reg 31(3); Employment Equality (Sexual Orientation) Regulations 2003/1661 reg 31(3).

[59] *R (KB) v South London and South and West Region Mental Health Review Tribunal* [2003] EWHC 193 (Admin), [2004] QB 936 [71]–[73]; *Anufrijeva v Southwark LBC* [2003] EWCA Civ 1406, [2004] QB 1124 [66]–[70].

[60] *Lonrho plc v Fayed (No 5)* [1993] 1 WLR 1489 (CA).

[61] *Fielding v Variety Inc* [1967] 2 QB 841 (CA) 850 (Lord Denning MR); *Joyce v Sengupta* [1993] 1 WLR 337 (CA) 351 (Sir Michael Kerr), where Sir Donald Nicholls (at 347–49), with whom Butler-Sloss LJ agreed, criticised the state of law but refrained from deciding the issue.

[62] [1997] AC 655 (HL) 707.

[63] For that question see PR Handford, *Mullany and Handford's Tort Liability for Psychiatric Damage*, 2nd edn (Sydney, 2006) [2.110]–[2.290].

addressing the compensability of distress where the claimant has suffered financial loss as well as distress and has a claim in negligence at least with regard to the
financial loss. Under those circumstances, distress has been compensated in a
number of cases. Most of these cases involved negligence on the part of a
solicitor[64] or surveyor[65] which resulted in the client moving into property that
was defective or otherwise unsuitable, causing the client significant discomfort.

Referring to these cases, Cooke P in the New Zealand Court of Appeal
pronounced in *Mouat v Clark Boyce* that 'when the plaintiff has a cause of action
for negligence, damages for distress, vexation, inconvenience and the like are
recoverable in both tort and contract, at least if reasonably foreseeable consequences of the breach of duty'.[66] It is unclear whether this statement was confined
to cases of concurrent liability in contract and negligence, or whether Cooke P
meant to say that foreseeable distress is compensable in negligence (provided that
the defendant's conduct is actionable) even where there is no concurrent liability
in contract. The latter proposition would appeal in terms of policy but might not
be a correct inference from the cases cited by Cooke P, for two reasons.

First, since in all those cases the solicitor or surveyor was concurrently liable
for breach of contract and since the client's distress was compensable in contract,[67] it could be argued that the tort claim was simply aligned with the contract
claim, the cases thus having no bearing on negligence standing alone.[68] This view
gains support from *Verderame v Commercial Union Assurance Co plc* where, in a
different situation of concurrent liability, it was held that the distress suffered
could only be compensated in the negligence action if it was compensable in the
contract action (which was denied *in casu*).[69] In *Hamilton-Jones v David & Snape*,
which again concerned distress damages in a case of concurrent liability, Neuberger J said that 'The logic of the reasoning in *Verderame* suggests, if anything,
that the approach to damages in tort in a case such as this is governed by the
approach to damages in contract'.[70]

Secondly, the discomfort of living in defective or otherwise unsuitable property may be qualified as physical in nature,[71] assigning the cases at issue to the
category of physical inconvenience.[72] Indeed, in *Ward v Cannock Chase District*

---

[64] *Buckley v Lane, Herdman & Co* [1977] CLY 3143; *Trask v Clark & Sons* [1980] CLY 2588;
Wapshott v Davis Donovan & Co [1996] PNLR 361 (CA).
[65] *Perry v Sidney Phillips & Son* [1982] 1 WLR 1297 (CA); *Cross v David Martin & Mortimer*
[1989] 10 EG 110, [1989] 1 EGLR 154; *Syrett v Carr & Neave* [1990] 48 EG 118; *Heatley v William
Brown Ltd* [1992] 1 EGLR 289; *Holder v Countrywide Surveyors Ltd* [2003] PNLR 3.
[66] [1992] 2 NZLR 559 (NZCA) 568. For the facts of the case see below ch 8, III.
[67] On the basis of the 'object of the contract' exception: below ch 7, V.
[68] A Burrows, *Remedies for Torts and Breach of Contract*, 3rd edn (Oxford, 2004) 338.
[69] [1992] BCLC 793 (CA) 803.
[70] [2003] EWHC 3147 (Ch), [2004] 1 WLR 924 [51].
[71] *Perry v Sidney Phillips & Son* [1982] 1 WLR 1297 (CA) 1307 (Kerr LJ); *Watts v Morrow* [1991] 1
WLR 1421 (CA) 1441–43, 1445; *Heatley v William Brown Ltd* [1992] 1 EGLR 289, 296; H Carty,
'Contract Theory and Employment Reality' (1986) 49 *MLR* 240, 245.
[72] Above II in this ch.

Council,[73] where the defendant authority negligently failed to maintain the plaintiff's house, Scott J awarded damages only for that part of the plaintiff's distress that was associated with his discomfort, and denied damages for other distress (on the ground of unforeseeability).

It may therefore be premature to suggest that the compensation of distress in the absence of personal injury or inconvenience is the rule in negligence cases. Michael Bridge suggests rather the opposite: 'In the most important of the torts, negligence, one sees a general resistance to liability for grief and emotional distress falling short of nervous shock'.[74] An example is *Behrens v Bertram Mills Circus Ltd*.[75] Two persons of short stature, husband and wife, were on exhibition in a booth when elephants of a nearby circus went out of control and knocked the booth over. The wife suffered personal injury, preventing the husband from working for some time. Devlin J awarded him damages for loss of earnings but not for the distress resulting from the frightening experience since he had suffered no physical or mental harm.[76] But Devlin J indicated that he would have awarded damages for distress had he been free from authority. This last statement is to be welcomed. There is no reason why significant distress should be left uncompensated in negligence or indeed any tort, provided the defendant's conduct is actionable.

V Bereavement

While at common law 'no damages are awarded for grief or sorrow caused by a person's death',[77] bereavement damages of currently £11,800 may be claimed under section 1A of the Fatal Accidents Act 1976 by the spouse, the civil partner or, under certain circumstances, the parent(s) of the deceased where a wrongful act causes death.[78]

---

[73] [1986] Ch 546, 579.
[74] MG Bridge, 'Contractual Damages for Intangible Loss: A Comparative Analysis' (1984) 62 *Can Bar Rev* 323, 329–30.
[75] [1957] 2 QB 1.
[76] ibid 27–28.
[77] *Hinz v Berry* [1970] 2 QB 40 (CA) 42 (Lord Denning MR).
[78] The term 'wrongful act' includes tort and breach of contract, in the view of GH Treitel, *Remedies for Breach of Contract: A Comparative Account* (Oxford, 1988) [155].

7

Non-Pecuniary Loss in Contract

I Overview of the Present Law

The law of England and Wales on the compensability of non-pecuniary loss in actions for breach of contract was authoritatively summarised by Bingham LJ in *Watts v Morrow*:

> A contract-breaker is not in general liable for any distress, frustration, anxiety, displeasure, vexation, tension or aggravation which his breach of contract may cause to the innocent party. This rule is not, I think, founded on the assumption that such reactions are not foreseeable, which they surely are or may be, but on considerations of policy.

> But the rule is not absolute. Where the very object of a contract is to provide pleasure, relaxation, peace of mind or freedom from molestation, damages will be awarded if the fruit of the contract is not provided or if the contrary result is procured instead. If the law did not cater for this exceptional category of case it would be defective ...

> In cases not falling within this exceptional category, damages are in my view recoverable for physical inconvenience and discomfort caused by the breach and mental suffering directly related to that inconvenience and discomfort.[1]

II The General Bar to Compensation

At least in England and Wales[2] and in Australia,[3] there exists a general rule excluding contractual damages for non-pecuniary loss. This rule is said[4] to have

---

[1] [1991] 1 WLR 1421 (CA) 1445. Approvingly quoted, eg, in *Johnson v Gore Wood & Co* [2002] 2 AC 1 (HL) 48–49 (Lord Cooke); *Farley v Skinner* [2001] UKHL 49, [2002] 2 AC 732, [14], [34], [47], [81].

[2] eg *Johnson v Gore Wood & Co* [2002] 2 AC 1 (HL) 37, 42, 49; *Farley v Skinner* [2001] UKHL 49, [2002] 2 AC 732 [16], [34], [47]; *Johnson v Unisys Ltd* [2001] UKHL 13, [2003] 1 AC 518, [69]; *Wiseman v Virgin Atlantic Airways Ltd* [2006] EWHC 1566 (QB) [16].

[3] eg *Thorpe v Lochel* [2005] WASCA 85 [23], [40], [138]; *Nikolich v Goldman Sachs J B Were Services Pty Ltd* [2006] FCA 784 [315].

[4] eg *Ruxley Electronics and Construction Ltd v Forsyth* [1996] AC 344 (HL) 374; *Johnson v Gore Wood & Co* [2002] 2 AC 1 (HL) 37, 42; *Johnson v Unisys Ltd* [2001] UKHL 13, [2003] 1 AC 518 [68]–[69]; F Dawson, 'General Damages in Contract for Non-pecuniary Loss' (1983) 10 *New Zealand*

been established in *Addis v Gramophone Co Ltd*,[5] where the defendants dismissed the plaintiff in an oppressive and discrediting way. In an action for wrongful dismissal, the jury reflected the manner of the dismissal in their award. The House of Lords, with Lord Collins dissenting, held that this had been wrong. Enonchong argues that the true *ratio* of *Addis* is nothing more than that a person aggrieved by a breach of contract may claim damages only for loss resulting from the breach itself and not for loss resulting from circumstances accompanying the breach.[6] Be that as it may, *Addis* has become the *locus classicus* for the general bar to contractual damages for non-pecuniary loss. In the following, therefore, this rule will be called the *Addis* rule. This rule has considerable exceptions, which are considered below.[7]

The Supreme Court of Canada initially adopted the *Addis* rule[8] but may have abolished it in two recent cases. The first was *Fidler v Sun Life Assurance Co of Canada*,[9] where the defendant insurance company initially refused to pay the disability benefits to which the claimant was entitled under an insurance contract. A week before the trial, the defendant paid all outstanding sums plus interest, and the trial concerned only the claimant's entitlement to damages other than compensation for financial loss. The trial judge awarded 'aggravated damages' of Can$20,000 on the ground that the contract in question had been one for 'peace of mind'. The Supreme Court of Canada upheld the award but rejected the label 'aggravated damages' and described the award as compensatory damages for the distress the defendant's breach of contract had caused the claimant.

The Court pointed to the principle, recognised throughout the Commonwealth, that non-pecuniary loss flowing from a breach of contract is compensable where the provision of 'peace of mind' was an object of the contract.[10] One object of a disability insurance contract, said the Court, is to provide psychological benefits such as the knowledge of income security in the event of disability.[11]

Universities Law Review 232, 233–34, 242; A Phang, 'The Crumbling Edifice? The Award of Contractual Damages for Mental Distress' [2003] *Journal of Business Law* 341.

[5] [1909] AC 488 (HL).

[6] N Enonchong, 'Breach of Contract and Damages for Mental Distress' (1996) 16 *Oxford Journal of Legal Studies* 617, 621–28. The distinction was described as 'conceptually attractive' but difficult to maintain in practice' by A Phang, 'The Crumbling Edifice? The Award of Contractual Damages for Mental Distress' [2003] *JBL* 341, 348. Lord Steyn supported Enonchong's view in *Malik v BCCI SA* [1998] AC 20 (HL) 51, but only in order to show that *Addis* is no bar to damages for the *financial* consequences of breach. That Lord Steyn had no intention of questioning *Addis* in relation to *non*-pecuniary loss is clear from his judgment in *Johnson v Unisys Ltd* [2001] UKHL 13, [2003] 1 AC 518 [15].

[7] Because of its abolition by the Law Reform (Miscellaneous Provisions) Act 1970 s 1, there will be no discussion of the action for breach of a promise of marriage where the damages awarded were allowed to reflect the claimant's injured feelings, wounded pride and the dishonour brought upon her family: *Berry v Da Costa* (1866) LR 1 CP 331; *Finlay v Chirney* (1888) LR 20 QBD 494 (CA) 506. See also *Addis v Gramophone Co Ltd* [1909] AC 488 (HL) 495, 498, 500.

[8] *Peso Silver Mines Ltd v Cropper* (1966) 58 DLR (2d) 1 (SCC) 10.

[9] 2006 SCC 30, [2006] 2 SCR 3.

[10] ibid [38]–[41].

[11] ibid [56].

Thus, the facts of *Fidler* fell squarely within one of the established exceptions to the *Addis* rule, and the case would be unspectacular were it not for the following. The Supreme Court of Canada opined that the *Addis* rule and the 'object of the contract' exception to it are merely applications of the *Hadley v Baxendale* principle according to which the recoverability of certain loss depends on whether it could have been contemplated at the time of the contract:

> In normal commercial contracts, the likelihood of a breach of contract causing mental distress is not ordinarily within the reasonable contemplation of the parties ... The matter is otherwise, however, when the parties enter into a contract, an object of which is to secure a particular psychological benefit.[12]

The Court concluded that 'there is only one rule by which compensatory damages *for breach of contract* should be assessed: the rule in *Hadley v Baxendale*. The *Hadley* test unites all forms of contractual damages under a single principle'.[13] Quoting this statement, the same Court said in *Honda Canada Inc v Keays* that 'in cases where parties have contemplated at the time of the contract that a breach in certain circumstances would cause the plaintiff mental distress, the plaintiff is entitled to recover'.[14] The latter case involved the wrongful dismissal of a disabled employee, and the Supreme Court held that while 'normal distress and hurt feelings resulting from dismissal are not compensable',[15] non-pecuniary loss can be compensated where it results from the manner of dismissal, for instance from the employer being untruthful, misleading or unduly sensitive.[16] This is a direct contradiction of *Addis*.

More significantly, describing the *Addis* rule and its exceptions as mere applications of the remoteness test amounts to an abolition of the *Addis* rule, for this rule is usually understood as a liability-restricting device additional to, and separate from, remoteness doctrine. While the Supreme Court of Canada may not have intended to generally widen the ambit of contractual damages for non-pecuniary loss, it does now allow such damages in the very situation in which *Addis* had denied it. This ambiguity, as McInnes points out, 'effectively invites claimants to demand compensation for reasonably foreseeable psychological injuries occasioned by contractual wrongs. The issue will not be laid to rest until the Supreme Court of Canada addresses the issue yet again'.[17]

---

[12] ibid [45] (McLachlin CJC and Abella J on behalf of the court).
[13] ibid [54] (McLachlin CJC and Abella J on behalf of the court). The same view had already been taken in *Vorvis v Insurance Corp of British Columbia* (1989) 58 DLR (4th) 193 (SCC) 218 (Wilson J, dissenting). The present remoteness regime in contract is discussed in ch 3.
[14] [2008] SCC 39, [2008] 2 SCR 362 [55] (Bastarache J on behalf of the majority).
[15] ibid [56] (Bastarache J on behalf of the majority).
[16] ibid [57]. The court held that the employer *in casu* had not acted in bad faith.
[17] M McInnes, 'Contractual Damages for Mental Distress—Again' (2009) 125 *Law Quarterly Review* 16, 19.

III   The Exception for Personal Injury

Where a breach of contract impairs the physical or mental[18] health of the aggrieved party, she may claim damages for the resultant non-pecuniary loss.[19] Just as in tort,[20] this loss consists of pain and suffering and loss of amenity.[21] Contractual damages for non-pecuniary loss consequent on personal injury have been awarded, for instance, where defective goods caused the buyer to become ill,[22] and where tenants suffered injury because their landlord had failed to repair defects in the property.[23]

IV   The Exception for Physical Inconvenience

Non-pecuniary loss is further recoverable where a breach of contract causes physical inconvenience or discomfort short of injury to the aggrieved party.[24] She may claim compensation not only for the physical inconvenience itself but also for the mental distress connected with it.[25] Damages were awarded, for instance, for the physical inconvenience of walking several miles home in a rainy night[26] and for the discomfort of living in cramped conditions[27] or in a defective property.[28] Courts should award a 'modest sum' however.[29]

---

[18]   *Malyon v Lawrence, Messer & Co* [1968] 2 Lloyd's Rep 539, 550–51; *Farley v Skinner* [2000] PNLR 441 (CA) [18].

[19]   Unless the illness is too remote: *Hobbs v London and South Western Railway Co* (1875) LR 10 QB 111, 117–19, 121–22, 123, 124–25; *Cook v Swinfen* [1967] 1 WLR 457 (CA) 461.

[20]   Above ch 6, I.

[21]   *Farley v Skinner* [2001] UKHL 49, [2002] 2 AC 732 [16] (Lord Steyn); HG Beale, 'Damages' in HG Beale (gen ed), *Chitty on Contracts, Vol 1: General Principles*, 30th edn (London, 2008) [26–082]; H McGregor, *McGregor on Damages*, 18th edn (London, 2009) [3–017]; F Dawson, 'General Damages in Contract for Non-pecuniary Loss' (1983) 10 *NZULR* 232, 248.

[22]   *Wren v Holt* [1903] 1 KB 610 (CA); *Grant v Australian Knitting Mills Ltd* [1936] AC 85 (PC); *Godley v Perry* [1960] 1 WLR 9.

[23]   *Griffin v Pillett* [1926] 1 KB 17; *Porter v Jones* [1942] 2 All ER 570 (CA); *Summers v Salford Co* [1943] AC 283 (HL).

[24]   *Burton v Pinkerton* (1867) LR 2 Exch 340; *Perera v Vandiyar* [1953] 1 WLR 672 (CA).

[25]   *McCall v Abelesz* [1976] QB 585 (CA) 594 (Lord Denning MR); *Watts v Morrow* [1991] 1 WLR 1421 (CA) 1445 (Bingham LJ); AS Burrows, 'Mental distress damages in contract—a decade of change' [1984] *Lloyd's Maritime and Commercial Law Quarterly* 119, 129–30.

[26]   *Hobbs v London and South Western Railway Co* (1875) LR 10 QB 111.

[27]   *Bailey v Bullock* [1950] 2 All ER 1167; *Wapshott v Davis Donovan & Co* [1996] PNLR 361 (CA).

[28]   *Calabar Properties Ltd v Stitcher* [1984] 1 WLR 287 (CA); *Watts v Morrow* [1991] 1 WLR 1421 (CA); *Wallace v Manchester City Council* (1998) 30 HLR 1111 (CA). See also *Perry v Sidney Phillips & Son* [1982] 1 WLR 1297 (CA) 1307 (Kerr LJ).

[29]   *Watts v Morrow* [1991] 1 WLR 1421 (CA) 1443. An award for a couple's discomfort of spending the weekends over eight months in a house under repair was reduced from £4,000 to £750.

It is clear that physical inconvenience attracts compensation. But it is unclear when inconvenience qualifies as physical. This came to light in *Farley v Skinner*.[30] The claimant, who was contemplating buying a certain house, engaged the defendant surveyor and specifically asked him to investigate aircraft noise. According to the defendant's report, aircraft noise was unlikely. The claimant bought the house, spent a large sum of money on modernisation and then discovered that the house was substantially affected by aircraft noise. He kept the house and claimed damages. His claim for diminution in value failed since the house, even with the noise, was worth the price paid. But the judge awarded the claimant £10,000 for distress and inconvenience caused by the noise, characterising the inconvenience as physical.[31]

The appellate courts discussed both the exception for physical inconvenience and the 'object of the contract' exception. Since the object exception will be discussed later,[32] the present discussion is confined to the exception for physical inconvenience. Before the Court of Appeal,[33] the claimant defended the categorisation of his inconvenience as physical on the ground that he heard the noise through his ears and thus experienced it through his senses. While Clarke LJ followed this argument,[34] the majority did not. Stuart-Smith LJ, with whom Mummery LJ agreed, admitted that persistent high levels of noise can cause physical discomfort. But he refused to accept this quality for every noise and in particular the noise at issue: 'All distress, annoyance, frustration, vexation and so on is a reaction to things perceived through the senses, usually of sight or hearing. But that does not make the distress physical'.[35]

The House of Lords missed the opportunity to enter a full-blown discussion and to clarify the law. Lord Steyn,[36] Lord Clyde[37] and Lord Hutton[38] said virtually no more than that the trial judge's decision had been open to him on the evidence. Only Lord Scott attempted a general definition of the category. He pointed to the difficulties in drawing the line: 'Is being awoken at night by aircraft noise "physical"? If it is, is being unable to sleep because of worry and anxiety "physical"?'[39] Building upon the claimant's argument, Lord Scott suggested that the cause, not the type, of the inconvenience should be decisive:

---

[30] [2000] PNLR 441 (CA); [2001] UKHL 49, [2002] 2 AC 732. See also *Johnson v Gore Wood & Co* [2002] 2 AC 1 (HL) 49–50 (Lord Cooke, dissenting): extreme financial embarrassment and estrangement from one's family are akin to physical discomfort.

[31] This is at least the way in which the appellate courts understood the judge's reasoning: [2000] PNLR 441 (CA) [15], [49]; [2001] UKHL 49, [2002] 2 AC 732 [38], [59].

[32] Below V in this chapter.

[33] After the initial two judges disagreed, the appeal was heard again by three other judges.

[34] [2000] PNLR 441 (CA) [60]–[63].

[35] ibid [17].

[36] [2001] UKHL 49, [2002] 2 AC 732 [30].

[37] ibid [38]. He said (at [35]) that the word 'physical' needs no further definition.

[38] ibid [60].

[39] ibid [85]. Lord Browne-Wilkinson agreed with both Lord Steyn and Lord Scott.

If the cause is no more than disappointment that the contractual obligation has been broken, damages are not recoverable even if the disappointment has led to a complete mental breakdown. But, if the cause of the inconvenience or discomfort is a sensory (sight, touch, hearing, smell etc) experience, damages can, subject to the remoteness rules, be recovered.[40]

Lord Scott's approach may explain the award of damages for inconvenience in cases where solicitors failed to advise their client that the property he contemplated buying as home was encumbered with a right of way in favour of the neighbour[41] or the public.[42] Even though it would not commonly be considered physical, the inconvenience of hearing or seeing people crossing in front of one's window stems from a sensory perception.

Lord Scott's approach is problematic however.[43] Since distress can often be said to result from a sensory experience, his approach considerably enlarges the scope of the exception for physical inconvenience and thus threatens the general rule, which the House of Lords still endorses. Conversely, his approach disregards physical inconvenience that exceptionally does not stem from a sensory experience. This leads to the basic problem of the exception for physical inconvenience. In the light of the progress in psychology and psychiatry over the past decades and the resultant increased awareness of mental illnesses, it may no longer be justifiable, or even feasible, to draw a clear line between physical and non-physical distress.[44]

V   The 'Object Of The Contract' Exception

Most awards of contractual damages for non-pecuniary loss are made on the basis that the provision of pleasure etc was an object of the contract broken. Consequently, Bingham LJ in *Watts v Morrow*[45] mentioned this exception first. Indeed, he went so far as to assert that the law would be defective without it. It may be inferred that the *Addis* rule is acceptable only because it is 'soothed' by the object exception.[46] This is somewhat surprising, for of all exceptions to the *Addis*

---

[40]   ibid. This statement can be justified on the basis of the 'scope of the duty' concept (above ch 2, VI). It is not the purpose of contractual obligations to prevent a mental breakdown of the promisee caused by mere disappointment about the breach.

[41]   *Piper v Daybell, Court-Cooper & Co* (1969) 210 EG 1047 (£50).

[42]   *Trask v Clark & Sons* [1980] CLY 2588 (£250).

[43]   A Phang, 'The Crumbling Edifice? The Award of Contractual Damages for Mental Distress' [2003] *JBL* 341, 380.

[44]   ibid 377–78; D Campbell, 'Exemplary damages' in D Harris, D Campbell, and R Halson, *Remedies in Contract and Tort*, 2nd edn (London, 2002) 596 fn 8 ('physical inconvenience as a specific ground of recovery cannot be given a coherent basis').

[45]   [1991] 1 WLR 1421 (CA) 1445. The relevant passage is quoted above I in this chapter.

[46]   E Macdonald, 'Contractual Damages for Mental Distress' (1994) 7 *Journal of Contract Law* 134, 142.

rule the object exception was the last to be established. It did not emerge until the 1970s. Before then the courts had strictly denied contractual damages for non-physical distress.[47]

The object exception originated in the Scottish case of *Diesen v Samson*, where a photographer who had failed to appear at a wedding as promised had to compensate the bride for the injury to her feelings caused by having no pictorial record of the wedding.[48] It was followed by Court of Appeal decisions granting holidaymakers damages for the distress and frustration they had suffered because the holidays had fallen short of the promised standard.[49] Another milestone was *Heywood v Wellers*,[50] where solicitors who had failed to obtain protection for their client against being molested by a man had to compensate her for the mental distress and upset caused by the continued molestation.[51]

These early cases were not straightforward in explaining why the non-pecuniary loss could be recovered. Some judgments said that the parties had or must have contemplated the non-pecuniary loss when making the contract.[52] Others said that the provision of pleasure, enjoyment and so on had been the very object of the contract.[53] The first explanation implies that mental distress is compensable whenever it satisfies the general remoteness test. This concept was expressly applied in some subsequent cases.[54] When the Court of Appeal later re-established that contractual liability for distress is subject to further limitations than remoteness alone,[55] the first explanation lost its validity and the second explanation moved into the limelight. The 'object of the contract' concept was born.

---

[47] *Hamlin v Great Northern Railway Co* [1856] 1 H & N 408, 411; 156 ER 1261, 1262; *Hobbs v London and South Western Railway Co* (1875) LR 10 QB 111, 122; *Groom v Crocker* [1939] 1 KB 194 (CA) 205, 224, where Sir Wilfrid Greene MR (at 206) and Scott LJ (at 225) regretted, however, that authority prevented them from awarding contractual damages for distress; *Bailey v Bullock* [1950] 2 All ER 1167, 1170; *Cook v Swinfen* [1967] 1 WLR 457 (CA) 461.

[48] 1971 SLT (Sh Ct) 49; approved in *Farley v Skinner* [2001] UKHL 49, [2002] 2 AC 732 [19] (Lord Steyn). A kind of precursor was *Wilson v United Counties Bank Ltd* [1920] AC 102 (HL) 112: below VI in this chapter.

[49] *Jarvis v Swans Tours Ltd* [1973] QB 233 (CA); *Jackson v Horizon Holidays Ltd* [1975] 1 WLR 1468 (CA); *Kemp v Intasun Holidays Ltd* [1987] 2 FTLR 234 (CA); *Peninsular & Oriental Steam Navigation Co* [1997] 2 Lloyd's Rep 136, 141 (CA).

[50] [1976] QB 446 (CA).

[51] Damages for the breach of a covenant not to molest were awarded without pecuniary loss proven in *Fearon v Earl of Aylesford* (1884) 12 QBD 539, 548.

[52] *Diesen v Samson* 1971 SLT (Sh Ct) 49, 50; *Jarvis v Swans Tours Ltd* [1973] QB 233 (CA) 240–41 (Stephenson LJ); *Heywood v Wellers* [1976] QB 446 (CA) 459 (Lord Denning MR), 462 (James LJ).

[53] *Jarvis v Swans Tours Ltd* [1973] QB 233 (CA) 237–38 (Lord Denning MR), 239 (Edmund Davies LJ); *Heywood v Wellers* [1976] QB 446 (CA) 463–64 (Bridge LJ).

[54] *Cox v Philips Industries Ltd* [1976] 1 WLR 638, 644; *McCall v Abelesz* [1976] QB 585 (CA) 594 (Lord Denning MR); *Buckley v Lane, Herdman & Co* [1977] CLY 3143; *Perry v Sidney Phillips & Son* [1982] 1 WLR 1297 (CA) 1302–303 (Lord Denning MR); *Vorvis v Insurance Corporation of British Columbia* [1989] 1 SCR 1085 (SCC) 1119–22 (Wilson J, dissenting); *Mouat v Clark Boyce* [1992] 2 NZLR 559 (NZCA) 569, 573.

[55] *Bliss v South East Thames RHA* [1985] IRLR 308 (CA) [59]; *Hayes v James & Charles Dodd* [1990] 2 All ER 815 (CA) 823–24, 826–27; *Watts v Morrow* [1991] 1 WLR 1421 (CA) 1440, 1445;

It has since been applied in various situations.[56] An example is *Raw v Croydon LBC*.[57] At the defendant authority's request, the claimant surrendered his exclusive burial rights in a certain plot at a cemetery, in exchange for exclusive rights in a different plot. The defendant undertook to transfer the remains of the claimant's father to the new plot. The claimant and his family continued to pay their respects to the deceased at the new site. After about 18 months it turned out that the defendant had transferred the remains of a different person to the new plot. An award of £1,250 for mental distress was made on the basis that the contract between the parties had been one for peace of mind.

The problem with the object exception is that the courts have not been able to come up with a consistent approach as to which contracts fall into this category. Some clarification was brought though by *Farley v Skinner* mentioned earlier.[58] The majority in the Court of Appeal took the view that it had not been the object of the contract *in casu* to protect the claimant against aircraft noise. Stuart-Smith LJ, with whom Mummery LJ agreed,[59] gave two reasons. First, the applicability of the object exception must be determined by the contract as a whole.[60] The contract *in casu* was an ordinary surveyor contract with the investigation into aircraft noise as a minor aspect only.[61] Secondly, it was not a contract to achieve a result but merely one to exercise reasonable care and skill.[62] Both arguments found disfavour in the House of Lords. The object exception applies, said their Lordships, whenever the provision of the amenity was a major or important part of the contract even if not its sole object.[63] It was further held immaterial that the

---

Branchett v Beaney [1992] 3 All ER 910 (CA) 916. See also *Farley v Skinner* [2000] PNLR 441 (CA) [42] (Mummery LJ); [2001] UKHL 49, [2002] 2 AC 732 [16] (Lord Steyn).

[56] 'I am satisfied that in the real life of our lower courts non-pecuniary damages are regularly awarded on the basis that the defendant's breach of contract deprived the plaintiff of the very object of the contract, viz pleasure, relaxation, and peace of mind. The cases arise in diverse contractual contexts, eg the supply of a wedding dress or double glazing, hire purchase transactions, landlord and tenant, building contracts, and engagement of estate agents and solicitors': *Farley v Skinner* [2001] UKHL 49, [2002] 2 AC 732 [20] (Lord Steyn).

[57] [2002] CLY 941.

[58] Above IV in this chapter.

[59] *Farley v Skinner* [2000] PNLR 441 (CA) [31], [41], adding some policy considerations at [32]–[34].

[60] ibid [22].

[61] ibid [24].

[62] ibid.

[63] *Farley v Skinner* [2001] UKHL 49, [2002] 2 AC 732 [23]–[24], [41]–[42] [51], [79]. Lord Hutton said (at [54]) that distress is recoverable 'where: (1) the matter in respect of which the individual claimant seeks damages is of importance to him, and (2) the individual claimant has made clear to the other party that the matter is of importance to him, and (3) the action to be taken in relation to the matter is made a specific term of the contract.' An extension of the object exception to cases where gaining a mental benefit was the main rather than the sole object of the contract had already been suggested in E Macdonald, 'Contractual Damages for Mental Distress' (1994) 7 *JCL* 134, 146.

contract-breaker did not guarantee achievement of a result but merely undertook to exercise reasonable care in achieving it.[64]

Farley v Skinner clarified what the object exception does not require, but it failed to clarify what it does require. A consistent approach is absent, as the cases dealing with solicitors' negligence demonstrate. Following *Heywood v Wellers*, the courts have awarded damages for mental distress in cases where solicitors' negligence resulted in the client being wrongly convicted of a crime[65] or declared bankrupt,[66] or in the client's children being abducted into a foreign country.[67] In *Hayes v James & Charles Dodd*,[68] by contrast, where the solicitors' negligence resulted in the clients buying property which was totally unsuitable for the business intended, the Court of Appeal denied damages for the ensuing distress on the ground that the solicitors had been consulted in a purely commercial matter. If a distinction between commercial and personal matters is decisive, where do we place divorce proceedings solely concerned with the division of the matrimonial assets? The improper handling of such proceedings with the result that the client failed to get an appropriate share of the assets was the subject matter of two cases, with different decisions as to the availability of mental distress damages.[69]

Also uncertain is the compensability of distress suffered by the buyer of a new car that has a number of severe defects during the first months. In *Alexander v Rolls Royce Motor Cars Ltd*,[70] the Court of Appeal, without clear explanation, denied compensation for such distress. This was despite accepting that 'the plaintiff had acquired the Rolls Royce car for his pleasure and to drive on social occasions so that he could enjoy the exceptional experience and ownership of such a prestigious car'.[71] By contrast, in *Jackson v Chrysler Acceptances Ltd*,[72] where the plaintiff had used the defective car during his family holidays in France, the same court awarded damages for spoilt holidays. It was held crucial that the car dealer had known about the plaintiff's holiday plans.

The last point suggests that the applicability of the object exception depends on whether or not the contract-breaker, when making the contract, knew that the

---

[64] [2001] UKHL 49, [2002] 2 AC 732 [25], [43], [53]. Somewhat differently from the other Lords, Lord Scott said (at [79], [86], [106]–[107]) that the claimant had been deprived of a contractual benefit.

[65] *McLeish v Amoo-Gottfried & Co* (1994) 10 PN 102 (£6,000). See also *McLoughlin v Grovers* [2001] EWCA Civ 1743, [2002] QB 1312.

[66] *Rey v Graham & Oldham* [2000] BPIR 354, 370 (£1,200).

[67] *Hamilton Jones v David & Snape* [2003] EWHC 3147 (Ch), [2004] 1 WLR 924 (£20,000).

[68] [1990] 2 All ER 815 (CA).

[69] Damages of £5,000 were awarded in *Dickinson v Jones Alexander & Co* (1989) 139 NLJ 1525. Damages were denied in *Channon v Lindley Johnstone* [2002] EWCA Civ 353, [2002] PNLR 41.

[70] [1996] RTR 95 (CA).

[71] ibid 101 (Beldam LJ).

[72] [1978] RTR 474 (CA) 481, 482. See also *Bernstein v Pamson Motors (Golders Green) Ltd* [1987] 2 All ER 220: On a cold day, the plaintiff's new car, having done about 140 miles, broke down on the motorway, and he had to be picked up by the emergency service. Rougier J (at 231) awarded him £150 'for a totally spoilt day, comprising nothing but vexation'.

other party expected a mental benefit from performance. Certainly, in the absence of such knowledge the non-pecuniary loss will be too remote.[73] But does that mean that the pure knowledge of the other party's expectation renders the contract-breaker liable for non-pecuniary consequences of breach? Ralph Gibson LJ in *Watts v Morrow* opined that there will be no liability unless the contract-breaker promised the mental benefit in question.[74] With respect, this cannot be the law, for pleasure as such will hardly ever be promised. A wedding photographer will not promise pleasure in watching the photos, and a tour operator will not promise enjoyment as such.[75]

It seems to be commonplace[76] that the object exception reflects the 'consumer surplus',[77] which is the subjective value to the promisee of the performance in question (measurable by the price for which she would have sold her contractual rights[78]) over and above its objective market value. This view finds support in *Ruxley Electronics and Construction Ltd v Forsyth*.[79] A swimming pool was built with a diving area that was 6 feet deep as opposed to the 7 feet 6 inches specified in the contract. Since the pool was still perfectly suitable for diving, the value of the house remained unaffected. The house owner claimed £20,000 as the estimated cost of rebuilding the pool to the specified depth. The judge found this out of proportion to the benefit sought and denied the claim. However, he qualified the contract as one 'for the provision of a pleasurable amenity' and awarded £2,500 for loss of amenity. The House of Lords approved.[80] Lord Mustill observed that the award reflected the consumer surplus.[81]

But even if there was a consumer surplus in all cases assigned to the object exception, the reverse is not true. By no means have the courts invoked the object exception in all situations in which a consumer surplus is present. Many

---

[73] E Macdonald, 'Contractual Damages for Mental Distress' (1994) 7 *JCL* 134, 144. Remoteness in contract is considered in ch 3.

[74] [1991] 1 WLR 1421 (CA) 1442: 'there was no express promise for the provision of peace of mind or freedom from distress and no such implied promise was alleged'.

[75] E Macdonald, 'Contractual Damages for Mental Distress' (1994) 7 *JCL* 134, 143.

[76] H Beale, 'Exceptional Measures of Damages in Contract' in P Birks (ed), *Wrongs and Remedies in the Twenty-First Century* (Oxford, 1996) 224; A Burrows, *Understanding the Law of Obligations: Essays on Contract, Tort and Restitution* (Oxford, 1998) 148; D Campbell, 'Exemplary damages' in D Harris, D Campbell, and R Halson, *Remedies in Contract and Tort*, 2nd edn (London, 2002) 597.

[77] The term was coined by D Harris, A Ogus and J Phillips, 'Contract Remedies and the Consumer Surplus' (1979) 95 *LQR* 581, 582, who defined it as 'the excess utility or subjective value obtained from a "good" over and above the utility associated with its market price' (citation omitted).

[78] F Dawson, 'General Damages in Contract for Non-pecuniary Loss' (1983) 10 *NZULR* 232, 252.

[79] [1996] AC 344 (HL).

[80] Thereby tacitly overruling *Knott v Bolton* (1995) 11 Const LJ 375 (CA), where compensation was denied for the distress a house owner had suffered by virtue of the architect failing to include the wide staircase and gallery requested. *Knott v Bolton* was expressly overruled in *Farley v Skinner* [2001] UKHL 49, [2002] 2 AC 732 [24], [41], [52], [93].

[81] [1996] AC 344 (HL) 360–361. The concept, but not the term consumer surplus, was also approved in *Farley v Skinner* [2001] UKHL 49, [2002] 2 AC 732 [21] (Lord Steyn).

employees will value their employment higher than their salary,[82] yet mental distress damages have been denied in cases of wrongful dismissal.[83] Many tenants will value the use of their property higher than the rent they pay, yet mental distress damages were denied *obiter* where a landlord had broken the covenant for quiet enjoyment.[84] Finally, mental distress damages were denied where a bank wrongfully dishonoured a cheque[85] or allowed unauthorised withdrawals through automatic telling machines.[86] Bank customers, it could be argued, expect peace of mind in respect to the operation of their day-to-day financial affairs.[87]

VI Loss of Reputation

While financial consequences of an injury to reputation are compensable,[88] the opposite is generally true for *non*-pecuniary consequences.[89] However, several groups of cases are said to form an exception to the latter rule.[90] The earliest group, apart from the outdated cases concerning the breach of promise of marriage,[91] is that of cases in which a bank wrongfully dishonoured a cheque written by its customer.[92] In these cases, the bank's action was held to have been so obviously injurious to the customer's credit and reputation that he was entitled to compensation for this injury without having to prove an actual pecuniary loss.[93] The principle was initially confined to customers who were

---

[82] E McKendrick, 'Breach of Contract and the Meaning of Loss' (1999) 52 *Current Legal Problems* 37, 44.

[83] *Addis v Gramophone Co Ltd* [1909] AC 488 (HL); *Shove v Downs Surgical plc* [1984] 1 All ER 7, 10; *Bliss v South East Thames RHA* [1985] IRLR 308 (CA) [58]–[59] (overruling *Cox v Phillips Industries Ltd* [1976] 1 WLR 638). *Dubitante Johnson v Gore Wood & Co* [2002] 2 AC 1 (HL) 50 (Lord Cooke).

[84] *Branchett v Beaney* [1992] 3 All ER 910 (CA) 916–918, disapproving Lord Denning's contrary dictum in *McCall v Abelesz* [1976] QB 585 (CA) 594.

[85] *Rae v Yorkshire Bank plc* [1988] BTLC 35 (CA).

[86] *McConville v Barclays Bank plc* [1993] 2 Bank LR 211.

[87] H Johnson, 'Distressed Customers' (1993) 12 *International Banking and Financial Law* 51.

[88] *Foaminol Laboratories Ltd v British Artid Plastics Ltd* [1941] 2 All ER 393, 399–400; *Spring v Guardian Assurance plc* [1995] 2 AC 296 (HL); *Malik v BCCI SA* [1998] AC 20 (HL) 40, 52–53. However, the restrictions of a statutory compensation scheme for unfair dismissal must not be circumvented: *Johnson v Unisys Ltd* [2001] UKHL 13, [2003] 1 AC 518; distinguished in *Eastwood v Magnox Electric plc* [2004] UKHL 35, [2005] 1 AC 503.

[89] eg *Withers v General Theatre Co Ltd* [1933] 2 KB 536 (CA) 545, 554; *Foaminol Laboratories Ltd v British Artid Plastics Ltd* [1941] 2 All ER 393, 399.

[90] JW Carter, E Peden and GJ Tolhurst, *Contract Law in Australia*, 5th edn (Chatswood, 2007) [36–10]; probably also HG Beale, 'Damages' in HG Beale (gen ed), *Chitty on Contracts, Vol 1: General Principles*, 30th edn (London, 2008) [26–086]–[26–087].

[91] This action was abolished by the Law Reform (Miscellaneous Provisions) Act 1970 s 1.

[92] *Rolin v Steward* (1854) 14 CB 595, 606–608, 139 ER 245, 249–50; *Gibbons v Westminster Bank Ltd* [1939] 2 KB 882, 888; *Kpohraror v Woolwich Building Society* [1996] 4 All ER 119 (CA). For an action in libel see *Davidson v Barclays Bank Ltd* [1940] 1 All ER 316.

[93] See *Wilson v United Counties Bank Ltd* [1920] AC 102 (HL) 112 (Lord Birkenhead LC).

'traders',[94] but Evans LJ, speaking for the Court of Appeal in *Kpohraror v Woolwich Building Society*, rejected this restriction: 'The credit rating of individuals is as important for their personal transactions, including mortgages and hire-purchase as well as banking facilities, as it is for those who are engaged in trade'.[95]

The 'cheque rule' was applied in different circumstances in *Wilson v United Counties Bank Ltd*.[96] A bank agreed with its customer to supervise the financial side of his business during his absence on military service and to take all reasonable steps to maintain his credit and reputation. Due to the bank's negligence, the customer became bankrupt. The jury awarded damages not only for the financial loss but also for the injury to the customer's credit and reputation. The House of Lords upheld the latter award, with Lord Birkenhead LC saying:

> If it be held that there is an irrebuttable presumption that the dishonour of a trader customer's cheque in the events supposed is injurious to him and may be compensated by other than nominal damages, the conclusion would appear to follow almost *a fortiori* that such damages may be given where the defendant has expressly contracted to sustain the financial credit of a trading customer and has committed a breach of this agreement.[97]

In another group of cases 'loss of publicity' was held to be compensable where, in breach of contract, the musical director of a theatre was not advertised or employed as such,[98] where an artist was not allowed to perform in a music hall,[99] where actors were not allowed to give the promised performance in a theatre,[100] and where the works of authors were not published as promised.[101] In *Withers v General Theatre Co Ltd*, the Court of Appeal restricted the ambit of recovery by holding that, while the actor may claim compensation for the missed opportunity to enhance his reputation, he cannot recover for the damage to his existing reputation.[102] This restriction was disapproved, on different facts but with an intention of general applicability, by the House of Lords in *Malik v BCCI SA*.[103]

---

[94] Emphasised in *Gibbons v Westminster Bank Ltd* [1939] 2 KB 882, 888.
[95] [1996] 4 All ER 119 (CA) 124.
[96] [1920] AC 102 (HL).
[97] ibid 112.
[98] *Bunning v Lyric Theatre Ltd* (1894) 71 LT 396.
[99] *Turpin v Victoria Palace Ltd* [1918] 2 KB 539, where damages were only denied because there had been no contractual obligation on the music hall to permit the artist to perform.
[100] *Marbe v George Edwardes (Daly's Theatre) Ltd* [1928] 1 KB 269 (CA); *Herbert Clayton & Jack Waller Ltd v Oliver* [1930] AC 209 (HL); *Withers v General Theatre Co Ltd* [1933] 2 KB 536 (CA).
[101] *Tolnay v Criterion Film Productions Ltd* [1936] 2 All ER 1625; *Joseph v National Magazine Co* [1959] Ch 14. See also *Malcolm v The Chancellor, Masters and Scholars of the University of Oxford* [1994] EMLR 17 (CA) 41 (Nourse LJ).
[102] [1933] 2 KB 536 (CA) 551, 554–55, 556. Followed in *Tolnay v Criterion Film Productions Ltd* [1936] 2 All ER 1625, 1626. The opposite view had been taken in *Marbe v George Edwardes (Daly's Theatre) Ltd* [1928] 1 KB 269 (CA) 281, 288.
[103] [1998] AC 20 (HL) 41, 51–52.

Finally, there have been cases where tradesmen who had been supplied defective goods were awarded damages for the injury to their commercial reputation,[104] where an apprentice wrongfully dismissed received damages for the 'loss of status',[105] and where a travel agent received damages for loss of goodwill from a shipowner who had failed to supply accommodation on a certain ship.[106] However, as a glance into the judgments reveals, the awards aimed to compensate a financial loss that could not be proven with accuracy.[107] For instance, in *GKN Centrax Gears Ltd v Matbro Ltd*, which involved defective goods, Stephenson LJ observed:

> The Court can and should draw inferences from the evidence called as to the probable extent of the total loss of business resulting from the original seller's breach of contract and must make its own moderate estimate without attempting perfect compensation.[108]

A thorough look at the 'cheque cases', *Wilson* and the 'loss of publicity' cases reveals that in all these cases too, the notional loss of reputation reflected in truth a financial loss the amount of which or the occurrence of which was difficult to prove with accuracy.[109] With regard to the 'cheque cases' and *Wilson*, Sir Wilfrid Greene MR observed in *Groom v Crocker*: 'In such cases it is the commercial credit of the customer that is injured, and the inference arises that pecuniary loss will necessarily ensue'.[110] Damages for 'loss of publicity' have been explained on the basis that the denial of publicity impaired the employment prospects of the artist.[111] There may thus be no exception to the *Addis* rule for mere loss of reputation.[112] As Evans LJ said *obiter* in *Kpohraror v Woolwich Building Society*: 'Damages for loss of reputation simpliciter are excluded, whether in contract or for torts other than defamation'.[113]

---

[104] *Cointat v Myham & Son* [1913] 2 KB 220, 222–24; *GKN Centrax Gears Ltd v Matbro Ltd* [1976] 2 Lloyd's Rep 555 (CA) 574, 577–78, 584–85.

[105] *Dunk v George Waller & Son* [1970] 2 QB 163 (CA).

[106] *Anglo-Continental Holidays Ltd v Typaldos Lines (London) Ltd* [1967] 2 Lloyd's Rep 61 (CA) 66, 67.

[107] F Dawson, 'General Damages in Contract for Non-pecuniary Loss' (1983) 10 *NZULR* 232, 243–45.

[108] [1976] 2 Lloyd's Rep 555 (CA) 578.

[109] A Burrows, *Remedies for Torts and Breach of Contract*, 3rd edn (Oxford, 2004) 313–15; E Peel, *Treitel on the Law of Contract*, 12th edn (London, 2007) [20–081]. With regard to *Wilson* also N Enonchong, 'Breach of Contract and Damages for Mental Distress' (1996) 16 *OJLS* 617, 623–24.

[110] [1939] 1 KB 194 (CA) 205. MacKinnon LJ said (at 230): 'In *Wilson's* case it was "credit as a trader," that is, a business asset that was lost or impaired'.

[111] See especially *Marbe v George Edwardes (Daly's Theatre) Ltd* [1928] 1 KB 269 (CA) 281–82; *Tolnay v Criterion Film Productions Ltd* [1936] 2 All ER 1625, 1626–27. An exception is *Bunning v Lyric Theatre Ltd* (1894) 71 LT 396, 398, where the court awarded damages for loss of reputation despite the finding that the plaintiff's employment prospects were unaffected.

[112] A Burrows, *Remedies for Torts and Breach of Contract*, 3rd edn (Oxford, 2004) 313, 317. See also H McGregor, *McGregor on Damages*, 18th edn (London, 2009) [3–031].

[113] [1996] 4 All ER 119 (CA) 125.

However, the 'object of the contract' exception considered before[114] could apply to loss of reputation, as suggested *obiter* by Ralph Gibson LJ in *Cambridge Nutrition Ltd v BBC*:

> I do not think that the decision in *Addis v Gramophone Co Ltd* is a bar to the recovery of damages for injury to reputation in an action for breach of contract, where the contractual provision proved to have been broken had as its purpose, or one of its purposes, the protection of the claimant against the sort of damage suffered.[115]

Indeed, the decisive factor in the 'loss of publicity' cases was the defendant's (express or implied) obligation to provide publicity.[116] Further, the fact that the bank expressly undertook to preserve the plaintiff's reputation grounded recovery in *Wilson*, as Lord Birkenhead's statement quoted earlier illustrates. But even if the object exception applies to loss of reputation, this principle would be part of the object exception itself and would not create another exception to the *Addis* rule.

VII   Need for Reform

Although generally proscribed, contractual damages for non-pecuniary loss are by no means uncommon. The awards made are commonly grouped into certain exceptions according to the type of loss and the nature of the obligation broken. But the two exceptions of practical significance—the physical inconvenience exception and the 'object of the contract' exception—are still unclear in their scope. All that can be said with certainty is that the scope of each exception has constantly widened, which starts to undermine the general rule.[117] Michael Bridge feels 'struck by the absence of structure and the conceptual underdevelopment of the subject',[118] and observes that 'odd cases are bundled together in an unclassified category of sundries'.[119] The law is a patchwork[120] and needs to be changed.[121] Tomain describes the similar situation in US law as:

---

[114] Above V in this chapter.

[115] [1990] 3 All ER 523 (CA) 540.

[116] *Turpin v Victoria Palace Ltd* [1918] 2 KB 539, 547 (where damages were denied because such an obligation had not been undertaken); *Bunning v Lyric Theatre Ltd* (1894) 71 LT 396, 397–98; *Marbe v George Edwardes (Daly's Theatre) Ltd* [1928] 1 KB 269 (CA) 283–87, 289.

[117] *Baltic Shipping Co v Dillon* (1993) 176 CLR 344 (HCA) 361 (Mason CJ).

[118] MG Bridge, 'Contractual Damages for Intangible Loss: A Comparative Analysis' (1984) 62 *Canadian Bar Review* 323, 327.

[119] ibid 328.

[120] MA Jones and AE Morris, 'The distressing effects of professional incompetence' (2004) 20 *Professional Negligence* 118, 137 (in relation to mental distress).

[121] Staughton LJ, in *Hayes v James & Charles Dodd* [1990] 2 All ER 815 (CA) 823, called for a clarification of the law by either the House of Lords or the Law Commission.

[A] classic example for the middle period in the development of a common law rule. Once a rule has been announced, its second stage begins during which cases are included within and without the rule, distinctions become fuzzy and sometimes contradictory, and reasoning is questionable. All of which leads to the demise and replacement of the rule.[122]

Considering that all attempts to clarify and contain the scope of the exceptions to the *Addis* rule have failed, the way forward, it seems, is indeed to abandon the rule altogether and to make non-pecuniary loss generally compensable in contract, just as it is in tort.[123] The Scottish Law Commission recommends such a reform for Scots law.[124] It needs to be investigated now whether there are cogent reasons for retaining the *Addis* rule.

VIII   Defensibility of the General Bar to Compensation

A   Avoiding Punishment

Is the *Addis* rule defensible?[125] In *Addis* itself, Lord Atkinson argued that to award damages for the non-pecuniary consequences of a breach of contract would overcompensate the aggrieved party and thus punish the contract-breaker, which is not the purpose of contractual remedies.[126] The view that damages for non-pecuniary harm are punitive in character was apparently shared by Lord Collins in *Addis*[127] and has since been judicially iterated,[128] most recently in *Farley v Skinner* where Mummery LJ said that 'the amount awarded is open to the trenchant criticisms that it is not truly or wholly compensatory, that it contains

---

[122] JP Tomain, 'Contract Compensation in Nonmarket Transactions' (1985) 46 *University of Pittsburgh Law Review* 867, 890–91; citation omitted.

[123] It would be completely unrealistic to call for a restriction of the scope of damages for non-pecuniary loss to 'bodily pain and suffering' in both contract and tort, as suggested by BS Jackson, 'Injured Feelings Resulting from Breach of Contract' (1977) 26 *International & Comparative Law Quarterly* 502, 513–15.

[124] Scottish Law Commission, 'Report on Remedies for Breach of Contract' (Scot Law Com No 174, 1999) Part 3, Appendix A, Draft Contract (Scotland) Bill s 2.

[125] For an outline of the major arguments *pro* and *con*, see WP Keeton (gen ed), *Prosser and Keeton on the Law of Torts*, 5th edn (St Paul, 1984) 360–61.

[126] *Addis v Gramophone Co Ltd* [1909] AC 488 (HL) 493–96. For the facts of Addis see above II in this chapter.

[127] [1909] AC 488 (HL) 497–501. He did approve the award *in casu*.

[128] *Herbert Clayton & Jack Waller Ltd v Oliver* [1930] AC 209 (HL) 220; *British Guiana Credit Corp v Da Silva* [1965] 1 WLR 248 (PC) 259. In *Seffert v Los Angeles Transit Lines* (1961) 56 Cal.2d 498 (SC of California) 511, Traynor J, dissenting, said that damages for pain and suffering 'originated under primitive law as a means of punishing wrongdoers and assuaging the feelings of those who had been wronged'. The same concept may stand behind the view of some US courts that the compensation of non-pecuniary loss is the domain of tort: see the cases cited by JP Tomain, 'Contract Compensation in Nonmarket Transactions' (1985) 46 *U Pitt L Rev* 867, 897 fns 123 and 124.

an impermissible punitive element'.[129] Indeed, the textbook by Harris, Campbell and Halson discusses contractual damages for distress, disappointment and loss of enjoyment within the chapter on exemplary damages.[130]

Even though exemplary damages and damages for non-pecuniary harm may indeed sometimes have the same practical effect,[131] there is a clear difference between compensation of the claimant's non-pecuniary harm and punishment of the defendant.[132] Non-pecuniary harm represents loss[133] and demands as such compensation under the compensatory principle[134] cherished by Lord Atkinson in *Addis*, unless there are cogent reasons to hold otherwise. It is thus not the general availability but the general unavailability of damages for non-pecuniary loss that conflicts with basic principle and needs to be justified.[135]

B Avoiding Excessive Awards

Even though damages for non-pecuniary loss do not aim at a punishment of the wrongdoer, a punitive side-effect could still result from an award of excessive sums.[136] In *Addis* itself, Lord Shaw feared an 'inflation of damages',[137] and the *Addis* rule has been defended by pointing to 'the United States practice of huge awards'.[138] Where juries fix the amount of damages, a fear of excessive awards may be justified,[139] as Scottish experience shows.[140] But in England and Wales

---

[129] [2000] PNLR 441 (CA) [34].

[130] D Harris, D Campbell and R Halson, *Remedies in Contract and Tort*, 2nd edn (London, 2002) ch 30. See also E Veitch, 'Sentimental Damages in Contract' (1977) 16 *University of Western Ontario Law Review* 227: the often unspoken function of contractual awards for intangible losses 'smacks of the punitive'.

[131] E Peel, *Treitel on the Law of Contract*, 12th edn (London, 2007) [20–015]; *Rookes v Barnard* [1964] AC 1129 (HL) 1221, where Lord Devlin observed that if one examines the cases in which the manner of committing a tort increased the amount of damages, 'it is not at all easy to say whether the idea of compensation or the idea of punishment has prevailed'.

[132] E Peel, ibid [20–073].

[133] *Watson, Laidlaw & Co Ltd v Pott, Cassels & Williamson* 1914 SC (HL) 18, 29 (Lord Shaw); *Rookes v Barnard* [1964] AC 1129 (HL) 1221; *Baltic Shipping Co v Dillon* (1993) 176 CLR 344 (HCA) 396 (McHugh J); RA Posner, *Economic Analysis of Law*, 7th edn (Austin, 2007) 196; N Enonchong, 'Breach of Contract and Damages for Mental Distress' (1996) 16 *OJLS* 617, 628.

[134] A Burrows, *Remedies for Torts and Breach of Contract*, 3rd edn (Oxford, 2004) 332.

[135] *Baltic Shipping Co v Dillon* (1993) 176 CLR 344 (HCA) 362 (Mason CJ); E Macdonald, 'Contractual Damages for Mental Distress' (1994) 7 *JCL* 134, 135, 141.

[136] A Phang, 'The Crumbling Edifice? The Award of Contractual Damages for Mental Distress' [2003] *JBL* 341, 345–46.

[137] *Addis v Gramophone Co Ltd* [1909] AC 488 (HL) 505.

[138] *Hayes v James & Charles Dodd* [1990] 2 All ER 815 (CA) 823 (Staughton LJ).

[139] JA Sebert, 'Punitive and Nonpecuniary Damages in Actions Based Upon Contract: Toward Achieving the Objective of Full Compensation' (1986) 33 *University of California at Los Angeles Law Review* 1565, 1599: juries would use the power to compensate annoyance or emotional distress 'to exercise their perceived redistributional tendencies in favor of individual plaintiffs and against corporate defendants, or to vent their collective spleens against defendants whom, despite contrary instructions from the judge, they believe deserve punishment'.

[140] In *Girvan v Inverness Farmers Dairy* 1994 SC 701, a jury award of £120,000 as *solatium* for an elbow fracture and lacerations suffered in a road accident was quashed as being excessive. When a

juries are no longer involved in contract cases since they have been largely removed from civil cases.[141] Judges can usually restrain themselves from making 'emotional' awards, as proven by the all in all reasonable amounts awarded for non-pecuniary loss in England[142] and other 'jury-free' jurisdictions.[143] Indeed, the Court of Appeal has called for an increase in the level of damages for pain, suffering and loss of amenity in personal injury cases.[144]

C   General Remoteness of Non-Pecuniary Loss

Contractual damages for non-pecuniary loss have sometimes been awarded on the ground that under the particular circumstances of the case the parties had or must have contemplated such loss when making the contract.[145] In those cases the foreseeability of the non-pecuniary loss was apparently regarded as something which made the instant case stand out from the usual scenario. It has indeed been argued that mental suffering on breach is not within the contemplation of the parties to ordinary, particularly commercial, contracts, so that the *Addis* rule is just an application of the *Hadley v Baxendale* foreseeability test.[146] This argument cannot be sustained. Considering that breaches of contract, commercial or otherwise, frequently cause non-pecuniary loss, such loss is 'surely' foreseeable, as Bingham LJ observed in *Watts v Morrow*.[147] This would be

---

second jury awarded £95,000, the appellate courts 'gave in' and upheld the award: *Girvan v Inverness Farmers Dairy (No 2)* 1996 SC 134 (CSIH); 1998 SC (HL) 1.

[141]   Supreme Court Act 1981 s 69.

[142]   KB Soh, 'Anguish, Foreseeability and Policy' (1989) 105 *LQR* 43, 45; E Macdonald, 'Contractual Damages for Mental Distress' (1994) 7 *JCL* 134, 139.

[143]   A Phang, 'The Crumbling Edifice? The Award of Contractual Damages for Mental Distress' [2003] *JBL* 341, 349–50; E Veitch, 'Sentimental Damages in Contract' (1977) 16 *UWOLR* 227, 240. For Canada *Vorvis v Insurance Corporation of British Columbia* [1989] 1 SCR 1085 (SCC) 1122 (Wilson J, dissenting); for New Zealand *Rowlands v Collow* [1992] 1 NZLR 178, 207.

[144]   *Heil v Rankin* [2001] QB 272 (CA): there should be a tapered increase of awards above £10,000 up to a maximum increase of one-third for the most severe injuries.

[145]   eg *Wilson v United Counties Bank Ltd* [1920] AC 102 (HL) 132 (Lord Atkinson). See also above V in this chapter.

[146]   eg *Johnson v Unisys Ltd* [2001] UKHL 13, [2003] 1 AC 518 [70] (Lord Millett); *Fidler v Sun Life Assurance Co of Canada* 2006 SCC 30, [2006] 2 SCR 3 [45]; *Kewin v Massachusetts Mutual Life Insurance Co* (1980) 409 Mich 401 (SC of Michigan) 414–19; H McGregor, *McGregor on Damages*, 18th edn (London, 2009) [3–020], [19–008]; D Campbell, 'Exemplary damages' in D Harris, D Campbell and R Halson, *Remedies in Contract and Tort*, 2nd edn (London, 2002) 600. See also *Turpin v Victoria Palace Ltd* [1918] 2 KB 539, 545; *Farley v Skinner* [2000] PNLR 441 (CA) [18] (Stuart-Smith LJ); [2001] UKHL 49, [2002] 2 AC 732 [75] (Lord Scott). The *Hadley v Baxendale* foreseeability test is discussed in ch 3.

[147]   [1991] 1 WLR 1421 (CA) 1445 (the relevant passage is quoted above I in this chapter). See also *Baltic Shipping Co v Dillon* (1993) 176 CLR 344 (HCA) 364 (Mason CJ), 380–81 (Deane J and Dawson J), 396 (McHugh J); F Dawson, 'General Damages in Contract for Non-pecuniary Loss' (1983) 10 *NZULR* 232, 255–56; N Enonchong, 'Breach of Contract and Damages for Mental Distress' (1996) 16 *OJLS* 617, 630–31; DW Greig and JLR Davis, *The Law of Contract* (Sydney, 1987) 1414; JA Sebert, 'Punitive and Nonpecuniary Damages in Actions Based Upon Contract: Toward Achieving the Objective of Full Compensation' (1986) 33 *UCLA LR* 1565, 1586–587.

even more so if the *Hadley* test were to be replaced by the *Wagon Mound* test, as suggested in this book.[148]

D   Assumption of Risk

For some commentators, it is just the foreseeability of non-pecuniary loss that explains the *Addis* rule. Anxiety and disappointment on breach, they say, is so obviously in the contemplation of contracting parties that they must be deemed to assume the risk of suffering it,[149] at least in the case of business people.[150] But why should parties to contracts, commercial or otherwise, 'acquiesce' in the suffering of a certain consequence of breach, and waive the right to compensation for it, when they know that they may normally claim compensation for all consequences of breach?[151] As Burrows says: 'If the risks of "losses" consequent on contract-breaking were truly accepted, no damages at all would be payable'.[152] If, however, the 'assumption of risk' argument means to say that contractual duties do not exist in order to avoid the usual disappointment and worry on breach, then the argument does have force. This issue will be considered later.[153]

E   Difficult Assessment

The general denial of compensation for inconvenience and injured feelings in contract has been explained on the ground that such loss is incapable of being appreciated or estimated.[154] It is certainly difficult to place a precise monetary value on inconvenience and distress,[155] but, as Lord Denning once said, 'it is no more difficult than the assessment which the courts have to make every day in

---

[148]   Above ch 4, IV F.

[149]   *Johnson v Unisys Ltd* [2001] UKHL 13, [2003] 1 AC 518 [70] (Lord Millett); H Carty, 'Contract Theory and Employment Reality' (1986) 49 *Modern Law Review* 240, 245; G Treitel, *The Law of Contract*, 11th edn (London, 2003) 992–93: 'anxiety is an almost inevitable concomitant of expectations based on promises, so that a contracting party must be deemed to take the risk of it'.

[150]   *Crump v Wala* [1994] 2 NZLR 331, 345–46; D Yates, 'Damages for Non-pecuniary Loss' (1973) 36 *MLR* 535, 538 ('disappointment as a consequence of breach is too obviously in the contemplation of the parties so that the businessman can be taken to have assumed the risk of disappointment in the event of breach whereas the private "consumer" may not').

[151]   *Baltic Shipping Co v Dillon* (1993) 176 CLR 344 (HCA) 362 (Mason CJ), 396 (McHugh J); N Enonchong, 'Breach of Contract and Damages for Mental Distress' (1996) 16 *OJLS* 617, 630; A Phang, 'The Crumbling Edifice? The Award of Contractual Damages for Mental Distress' [2003] *JBL* 341, 350.

[152]   A Burrows, *Remedies for Torts and Breach of Contract*, 3rd edn (Oxford, 2004) 333.

[153]   Below VIII G in this chapter.

[154]   *Hamlin v Great Northern Railway Co* [1856] 1 H & N 408, 411; 156 ER 1261, 1262 (Pollock CB); *Farley v Skinner* [2000] PNLR 441 (CA) [18] (Stuart-Smith LJ), [33]–[34] (Mummery LJ). See also E Macdonald, 'Contractual Damages for Mental Distress' (1994) 7 *JCL* 134, 141, 155.

[155]   Or the 'consumer surplus' (above V in this chapter): MG Bridge, 'Contractual Damages for Intangible Loss: A Comparative Analysis' (1984) 62 *Can Bar Rev* 323, 367; A Phang, 'The Crumbling Edifice? The Award of Contractual Damages for Mental Distress' [2003] *JBL* 341, 349.

personal injury cases for loss of amenities'.[156] Moreover, the argument clashes with the established principle that: 'Where there has been an actual loss of some sort, the common law does not permit difficulties of estimating the loss in money to defeat the only remedy it provided for breach of contract, an award of damages'.[157] Considering also that distress and inconvenience have attracted tortious damages,[158] there must be a good reason why a difficult assessment should bar compensation just for *non*-physical inconvenience or distress in *contract* (and not in tort).

In the decision by the High Court of Australia in *Baltic Shipping Co v Dillon*,[159] Brennan J saw such a reason in the prevention of an indeterminate liability for breach of contract. The institution of contract, he said, can operate only if parties entering a contract are able to estimate the extent of their liability in the event of breach. Such estimation would be impossible if the subjective mental reaction of the aggrieved party were added on as further damage, since liability for breach would fluctuate according to the personal situation of the aggrieved party. In a similar vein, Francis Dawson has argued that the *Addis* rule 'finds its justification in the need to maintain certainty and predictability in commercial affairs'.[160]

Two objections must be made. First, the ability to estimate the extent of liability is as important in tort as it is in contract. Economists conceive negligence as the infliction of an injury that could have been avoided at less cost than the expected cost of that injury, the latter being the product of the probability of the injury and the magnitude of the expected loss.[161] Someone who contemplates performing a potentially dangerous action is able to determine the efficiency of (additional) precautions only if the loss in the event of an accident can be estimated with some certainty. Indemnity insurers are able to calculate the appropriate premium for an insured risk only if they can estimate the extent of liability should the risk materialise.

Secondly, a reversal of the *Addis* rule would lead to the uncertainty feared only if non-physical distress then became compensable for the first time, and the courts had to start from scratch in placing a monetary value on such loss. But non-physical distress has already been compensated in tort, and exceptionally also in contract, in a number of instances, so that some guidance as to the valuation of such loss is available.[162] And the more cases come before the courts,

---

[156] *Jarvis v Swans Tours Ltd* [1973] QB 233 (CA) 238. See also H Beale, 'Exceptional Measures of Damages in Contract' in P Birks (ed), *Wrongs and Remedies in the Twenty-First Century* (Oxford, 1996) 225; A Burrows, *Remedies for Torts and Breach of Contract*, 3rd edn (Oxford, 2004) 333.

[157] *Fink v Fink* (1947) 74 CLR 127 (HCA) 143 (Dixon J and McTiernan J). See also *Chaplin v Hicks* [1911] 2 KB 786 (CA) 792; *Turpin v Victoria Palace Ltd* [1918] 2 KB 539, 545; *Ruxley Electronics and Construction Ltd v Forsyth* [1996] AC 344 (HL) 360–61.

[158] Above ch 6, II and IV.

[159] (1993) 176 CLR 344 (HCA) 369.

[160] F Dawson, 'General Damages in Contract for Non-pecuniary Loss' (1983) 10 *NZULR* 232, 234.

[161] eg R Cooter and T Ulen, *Law and Economics*, 5th edn (Boston, 2008) 342–44, 349–51; RA Posner, *Economic Analysis of Law*, 7th edn (Austin, 2007) 167–70.

[162] N Enonchong, 'Breach of Contract and Damages for Mental Distress' (1996) 16 *OJLS* 617, 629.

the larger the material becomes with which future cases can be compared. Over time there might, and indeed should,[163] develop a tariff system for non-physical distress akin to the one used in personal injury cases.[164]

F Lower Cost of Contracting

Greig and Davis argue that the general award of even modest compensation for distress resulting from breach of contract 'would lead to an increase in the cost of entering into a contract, without any substantial benefit being derived therefrom'.[165] Sharing this view, David Campbell argues that if non-pecuniary loss were generally compensable in the case of a sale of goods to consumers, where a contractual limitation of the seller's liability must pass muster under the unfair-terms legislation, 'the pricing of consumer goods might [then] be radically shifted in ways courts acting on their own initiative cannot possibly understand or evaluate'.[166]

The assertion of an increase in the cost of contracting is true *ceteris paribus*, that is, if all other circumstances remain unchanged. The assessment and award of damages, or the bargaining for an out-of-court settlement, produces cost, especially where the loss in question is difficult to assess,[167] and this cost will *ceteris paribus* increase the price for goods and services. But compensating distress would save the cost of suffering it[168] and would do justice,[169] and either effect may well form the 'substantial benefit' that Greig and Davis are missing.

Moreover, it is not certain that a reversal of *Addis* would increase the cost of contracting if all effects of such a change are taken into account. If significant distress resulting from a breach of contract is compensated, consumers may more readily enter into contracts the breach of which is prone to cause significant distress, such as contracts for holidays.[170] This promotional effect may reduce the supplier's cost for the individual contract because a larger number of the same product is sold or because marketing can be reduced, and these savings may outweigh the additional cost of increased litigation.[171]

---

[163] MG Bridge, 'Contractual Damages for Intangible Loss: A Comparative Analysis' (1984) 62 *Can Bar Rev* 323, 369.

[164] See Judicial Studies Board, *Guidelines for the Assessment of General Damages in Personal Injury Cases*, 9th edn (Oxford, 2008).

[165] DW Greig and JLR Davis, *The Law of Contract* (Sydney, 1987) 1414.

[166] D Campbell, 'Exemplary damages' in D Harris, D Campbell and R Halson, *Remedies in Contract and Tort*, 2nd edn (London, 2002) 597 fn 14.

[167] E Macdonald, 'Contractual Damages for Mental Distress' (1994) 7 *JCL* 134, 146–47.

[168] ibid, where Macdonald calls for an empirical investigation into which cost is higher.

[169] *Baltic Shipping Co v Dillon* (1993) 176 CLR 344 (HCA) 396 (McHugh J); N Enonchong, 'Breach of Contract and Damages for Mental Distress' (1996) 16 *OJLS* 617, 632; A Phang, 'The Crumbling Edifice? The Award of Contractual Damages for Mental Distress' [2003] *JBL* 341, 373.

[170] N Enonchong, ibid, referring to the plaintiff's hesitation of booking a holiday in *Jackson v Horizon Holidays Ltd* [1975] 1 WLR 1468 (CA). Sympathetic to this argument is A Phang, ibid 347.

[171] See also the similar discussion in the context of exemplary damages below ch 16, I E.

G   Avoiding a Flood of Claims

In *Hayes v James & Charles Dodd* Staughton LJ remarked that he 'would not view with enthusiasm the prospect that every shipowner in the Commercial Court, having successfully claimed for unpaid freight or demurrage, would be able to add a claim for mental distress suffered while he was waiting for his money'.[172] This statement voiced the fear that making non-pecuniary loss, particularly distress, generally compensable in contract would open the gates to a flood of claims.[173] This fear is said to be the chief reason why the courts still cling to *Addis*.[174] Indeed, the floodgate argument enjoys great popularity whenever a remedy is denied.

But the floodgate argument is as weak as it is common. Where a particular remedy should in principle be available, it makes little sense to deny it on the ground that, if available, it would actually be pursued.[175] In the present context the fear is unfounded too. Subject to the unfair-terms legislation,[176] liability for non-pecuniary loss can be excluded through a provision in the contract.[177] In addition, the usual hazards of litigation will always deter a number of victims of breach from going to court, in particular where the claim is small.[178] Most importantly, many breaches of contract are simply unable to produce compensable non-pecuniary loss, for two reasons. First, a large number of parties to contracts are companies, which have no feelings and are consequently incapable of suffering non-pecuniary harm.[179] This factor will already eliminate most of Staughton LJ's shipowners.[180]

---

[172]   [1990] 2 All ER 815 (CA) 823.

[173]   This fear is shared by J Swanton and B McDonald, 'Measuring contractual damages for defective building work' (1996) 70 *Australian Law Journal* 444, 449.

[174]   Especially, A Phang, 'The Crumbling Edifice? The Award of Contractual Damages for Mental Distress' [2003] *JBL* 341, 350. See also H Beale, 'Exceptional Measures of Damages in Contract' in P Birks (ed), *Wrongs and Remedies in the Twenty-First Century* (Oxford, 1996) 225; A Burrows, *Remedies for Torts and Breach of Contract*, 3rd edn (Oxford, 2004) 330 ('widely-held fear'); K Swinton, 'Foreseeability: Where Should the Award of Contract Damages Cease?' in BJ Reiter and J Swan (eds), *Studies in Contract Law* (Toronto, 1980) 81–82; E Veitch, 'Sentimental Damages in Contract' (1977) 16 *UWOLR* 227, 231.

[175]   KB Soh, 'Anguish, Foreseeability and Policy' (1989) 105 *LQR* 43, 45.

[176]   Unfair Contract Terms Act 1977; Unfair Terms in Consumer Contracts Regulations 1999.

[177]   JA Sebert, 'Punitive and Nonpecuniary Damages in Actions Based Upon Contract: Toward Achieving the Objective of Full Compensation' (1986) 33 *UCLA LR* 1565, 1656.

[178]   ibid. See also JP Tomain, 'Contract Compensation in Nonmarket Transactions' (1985) 46 *U Pitt L Rev* 867, 921.

[179]   *Lonrho plc v Fayed (No 5)* [1993] 1 WLR 1489 (CA) 1505; *Firsteel Cold Rolled Products Ltd v Anaco Precision Pressings Ltd, The Times,* 21 November 1994 (where it was also held that distress suffered by a company's directors or other employees cannot be attributed to the company); H Beale, 'Exceptional Measures of Damages in Contract' in P Birks (ed), *Wrongs and Remedies in the Twenty-First Century* (Oxford, 1996) 225; A Burrows, *Remedies for Torts and Breach of Contract*, 3rd edn (Oxford, 2004) 333. Aggravated and exemplary damages are awardable to companies: *Messenger Newspapers Group Ltd v National Graphical Association (1982)* [1984] IRLR 397 [77]. Trading companies may sue for injury to their business reputation: *Lonrho plc v Fayed (No 5)* [1993] 1 WLR 1489 (CA) 1502.

[180]   Scottish Law Commission, 'Report on Remedies for Breach of Contract' (Scot Law Com No 174, 1999) [3.3].

Secondly, non-pecuniary loss must apparently pass a certain threshold before the court pays attention to it, for a case where negligible non-pecuniary loss was compensated can hardly be found, not even in tort which shows a generous attitude towards non-pecuniary loss.[181] Bridge ascribes this fact to 'a strong current of sentiment that emotional bruises are an inevitable consequence of human existence and that a certain degree of personal robustness should be cultivated'.[182] This is but another way of saying that the law, in the area of non-pecuniary loss, does not concern itself with trifles or, as the ancient Romans said, *de minimis non curat lex*. It can safely be assumed that the courts would apply this rule equally, if not even more strictly, to non-pecuniary loss currently uncompensable per se.[183] Indeed, because of the *de minimis* principle, a reversal of the rule in *Addis* may have no significant impact at all, at least in the area of mental distress. It has been suggested that distress will normally be negligible unless it proceeds from physical inconvenience or the provision of a mental benefit was a major object of the contract.[184] In those two situations, mental distress damages are already available today.[185]

Moreover, even if liability for non-pecuniary loss were no longer specifically barred, it would still remain subject to the principles limiting liability in general, for any loss.[186] The mitigation principle,[187] for instance, excludes liability inasmuch as the aggrieved party had a reasonable opportunity to avoid the non-pecuniary loss suffered,[188] or to bring it down to a level that is *de minimis*.[189] And the remoteness principle discussed in Part 1 excludes liability where the kind of

---

[181] With regard to damages under the Human Rights Act 1998 s 8, it has expressly been held that frustration and distress must be significant to be compensable: *R (KB) v South London and South and West Region Mental Health Review Tribunal* [2003] EWHC 193 (Admin), [2004] QB 936, [71]–[73]; *Anufrijeva v Southwark LBC* [2003] EWCA Civ 1406, [2004] QB 1124, [66]–[70].

[182] MG Bridge, 'Contractual Damages for Intangible Loss: A Comparative Analysis' (1984) 62 *Can Bar Rev* 323, 329.

[183] ibid, 359–60 (citation omitted): 'The examples in mind concern parents who keenly feel their children's disappointment when Christmas toys do not work; married couples finding on the occasion of their anniversary that the wine they bought is 'corked'; customers upset by abusive altercations with a gas pump attendant; women whose hair is badly cut by their hairdressers; and restaurant clients who are served inferior meals'.

[184] *Baltic Shipping Co v Dillon* (1993) 176 CLR 344 (HCA) 365 (Mason CJ); N Enonchong, 'Breach of Contract and Damages for Mental Distress' (1996) 16 *OJLS* 617, 634–37. See also E Macdonald, 'Contractual Damages for Mental Distress' (1994) 7 *JCL* 134, 146.

[185] Above IV and V in this chapter.

[186] Emphasised by AS Burrows, 'Mental distress damages in contract—a decade of change' [1984] *LMCLQ* 119, 131; N Enonchong, 'Breach of Contract and Damages for Mental Distress' (1996) 16 *OJLS* 617, 636. See also H Beale, 'Exceptional Measures of Damages in Contract' in P Birks (ed), *Wrongs and Remedies in the Twenty-First Century* (Oxford, 1996) 225; E Macdonald, 'Contractual Damages for Mental Distress' (1994) 7 *JCL* 134, 136; A Phang, 'The Crumbling Edifice? The Award of Contractual Damages for Mental Distress' [2003] *JBL* 341, 346.

[187] Below ch 10, VI C.

[188] *Cross v David Martin & Mortimer* [1989] 10 EG 110, 118; [1989] 1 EGLR 154, 159; H Beale, 'Exceptional Measures of Damages in Contract' in P Birks (ed), *Wrongs and Remedies in the Twenty-First Century* (Oxford, 1996) 226.

[189] *Hobbs v London and South Western Railway Co* (1875) LR 10 QB 111, 123; N Enonchong, 'Breach of Contract and Damages for Mental Distress' (1996) 16 *OJLS* 617, 639.

non-pecuniary loss suffered is outside the scope of the duty breached,[190] which is particularly the case where such loss could not have been contemplated,[191] or could have been contemplated to a negligible extent only.[192]

Both the *de minimis* principle and the duty to mitigate non-pecuniary loss are illustrated by the Australian case of *Falko v James McEwan & Co Pty Ltd*.[193] The defendant undertook to supply and install an oil heater in the complainant's home. When the heater was delivered it turned out that, in order to supply the heater with electricity, a new power point was required. In breach of contract, the defendant refused to install a new power point, as a result of which the complainant could not use the heater for several months. The magistrate awarded Aus$400 for inconvenience and distress suffered. When asked on what basis he arrived at this figure, he replied: 'Pick a number'. The Supreme Court of Victoria quashed the award on two grounds. First, the complainant could have avoided the inconvenience and distress by having a new power point installed, which could be done in about 20 to 30 minutes at a cost of no more than Aus$11. In not doing so, the complainant acted unreasonably, and the mitigation principle barred compensation for the resultant loss.[194] Secondly, the inconvenience and distress was minimal both in nature and duration.[195]

What the defenders of the *Addis* rule probably fear most is that without the rule every victim of a breach of contract could and would claim damages for the mere disappointment about the breach occurring.[196] This fear is unfounded. Mere disappointment about a breach will never be compensable,[197] which can be explained in three not mutually exclusive ways. First, disappointment alone will almost always be *de minimis*.[198] Secondly, contractual duties may be said not to aim at the prevention of the mere disappointment of them being broken, so that such disappointment falls outside the scope of the duty breached and is hence

---

[190] A Kramer, 'The New Test of Remoteness in Contract' (2009) 125 *LQR* 408, 414, who sees no need for a specific bar to damages for non-pecuniary loss in addition to the 'scope of the duty' concept.

[191] *Farley v Skinner* [2001] UKHL 49, [2002] 2 AC 732 [84] (Lord Scott); E Macdonald, 'Contractual Damages for Mental Distress' (1994) 7 *JCL* 134, 144. See also Scottish Law Commission, 'Report on Remedies for Breach of Contract' (Scot Law Com No 174, 1999) [3.5]; I Ramsay, Note (1977) 55 *Can Bar Rev* 169, 176.

[192] A Phang, 'The Crumbling Edifice? The Award of Contractual Damages for Mental Distress' [2003] *JBL* 341, 356, who throughout his article stresses the efficiency and sufficiency of the remoteness principle to bar liability for non-pecuniary loss.

[193] [1977] VR 447 (VSC).

[194] ibid 452.

[195] ibid 453.

[196] This fear is voiced by JW Carter, E Peden and GJ Tolhurst, *Contract Law in Australia*, 5th edn (Chatswood, 2007) [36–08].

[197] See *Wapshott v Davis Donovan & Co* [1996] PNLR 361 (CA) 378, where Beldam LJ drew a distinction between 'mere disappointment at the failure of the other party to the contract to fulfil his bargain' and 'actual discomfort and inconvenience and distress'.

[198] *Baltic Shipping Co v Dillon* (1993) 176 CLR 344 (HCA) 404 (McHugh J), also observing though that the disappointment may exceptionally be significant.

uncompensable.[199] This may have been meant by Lord Cooke when he said in *Johnson v Gore Wood & Co*: 'Contract-breaking is treated as an incident of commercial life which players in the game are expected to meet with mental fortitude'.[200]

Burrows offers a third explanation.[201] Where the aggrieved party expected solely a financial benefit from the performance not rendered, the disappointment at not receiving this benefit is incidentally compensated by an award of damages for the financial loss. Where a mental benefit was expected, the disappointment on breach does still not attract damages if substitute performance is available, for the duty to mitigate will normally require the aggrieved party to buy substitute performance from the damages awarded and thus receive the expected mental benefit. Burrows therefore sees room for disappointment to be compensated only where the aggrieved party expected a mental benefit and where substitute performance is unavailable or impossible, such as in the spoilt holidays cases. And in this situation, one may add, mental distress damages are to compensate the lost benefit, the 'consumer surplus',[202] rather than the mere disappointment about breach.

Now the floodgate argument could be presented in the form that if non-pecuniary loss became generally compensable in contract, the courts would face (more) claims for compensation of such loss where there is no financial loss (or where the financial loss has already been paid for). In other words, litigation would arise only because of non-pecuniary loss being compensable. But even if presented in this form, the floodgate argument cannot convince. The *de minimis* rule and the hazards of litigation will prevent many victims of a breach of contract from going to court with non-pecuniary loss alone, and where a victim does go to court, the loss in suit will probably be more than negligible and should be compensated if justice is to be done.

H   Avoiding Bogus Claims

The *Addis* rule might be defended with the argument that its reversal would lead not only to a flood of legitimate claims—the argument just dealt with—but also

---

[199]   See A Kramer, 'An Agreement-Centred Approach to Remoteness and Contract Damages' in N Cohen and E McKendrick (eds), *Comparative Remedies for Breach of Contract* (Oxford, 2005) 278. The 'scope of the duty' concept is discussed above ch 2 VI.

[200]   [2002] 2 AC 1 (HL) 49. He had made a similar statement as President of the New Zealand Court of Appeal in *Mouat v Clark Boyce* [1992] 2 NZLR 559 (NZCA) 569: 'Ordinary commercial contracts are not intended to shelter the parties from anxiety'. See also MJ Tilbury, *Civil Remedies, Vol 1: Principles of Civil Remedies* (Sydney, 1990) [3099].

[201]   AS Burrows, 'Mental distress damages in contract—a decade of change' [1984] *LMCLQ* 119, 123, 125.

[202]   Above V in this chapter.

to a flood of bogus claims.[203] Indeed, since non-pecuniary loss is intangible and thus subjective, making it generally compensable in contract could tempt some victims of breach to allege such loss where it has not actually occurred. But if the possibility of bogus claims were a valid reason for keeping non-pecuniary loss generally uncompensable, such loss would have to be uncompensable in all causes of action, including tort. Nobody has ever called for an exclusion of tortious liability for non-pecuniary loss on the ground that there could be bogus claims. Moreover, the claimant bears the onus of proof. She needs to convince the court that she has actually suffered non-pecuniary loss that is not *de minimis.*[204] 'The credibility of the parties will be assessed by their testimony, and their greed will be tempered accordingly.'[205] We should trust in the courts' ability to separate the grain from the chaff.[206]

IX Way of Reform

Since the *Addis* rule cannot be justified on principle,[207] it should be abandoned.[208] Such a development would align contract with tort, and would further align the law of England and Wales with international standards. Article 9.501(2)(a) of the Principles of European Contract Law provides for the compensation of non-pecuniary loss flowing from non-performance. The official comment lists 'pain and suffering, inconvenience and mental distress' as examples, and mentions spoilt package holidays as a scenario where non-pecuniary loss will

---

[203] For this argument and its rejection see AS Burrows, 'Mental distress damages in contract—a decade of change' [1984] *LMCLQ* 119, 133; N Enonchong, 'Breach of Contract and Damages for Mental Distress' (1996) 16 *OJLS* 617, 629; WP Keeton (gen ed), *Prosser and Keeton on the Law of Torts*, 5th edn (St Paul, 1984) 360–61; I Ramsay, Note (1977) 55 *Can Bar Rev* 169, 172–73.

[204] A Burrows, *Remedies for Torts and Breach of Contract*, 3rd edn (Oxford, 2004) 333. The application of a 'clear and convincing evidence standard of proof' is called for by JA Sebert, 'Punitive and Nonpecuniary Damages in Actions Based Upon Contract: Toward Achieving the Objective of Full Compensation' (1986) 33 *UCLA LR* 1565, 1655.

[205] JP Tomain, 'Contract Compensation in Nonmarket Transactions' (1985) 46 *U Pitt L Rev* 867, 899. In *Mouat v Clark Boyce* [1992] 2 NZLR 559 (NZCA) 574, Richardson J said that 'the Courts can be expected to examine claims of this kind with appropriate rigour'.

[206] AS Burrows, 'Mental distress damages in contract—a decade of change' [1984] *LMCLQ* 119, 133; A Phang, 'The Crumbling Edifice? The Award of Contractual Damages for Mental Distress' [2003] *JBL* 341, 349.

[207] 'If the objective of contract damage rules is to provide full compensation for breach, then courts should recognize that emotional distress will often be an actual, substantial, and foreseeable consequence of breach in a wide variety of contracts': JA Sebert, 'Punitive and Nonpecuniary Damages in Actions Based Upon Contract: Toward Achieving the Objective of Full Compensation' (1986) 33 *UCLA LR* 1565, 1591.

[208] H Beale, 'Exceptional Measures of Damages in Contract' in P Birks (ed), *Wrongs and Remedies in the Twenty-First Century* (Oxford, 1996) 225–26; A Burrows, *Remedies for Torts and Breach of Contract*, 3rd edn (Oxford, 2004) 332–33; N Enonchong, 'Breach of Contract and Damages for Mental Distress' (1996) 16 *OJLS* 617, 636, 639–40; A Phang, 'The Crumbling Edifice? The Award of Contractual Damages for Mental Distress' [2003] *JBL* 341, 347–48, 360–61, 372–74.

be compensated.[209] The European Union's Draft Common Frame of Reference contains the same principle. Article III-3:701(1) gives a right to damages for loss caused by the non-performance of an obligation. Article III-3:701(3) provides that loss includes 'economic and non-economic loss', and that non-economic loss includes 'pain and suffering and impairment of the quality of life.' To the same effect, Article 7.4.2(2) of the UNIDROIT Principles of International Commercial Contracts 2004 provides that the compensable harm resulting from non-performance 'may be non-pecuniary and includes, for instance, physical suffering or emotional distress'.

McGregor suggests, however, that the *Addis* rule should stay in place for contracts that affect the aggrieved party's 'business interests' and should be abolished only for contracts that affect the aggrieved party's 'personal, social and family interests'.[210] Despite being supported by other commentators[211] and by courts outside England and Wales,[212] 'the soundness and practicability of that distinction is doubtful'.[213] The line between the two types of contract is by no means easy to draw.[214] In which category do consumer contracts belong where one party acts in the course of a business and the other does not?[215] Here the two parties take different views about the nature of the contract. People who book a package holiday or buy a new car for private use do not consider the contract commercial in nature but the travel agent or car dealer certainly does. Even if the viewpoint of the aggrieved party is always decisive, which seems to be McGregor's approach,[216] the classification will still be difficult where the aggrieved party has

---

[209]   O Lando and H Beale (eds), *Principles of European Contract Law, Parts I and II, Combined and Revised* (The Hague, 2000) 436.

[210]   H McGregor, *McGregor on Damages*, 18th edn (London, 2009) [3–020].

[211]   AI Ogus, *The Law of Damages* (London, 1973) 309; I Ramsay, Note (1977) 55 *Can Bar Rev* 169, 173–74, 177. A presumption to the same effect is suggested by A Phang, 'The Crumbling Edifice? The Award of Contractual Damages for Mental Distress' [2003] *JBL* 341, 353–55; JA Sebert, 'Punitive and Nonpecuniary Damages in Actions Based Upon Contract: Toward Achieving the Objective of Full Compensation' (1986) 33 *UCLA LR* 1565, 1594–96.

[212]   Australia: *Falko v James McEwan & Co Pty Ltd* [1977] VR 447 (VSC) 450–53.
Canada: *Brown v Waterloo (City) Regional Commissioners of Police* (1982) 136 DLR (3d) 49, 56.
New Zealand: *Mouat v Clark Boyce* [1992] 2 NZLR 559 (NZCA) 569 (Cooke P); *Crump v Wala* [1994] 2 NZLR 331, 345–46. Scotland: *Diesen v Samson* 1971 SLT (Sh Ct) 49, 50. US: *Roberson v Dale* (1979) 464 F.Supp 680, 683–84; *Kewin v Massachusetts Mutual Life Insurance Co* (1980) 409 Mich 401 (SC of Michigan), 414–19. Perhaps also *Hayes v James & Charles Dodd* [1990] 2 All ER 815 (CA) 824 (Staughton LJ).

[213]   Scottish Law Commission, 'Report on Remedies for Breach of Contract' (Scot Law Com No 174, 1999) [3.3].

[214]   *Baltic Shipping Co v Dillon* (1993) 176 CLR 344 (HCA) 365–66 (Mason CJ); BS Jackson, 'Injured Feelings Resulting from Breach of Contract' (1977) 26 *ICLQ* 502, 515. See also E Macdonald, 'Contractual Damages for Mental Distress' (1994) 7 *JCL* 134, 153.

[215]   The difficulty is acknowledged by I Ramsay, Note (1977) 55 *Can Bar Rev* 169, 174; JA Sebert, 'Punitive and Nonpecuniary Damages in Actions Based Upon Contract: Toward Achieving the Objective of Full Compensation' (1986) 33 *UCLA LR* 1565, 1594–595.

[216]   And is certainly the approach of AI Ogus, *The Law of Damages* (London, 1973) 309. The 'good sense of the judge' is relied upon by I Ramsay, ibid, 177.

combined commercial and non-commercial purposes. A businessman may, for instance, take his family to a business trip or buy a car for both business and private use.

To avoid difficulties of categorisation, McGregor's approach could be developed into, or perhaps merely reformulated as, the concept that the *Addis* rule stays in place only for contracts *undoubtedly* commercial such as the sale of a machine from one factory to another or the shipping of such a machine. Retaining the *Addis* rule for undoubtedly commercial contracts is, however, unnecessary to avoid what McGregor and his followers obviously fear, namely a proliferation of damages for non-pecuniary loss in purely commercial relations. The breach of a purely commercial contract will rarely give rise to compensable non-pecuniary loss, as explained earlier.[217] Where the breach of a purely commercial contract does give rise to significant non-pecuniary loss—where, for instance, the businessman aggrieved by the breach suffers significant distress because he has sunk from an affluent life to a life on social benefits and has become estranged from wife and son[218]—there is no justification for leaving such loss uncompensated while consumers enjoy full protection by the law.[219]

---

[217] Above VIII G in this chapter.

[218] These were the (alleged) facts in *Johnson v Gore Wood & Co* [2002] 2 AC 1 (HL), where only Lord Cooke (at 49–50), dissenting, allowed the claim for mental-distress damages to proceed.

[219] Criticising the denial of mental-distress damages in *Hayes v James & Charles Dodd* [1990] 2 All ER 815 (CA), Thomas J, in *Rowlands v Collow* [1992] 1 NZLR 178, 207, said that 'it would be a pity if the Courts lacked the sensibility to distinguish between an impersonal shipping magnate who is a party to a freight contract on the one hand, and a husband and wife team seeking professional advice from their solicitors on whom they relied implicitly on the other. Notwithstanding that the plaintiffs [in *Hayes*] were conducting a business and sustained a business loss for which they were eventually compensated, their personal suffering was of a character which should attract damages.'

8

Non-Pecuniary Loss in Equity

Equity's attitude towards the compensation of non-pecuniary loss can be summarised as follows. Non-pecuniary loss is likely to be compensable in cases of
breach of confidence in its core meaning involving information that was
imparted in a confidential manner. The courts and Parliament have classified this
wrong as an equitable one. Non-pecuniary loss is clearly compensable in cases of
breach of confidence in its extended meaning covering invasion of privacy. It is
controversial, however, whether this new branch of the action for breach of
confidence is a new tort or still an equitable wrong. Compensation for non-
pecuniary loss has rarely been awarded for equitable wrongs other than breach of
confidence (or breach of privacy). However, there is no reason for equity
proscribing per se the compensation of non-pecuniary loss that is not *de minimis*
and is within the scope of the particular duty breached. All these propositions
will now be elaborated.

I Breach of Confidence in its Core Meaning

A breach of confidence in its core meaning occurs where secret information that
has been confidentially imparted by one person (the confider) to another (the
confidant) is used by the latter to the detriment of the former without legal
justification. As Megarry J laid down in *Coco v AN Clark (Engineers) Ltd*:

> First, the information ... must 'have the necessary quality of confidence about it'.
> Secondly, that information must have been imparted in circumstances importing an
> obligation of confidence. Thirdly, there must be an unauthorised use of that informa-
> tion to the detriment of the party communicating it.[1]

---

[1] [1968] FSR 415, 419; [1969] RPC 41, 47. Approvingly quoted, eg, in *Attorney-General v
Observer Ltd, sub nom Attorney-General v Guardian Newspapers Ltd (No 2)* [1990] 1 AC 109, 233 (HL)
268 (Lord Griffiths); *OBG Ltd v Allan* [2007] UKHL 21, [2008] 1 AC 1 [111] (Lord Hoffmann).

Even though areas of law other than equity may have contributed to the emergence of the action for breach of confidence,[2] the courts have persistently classified breach of confidence in the core meaning as an equitable wrong. In *Kitechnology BV v Unicor GmbH Plastmaschinen,* for instance, Evans LJ observed that even though claims for breach of confidence in its core meaning 'are certainly non-contractual', they 'do not arise in tort' but in equity.[3] Parliament has taken the same view, for section 171(1)(e) of the Copyright, Designs and Patents Act 1988 reads: 'Nothing in this Part [on copyright] affects ... the operation of any rule of equity relating to breaches of trust or confidence'.

Cases of breach of confidence in its core meaning normally involve business or trade secrets where the focus is on financial loss caused by the breach. However, the courts have occasionally faced confidential information of private nature and been asked to compensate the distress which a disclosure of such information has caused the confider. The first of these cases was *W v Egdell,*[4] which involved the disclosure of a psychiatrist's medical report to third parties. Scott J denied liability on the ground that the disclosure was in the public interest. He went on to state that even if the disclosure had constituted a breach of confidence, he would still have denied compensation for the distress which the disclosure had caused the patient. Referring to *Bliss v South East Thames RHA,*[5] where the Court of Appeal had re-established the general exclusion of damages for distress in contract, Scott J said: 'I do not see any reason, on this point, why equity should not follow the law'.[6]

Subsequent decisions have taken the opposite view, however. The 'breakthrough' came in *Cornelius v De Taranto,*[7] which again involved the disclosure of a psychiatrist's medical report to third parties. Morland J found a breach of confidence and awarded £3,000 for the distress which it had caused the patient. Acknowledging that Scott J in *W v Egdell* had expressed a different view, Morland J observed that 'recovery of damages for mental distress caused by breach of confidence, when no other substantial remedy is available, would not be inimical

---

[2] 'Property, contract, bailment, trust, fiduciary relationship, good faith, unjust enrichment, have all been claimed, at one time or another, as the basis of judicial intervention': G Jones, 'Restitution of Benefits Obtained in Breach of Another's Confidence' (1970) 86 *Law Quarterly Review* 463. See also A Burrows, *Remedies for Torts and Breach of Contract,* 3rd edn (Oxford, 2004), 606–609.

[3] [1995] FSR 765 (CA) 777–78; Sir Donald Nicholls VC and Waite LJ agreed. See also *Seager v Copydex Ltd* [1967] 1 WLR 923 (CA) 931 (Lord Denning MR); *Attorney-General v Observer Ltd, sub nom Attorney-General v Guardian Newspapers Ltd (No 2)* [1990] 1 AC 109 (HL) 255, 268, 281; W Cornish and D Llewelyn, *Intellectual Property: Patents, Copyright, Trademarks and Allied Rights,* 6th edn (London, 2007) [8–06]–[8–07]; R Plibersek, 'Assessment of Damages for Breach of Confidence in England and Australia' (1991) 13 *European Intellectual Property Review* 283 ff. A cause of action *sui generis* is suggested by L Bently and B Sherman, *Intellectual Property Law,* 3rd edn (Oxford, 2009) 1005.

[4] [1990] Ch 359.

[5] [1985] IRLR 308 (CA).

[6] [1990] Ch 359, 398.

[7] [2001] EMLR 329; upheld on appeal without discussion of the point: [2001] EWCA Civ 1511, [2002] EMLR 112.

to considerations of policy but indeed to refuse such recovery would illustrate that something was wrong with the law'.[8] As justification for this novel step, Morland J relied on the right to private and family life guaranteed by Article 8 of the European Convention on Human Rights. He said that:

> [I]t would be a hollow protection of that right if in a particular case in breach of confidence without consent details of the confider's private and family life were disclosed by the confidant to others and the only remedy that the law of England allowed was nominal damages.[9]

Cornelius v De Taranto has been followed in several cases. In *Archer v Williams*,[10] where the former private secretary of a well-known scientist published confidential information, a sum of £2,500 was awarded for injury to feelings. In *McKennitt v Ash*,[11] where a former close friend and travel companion of a well-known folk singer published confidential information, a sum of £5,000 was awarded for hurt feelings and distress. In the Australian case *Giller v Procopets*,[12] the de facto relationship between the plaintiff and the defendant broke down and the defendant, without the plaintiff's consent, showed third parties a videotape depicting the couple's sexual activities. The Victorian Court of Appeal unanimously recognised the compensability of mental distress in the core situation of breach of confidence, and the majority awarded damages in the sum of Aus$40,000, including Aus$10,000 in aggravated damages.[13] It seems established now that non-pecuniary loss is compensable in the core situation of breach of confidence.[14]

II Breach of Confidence in its Extended Meaning ('Breach of Privacy')

In its core meaning, breach of confidence requires that the information at issue was confidentially imparted by one person to another. It is now recognised, however, that a person can be under an obligation not to disclose certain information, in particular on aspects of another person's private life, even though

---

  [8] [2001] EMLR 329 [69].

  [9] ibid [66].

  [10] [2003] EWHC 1670 (QB), [2003] EMLR 869.

  [11] [2005] EWHC 3003 (QB), [2006] EMLR 178; confirmed in [2006] EWCA Civ 1714, [2008] QB 73.

  [12] [2008] VSCA 236, (2008) 40 Fam LR 378.

  [13] ibid [446] (Neave JA). Maxwell P concurred. Ashley JA opined (at 160]) that 'any award beyond $27,500—this including an amount of about $7,500 for what would be called aggravated damages in an action at law—would step into the impermissible realm of punishment'.

  [14] L Clarke, 'Remedial Responses to Breach of Confidence: The Question of Damages' (2005) 24 *Civil Justice Quarterly* 316, 324; N Witzleb, 'Monetary remedies for breach of confidence in privacy cases' (2007) 27 *Legal Studies* 430, 444–47.

that information was never confidentially imparted but was acquired by other means such as eavesdropping or surreptitiously taking photographs. In *Attorney-General v Observer Ltd, sub nom Attorney-General v Guardian Newspapers Ltd (No 2)*, Lord Goff recognised a duty of confidentiality

> where an obviously confidential document is wafted by an electric fan out of a window into a crowded street, or where an obviously confidential document, such as a private diary, is dropped in a public place, and is then picked up by a passer-by.[15]

Subsequent cases have firmly established that concept. This development is a product of countervailing forces. On the one hand, the courts have persistently refused to recognise a full-blown tort of privacy.[16] On the other hand, the Human Rights Act 1998 has forced the courts to afford adequate protection to the right to private and family life, laid down in Article 8 of the European Convention on Human Rights. This right has to be balanced against freedom of expression, laid down in Article 10 of the Convention. The courts have 'shoehorned'[17] this balancing exercise into the action for breach of confidence.

In applying the action for breach of confidence to the unauthorised publication of private information *not* obtained from the person concerned, the courts have dropped the traditional requirement of a pre-existing relationship of confidentiality between the parties.[18] Instead, they ask whether the defendant knew or ought to have known that the claimant had a reasonable expectation of privacy, and whether the claimant's interest in privacy is outweighed by the defendant's freedom of speech or any other competing interest.[19] As Buxton LJ summarised in *McKennitt v Ash*:

> [W]here the complaint is of the wrongful publication of private information, the court has to decide two things. First, is the information private in the sense that it is in principle protected by article 8? If 'no', that is the end of the case. If 'yes', the second question arises: in all the circumstances, must the interest of the owner of the private information yield to the right of freedom of expression conferred on the publisher by article 10?[20]

---

[15] [1990] 1 AC 233 (HL) 281. See also *Hellewell v Chief Constable of Derbyshire* [1995] 1 WLR 804, 807.

[16] *Malone v Metropolitan Police Commissioner* [1979] Ch 344, 372–73; *Kaye v Robertson* [1991] FSR 62 (CA); *Wainwright v Home Office* [2003] UKHL 53, [2004] 2 AC 406 [31]–[34]; *Campbell v MGN Ltd* [2004] UKHL 22, [2004] 2 AC 457 [11], [43], [133]–[134].

[17] *Douglas v Hello! Ltd (No 3)* [2005] EWCA Civ 595, [2006] QB 125 [53] (Lord Phillips MR); *McKennitt v Ash* [2006] EWCA Civ 1714, [2008] QB 73 [8] (Buxton LJ).

[18] The breakthrough came with *Campbell v MGN Ltd* [2004] UKHL 22, [2004] 2 AC 457; *Douglas v Hello! Ltd (No 3)* [2005] EWCA Civ 595, [2006] QB 125.

[19] *A v B plc* [2002] EWCA Civ 337, [2003] QB 195 [11]; *Campbell v MGN Ltd* [2004] UKHL 22, [2004] 2 AC 457 [21], [85], [137]; *Douglas v Hello! Ltd (No 3)* [2005] EWCA Civ 595, [2006] QB 125 [82]; *Mosley v News Group Newspapers Ltd* [2008] EWHC 1777 (QB), [2008] EMLR 679 [7]–[15].

[20] [2006] EWCA Civ 1714, [2008] QB 73 [11]. Latham LJ and Longmore LJ concurred.

The new branch of the action for breach of confidence protects autonomy, dignity and self-esteem rather than confidence.[21] In *Campbell v MGN Ltd*, both Lord Phillips MR,[22] who delivered the judgment of the Court of Appeal, and Lord Nicholls[23] in the House of Lords called the new wrong in passing a 'tort' as opposed to an equitable wrong. Lord Phillips MR spoke of 'breach of privacy',[24] and Lord Nicholls spoke of 'misuse of private information'.[25] Books on tort law cover the new wrong,[26] and McGregor suggests that its classification as a tort 'must come to be accepted'.[27] Cases decided subsequent to *Campbell v MGN Ltd* demonstrate, however, that the classification of the new wrong as a tort is not (yet) accepted.

In *OBG Ltd v Allan*, Lord Nicholls avoided the term 'tort' and said instead that 'breach of confidence, or misuse of confidential information, now covers two distinct causes of action, protecting two different interests: privacy, and secret ('confidential') information'.[28] A classification of breach of privacy as a tort was clearly rejected in *Douglas v Hello! Ltd (No 3)*[29] where the Court of Appeal refused to apply to that wrong section 9 of the Private International Law (Miscellaneous Provisions) Act 1995, which governs choice of law in tort. Similarly, in the 'breach of privacy' case *Mosley v News Group Newspapers Ltd*,[30] the availability of exemplary damages was denied on the ground that they are unavailable in equity and that breach of privacy must still be classified as an equitable wrong rather than a tort. For the time being, therefore, both branches of breach of confidence must still be regarded as equitable wrongs.

Even though the new branch of the action for breach of confidence may protect the interest in commercially exploiting certain private information,[31] its main effect has been to open the door to compensation for non-pecuniary loss. As McGregor observes, 'when it comes to damages for an invasion of privacy, non-pecuniary loss by way of an injury to feelings and mental distress predominates'.[32] This is demonstrated by the very cases that firmly established the extended meaning of breach of confidence.

---

[21] *Campbell v MGN Ltd* [2004] UKHL 22, [2004] 2 AC 457 [51] (Lord Hoffmann); *Mosley v News Group Newspapers Ltd* [2008] EWHC 1777 (QB), [2008] EMLR 679 [7].

[22] [2002] EWCA Civ 1373, [2003] QB 633 [61].

[23] [2004] UKHL 22, [2004] 2 AC 457 [14]–[15].

[24] [2002] EWCA Civ 1373, [2003] QB 633 [69]–[70].

[25] [2004] UKHL 22, [2004] 2 AC 457 [14]. This term is also preferred by H McGregor, *McGregor on Damages*, 18th edn (London, 2009) [42–002].

[26] eg S Deakin, A Johnston and B Markesinis, *Markesinis and Deakin's Tort Law*, 6th edn (Oxford, 2008) ch 22; WVH Rogers, *Winfield and Jolowicz on Tort*, 17th edn (London, 2006) [12.76].

[27] H McGregor, *McGregor on Damages*, 18th edn (London, 2009) [42–017].

[28] [2007] UKHL 21, [2008] 1 AC 1 [255].

[29] [2005] EWCA Civ 595, [2006] QB 125 [96].

[30] [2008] EWHC 1777 (QB), [2008] EMLR 679 [181]–[190]. On exemplary damages in equity see below ch 14, VIII.

[31] *OBG Ltd v Allan* [2007] UKHL 21, [2008] 1 AC 1.

[32] H McGregor, *McGregor on Damages*, 18th edn (London, 2009) [42–003].

The first case was *Campbell v MGN Ltd*,[33] which involved the publication by the newspaper *The Mirror* of a photo of the famous fashion model Naomi Campbell leaving a meeting of a drug addiction self-help group. Morland J held that the publication had not only contravened the Data Protection Act 1998 but also constituted a breach of confidence.[34] He awarded £2,500 for distress and injury to feelings as well as £1,000 aggravated damages to reflect the 'highly offensive and hurtful manner' of the publication.[35] In respect of the claim for breach of confidence, Morland J regarded the traditional requirement of an imparting of the information as satisfied. *The Mirror*, he said, must have been 'tipped off' by another member of the self-help group or by one of Naomi Campbell's staff, and that person had 'owed her an obligation of confidence in relation to the information'.[36] A majority in the House of Lords upheld the finding of a breach of confidence, but this decision was based on a reasonable expectation of privacy on Naomi Campbell's part rather than an imparting of the information by her to the person who 'tipped off' *The Mirror*.[37]

The second milestone case was *Douglas v Hello! Ltd (No 3)*,[38] which involved the publication by the magazine *Hello!* of photos surreptitiously taken at the wedding of the actors Michael Douglas and Catherine Zeta-Jones, who had sold the exclusive right to publish photos of their wedding to the magazine *OK!* and had taken elaborate measures to prevent the unauthorised taking of photos at their wedding. Lindsay J held that the publication had been a breach of confidence, and awarded £3,750 each for the distress caused by the publication of the unauthorised photographs. He regarded the traditional requirement of an imparting of the information as satisfied on the ground that the events at the wedding had been confidentially imparted to those present, including the 'paparazzo' photographer.[39] The Court of Appeal upheld the finding of a breach of confidence, but this decision was based on a reasonable expectation of privacy on the part of the Douglases rather than an imparting of confidential information.[40]

The awards of compensation for distress in the cases mentioned so far were very modest. Much higher awards are, however, possible. A record sum of £60,000 was awarded in *Mosley v News Group Newspapers Ltd*,[41] where a newspaper published written accounts and video footage of a private sex party involving the president of the International Automobile Federation. In the

---

[33] [2004] UKHL 22, [2004] 2 AC 457.
[34] [2002] EWHC 499 (QB), [2002] EMLR 617.
[35] ibid [169].
[36] ibid [42].
[37] [2004] UKHL 22, [2004] 2 AC 457.
[38] [2005] EWCA Civ 595, [2006] QB 125.
[39] [2003] EWHC 786 (Ch), [2003] 3 All ER 996 [197].
[40] [2005] EWCA Civ 595, [2006] QB 125. This decision was not appealed before the House of Lords, which was solely concerned with the claim brought by *OK!* against *Hello!*: *OBG Ltd v Allan* [2007] UKHL 21, [2008] 1 AC 1.
[41] [2008] EWHC 1777 (QB), [2008] EMLR 679.

Australian case *Doe v ABC*, a rape victim was identified as such in radio news and obtained Aus$25,000 'as compensation for the hurt, distress, embarrassment, humiliation, shame and guilt experienced as a result of the broadcasts'.[42]

In conclusion, 'it can now no longer be seriously doubted that compensation is available where a breach of privacy causes injury to feelings'.[43]

III Other Equitable Wrongs

Compensation for non-pecuniary loss has rarely been awarded for equitable wrongs other than breach of confidence (or breach of privacy). A few Canadian and New Zealand cases form an exception.

In the Canadian case *Szarfer v Chodos*,[44] a solicitor had a sexual affair with his client's wife, causing the client to suffer reactive depression and anxiety. The solicitor was held to have breached his fiduciary duty towards his client, and general damages in the sum of Can$30,000 were awarded. In *M (K) v M (H)*, where the plaintiff sued her father for sexually abusing her when she had been a child, the Supreme Court of Canada held that the father's conduct had constituted not only a tort but also a breach of fiduciary duty, and that the plaintiff's non-pecuniary loss was compensable in both causes of action.[45]

While those two cases support the compensability of non-pecuniary loss caused by a breach of fiduciary duty, they may not be very significant beyond the particular situations decided. Both cases involved personal injury, where the compensability of non-pecuniary loss should be uncontroversial even in equity. But equitable wrongs rarely cause personal injury. Furthermore, the concept of breach of fiduciary duty was given a very wide scope in those two cases. A fiduciary relationship was clearly present in *Szarfer v Chodos*, but it is questionable whether the solicitor's choice of sexual partner can properly be regarded as a breach of fiduciary duty. With regard to *M (K) v M (H)*, it is questionable whether the parental obligation not to inflict personal injury upon the child can be properly classified as fiduciary in nature. As the Federal Court of Australia said in *Paramisavam v Flynn*:

> [T]here can be no doubt that that is a fundamental aspect of a parent's obligation; and it is one which should be, and is, appropriately protected by law. It does not follow,

---

[42] [2007] VCC 281 [186] (Hampel J).

[43] N Witzleb, 'Monetary remedies for breach of confidence in privacy cases' (2007) 27 *LS* 430, 447.

[44] (1986) 27 DLR (4th) 388.

[45] [1992] 3 SCR 6 (SCC) 80–82. The decision is welcomed by L Hoyano, 'The Flight to the Fiduciary Haven' in P Birks (ed), *Privacy and Loyalty* (Oxford, 1997) 247.

however, that 'fiduciary' is the right label for it, still less that equitable intervention is necessary, appropriate or justified by any principled development of equity's doctrines.[46]

Non-pecuniary loss not resulting from personal injury has been compensated in equity in two New Zealand cases. The first was *McKaskell v Benseman*,[47] where the plaintiffs instructed one of the defendants, a solicitor in sole practice, to act for them in a dispute with their neighbours. Their work was attended by a solicitor employed by that defendant. The neighbours' solicitor sent a letter to the plaintiffs' solicitor containing an offensive passage. Without consulting them, the plaintiffs' solicitor returned the letter to the neighbours' solicitor and suggested that it be rewritten. The neighbours' solicitor apologised and rewrote the letter, deleting the offensive passage. Several months later, the plaintiffs became aware of the first letter and the offensive passage. They sued their principal solicitor and the employee solicitor handling their case, arguing that the two solicitors had been obliged to show the offensive letter to the plaintiffs as soon as they received it. Jeffries J held the solicitors liable for breach of fiduciary duty and awarded the plaintiffs NZ$1,000 against each of them for emotional stress.

The second case was *Mouat v Clark Boyce*,[48] where the plaintiff, an elderly widow, granted a mortgage over her home as security for a loan made to her son. The defendant solicitor acted in the matter for both her and her son. He sought no information on the financial situation of either of them and never discussed the matter with the plaintiff in the absence of her son. When the plaintiff's son later defaulted and became bankrupt, the plaintiff was called on to pay the debt secured by the mortgage. The defendant was held liable for negligence and breach of fiduciary duty,[49] and the plaintiff obtained compensation for both financial loss and mental distress.[50] The New Zealand Court of Appeal took the view that whenever a tortious or contractual duty of care or a fiduciary duty is breached, compensation may be awarded for non-pecuniary loss that was foreseeable at the time of the breach. Cooke P said that

> there are many tort, contract or statutory status cases in New Zealand in which foreseeable distress has been an ingredient in the award ... There appears to be no solid ground for denying that equitable compensation can likewise extend so far. It would be anachronistic to draw distinctions in this respect between the various sources of liability, dictated as they are by the same considerations of policy.[51]

---

[46] (1998) 90 FCR 489 (FCA) 506 (Miles J, Lehane J and Weinberg J). Things may be different for a guardian: *Williams v Minister, Aboriginal Land Rights Act 1983* (1994) 35 NSWLR 497 (NSWCA) 511 (Kirby P); *Trevorrow v South Australia* [2007] SASC 285 [1010]–[1011].

[47] [1989] 3 NZLR 75.

[48] [1992] 2 NZLR 559 (NZCA).

[49] The finding of liability was reversed on appeal: [1994] 1 AC 428 (PC).

[50] The award was reduced by one half on the ground of contributory negligence. On that issue see below ch 11.

[51] [1992] 2 NZLR 559 (NZCA) 569. See also *Frame v Smith* [1987] 2 SCR 99 (SCC) 151 (Wilson J, dissenting).

In the subsequent case *Watson v Dolmark Industries Ltd*, Cooke P thought that an award of equitable compensation for injury to feelings is 'prima facie inappropriate' in a 'commercial case'.[52] But a fundamental distinction between commercial and other contexts is as problematic in equity as it is in contract.[53]

The fact that non-pecuniary loss has rarely been compensated in equitable actions other than breach of confidence (or breach of privacy) is not necessarily evidence of such non-pecuniary loss being uncompensable per se. The rarity of awards may simply be due to the fact that the remedy of equitable compensation until fairly recently lived in the shadows, and the fact that equitable wrongs other than breach of confidence (or breach of privacy) rarely cause personal injury or emotional harm, so that any non-pecuniary loss is usually either *de minimis* or outside the scope of the particular duty breached. Where an equitable wrong causes non-pecuniary loss that is not *de minimis* and is within the scope of the duty breached, there is no reason why compensation for that loss should be denied. Considering that the extent of liability has traditionally been wider in equity than at common law, illustrated by equity's traditional refusal to limit liability on grounds of remoteness[54] or contributory negligence,[55] it would be paradoxical if non-pecuniary loss were less likely to be compensated in equity than at common law, particularly in tort.

In conclusion, non-pecuniary loss that is within the scope of the duty breached and is not *de minimis* should be compensable in contract, tort and equity.

---

[52] [1992] 3 NZLR 311 (NZCA) 316. The view is shared by C Rickett, 'Compensating for Loss in Equity—Choosing the Right Horse for Each Course' in P Birks and F Rose (eds), *Restitution and Equity, Vol 1: Resulting Trusts and Equitable Compensation* (London, 2000) 183.

[53] Above ch 7, IX.

[54] Above ch 5.

[55] Below ch 11.

Part 3

Contributory Negligence

9

Contributory Negligence in Tort

The claimant may contribute to the occurrence of the defendant's wrong or the ensuing loss by acting unreasonably. Unreasonable behaviour occurring once the claimant is aware of the wrong is addressed through the mitigation principle, according to which the claimant cannot recover for loss that she could have avoided by taking reasonable steps.[1] Unreasonable behaviour prior to that date is called contributory negligence. At common law, contributory negligence is a complete defence to many torts. For this reason, some textbooks on damages leave the issue out on the ground that it relates to the existence rather than the extent of liability.[2] However, the Law Reform (Contributory Negligence) Act 1945 replaced the complete defence with a proportionate reduction in the damages. The issue of contributory negligence has thus become a proper part of the law of damages. It features in most textbooks on damages[3] or remedies in general.[4]

I The Position Apart from the 1945 Act

Even though the effect of contributory negligence in tort is almost entirely governed by the Law Reform (Contributory Negligence) Act 1945, a glance at the position apart from that Act is necessary to understand the thrust of the Act and its references to the common law. Usually, the position apart from the 1945 Act is described in the past tense, suggesting a 'freezing' of the common law at its state in 1945. But there is

---

[1] Below ch 10, VI C.

[2] SM Waddams, *The Law of Damages*, 3rd edn (Toronto, 1997) [15.20]. The issue is also left out by H Street, *Principles of the Law of Damages* (London, 1962).

[3] H McGregor, *McGregor on Damages*, 18th edn (London, 2009) ch 5; AI Ogus, *The Law of Damages* (London, 1973) 103–107.

[4] A Burrows, *Remedies for Torts and Breach of Contract*, 3rd edn (Oxford, 2004) 129–44; D Harris, D Campbell and R Halson, *Remedies in Contract and Tort*, 2nd edn (London, 2002) 86–87, 308–309, 578.

no reason why the common law should not still be able to develop alongside the 1945 Act.[5] For this reason, the following outline will be made in the present tense.

The 1945 Act aside, contributory negligence is a complete defence to many torts. The defendant defeats the action if he demonstrates that the claimant was the author of her injury through her own carelessness.[6] A good illustration is *Butterfield v Forrester,*[7] where the plaintiff rode 'as fast as his horse could go' through Derby and hit a pole put up across the road by the defendant. The plaintiff was thrown down and suffered injury. Liability was denied as a person riding with reasonable and ordinary care would have seen and avoided the obstruction. As a result of contributory negligence being a defence, the slightest unreasonable action on the claimant's part completely exonerates the defendant.

In order to alleviate the harsh effect of this concept, the claimant's carelessness has been held irrelevant where the defendant had the 'last opportunity' to avoid the accident. The leading case is *Davies v Mann,*[8] where the defendant's servant, by driving his wagon at a 'smartish pace' along a highway, ran over and killed a donkey belonging to the plaintiff, which the latter had negligently left on the road so hobbled that it could not get out of the way. It was held that the carelessly fast driving of the wagon had caused the accident, and that the plaintiff could recover damages, notwithstanding that he, at an earlier stage, had been negligent in leaving the donkey hobbled on the road. This case gave rise to the following rule: 'when both parties are careless, the party which has the last opportunity of avoiding the results of the other's carelessness is alone liable'.[9] However, the 'last opportunity' rule has faced criticism,[10] and has been said to be in demise[11] or even abandoned.[12]

---

[5] *Standard Chartered Bank v Pakistan National Shipping Corp (No 4)* [2001] QB 167 (CA) [107] (Ward LJ); *Dairy Containers Ltd v NZI Bank Ltd* [1995] 2 NZLR 30, 110–11; A Burrows, *Remedies for Torts and Breach of Contract,* 3rd edn (Oxford, 2004) 135.

[6] The defendant bears the onus of proof: *Wakelin v London and South Western Railway Co* (1887) LR 12 App Cas 41 (HL) 47, 51–52.

[7] (1809) 11 East 60, 61; 103 ER 926, 927. See also *Tuff v Warman* (1858) 5 CBNS 573, 141 ER 231; *Radley v London and North Western Railway Co* (1876) 1 App Cas 754 (HL) 759; *Cayzer, Irvine & Co v Carron Co* (1884) 9 App Cas 873 (HL) 881; *Wakelin v London and South Western Railway Co* (1887) LR 12 App Cas 41 (HL) 45, 47, 51.

[8] (1842) 10 M & W 546, 548–49; 152 ER 588, 589.

[9] *The Boy Andrew* [1948] AC 140 (HL) 149 (Viscount Simon). See also *Radley v London and North Western Railway Co* (1876) 1 App Cas 754 (HL) 759–60; *The Volute* [1922] 1 AC 129 (HL) 139; *Anglo-Newfoundland Development Co Ltd v Pacific Steam Navigation Co Ltd* [1924] AC 406 (HL) 420 (Lord Shaw); *The Eurymedon* [1938] P 41 (CA) 49–50 (Greer LJ).

[10] *The Boy Andrew* [1948] AC 140 (HL) 149 (Viscount Simon): 'The suggested test of "last opportunity" seems to me inaptly phrased and likely in some cases to lead to error, as the Law Revision Committee said in their report (Cmd 6032 of 1939, p 16): "In truth, there is no such rule—the question, as in all questions of liability for a tortious act, is, not who had the last opportunity of avoiding the mischief, but whose act caused the wrong?"' See also *Grant v Sun Shipping Co Ltd* [1948] AC 549 (HL) 563 (Lord du Parcq); *The Ouro Fino* [1988] 2 Lloyd's Rep 325 (CA) 329 (O'Connor LJ).

[11] *Davies v Swan Motor Co (Swansea) Ltd* [1949] 2 KB 291 (CA) 318 (Evershed LJ).

[12] ibid 321 (Denning LJ: 'dead'); *The Ouro Fino* [1988] 2 Lloyd's Rep 325 (CA) 329 (O'Connor LJ).

The common law defence of contributory negligence applies to the torts of negligence,[13] nuisance on the highway,[14] breach of statutory duty,[15] and probably also *Rylands v Fletcher*.[16] The defence does not apply to intentional torts,[17] for it seems unjust to completely exonerate a defendant who intended the damage caused, only because the claimant was slightly careless.

II   The Ambit of the 1945 Act

Section 1(1) of the Law Reform (Contributory Negligence) Act 1945 provides:

> Where any person suffers damage[18] as the result partly of his own fault and partly of the fault of any other person or persons, a claim in respect of that damage shall not be defeated by reason of the fault of the person suffering the damage, but the damages recoverable in respect thereof shall be reduced to such extent as the court thinks just and equitable having regard to the claimant's share in the responsibility for the damage [.][19]

In consequence of this provision, contributory negligence no longer serves as a complete defence to an action in tort. Instead, the court is called upon to weigh each party's responsibility for the damage and apportion liability accordingly. The defendant still bears the onus of pleading[20] and proving[21] contributory negligence.

Some statutes expressly exclude[22] or provide for[23] an application of the 1945 Act to particular torts. Does the Act otherwise apply to all torts, or only to those torts in which the contributory negligence defence may be raised at common law?

---

[13]   *Radley v London and North Western Railway Co* (1876) 1 App Cas 754 (HL) 759; *Cayzer, Irvine & Co v Carron Co* (1884) 9 App Cas 873 (HL) 881; *Wakelin v London and South Western Railway Co* (1887) LR 12 App Cas 41 (HL) 45, 47, 51.

[14]   *Butterfield v Forrester* (1809) 11 East 60, 61; 103 ER 926, 927.

[15]   *Caswell v Powell Duffryn Associated Collieries Ltd* [1940] AC 152 (HL).

[16]   *Dunn v Birmingham Canal Navigation Co* (1872) LR 7 QB 244, 260 (Cockburn CJ).

[17]   *Alliance & Leicester Building Society v Edgestop Ltd* [1993] 1 WLR 1462, 1474; *Nationwide Building Society v Balmer Radmore* [1999] PNLR 606, 677; *Nationwide Building Society v Thimbleby* [1999] PNLR 733, 756–57; *Ward v Chief Constable of the RUC* [2000] NI 543, 550. See also *Quinn v Leathem* [1901] AC 495 (HL) 537 (Lord Lindley).

[18]   Pursuant to s 4 of the 1945 Act, 'damage' includes loss of life and personal injury.

[19]   In relation to accidents at sea, an apportionment of liability is provided for by the Merchant Shipping Act 1995 s 187.

[20]   *Fookes v Slaytor* [1978] 1 WLR 1293 (CA). For Scotland *Taylor v Simon Carves Ltd* 1958 SLT (Sh Ct) 23.

[21]   'In such cases, as in every other case where contributory negligence is alleged, the burden of proving on the balance of probabilities that a plaintiff has contributed to the cause of damage suffered lies upon he who alleged it, namely, the defendant': *Owens v Brimmel* [1977] QB 859, 864 (Watkins J).

[22]   Torts (Interference with Goods) Act 1977 s 11(1) for conversion and intentional trespass to goods. The exemption of non-intentional conversion from the ambit of the 1945 Act is criticised by A Burrows, *Remedies for Torts and Breach of Contract*, 3rd edn (Oxford, 2004) 135.

[23]   Crown Proceedings Act 1947 s 4(3); Animals Act 1971 s 10; Banking Act 1979, s 47 (which restricts the exclusion mentioned in the previous footnote); Consumer Protection Act 1987 s 6(4). An apportionment of liability by virtue of contributory negligence is also provided for by the Fatal Accidents Act 1976 s 5.

What the scope of the Act *should* be will be considered first. Since it is the thrust of the 1945 Act to replace the complete defeat of the claimant's action by virtue of contributory negligence with an apportionment regime, it seems at first sight appropriate to apply the Act only where, leaving it aside, the claimant's action would in fact be defeated.[24] However, 'the common law is largely undeveloped or unsettled',[25] which makes it unwise to chain the applicability of the Act to the position at common law. More importantly, the idea that a claimant who contributed to her loss should bear a part of it is of immediate appeal. It is fair and just, and it fosters efficiency, for it gives the claimant an incentive to take cost-efficient precautions.[26]

For these reasons, the 1945 Act should apply to all torts unless statute provides otherwise. In particular, the Act should apply to all intentional torts[27] including deceit[28] and trespass to the person.[29] Of course, the liability of an intentional tortfeasor should not easily be reduced on account of the victim's carelessness. But the victim may have provoked the tort[30] or otherwise substantially contributed to the damage suffered. Instead of exempting intentional torts per se from the ambit of the 1945 Act, the courts should be allowed to judge each case on its merits. They still retain the power to refuse any reduction in the claim where they find this appropriate.[31]

But does the wording of the Act allow such a wide application of it? Pursuant to section 1(1), the Act applies where both parties to the action were at fault. Section 4 defines 'fault' as 'negligence, breach of statutory duty or other act or omission which gives rise to a liability in tort or would, apart from this Act, give rise to the defence of contributory negligence'. The construction of this passage is

---

[24] NE Palmer and PJ Davies, 'Contributory Negligence and Breach of Contract—English and Australasian Attitudes Compared' (1980) 29 *International & Comparative Law Quarterly* 415, 417.

[25] MJ Tilbury, *Civil Remedies, Vol 1: Principles of Civil Remedies* (Sydney, 1990) [3139].

[26] In the view of RA Posner, *Economic Analysis of Law*, 7th edn (Austin, 2007) 172–75, apportionment is more efficient than giving full damages to the victim but less efficient than giving no damages because of the administrative costs generated by transfer payments.

[27] The law was held to be otherwise in *Nationwide Building Society v Thimbleby* [1999] PNLR 733, 749–60.

[28] The courts have held otherwise: *Alliance & Leicester Building Society v Edgestop Ltd* [1993] 1 WLR 1462, 1474–1477; *Corporacion Nacional del Cobre de Chile v Sogemin Metals Ltd* [1997] 1 WLR 1396, 1400–1401; *Standard Chartered Bank v Pakistan National Shipping Corp (Nos 2 and 4)* [2001] QB 167 (CA) [60]–[71], [102]–[120]; [2002] UKHL 43, [2003] 1 AC 959 [12]–[18], [42]–[44]; *Bank of Tokyo-Mitsubishi UFJ Ltd v Başkan Gida Sanayi Ve Pazarlama AS* [2009] EWHC 1276 (Ch) [1006].

[29] This seems to be the law: *Murphy v Culhane* [1977] QB 94 (CA) 98–99; *Wasson v Chief Constable of the RUC* [1987] 8 NIJB 34; *Tumelty v MoD* [1988] 3 NIJB 51; *Ward v Chief Constable of the RUC* [2000] NI 543, 550. The opposite view seems to have been taken in *Lane v Holloway* [1968] 1 QB 379 (CA) 392–93.

[30] This actually happened in all the cases cited in the previous footnote.

[31] Below VI in this chapter.

controversial.[32] The starting point is the core part 'other act or omission which gives rise to a liability in tort or would, apart from this Act, give rise to the defence of contributory negligence'. Shortly after the Act came into force, Glanville Williams suggested that the first limb of the relative clause (down to 'tort') be taken as defining the defendant's liability and the second limb (from 'would' onwards) as defining the claimant's fault.[33] Apart from a few dicta suggesting an application of *both* limbs to the claimant,[34] the courts have adopted Williams' approach.[35] However, a split application of the relative clause, convenient though it would be, is semantically impossible. Section 4 defines 'fault' for both claimant and defendant in a single sentence. The relative clause, and thus both alternatives of it, must be applied to the claimant and the defendant alike.

To start with the defendant then, he was at 'fault' if he committed a tort—which is just the premise at the present stage—or if his conduct would, apart from the Act, give rise to the defence of contributory negligence. The second alternative has been opposed on the ground that, since contributory negligence does not at common law[36] presuppose a duty of care, the defendant would be liable to pay damages even though he did not at common law break a duty of care.[37] True, an application of the second limb to the defendant renders the definition of 'fault' on the defendant's part too wide. But this does not produce the effect feared. It is clear that the 1945 Act was not intended to create new torts,[38] and comes into play only where the defendant is liable independently of the Act or would be liable if there was no contributory negligence. There is thus no harm in applying the second limb of the relative clause to the defendant.

An application of the first limb to the claimant has also been criticised. Blaming the claimant for conduct that was not negligent and would therefore not

---

[32] All possible interpretations are listed by P Giliker, 'General Defences' in K Oliphant (gen ed), *The Law of Tort*, 2nd edn (London, 2007) [5.4] fn 2.

[33] GL Williams, *Joint Torts and Contributory Negligence* (London, 1951) 318.

[34] *Forsikringsaktieselskapet Vesta v Butcher* [1989] AC 852 (CA) 862 (O'Connor LJ); *Alliance & Leicester Building Society v Edgestop Ltd* [1993] 1 WLR 1462, 1474; *Barings plc v Coopers & Lybrand* [2003] EWHC 1319 (Ch), [2003] PNLR 34 [896]. See also *Murphy v Culhane* [1977] QB 94 (CA) 99 (Lord Denning MR).

[35] *Basildon DC v JE Lesser (Properties) Ltd* [1985] QB 839, 847–49; *The Shinjitsu Maru No 5* [1985] 1 WLR 1270, 1288; *Barclays Bank plc v Fairclough Building Ltd (No 1)* [1995] QB 214 (CA) 228; *Reeves v Metropolitan Police Commissioner* [2000] 1 AC 360 (HL) 369 (Lord Hoffmann), 382 (Lord Hope); *Standard Chartered Bank v Pakistan National Shipping Corp (Nos 2 and 4)* [2001] QB 167 (CA) [30]–[34], [53]–[57], [84]–[87]; [2002] UKHL 43, [2003] 1 AC 959 [11], [42].

[36] Nor under the 1945 Act: below IV in this chapter.

[37] GL Williams, *Joint Torts and Contributory Negligence* (London, 1951) 318; AH Hudson, 'Contributory negligence as a defence to battery' (1984) 4 *Legal Studies* 332, 337–38; NE Palmer and PJ Davies, 'Contributory Negligence and Breach of Contract—English and Australasian Attitudes Compared' (1980) 29 *ICLQ* 415, 416 fn 7; *Standard Chartered Bank v Pakistan National Shipping Corp (No 4)* [2001] QB 167 (CA) [54] (Aldous LJ). See also A Burrows, *Remedies for Torts and Breach of Contract*, 3rd edn (Oxford, 2004) 137.

[38] *Drinkwater v Kimber* [1952] 2 QB 281 (CA) 288 (Singleton LJ: 'does not create a right of action'), 292 (Morris LJ: 'does not purport to create any new variety of claim'); AS Taylor, 'Contributory Negligence—A Defence to Breach of Contract?' (1986) 49 *Modern Law Review* 102, 105.

raise the contributory negligence defence at common law, only because it amounts to a tort, has been said to be 'contrary to the "feel" of the defence of contributory *negligence*'.[39] But if the claimant is blamed for harming herself, she must a fortiori be blamed for harming the defendant. Another criticism was made by Bray CJ (dissenting) in the decision by the Supreme Court of South Australia in *Venning v Chin*.[40] He argued that a party to a traffic accident caused solely by another party's carelessness must not face a reduction in his damages on the ground that he was driving a stolen car, thereby committing an act 'which gives rise to a liability in tort'. Bray CJ was, with respect, right, but an application of the first limb to the claimant does not have the effect he feared. Even if the claimant's conduct counts as 'fault' pursuant to section 4 of the 1945 Act, it is still necessary that the conduct contributed to the risk that led to the damage,[41] and this is not the case in Bray CJ's example.

It follows that the claimant is at 'fault' if she committed a tort *against the defendant*,[42] or if her conduct would, apart from the 1945 Act, give rise to the defence of contributory negligence. According to a widespread view, the second alternative brings into the ambit of the Act only those torts in which the contributory negligence defence may be raised at common law.[43] This is true if the claimant's conduct is required to ground the common law defence in the particular tort concerned. However, as Burrows points out,[44] another interpretation is that the claimant's conduct must be of the sort that at common law would give rise to the contributory negligence defence if she were suing for a tort to which the common law defence indisputably applies, for instance negligence. This interpretation brings all torts into the ambit of the Act. As a result, the desirable general applicability of the 1945 Act may be achieved through a possible, if stretched, interpretation of the core part of the definition of 'fault' in section 4.

Another way to the same end follows from a consideration of the other parts of the definition. Prior to its core part, the definition mentions 'negligence [or] breach of statutory duty'. The relative clause (from 'which' onwards) can be understood as limiting only the phrase 'other act or omission' and not also 'negligence [or] breach of statutory duty', and the then free-standing word

---

[39] NE Palmer and PJ Davies, 'Contributory Negligence and Breach of Contract—English and Australasian Attitudes Compared' (1980) 29 *ICLQ* 415, 416 fn 7.

[40] (1974) 10 SASR 299 (SASC) 316–17.

[41] Below IV in this chapter.

[42] G Treitel, *The Law of Contract*, 11th edn (London, 2003) 987 fn 82.

[43] *Standard Chartered Bank v Pakistan National Shipping Corp (Nos 2 and 4)* [2001] QB 167 (CA) [35], [60], [107]–[120]; [2002] UKHL 43, [2003] 1 AC 959 [13], [42] (HL); GL Williams, *Joint Torts and Contributory Negligence* (London, 1951) 318 fn 3. Note that the common law defence may still widen its ambit: *Standard Chartered Bank v Pakistan National Shipping Corp (No 4)* [2001] QB 167 (CA) [107] (Ward LJ); *Dairy Containers Ltd v NZI Bank Ltd* [1995] 2 NZLR 30, 110.

[44] A Burrows, *Remedies for Torts and Breach of Contract*, 3rd edn (Oxford, 2004) 135, 138.

'negligence' can be understood as lack of care as opposed to the whole tort.[45] It has been objected that the phrase 'other act or omission' indicates that 'negligence' (and 'breach of statutory duty') must also be something 'which gives rise to a liability in tort'.[46] But this effect of the word 'other' is not the only semantic possibility. If the word 'negligence' is given its widest possible meaning, any lack of care on the claimant's part renders the 1945 Act applicable irrespective of whether it constitutes a tort or gives rise to the contributory negligence defence at common law. The same interpretation must logically be made for the defendant. Any lack of care on the part of the defendant counts as a 'fault' for the purposes of the 1945 Act regardless of whether the conduct constitutes a tort. This might be rejected as being too wide but, again, an over-inclusive definition of 'fault' in section 4 is unproblematic as the 1945 Act does not create new torts. In summary, the 1945 Act can,[47] and should, apply to all torts unless statute provides otherwise.

III Causation

Both the claimant's conduct and the defendant's conduct must have been a factual cause of the occurrence of the damage or its extent in the 'but for' sense. Otherwise the damage would not be the result partly of the claimant's fault and partly of the defendant's fault, as required by section 1(1) of the 1945 Act.[48] Furthermore, where the defendant's conduct was no factual cause of the damage, there is no liability in the first place. And where the claimant's conduct was no cause of the damage, there is no reason why liability should be reduced on account of this conduct. The claimant's conduct, it should be clarified, is not required to be a cause of the *accident* but only a cause of the *damage*. The failure to wear a seat belt, for instance, amounts to contributory negligence where it increased the injuries sustained even though it made no contribution to the other party's negligent driving. As Lord Denning MR said in *Froom v Butcher*:

> The question is not what was the cause of the accident. It is rather what was the cause of the damage ... The *accident* is caused by the bad driving. The *damage* is caused in part

---

[45] *Mouat v Clark Boyce* [1992] 2 NZLR 559 (NZCA) 564–65 (Cooke P); GL Williams, *Joint Torts and Contributory Negligence* (London, 1951) 294, 329–30.

[46] *Nationwide Building Society v Thimbleby* [1999] PNLR 733, 749–54; *Standard Chartered Bank v Pakistan National Shipping Corp (No 4)* [2001] QB 167 (CA) [54] (Aldous LJ); *AS James Pty Ltd v CB Duncan* [1970] VR 705 (VSC) 725–26; A Burrows, *Remedies for Torts and Breach of Contract*, 3rd edn (Oxford, 2004) 139; NE Palmer and PJ Davies, 'Contributory Negligence and Breach of Contract— English and Australasian Attitudes Compared' (1980) 29 *ICLQ* 415, 417; AS Taylor, 'Contributory Negligence—A Defence to Breach of Contract?' (1986) 49 *MLR* 102, 107.

[47] MA Jones, 'General Defences' in AM Dugdale and MA Jones, *Clerk & Lindsell on Torts*, 19th edn (London, 2006) [3–39].

[48] *Jones v Livox Quarries Ltd* [1952] 2 QB 608 (CA) 615 (Denning LJ).

by the bad driving of the defendant, and in part by the failure of the plaintiff to wear a seat belt. If the plaintiff was to blame in not wearing a seat belt, the damage is in part the result of his own fault.[49]

But is a factual 'but for' contribution by each party sufficient to bring the case into the ambit of the 1945 Act, or is it necessary that each party's conduct was a *legal* cause of the damage under the doctrines of legal causation and *novus actus interveniens*? It should first be noted that the applicability of the 1945 Act is not dependent on who had the last opportunity to avoid the accident.[50] The 'last opportunity' rule developed at common law in order to alleviate the harsh effect of the all-or-nothing defence,[51] and thus lost its raison d'être with the introduction of apportionment.[52]

Notwithstanding the downfall of the 'last opportunity' rule, the courts have not refrained from applying legal causation doctrine to cases otherwise within the ambit of the 1945 Act.[53] A good example is *Norris v Moss & Sons*.[54] In breach of health and safety regulations, the defendants erected scaffolding where one of the uprights was not vertical but was inclining away from the building. The plaintiff, an employee of the defendants, decided to remedy this defect but did so in a 'fantastically wrong' way, as a result of which the scaffolding collapsed and injured him. Since the injury would not have happened had the scaffolding not been defective in the first place, the defendants' breach of statutory duty was a cause of the injury in the 'but for' sense. Nevertheless, the plaintiff's carelessness was held to be the sole legal cause of the injury.

However, in other cases where an employer contravened health and safety regulations and where a workman was injured because he undertook repair in a 'very foolish' way, the workman's 'foolish' behaviour was not held to be the sole cause of the accident but led to a substantial reduction in the damages by virtue of the 1945 Act.[55] The impact of the 1945 Act on legal causation doctrine was also emphasised by Denning LJ in *Jones v Livox Quarries Ltd*:

> In the course of the argument my Lord suggested that before the Act of 1945 he would have regarded this case as one where the plaintiff should recover in full. That would be

---

[49]   [1976] QB 286 (CA) 292.

[50]   *Davies v Swan Motor Co (Swansea) Ltd* [1949] 2 KB 291 (CA) 318, 321–24; *Jones v Livox Quarries Ltd* [1952] 2 QB 608 (CA) 615 (Denning LJ: 'It can now be safely asserted that the doctrine of last opportunity is obsolete'); *Gorham v British Telecommunications plc* [2000] 1 WLR 2129 (CA) 2148 (Sir Murray Stuart-Smith: 'the last opportunity rule is no longer good law').

[51]   Above I in this chapter.

[52]   *Davies v Swan Motor Co (Swansea) Ltd* [1949] 2 KB 291 (CA) 318, 322. The issue of last opportunity remains a factor in weighing each party's blameworthiness: MA Jones, 'General Defences' in AM Dugdale and MA Jones, *Clerk & Lindsell on Torts*, 19th edn (London, 2006) [3–36].

[53]   The continued applicability of legal causation doctrine under the 1945 Act was emphasised in *Davies v Swan Motor Co (Swansea) Ltd* [1949] 2 KB 291 (CA) 323 (Denning LJ).

[54]   [1954] 1 WLR 346 (CA). Similarly *Manwaring v Billington* [1952] 2 All ER 747 (CA); *Rushton v Turner Brothers Asbestos Co Ltd* [1960] 1 WLR 96.

[55]   *Mitchell v Westin Ltd* [1965] 1 WLR 297 (CA): reduction by 80%; Sellers LJ and Pearson LJ favouring a reduction to nil; *Jayes v IMI (Kynoch) Ltd* [1985] ICR 155 (CA): reduction to nil.

because the negligence of the dumper driver would then have been regarded as the predominant cause. Now, since the Act, we have regard to all the causes, and one of them undoubtedly was the plaintiff's negligence in riding on the towbar of the traxcavator.[56]

It seems indeed preferable to apply the Act whenever either party's fault was a factual cause of the risk involved, and to consider the factors relating to legal causation within apportionment. Why force an all-or-nothing decision under legal causation doctrine when a flexible apportionment regime is available? Even where the 1945 Act applies, the outcome does not necessarily have to lie *between* all and nothing. Where the defendant's contribution to the damage is so dominant as to form the sole *legal* cause of it, the court, in exercising its discretion under the 1945 Act, may refuse to make any reduction in the defendant's liability. Conversely, although this is controversial, where the claimant's contribution to the damage is so dominant as to form the sole *legal* cause of it, the court, in weighing the parties' responsibility under the 1945 Act, may reduce the defendant's liability to nil.[57]

IV The Claimant's Fault

For the purposes of the 1945 Act, the claimant was at fault if she failed to take reasonable care of her own interests, in other words, if she broke a 'duty to herself'.[58] It is not required that the claimant owed the defendant a duty of care.[59] In this respect, the term contributory *negligence* is misleading; the term contributory *fault* would be more accurate.[60] If carelessness counts as fault, so too must a fortiori intentional self-harm.[61]

---

[56] [1952] 2 QB 608 (CA) 617.

[57] Below VI in this chapter.

[58] 'When a man steps into the road he owes a duty to himself to take care for his own safety, but he does not owe any duty to a motorist who is going at an excessive speed to avoid being run down. Nevertheless, if he does not keep a good lookout, he is guilty of contributory negligence': *Davies v Swan Motor Co (Swansea) Ltd* [1949] 2 KB 291 (CA) 324 (Denning LJ).

[59] '[W]hen contributory negligence is set up as a defence, its existence does not depend on any duty owed by the injured party to the party sued, and all that is necessary to establish such a defence is to prove to the satisfaction of the jury that the injured party did not in his own interest take reasonable care of himself and contributed, by this want of care, to his own injury': *Nance v British Columbia Electric Railway Co Ltd* [1951] AC 601 (PC) 611 (Viscount Simon). See also B Coote, 'Contributory Negligence Reform and the Right to Rely on a Contract' [1992] *New Zealand Recent Law Review* 313, 316.

[60] *Reeves v Metropolitan Police Commissioner* [2000] 1 AC 360 (HL) 383 (Lord Hope); WP Keeton (gen ed), *Prosser and Keeton on the Law of Torts*, 5th edn (St Paul, 1984) 453.

[61] *Reeves v Metropolitan Police Commissioner* [1999] QB 169 (CA) 194, 198; [2000] 1 AC 360 (HL) 369–370, 376–377, 382–383, 385; J Edelman and J Davies, 'Torts and Equitable Wrongs' in A Burrows (ed), *English Private Law*, 2nd edn (Oxford, 2007) [17.202]; GL Williams, *Joint Torts and*

Even though contributory negligence does not import any notion of owing the defendant a duty of care, reasonableness on the part of the claimant is in general decided under the same principles used to determine the breach of a duty of care towards another person. The claimant will thus be measured against the standard of the reasonable person.[62] However, as Glanville Williams notes, 'the reasonable defendant is not allowed to have lapses, but the reasonable plaintiff is'.[63] Another requirement is foreseeability of harm.[64] This should relate not to *any* harm but to the (type of) harm that actually occurred.[65]

Finally, the harm that has occurred must be within the scope of the risk created by the claimant's fault.[66] This is demonstrated by *Jones v Livox Quarries Ltd*,[67] where the plaintiff was standing on the tow bar at the back of a traxcavator in defiance of orders not to do so, and suffered injury when another vehicle was negligently driven into his back. The Court of Appeal held that contributory negligence could not be based on the fact that the plaintiff had exposed himself to the risk of falling off the vehicle since this had not actually happened. It was necessary to ask whether the plaintiff had exposed himself to the risk of being run into by a following vehicle, which was eventually answered in the affirmative. But there would have been no contributory negligence, said the Court, if the plaintiff, whilst riding on the tow bar, had been shot in the eye by a negligent sportsman.[68]

V Damage

Section 1(1) of the Law Reform (Contributory Negligence) Act 1945 refers to damage partly caused by the claimant's conduct and partly caused by the defendant's conduct, and provides that a claim in respect of that damage may be

---

Contributory Negligence (London, 1951) 199–200 ('contributory *intention*'). See also *Pallister v Waikato Hospital Board* [1975] 2 NZLR 725 (NZCA) 736 (Richmond J).

[62] *Caswell v Powell Duffryn Associated Collieries Ltd* [1940] AC 152 (HL) 164, 186–87; *Jones v Livox Quarries Ltd* [1952] 2 QB 608 (CA) 614, 615; *AC Billings & Sons Ltd v Riden* [1958] AC 240 (HL) 251–55 (Lord Reid). For details see P Giliker, 'General Defences' in K Oliphant (gen ed), *The Law of Tort*, 2nd edn (London, 2007) [5.13]–[5.16]; MA Jones, 'General Defences' in AM Dugdale and MA Jones, *Clerk & Lindsell on Torts*, 19th edn (London, 2006) [3–51]–[3–64].

[63] GL Williams, *Joint Torts and Contributory Negligence* (London, 1951) 353.

[64] eg *Jones v Livox Quarries Ltd* [1952] 2 QB 608 (CA) 615 (Denning LJ); *O'Connell v Jackson* [1972] 1 QB 270 (CA) 275 (Edmund Davies LJ).

[65] In analogy to the requirements of establishing negligence: above ch 2, II and III. A consideration of that issue within apportionment is suggested by P Giliker, 'General Defences' in K Oliphant (gen ed), *The Law of Tort*, 2nd edn (London, 2007) [5.28].

[66] A Burrows, *Remedies for Torts and Breach of Contract*, 3rd edn (Oxford, 2004) 130; D Harris, 'Causation, mitigation and contributory negligence' in D Harris, D Campbell and R Halson, *Remedies in Contract and Tort*, 2nd edn (London, 2002) 308–309; WVH Rogers, *Winfield and Jolowicz on Tort*, 17th edn (London, 2006) [6–46].

[67] [1952] 2 QB 608 (CA).

[68] ibid 616, 618.

reduced according to the claimant's share in the responsibility for the damage. Where the same accident generates damage caused by both parties and other damage caused by one party alone, the 1945 Act can only apply to the former damage. Consider, for instance, a road accident victim who failed to wear a seat belt. It has consistently been held that the 1945 Act applies to that situation only insofar as wearing a seat belt would actually have prevented or lessened the injuries sustained.[69] Where some of the injuries would have been prevented or lessened by wearing a seat belt and others not, the 1945 Act applies only to the former.[70] As Edmund Davies LJ said in *O'Connell v Jackson*, where the plaintiff moped driver had failed to wear a crash helmet:

> It must be borne in mind that, for so much of the injuries and damage as would have resulted from the accident even if a crash helmet had been worn, the defendant is wholly to blame, and the plaintiff not at all. For the additional injuries and damage which would not have occurred if a crash helmet had been worn, the defendant, as solely responsible for the accident, must continue in substantial measure to be held liable, and it is only in that last field of additional injuries and damage that the contributory negligence of the plaintiff has any relevance.[71]

This clear and logical concept is somewhat threatened by the decision of the Court of Appeal in *Platform Home Loans Ltd v Oyston Shipways Ltd*.[72] A credit institute lent money on mortgage, relying on a valuation of the property securing the loan which later turned out to have negligently overvalued the property. The issues in that case were whether certain conduct on the part of the lender amounted to contributory negligence, and how the 1945 Act interacts with the limitation of a valuer's liability established in *SAAMCO*.[73] An exploration of those detailed issues goes beyond the scope of the present discussion and is not relevant for the interpretation of the 1945 Act in general. What does bear relevance beyond the case of negligent valuation are certain remarks made by Morritt LJ on behalf of the Court of Appeal. The 1945 Act applies, he said, where one part of the whole damage was caused solely by the claimant and another part solely by the defendant:

---

[69] *Lertora v Finzi* [1973] RTR 161; *Pasternack v Poulton* [1973] 1 WLR 476, 482; *Smith v Blackburn* [1974] 2 Lloyd's Rep 229, 234; *Challoner v Williams* [1974] RTR 221; *Drage v Smith* [1975] 1 Lloyd's Rep 438, 440; *Owens v Brimmel* [1977] QB 859, 863–64.

[70] *Froom v Butcher* [1976] QB 286 (CA) 296.

[71] [1972] 1 QB 270 (CA) 277–78. Notwithstanding the clear distinction between the part of the damage to which the 1945 Act applies and the part to which the Act does not apply, the court reduced the plaintiff's overall damages by 15%. But this followed simply from the fact that the court was unable, on the evidence, to separate the two parts of the damage in the case at hand. This problem is not uncommon; see for instance *Toperoff v Mor* [1973] RTR 419, 421.

[72] [1998] Ch 466 (CA).

[73] *South Australia Asset Management Corp v York Montague Ltd* [1997] AC 191 (HL); above ch 2, VI.

It is as consistent with the words used [in section 1(1)] that half the damage should be solely the fault of the claimant and the other half solely the fault of the other person as with a requirement that all the damage should be partly caused by the fault of each.[74]

This was a far-reaching departure from the interpretation of section 1(1) established in the seat belt cases. Startlingly, Morritt LJ referred just to the seat belt cases as an authority for his proposition. But he named only one case specifically: *Froom v Butcher*.[75] That case will now be examined.

In a traffic accident caused solely by the defendant's negligence, the plaintiff, who did not wear a seat belt, suffered head and chest injuries and a broken finger. Had he worn a seat belt, the head and chest injuries would have been completely prevented, but the finger would still have broken. The judge refused to regard the failure to wear a seat belt as contributory negligence, but said that had he taken the opposite view, he would have reduced the plaintiff's damages by 20 per cent. The Court of Appeal did regard the failure to wear a seat belt as contributory negligence.[76]

On the issue of apportionment, the Court of Appeal suggested that the victim's share in the responsibility for injuries which would have been prevented by wearing a seat belt should generally be assessed at 25 per cent. Accordingly, said the Court, the plaintiff's damages in respect of the head and chest injuries should be reduced by 25 per cent whereas the damages in respect of the broken finger should not be reduced at all, as the finger would still have broken even if the plaintiff had worn a seat belt.[77] However, since both parties had accepted the judge's decision on apportionment, the Court of Appeal felt bound by it and reduced the plaintiff's overall damages by 20 per cent.

Morritt LJ in *Platform* regarded *Froom v Butcher* as an example of a case where one part of the damage was caused solely by the claimant and another part solely by the defendant:

Had the plaintiff been wearing a seat belt he would only have sustained a broken finger. Thus the fault of neither party caused all the damage sustained ... Thus the 'damage' for the purpose of section 1(1) in that case included damage for which the claimant was exclusively responsible[.][78]

In other words, the head and chest injuries were caused solely by the plaintiff, the broken finger was caused solely by the defendant, yet the Court applied the 1945 Act to all injuries. With respect, this was a misreading of *Froom v Butcher*.[79] First, the head and chest injuries were not caused solely by the plaintiff. True, had he worn a seat belt, those injuries would not have occurred. But the injuries would not have occurred either had the defendant driven carefully. It follows that the

[74] [1998] Ch 466 (CA) 478.
[75] [1976] QB 286 (CA).
[76] ibid 290–95.
[77] ibid 296.
[78] [1998] Ch 466 (CA) 478.
[79] J Stapleton, 'Risk-Taking by Commercial Lenders' (1999) 115 *Law Quarterly Review* 527, 528.

head and chest injuries were caused by both parties.[80] Secondly, the Court of Appeal in *Froom v Butcher* did not apply the 1945 Act to all of the plaintiff's injuries, including the broken finger which had been caused by the defendant alone. It was expressly said that the broken finger did not fall within the ambit of the Act. The reduction in the plaintiff's overall damages followed simply from the parties' acceptance of the judge's decision to that effect.

Since Morritt LJ's interpretation of section 1(1) of the 1945 Act resulted from a profound misunderstanding of *Froom v Butcher*, the only case he specifically named as authority, his proposition bears little weight. It should also be noted that the House of Lords (Lord Cooke dissenting) in *Platform* reversed the Court of Appeal's decision on the main issue involved, the interaction between the 1945 Act and the *SAAMCO* concept.[81] While their Lordships did not expressly reject Morritt LJ's interpretation of section 1(1), they did not endorse it either. Therefore, it is suggested, the courts should follow the seat belt cases rather than *Platform* for the definition of 'damage' in section 1(1).[82] Only that part of the whole damage which was caused by both parties falls within the ambit of the 1945 Act.

VI Apportionment

If certain damage falls into the ambit of the 1945 Act, section 1(1) provides that 'the damages recoverable in respect thereof shall be reduced to such extent as the court thinks just and equitable having regard to the claimant's share in the responsibility for the damage'. 'Responsibility' is allocated according to the causative potency and the blameworthiness of each party's conduct.[83] While the former has been described as the dangerousness of a conduct according to its statistical tendency to produce harm,[84] the latter relates to moral culpability,[85] considering the degree of awareness of the risk involved[86] (which in turn depends on the age of the actor[87]) and whether the defendant had a duty to prevent the

---

[80] ibid.

[81] [2000] 2 AC 190 (HL).

[82] P Giliker, 'General Defences' in K Oliphant (gen ed), *The Law of Tort*, 2nd edn (London, 2007) [5.20]; J Stapleton, 'Risk-Taking by Commercial Lenders' (1999) 115 *LQR* 527, 528–29.

[83] *Corr v IBC Vehicles Ltd* [2008] UKHL 13, [2008] 1 AC 884 [44], [48]; *Calvert v William Hill Credit Ltd* [2008] EWCA Civ 1427, [2009] Ch 330 [69]; *St George v Home Office* [2008] EWCA Civ 1068, [2009] 1 WLR 1670 [50], [63]. See also below ch 10, VI A.

[84] HLA Hart and T Honoré, *Causation in the Law*, 2nd edn (Oxford, 1985) 233.

[85] ibid 234; S Chapman, 'Apportionment of Liability Between Tortfeasors' (1948) 64 *LQR* 26, 27.

[86] *C v Imperial Design Ltd* [2001] Env LR 33 (CA) [32]–[33], [44].

[87] ibid [32]–[33], [41]; *Hughes v Lord Advocate* 1963 SC (HL) 31, 40 (Lord Jenkins); *Yachuk v Blais Co Ltd* [1949] AC 386 (PC).

very acts of contributory negligence.[88] In cases of strict liability, the absence of carelessness on the defendant's part cannot have the effect that the slightest carelessness on the claimant's part shifts the whole responsibility onto the latter. Probably the best approach in that case is to allocate responsibility according to the degree to which each party has departed from the standard imposed by law.[89]

As a result of weighing each party's responsibility, the court awards the claimant a certain percentage of the damages she would obtain had there not been contributory negligence. Does the percentage have to lie *between* nil and 100, or is either extreme also possible?[90] It seems established that the court may consider the contributory fault *de minimis* and award full damages. This power has been recognised in many cases.[91] It was denied in one case with a reference to the wording of section 1(1).[92] True, according to this provision the damages 'shall be reduced'. But they shall be reduced 'to such extent as the court thinks just and equitable'. Where the court does not consider any reduction 'just and equitable' because the claimant's blame is *de minimis*, the wording of section 1(1) is consistent with a full damages award.

With regard to the possibility of reducing the damages to nil,[93] the Court of Appeal has made several decisions for[94] and against,[95] most of which did not

---

[88] *Staveley Iron & Chemical Co Ltd v Jones* [1956] AC 627 (HL) 648 (Lord Tucker); *Reeves v Metropolitan Police Commissioner* [1999] QB 169 (CA) 181–83 (Buxton LJ); [2000] 1 AC 360 (HL) 372 (Lord Hoffman); *C v Imperial Design Ltd* [2001] Env LR 33 (CA) [31].

[89] AI Ogus, *The Law of Damages* (London, 1973) 105. A different view is taken by WVH Rogers, *Winfield and Jolowicz on Tort*, 17th edn (London, 2006) [6–53]: only the claimant's conduct should be relevant.

[90] Note that the indemnification for a mistake by the land registrar may be reduced by reason of the claimant's lack of proper care: Land Registration Act 2002 sch 8 para 5(2). The reduction 'may be anything from nil to total': *Prestige Properties Ltd v Scottish Provident Institution* [2002] EWHC 330 (Ch), [2003] Ch 1 [35] (Lightman J), on the predecessor of the current statute.

[91] *Hawkins v Ian Ross (Castings) Ltd* [1970] 1 All ER 180, 188; *Stocker v Norprint Ltd* (1970) 10 KIR 10 (CA) 14 (Phillimore LJ); *Vacwell Engineering Co Ltd v BDH Chemicals Ltd* [1971] 1 QB 88, 110; *Sahib Foods Ltd v Paskin Kyriakides Sands (a firm)* [2003] EWCA Civ 1832, [2004] PNLR 22 [69]; *St George v Home Office* [2008] EWCA Civ 1068, [2009] 1 WLR 1670 [63].

[92] *Boothman v British Northrop Ltd* (1972) 13 KIR 112 (CA) 121. The view is shared by MJ Tilbury, *Civil Remedies, Vol 1: Principles of Civil Remedies* (Sydney, 1990) [3150].

[93] In Case C-537/03 *Candolin v Vahinkovakuutusosakeyhtio Pohjola* [2005] ECR I-5745, the European Court of Justice held that the EC Motor Insurance Directives, which aim to ensure that victims of motor vehicle accidents can claim compensation under compulsory insurance, preclude national law from excluding or disproportionately limiting such compensation by virtue of contributory negligence. There can thus be no reduction to nil in that situation.

[94] *Mitchell v Westin Ltd* [1965] 1 WLR 297 (CA) 305 (Sellers LJ), 308–309 (Pearson LJ); *Jayes v IMI (Kynoch) Ltd* [1985] ICR 155 (CA) 158–59; *Reeves v Metropolitan Police Commissioner* [1999] QB 169 (CA) 194–95 (Morritt LJ). See also *Nitrigin Eireann Teoranta v Inco Alloys Ltd* [1992] 1 WLR 498, 506.

[95] *Pitts v Hunt* [1991] 1 QB 24 (CA) 48, 51, 52; *Dean v Railtrack plc* [2001] EWCA Civ 835 [9], [11]; *Anderson v Newham College of Further Education* [2002] EWCA Civ 505, [2003] ICR 212; *Buyukardicli v Hammerson UK Properties plc* [2002] EWCA Civ 683 [7]. Perhaps also *McCreesh v Courtaulds plc* [1997] PIQR P421 (CA) 424–25.

discuss the issue nor even referred to previous cases. In an attempt at reconciliation, Lord Bingham CJ, in *Reeves v Metropolitan Police Commissioner*, said about the cases in which a reduction to nil had been made:

> I think perhaps such cases are properly to be understood as based on causation: the court has found that the defendant was negligent or in breach of statutory duty but has nevertheless concluded that such negligence or breach was not to any degree causative of the plaintiff's injury or damage.[96]

It is indeed possible to reinterpret all cases in which a reduction to nil has been made as instances where the defendant's conduct was no legal cause of the damage occurred. But why should such a reinterpretation be made? Why should an outcome achieved on the firm ground of applying the 1945 Act be pushed onto the shaky ground of legal causation?

Beldam LJ in *Pitts v Hunt* advanced four arguments against a reduction to nil, based on the wording of section 1(1) of the 1945 Act.[97] First, he said, a reduction to nil implies that the claimant alone caused the damage, which is at odds with the requirement that the damage be 'the result' partly of the defendant's fault.[98] But factual causation in the 'but for' sense should be sufficient to make the damage 'the result' of either party's fault.[99] Factors normally considered in the context of legal causation and remoteness should be weighed within apportionment. It is therefore logically possible that the claimant bears sole responsibility because of her overwhelming blame even though the defendant's fault was a factual cause of the damage.[100]

Secondly, Beldam LJ argued, section 1(1) provides that the claim 'shall not be defeated' by reason of contributory negligence; a reduction to nil effectively defeats the claim.[101] But this phrase simply intends to remove the position at common law where the slightest fault on the part of the claimant defeats her claim completely.[102] It follows that section 1(1) merely prohibits the claim from being defeated per se, but it does not necessarily prohibit the claim from being defeated de facto because of the claimant's overwhelming blameworthiness.

Thirdly, Beldam LJ argued, the formulation in section 1(1) that the 'damages recoverable … shall be reduced' presupposes that the claimant will recover some

---

[96] [1999] QB 169 (CA) 198. This interpretation seems to have been followed in *Pratt v Intermet Refractories Ltd*, LEXIS Transcript 21 January 2000 (CA) (May LJ); *Billington v Maguire* [2001] EWCA Civ 273 [26] (Sir Anthony Evans).

[97] [1991] 1 QB 24 (CA) 48. Approvingly quoted in *Anderson v Newham College of Further Education* [2002] EWCA Civ 505, [2003] ICR 212 [14].

[98] The same argument was made, with regard to the virtually identical contributory negligence legislation of New South Wales, in *Wynbergen v Hoyts Co Pty Ltd* (1997) 149 ALR 25 (HCA) 29–30.

[99] Above III in this chapter.

[100] P Giliker, 'General Defences' in K Oliphant (gen ed), *The Law of Tort*, 2nd edn (London, 2007) [5.38].

[101] This argument is supported by S Deakin, A Johnston and B Markesinis, *Markesinis and Deakin's Tort Law*, 6th edn (Oxford, 2008) 900, who go so far as to suggest that 'the court should strive to avoid awarding a deduction *approaching* 100 per cent'.

[102] *McEwan v Lothian Buses plc* 2006 SCLR 592 (CSOH) [33].

damages. It is unclear whether Beldam LJ relied on the word 'recoverable' or the word 'reduced'. Neither word supports his conclusion. A reduction by the full amount is still a 'reduction'. What is subject to reduction is the amount of damages that would be awarded had the claimant not been at fault. Incidentally, section 1(2) of the Act obliges the court to record the amount of the total damages. The word 'recoverable' in section 1(1) simply means that the starting point for the calculation is not the whole loss suffered (including irrecoverable items) but the total damages that would actually be awarded had there not been contributory negligence. It does not imply that something recoverable must be left *after* the reduction has been made.

Finally, Beldam LJ said, section 1(1) provides for an apportionment according to 'the claimant's share in the responsibility for the damage'; to hold the claimant 100 per cent responsible is not to hold that he 'shares' in the responsibility. This argument seems very formalistic. A person who is the only shareholder in a company owns a share of 100 per cent. In conclusion, there are no compelling reasons why a court should be prohibited from reducing the damages to nil where appropriate. This is the view that the Court of Session has pronounced *obiter* for the application of the 1945 Act in Scotland.[103]

---

[103] ibid [32]–[34].

10

Contributory Negligence in Contract

I The Position Apart from the 1945 Act

The Law Reform (Contributory Negligence) Act 1945 aside, liability for breach of contract is in general not affected by unreasonable behaviour on the claimant's part.[1] Contracting parties, it is said, are not expected to take precautions against breach,[2] for 'a man is entitled to act in the faith that the other party to a contract is carrying out his part of it properly'.[3] Some commentators suggest an exception where the claimant's behaviour amounts to an independent legal wrong against the defendant,[4] and where the defendant breaks a duty of care concurrent in contract and tort.[5] Examples for the latter situation include the liability of a carrier for injury to the passenger, of an innkeeper for loss of the guest's goods, and of a landlord for a failure to keep the property in repair. In these cases, it is argued, the claimant cannot circumvent the complete defence she faces in tort by simply pleading her case in contract. Others 'remain quite unconvinced that contributory negligence, as such, at common law had any relevance in a claim in

---

[1] *Forsikringsaktieselskapet Vesta v Butcher* [1989] AC 852 (CA) 879 (Sir Roger Ormrod: 'Had contributory negligence been a defence at common law to a claim for damages for breach of contract the reports and the textbooks prior to 1945 would have been full of references to it.'); *Astley v Austrust Ltd* (1999) 197 CLR 1 (HCA) [76] (Gleeson CJ, McHugh J, Gummow J and Hayne J: 'No case can be found in the books where contributory negligence, as such, was ever held to be a defence to an action for breach of contract.'); GL Williams, *Joint Torts and Contributory Negligence* (London, 1951) 216–22; PA Chandler, 'Contributory Negligence and Contract: Some Underlying Disparities' (1989) 40 *Northern Ireland Legal Quarterly* 152, 154–62.

[2] E Peel, *Treitel on the Law of Contract*, 12th edn (London, 2007) [20–106]; GL Williams, ibid 214.

[3] *Compania Naviera Maropan S/A v Bowaters Lloyd Pulp and Paper Mills Ltd* [1955] 2 QB 68, 77 (Devlin J). Approvingly quoted in *Reardon Smith Line Ltd v Australian Wheat Board* [1956] AC 266 (PC) 282 (Lord Somervell); *Barclays Bank plc v Fairclough Building Ltd (No 1)* [1995] QB 214 (CA) 229–30 (Beldam LJ).

[4] E Peel, *Treitel on the Law of Contract*, 12th edn (London, 2007) [20–111].

[5] ibid [20–106]; GL Williams, *Joint Torts and Contributory Negligence* (London, 1951) 214–15.

contract'.[6] They ascribe the results in the seemingly deviating cases to causation[7] or the substantially tortious nature of liability.[8]

All this relates to the law as it stood when the 1945 Act was passed. There seems to be a widespread view that the common law became 'frozen' at that time, evidenced by the use of the past tense in describing the position apart from the 1945 Act. The same is true for tort, with regard to which it has been argued that the existence of legislation is no reason why the common law should not still be able to develop.[9] There is even less reason in contract where, as it will be shown, the 1945 Act is held to be largely inapplicable. It follows that if an apportionment of liability is considered desirable, as the following study attempts to demonstrate, but impossible under the wording of the 1945 Act, apportionment may be recognised as being available at common law.[10] The courts in Ontario and New Brunswick have done so.[11]

II The Impact of the 1945 Act—Overview

Even though the Law Reform (Contributory Negligence) Act 1945 'was of course passed with tort rather than contract in mind',[12] it did have some impact on contract. After over 40 years of uncertainty,[13] the law was effectively settled in *Forsikringsaktieselskapet Vesta v Butcher*.[14] Vesta, a Norwegian insurance company, insured a fish farm for lost fish and sought to reinsure 90 per cent of the

[6] *Forsikringsaktieselskapet Vesta v Butcher* [1989] AC 852 (CA) 879 (Sir Roger Ormrod). See also *AS James Pty Ltd v CB Duncan* [1970] VR 705 (VSC) 722–25.

[7] ibid; AS Taylor, 'Contributory Negligence—A Defence to Breach of Contract?' (1986) 49 *Modern Law Review* 102, 103–104. See also J Swanton, 'Contributory Negligence as a Defence to Actions for Breach of Contract' (1981) 55 *Australian Law Journal* 278, 281.

[8] PA Chandler, 'Contributory Negligence and Contract: Some Underlying Disparities' (1989) 40 *NILQ* 152, 156–62; NE Palmer and PJ Davies, 'Contributory Negligence and Breach of Contract—English and Australasian Attitudes Compared' (1980) 29 *International & Comparative Law Quarterly* 415, 420.

[9] Above ch 9, I.

[10] In favour of such a development are G Davis and J Knowler, 'Astley v Austrust Ltd' (1999) 23 *Melbourne University Law Review* 795, 812–16; TM FitzPatrick, 'Contributory Negligence and Contract—A Critical Reassessment' (2001) 30 *Common Law World Review* 412 ff; M Tilbury and JW Carter, 'Converging Liabilities and Security of Contract: Contributory Negligence in Australian Law' (2000) 16 *Journal of Contract Law* 78, 97–98. In *Dairy Containers Ltd v NZI Bank Ltd* [1995] 2 NZLR 30, 110–11, Thomas J assumed *obiter* that in the absence of the apportionment legislation the common law would have developed towards allowing apportionment in conversion.

[11] See the cases cited by G Davis and J Knowler, ibid fns 117 and 119; TM FitzPatrick, ibid 413–15. In *Canadian Western Natural Gas Co Ltd v Pathfinder Surveys Ltd* (1980) 21 AR 459 (ABCA) [68], Prowse JA pointed out that if he had held the apportionment legislation inapplicable to the contract action at hand, he 'would not have considered it beyond the scope of the common law' to apportion liability at common law.

[12] H McGregor, *McGregor on Damages*, 18th edn (London, 2009) [5–003].

[13] See NE Palmer and PJ Davies, 'Contributory Negligence and Breach of Contract—English and Australasian Attitudes Compared' (1980) 29 *ICLQ* 415, 422–31.

[14] [1986] 2 All ER 488 (Hobhouse J); [1989] AC 852 (CA and HL).

risk with Lloyd's. Vesta asked their brokers to arrange the reinsurance contract. In a telephone call Vesta told the brokers that the reinsurance contract was not to contain a term requiring a 24-hour watch over the fish because such a watch did not take place. In breach of their (contractual and tortious) duty of care, the brokers failed to delete that term in the reinsurance contract. When the fish farm suffered a large loss of fish caused by a severe storm, the underwriter at Lloyd's refused to pay the amount reinsured on the ground that the 24-hour watch term had not been complied with. Vesta sued the underwriter under the reinsurance contract and, alternatively, the brokers for breach of contract and negligence.

The underwriter was ultimately held liable to pay the amount reinsured irrespective of the 24-hour watch term. With regard to the eventually irrelevant alternative claim the brokers argued that Vesta had been contributorily negligent in relying on a single telephone call to bring about the deletion of a crucial contract term. Vesta was indeed held to have been careless, but the question arose whether this was material to Vesta's *contractual* claim against the brokers. In discussing the applicability of the 1945 Act to contract, Hobhouse J identified the following three categories of a breach of contract:

(1) Where the defendant's liability arises from some contractual provision which does not depend on negligence on the part of the defendant.
(2) Where the defendant's liability arises from a contractual obligation which is expressed in terms of taking care (or its equivalent) but does not correspond to a common law duty to take care which would exist in the given case independently of contract.
(3) Where the defendant's liability in contract is the same as his liability in the tort of negligence independently of the existence of any contract.[15]

The case at hand fell into category 3 in which Hobhouse J held the 1945 Act applicable.[16] The Court of Appeal approved his decision[17] (the House of Lords dismissed the appeal without going into the issue of contributory negligence[18]). Even though neither Hobhouse J[19] nor the majority[20] in the Court of Appeal clearly rejected an application of the 1945 Act to category 1 and 2, *Vesta* has been

[15] [1986] 2 All ER 488, 508. The distinction had already been suggested by J Swanton, 'Contributory Negligence as a Defence to Actions for Breach of Contract' (1981) 55 *ALJ* 278 ff; AS Taylor, 'Contributory Negligence—A Defence to Breach of Contract?' (1986) 49 *MLR* 102, 106–108.

[16] [1986] 2 All ER 488, 510.

[17] [1989] AC 852 (CA) 860–67, 875, 879. Sir Roger Ormrod's judgment is somewhat ambiguous, however, as he suggested (at 879) that the brokers were essentially liable in tort.

[18] [1989] AC 852, 880 (HL) 890.

[19] Who left the position expressly open in respect to category 2 ([1986] 2 All ER 488, 510) and said in respect to category 1 that 'one would not expect there to be much dispute that the Act does not apply, but in any event the primary question must be a question of the construction of the relevant contract, not of the statute': [1986] 2 All ER 488, 508–509.

[20] Sir Roger Ormrod impliedly rejected an application of the 1945 Act to category 1 or 2 by saying that 'the Act is concerned only with tortious liability': [1989] AC 852 (CA) 879.

interpreted to that effect,[21] and has in this interpretation been applied by the Court of Appeal[22] and lower courts. Subject to an intervention by the House of Lords, the division between the three types of breach of contract and the applicability of the 1945 Act to category 3 only is 'now clear law'.[23]

Where a party to a contract breaks several obligations arising from the same contract, each breach has to be categorised separately. Hobhouse J clarified this issue, even before the appeal against his decision in *Vesta* was decided, in *The Good Luck*.[24] The defendant broke two obligations arising from the same contract: a strict obligation and an implied duty to take care coexistent with an identical duty in tort. Hobhouse J assigned the breach of the first obligation to category 1 and the breach of the second obligation to category 3. Accordingly, the damages recoverable in respect of the first breach were not reduced on account of contributory negligence (the second breach caused no loss). The Court of Appeal, while reversing his decision on other grounds, expressly approved Hobhouse J's approach to contributory negligence.[25]

The three categories will now be explored in greater detail.

III   Breach of a Duty of Care Co-Extensive In Contract and Tort

Category 3 concerns the breach of a contractual duty of care co-existent with an identical duty in tort. In other words, it concerns concurrent liability in contract and tort where the contractual liability is not strict but depends on a failure to exercise reasonable care.[26] Category 3 covers, for instance, the breach of the duty of care owed by solicitors and other professionals to their clients.[27]

---

[21]   HG Beale, 'Damages' in HG Beale (gen ed), *Chitty on Contracts, Vol 1: General Principles*, 30th edn (London, 2008) [26–049]; A Burrows, 'Limitations on Compensation' in A Burrows and E Peel (eds), *Commercial Remedies: Current Issues and Problems* (Oxford, 2003) 38; B Coote, 'Contributory Negligence Reform and the Right to Rely on a Contract' [1992] *New Zealand Recent Law Review* 313, 315; A Porat, 'Contributory Negligence in Contract Law: Toward a Principled Approach' (1994) 28 *University of British Columbia Law Review* 141; J Swanton, 'Contributory Negligence is Not a Defence to Actions for Breach of Contract in Australian Law—Astley v Austrust Ltd' (1999) 14 *JCL* 251, 254.

[22]   See especially, *Barclays Bank plc v Fairclough Building Ltd (No 1)* [1995] QB 214 (CA); below V in this chapter.

[23]   A Burrows, *Remedies for Torts and Breach of Contract*, 3rd edn (Oxford, 2004) 139.

[24]   *Bank of Nova Scotia v Hellenic Mutual War Risks Association (Bermuda) Ltd (The Good Luck)* [1988] 1 Lloyd's Rep 514, 555.

[25]   [1990] 1 QB 818 (CA) 904. The House of Lords did not deal with this issue: [1992] 1 AC 233 (HL) 266.

[26]   Strict contractual liability concurrent with tortious liability falls into category 1: below V in this chapter.

[27]   See R Halson, 'The protected contractual interests' in D Harris, D Campbell and R Halson, *Remedies in Contract and Tort*, 2nd edn (London, 2002) 87 fn 12, and the cases cited there.

The first notable category 3 case decided after the passing of the 1945 Act was *Sayers v Harlow UDC*.[28] A woman found herself locked in the cubicle of a public toilet (for the use of which she had paid) due to the defective state of the lock. In an attempt to climb over the door, she placed a foot onto a revolving toilet roll. She fell to the ground and sustained injury. The Court of Appeal held the local authority operating the toilet liable for breach of a duty of care, but found contributory negligence of 25 per cent and reduced the damages accordingly. The applicability of the 1945 Act was not discussed; it was taken for granted. Indeed, since the authority had in principle accepted its liability, the Court left open whether liability rooted in contract or tort or both.[29] Concurrent liability would have been the correct view. The toilet visitor was a contractual invitee.[30]

After *Sayers* several dicta rejected an application of the 1945 Act to a category 3 breach of contract[31] until *Vesta* settled the law in favour of apportionment.[32] It has since been clarified that the applicability of the Act does not require the claim to be in substance a claim in tort.[33] Given that concurrent duties in contract and tort may well be characterised as one duty generating alternative causes of action,[34] it would indeed be difficult to determine whether liability for breach of such a duty is in substance tortious or contractual,[35] and 'it would be anomalous if the claimant could avoid the apportionment provisions of the Act by the simple device of suing only in contract'.[36]

---

[28] [1958] 1 WLR 623 (CA).

[29] ibid 625 (Lord Evershed MR): 'Nothing turns upon the foundation of liability'.

[30] *Forsikringsaktieselskapet Vesta v Butcher* [1989] AC 852 (CA) 866 (O'Connor LJ).

[31] *Sole v WJ Hallt Ltd* [1973] QB 574; *Acrecrest Ltd v WS Hattrell & Partners* [1983] QB 260 (CA) 281 (Donaldson LJ); *The Shinjitsu Maru No 5* [1985] 1 WLR 1270, 1288; *AS James Pty Ltd v CB Duncan* [1970] VR 705 (VSC) 726.

[32] *UCB Bank plc v Hepherd Winstanley & Pugh* [1999] Lloyd's Rep PN 963 (CA); above II in this chapter.

[33] *Youell v Bland Welch & Co Ltd (No 2)* [1990] 2 Lloyd's Rep 431, 459–60.

[34] JG Fleming, *The Law of Torts*, 9th edn (Sydney, 1998) 203 fn 426; followed in *Mouat v Clark Boyce* [1992] 2 NZLR 559 (NZCA) 565 (Cooke P).

[35] The opposite view is taken by PA Chandler, 'Contributory Negligence and Contract: Some Underlying Disparities' (1989) 40 *NILQ* 152, 168–70.

[36] HG Beale, 'Damages' in HG Beale (gen ed), *Chitty on Contracts, Vol 1: General Principles*, 30th edn (London, 2008) [26–049]. See also Law Commission, 'Contributory Negligence as a Defence in Contract' (Law Com No 219, 1993) [3.42]; B Coote, 'Contributory Negligence Reform and the Right to Rely on a Contract' [1992] *NZLR Rev* 313, 317; R Halson, 'The protected contractual interests' in D Harris, D Campbell and R Halson, *Remedies in Contract and Tort*, 2nd edn (London, 2002) 87; MJ Tilbury, *Civil Remedies, Vol 1: Principles of Civil Remedies* (Sydney, 1990) [3143]. Vivid examples are given by J Swanton, 'Contributory Negligence is Not a Defence to Actions for Breach of Contract in Australian Law—Astley v Austrust Ltd' (1999) 14 *JCL* 251, 261–62; GL Williams, *Joint Torts and Contributory Negligence* (London, 1951) 328–29.

On similar grounds, apportionment has been held available in actions under s 2(1) of the Misrepresentation Act 1967 where there is a concurrent action in negligence at common law: *Gran Gelato Ltd v Richcliff (Group) Ltd* [1992] Ch 560, 572–74.

While the New Zealand Court of Appeal has followed *Vesta*,[37] the High Court of Australia (Callinan J dissenting) took a different view in *Astley v Austrust Ltd*.[38] The claimant's choice of action, said the majority, determines the decision on other issues too, for instance on remoteness of damage, statutory prescription and the maintainability of an action against a defendant outside the jurisdiction. This is true, but all these differences are themselves questionable.[39] It was further argued that differences between the contractual and the tortious claim may result from the terms of the contract. True again, but the parties' ability to create, by their agreement, differences between contract and tort is no justification for maintaining such differences as the default rule. Furthermore, parties are unlikely to actually create differences. An exclusion of liability for breach, for instance, will normally exclude liability on any ground, be it contract, tort or equity, for a restriction to certain grounds would render the exclusion clause ineffective. In response to *Astley v Austrust Ltd*, all Australian jurisdictions have amended their apportionment legislation so as to include a category 3 breach of contract (and in South Australia also a category 2 breach).[40]

This raises the question of whether the wording of the 1945 Act (UK) actually allows for its application to a category 3 breach of contract. Surprisingly, this question found no serious attention in *Vesta*[41] from either Hobhouse J[42] or the Court of Appeal. Both instances felt bound by the Court of Appeal's decision in *Sayers* where the wording of the Act had not been scrutinised either.[43] However, both O'Connor LJ and Neill LJ in *Vesta*[44] referred to the New Zealand case of *Rowe v Turner Hopkins & Partners* where Pritchard J had explained the applicability of the apportionment legislation to a category 3 case in the following way.[45]

---

[37] *Mouat v Clark Boyce* [1992] 2 NZLR 559 (NZCA) 564–65 (Cooke P), 574–75 (Gault J). Cooke P's statement was *obiter* as he denied contractual liability *in casu*.

[38] (1999) 197 CLR 1 (HCA) [60].

[39] The differences between contract and tort with regard to remoteness of damage are challenged above ch 4, IV.

[40] Australian Capital Territory: Law Reform (Miscellaneous Provisions) Act 1955 s 10. New South Wales: Law Reform (Miscellaneous Provisions) Act 1965 s 8. Northern Territory: Law Reform (Miscellaneous Provisions) Act s 15. Queensland: Law Reform Act 1995 s 5. South Australia: Law Reform (Contributory Negligence and Apportionment of Liability) Act 2001 ss 3, 4(1)(b). Tasmania: Wrongs Act 1954 s 2. Victoria: Wrongs Act 1958 s 25. Western Australia: Law Reform (Contributory Negligence and Tortfeasors' Contribution) Act 1947 s 3A.

[41] Noted by TM FitzPatrick, 'Contributory Negligence and Contract—A Critical Reassessment' (2001) 30 *CLWR* 255, 261–65.

[42] Who expressly refrained from commenting on Neill LJ's statement in *The Shinjitsu Maru No 5* [1985] 1 WLR 1270, 1288, that the wording of the 1945 Act does not allow its application to any claim in contract: [1986] 2 All ER 488, 510.

[43] Since *Sayers* was silent on that issue, it was not binding on the Court of Appeal in *Vesta*, says TM FitzPatrick, 'Contributory Negligence and Contract—A Critical Reassessment' (2001) 30 *CLWR* 255, 263–64.

[44] [1989] AC 852 (CA) 865–66 (O'Connor LJ), 875 (Neill LJ).

[45] [1980] 2 NZLR 550, 555–56. See also NE Palmer and PJ Davies, 'Contributory Negligence and Breach of Contract—English and Australasian Attitudes Compared' (1980) 29 *ICLQ* 415, 445; AS Taylor, 'Contributory Negligence—A Defence to Breach of Contract?' (1986) 49 *MLR* 102, 107; GL Williams, *Joint Torts and Contributory Negligence* (London, 1951) 330, who alternatively suggests

The requirement in the first limb of the definition of 'fault' that the defendant be liable in tort is fulfilled.[46] It does no harm that the defendant is concurrently liable in contract. The requirement in the second limb that the claimant's conduct give rise to the contributory negligence defence at common law is also fulfilled because it does so in respect to the defendant's liability in tort. Such an interpretation is perfectly consistent with the wording of the 1945 Act. Another way of bringing category 3 into the ambit of the 1945 Act is the interpretation discussed in the context of category 2.[47]

The High Court of Australia in *Astley v Austrust Ltd* took a different view,[48] arguing that contributory negligence is no defence to a contractual action at common law, and pointing to the fact that the apportionment legislation under consideration provided that the claim 'shall not be defeated' by reason of contributory negligence, a phrase still to be found in the 1945 Act (UK). But this is no insurmountable obstacle to an application of the 1945 Act to a category 3 breach of contract. Some commentators suggest that contributory negligence defeats a contractual claim at common law whenever a concurrent tortious claim is so defeated.[49] In any event, the Act does not actually require that the claim be defeated at common law. Consequently, liability may indeed be apportioned in category 3 cases. A legislative clarification to this effect, as proposed by the Law Commission,[50] would nonetheless be welcome.

IV Breach of a Purely Contractual Duty of Care

Category 2 concerns the breach of a contractual duty of care *not* accompanied by a co-extensive duty in tort. Since it has been established that contract and tort may overlap, especially in the area of professional liability, and that pure economic loss may, under certain conditions, be recovered in negligence,[51] 'very few cases fall within category two and not category three'.[52] Prior to *Vesta* there

---

interpreting the word 'fault' in s 1(1) of the 1945 Act independently of its definition in s 4. But to ignore a statutory definition is problematic, which is why Williams' suggestion was rejected in *AS James Pty Ltd v CB Duncan* [1970] VR 705 (VSC) 726–27.

[46] Pritchard J adopted the common doctrine of applying the first limb of that definition to the defendant's liability and the second limb to contributory negligence: above ch 9, II.

[47] Below IV in this chapter.

[48] (1999) 197 CLR 1 (HCA) [80].

[49] Above I in this chapter.

[50] Law Commission, 'Contributory Negligence as a Defence in Contract' (Law Com No 219, 1993) [4.7]–[4.15], Appendix A, Draft Contributory Negligence Bill s 1(1).

[51] Above ch 1, III.

[52] A Burrows, *Remedies for Torts and Breach of Contract*, 3rd edn (Oxford, 2004) 143. According to R Halson, 'The protected contractual interests' in D Harris, D Campbell and R Halson, *Remedies in Contract and Tort*, 2nd edn (London, 2002) 87 fn 11, a category 2 case is the failure to act with reasonable care and skill contrary to the Supply of Goods and Services Act 1982 s 13.

had been conflicting first instance decisions as to whether the 1945 Act applies to category 2.[53] *Vesta* settled the controversy in favour of the non-applicability of the Act.[54]

This position is untenable.[55] Since a co-extensive duty of care in tort brings the case into category 3, which is subject to the 1945 Act, the applicability of the Act to the breach of a contractual duty of care depends on whether there is concurrent liability in tort. Accordingly, for the sole purpose of determining the applicability of the 1945 Act, *Vesta* forces both the court[56] and the parties to raise tort issues in what is meant to be a purely contractual action. 'Litigation for such a purpose seems wasteful'.[57] This effect could still be acceptable though if liability in tort were always easy to determine. But the opposite is true.[58] Particularly in the case of pure economic loss it is often difficult to predict whether a tortious duty of care will be recognised. *Vesta* chains the outcome in a contract action to these uncertainties in tort law.

Furthermore, as some commentators point out, *Vesta* encourages an 'odd reversal of roles'.[59] Imagine an action for the breach of a contractual duty of care where the claimant has contributed to the loss through her own carelessness. Now the defendant seeks an apportionment of liability on the ground of contributory negligence, and knows that the court can do so if there is concurrent liability in tort (category 3). Consequently, the defendant will argue that he is liable in tort too. In other words, the defendant will be keen on demonstrating the severity of his wrong in order to reduce his liability.[60] By the same token, the claimant seeks to avoid apportionment, and knows that apportionment is barred if there is no concurrent liability in tort (category 2). Consequently, the claimant will argue that the defendant is *not* liable in tort. In other words, the claimant will be keen on 'downgrading' the wrong in order to increase her damages. This is

---

[53] In favour of an application of the Act: *De Meza v Apple* [1974] 1 Lloyd's Rep 508, 519; the issue was not argued on appeal: [1975] 1 Lloyd's Rep 498 (CA). Perhaps also *Artingstoll v Hewen's Garages Ltd* [1973] RTR 197, 201. Against an application of the Act: *The Shinjitsu Maru No 5* [1985] 1 WLR 1270, 1288.

[54] *Raflatac Ltd v Eade* [1999] 1 Lloyd's Rep 506, 510; above II in this chapter.

[55] The opposite view is taken by PA Chandler, 'Contributory Negligence and Contract: Some Underlying Disparities' (1989) 40 *NILQ* 152, 174–75.

[56] B Coote, 'Contributory Negligence Reform and the Right to Rely on a Contract' [1992] *NZRL Rev* 313, 317.

[57] J Swanton, 'Contributory Negligence as a Defence to Actions for Breach of Contract' (1981) 55 *ALJ* 278, 285.

[58] Law Commission, 'Contributory Negligence as a Defence in Contract' (Law Com No 219, 1993) [3.27].

[59] A Burrows, *Remedies for Torts and Breach of Contract*, 3rd edn (Oxford, 2004) 141; A Burrows, *Understanding the Law of Obligations: Essays on Contract, Tort and Restitution* (Oxford, 1998) 150. See also PL Newman, 'The Law Reform Act 1945 and Breaches of Contract' (1990) 53 *MLR* 201, 203. In the view of PA Chandler, 'Contributory Negligence and Contract: Some Underlying Disparities' (1989) 40 *NILQ* 152, 167–70, the problem should be solved by not applying the 1945 Act even in category 3 if the action is in substance contractual.

[60] This effectively happened in the Scottish case *Deans v Glasgow Housing Association Ltd* [2009] Hous LR 82 [17]–[18].

odd indeed. To avoid the oddity, categories 2 and 3 must be treated identically as to whether apportionment is available. Since the availability of apportionment in category 3 is firmly established, for good reasons,[61] apportionment must also be allowed in category 2.

The Law Commission has proposed legislation to this effect.[62] New legislation is certainly desirable but for the foreseeable future we have to manage with the 1945 Act. Does the Act allow the desirable apportionment in category 2? Again, this depends on how the definition of 'fault' in section 4 is interpreted.[63] The initial word 'negligence' may be regarded as not being qualified by the phrase 'other act or omission which ...', and may be understood as lack of care as opposed to the tort of negligence. Under this interpretation, any careless breach of contract—and category 2 concerns careless breach—counts as 'fault' on the defendant's part, and any careless contribution to the damage counts as 'fault' on the claimant's part.[64]

If one takes the view that only the second limb of the relative clause defines the claimant's 'fault', it becomes relevant whether the claimant's conduct 'would, apart from this Act, give rise to the defence of contributory negligence'. If this is understood as requiring that the claimant's conduct give rise to the common law defence *in the particular cause of action*,[65] the condition is not satisfied since contributory negligence affords no defence at common law in category 2 cases.[66] However, the second limb may be understood more broadly as requiring only that the claimant's conduct be of the sort that at common law gives rise to the contributory negligence defence if the claimant were suing for a cause of action to which this defence clearly applies, for instance negligence.[67] On this interpretation, the 1945 Act may be applied in category 2 cases.

V Strict Contractual Liability – The Present Law

Category 1 comprises cases where contractual liability does not depend on fault, in other words, where a strict contractual obligation such as the obligation to pay

---

[61] Above III in this chapter.

[62] Law Commission, 'Contributory Negligence as a Defence in Contract' (Law Com No 219, 1993) [4.7]–[4.15], Appendix A, Draft Contributory Negligence Bill, s 1(1).

[63] Above ch 9, II.

[64] *Mouat v Clarke Boyce* [1992] 2 NZLR 559 (NZCA) 564–65 (Cooke P); NH Andrews, 'No Apportionment for Contributory Negligence in Contract' [1986] *CLJ* 8, 9–10.

[65] In favour of such a requirement: *The Shinjitsu Maru No 5* [1985] 1 WLR 1270, 1288; NE Palmer and PJ Davies, 'Contributory Negligence and Breach of Contract—English and Australasian Attitudes Compared' (1980) 29 *ICLQ* 415, 417–18.

[66] Above I in this chapter.

[67] A Burrows, *Remedies for Torts and Breach of Contract*, 3rd edn (Oxford, 2004) 135, 138. See also above ch 9, II.

money or to deliver goods is breached.[68] It has long been held that the 1945 Act does not apply in such a situation.[69] This position is said[70] to have been affirmed in *Vesta* and has clearly been affirmed in subsequent cases, most prominently in *Barclays Bank plc v Fairclough Building Ltd (No 1)*.[71]

The defendant contractor undertook, for a sum of some £130,000, to clean and treat the asbestos roofs of the plaintiff's warehouses. In breach of the Control of Asbestos at Work Regulations 1987, the defendant's subcontractor cleaned the roofs with high-pressure water without taking essential precautions. This caused heavy asbestos contaminations in the buildings. Extensive remedial works were necessary at a cost of some £4m. In the plaintiff's action for breach of contract, the judge found that the defendant had failed to exercise reasonable care and skill. He also found that the plaintiff should have supervised the work so as to prevent the defendant's fault, and accordingly reduced the damages by 40 per cent.

The Court of Appeal awarded full damages. Leaving open whether the plaintiff had in fact been at fault, Beldam LJ, giving the leading judgment, held the 1945 Act inapplicable[72] on the ground that the defendant's liability was one of strict liability, not merely failure to take care,[73] so that the case fell within category 1. According to a term in the contract, the defendant's workmanship had to be the best of its kind. This term, Beldam LJ said, required a standard to be achieved, not only reasonable care to try to attain the standard. Another instance of strict liability was found in the breach of the contractual term requiring the defendant to comply with any statute, statutory instrument or regulation applicable to the works.

The defendant, it should also be noted, tried to render the 1945 Act applicable by asserting concurrent liability in tort (negligence, nuisance and/or trespass). While Beldam LJ flatly rejected any such liability, Simon Brown LJ held the Act inapplicable even on the assumption that tortious liability did exist. Although he considered this case covered by the language of the Act,[74] he found an implied contracting-out: 'there seem to me compelling reasons why the contract, even assuming it is silent as to apportionment, should be construed as excluding the operation of the Act of 1945'.[75] Otherwise, he said, the defendant would benefit

---

[68] See the cases cited by the Law Commission, 'Contributory Negligence as a Defence in Contract' (Law Com No 219, 1993) [3.24] fns 65–69.

[69] *Quinn v Burch Bros (Builders) Ltd* [1966] 2 QB 370, 377–81; *Basildon DC v JE Lesser (Properties) Ltd* [1985] QB 839; *The Shinjitsu Maru No 5* [1985] 1 WLR 1270, 1288.

[70] *Banque Keyser Ullmann SA v Skandia (UK) Insurance Co Ltd* [1990] 1 QB 665 (CA) 720–21; above II in this chapter.

[71] [1995] QB 214 (CA). Further *Bank of Nova Scotia v Hellenic Mutual War Risks Association (Bermuda) Ltd (The Good Luck)* [1988] 1 Lloyd's Rep 514, 555 (Hobhouse J); [1990] 1 QB 818 (CA) 904.

[72] [1995] QB 214 (CA) 230.

[73] ibid 223.

[74] ibid 232.

[75] ibid 233.

from an assertion of his own liability in tort while the claimant would seek to exonerate him.[76] Consequently, the 1945 Act never applies to the breach of a strict contractual obligation even where the defendant is also liable in tort.[77]

Does the language of the 1945 Act bar its application to all category 1 cases? It has been shown that where a contract-breaker is concurrently liable in tort, the tort aspect of the case may be said to 'draw' the contract aspect into the ambit of the Act.[78] It has further been shown that the word 'negligence' in the definition of 'fault' may be interpreted as encompassing the breach of a purely contractual duty of care.[79] One could go a step further and include into 'negligence' also the negligent breach of a strict contractual obligation.[80] Accordingly, the wording of the Act allows its application to the breach of a strict contractual obligation where the contract-breaker is also liable in tort[81] or has been at fault. Where neither is the case, and this will be the usual situation in category 1, it is impossible to bring the facts within the language of the Act even where the claimant has broken a duty of care towards the defendant.[82]

VI Need for Apportionment in Cases of Strict Liability

The unavailability of apportionment in the bulk of category 1 cases would not be alarming if there were no practical need for it. But there is. Desperate not to let the claimant get away with her contribution to the loss, the courts occasionally resort to causation, remoteness or mitigation doctrine. But since the claimant

---

[76] ibid. The same paradox looms in category 2 cases: above IV in this chapter.

[77] Law Commission, 'Contributory Negligence as a Defence in Contract' (Law Com No 219, 1993) [3.29]. This view had already been taken, without discussing the issue, by in *Banque Keyser Ullmann SA v Skandia (UK) Insurance Co Ltd* [1990] 1 QB 665, 720–21 (Steyn J). The opposite view seems to have been taken *obiter* in the pre-*Vesta* case *Vacwell Engineering Co Ltd v BDH Chemicals Ltd* [1971] 1 QB 88, 110.

[78] Above III in this ch.

[79] Above IV in this ch.

[80] Against an application of the Act in that situation: *Quinn v Burch Bros (Builders) Ltd* [1966] 2 QB 370, 380–81; NE Palmer and PJ Davies, 'Contributory Negligence and Breach of Contract—English and Australasian Attitudes Compared' (1980) 29 *ICLQ* 415, 426; J Swanton, 'Contributory Negligence as a Defence to Actions for Breach of Contract' (1981) 55 *ALJ* 278, 287.

[81] An application of the Act to that case is supported by NE Palmer and PJ Davies, 'Contributory Negligence and Breach of Contract—English and Australasian Attitudes Compared' (1980) 29 *ICLQ* 415, 446–47. For the opposite view, which concedes the linguistic possibility of applying the Act, see *Barclays Bank plc v Fairclough Building Ltd (No 1)* [1995] QB 214 (CA) 233 (Simon Brown LJ); G Davis and J Knowler, 'Astley v Austrust Ltd' (1999) 23 *MULR* 795, 811–12; TM FitzPatrick, 'Contributory Negligence and Contract—A Critical Reassessment' (2001) 30 *CLWR* 255, 266 ff; J Swanton, 'Contributory Negligence as a Defence to Actions for Breach of Contract' (1981) 55 *ALJ* 278, 288.

[82] Apportionment in the latter case is called for by B Coote, 'Contributory Negligence Reform and the Right to Rely on a Contract' [1992] *NZRL Rev* 313, 317–19.

gets either all or nothing under these concepts, they do not obviate the need for an apportionment regime,[83] as will now be demonstrated.

A   Resorting to Causation Doctrine

Since causation is a doctrine independent of contributory negligence, one would not expect the doctrine to vary depending on whether or not apportionment by virtue of contributory negligence is available. However, the courts have displayed a greater willingness to regard the chain of causation as being broken by the claimant's unreasonable behaviour in circumstances in which the 1945 Act is not applicable.[84]

An example is *Quinn v Burch Bros (Builders) Ltd*.[85] When the defendants, in breach of contract, failed to supply the plaintiff with a stepladder he made do with a folded trestle that was not footed. He fell to the ground and was injured. Paull J considered the use of the trestle unreasonable and said: 'Apart from the Act of 1945, a man's own contributory negligence breaks the [causal] link in tort as well as in contract'.[86] Since it was a case of strict contractual liability where Paull J, anticipating *Vesta*, held the 1945 Act inapplicable, he considered the chain of causation broken and denied the claim. He clarified that he would have apportioned liability under the 1945 Act if the action had been in tort.[87] In *Sole v WJ Hallt Ltd*, where damages were apportioned in a case of concurrent liability in contract and tort, Swanwick J remarked that had the action been in contract alone, he would have felt compelled by *Quinn* to regard the chain of causation as being broken by the plaintiff's contributory negligence.[88]

Unreasonable behaviour on the claimant's part will not, however, break the chain of causation in every single case that lies outside the ambit of the 1945 Act. In *The Good Luck*,[89] for instance, the judge held the plaintiffs one-third to blame for their loss but could not apportion liability as the relevant breach of contract fell into category 1. He still found the breach had caused the loss, a decision affirmed by the appellate courts.[90]

---

[83]   TM FitzPatrick, 'Contributory Negligence and Contract—A Critical Reassessment' (2001) 30 *CLWR* 412, 428. With regard to categories 2 and 3 also Law Commission, 'Contributory Negligence as a Defence in Contract' (Law Com No 219, 1993) [3.8], [3.15], [3.18], [3.21]. The opposite view is taken by NE Palmer and PJ Davies, 'Contributory Negligence and Breach of Contract—English and Australasian Attitudes Compared' (1980) 29 *ICLQ* 415, 447–51.

[84]   As noted by the Law Commission, ibid [3.10].

[85]   [1966] 2 QB 370. See also *Lexmead (Basingstoke) Ltd v Lewis* [1982] AC 225, 277; *Arkin v Borchard Lines Ltd* [2003] 2 Lloyd's Rep 225, 310.

[86]   [1966] 2 QB 370, 378.

[87]   ibid 375. The decision was upheld on appeal without indication as to what the outcome would have been had the action been in tort: ibid 381 (CA) 388 ff.

[88]   [1973] QB 574, 582.

[89]   *Bank of Nova Scotia v Hellenic Mutual War Risks Association (Bermuda) Ltd (The Good Luck)* [1988] 1 Lloyd's Rep 514, 554–55; above II in this chapter.

[90]   [1990] 1 QB 818 (CA) 903–904; [1992] 1 AC 233 (HL) 266–67.

Quinn and *The Good Luck* demonstrate the all-or-nothing effect of causation doctrine. Either the claimant's conduct does not break the chain of causation and she gets all the damages (as in *The Good Luck*), or the claimant's conduct does break the chain of causation and she gets nothing at all (as in *Quinn*). For this reason, causation doctrine is no adequate substitute for apportionment.[91]

The unsatisfactory situation of awarding either all or nothing prompted an apportionment of liability *as a matter of causation* in *Tennant Radiant Heat Ltd v Warrington Development Corp.*[92] Due to want of maintenance the roof of a leased warehouse collapsed, which damaged the building as well as the lessee's goods. Owner and lessee sued each other for damages. The owner was found liable in negligence and nuisance; the lessee was found liable for breach of a repairing covenant but not in tort. The Court of Appeal held the 1945 Act inapplicable to either claim or counterclaim on the ground that since the lessee was only guilty of breaking a strict contractual obligation, the conduct of neither party would at common law give rise to a defence of contributory negligence. Nevertheless, the Court felt able to apportion responsibility by having regard to the extent to which each party's failure to maintain the roof had caused the damage. Liability was apportioned as 90 per cent to the owner and 10 per cent to the lessee. This, the Court admitted, was exactly the result the 1945 Act would have produced.

Can causation doctrine fill the gap left by the 1945 Act as *Tennant* suggests?[93] Some say that causation doctrine is only able to determine a cause of the loss but not to weigh various causes against each other, so that an apportionment on the basis of causation alone must always lead to equal shares.[94] This critique may go too far. In distributing loss under the 1945 Act, the courts have regard to both the blameworthiness and the causative potency of each party's conduct,[95] the latter being described as the dangerousness of an act according to its statistical tendency to produce harm.[96] Hence the courts do distinguish different degrees of

---

[91] TM FitzPatrick, 'Contributory Negligence and Contract—A Critical Reassessment' (2001) 30 *CLWR* 412, 428; Scottish Law Commission, 'Report on Remedies for Breach of Contract' (Scot Law Com No 174, 1999) [4.1], [4.8], [4.10]. For categories 2 and 3 also Law Commission, 'Contributory Negligence as a Defence in Contract' (Law Com No 219, 1993) [3.12], [3.15].

[92] [1988] 11 EG 71; [1988] 1 EGLR 41 (CA). The appeal was heard only days after the Court of Appeal's decision in *Vesta*. *Tennant* was followed in *W Lamb Ltd v J Jarvis & Sons plc* (1998) 60 Con LR 1, where it could not be established whether the damage had been caused by the plaintiff's fault or the defendant's fault or both.

[93] Affirmatively PL Newman, 'The Law Reform Act 1945 and Breaches of Contract' (1990) 53 *MLR* 201, 203. Probably also KR Handley, 'Reduction of Damages Awards' in PD Finn (ed), *Essays on Damages* (Sydney, 1992) 125. An application of the *Tennant* principle where both parties are in breach of contract is suggested by PA Chandler, 'Contributory Negligence and Contract: Some Underlying Disparities' (1989) 40 *NILQ* 152, 176–77; E Peel, *Treitel on the Law of Contract*, 12th edn (London, 2007) [20–111].

[94] S Chapman, 'Apportionment of Liability Between Tortfeasors' (1948) 64 *Law Quarterly Review* 26, 28. Sympathising with this argument T Hervey, '"Responsibility" Under the Civil Liability (Contribution) Act 1978' (1979) 129 *New Law Journal* 509, 510; Law Commission, 'Contributory Negligence as a Defence in Contract' (Law Com No 219, 1993) [3.14], [4.19].

[95] Above ch 9, VI.

[96] HLA Hart and T Honoré, *Causation in the Law*, 2nd edn (Oxford, 1985) 233.

causation. What defeats the *Tennant* concept nonetheless is that a consideration of the degrees of causation *alone*[97] neglects the mental attitude and moral culpability of the parties,[98] which may lead to unjust results.[99] Where a car crash is caused by both the driver's excessive speeding and the previous failure by the garage to rectify a steering fault, the actions of each side may be of equal causative potency but the driver bears greater culpability.[100] And the culpability of a nurse who grossly negligently puts poison into a food jar from which the patient eats may far outweigh the culpability of the doctor who subsequently fails the difficult task of diagnosing food poisoning.[101]

B   Resorting to Remoteness Doctrine

Sometimes the claimant's unreasonable conduct is addressed by qualifying the ensuing damage as being too remote.[102] Take, for instance, *Berryman v Hounslow LBC*.[103] The plaintiff lived on the fifth floor in the defendant council's block of flats, in which there were two lifts. While one lift was out of service for refurbishment, the plaintiff descended with her two children in the other lift, and returned shortly afterwards with the children and five bags of shopping. Neither lift worked. She carried the bags upstairs one at a time, having her baby constantly on her hip. As a result of the strain, she suffered a slipped disc. The council was found to have breached its contractual duty to keep the lifts in reasonable repair—it was left open whether there was also liability under the Occupiers' Liability Act 1957[104]—but the Court of Appeal considered the injury unforeseeable and thus too remote 'given that anyone climbing the stairs would be likely to lessen the load, to take it in stages, to take their time and/or to get

---

[97]   As in the context of contribution between two tortfeasors in *Smith v Bray* (1939) 56 TLR 200; *Collins v Hertfordshire County Council* [1947] KB 598, 624. Today, contribution depends also on blameworthiness: *Randolph v Tuck* [1962] 1 QB 175, 185.

[98]   HLA Hart and T Honoré, *Causation in the Law*, 2nd edn (Oxford, 1985) 234.

[99]   'To attempt to apportion damages by reference to degree of participation in the chain of causation is a hopeless enterprise, for it has no necessary connection with anything that would appeal to the ordinary person as being just and equitable': G Williams, 'The Two Negligent Servants' (1954) 17 *MLR* 66, 69. Approvingly quoted by the Law Commission, 'Contributory Negligence as a Defence in Contract'. (Law Com No 219, 1993) [4.20] fn 64. Note that the Court of Appeal has required 'substantial argument' for a reapplication of *Tennants*: *Bank of Nova Scotia v Hellenic Mutual War Risks Association (Bermuda) Ltd (The Good Luck)* [1990] 1 QB 818 (CA) 904.

[100]   Example by the Law Commission, ibid [4.20].

[101]   Example by G Williams, 'The Two Negligent Servants' (1954) 17 *MLR* 66, 69.

[102]   Whether the aggrieved party's unreasonable behaviour rendered the damage too remote was discussed, eg, in *Mowbray v Merryweather* [1895] 2 QB 640 (CA); *The Kate* [1935] P 100. In *Youell v Bland Welch & Co Ltd (No 2)* [1990] 2 Lloyd's Rep 431, 462, Phillips J said that the claimant's negligent failure to detect the breach constitutes contributory negligence, but the loss is too remote if it is not reasonably foreseeable that the claimant will remain ignorant of the breach. The present remoteness test in contract is considered in ch 3.

[103]   [1997] PIQR P83 (CA).

[104]   Since the contractual obligation was strict, concurrent liability in tort would not, in any event, have transported the case from category 1 into category 3: above V in this chapter.

help'.[105] In other words, it was not foreseeable that there could be unreasonable behaviour on the plaintiff's part leading to serious injury.

But if it were really the case that a wrongdoer does not have to reckon with unreasonable behaviour on the victim's part, contributory negligence would always render the damage too remote[106] and the 1945 Act would never come into play. There are two further reasons[107] why contributory negligence cannot adequately be dealt with under the guise of remoteness. First, remoteness doctrine considers what the parties contemplated when making the contract[108] and not their comparative fault in causing the damage. Secondly, remoteness doctrine compels an all-or-nothing decision rather than an apportionment of liability. The damage is either too remote or not. True, the claimant may recover the lower amount of loss that the parties did contemplate[109] but, again, the extent of liability in that case depends on the parties' contemplation at the time of the contract and not their comparative blameworthiness in causing the damage.

The superiority of apportionment to an all-or-nothing decision under remoteness doctrine is illustrated by *Sayers v Harlow UDC* mentioned earlier.[110] While the judge did indeed consider the loss too remote on the ground that the toilet visitor's unreasonable attempt to climb over the door had not been foreseeable, the Court of Appeal took a different view[111] and was thus able to allocate three quarters of the loss to the authority whose failure to keep the toilet lock in good repair had triggered the accident. In *Berryman*, too, it would have been more just to let the council bear a part of the plaintiff's loss, provided that the plaintiff's injury is regarded as falling within the protective scope of the council's duty to keep the lifts in reasonable repair.[112]

C   Resorting to Mitigation Doctrine

Where a claimant, knowing that a tort or breach of contract has been committed against her, increases the ensuing loss through unreasonable behaviour, she cannot recover damages for the extra loss which reasonable behaviour would

---

[105]   [1997] PIQR P83 (CA) P89 (Henry LJ, with whom the other members of the bench agreed).

[106]   In *Bank of Nova Scotia v Hellenic Mutual War Risks Association (Bermuda) Ltd (The Good Luck)* [1992] 1 AC 233 (HL), the defendant argued that the plaintiff's unreasonable behaviour rendered the loss too remote as it had not been in the contemplation of the parties. Lord Goff said (at 267–68) that this was an issue of causation rather than remoteness.

[107]   Noted by TM FitzPatrick, 'Contributory Negligence and Contract—A Critical Reassessment' (2001) 30 *CLWR* 412, 428. For categories 2 and 3 also Law Commission, 'Contributory Negligence as a Defence in Contract' (Law Com No 219, 1993) [3.17].

[108]   Above ch 3.

[109]   *Cory v Thames Ironworks and Shipbuilding Co Ltd* (1868) LR 3 QB 181; *Victoria Laundry (Windsor) Ltd v Newman Industries Ltd* [1949] 2 KB 528 (CA) 543 (above ch 3, II).

[110]   [1958] 1 WLR 623 (CA); above III in this chapter.

[111]   [1958] 1 WLR 623 (CA) 625–28, 630–31, 632–33.

[112]   The view that the plaintiff's injury fell outside the scope of the council's duty is taken by A Tettenborn, 'Hadley v Baxendale Foreseeability: a Principle Beyond Its Sell-by Date?' (2007) 23 *Journal of Contract Law* 120, 141.

have avoided.[113] This 'duty to mitigate' has been invoked to reduce a contract-breaker's liability where apportionment by virtue of contributory negligence was unavailable. An example is *Schering Agrochemicals Ltd v Resibel NV SA*.[114]

Schering produced and bottled highly inflammable chemicals. Resibel supplied Schering with equipment that heat-sealed caps onto bottles. The equipment contained a safety device whose purpose was to switch off the heat sealer and sound an alarm if a bottle was stationary under the heat sealer for too long and thereby exposed to excessive heat. On 30 September 1987, more than one month after the equipment had been put into operation, a disastrous fire broke out in Schering's factory owing to a defect in the safety device of the heat sealer. Resibel admitted being in breach of contract for delivering equipment of unsatisfactory quality, contrary to section 14(3) of the Sale of Goods Act 1979. Now the twist in the case was that on 8 September two of Schering's workers noticed that the safety device did not switch off the heat sealer when it should have done. This incident, which caused no damage, was reported to a supervisor who took no action. If Schering had investigated the incident, the defect in the safety device would have been discovered and the fire prevented.

Referring to Schering's failure to investigate this incident, Resibel denied full liability. Since Resibel was in breach of a strict contractual obligation, Hobhouse J, applying his own concept set out in *Vesta*, denied apportionment by virtue of contributory negligence.[115] He also held that neither causation nor remoteness doctrine could assist Resibel. However, he saw a failure on Schering's part to mitigate the loss once its employees became aware of Resibel's breach of contract, which was on 8 September. He accordingly limited Schering's damages to those losses that could not have been avoided even if the incident of 8 September had been investigated and the fire prevented. Schering recovered only the cost that would have been incurred by an investigation of the incident and the consequential temporary production stop.

The Court of Appeal upheld that decision.[116] However, Nolan LJ observed that Resibel was fortunate that the 1945 Act could not be applied, for he would have preferred an apportionment of responsibility to an unsatisfactory all-or-nothing decision under causation, remoteness or mitigation doctrine.[117] His remark highlights that the duty to mitigate, like the concepts of causation and remoteness, is no adequate substitute for an application of the 1945 Act because it

---

[113] eg *Peters v East Midlands SHA* [2009] EWCA Civ 145, [2009] 3 WLR 737 [33]; H McGregor, *McGregor on Damages*, 18th edn (London, 2009) [7–004], [7–014]–[7–090]; Law Commission, 'Contributory Negligence as a Defence in Contract' (Law Com No 219, 1993) [3.19]–[3.21].

[114] 4 June 1991, unreported (Hobhouse J); 26 November 1992, unreported (CA).

[115] 4 June 1991, unreported. He left open whether Resibel was also liable in negligence. Such liability would not have moved the case from category 1 to category 3: above V in this chapter.

[116] 26 November 1992, unreported (CA). However, Scott LJ held mitigation doctrine inapplicable and based his decision instead on causation doctrine, whereas Purchas LJ and Nolan LJ took the view that the judge's decision could be upheld on either ground.

[117] An apportionment of liability in the *Schering* scenario is also preferred by A Burrows, *Remedies for Torts and Breach of Contract*, 3rd edn (Oxford, 2004) 142.

compels an all-or-nothing decision.[118] True, the mitigation principle bars recovery only for the loss avoidable through reasonable behaviour. But in relation to *that* loss, it is all or nothing.[119] Another reason why mitigation doctrine cannot fill the gap left by the 1945 Act is the fact that the doctrine does not deal with the claimant's behaviour prior to the defendant's wrong.

Schering also demonstrates the illogicality of separating contributory negligence and the duty to mitigate. Both concepts address the claimant's contribution to the loss through unreasonable behaviour, but the ambit of the concepts differs. While the victim of any (common law) wrong is under a duty to mitigate the loss, the 1945 Act is not applied to all torts[120] and cannot be applied to all breaches of contract.[121] The difference in the ambit of the two concepts means that the effect of the claimant's unreasonable conduct on the defendant's liability may depend on where the demarcation line between the two concepts lies. If the duty to mitigate arose only once damage has occurred, Resibel's liability in *Schering* would have been unaffected as no damage occurred before 30 September. Hobhouse J was only able to limit Resibel's liability because he recognised a duty to mitigate from the time the aggrieved party becomes aware of the breach[122] irrespective of whether damage has already occurred.

Setting the demarcation line between mitigation and contributory negligence at a time prior to the occurrence of the loss is, however, not possible in torts only actionable on proof of damage.[123] Here it is illogical that the relevance of the claimant's unreasonable behaviour should depend on the coincidence of when the damage occurs.[124] Consequently, as Glanville Williams has suggested, the two concepts should no longer be separated but the duty to mitigate should be assimilated into a broader concept of contributory negligence.[125] This would be

---

[118] Law Commission, 'Contributory Negligence as a Defence in Contract' (Law Com No 219, 1993) [3.21] (for categories 2 and 3).

[119] A Porat, 'Contributory Negligence in Contract Law: Toward a Principled Approach' (1994) 28 *UBC Law Rev* 141, 159.

[120] An application to all torts is advocated above ch 9, II.

[121] Above V in this chapter.

[122] Whether the aggrieved party's unreasonable failure to detect the breach is an issue of contributory negligence or mitigation doctrine is controversial. In favour of contributory negligence: *Youell v Bland Welch & Co Ltd (No 2)* [1990] 2 Lloyd's Rep 431, 462; A Porat, 'Contributory Negligence in Contract Law: Toward a Principled Approach' (1994) 28 *UBC Law Rev* 141, 166–69; J Swanton, 'Contributory Negligence as a Defence to Actions for Breach of Contract' (1981) 55 *ALJ* 278, 287. In favour of mitigation doctrine: *Toepfer v Warinco AG* [1978] 2 Lloyd's Rep 569, 578; A Burrows, 'Contributory Negligence in Contract: Ammunition for the Law Commission' (1993) 109 *LQR* 175, 176, who calls this the majority view; DR Harris 'The Remedies of the Buyer' in AG Guest (gen ed), *Benjamin's Sale of Goods*, 7th edn (London, 2006) [17–060]; E Peel, *Treitel on the Law of Contract*, 12th edn (London, 2007) [20–098]; GL Williams, *Joint Torts and Contributory Negligence* (London, 1951) 290.

[123] B Coote, 'Contributory Negligence Reform and the Right to Rely on a Contract' [1992] *NZRL Rev* 313, 316.

[124] Vivid illustrations are provided by GL Williams, *Joint Torts and Contributory Negligence* (London, 1951) 288–90.

[125] ibid 291.

consistent with the wording of the 1945 Act.[126] It would, of course, necessitate a harmonisation of the ambit. This can only be done by recognising that contributory negligence, just like mitigation, is a doctrine relevant to all wrongs.

VII   Defensibility of Denying Apportionment in Cases of Strict Liability

A   No Duty to Supervise the Defendant

What are the arguments in support of the present position in category 1? One argument is that if the claimant's unreasonable behaviour was allowed to affect strict contractual liability, the claimant would come under a duty to supervise the defendant's performance, which would undermine the strict nature of the latter's obligation.[127] The Law Commission is particularly concerned about the reliability upon the warranty given by a seller of goods.[128] It provides the examples of a farmer who suffers a car accident as a result of a defective coupling,[129] a restaurant owner who buys a defective deep fat fryer that causes a fire,[130] and a builder who falls from a step-ladder because a rung is badly cracked.[131] In all these scenarios the buyer would have discovered the defect had he checked the product before use. Nevertheless, says the Law Commission, the buyer was entitled to rely on the seller's warranty.

However, the Commission concedes that where the claimant is a consumer, 'it is likely that the court would, in any event, find that it was reasonable, and not contributorily negligent, for him to rely on the defendant's warranty'.[132] The Commission is further confident that in category 2 and 3 cases no duty to supervise the defendant's performance will usually be imposed onto the claimant, consumer or otherwise, as the court will respect the allocation of risk in the

---

[126]   ibid 293–94. In *The Calliope* [1970] P 172, 182–83, Brandon J said *obiter* that the wording of the 1945 Act allows its application to the claimant's behaviour subsequent to the casualty.

[127]   PA Chandler, 'Contributory Negligence and Contract: Some Underlying Disparities' (1989) 40 *NILQ* 152, 172.

[128]   'If the defendant commits himself to a strict obligation regardless of fault, the plaintiff should be able to rely on him fulfilling his obligation and should not have to take precautions against the possibility that a breach might occur': Law Commission, 'Contributory Negligence as a Defence in Contract' (Law Com No 219, 1993) [4.2]; citation omitted.

[129]   ibid [4.3]. The example is based on *Lexmead (Basingstoke) Ltd v Lewis* [1982] AC 225 (HL).

[130]   Law Commission, 'Contributory Negligence as a Defence in Contract' (Law Com No 219, 1993) [4.4].

[131]   ibid.

[132]   ibid [4.3]. Note that the claimant's knowledge of the defects will render the whole warranty ineffective: *Ingham v Emes* [1955] 2 QB 366 (CA); *Lexmead (Basingstoke) Ltd v Lewis* [1982] AC 225 (HL) 276–77.

contract.[133] What the Commission suggests then is that, if contributory negligence were generally relevant in contract, the courts would discriminate between a category 2 or 3 claimant, and a category 1 consumer-claimant on the one hand and a category 1 business-claimant on the other. Is this conceivable? Authority suggests otherwise.[134] To be safe, a statute that generally permits an apportionment in contract could expressly provide that the parties' allocation of risk shall be respected. Indeed, the draft bill proposed by the Law Commission (in relation to categories 2 and 3) does so[135] by obliging the court to 'have regard to the nature of the contract and the mutual obligations of the parties'.[136]

Moreover, any fear of the claimant coming under a duty to supervise is no justification for withholding apportionment where the claimant's fault consists in something other than a failure to check on the defendant's performance.[137] In the Law Commission's examples, the farmer may increase the damage by failing to wear a seat belt,[138] the restaurant owner may increase the damage by not having any fire extinguishers, and the builder's inability to hold himself on the stepladder when the rung gives way may result from him being drunk. In all these scenarios it would be unjust to shift the whole loss onto the seller of the defective product. The mitigation principle which the Law Commission says may sometimes step in for apportionment[139] cannot help in these scenarios because, as the Law Commission recognises,[140] it requires the claimant's awareness of the defendant's breach. Causation or remoteness doctrine may help[141] but compels an all-or-nothing decision.[142] In the three scenarios it would be equally unjust to shift the whole loss onto the buyer.

---

[133] 'In practice, we would not expect a court to hold that failure to supervise constituted a failure by the plaintiff to take reasonable care of his own interests unless it was very clear in the circumstances that he should have done so': Law Commission, 'Contributory Negligence as a Defence in Contract' (Law Com No 219, 1993) [4.13].

[134] eg *Mowbray v Merryweather* [1895] 2 QB 640 (CA), where the failure by the plaintiff stevedores to check the defective chain supplied by the defendant was considered irrelevant on the ground that they had been entitled to rely on the defendant's warranty. The principle was extended to the covenant to keep a thing in repair in *The Kate* [1935] P 100.

[135] This is at least the Law Commission's expectation: Law Commission, 'Contributory Negligence as a Defence in Contract' (Law Com No 219, 1993) [4.29].

[136] ibid Appendix A, Draft Contributory Negligence Bill s 1(3)(b). Similar proposals by the New Zealand Law Commission are reported by B Coote, 'Contributory Negligence Reform and the Right to Rely on a Contract' [1992] *NZRL Rev* 313, 320–21.

[137] TM FitzPatrick, 'Contributory Negligence and Contract—A Critical Reassessment' (2001) 30 *CLWR* 412, 430–31.

[138] ibid.

[139] Law Commission, 'Contributory Negligence as a Defence in Contract' (Law Com No 219, 1993) [4.2].

[140] ibid [3.19]–[3.20], [4.2].

[141] For causation see E Peel, *Treitel on the Law of Contract*, 12th edn (London, 2007) [20–108].

[142] For the unsuitability of causation, remoteness and mitigation doctrine to deal with contributory negligence see above VI in this chapter.

B   Distribution of Blame is Difficult

The Law Commission further argues that 'where the defendant is in breach of a strict contractual duty, fault is immaterial, and it would be difficult and inappropriate to compare his blameworthiness with that of the plaintiff'.[143] Why would it be inappropriate? The 'innocent' contract-breaker ought not to be in a worse position than the culpable one. Moreover, a category 1 contract-breaker is not necessarily 'innocent'. Although in that case liability does not depend on fault, the individual defendant may actually have been at fault. The Law Commission opposes an apportionment even in that case, describing it again as 'inappropriate' to consider the defendant's blameworthiness where it is irrelevant to his liability.[144] But even if it is irrelevant to his liability in principle, it may well be relevant to the question of which party bears more blame for causing the damage.

And why would it be difficult to compare an 'innocent' defendant with a 'culpable' claimant? Such a comparison has to be made in the case of strict liability in tort. Indeed, the Consumer Protection Act 1987, which imposes strict liability for defective products,[145] expressly provides for an application of the 1945 Act. In those situations, it is suggested, responsibility should be allocated according to the degree to which each party has departed from the standard imposed by law.[146] The same method can be applied to a category 1 breach of contract.[147] An analogy to tort has been rejected, however, on two grounds.

The first ground is the fact that a contract-breaker, unlike a tortfeasor, had the opportunity to negotiate with the other party for an apportionment on account of contributory negligence.[148] This is true, but it is equally true that, subject to the unfair-terms legislation, parties entering a contract may exclude apportionment where apportionment is the default set by law.[149] The issue is what the default ought to be.

---

[143] Law Commission, 'Contributory Negligence as a Defence in Contract' (Law Com No 219, 1993) [3.24]; citation omitted. Concurring G Davis and J Knowler, 'Astley v Austrust Ltd' (1999) 23 *MULR* 795, 812. Similarly NH Andrews, 'No Apportionment for Contributory Negligence in Contract' [1986] *CLJ* 8, 10.

[144] Law Commission, 'Contributory Negligence as a Defence in Contract' (Law Com No 219, 1993) [3.24] fn 70.

[145] Since s 4(1)(e) of the Act excludes liability if the defect was undiscoverable according to the scientific and technical knowledge at the relevant time, a difference to strict contractual liability is seen by the Law Commission, 'Contributory Negligence as a Defence in Contract' (Law Com No 219, 1993) [3.40]. But there is a greater difference to fault-based liability as a fault by the individual producer is not required.

[146] Above ch 9, VI.

[147] An apportionment 'in light of all the circumstances of the case' is suggested by TM FitzPatrick, 'Contributory Negligence and Contract—A Critical Reassessment' (2001) 30 *CLWR* 412, 432.

[148] Law Commission, 'Contributory Negligence as a Defence in Contract' (Law Com No 219, 1993) [3.25]; *Astley v Austrust Ltd* (1999) 197 CLR 1 (HCA) [86]; PA Chandler, 'Contributory Negligence and Contract: Some Underlying Disparities' (1989) 40 *NILQ* 152, 174.

[149] Scottish Law Commission, 'Report on Remedies for Breach of Contract' (Scot Law Com No 174, 1999) [4.7]. The Law Commission for England and Wales recommends a statutory clarification

The second ground for rejecting an equal treatment of contract and tort is the fact that the contractual claimant, unlike the tortious one, has given consideration for the defendant's promise.[150] True again, but that does not mean that the defendant has promised to compensate the claimant in full even where the latter contributes to the damage through unreasonable conduct.[151]

C Uncertainty

The Law Commission further sees uncertainty created by an introduction of apportionment into category 1,[152] in two respects. First, it would become necessary to investigate the quality of the defendant's conduct, which is, at present, irrelevant as liability does not depend on it.[153] True, the quality of the defendant's conduct is currently no issue. But to investigate that issue seems to be much easier and clearer[154] than to determine, as is currently necessary,[155] whether the claimant's conduct breaks the chain of causation or renders the damage too remote or constitutes a failure to mitigate the loss. Furthermore, making apportionment available for all kinds of breach of contract would obviate the need to determine for the purpose of contributory negligence whether or not the defendant's liability is dependent on fault.

Secondly, the Law Commission fears uncertainty as to the quantum of apportionment.[156] It reports the suggestion by a respondent that the introduction of apportionment into category 1 would give rise to a large number of cases where the sole issue in dispute is the amount of contribution payable by the claimant. Even though the outcome of cases would become more predictable over time, says the Commission, the law would always be too uncertain for business people,

---

of the right to exclude apportionment in the contract: Law Commission, 'Contributory Negligence as a Defence in Contract' (Law Com No 219, 1993) [4.23]–[4.27], Appendix A, Draft Contributory Negligence Bill s 1(2).

[150] *Astley v Austrust Ltd* (1999) 197 CLR 1 (HCA) [85]–[87].

[151] G Davis and J Knowler, 'Astley v Austrust Ltd' (1999) 23 *MULR* 795, 810–811; M Tilbury and JW Carter, 'Converging Liabilities and Security of Contract: Contributory Negligence in Australian Law' (2000) 16 *JCL* 78, 91; TM FitzPatrick, 'Contributory Negligence and Contract—A Critical Reassessment' (2001) 30 *CLWR* 412, 424–25, who points out that if the payment of consideration were decisive, apportionment would have to be allowed in the case of a gratuitous promise (in a deed), and denied in a negligence case where the claimant has actually paid for the defendant's services; neither of these is the law.

[152] Law Commission, 'Contributory Negligence as a Defence in Contract' (Law Com No 219, 1993) [3.30]–[3.32], [4.5]–[4.6]. Concurring *Barclays Bank plc v Fairclough Building Ltd (No 1)* [1995] QB 214 (CA) 230 (Beldam LJ).

[153] Law Commission, ibid [3.30], [4.5]–[4.6].

[154] Scottish Law Commission, 'Report on Remedies for Breach of Contract' (Scot Law Com No 174, 1999) [4.8].

[155] Above VI in this chapter.

[156] Law Commission, 'Contributory Negligence as a Defence in Contract' (Law Com No 219, 1993) [3.31]–[3.33], [4.5]–[4.6]. In order to dispel this concern, a restriction of the possible deduction to a few fixed percentages (such as 25%, 50% and 75%) is suggested by A Burrows, *Remedies for Torts and Breach of Contract*, 3rd edn (Oxford, 2004) 143–44.

who rarely provide for apportionment in their contracts. The assertion that 'Commercial people in particular prefer the certainty of fixed rules to the vagueness of concepts such as "just and equitable"'[157] has been challenged.[158] In any event, the fear of a flood of disputes on the quantum of apportionment seems unfounded given that no such flood has deluged Ireland[159] where the contributory negligence legislation has referred to contract since it was passed in 1961.[160] Furthermore, why is no uncertainty feared in category 2 or 3? The Commission attempts to explain the distinction on the ground that the distribution of blame is particularly intricate where the defendant's liability is strict. This argument has already been rejected.[161]

D   Inequalities of Bargaining Power

Finally, the Law Commission argues that a defendant who is the financially stronger party would gain even more power if apportionment on the ground of contributory negligence were available: 'It would give such a defendant another potential weapon with which to resist the plaintiff's claim and drag the case out until the plaintiff had neither the resources nor the energy to pursue it further'.[162] The Commission considers this particularly problematic in consumer contracts.[163] In similar vein, others argue that an introduction of apportionment into category 1 'would place an onus on consumers to seek inclusion of express disclaimers regarding their own contributory fault'.[164] The argument is flawed.

Where the law does not provide for apportionment as the default rule, a defendant with superior bargaining power may successfully push for a clause in the contract providing for apportionment. Such a clause should in general pass muster with the unfair-terms legislation,[165] for it can hardly be said to be not fair and reasonable to reduce the claimant's damages according to her share in the responsibility for the loss. An exception exists where the stronger party acted in the course of a business, was at fault and caused death or personal injury to the

---

[157]   *Astley v Austrust Ltd* (1999) 197 CLR 1 (HCA) [85] (Gleeson CJ, McHugh J, Gummow J and Hayne J).
[158]   TM FitzPatrick, 'Contributory Negligence and Contract—A Critical Reassessment' (2001) 30 *CLWR* 412, 426–27; M Tilbury and JW Carter, 'Converging Liabilities and Security of Contract: Contributory Negligence in Australian Law' (2000) 16 *JCL* 78, 96–97.
[159]   Indeed, an absence of reported cases prior to 1992 is noted by B Coote, 'Contributory Negligence Reform and the Right to Rely on a Contract' [1992] *NZRL Rev* 313, 314.
[160]   Civil Liability Act 1961 ss 2(1), 34–42.
[161]   Above VII B in this chapter.
[162]   Law Commission, 'Contributory Negligence as a Defence in Contract' (Law Com No 219, 1993) [3.35].
[163]   ibid [3.36].
[164]   PA Chandler, 'Contributory Negligence and Contract: Some Underlying Disparities' (1989) 40 *NILQ* 152, 174.
[165]   Unfair Contract Terms Act 1977; Unfair Terms in Consumer Contracts Regulations 1999.

weaker party. Liability in that situation cannot be excluded or even restricted.[166] But personal injury is not the usual concern of contractual liability. It follows that the only effective means of protecting a financially weaker claimant against an unmeritorious defence of contributory negligence is to prohibit apportionment clauses in the contract. Not even the Law Commission is prepared to go that far.

Secondly, if apportionment poses a problem in cases of unequal bargaining power, it must do so regardless of which category the defendant's breach belongs to. Yet, the Law Commission sees no problems with unequal bargaining power in category 2 or 3. The explanation given is that 'the defendant can only undermine the plaintiff's position by raising an unmeritorious defence if the legal position is sufficiently uncertain', which it is not in category 2 and 3.[167] In category 1, the availability of apportionment would not create alarming uncertainty either.[168]

VIII   Way of Reform

An apportionment of liability on the ground of contributory negligence is already available in category 3.[169] This being the case, it is untenable to withhold apportionment from category 2.[170] Finally, there are cogent reasons for allowing apportionment in category 1 too.[171] Apportionment should therefore be available in all actions for breach of contract,[172] as recommended for Scots law by the Scottish Law Commission.[173] Such a reform would align the general law of contract with employment law, where the compensation awarded to an employee for unfair dismissal or other unfair treatment may be reduced on account of her contribution to the employer's action.[174] The reform would further align the law of England and Wales (and Scots law) with the position under the Principles of

---

[166] Unfair Contract Terms Act 1977 ss 1, 2(1).

[167] Law Commission, 'Contributory Negligence as a Defence in Contract' (Law Com No 219, 1993) [3.37].

[168] Above VII C in this chapter.

[169] Above III in this chapter.

[170] Above IV in this chapter.

[171] Above VII in this chapter.

[172] A Burrows, *Remedies for Torts and Breach of Contract*, 3rd edn (Oxford, 2004) 141–44.

[173] Scottish Law Commission, 'Report on Remedies for Breach of Contract' (Scot Law Com No 174, 1999) Part 4, Appendix A, Draft Contract (Scotland) Bill s 3.

[174] Employment Rights Act 1996 ss 49(5), 123(6); Trade Union and Labour Relations (Consolidation) Act 1992 s 149(6). Pursuant to the Employment Rights Act 1996 s 116(1)(c), (3)(c) the employee's contribution to her dismissal is also relevant to the decision on reinstatement or re-engagement.

European Contract Law,[175] the European Code of Contract,[176] the European Union's Draft Common Frame of Reference,[177] and the UNIDROIT Principles of International Commercial Contracts 2004.[178]

[175] Art 9.504: 'The non-performing party is not liable for loss suffered by the aggrieved party to the extent that the aggrieved party contributed to the non-performance or its effects'. One of the main illustrations given is a category 1 case: O Lando and H Beale (eds), *Principles of European Contract Law, Parts I and II, Combined and Revised* (The Hague, 2000) 444.

[176] Art 167(3): 'If an act or omission of the creditor has contributed to causing the damage, damages are reduced in keeping with the consequences resulting from the act or omission'. An English version of the European Code of Contract was published as a Special Issue of the Edinburgh Law Review 2004.

[177] Art. III-3:704: 'The debtor is not liable for loss suffered by the creditor to the extent that the creditor contributed to the non-performance or its effect.'

[178] Art 7.4.7: 'Where the harm is due in part to an act or omission of the aggrieved party or to another events as to which that party bears the risk, the amount of damages shall be reduced to the extent that these factors have contributed to the harm, having regard to the conduct of each of the parties'. The United Nations Convention on Contracts for the International Sale of Goods does not address contributory negligence in general but contains the mitigation principle (Art 77) and excludes liability where one party causes the other party to breach (Art 80).

11

Contributory Negligence in Equity

Equity, as the name indicates, aims to do equity between the parties. It is governed by maxims such as 'He who seeks equity must do equity' and 'He who seeks equity must come with clean hands'.[1] It should go without saying that the equitable compensation payable by a defaulting trustee or fiduciary may be reduced according to the degree by which the principal has contributed to the wrong or the ensuing loss.[2] There has been judicial support for such apportionment in New Zealand and Canada.

The breakthrough came in the New Zealand case *Day v Mead*.[3] Day was a surveyor and Mead was his solicitor for 25 years. Mead was also a director and shareholder of a company. In July 1977, on Mead's advice, Day purchased 20,000 shares in that company at NZ$1 per share, knowing of Mead's involvement in the company. Day took an interest in the company's business, regularly visited its factory and attended a few directors' meetings as an onlooker. In December 1977, once again acting on Mead's advice, Day purchased further 80,000 shares at NZ$1 per share. Mead acted as Day's solicitor in both transactions. In March 1978, the company went into receivership and Day lost both investments.

It was held that Mead had breached his fiduciary and contractual duty towards Day by failing to refer him to an independent solicitor and to inform him of the company's financial difficulties. It was further held that Day was equally to blame for the loss of his second investment due to his business experience and the fact that he had attended a directors' meeting in October 1977 where the company's financial difficulties were discussed. Day's compensation with regard to his second investment was reduced by one half. The New Zealand Court of Appeal accepted the trial judge's view that equitable compensation may be apportioned on the ground of contributory negligence. Cooke P said that

---

[1] For these maxims see *Day v Mead* [1987] 2 NZLR 443 (NZCA) 451 (Cooke P); WMC Gummow, 'Compensation for Breach of Fiduciary Duty' in TG Youdan (ed), *Equity, Fiduciaries and Trusts* (Toronto, 1989) 75.

[2] PW Michalik, 'The availability of compensatory and exemplary damages in equity: A note on the *Aquaculture* decision' (1991) 21 *Victoria University of Wellington Law Review* 391, 408. The misapplication of trust funds by a trustee, where the beneficiary will rarely contribute to the loss, is outside the scope of the discussion: above ch 5, I.

[3] [1987] 2 NZLR 443 (NZCA).

there appears to be no solid reason for denying jurisdiction to follow that obviously just course, especially now that law and equity have mingled or are interacting. It is an opportunity for equity to show that it has not petrified and to live up to the spirit of its maxims.[4]

The New Zealand Court of Appeal confirmed its view in *Mouat v Clark Boyce*,[5] where the plaintiff, an elderly widow, granted a mortgage over her home as security for a loan made to her son. The defendant solicitor acted in the matter for both her and her son. He told the plaintiff that she should have independent advice, but the plaintiff said that she did not need it as she trusted her son. She did in fact have misgivings but did not want to show her feelings before a stranger. The defendant sought no information on the financial state of either the plaintiff or her son and never discussed the matter with the plaintiff in the absence of her son. When the plaintiff's son later defaulted and became bankrupt, the plaintiff was called on to pay the debt secured by the mortgage. The defendant was held liable for negligence and breach of fiduciary duty,[6] but the plaintiff was held to have acted unreasonably in failing to take independent advice and concealing her doubts from the defendant. For that reason, the trial judge reduced the damages by two thirds.[7] The New Zealand Court of Appeal changed the reduction to one half but, crucially, confirmed the possibility of 'abating' equitable compensation on the ground of contributory negligence. Cooke P said that

> it is not easy to think of any reason why he or she who claims compensation because someone else has broken a duty of care or a fiduciary duty, however arising, should not at the same time accept some responsibility for his or her own actions. Short of contract to the contrary, surely none of us should be wholly free of responsibility for consequences to ourselves to which we have carelessly contributed.[8]

Even though both *Day v* Mead and *Mouat v Clark Boyce* involved concurrent liability in equity and at common law, the New Zealand Court of Appeal had no intention in either case to confine the possibility of apportioning equitable compensation to cases of concurrent liability. In *Canson Enterprises Ltd v Boughton & Co*,[9] La Forest J in the Supreme Court of Canada said *obiter* that he agreed with the approach taken in *Day v Mead*.

---

[4] ibid 451. He further said (at 452): 'Contribution is now consistent with prevailing theories of both the law and the market-place. And it meets our sense of fairness'.

[5] [1992] 2 NZLR 559 (NZCA).

[6] The finding of liability was reversed on appeal: [1994] 1 AC 428 (PC).

[7] The damages before reduction included NZ$25,000 for mental distress. On that issue see above ch 8, III.

[8] [1992] 2 NZLR 559 (NZCA) 566.

[9] [1991] 3 SCR 534 (SCC) 585. Sopinka J, Gonthier J and Cory J concurred.

While the courts in England and Wales have pointed out that the principal's unreasonable contribution to her loss may lead to a denial of equitable compensation by virtue of causation[10] or remoteness doctrine,[11] there appears to be no case in which equitable compensation was apportioned or the possibility of apportionment recognised.[12] On the contrary, Blackburne J rejected the possibility of apportioning equitable compensation on the ground of contributory negligence in *Nationwide Building Society v Balmer Radmore*.[13] A building society suffered large losses when some 400 residential mortgagors defaulted and the properties concerned were repossessed and sold at a loss. In each case the same firm of solicitors had acted for both the borrower and the society. In the course of investigating title, the solicitors became aware of a substantial overvaluation of the properties by surveyors and other irregularities but failed to inform the society of this. Blackburne J held the solicitors liable for negligence and breach of contract and, where they had *intentionally* withheld important information from the society, also for breach of fiduciary duty. With regard to the effect of contributory negligence on the society's part, he held that liability could be apportioned at common law but not in equity.

While the principal's conduct, he said, may be relevant in the context of remoteness and 'as a factor determining the loss for which he can recover',[14] equitable compensation cannot be apportioned. He expressed this view 'with some diffidence', acknowledging that this was 'a highly contentious topic'.[15] He noted *Day v Mead* but distinguished it on the ground that the breach of fiduciary duty in that case had been an innocent one whereas the breaches before him (if established) had been intentional.

Blackburne J explained his denial of apportionment in the case of a consciously disloyal fiduciary with two arguments. First, he said, contributory negligence has no effect in an intentional tort, and there is no reason why equity should adopt a less rigorous approach.[16] The premise of that argument, namely that the 1945 Act has no application to intentional torts, has already been challenged.[17] Secondly, he said, allowing apportionment by reason of contributory negligence 'risks subverting the fundamental principle of undivided and

---

[10]   *Lipkin Gorman v Karpnale Ltd* [1987] 1 WLR 987, 1019; *Corporacion Nacional Del Cobre De Chile v Sogemin Metals Ltd* [1997] 1 WLR 1396, 1402–404. See also *Canson Enterprises Ltd v Boughton & Co* [1991] 3 SCR 534 (SCC) 554 (McLachlin J).

[11]   *Nationwide Building Society v Balmer Radmore* [1999] PNLR 606, 677.

[12]   As noted in *Corporacion Nacional Del Cobre De Chile v Sogemin Metals Ltd* [1997] 1 WLR 1396, 1402.

[13]   [1999] PNLR 606.

[14]   ibid 676–77. The decision is embraced by C Rickett, 'Compensating for Loss in Equity—Choosing the Right Horse for Each Course' in P Birks and F Rose (eds), *Restitution and Equity, Vol 1: Resulting Trusts and Equitable Compensation* (London, 2000) 186–87.

[15]   ibid 676.

[16]   [1999] PNLR 606, 677. The same argument is made by L Ho, 'Attributing losses to a breach of fiduciary duty' (1998) 12 *Trust Law International* 66, 75.

[17]   Above ch 9, II.

unremitting loyalty which is at the core of the fiduciary's obligation'.[18] He pointed to the 'unwisdom of entangling the already complex law as to fiduciary duties with notions of contributory negligence'.[19] But to determine each party's responsibility for the damage may be easier than to apply remoteness doctrine. Moreover, the unavailability of apportionment of liability on the ground of contributory negligence bears the risk that unreasonable conduct on a principal's part may lead to a complete exoneration of the fiduciary on grounds of causation or remoteness. Thus, as Vann points out, the 'fear that allowing a plea of contributory negligence would relieve defendants of liability is paradoxically realised by *not* allowing such a plea'.[20]

Edelman and Davies oppose an apportionment of liability for *any* breach of fiduciary duty with the argument that 'It is of the essence of a fiduciary relationship that the beneficiary is relieved of the need to watch over his own affairs and monitor the fiduciary'.[21] With regard to the 'duty' to watch one's own affairs, it must be asked why the principal should be relieved from that 'duty' in every aspect. She must of course be relieved insofar as the fiduciary possesses greater skill, knowledge or experience. She may, however, be required to take the precautions that a reasonable person with her skill, knowledge and experience would take.

With regard to the duty to monitor the fiduciary, it must be objected that such a duty would rarely be imposed even if apportionment were available, for the principal is in general entitled to trust the fiduciary[22] just as a buyer is entitled to rely on the seller's warranty.[23] Burrows points out that 'the content of the trustee's duty—to look after the trust property for the benefit of the beneficiary—means that a beneficiary could rarely, if ever, be regarded as "at

---

[18] [1999] PNLR 606, 677, paraphrasing WMC Gummow, 'Compensation for Breach of Fiduciary Duty' in TG Youdan (ed), *Equity, Fiduciaries and Trusts* (Toronto, 1989) 86. See also *Pilmer v Duke Group Ltd* (2001) 207 CLR 165 (HCA) 230–31 (Kirby J).

[19] [1999] PNLR 606, 677, quoting WMC Gummow, ibid 87.

[20] V Vann, *Equitable Compensation in Australia: Principles and Problems* (Saarbrücken, 2009) 334, who argues that a careful consideration of the risk allocation between the parties obviates the need to resort to contributory negligence.

[21] J Edelman and J Davies, 'Torts and Equitable Wrongs' in A Burrows (ed), *English Private Law*, 2nd edn (Oxford, 2007) [17.211]. See also *Carl B Potter Ltd v Mercantile Bank of Canada* [1980] 2 SCR 343 (SCC) 352 (Ritchie J: 'I know of no authority for the proposition that a *cestui que trust* owes a duty to its trustee to ensure that the terms of the trust are observed'.); *Pilmer v Duke Group Ltd* (2001) 207 CLR 165 (HCA) 231 (Kirby J); KR Handley, 'Reduction of Damages Awards' in PD Finn (ed), *Essays on Damages* (Sydney, 1992) 127; RP Meagher, JD Heydon and MJ Leeming, *Meagher, Gummow and Lehane's Equity: Doctrines and Remedies*, 4th edn (Australia, 2002) [23–020]; S Worthington, 'Review of *Hochelaga Lectures. Fusing Common Law and Equity: Remedies, Restitution and Reform* by Andrew Burrows' (2003) 119 *Law Quarterly Review* 519, 521.

[22] J Beatson, 'Unfinished Business: Integrating Equity' in J Beatson, *The Use and Abuse of Unjust Enrichment: Essays on the Law of Restitution* (Oxford, 1991) 256.

[23] Above ch 10, VII A.

fault", compared with the trustee, in relation to that property'.[24] Where a principal has reason to be suspicious, it may be justified to require her to carry out checks readily available.[25]

Day v Mead vividly demonstrates the need for apportionment on the ground of contributory negligence being available in equity. Day had business experience and had become aware of the company's financial difficulties before his second investment. It was unreasonable for him to make that investment without further investigation or independent advice. Indeed, Somers J in the New Zealand Court of Appeal remarked that had it not been for the fact that Day's judgment must have been 'dulled or overlaid' by his confidence in Mead, there would have been 'much to be said for the view that his responsibility for this loss was almost total'.[26] It would have been anything but equitable to grant him full compensation.

In summary, there are no cogent reasons for disallowing an apportionment of equitable compensation on the ground of contributory negligence. But there exists a good reason for allowing it, namely the fact that equitable liability is often concurrent with liability at common law, where apportionment is available in many instances and should be available where it currently is not. It would be illogical if the claimant could circumvent the apportionment looming at common law by pleading her case in equity. That would have happened in *Day v Mead* and *Mouat v Clark Boyce* had apportionment been denied in equity. If, accordingly, apportionment is possible in instances of concurrent liability, it should also be possible in all other instances of equitable liability, for otherwise the defendant would be keen on demonstrating his concurrent liability at common law while the claimant would be keen on exonerating the defendant in that respect.[27]

Contract, tort and equity should therefore share the following general principle: Where the claimant has contributed to the occurrence of the defendant's wrong or the ensuing loss through unreasonable behaviour, the court may apportion liability according to each party's share in the responsibility for the loss.

---

[24] A Burrows, 'Remedial Coherence and Punitive Damages in Equity' in S Degeling and J Edelman (eds), *Equity in Commercial Law* (Sydney, 2005) 384.

[25] D Hayton, 'Fiduciaries in Context: An Overview' in P Birks (ed), *Privacy and Loyalty* (Oxford, 1997) 284, referring to *Lipkin Gorman v Karpnale Ltd* [1987] 1 WLR 987, where a firm whose partner had stolen money from it and gambled it away was denied any relief for loss sustained after the firm had reason to be suspicious but failed to undertake even a modest investigation.

[26] [1987] 2 NZLR 443 (NZCA) 457.

[27] A similar oddity may occur in a category 2 contract case: above ch 10, IV.

Part 4

Gain-Based Relief

12

The Present Law of 'Restitution for Wrongs'

I Terminology

Parts 1 to 3 examined certain aspects of compensatory damages, being concerned with the loss a wrong has inflicted upon the victim. The focus now shifts from the victim's loss to the gain the wrongdoer has made from the wrong. 'It is increasingly recognised today that the ends of justice sometimes go beyond compensating a plaintiff for his loss and may extend to stripping a defendant of his profits.'[1] This Part investigates whether and when the victim of a wrong is, or should be, entitled to claim the wrongdoer's gain.[2] That investigation necessitates entering a minefield of conceptual and terminological controversies. In particular, the meaning of 'restitution' and 'unjust enrichment' is controversial.

Under the 'quadration' theory, 'the law of restitution and the principle against unjust enrichment are two sides of the same coin'.[3] 'Restitutionary liability means that there has been unjust enrichment and *vice versa*'.[4] A defendant's unjust enrichment can be at the claimant's expense in two ways: by subtraction from the claimant or by a wrong to the claimant.[5] There is thus a division between unjust enrichment by subtraction and unjust enrichment by wrongdoing. Alternative terms used are autonomous and parasitic unjust enrichment in order to signify that the availability of restitution depends on a wrong in the latter category but not in the former.

Another school opposes the concept of gain-based relief for wrongs being part of the law of unjust enrichment (in a substantive sense).[6] Gain-based relief for

---

[1] *Dubai Aluminium Co Ltd v Salaam* [2002] UKHL 48, [2003] 2 AC 366 [164] (Lord Millett).
[2] This Part will not discuss when ill-gotten gains are, or should be, held on constructive trust for the claimant.
[3] A Burrows, *The Law of Restitution*, 2nd edn (London, 2002) 5.
[4] C Webb, 'What is Unjust Enrichment?' (2009) 29 *Oxford Journal of Legal Studies* 215, 242.
[5] A Burrows, *The Law of Restitution*, 2nd edn (London, 2002) 5–6; H McGregor, *McGregor on Damages*, 18th edn (London, 2009) [12–002].
[6] P Birks, 'Misnomer' in WR Cornish and others, *Restitution: Past, Present and Future* (Oxford, 1998) 1; J Edelman, *Gain-Based Damages: Contract, Tort, Equity and Intellectual Property* (Oxford,

wrongs is seen as part of the law of wrongs, and the law of unjust enrichment is confined to what the 'quadrationists' call autonomous unjust enrichment. On this view, contrary to the 'quadration' theory, a restitutionary award does not always reverse unjust enrichment. Some advocates of this school use the term 'disgorgement' rather than 'restitution' to denote either all gain-based awards for wrongs[7] or those gain-based awards for wrongs that are made irrespective of a transfer of value from the claimant to the defendant.[8]

A third school takes the completely opposite view and rejects the concept of parasitic unjust enrichment.[9] According to this school, the instances of gain-based relief that are said to arise from wrongs are in fact instances of autonomous unjust enrichment or fall even outside the law of unjust enrichment. In those instances, gain-based relief flows not from the commission of a wrong as such but from other factors, in particular the unjustified appropriation of property or rights akin to property.

Since the first two schools recognise gain-based awards responding to a wrong as such, they can, but do not have to,[10] regard those awards as a type of 'damages'. The third school, by contrast, avoids the term 'damages' to describe gain-based relief because that term should be reserved for monetary awards responding to a wrong as such, which is not the case for gain-based awards according to that school. Under the third school, therefore, gain-based awards should not strictly be discussed in a book on damages. It might thus seem paradoxical that this Part will support the third school. The inclusion of gain-based relief in this book is still justified because the third school is a minority view and because the courts regard most gain-based awards as a response to wrongs as such. The following overview of the present law will adopt judicial parlance, and the term 'restitution for wrongs' (in inverted commas) will be used to denote the subject matter of this Part. Otherwise this Part speaks of 'gain-based relief' and avoids in that context the terms 'damages' (with any epithet) and 'restitution'.

2002) 36–41; LD Smith, 'The Province of the Law of Restitution' (1992) 71 *Canadian Bar Review* 672, 683–94; G Virgo, *The Principles of the Law of Restitution*, 2nd edn (Oxford, 2006) 8–10, 425–28.

[7] LD Smith, ibid 694–699.

[8] J Edelman, *Gain-Based Damages: Contract, Tort, Equity and Intellectual Property* (Oxford, 2002) 3, 72, 78–79; J Edelman, 'Gain-Based Damages and Compensation' in A Burrows and Lord Rodger of Earlsferry (eds), *Mapping the Law: Essays in Memory of Peter Birks* (Oxford, 2006) 141, 147–52.

[9] J Beatson, 'The Nature of Waiver of Tort' in J Beatson, *The Use and Abuse of Unjust Enrichment: Essays on the Law of Restitution* (Oxford, 1991) 206–43; D Friedmann, 'Restitution for Wrongs: The Basis of Liability' in WR Cornish and others, *Restitution: Past, Present and Future* (Oxford, 1998) 133; J Stapleton, 'A New "Seascape" for Obligations: Reclassification on the Basis of Measure of Damages' in P Birks (ed), *The Classification of Obligations* (Oxford, 1997) 207, 221, 225; S Worthington, 'Reconsidering Disgorgement for Wrongs' (1999) 62 *Modern Law Review* 218.

[10] H McGregor, *McGregor on Damages*, 18th edn (London, 2009) [12–002].

II   The Inclusion of Hypothetical-Fee Awards

In line with the practice of textbooks in this area, the following overview of the present law of 'restitution for wrongs' includes instances of the so-called 'user principle'.[11] In the case of certain wrongs, particularly the temporary misappropriation of property, damages can be assessed by reference to the fee that the defendant would have reasonably had to pay for a licence by the claimant. Damages can be assessed in this way even where the parties would not in fact have negotiated a licence agreement had they met beforehand. It is highly contentious whether those awards are best characterised as compensatory, gain-based, a hybrid or rights-based. Some judgments are ambiguous, and those that express a clear view split roughly equally between a compensatory[12] and a gain-based analysis.[13] Academic opinion is also divided.

Some commentators argue that hypothetical-fee awards cannot be based on the defendant's gain because they differ in amount from the actual profit the defendant has made from the wrong: The profit may be higher or lower than the hypothetical licence fee.[14] This argument is misconceived. Where the defendant has used the claimant's property without permission (the core area of application of the user principle), the defendant's primary gain is not the profit derived from such use but the use itself. Since the use cannot be given up in kind, its monetary value must be assessed. Taking the profit the defendant has derived from the use is just one of several methods of assessment. Another method is to ask what the defendant would have reasonably had to pay for the use. A gain-based analysis of hypothetical-fee awards is therefore possible whether or not alternative analyses are also possible.[15]

---

[11]   Coined in *Stoke-on-Trent City Council v W & J Wass Ltd* [1988] 1 WLR 1406 (CA) 1416 (Nicholls LJ). Recent examples are *Sinclair v Gavaghan* [2007] EWHC 2256 (Ch) and *Field Common Ltd v Elmbridge BC* [2008] EWHC 2079 (Ch), [2009] 1 P & CR 1, both involving trespass to land.

[12]   eg ibid; *Jaggard v Sawyer* [1995] 1 WLR 269 (CA) 281, 291; *Attorney-General v Blake (Jonathan Cape Ltd Third Party)* [2001] 1 AC 268 (HL) 298 (Lord Hobhouse); *Severn Trent Water Ltd v Barnes* [2004] EWCA Civ 570 [23], [35]; *WWF-World Wide Fund for Nature v World Wrestling Federation Entertainment Inc* [2007] EWCA Civ 286, [2008] 1 WLR 445 [29].

[13]   eg *Penarth Dock Engineering Co Ltd v Pounds* [1963] 1 Lloyd's Rep 359, 361–62; *Ministry of Defence v Ashman* (1993) 25 HLR 513 (CA) 519 (Hoffmann LJ); *Surrey CC v Bredero Homes Ltd* [1993] 1 WLR 1361 (CA) 1369 (Steyn LJ); *Attorney-General v Blake (Jonathan Cape Ltd Third Party)* [2001] 1 AC 268 (HL) 278–85 (Lord Nicholls); *Gondal v Dillon Newsagents Ltd* [2001] RLR 221 (CA) 228.

[14]   D Pearce and R Halson, 'Damages for Breach of Contract: Compensation, Restitution and Vindication' (2008) 28 *OJLS* 73, 90, 93.

[15]   In *Inverugie Investments Ltd v Hackett* [1995] 1 WLR 713 (PC) 718, Lord Lloyd said that the user principle 'need not be characterised as exclusively compensatory, or exclusively restitutionary; it combines elements of both'. See also M McInnes, 'Account of Profits for Common Law Wrongs' in S Degeling and J Edelman (eds), *Equity in Commercial Law* (Sydney, 2005) 418–19; G Virgo, 'Restitutionary Remedies for Wrongs: Causation and Remoteness' in CEF Rickett (ed), *Justifying Private Law Remedies* (Oxford, 2008) 315–16; N Witzleb, 'Monetary remedies for breach of confidence in privacy cases' (2007) 27 *Legal Studies* 430, 442.

It is, moreover, suggested that a gain-based analysis is superior to the alternative analyses. There is no need here for undertaking a full-blown review of the alternative analyses. Others have already done so and have convincingly rejected them.[16] The following is a brief outline of that debate.

The traditional compensatory analysis argues that hypothetical-fee awards compensate the claimant for the lost opportunity to bargain with the defendant.[17] This analysis works where the parties would in fact have negotiated a licence agreement had they met beforehand.[18] But this is not always the case. The claimant cannot be said to have lost an opportunity to bargain where either the defendant would not have been willing to pay for a licence[19] or the claimant would not have been willing to grant the defendant a licence.[20]

A similar objection faces the attempt to see a loss suffered by the claimant in the lost ability to obtain an injunction.[21] It works where the claimant would have obtained an injunction had she gone to court in time, and where she was not able to go to court in time because, for instance, she was not aware of the defendant's conduct. But the claimant cannot be said to have lost the ability to obtain an

---

[16] See especially, A Burrows, 'Are "Damages on the *Wrotham Park* Basis" Compensatory, Restitutionary or Neither?' in D Saidov and R Cunnington (eds), *Contract Damages: Domestic and International Perspectives* (Oxford, 2008) 165; C Rotherham, '"*Wrotham Park* damages" and accounts of profits: compensation or restitution?' [2008] *Lloyd's Maritime and Commercial Law Quarterly* 25.

[17] This argument was first elaborated by RS Sharpe and SM Waddams, 'Damages for lost opportunity to bargain' (1982) 2 *OJLS* 290. Support for the argument includes *Tito v Waddell (No 2)* [1977] Ch 106, 335; *Attorney-General v Blake (Jonathan Cape Ltd Third Party)* [2001] 1 AC 268 (HL) 298 (Lord Hobhouse); *Severn Trent Water Ltd v Barnes* [2004] EWCA Civ 570 [35]; *WWF-World Wide Fund for Nature v World Wrestling Federation Entertainment Inc* [2007] EWCA Civ 286, [2008] 1 WLR 445 [29]; C Smith, 'Recognising a Valuable Lost Opportunity to Bargain when a Contract is Breached' (2005) 21 *Journal of Contract Law* 250; Lord Scott, 'Damages' [2007] *LMCLQ* 465, 467–68; DM Fox, 'Remedies for Interference with a Prescriptive Right to Light' [2007] *Cambridge Law Journal* 267, 270.

[18] An example is *Severn Trent Water Ltd v Barnes* [2004] EWCA Civ 570 especially [35].

[19] C Rotherham, '"*Wrotham Park* damages" and accounts of profits: compensation or restitution?' [2008] *LMCLQ* 25, 34–35. See also *Field Common Ltd v Elmbridge BC* [2008] EWHC 2079 (Ch), [2009] 1 P & CR 1 [90]. An example is *Strand Electric and Engineering Co Ltd v Brisford Entertainments Ltd* [1952] 2 QB 246 (CA), discussed below IV B in this chapter.

[20] eg J Beatson, 'The Nature of Waiver of Tort' in J Beatson, *The Use and Abuse of Unjust Enrichment: Essays on the Law of Restitution* (Oxford, 1991) 233; A Burrows, 'Are "Damages on the *Wrotham Park* Basis" Compensatory, Restitutionary or Neither?' in D Saidov and R Cunnington (eds), *Contract Damages: Domestic and International Perspectives* (Oxford, 2008) 169–71; R Cunnington, 'The Assessment of Gain-Based Damages for Breach of Contract' (2008) 71 *MLR* 559, 562; H McGregor, *McGregor on Damages*, 18th edn (London, 2009) [12–009]; D Pearce and R Halson, 'Damages for Breach of Contract: Compensation, Restitution and Vindication' (2008) 28 *OJLS* 73, 89, 92–93; R Stevens, *Torts and Rights* (Oxford, 2007) 68; G Virgo, 'Restitutionary Remedies for Wrongs: Causation and Remoteness' in CEF Rickett (ed), *Justifying Private Law Remedies* (Oxford, 2008) 313–314. An example is *Penarth Dock Engineering Co Ltd v Pounds* [1963] 1 Lloyd's Rep 359, discussed below IV C in this chapter.

[21] This analysis was accepted as correct by both parties in *Tamares (Vincent Square) Ltd v Fairpoint Properties (Vincent Square) Ltd (No 2)* [2007] EWHC 212 (Ch), [2007] 1 WLR 2167, as the judge noted at [3].

injunction where the court would never have granted an injunction for discretionary reasons or where the claimant failed to seek an injunction (in time) even though she was aware of the defendant's conduct.[22]

A new trend among commentators is to conceptualise hypothetical-fee awards as a remedy for breaches of rights per se rather than compensation for financial loss consequent upon such breach.[23] Hypothetical-fee awards are described as compensation for a 'detriment' (as opposed to 'patrimonial loss')[24], as compensation for the loss of '*dominium* (*ie* the right to control access and use)',[25] as 'vindicatory damages' representing the intrinsic value of the right infringed rather than the amount of consequential gain or loss,[26] or as 'damages awarded as a substitute for the right infringed' as opposed to 'consequential damages as compensation for loss to the claimant, or gain to the defendant, consequent upon this infringement'.[27]

This new trend faces two major objections.[28] First, 'it is hard to see in principle why a claimant should receive compensation that does not reflect the evidence as to its own position'.[29] Secondly, the concept of remedying breaches of rights per se cannot logically be confined to the rights for which hypothetical-fee awards are recognised but would also apply to other rights such as bodily integrity, the right to freedom and the right to contractual performance. That is not the present law.[30]

The following overview of the present law of 'restitution for wrongs' is ordered according to types of wrong since the courts have recognised or refused gain-based relief for individual wrongs. The overview will start with equitable wrongs, for which the availability of gain-based relief is largely settled. It will then look at

---

[22] A Burrows, 'Are "Damages on the *Wrotham Park* Basis" Compensatory, Restitutionary or Neither?' in D Saidov and R Cunnington (eds), *Contract Damages: Domestic and International Perspectives* (Oxford, 2008) 171–72; R Cunnington, 'The Assessment of Gain-Based Damages for Breach of Contract' (2008) 71 *MLR* 559, 563.

[23] R Nolan, 'Remedies for Breach of Contract: Specific Enforcement and Restitution' in FD Rose (ed), *Failure of Contracts: Contractual, Restitutionary and Proprietary Consequences* (Oxford, 1997) 47; A Tettenborn, 'Gain, loss and damages for breach of contract: what's in an acronym?' (2006) 14 *Restitution Law Review* 112, 113; and the works cited in the next four footnotes.

[24] F Giglio, *The Foundations of Restitution for Wrongs* (Oxford, 2007) 194.

[25] M McInnes, 'Gain, Loss and the User Principle' (2006) 14 *RLR* 76, 85. Adopted, with regard to rights held for non-commercial purposes, by J Edelman, 'Gain-Based Damages and Compensation' in A Burrows and Lord Rodger of Earlsferry (eds), *Mapping the Law: Essays in Memory of Peter Birks* (Oxford, 2006) 153–58. See also J Stapleton, 'A New "Seascape" for Obligations: Reclassification on the Basis of Measure of Damages' in P Birks (ed), *The Classification of Obligations* (Oxford, 1997) 227.

[26] D Pearce and R Halson, 'Damages for Breach of Contract: Compensation, Restitution and Vindication' (2008) 28 *OJLS* 73, 90–92.

[27] R Stevens, *Torts and Rights* (Oxford, 2007) 60.

[28] For further objections see A Burrows, 'Are "Damages on the *Wrotham Park* Basis" Compensatory, Restitutionary or Neither?' in D Saidov and R Cunnington (eds), *Contract Damages: Domestic and International Perspectives* (Oxford, 2008) 172–76, 181–85; C Rotherham, '"*Wrotham Park* damages" and accounts of profits: compensation or restitution?' [2008] *LMCLQ* 25, 42–52.

[29] A Burrows, ibid 176.

[30] ibid 173, 181–82.

those torts for which the courts have expressly considered the availability of gain-based relief. Finally, it will look at breach of contract, for which the scope of gain-based relief is still unsettled.

III Equity

The availability of gain-based relief is firmly established for breach of confidence (at least in its core meaning) and breach of fiduciary duty, both of which are considered below. The High Court of Australia has awarded an account of profits for dishonestly assisting a breach of fiduciary duty.[31] In England and Wales, the same approach has been favoured by commentators[32] and *obiter* in *Fyffes Group Ltd v Templeman*, where Toulson J saw 'cogent grounds, in principle and in practical justice, for ... holding that the briber of an agent may be required to account to the principal for benefits obtained from the corruption of the agent'.[33]

A Breach of Fiduciary Duty

In *Bristol and West Building Society v Mothew*, Millett LJ provided the following oft-cited description of a fiduciary's duty of loyalty:

> A fiduciary must act in good faith; he must not make a profit out of his trust; he must not place himself in a position where his duty and his interest may conflict; he may not act for his own benefit or the benefit of a third person without the informed consent of his principal.[34]

A fiduciary breaching the duty of loyalty has to account to the principal for all profit made from the breach. Three cases may illustrate this well-established principle. The first is *Regal (Hastings) Ltd v Gulliver*,[35] where the claimant company ('Regal') decided to set up a subsidiary company ('Amalgamated') with a registered capital of £5,000 in £1 shares. Regal subscribed for £2,000 of Amalgamated's capital, but subscription for the entire capital was needed to get Amalgamated into business. Since Regal lacked the funds to acquire more than 2,000 shares, Regal's directors acquired the remaining 3,000 shares personally with their own money. Shortly afterwards, they sold those shares at a substantial profit. It was held that the directors had broken their fiduciary duty towards

---

[31] *Warman International Ltd v Dwyer* (1995) 182 CLR 544 (HCA).

[32] A Burrows, *Remedies for Torts and Breach of Contract*, 3rd edn (Oxford, 2004) 611–12; G Jones, *Goff & Jones: The Law of Restitution*, 7th edn (London, 2007) [33–033]; G Virgo, *The Principles of the Law of Restitution*, 2nd edn (Oxford, 2006) 536.

[33] [2000] 2 Lloyd's Rep 643, 672.

[34] [1998] Ch 1 (CA) 18; Otton LJ concurring. For company directors see Companies Act 2006 ss 175–77.

[35] [1942] 1 All ER 378, [1967] 2 AC 134 (HL).

Regal by acquiring the shares and that Regal could claim the profit that the directors had made from that investment.

The second case is *Boardman v Phipps*,[36] where a trust held shares in a company. One of the beneficiaries and the trust's solicitor bought, personally and with their own money, the majority of shares in the company. Subsequently, the company did well and paid substantial dividends to its shareholders. It was held that the beneficiary and the solicitor had been under a fiduciary duty towards the trust, that they had broken that duty by acquiring the shares and that the trust could claim the profit made by them subject to a liberal allowance for their work and skill.

The third and final case is *Industrial Development Consultants Ltd v Cooley*.[37] Mr Cooley was the managing director of the plaintiff company (IDC), which provided construction consultancy services. He offered IDC's services to a public gas board for a certain project. The gas board declined to employ IDC but, since Mr Cooley was a distinguished architect, offered the contract to him personally. Mr Cooley accepted this offer and obtained his release from IDC's services by falsely representing to IDC that he was ill. It was held that he had broken his fiduciary duty towards IDC and had to account to IDC for all the remuneration received from the gas board.

These three cases demonstrate not only the general availability of an account of profits in the case of a breach of fiduciary duty but also that a breach of fiduciary duty may occur even though the fiduciary acted in good faith (*Regal (Hastings)* and *Boardman*),[38] the transaction benefited the principal (*Regal (Hastings)* and *Boardman*), and the principal could not have made the gain that the fiduciary has made (*Regal (Hastings)*, *Cooley* and probably also *Boardman*).[39] Such a harsh liability is said to be necessary for the 'safety of mankind'[40] as fiduciaries would otherwise feel 'a temptation to refrain from exerting their strongest efforts on behalf of the [principal]'.[41]

In the recent case of *Murad v Al-Saraj*,[42] the Court of Appeal criticised the inability to ever limit or exclude an account of profits where the fiduciary acted in good faith or where the principal, if asked in advance, would have allowed the fiduciary to make the profit in question.[43] In the light of *Regal (Hastings) Ltd v*

---

[36]   [1967] 2 AC 46 (HL).

[37]   [1972] 1 WLR 443.

[38]   In *Bray v Ford* [1896] AC 44 (HL) 52, Lord Herschell emphasised that the duty of loyalty may be violated 'without any breach of morality, without any wrong being inflicted, and without any consciousness of wrong-doing'.

[39]   For company directors see now also Companies Act 2006 s 175(2).

[40]   *Parker v McKenna* (1874) LR 10 Ch App 96 (DC) 125 (James LJ).

[41]   *Irving Trust Co v Deutsch* (1934) 73 F.2d 121 (US CA for 2nd Circuit) 124 (Swan J).

[42]   [2005] EWCA Civ 959, [2005] WTLR 1573 [82] (Arden LJ), [121] (Jonathan Parler LJ), [141] ff (Clarke LJ).

[43]   Similarly, in *Strother v 3464920 Canada Inc* [2007] SCC 24, [2007] 2 SCR 177 [155], McLachlin CJ, dissenting, doubted the availability of an account of profits where the principal could not have personally made the profit that the fiduciary has made.

Gulliver[44] and *Boardman v Phipps*,[45] however, the majority in *Murad* took the view that only the House of Lords could relax the strict rule.[46]

Like all equitable remedies, an account of profits is discretionary,[47] but 'it is granted or withheld according to settled principles'.[48] The obligation to account extends to the net profit,[49] deducting from the fiduciary's gross profit 'all proper disbursements and expenses which he may have, or which may have been, properly incurred'.[50] Thus, an account of profits does not generally put the fiduciary in a worse position than without the breach[51] unless such worsening is seen in lost remuneration from alternative, lawful transactions which the fiduciary could have entered into during the time he spent on the impugned transaction.

But even the possibility of alternative business does not necessarily mean that an account of profits puts the fiduciary in a worse position than without the breach, for the court ordering an account of profits in response to a breach of fiduciary duty may allow the fiduciary to keep a part of the net profit as an allowance for the work and skill employed in obtaining the profit.[52] Such an allowance was made in *Boardman v Phipps* on the ground that 'it would be inequitable now for the beneficiaries to step in and take the profit without paying for the skill and labour which has produced it'.[53]

In *Warman International Ltd v Dwyer*,[54] where a company manager set up his own business and competed with his principal, the High Court of Australia awarded the company an account of profits only for the net profit that the manager's new business had made in its first two years. However, an allowance for work and skill is rarely made in order to deter fiduciaries from acting in breach of fiduciary duty.[55] It is unlikely to be made, albeit not completely ruled out, where the fiduciary has acted dishonestly or been involved in surreptitious dealing.[56]

---

[44] [1967] 2 AC 134 (HL).

[45] [1967] 2 AC 46 (HL).

[46] [2005] EWCA Civ 959, [2005] WTLR 1573 [82]–[83] (Arden LJ), [121] (Jonathan Parker LJ).

[47] eg *Attorney-General v Blake (Jonathan Cape Ltd Third Party)* [2001] 1 AC 268 (HL) 279 (Lord Nicholls); *Forsyth-Grant v Allen* [2008] EWCA Civ 505, [2008] Env LR 41 [40].

[48] *Warman International Ltd v Dwyer* (1995) 182 CLR 544 (HCA) 559 (Mason CJ, Brennan J, Deane J, Dawson J and Gaudron J).

[49] *Regal Hastings Ltd v Gulliver* [1967] 2 AC 134 (HL) 154 (Lord Wright); *Patel v Brent LBC* [2003] EWHC 3081 (Ch), [2004] WTLR 577 [29].

[50] *De Bussche v Alt* (1878) LR 8 Ch D 286 (Ch) 307 (Hall VC). See also *Badfinger Music v Evans* [2001] WTLR 1; *Warman International Ltd v Dwyer* (1995) 182 CLR 544 (HCA) 561.

[51] M Conaglen 'Strict Fiduciary Loyalty and Accounts of Profits' [2006] *CLJ* 278, 280; V Vann 'Causation and Breach of Fiduciary Duty' [2006] *Singapore Journal of Legal Studies* 86, 97.

[52] eg *Boardman v Phipps* [1967] 2 AC 46 (HL) 104, 112; *O'Sullivan v Management Agency and Music Ltd* [1985] QB 428 (CA) 459, 468, 472–73.

[53] [1964] 1 WLR 993 (Ch) 1018 (Wilberforce J).

[54] (1995) 182 CLR 544 (HCA).

[55] *Guinness plc v Saunders* [1990] 2 AC 663 (HL) 701 (Lord Goff). See also *Say-Dee Pty Ltd v Farah Constructions Pty Ltd* [2005] NSWCA 309 [252].

[56] *O'Sullivan v Management Agency and Music Ltd* [1985] QB 428 (CA) 468 (Fox LJ); *Badfinger Music v Evans* [2001] WTLR 1; *Crown Dilmun v Sutton* [2004] EWHC 52 (Ch), [2004] WTLR 497 [213].

B   Breach of Confidence Including Breach of Privacy

A breach of confidence in its core meaning occurs where secret information that has been confidentially imparted by one person (the confider) to another (the confidant) is used by the latter to the detriment of the former without legal justification.[57] Where a confidant has deliberately broken confidence, the confider may claim an account of all the profits the confidant has made from the breach. Authority for that rule is *Peter Pan Manufacturing Corp v Corsets Silhouette Ltd*,[58] where the claimant (Peter Pan), a manufacturer of brassieres, granted the defendant (Silhouette) a licence to manufacture and sell Peter Pan brassieres in the UK. Peter Pan showed Silhouette, in confidence, the design and manufacture technique of certain brassieres. After the licence agreement had expired, Silhouette continued to manufacture and sell brassieres, using the confidential information provided by Peter Pan. Pennycuick J regarded this as a breach of confidence and ordered Silhouette to account to Peter Pan for the profit made from the breach, the profit being the difference between the receipts from the sale of the offending brassieres and the cost of their manufacture.

A duty of confidentiality, and liability to account for the profits made from breach of confidence, extends to third parties who have received the information at issue from the confidant and know about its confidential nature. Authority for that rule is *Attorney-General v Observer Ltd, sub nom Attorney-General v Guardian Newspapers Ltd (No 2)*,[59] where Peter Wright, a former member of the British Security Service MI5, wrote a book entitled *Spycatcher* about his spying activities and published it in the United States. Two days before the book's publication, the *Sunday Times* published extracts from the book in the UK. It was held that Peter Wright had broken his duty towards the Crown not to disclose secret information obtained while working for MI5, and that the *Sunday Times*, who knew the information at issue to be confidential, had also committed a breach of confidence since the information had not yet been in the public domain and no countervailing public interests had justified disclosure. The *Sunday Times* was ordered to account to the Crown for the profit made from the breach of confidence, the profit being the extra receipts made from an increase in the newspaper's circulation attributable to the *Spycatcher* extract.[60]

According to *Seager v Copydex Ltd (No 1)*,[61] an account of profits may not be available for a breach of confidence committed unconsciously. Mr Seager owned the patent for a carpet grip and negotiated with Copydex with a view to Copydex

---

[57]   eg *Coco v AN Clark (Engineers) Ltd* [1968] FSR 415, 419; [1969] RPC 41, 47; above ch 8, I.

[58]   [1964] 1 WLR 96.

[59]   [1990] 1 AC 109 (Ch), 174 (CA), 233 (HL). An injunction may also be granted against the third party; eg *English & American Insurance Co Ltd v Herbert Smith* [1988] FSR 232; *Hoechst UK Ltd v Chemiculture Ltd* [1993] FSR 270.

[60]   Lord Brightman considered awarding a 'due proportion' of the entire net profit made from the newspaper issue containing the *Spycatcher* extract: [1990] 1 AC 109, 233 (HL) 266.

[61]   [1967] 1 WLR 923 (CA).

marketing the grip. During the negotiations, which came to nothing, Mr Seager told Copydex, in confidence, about his idea for an alternative grip with a V tang and strong-point. After the negotiations had ended, Copydex made a carpet grip with a V tang and strong-point, using Mr Seager's idea. In a decision on liability in principle, the Court of Appeal held Copydex liable for breach of confidence even though the Court accepted that Copydex had honestly believed that it was acting lawfully since the new grip did not infringe Mr Seager's patent. Lord Denning MR remarked that it 'may not be a case for ... an account'.[62] The unexpressed reason for this seems to have been the fact that the breach of confidence *in casu*, unlike the breach in the earlier *Peter Pan* case, had been unintentional.[63] It is surprising however, that mere ignorance of the law should suffice to exclude an account of profits.[64]

Be that as it may, the confider seems to be able to claim damages based on the market value of the confidential information, whether or not the breach of confidence was intentional. This was established in *Seager v Copydex Ltd (No 2)*,[65] which concerned the measure of damages claimed by Mr Seager. With regard to the value of the information used by Copydex in breach of confidence, the Court of Appeal distinguished: if there was nothing special about the information, that is if it involved no inventive step, its value was the fee that a consultant would charge for providing it; if the information was special, that is if it involved an inventive step, its value would be the price that a willing buyer would pay for it. The first measure is gain-based as it refers to an expense saved by the confidant, not a loss suffered by the confider.[66] The second measure too is preferably analysed as being gain-based,[67] although it could be analysed as being loss-based, compensating the confider for the loss of a licence fee.[68]

Further authority for the availability of gain-based relief for breach of confidence in its core meaning is found in *Universal Thermosensors Ltd v Hibben*.[69] The defendants left their employment with the plaintiff company and set up a rival business, wrongfully using confidential information obtained in their former employment. On a cross-undertaking in damages, the plaintiff obtained an interim injunction, which eventually proved too wide, restraining the defendants from lawful conduct. In calculating the damages the defendants could claim under the cross-undertaking, Sir Donald Nicholls VC took into consideration that they

---

[62] ibid 932.
[63] A Burrows, *Remedies for Torts and Breach of Contract*, 3rd edn (Oxford, 2004) 624.
[64] A categorical exclusion of an account for every unconscious breach of confidence is seen as 'undesirable' by G Jones, *Goff & Jones: The Law of Restitution*, 7th edn (London, 2007) [34–021].
[65] [1969] 1 WLR 809 (CA).
[66] A Burrows, *Remedies for Torts and Breach of Contract*, 3rd edn (Oxford, 2004) 624.
[67] Above II in this chapter.
[68] A Burrows, *Remedies for Torts and Breach of Contract*, 3rd edn (Oxford, 2004) 624.
[69] [1992] 1 WLR 840.

ought to pay compensation to the plaintiff for the benefits they derived from the wrongful use of its confidential information, in particular, but not exclusively, by saving themselves the time, trouble and expense of compiling their own list of contacts without reference to the plaintiff's records.[70]

Even though Sir Donald Nicholls VC was speaking of 'compensation', his reference to 'benefits' and saved efforts means that the plaintiff's claim must have been gain-based. Indeed, with reference to *Seager v Copydex Ltd (No 1)* he said:

An award of damages in such circumstances would not be a novelty. There are several fields where the courts have awarded damages to a plaintiff whose property is wrongfully used by another even though the plaintiff has not suffered any pecuniary loss by such user.[71]

Breach of confidence is now also the concept used to address invasions of privacy. In applying the concept of breach of confidence to invasions of privacy, the courts do not require the information at issue to have been confidentially imparted. Instead, they ask whether the defendant knew or ought to have known that the claimant had a reasonable expectation of privacy, and whether the claimant's interest in privacy is outweighed by the defendant's freedom of speech or any other competing interest. Even though this new wrong has been called 'breach of privacy' and is covered in textbooks on tort, the courts still regard it as an equitable wrong in the same way as breach of confidence in its core meaning.[72]

If breach of privacy is regarded as a specific type of breach of confidence, gain-based relief should be available for the former as it is for the latter. Indeed, the availability of gain-based relief for breach of privacy was effectively recognised, even though it was denied *in casu*, by the Court of Appeal in *Douglas v Hello! Ltd (No 3)*.[73] That case arose out of the publication by the magazine *Hello!* of photos surreptitiously taken at the wedding of the actors Michael Douglas and Catherine Zeta-Jones, who had sold the exclusive right to publish photos of their wedding to the magazine *OK!* and had taken elaborate measures to prevent the unauthorised taking of photos at their wedding. In the Douglases' claim against *Hello!* for breach of privacy, the Court of Appeal made clear that it 'would have had no hesitation' to award an account of profits had *Hello!* made a profit from the publication.[74]

The Court did reject an award of damages calculated by reference to a hypothetical licence fee, but this rejection was not based on the view that such an award is in principle unavailable in an action for breach of privacy. Rather, the Court rejected a hypothetical-fee award on the ground that the Douglases would

---

[70]   ibid 858–59.
[71]   ibid 856.
[72]   *Douglas v Hello! Ltd (No 3)* [2005] EWCA Civ 595, [2006] QB 125 [96]; *Mosley v News Group Newspapers Ltd* [2008] EWHC 1777 (QB) [181]–[197]; above ch 8, II.
[73]   [2005] EWCA Civ 595, [2006] QB 125.
[74]   ibid [249].

never have permitted *Hello!* to publish the unauthorised photographs and had indeed been prevented from giving such permission by the exclusive licence granted to *OK!*, which also made it difficult to assess the hypothetical licence fee.[75] *Douglas v Hello! Ltd (No 3)* thus recognised the availability of an account of profits, and did not rule out a hypothetical-fee award where the claimant, if asked in advance, would have permitted the invasive act in question.

IV Tort

A Historical Development

Gain-based relief is not available for every tort,[76] for instance not for trespass to the person[77] or defamation.[78] It is available for some torts, in particular the proprietary torts. However, the law has not developed in a coherent and rational way. Different types of gain-based awards have been made for different torts; for instance awards of 'mesne profits' in cases of unauthorised occupation of land, and 'wayleave' awards in other cases of unauthorised use of land.[79] In other cases, for instance conversion, the claimant was allowed to bring an action in *indebitatus assumpsit* for money had and received. But this route to gain-based relief was, for a long time, bedevilled by two related fictions. First, it was said that the defendant, by committing a tort against the claimant, impliedly promised the latter to pay to him the proceeds of the tort.[80] Secondly, in order to prevent the claimant from seeking remedies for both the tort and the implied contract, the claimant was said to 'waive the tort' by bringing an action in *indebitatus assumpsit*. Thus, in *Lamine v Dorrell*, which involved the wrongful sale of debentures, Powell J said that 'the plaintiff may dispense with the wrong, and suppose the sale made by his consent, and bring an action for the money they were sold for, as money received to his use'.[81]

Both fictions survived until 1941 when they were finally laid to rest by the House of Lords in *United Australia Ltd v Barclays Bank Ltd*.[82] U received a cheque payable to U or order. U's secretary invalidly indorsed the cheque so as to make it

---

[75] ibid [246]–[248]. The court's reasons are criticised by G Jones, *Goff & Jones: The Law of Restitution*, 7th edn (London, 2007) [34–023].

[76] For the view that gain-based relief should in principle be available for every tort, see G Jones ibid [36–006]; H Street, *Principles of the Law of Damages* (London, 1962) 254.

[77] *United Australia Ltd v Barclays Bank Ltd* [1941] AC 1 (HL) 13 (Viscount Simon LC).

[78] ibid; *Hart v EP Dutton & Co Inc* (1949) 93 NYS 2d 871 (NY SC).

[79] Below IV C in this chapter.

[80] eg *Arris v Stukely* (1678) 2 Mod 260, 86 ER 1060; *Shuttleworth v Garnet* (1688) 3 Mod 239, 87 ER 156; *Foster v Stewart* (1814) 3 M & S 191, 105 ER 582.

[81] (1701) 2 Ld Raym 1216, 92 ER 303.

[82] [1941] AC 1 (HL).

payable to M. M indorsed the cheque and paid it into its account with bank B. B collected the proceeds of the cheque and placed them to the credit of M's account. The conduct of both B and M constituted the tort of conversion. U brought an action against M for the amount of the cheque either as money lent or as money had and received to the use of U, but U discontinued that action without obtaining final judgment. U then brought an action against B for conversion of the cheque. B argued that U, by initiating proceedings against M for money lent or for money had and received, had elected to waive the tort so as to be precluded from bringing a tort action against B. The House of Lords rejected that argument.

Their Lordships pointed out that the concept of 'waiver of tort' had emerged when the forms of action prevented a claimant from simultaneously seeking contractual and tortious remedies, so that the choice of one form of action could be interpreted as an election between alternative remedies. Today, they said, alternative remedies can be sought in the same action, and the right to claim damages for the tort is lost only if the claimant has obtained final judgment in an action for money had and received. The mere initiation of proceedings for money had and received does not constitute a true waiver of the tort so as to ratify the defendant's conduct.[83] U's discontinued action against M for money had and received would thus have been no bar to an action for conversion even against M, let alone B.

But their Lordships went further and emphasised that U could have brought an action for conversion against B even if U's discontinued action against M for money had and received *had* barred an action for conversion against M. They rejected the idea that the action for money had and received had been based on an implied contract between U and M, ratifying M's conduct and thus B's conduct too.[84] The fiction of an implied promise, they said, had been necessary under the forms of action because there was only the choice between an action for tort and one for debt or *assumpsit*. Today, they said, the substance of the claim for money had and received is the right of the claimant to recover property or its proceeds from one who has wrongfully received them. It has subsequently been clarified that the commission of a tort against the claimant remains 'a sine qua non' for the action for money had and received.[85]

---

[83] Most vivid was Lord Atkin, ibid 29: 'If I find that a thief has stolen my securities and is in possession of the proceeds, when I sue him for them I am not excusing him. I am protesting violently that he is a thief and because of his theft I am suing him.'

[84] Most vivid was again Lord Atkin, ibid 27: 'The cheat or the blackmailer does not promise to repay to the person he has wronged the money which he has unlawfully taken: nor does the thief promise to repay the owner of the goods stolen the money which he has gained from selling the goods.'

[85] *Chesworth v Farrar* [1967] 1 QB 407, 417 (Edmund Davies J).

B   Wrongful Interference with Goods

Wrongful interference with someone else's goods may occur by using or selling the goods. Gain-based damages have long been recognised, in substance but not name, for both forms. In the case of wrongful sale, the claimant may claim the price at which the defendant sold.[86] Where the defendant sold at the market price of the goods, the claim may be classified as one for compensation of the claimant's loss. But where the defendant sold above the market value at a price that the claimant could not personally have achieved, the claim must be classified as being based on the defendant's gain.

In the case of wrongfully using someone else's goods (called 'wrongful user'), it has long been recognised that the victim may claim damages even though she would not have used the goods herself. As the Earl of Halsbury LC asked rhetorically in *The Mediana*:

> Supposing a person took away a chair out of my room and kept it for twelve months, could anybody say you had a right to diminish the damages by shewing that I did not usually sit in that chair, or that there were plenty of other chairs in the room?[87]

Lord Shaw gave a similar illustration in the Scottish case *Watson, Laidlaw & Co Ltd v Pott, Cassels & Williamson*:

> If A, being a liveryman, keeps his horse standing idle in the stable, and B, against his wish or without his knowledge, rides or drives it out, it is no answer to A for B to say: 'Against what loss do you want to be restored? I restore the horse. There is no loss. The horse is none the worse; it is the better for the exercise.'[88]

The principle was applied in *Strand Electric and Engineering Co Ltd v Brisford Entertainments Ltd*.[89] A theatre hired portable switchboards from the plaintiff. When the defendant took over the theatre, it refused to return the switchboards to the plaintiff and kept them in use. In an action for detinue,[90] the Court of Appeal held the plaintiff entitled to the full market rate of hire of such switchboards for the whole period of detention. It was held immaterial that the plaintiff might not actually have realised the full hire during the whole detention period due to the fact that only 75 per cent of the plaintiff's stock was out on hire at any one time and that stock was sometimes loaned gratis or accidentally destroyed. Denning LJ justified the decision by recognising that the damages were based on the defendant's gain rather than the plaintiff's loss:

> The claim for a hiring charge is therefore not based on the loss to the plaintiff, but on the fact that the defendant has used the goods for his own purposes. It is an action

---

[86]   *Lamine v Dorrell* (1701) 2 Ld Raym 1216, 92 ER 303, using the 'waiver of tort' doctrine.
[87]   [1900] AC 113 (HL) 117.
[88]   1914 SC (HL) 18, 31.
[89]   [1952] 2 QB 246 (CA).
[90]   The tort of detinue is now abolished: Torts (Interference with Goods) Act 1977 s 2(1).

against him because he has had the benefit of the goods. It resembles, therefore, an action for restitution rather than an action of tort.[91]

Romer LJ and Somervell LJ, by contrast, described the damages award as being based on the plaintiff's loss. They held the plaintiff entitled to an irrebuttable assumption that it would have realised the full hire absent the wrongful detention. On the argument that the plaintiff might not have found a hirer, Romer LJ said that

> a defendant who has wrongfully detained and profited from the property of someone else cannot avail himself of a hypothesis such as this. It does not lie in the mouth of such a defendant to suggest that the owner might not have found a hirer; for in using the property he showed that he wanted it and he cannot complain if it is assumed against him that he himself would have preferred to become the hirer rather than not have had the use of it at all.[92]

Since Romer LJ and Somervell LJ described the damages award as loss-based, they expressly reserved their opinion as to whether the same award would have been made had the switchboards not been profit-earning or never applied by the plaintiff to remunerative purposes.[93]

In *Kuwait Airways Corp v Iraqi Airways Co (Nos 4 and 5)* Lord Nicholls expressly acknowledged the availability of gain-based damages for conversion:

> Sometimes, when the goods or their equivalent are returned, the owner suffers no financial loss. But the wrongdoer may well have benefited from his temporary use of the owner's goods. It would not be right that he should be able to keep this benefit. The court may order him to pay damages assessed by reference to the value of the benefit he derived from his wrongdoing.[94]

C Trespass to Land

Gain-based relief is also recognised for trespass to land. The aggrieved land owner can claim the rent value of the user even though she would not have personally used the land in the way the trespasser did, or offered the use to anyone for rent. An early example is *Whitwham v Westminster Brymbo Coal and Coke Co*,[95] where the defendant's colliery, over several years, dumped waste onto the neighbouring land owned by the plaintiff. The Court of Appeal held that the plaintiff was entitled not only to compensation for the diminution in value that the waste had caused to the land but also to a 'wayleave' award reflecting the value of using the land for dumping waste. Even though the Court spoke of

---

[91] [1952] 2 QB 246 (CA) 254–55.
[92] ibid 257.
[93] ibid 252 (Somervell LJ), 257 (Romer LJ).
[94] [2002] UKHL 19, [2002] 2 AC 883, 1066 [87].
[95] [1896] 2 Ch 538 (CA). Other cases include *Martin v Porter* (1839) 5 M & W 351, 151 ER 149; *Jegon v Vivian* (1871) LR 6 Ch App 742.

'compensation', a hypothetical-fee award is best classified as gain-based.[96] Indeed, Lindley LJ might have alluded to the award being gain-based by saying that 'if one person has without leave of another been using that other's land for his own purposes, he ought to pay for such user'.[97]

An award expressly based on the defendant's gain was made in *Penarth Dock Engineering Co Ltd v Pounds*,[98] where the defendant committed a breach of contract and a trespass by failing to remove their pontoon from the plaintiff's dock. Lord Denning MR, sitting as a single judge, found that the plaintiff 'would not seem to have suffered any damage to speak of'[99] as the pontoon had not caused the plaintiff to incur any extra cost, and the plaintiff would not have made money out of the dock absent the trespass. Nevertheless, relying on *Whitwham* mentioned before and on his own comments in *Strand Electric*,[100] Lord Denning pronounced that 'in a case of this kind ... the test of the measure of damages is not what the plaintiffs have lost, but what benefit the defendant obtained by having the use of the berth'.[101]

A hypothetical-fee award was also made in *Bracewell v Appleby*,[102] where the defendant could access his newly-built house only by wrongfully using the plaintiffs' road. An injunction stopping the trespass was refused on the ground that the plaintiffs had unduly delayed proceedings, but the plaintiffs obtained (equitable) damages in lieu under Lord Cairns' Act. Those damages were measured by reference to the sum that the plaintiffs would have accepted for granting the defendant a right of way over their road.

The availability of gain-based relief for trespass to land enjoys further support from cases where a tenant wrongfully held over after the end of the lease, and where the landlord obtained damages exceeding his actual loss (mesne profits). An example is *Swordheath Properties Ltd v Tabet*,[103] where the Court of Appeal held the landlord entitled to damages based on the 'ordinary letting value' of the premises even though there was no evidence that the landlord could or would have let the premises to someone else in the relevant period.

Gain-based relief was clearly recognised by a majority in the Court of Appeal in *Ministry of Defence v Ashman*.[104] The deserted wife of an RAF serviceman and her children wrongfully remained in occupation of RAF accommodation, which was let to RAF personnel and their families at a concessionary rate and was not

---

[96] Above II in this chapter.
[97] [1896] 2 Ch 538 (CA) 541–42.
[98] [1963] 1 Lloyd's Rep 359.
[99] ibid 361.
[100] [1952] 2 QB 246 (CA); above IV B in this chapter.
[101] [1963] 1 Lloyd's Rep 359, 361–62.
[102] [1975] Ch 408.
[103] [1979] 1 WLR 285 (CA). Followed in *Inverugie Investments Ltd v Hackett* [1995] 1 WLR 713 (PC); *Lawson v Hartley-Brown* (1996) 71 P & CR 242 (CA); *Jones v Merton LBC* [2008] EWCA Civ 660, [2009] 1 P & CR 3 [24].
[104] (1993) 25 HLR 513 (CA). Followed in *Ministry of Defence v Thompson* (1993) 25 HLR 552 (CA), which had similar facts.

let on the open market. When the RAF claimed mesne profits for trespass, the question arose whether the award was to be calculated by reference to the concessionary rate or the higher rate that the wife would have had to pay for local authority accommodation in the relevant period. The former was the RAF's loss, the latter was the wife's gain from the trespass. Hoffmann LJ and Kennedy LJ held the RAF entitled to a gain-based award. Hoffmann LJ summarised the law as follows:

> A person entitled to possession of land can make a claim against a person who has been in occupation without his consent on two alternative bases. The first is for the loss which he has suffered in consequence of the defendant's trespass … The second is the value of the benefit which the occupier has received. This is a claim for restitution … It is true that in the earlier cases it has not been expressly stated that a claim for mesne profit for trespass can be a claim for restitution. Nowadays I do not see why we should not call a spade a spade.[105]

Lloyd LJ dissented, opining that, where a tenant holds over after the end of the lease, the landlord can only claim his loss, but not the tenant's gain, unless the landlord consented to the holding over.[106] He primarily relied on *Phillips v Homfray (No 2)*.[107]

In that case, the deceased had trespassed by using roads and passages under the plaintiff's land to transport coal. In an action against the then living tortfeasor, the plaintiff was held entitled to a wayleave for the trespass and an inquiry to ascertain its amount was ordered.[108] Before that inquiry was completed, the tortfeasor died. His executrix moved to stay proceedings under the then existing rule that tortious liability did not survive the tortfeasor's death (*actio personalis moritur cum persona*).[109] Since claims in unjust enrichment did survive the death of the person liable, the question arose whether the plaintiff's claim was one in tort or in unjust enrichment. Bowen LJ and Cotton LJ held (Baggallay LJ dissenting) that the plaintiff's claim had not survived the deceased's death. It would only have survived, they said, if the deceased had appropriated the plaintiff's property or proceeds thereof. But the deceased simply saved the expense of paying the plaintiff for the use or finding an alternative mode of transport.

Phillips v Homfray (No 2) has been cited, by Lloyds LJ in *Ministry of Defence v Ashman* and others, as a bar to gain-based damages for trespass to land where the defendant did not obtain a positive benefit. However, *Phillips v Homfray (No 2)* can be no such bar, for two reasons. First, it has been ignored in many modern cases awarding gain-based damages, for example, by a majority in the Court of

---

[105] (1993) 25 HLR 513 (CA) 519.
[106] ibid 520–21.
[107] (1883) LR 24 Ch D 439 (CA).
[108] *Phillips v Homfray (No 1)* (1871) LR 6 Ch App 770 (CA).
[109] The *actio personalis* rule was abolished by the Law Reform (Miscellaneous Provisions) Act 1934 s 1.

Appeal in *Ministry of Defence v Ashman*. Secondly, *Phillips v Homfray (No 2)* has been subject to an intense scholarly criticism and scrutiny, and there is now widespread agreement among commentators that that case is no bar to gain-based relief today because it was 'wrongly decided',[110] its reasons 'can no longer be supported',[111] or it was only concerned with the *actio personalis* rule now abolished.[112]

If the availability of gain-based relief for trespass to land was still in doubt, the doubts were removed by Lord Nicholls in his leading speech in *Attorney-General v Blake (Jonathan Cape Ltd Third Party)*:

> A trespasser who enters another's land may cause the landowner no financial loss. In such a case damages are measured by the benefit received by the trespasser, namely, by his use of the land. The same principle is applied where the wrong consists of the use of another's land for depositing waste, or by using a path across the land or using passages in an underground mine. In this type of case the damages recoverable will be, in short, the price a reasonable person would pay for the right of user[.][113]

Lord Nicholls' lucid statement has led the courts to clearly recognise the availability of gain-based relief for trespass to land. A recent example is *Field Common Ltd v Elmbridge BC*,[114] where the defendant council, wrongfully exceeding an existing right of way, laid tarmac over a part of the claimant's land in order to provide access to an adjoining industrial estate owned by the council and let to tenants. The council was held liable for the trespass committed by its tenants by driving over the claimant's land. Damages were awarded and assessed by reference to 'the amount which the Council would have been prepared to pay for a licence to do what it did do'.[115]

D   Intellectual Property Wrongs

In actions for intellectual property wrongs, gain-based awards can be made not only through an account of profits (ordering the defendant to disgorge all profits made from the infringement[116]) but also through an award of damages, in two

---

[110]   G Virgo, *The Principles of the Law of Restitution*, 2nd edn (Oxford, 2006) 463, 464.

[111]   G Jones, *Goff & Jones: The Law of Restitution*, 7th edn (London, 2007) [36–003].

[112]   W Swadling, 'The Myth of *Phillips v Homfray*' in W Swadling and G Jones (eds), *The Search for Principle: Essays in Honour of Lord Goff of Chieveley* (Oxford, 1999) 277; J Edelman, *Gain-Based Damages: Contract, Tort, Equity and Intellectual Property* (Oxford, 2002) 133; RJ Sharpe and SM Waddams, 'Damages for lost opportunity to bargain' (1982) 2 *OJLS* 290, 294–95; EJ Weinrib, 'Restitutionary Damages as Corrective Justice' (2000) 1 *Theoretical Inquiries in Law* 1, 15. See also P Birks, *An Introduction to the Law of Restitution*, revised edn (Oxford, 1989) 323–25.

[113]   [2001] 1 AC 268 (HL) 278.

[114]   [2008] EWHC 2079 (Ch), [2009] 1 P & CR 1.

[115]   ibid [85]. See also *Gondal v Dillon Newsagents Ltd* [2001] RLR 221 (CA) 228; *Horsford v Bird* [2006] UKPC 3, [2006] 1 EGLR 75; *Sinclair v Gavaghan* [2007] EWHC 2256 (Ch).

[116]   The court may make an allowance for the skill and labour exercised by the infringer in making the profits: *Redwood Music Ltd v Chappell & Co Ltd* [1982] RPC 109, 132 (for copyright); *Spring Form Inc v Toy Brokers Ltd* [2002] FSR 17 [10] (for patent).

ways. First, damages may be assessed by reference to a hypothetical reasonable royalty,[117] that is 'the royalty that a willing licensor and a willing licensee would have agreed'.[118] Such awards are best classified as gain-based.[119] Secondly, where 'the defendant knew, or had reasonable grounds to know, that he engaged in infringing activity', Regulation 3 of the Intellectual Property (Enforcement, etc.) Regulations 2006[120] requires a court assessing damages to take into account, among others, 'any unfair profits made by the defendant'. While this should not normally lead to damages awards being based on the defendant's whole profit, for this would render the alternative remedy account of profits largely redundant, it does mean that an award of damages may exceed the claimant's loss.

A court can generally respond to an intellectual property wrong by awarding either an account of profits or damages, but not both for the same wrong.[121] Both remedies have long been recognised for passing-off[122] and are listed in section 61(1) of the Patents Act 1977 as remedies available for patent infringement. With regard to copyright,[123] performers' property rights,[124] trademark,[125] EC design,[126] UK registered design[127] and UK unregistered design,[128] literally identical statutory provisions provide: 'In an action for infringement ... all such relief by way of damages, injunctions, accounts or otherwise is available ... as is available in respect of the infringement of any other property right'.

Interpreting the analogy with tangible property in a loose way, the courts are willing to respond to the intellectual property wrongs in question by awarding not only damages but also an account of profits.[129] However, 'accounts of profits

---

[117] eg *General Tire & Rubber Co v Firestone Tyre & Rubber Co Ltd* [1975] 1 WLR 819 (HL) (for patent); *Blayney v Clogau St David's Gold Mines Ltd* [2002] EWCA Civ 1007, [2003] FSR 19 [10]–[20] (for copyright); *Reed Executive plc v Reed Business Information Ltd* [2002] EWHC 2772 (Ch) [13], [23] (for trademark and passing-off); *Irvine v Talksport Ltd* [2003] EWCA Civ 423, [2003] FSR 35 [104] (for passing-off); Intellectual Property (Enforcement, etc.) Regulations 2006 SI 2006/1028 reg 3 (for culpable infringements of intellectual property rights).

[118] *Ultraframe (UK) Ltd v Eurocell Building Plastics Ltd* [2006] EWHC 1344 (Pat) [47] (Kitchin J).

[119] Above II in this chapter.

[120] SI 2006/1028, implementing Directive 2004/48/EC of the European Parliament and of the Council of 29 April 2004 on the enforcement of intellectual property rights [2004] OJ L195/16.

[121] Patents Act 1977 s 61(2) (for patent); *MacDonald v French Connection Group plc* [2006] EWHC 3695 (Ch) [15] (for copyright).

[122] eg *Hogg v Kirby* (1803) 8 Ves Jun 215, 223; 32 ER 336, 339; *AG Spalding & Bros v AW Gamage Ltd* (1915) 32 RPC 273 (HL) 283.

[123] Copyright, Designs and Patents Act 1988 s 96(2).

[124] Copyright, Designs and Patents Act 1988 s 191I(2).

[125] Trade Marks Act 1994 s 14(2). This provision applies not only to UK trademarks but also to Community trademarks: Council Regulation (EC) 40/1994 of 20 December 1993 on the Community trade mark [1994] OJ L11/1 art 14.

[126] Community Design Regulations 2005 SI 2005/2339 reg 1A(2), inserted by the Intellectual Property (Enforcement, etc.) Regulations 2006 SI 2006/1028 sch 3.

[127] Registered Designs Act 1949 s 24A(2), inserted by the Intellectual Property (Enforcement, etc.) Regulations 2006 SI 2006/1028 sch 1.

[128] Copyright, Designs and Patents Act 1988 s 229(2).

[129] eg *Taylor v Rive Droite Music Ltd* [2005] EWCA Civ 1300, [2006] EMLR 52 [56] (for copyright); *Doncaster Pharmaceuticals Group Ltd v The Bolton Pharmaceutical Co 100 Ltd* [2006]

are intrinsically difficult to take, uncertain and expensive' and 'have not been common in infringement cases, whether of patents, trade marks, copyright or design, nor in passing off cases'.[130] Another factor for the unpopularity of an account of profits may be the ruling by the House of Lords[131] that an account cannot be combined with 'additional damages', which are available for the infringement of copyright, performers' property rights and UK unregistered design.[132]

Depending on the particular intellectual property right, an account of profits and/ or damages may be unavailable where the defendant was not aware, and had no reasonable ground for supposing, that the right in question existed. An exclusion of 'damages' by virtue of the defendant's innocence must encompass an exclusion of 'restitutionary damages' in the form of a hypothetical-royalty award.[133]

Innocence has the strongest effect where an article infringing a UK unregistered design is imported or dealt with. This constitutes a secondary infringement of the design right only if the importer or dealer 'knows or has reason to believe' that the article in question is an infringing article.[134] An innocent importer or dealer is thus not liable at all. Even where the defendant knows, or should know, that the article in question is an infringing article, liability is restricted to 'damages not exceeding a reasonable royalty' if the defendant shows that 'the infringing article was innocently acquired by him or a predecessor in title of his'.[135]

Less protection is afforded to the innocent infringer of a patent or a UK registered design. Neither an account of profits nor an award of damages is available[136] but other remedies such as an injunction[137] are.

Even less protection is afforded to the innocent infringer of certain other intellectual property rights. In the case of passing-off, innocence may exclude an account of profits[138] but not damages.[139] Just the opposite is true for copyright,

---

EWCA Civ 661, [2007] FSR 3 [19] (for trademark); *J Choo (Jersey) Ltd v Towerstone Ltd* [2008] EWHC 346 (Ch), [2008] FSR 19 [37] (for design).

[130]   *Spring Form Inc v Toy Brokers Ltd* [2002] FSR 17 [6] (Pumfrey J).

[131]   *Redrow Homes Ltd v Bett Brothers plc* 1998 SC (HL) 64.

[132]   Copyright, Designs and Patents Act 1988 ss 97(2), 191J(2) and 229(3) respectively. The nature of 'additional damages' is mentioned below ch 14, V.

[133]   J Edelman, *Gain-Based Damages: Contract, Tort, Equity and Intellectual Property* (Oxford, 2002) 231–232; C Rotherham, 'The Conceptual Structure of Restitution for Wrongs' [2007] *CLJ* 172, 192.

[134]   Copyright, Designs and Patents Act 1988 s 227(1).

[135]   Copyright, Designs and Patents Act 1988 s 233(2).

[136]   Patents Act 1977 s 62(1); Registered Designs Act 1949 s 24B(1), inserted by the Intellectual Property (Enforcement, etc.) Regulations 2006 SI 2006/1028 sch 1.

[137]   Expressly preserved by Registered Designs Act 1949 s 24B(3), inserted by the Intellectual Property (Enforcement, etc.) Regulations 2006 SI 2006/1028 sch 1.

[138]   *AG Spalding & Bros v AW Gamage Ltd* (1915) 32 RPC 273 (HL) 283; *Young & Co Ltd v Holt* (1948) 65 RPC 25.

[139]   *Gillette UK Ltd v Edenwest Ltd* [1994] RPC 279, 291–93; *Reed Executive plc v Reed Business Information Ltd* [2004] EWCA Civ 159, [2004] RPC 40 [131]–[136].

performers' property rights and the primary infringement of a UK unregistered design by making articles to that design. If the infringer did not know, and had no reason to believe, that the intellectual property right in question existed, 'the plaintiff is not entitled to damages against him, but without prejudice to any other remedy'.[140] An account of profits is thus available.

In respect of EC design and trademark, the relevant legislation contains no defence of innocence so that the court is free to award either an account of profits or damages against an innocent infringer.[141] In one trademark case, the infringer's initial innocence was one of the factors that led to an account of profits being refused on discretionary grounds.[142] However, the legislator's conscious decision against a defence of innocence should usually prevail.

E Nuisance

In three cases, the Court of Appeal has rejected the general availability of gain-based relief for nuisance. The first case is *Stoke-on-Trent City Council v W & J Wass Ltd* (*Wass*),[143] where the defendant committed a nuisance by knowingly and repeatedly operating a market in close proximity to the plaintiff's market, thereby infringing the plaintiff's exclusive right to hold a market in that area. The plaintiff obtained a permanent injunction restraining the defendant from further operating its market. On the claim for damages for the period in which the defendant had operated its market, the trial judge found that the defendant's market had not affected the custom of the plaintiff's market. He still awarded damages by reference to the licence fee that the plaintiff could have reasonably required for allowing the defendant's market.

The Court of Appeal restricted the plaintiff to nominal damages. A hypothetical licence fee, the Court acknowledged, could be claimed in actions for trespass to land, wrongful interference with goods, patent infringement and breach of a restrictive covenant. Nicholls LJ, with whom Mann LJ agreed, called this the 'user principle'.[144] But the Court refused to apply that principle *in casu*. Nicholls LJ opined that a market right merely protects the owner against a disturbance of the

---

[140] Copyright, Designs and Patents Act 1988 ss 97(1), 191J(1), and 233(1) for copyright, performers' property rights and UK unregistered design respectively.

[141] *Waterford Wedgwood plc v David Nagli Ltd* [1998] FSR 92, 100 (for trademark); *J Choo (Jersey) Ltd v Towerstone Ltd* [2008] EWHC 346 (Ch), [2008] FSR 19 [37] (for EC design). In the latter case, Floyd J saw 'no possible policy reason' for the difference between EC and UK designs as to innocent infringement (at [33]) but he was confident that Parliament had intended that difference (at [34]–[36]).

[142] *Conran v Mean Fiddler Holdings Ltd* [1997] FSR 856, 861.

[143] [1988] 1 WLR 1406 (CA).

[144] ibid 1416 (Nicholls LJ).

lawful market such as loss of stallage or tolls. Absent such disturbance, he said, an award of damages would be an 'anomaly' even though an injunction may still be granted.[145]

Nourse LJ, with whom Mann LJ also agreed, acknowledged that (by then) one case had recognised the user principle for the infringement of a right to light,[146] but he pointed out that the plaintiff in that case had suffered loss.[147] In the absence of loss, he said, the user principle had only been recognised for trespass to land, wrongful interference with goods and breach of a restrictive covenant. He did not feel empowered to widen the scope of the user principle in the absence of loss, even though he admitted that 'there may be a logical difficulty in making a distinction between the present case and the way-leave cases'.[148] If, in the absence of loss, the user principle were applied to the infringement of a market right, he said, it would also have to be applied to the obstruction of a right to light or a right to way and perhaps even to defamation.[149] He did recognise the possibility of the user principle gaining a wider scope in future:

> It is possible that the English law of tort, more especially of the so-called 'proprietary torts,' will in due course make a more deliberate move towards recovery based not on loss suffered by the plaintiff but on the unjust enrichment of the defendant … But I do not think that that process can begin in this case and I doubt whether it can begin at all at this level of decision.[150]

The second case in which the Court of Appeal rejected the general availability of gain-based relief for nuisance is *Forsyth-Grant v Allen*,[151] where the defendant built two semi-detached houses next to the claimant's hotel, thereby infringing the claimant's right of light acquired by prescription. Prior to the construction of the two houses, the defendant made the claimant several offers to pay 'reasonable compensation' for any loss of light. The claimant did not reply to these offers and indeed refused the defendant's architect entry to her hotel. When the two houses were completed, the claimant brought an action in nuisance and claimed the profit that the defendant had made from the infringement of her right of light. The Court of Appeal rejected that claim.

Primarily relying on *Wass*, Patten J, with whom Mummery LJ agreed, considered an account of profits unavailable in nuisance.[152] Toulson LJ expressly left open the possibility of an account of profits being awarded in nuisance in an appropriate case, but he quickly added that the present case was not such a case because of the claimant's unreasonable failure to cooperate with the defendant.[153]

---

[145]   ibid 1418–19.
[146]   *Carr-Saunders v Dick McNeil Associates Ltd* [1986] 1 WLR 922, 931.
[147]   [1988] 1 WLR 1406 (CA) 1413.
[148]   ibid 1415.
[149]   ibid.
[150]   ibid.
[151]   [2008] EWCA Civ 505, [2008] Env LR 41.
[152]   ibid [32]–[33].
[153]   ibid [47].

Even though the claimant had not raised the issue, the Court also touched upon the possibility of assessing damages by reference to the price that the defendant might reasonably have been required to pay for a relaxation of the claimant's right to light. While Toulson LJ considered such an assessment possible 'in an appropriate case',[154] Patten J expressed doubts.[155]

The third case in which the Court of Appeal rejected the general availability of gain-based relief for nuisance is *Devenish Nutrition Ltd v Sanofi-Aventis SA (France)* *(Devenish)*.[156] That case did not actually involve nuisance, but anti-competitive practices. In breach of Article 81(1) of the EC Treaty, certain vitamin manufacturers formed worldwide cartels to fix the prices for their products and allocate sales quota. The claimant (Devenish) purchased vitamins from cartel members and used them to make animal feedstuffs, which it sold on to custom-ers. After the European Commission had imposed fines on the cartel members, Devenish brought a civil follow-on action and claimed, inter alia, a restitutionary award in the amount of the overcharge, that is the amount by which the prices charged by the cartel members exceeded the prices that would have been charged had there been no cartels. The Court of Appeal rejected that claim.

While Longmore LJ based this rejection primarily on the ground that Deven-ish had passed the overcharge on to its customers,[157] Arden LJ, with whom Tuckey LJ agreed on this point,[158] rejected in principle the availability of gain-based relief for 'non-proprietary' torts such as nuisance or breach of competition law. Arden LJ conceded[159] that to allow gain-based recovery in exceptional cases of non-proprietary torts would be consistent with *Attorney-General v Blake (Jonathan Cape Ltd Third Party)*,[160] where the House of Lords recognised the availability of an account of profits in exceptional cases of breach of contract. But she opined that *Wass* had excluded gain-based recovery in non-proprietary torts and that *Blake* had not overruled *Wass*.[161] In relation to nuisance, therefore, the Court of Appeal in *Devenish* declared gain-based recov-ery unavailable unless and until the House of Lords holds otherwise.

It would be futile to go into the niceties of what the ratio of each of these three cases was. Their combined effect is a general proscription of gain-based relief in nuisance actions. An exception may be the infringement of a right to light, in which situation gain-based relief has been awarded in one first-instance

---

[154] ibid [38].
[155] ibid [32].
[156] [2008] EWCA Civ 1086.
[157] ibid [146].
[158] ibid [155].
[159] ibid [57].
[160] [2001] 1 AC 268 (HL); below IV B in this chapter.
[161] [2008] EWCA Civ 1086 [75].

decision[162] and recognised *obiter* in two others.[163] These cases may still stand since they were noted without disapproval in *Forsyth-Grant v Allen*[164] and not mentioned at all in *Devenish*. What is true for a right to light should equally apply to other easements such as a right of way. This raises the question of whether a hypothetical-fee award is available only where the claimant has suffered loss (the question is academic for a right to light where there will always be loss of amenity). Nourse LJ in *Wass* supported such a limitation. But his observations were *obiter* for all rights other than market rights, and the Court of Appeal in *Forsyth-Grant v Allen* did not mention such a limitation at all. Where an easement is infringed, therefore, damages calculated by reference to a hypothetical relaxation fee may be available whether or not the claimant has suffered loss.

F Deceit and Fraud

Deceit is a fraudulent misrepresentation that induces the other party to enter into a contract.[165] The victim is generally entitled to rescind the contract in question[166] and then recover money and (the value of) property transferred under the contract.[167] This claim is simply based on the absence of a valid contract justifying the transfer. It is indisputably a claim in (autonomous) unjust enrichment (or enrichment by subtraction)[168] and thus irrelevant in the present context. What is of interest here is 'restitution for wrongs', that is gain-based relief in the absence of rescission. Such relief was awarded in an old case[169] on the basis of the now rejected implied-contract theory,[170] but was denied by the Court of Appeal in *Halifax Building Society v Thomas*.[171]

Mr Thomas obtained a mortgage advance from Halifax by fraudulently misrepresenting his identity and creditworthiness, which was a criminal offence. He used the money to purchase a flat. After he had defaulted on his interest payments and Halifax had discovered his true identity, Halifax exercised its right to sell the flat. The proceeds of the sale exceeded the loan. Halifax sought a declaration that it was entitled to keep the surplus as it constituted a benefit that Mr Thomas had obtained from his tort against Halifax. If made out, Halifax' claim would have defeated the Crown's claim to confiscate the surplus under a confiscation order made in criminal proceedings against Mr Thomas.

---

[162]   *Tamares (Vincent Square) Ltd v Fairpoint Properties (Vincent Square) Ltd (No 2)* [2007] EWHC 212 (Ch), [2007] 1 WLR 2167.
[163]   *Carr-Saunders v Dick McNeil Associates Ltd* [1986] 1 WLR 922, 931; *Deakins v Hookings* [1994] 1 EGLR 190, 195–96.
[164]   [2008] EWCA Civ 505, [2008] Env LR 41 [26], [38].
[165]   *Derry v Peek* (1889) LR 14 App Cas 337 (HL).
[166]   eg *Cobbe v Yeoman's Row Management Ltd* [2008] UKHL 55, [2008] 1 WLR 1752 [4].
[167]   eg *Redgrave v Hurd* (1881) LR 20 Ch D 1 (CA).
[168]   See above I in this chapter.
[169]   *Hill v Perrott* (1810) 3 Taunt 274, 128 ER 109.
[170]   For that theory and its rejection see above IV A in this chapter.
[171]   [1996] Ch 217 (CA).

The Court of Appeal rejected Halifax' claim primarily on the ground that Halifax, by exercising its rights as mortgagee and selling the flat, had affirmed the mortgage and thus truly waived the tort of deceit.[172] But Peter Gibson LJ, who delivered the leading judgment, gave another reason which was apparently independent of the ratification argument:

> Further I am not satisfied that in the circumstances of the present case it would be right to treat the unjust enrichment of Mr Thomas as having been gained 'at the expense of' the society … I do not overlook the fact that the policy of law is to view with disfavour a wrongdoer benefiting from his wrong, the more so when the wrong amounts to fraud, but it cannot be suggested that there is a universally applicable principle that in every case there will be restitution of benefit from a wrong … On the facts of the present case, in my judgment, the fraud is not in itself a sufficient factor to allow the society to require Mr Thomas to account to it.[173]

In *Murad v Al-Saraj*,[174] where a fiduciary made a fraudulent misrepresentation towards his principals, Etherton J seems to have awarded an account of profits not only for breach of fiduciary duty but also for the tort of deceit. Indeed, he proclaimed that the availability of an account of profit for deceit is 'now well established'.[175] He distinguished *Halifax Building Society v Thomas* on the ground that Halifax had suffered no loss.[176] The Court of Appeal in *Murad v Al-Saraj*[177] dealt with the relevance of the principals' hypothetical consent[178] and voiced no support for the idea of an account of profits being available for deceit. On the contrary, Arden LJ was keen to clarify that the account of profits awarded by Etherton J found its basis in the fiduciary relationship and not in the tort of deceit:

> It would be tempting to jump to the conclusion … that in this case the judge took the novel step of awarding the equitable remedy of account for the common law tort of deceit (cf *Attorney General v Blake* [2001] 1 AC 268), but that is not in my judgment the true interpretation of the judge's judgment. The judge gave a remedy of account because there was a fiduciary relationship. For wrongs in the context of such a relationship, an order for an account of profits is a conventional remedy.[179]

In recent cases, *Halifax Building Society v Thomas* has still been regarded as binding authority for the unavailability of gain-based relief against a 'fraudster who is not a fiduciary and whose gains cannot be said to derive from his

---

[172] ibid 226–27. This reasoning is criticised as being 'incorrect' by C Mitchell, 'No Account of Profits for a Victim of Deceit' [1996] *LMCLQ* 314, 316; G Virgo, *The Principles of the Law of Restitution*, 2nd edn (Oxford, 2006) 474.

[173] [1996] Ch 217 (CA) 227–28.

[174] [2004] EWHC 1235 (Ch).

[175] ibid [342]. The same claim is made by G Jones, *Goff & Jones: The Law of Restitution*, 7th edn (London, 2007) [36–005].

[176] [2004] EWHC 1235 (Ch) [346].

[177] [2005] EWCA Civ 959, [2005] WTLR 1573.

[178] See S Harder, 'Is a Defaulting Fiduciary Exculpated by the Principal's Hypothetical Consent?' (2008) 8 *Oxford University Commonwealth Law Journal* 25, 31–32.

[179] [2005] EWCA Civ 959, [2005] WTLR 1573 [46].

wrongful use of the claimant's property'.[180] It must be concluded that a victim of fraudulent misrepresentation cannot, without rescinding the contract in question, claim the profit the swindler has made as a result of the deceit.

By contrast, gain-based relief in the absence of rescission is available in cases of fraud by way of bribery. An agent accepting a bribe breaches his fiduciary duty of loyalty towards his principal, and the latter has an equitable claim against the former for the amount of the bribe.[181] There are remedies at common law too. Lord Diplock, delivering the Privy Council's decision in *Mahesan S/O Thambiah v Malaysia Government Officers' Co-Operative Housing Society Ltd*, pronounced that

> both as against the briber and the agent bribed the principal has these alternative remedies: (1) for money had and received under which he can recover the amount of the bribe as money had and received or, (2) for damages for fraud, under which he can recover the amount of the actual loss sustained in consequence of his entering into the transaction in respect of which the bribe was given ...[182]

Even though the juxtaposition, made in this passage and subsequent cases,[183] between 'money had and received' and 'damages for fraud' suggests that the former is a claim in autonomous unjust enrichment and not fraud,[184] some scholars opine that the claim for money had and received, like the claim for compensatory damages, arises from the tort of fraud and is thus a claim in parasitic unjust enrichment.[185] Be that as it may, the principal's common law claim against the briber is limited to the amount of the bribe or the principal's loss, whichever is greater; the principal has no common law claim for the whole profit that the briber has made from the contract obtained by the bribe.[186]

---

[180] *Sinclair Investment Holdings SA v Versailles Trade Finance Ltd* [2007] EWHC 915 (Ch), [2007] 2 All ER (Comm) 993 [127] (Rimer J). See also *Renault UK Ltd v Fleetpro Technical Services Ltd* [2007] EWHC 2541 (QB), [2007] All ER (D) 208 [157]; *Devenish Nutrition Ltd v Sanofi-Aventis SA (France)* [2008] EWCA Civ 1086 [85] (Arden LJ).

[181] *Fawcett v Whitehouse* (1829) 1 Russ & M 132, 39 ER 51; *Boston Deep Sea Fishing and Ice Co v Ansell* (1888) LR 39 Ch D 339, 349 (CA) 367–68 (Bowen LJ); *Reading v Attorney-General* [1951] AC 507 (HL). In *Attorney-General for Hong Kong v Reid* [1994] 1 AC 324 (PC), it was held that the agent holds the bribe on constructive trust for the principal.

[182] [1979] AC 374 (PC) 383.

[183] *Armagas Ltd v Mundogas SA* [1986] AC 717 (CA) 743 (Goff LJ); *Petrotrade Inc v Smith* [2000] 1 Lloyd's Rep 486, 490; *Fyffes Group Ltd v Templeman* [2000] 2 Lloyd's Rep 643, 660.

[184] Such classification is favoured by J Beatson, 'The Nature of Waiver of Tort' in J Beatson, *The Use and Abuse of Unjust Enrichment: Essays on the Law of Restitution* (Oxford, 1991) 223.

[185] P Birks, *An Introduction to the Law of Restitution*, revised edn (Oxford, 1989) 338, 339, who concedes that the claim against the briber, but not the agent, may equally-well be classified as one in autonomous unjust enrichment; J Edelman, *Gain-Based Damages: Contract, Tort, Equity and Intellectual Property* (Oxford, 2002) 142.

[186] A Berg, 'Bribery—transaction validity and other civil law implications' [2001] *LMCLQ* 27, 60, who argues (at 61) that the law should develop towards recognising a tortious claim for the whole profit. For the question of whether such a claim lies in equity see A Berg (at 57–60) and above III, before A, in this chapter.

V Contract

Traditionally, damages for breach of contract could never be based on the defendant's gain but only on the claimant's loss. A vivid example is *Tito v Waddell (No 2)*,[187] where the defendants saved considerable expense by not fulfilling their contractual obligation to replant a large part of Ocean Island after mining operations had ceased. In an action by the landowners, an award of cost-of-cure damages was considered inappropriate, and the diminution in the land's value was nil as a replanting would not have increased its value. Consequently, the claimants obtained only nominal damages. In passing, Megarry VC rejected gain-based damages (which had not been claimed) by saying that

> it is fundamental to all questions of damages that they are to compensate the plaintiff for his loss or injury by putting him as nearly as possible in the same position as he would have been in had he not suffered the wrong. The question is not one of making the defendant disgorge what he has saved by committing the wrong, but one of compensating the plaintiff.[188]

However, the traditional exclusion of gain-based damages for breach of contract has experienced significant inroads, in two ways. In one line of cases, starting with *Wrotham Park Estate Co Ltd v Parkside Homes Ltd*,[189] the courts have assessed damages by reference to the fee that the contract-breaker would have had to pay for a relaxation of the obligation at issue. Such awards are best characterised as gain-based.[190] In a second line of cases, starting with *Attorney-General v Blake (Jonathan Cape Ltd Third Party)*,[191] the courts have awarded an account of profits, ordering the contract-breaker to disgorge all profits made from the breach. Both lines of cases will now be presented.

A   Hypothetical-Fee Award ('*Wrotham Park* Damages')

In *Wrotham Park Estate Co Ltd v Parkside Homes Ltd*,[192] a development company (Parkside) built houses on certain land in breach of a restrictive covenant, registered as a land charge, which made the development of the land subject to approval by the neighbouring Wrotham Park Estate (Estate). In an action for breach of contract against Parkside and the purchasers of the houses, the Estate sought a mandatory injunction for the demolition of the houses, but no interim injunction. By the time of the trial, the houses had been completed and occupied

---

[187]   [1977] Ch 106.
[188]   ibid 332. See also *Teacher v Calder* [1899] AC 451 (HL(Sc)) 467–68.
[189]   [1974] 1 WLR 798.
[190]   Above II in this chapter.
[191]   [2001] 1 AC 268 (HL).
[192]   [1974] 1 WLR 798.

by the purchasers. Brightman J refused a mandatory injunction on the ground that it would 'be an unpardonable waste of much needed houses to direct that they now be pulled down'.[193]

He awarded equitable damages in lieu of an injunction under the Chancery Amendment Act 1858 ('Lord Cairns' Act'). Even though the value of the Wrotham Park Estate was 'not diminished by one farthing',[194] he said, the defendants should not 'be left in undisturbed possession of the fruits of their wrongdoing'.[195] Referring to the user principle in tort,[196] he held the defendants liable to pay such a sum 'as might reasonably have been demanded by the [Estate] from Parkside as a quid pro quo for relaxing the covenant'[197] even though the Estate 'would clearly not have granted any relaxation'.[198] He fixed that hypothetical fee at 5 per cent of the profit Parkside had anticipated to make, and had made, from the development.[199]

For a long time, *Wrotham Park* was 'a solitary beacon'.[200] Indeed, the Court of Appeal rejected an assessment of contractual damages by reference to a hypothetical relaxation fee in *Surrey CC v Bredero Homes Ltd.*[201] Two local councils sold certain land to a development company (Bredero) subject to a covenant by Bredero to adhere to an existing planning permission, which prescribed a maximum of 72 houses on that land. In breach of that covenant, Bredero built 77 houses, as allowed by a later planning permission. Although aware of the development, the two councils did nothing to prevent it but waited until its completion and then sought damages. They conceded not to have suffered any loss by virtue of Bredero's breach but claimed the fee that they would have demanded for a relaxation of the covenant.

Reinforcing the traditional unavailability of gain-based damages for breach of contract, the Court of Appeal upheld an award of nominal damages only. *Wrotham Park* was distinguished, but each judge gave a different reason. Dillon LJ distinguished *Wrotham Park* on the ground that the award made in that case had been one of equitable damages under Lord Cairns' Act whereas the present case concerned damages at common law.[202] Steyn LJ distinguished *Wrotham Park* on the ground that that case had involved the wrongful use of property in a wide

---

[193] ibid 811.

[194] ibid 812.

[195] ibid.

[196] Brightman J, ibid 813–14, cited the following cases, all of which are considered above IV B and C in this chapter: *Whitwham v Westminster Brymbo Coal & Coke Co* [1896] 2 Ch 538 (CA); *Watson, Laidlaw & Co Ltd v Pott, Cassels & Williamson* 1914 SC (HL) 18; *Strand Electric and Engineering Co Ltd v Brisford Entertainments Ltd* [1952] 2 QB 246 (CA); *Penarth Dock Engineering Co Ltd v Pounds* [1963] 1 Lloyd's Rep 359.

[197] [1974] 1 WLR 798, 815.

[198] ibid.

[199] ibid 815–16.

[200] *Attorney-General v Blake (Jonathan Cape Ltd Third Party)* [2001] 1 AC 268 (HL) 283 (Lord Nicholls).

[201] [1993] 1 WLR 1361 (CA).

[202] ibid 1366–67.

sense, which the present case did not.[203] Rose LJ distinguished *Wrotham Park* on the ground that the claimant in that case had objected to the development as soon as it learnt of it whereas the claimants in the present case had never objected to the development.[204]

Subsequently, in *Jaggard v Sawyer*,[205] the Court of Appeal 'revived' *Wrotham Park* damages by classifying them as compensatory. The case concerned a residential development of 10 properties lining a private cul-de-sac. Each plot, including the area of roadway immediately in front of it, was conveyed subject to covenants not to use any part of the unbuilt land other than as a private garden. The defendants bought one plot and additional land behind it, on which they built another house. Access to the new house was by means of a driveway over the defendants' original plot, thus breaching the restrictive covenant in favour of the other nine plots. When the defendants' building work was at an advanced stage, the owner of another plot sought an injunction restraining the use of the defendants' original plot as a driveway to their new house.

The trial judge refused an injunction but awarded damages *in lieu* (under section 50 of the Supreme Court Act 1981) and, relying on *Wrotham Park*, assessed the damages by reference to what the defendants might reasonably have paid for a relaxation of the covenant. The Court of Appeal upheld the damages award and 'sidestepped' the (seeming) disapproval of *Wrotham Park* in *Surrey CC v Bredero Homes Ltd* by arguing that *Wrotham Park* damages are not in fact gain-based but rather compensate the claimant for a lost opportunity to bargain.[206]

Surrey CC v Bredero Homes Ltd was finally laid to rest in *Attorney-General v Blake (Jonathan Cape Ltd Third Party)*,[207] where both Lord Nicholls,[208] giving the leading speech, and Lord Hobhouse,[209] dissenting, observed that *Wrotham Park* 'is to be preferred' over *Surrey CC v Bredero Homes Ltd*. Lord Nicholls regarded *Wrotham Park* damages as gain-based[210] whereas Lord Hobhouse regarded them as compensatory.[211]

Wrotham Park damages have since flourished in cases involving the breach of a restrictive covenant,[212] breach of a landlord's covenant for quiet enjoyment,[213] and other cases. One example for the last category is *Lane v O'Brien Homes Ltd*,[214]

---

[203]   ibid 1369–71.
[204]   ibid 1371.
[205]   [1995] 1 WLR 269 (CA).
[206]   ibid 281–82, 291. See also *Gafford v Graham* (1999) 77 P & CR 73 (CA) 86.
[207]   [2001] 1 AC 268 (HL); below V B in this chapter.
[208]   [2001] 1 AC 268 (HL) 283.
[209]   ibid 298.
[210]   ibid 283–84.
[211]   ibid 298.
[212]   *Amec Developments Ltd v Jury's Hotel Management (UK) Ltd* (2001) 82 P & CR 22 [11].
[213]   *Lunn Poly Ltd v Liverpool & Lancashire Properties Ltd* [2006] EWCA Civ 430, [2006] 2 EGLR 29.
[214]   [2004] EWHC 303 (QB).

where the defendant built four houses on its land even though a contract between the defendant and the neighbouring landowner allowed only three houses on the defendant's land. It was not argued by either counsel that *Wrotham Park* damages were unavailable because the contract in question was a collateral agreement rather than a restrictive covenant.[215]

Another example for an award of *Wrotham Park* damages outside restrictive-covenant situations is *Experience Hendrix LLC v PPX Enterprises Inc.*[216] In 1973, the estate of the guitarist, singer and songwriter Jimi Hendrix and PPX Enterprises Inc (PPX) settled a copyright dispute by agreeing that PPX was entitled to certain masters, listed in a schedule, and was entitled to honour the then existing licences for other masters, but was not entitled to grant new licences for masters not listed in the schedule. Deliberately breaching that agreement, PPX did grant new licences for masters not listed in the schedule. In an action for breach of contract, the Court of Appeal did not consider the case so exceptional as to apply *Blake* and order PPX to account for all profits made from the infringing licences, but the Court did apply *Wrotham Park* and awarded damages in the amount of such a sum as Jimi Hendrix' estate might reasonably have demanded for permitting the infringing licences, even though the estate would not in fact have given permission.

In conclusion, it is now established that damages for breach of contract can, in certain circumstances, be assessed by reference to a hypothetical relaxation fee. It seems further established that hypothetical-fee awards are available not only *in lieu* of an injunction (under section 50 of the Supreme Court Act 1981) but also at common law.[217] What is unclear are the circumstances in which hypothetical-fee awards are available. Virgo is probably correct in suggesting that they are only available where a compensatory award is inadequate and are 'more likely to be granted where the contractual right is related to a property right in some way'.[218]

B   Account of Profits ('*Blake* Damages')

In *Attorney-General v Blake (Jonathan Cape Ltd Third Party)*,[219] the former double agent George Blake published an autobiography containing information that he had acquired while working for the Secret Intelligence Service (SIS). When he had joined the SIS, Blake expressly undertook not to divulge, either

---

[215]   ibid [21].

[216]   [2003] EWCA Civ 323, [2003] FSR 46. *Wrotham Park* damages were further held available, but denied on procedural grounds, in *WWF-World Wide Fund for Nature v World Wrestling Federation Entertainment Inc* [2007] EWCA Civ 286, [2008] 1 WLR 445.

[217]   *WWF-World Wide Fund for Nature v World Wrestling Federation Entertainment Inc* [2007] EWCA Civ 286, [2008] 1 WLR 445 [54]; *Field Common Ltd v Elmbridge BC* [2008] EWHC 2079 (Ch), [2009] 1 P & CR 1 [67]. See also *Attorney-General v Blake (Jonathan Cape Ltd Third Party)* [2001] 1 AC 268 (HL) 282–84 (Lord Nicholls).

[218]   G Virgo, *The Principles of the Law of Restitution*, 2nd edn (Oxford, 2006) 492.

[219]   [2001] 1 AC 268 (HL).

during or after his employment with the SIS, any official information gained as a result of that employment. Blake published his autobiography without seeking permission from the Crown. The publisher undertook to pay Blake £150,000 as an advance against royalties. After £60,000 of that sum had been paid to Blake, the Crown brought an action against him seeking to prevent Blake from obtaining the outstanding £90,000 and for that sum to be paid to the Crown instead. The Crown based its claim on several causes of action but only the action for breach of contract succeeded in the House of Lords where the majority (Lord Hobhouse dissenting) ordered Blake to account to the Crown for the profits he had made from his autobiography.

Lord Nicholls, giving the leading speech, noted the availability of an account of profits for certain equitable wrongs and torts, and he also noted the contractual gain-based award made in *Wrotham Park*. In the light of these authorities, he said, it was 'only a modest step' to recognise the exceptional availability of an account of profits for breach of contract.[220] An account was warranted *in casu* because Blake's undertaking of secrecy 'was closely akin to a fiduciary obligation',[221] and an account of profits would have been awarded 'almost as a matter of course' had the information divulged by Blake still been confidential.[222] Lord Nicholls clarified that, in actions for breach of contract, an 'account of profits will be appropriate only in exceptional circumstances'.[223] On the question of when circumstances are exceptional, he said that a 'useful general guide, although not exhaustive, is whether the plaintiff had a legitimate interest in preventing the defendant's profit-making activity'.[224] He went on to list three facts which, individually, would *not* justify ordering an account of profits:

> [T]he fact that the breach was cynical and deliberate; the fact that the breach enabled the defendant to enter into a more profitable contract elsewhere; and the fact that by entering into a new and more profitable contract the defendant put it out of his power to perform his contract with the plaintiff.[225]

Even though Lord Nicholls emphasised the exceptional character of awarding an account of profits for breach of contract, an account was held available less than 16 months after *Blake* in *Esso Petroleum Co Ltd v Niad Ltd*.[226] Niad ran a petrol station exclusively selling Esso's petrol and joined a pricing agreement, called Pricewatch, made between Esso and its dealers. Under that agreement, the petrol station undertook to sell petrol at the prices 'recommended' by Esso, and Esso undertook to provide financial support in recompense. On four occasions, Niad deliberately breached the Pricewatch agreement by selling petrol at a higher price

---

[220] ibid 285.
[221] ibid 287.
[222] ibid.
[223] ibid 285.
[224] ibid.
[225] ibid 286.
[226] [2001] EWHC 6 (Ch), [2001] All ER (D) 324.

than recommended by Esso, but Niad still received the financial support from Esso. Esso brought an action for breach of contract and claimed an account of the profits Niad had made from charging a higher price than recommended by Esso. Applying *Blake*, it was held that the facts were sufficiently exceptional to warrant ordering an account of profits because it was almost impossible to attribute lost sales to Niad's breach of contract; Niad's breach had undermined the whole Pricewatch scheme; and Esso had a legitimate interest in preventing Niad from profiting from its breach.[227]

The immediate application of *Blake* might have been taken as a sign that awards of an account of profits would now proliferate in contract cases. But this has not in fact happened in the decade since *Blake* was decided. In several contract cases, the award of an account of profits in accordance with *Blake* was considered but eventually refused.[228] Those cases demonstrate that the award of an account of profits for breach of contract remains the exception, but they have failed to clarify which circumstances are sufficiently exceptional.

---

[227] ibid [63].
[228] *WWF-World Wide Fund for Nature v World Wrestling Federation Entertainment Inc* [2002] FSR 32 [63]; *AB Corp v CD Co (The Sine Nomine)* [2002] 1 Lloyd's Rep 805; *Experience Hendrix LLC v PPX Enterprises Inc* [2003] EWCA Civ 323, [2003] FSR 46 [44]; *Harris v Williams-Wynne* [2005] EWHC 151 (Ch) [34]–[35], affirmed in [2006] EWCA Civ 104, [2006] 2 P & CR 27.

13

The Proper Scope of 'Restitution for Wrongs'

I Existing Theories

Having examined the present law of 'restitution for wrongs', the focus now shifts to the question of when gain-based relief in this area *ought* to be available. The Law Commission has considered this question but concluded that 'development of the law on restitution for wrongs is most appropriately left to the courts'.[1] A legislative reform of 'restitutionary damages' is recommended only to the extent to which this is necessary as a by-product of the recommended reform of exemplary (or punitive) damages, which are considered in Part 5 of this book. In the Law Commission's view, punitive damages ought to be available whenever a civil wrong other than breach of contract has been committed with a 'deliberate and outrageous disregard of the plaintiff's rights',[2] and legislation should not provide for punitive damages in this situation without also allowing 'the less extreme remedy of restitution for a wrong'.[3] But the courts are to be free to recognise 'restitution for wrongs' in other situations.[4]

There is a plethora of scholarly theories comprehensively setting out when 'restitution for wrongs' should be available, and the theories of the main participants in that debate will now be described. Subsequently, the theory advocated in this book will be presented. The explanation of the theory advocated here will expressly or impliedly take a stand on the existing theories. For that reason, the following description of the main existing theories is free from comments or criticism.

---

[1] Law Commission, 'Aggravated, Exemplary and Restitutionary Damages' (Law Com No 247, 1997) [3.38].
[2] ibid [5.42]–[5.77].
[3] ibid [3.51].
[4] ibid [3.52]–[3.53].

A   Birks

According to Birks, gain-based recovery is, or should be, available for three types of wrongs: where the defendant has deliberately set out to enrich himself by committing the wrong; where the duty broken aims to prevent the enrichment in question; and where the availability of gain-based recovery is a prophylactic measure to prevent certain enrichment or harm.[5]

The first category (deliberate exploitation of wrongdoing) comprises bribery, for which the availability of gain-based recovery is already recognised, but also instances in which the availability of gain-based recovery is yet to be (fully) recognised, such as a breach of contract committed deliberately with a view to make profit.[6]

The second category (anti-enrichment wrongs) comprises wrongful interference with goods, trespass to land, breach of a restrictive covenant, breach of confidence, and breach of fiduciary duty by making a profit which the principal might otherwise have made herself. A major purpose of regarding these instances as wrongs is to prevent enrichment. By contrast, defamation, negligence, nuisance and interference with contractual relations are anti-harm wrongs, not anti-enrichment wrongs, so there is no gain-based recovery unless those wrongs are committed with a profit-making motive and thus fall into the first category.

The third category (prophylaxis) concerns breach of fiduciary duty by making a profit which the principal could not have made herself. Here, gain-based recovery is available not to prevent the enrichment as such but to remove the danger of the fiduciary giving bad advice, and thus causing loss, to the principal.

B   Edelman

Edelman distinguishes two types of gain-based damages for civil wrongs, which he calls 'restitutionary damages' and 'disgorgement damages'.[7] Restitutionary damages reverse a wrongful transfer of value from the claimant to the defendant. An example is a hypothetical-fee award for the wrongful use of another's property. Such an award reverses the transfer from the claimant to the defendant of the market value of the use. 'Disgorgement damages', by contrast, do not require such a transfer of value. They strip the defendant of profits made as a

---

[5]   P Birks, *An Introduction to the Law of Restitution*, revised edn (Oxford, 1989) 326–46.

[6]   Birks, ibid 334, exemplifies this by the facts of *City of New Orleans v Firemen's Charitable Association* (1891) 43 La Ann 447, 9 So 486 (SC of Louisiana), discussed below V B in this chapter. The availability of gain-based relief for every wrong committed with a view to make profit is also supported by H McGregor, 'Restitutionary Damages' in P Birks (ed), *Wrongs and Remedies in the Twenty-First Century* (Oxford, 1996) 208–10, 214–15.

[7]   J Edelman, *Gain-Based Damages: Contract, Tort, Equity and Intellectual Property* (Oxford, 2002) 2–3, 65–93; J Edelman, 'Gain-Based Damages and Compensation' in A Burrows and Lord Rodger of Earlsferry (eds), *Mapping the Law: Essays in Memory of Peter Birks* (Oxford, 2006) 141, 147–52.

result of the wrong, irrespective of the source of the profit. An example is the award of an account of profits for breach of fiduciary duty, which is available even where the fiduciary acted in good faith, the breach benefitted the principal, and the principal could not have made the profit herself.

By reversing a transfer of value from the claimant to the defendant, 'restitutionary damages' operate in an identical manner to restitution for (autonomous) unjust enrichment. Their rationale is Aristotelian corrective justice, and they should be available for every civil wrong. 'Disgorgement damages', by contrast, aim to provide deterrence where a compensatory award fails to do so sufficiently. This is in two situations. One is breach of fiduciary duty, where 'disgorgement damages' are, and should remain, available even for innocent breaches in order to protect the institution of trust inherent in fiduciary relationships. 'Disgorgement damages' are further appropriate where a wrong is committed with a view to make profit exceeding the victim's loss. Edelman acknowledges that, contrary to the principle he suggests, 'disgorgement damages' are available for an innocent infringement of certain intellectual property rights, which he describes as an anomaly, and are not available for every cynical breach of contract.

C Friedmann

Friedmann recognises two situations of gain-based recovery, one of which is the commission of a wrong in circumstances where considerations of deterrence and punishment call for gain-based recovery.[8] The prime example of such a wrong is breach of fiduciary duty. The other, and more common, situation of gain-based recovery is the 'appropriation' of a property or quasi-property interest. 'Property' for this purpose comprises not only tangible and intangible property in its actual sense, but also other exclusive rights such as the right to publicity, privacy, reputation and bodily integrity. Any 'appropriation' of such 'property' triggers gain-based recovery, whether or not the appropriation amounts to a tort.

Quasi-property rights are protected interests in ideas, information, trade secrets and opportunity. Since they lack the element of exclusiveness, gain-based recovery is not triggered by every appropriation. Additional factors are required such as the wrongfulness of the appropriation. Gain-based recovery in the quasi-property category should also be available for certain breaches of contract, in particular: where the defendant undertook to sell certain property to the claimant but then sold it at a higher price to a third party; where the defendant delayed the transfer of property, deriving profit from its use in the meantime; where the defendant saved expenses by not performing as he should have. In those situations, gain-based recovery should also be available against a third party inducing the breach of contract.

---

[8] D Friedmann, 'Restitution of Benefits Obtained Through the Appropriation of Property or the Commission of a Wrong' (1980) 80 *Columbia Law Review* 504.

D Jackman

In Jackman's view, an award of gain-based damages for proprietary torts, breach of a restrictive covenant, breach of fiduciary duty and breach of confidence protects the 'facilitative institutions' of property and relationships of trust and confidence.[9] Gain-based damages redress harm to the facilitative institution where this cannot be done by compensatory damages because the individual victim has suffered no loss. Another facilitative institution recognised by Jackman is contract. At the time of his article (1989), *Wrotham Park* was still the only case recognising gain-based damages for breach of contract. Jackman explains *Wrotham Park* by pointing to the proprietary nature of restrictive covenants, and explains the (then) complete unavailability of gain-based damages for other breaches of contract on the ground that compensatory damages are normally sufficient to protect the institution of contract. Additional protection in the form of an account of profits might be required, however, where a contract is deliberately broken for the sake of making a gain.

E Jaffey

Like Edelman, Jaffey makes a sharp distinction between hypothetical-fee awards, which Jaffey calls the 'use claim', and disgorgement of profits.[10] Unlike Edelman, however, Jaffey is not of the view that the use claim always reverses a transfer of value. Jaffey differs from Edelman further in respect of the scope of the two types of gain-based awards. For Jaffey, the use claim arises not from a wrong but from an imputed contract that effects an exchange of payment for benefit. A contract is imputed where the defendant infringed the claimant's exclusive right to exploit the asset in question. Instances of this are the use of tangible and intellectual property, breach of restrictive covenants and forced labour, but not defamation, trespass to the person, deceit or (ordinary) breach of contract.

Jaffey regards disgorgement of profits as a form of civil punishment for wrongs. It should be available for all wrongs but not generally for breach of contract. For Jaffey, breach of contract is not generally a wrong because a contract generally imposes liability for the other party's reliance interest only but no duty to perform. Where (compensatory) damages are inadequate, a duty to perform does exist and disgorgement of profits should thus be available. This is the case where the defendant is the only source of supply for the claimant's business, where the defendant is under a negative obligation (that is an obligation *not* to do something) or where the defendant undertook to obviate a risk to the claimant.

---

[9] IM Jackman, 'Restitution for Wrongs' [1989] *Cambridge Law Journal* 302.
[10] P Jaffey, *The Nature and Scope of Restitution: Vitiated Transfers, Imputed Contracts and Disgorgement* (Oxford, 2000), especially chs 1, 2, 4, 11, 12 and 13.

Jaffey classifies all fiduciary relationships as contractual but justifies the availability of disgorgement for every breach of fiduciary duty on the ground that a fiduciary is under an actual duty to promote the principal's interests since specific performance and compensation are inadequate to protect the principal's reliance interest.

F   Tettenborn

Tettenborn favours the availability of gain-based relief for two types of wrongs.[11] The first is the infringement of a property right or another right that exists at least partly for the purpose of being traded or turned into money. Gain-based relief is appropriate in this situation as the defendant should not be able to escape the bargaining process. An example of a right that does not exist to be bought or sold is the right not to be assaulted or injured. Gain-based relief is therefore inappropriate where a third party paid the defendant to beat the claimant up. Since restrictive covenants are normally entered into with one eye on their release for money, their breach falls into the first category. Other breaches of contract should not attract gain-based relief (unless they involve breach of fiduciary duty) since the breach may be economically efficient[12] and since the aggrieved party could have stipulated for a clause in the contract allowing gain-based relief in the event of breach.

The second type of wrong which should allow gain-based relief in Tettenborn's view is the breach of an obligation of loyalty. Fiduciaries are under an obligation to exercise a power in the principal's interest and not to turn it to their own advantage. There is thus built into fiduciary relationships an understanding that benefits accruing as a result of the fiduciary's efforts are to accrue, in whole or in part, to the principal. Gain-based relief gives full effect to that understanding.

G   Weinrib

In Weinrib's view, the proper framework for understanding private law is the idea of corrective justice: 'The two parties are correlatively situated as the doer and sufferer of an injustice that is itself undone by the corresponding remedy.'[13] This idea explains why gain-based damages are not available for every wrong. The mere fact that the gain results from a wrong is insufficient to justify gain-based damages, in the same way in which factual causation alone is insufficient to justify compensatory damages. What matters is not the historical connection of

---

[11]   A Tettenborn, *Law of Restitution in England and Ireland*, 3rd edn (London, 2002) [11–7]–[11–10], [11–21].

[12]   The theory of efficient breach is discussed below ch 16, I A and B.

[13]   EJ Weinrib, 'Restitutionary Damages as Corrective Justice' (2000) 1 *Theoretical Inquiries in Law* 1, 5. See also EJ Weinrib, *The Idea of Private Law* (Cambridge, Mass, 1995) especially ch 3.

gain to wrong, but whether the gain partakes of the wrong's normative quality. Gain-based damages are justified where the defendant's gain is of something that lies within the right of the claimant, for then the gain stands as the present embodiment of the wrong rather than just a sequel to it. This is the case in at least three situations: the misappropriation of another's property, the violation of the right to bodily integrity, and breach of fiduciary duty.

Since the right of a property owner to set the terms for the transfer or use of the property implies a correlative duty on others to abstain from transferring or using it, the owner's right to the profits from the transfer or use of the property imports a correlative duty on others to abstain from those profits. An unauthorised gain is the continuing embodiment of an injustice as between the property owner and the wrongdoer, and the injustice is undone when the gain is restored to the owner of the object from which the gain accrued.[14] The same applies to a violation of the right to bodily integrity. The fact that this right, unlike virtually all property rights, cannot be acquired or alienated is irrelevant because the defendant has in fact treated the claimant's right as a commodity.[15] Finally, a fiduciary's loyalty is an entitlement of the principal. Since the duty of loyalty means that the fiduciary cannot profit from the relationship, unauthorised gains can be regarded as the material embodiment of the breach of duty.[16]

H Worthington

Worthington recognises two different types of gain-based relief in two different situations.[17] First, the unauthorised use of certain assets entitles the asset-holder to claim the 'use value' of the asset but not disgorgement of all profits made from the use. Qualifying assets are intangible and tangible property (including money) and protected information but not personal rights. Secondly, disgorgement of all ill-gotten profits is available where an equitable obligation of good faith or loyalty has been broken. 'The aim is to exact particular standards of conduct in protected relationships.'[18] It is noteworthy that Worthington regards neither situation as one of dependent or parasitic unjust enrichment. In her view, the unauthorised use of property or protected information is an instance of autonomous or subtractive unjust enrichment, and the equitable wrongs fall outside the law of unjust enrichment altogether.

---

[14] EJ Weinrib, 'Restitutionary Damages as Corrective Justice' ibid, 12; EJ Weinrib, *The Idea of Private Law* ibid, 141.

[15] EJ Weinrib, 'Restitutionary Damages as Corrective Justice' ibid, 34.

[16] ibid 33; EJ Weinrib, *The Idea of Private Law* (Cambridge, Mass, 1995) 141.

[17] S Worthington, 'Reconsidering Disgorgement for Wrongs' (1999) 62 *Modern Law Review* 218.

[18] ibid 237.

II The Significance of Exclusive Entitlements

Many judges and commentators have justified 'restitution for wrongs' with the maxim 'wrongdoers must not profit from their wrongs'. On a superficial level, this maxim sounds convincing. On a closer look, however, the maxim has little substance. The fundamental problem with the maxim is the definition of 'wrong'. If 'wrong' is defined as 'an action that brings the actor under an obligation to give up the profit made from the action', the maxim 'wrongdoers must not profit from their wrongs' means that 'where an action brings the actor under an obligation to give up the profit made from the action, the actor must not profit from that action'. The latter statement is plainly correct but also plainly circular.

Indeed, the advocates of the maxim 'wrongdoers must not profit from their wrongs' define 'wrong' in a different way, namely as a breach of duty.[19] A strong indicator for certain conduct constituting a breach of duty, they say, is the availability of compensation if that conduct has caused loss to the victim.[20] In effect, therefore, they define 'wrong' as 'an action that, if it causes loss to another, brings the actor under an obligation to compensate that loss', and the maxim 'wrongdoers must not profit from their wrongs' translates as 'where an action, if it causes loss to another, brings the actor under an obligation to compensate that loss, the actor must not profit from that action'. The last statement is not circular, but it is not immediately convincing either. It is not clear why the actor should have to give up profit that is left after compensating the loss inflicted upon the victim.[21] If 'wrong' is essentially defined as loss-causing action, it is not clear why the commission of a wrong should generate gain-based as well as loss-based remedies.

Where a claimant has suffered loss and seeks compensation from the defendant, the law must find a reason why the defendant should compensate the claimant's loss. The law must find a connection between the defendant and the loss, which usually means that the defendant (or someone for whose conduct the defendant is responsible) has caused the loss and that the defendant promised not to cause such loss, or was at fault in causing the loss, or caused the loss through an activity to which the law ties strict liability.

Where a claimant brings an action to obtain a gain made by the defendant, the law must find a reason why the claimant should obtain that gain. The law must

---

[19] P Birks, *An Introduction to the Law of Restitution*, revised edn (Oxford, 1989) 313; A Burrows, 'Remedial Coherence and Punitive Damages in Equity' in S Degeling and J Edelman (eds), *Equity in Commercial Law* (Sydney, 2005) 387. The definition is criticised by P Cane, 'Exceptional Measures of Damages: A Search for Principles' in P Birks (ed), *Wrongs and Remedies in the Twenty-First Century* (Oxford, 1996) 314–15.

[20] A Burrows, ibid; J Edelman, *Gain-Based Damages: Contract, Tort, Equity and Intellectual Property* (Oxford, 2002) 32–33, 42–44. The definition of 'wrong' by reference to the availability of compensation is criticised by P Cane, ibid 318–20.

[21] EJ Weinrib, 'Restitutionary Damages as Corrective Justice' (2000) 1 *Theoretical Inquiries in Law* 1, 11.

find a connection between the claimant and the defendant's gain. Such a connection cannot lie in the mere fact that the defendant has derived the gain from a wrong against the claimant, that is from an activity that has inflicted loss upon the claimant.[22] As Weinrib points out, factual causation alone can justify gain-based relief no more than it can justify compensatory damages.[23]

Friedmann[24] and Weinrib[25] are correct in maintaining that gain-based relief is appropriate where the law allocates the defendant's gain to the claimant. This happens where the defendant has derived the gain from an asset (in a wide sense) the exploitation of which is exclusively reserved for the claimant, and the defendant did not have the claimant's permission or any other legal justification. Gain-based relief should thus be triggered by the unauthorised exploitation of an asset exclusively reserved for another person or, shortly, by the unauthorised use of an exclusive entitlement.[26] Which rights and interests ought to be classified as exclusive entitlements in this respect will be discussed below.[27]

The exclusive-entitlement theory advocated here is a combination of the theories advanced by Friedmann and Weinrib. There are differences to both theories, however. Friedmann regards the appropriation of property or quasi-property as a sufficient condition for gain-based relief, but not as a necessary condition because he sees breach of fiduciary duty as being beyond the reach of the property theory and still endorses the availability of gain-based relief in that case.[28] Weinrib, conversely, regards the violation of property or a property-like right as a necessary condition for gain-based relief (outside mistaken payments and the like), but not as a sufficient condition because he also requires that such violation constitute a wrong. The present book suggests that the unauthorised use of another person's exclusive entitlement should be both necessary (outside mistaken payments and the like) and in principle sufficient to justify gain-based relief.

---

[22] The opposite view is taken by G Jones, *Goff & Jones: The Law of Restitution*, 7th edn (London, 2007) [36–006], who calls for gain-based relief being available for every tort.

[23] EJ Weinrib, 'Restitutionary Damages as Corrective Justice' (2000) 1 *Theoretical Inquiries in Law* 1, 8–11; above I G in this chapter. For compensatory damages see Part1, especially ch 2 I and VI.

[24] D Friedmann, 'Restitution of Benefits Obtained Through the Appropriation of Property or the Commission of a Wrong' (1980) 80 *Colum L Rev* 504, especially 506–508; above I C in this chapter.

[25] EJ Weinrib, 'Restitutionary Damages as Corrective Justice' (2000) 1 *Theoretical Inquiries in Law* 1, especially 12; EJ Weinrib, *The Idea of Private Law* (Cambridge, Mass, 1995) 141–42.

[26] It could be argued that if the *exploitation* of an exclusive right without the right-holder's consent triggers gain-based relief, so should *a fortiori* the *acquisition* of an exclusive right without the right-holder's (proper) consent. The notion of an exclusive entitlement could thus be employed beyond 'restitution for wrongs' in some (other) instances of unjust enrichment. Indeed, it has been argued that '[w]here a claimant has or can establish an exclusive entitlement to a particular asset, it follows that he should have a claim if that asset then comes into the defendant's hands without the claimant's consent': C Webb, 'Property, Unjust Enrichment, and Defective Transfers' in R Chambers, C Mitchell and J Penner (eds), *Philosophical Foundations of the Law of Unjust Enrichment* (Oxford, 2009) 368.

[27] III–V in this chapter.

[28] D Friedmann, 'Restitution of Benefits Obtained Through the Appropriation of Property or the Commission of a Wrong' (1980) 80 *Colum L Rev* 504, 508–10, 551–53.

Like Weinrib,[29] this book suggests that a breach of fiduciary duty can be classified as the unauthorised use of an exclusive entitlement enjoyed by the principal.[30] Unlike Friedmann, therefore, this book sees no need to make an exception to the property theory in order to explain gain-based relief against defaulting fiduciaries.

Unlike Weinrib, this book suggests that the unauthorised use of another person's exclusive entitlement may allow gain-based relief even where that use does not constitute a wrong in the sense of a compensation-triggering breach of duty. As Friedmann points out, conduct otherwise constituting a wrong may be exculpated on certain grounds such as incapacity, and those grounds are not necessarily relevant to gain-based relief.[31] Compensatory and gain-based remedies may rest on different policy considerations and may thus have different requirements as to factors such as culpability.

That is not to say that gain-based relief should never depend on culpability as an additional requirement to the violation of an exclusive entitlement.[32] But the relevance of culpability for gain-based relief should not depend on whether an innocent infringer should be liable to compensation, but solely on whether he should be liable to gain-based relief. An excellent example for a differentiation between compensatory and gain-based remedies on the basis of culpability is the sophisticated regime of remedies for intellectual property wrongs. Depending on the right infringed, the defendant's innocence excludes only an account of profits, only damages, both, or neither.[33] The ability to tailor the remedies according to the policy considerations would be lost if the availability of gain-based relief depended on compensation being available.

It follows that the present book rejects the concept of gain-based relief *for* wrongs (dependent or parasitic unjust enrichment). The unauthorised use of another person's exclusive entitlement should be regarded as an independent justification for gain-based relief and thus as an instance of autonomous unjust enrichment. The present book further rejects Edelman's fundamental distinction within gain-based relief between an award of a hypothetical licence fee ('restitutionary damages') and disgorgement of the whole profit derived from a certain activity.[34] Where the defendant has made unauthorised use of an exclusive entitlement enjoyed by the claimant, the defendant's primary gain is neither the

---

[29] EJ Weinrib, 'Restitutionary Damages as Corrective Justice' (2000) 1 *Theoretical Inquiries in Law* 1, 33; EJ Weinrib, *The Idea of Private Law* (Cambridge, Mass, 1995) 141.

[30] Below IV D in this chapter.

[31] D Friedmann, 'The Protection of Entitlements via the Law of Restitution—Expectancies and Privacy' (2005) 121 *Law Quarterly Review* 400, 403.

[32] The relevance of fault to the availability of gain-based relief in different situations is discussed by C Rotherham, 'The Conceptual Structure of Restitution for Wrongs' [2007] *CLJ* 172, 189–98.

[33] Above ch 12, IV D.

[34] J Edelman, *Gain-Based Damages: Contract, Tort, Equity and Intellectual Property* (Oxford, 2002) 2–3, 65–93; J Edelman, 'Gain-Based Damages and Compensation' in A Burrows and Lord Rodger of Earlsferry (eds), *Mapping the Law: Essays in Memory of Peter Birks* (Oxford, 2006) 141, 147–52; above I B in this chapter.

profit derived from such use nor the licence fee the defendant has saved. The defendant's primary gain is the use of the claimant's asset. Of course, the defendant cannot give up the use in kind but can only pay its value, and the value of the use may be assessed by reference to the profit the defendant has derived from the use or the licence fee the defendant would have reasonably had to pay.

But the value of the use may be assessed in other ways too. In some cases involving the infringement of a restrictive covenant or a right to light, the value of the unauthorised use was assessed at a proportion of the profit the defendant had anticipated to make from the infringing development.[35] Furthermore, when awarding an account of profits against a defaulting fiduciary, the courts may make an allowance for work and skill, particularly where the fiduciary acted in good faith. In other situations too, an allowance for work and skill might be made[36] or the defendant's (lack of) culpability might otherwise influence the amount of recovery.[37] The claimant's conduct might also influence the amount.[38] This is not to say that courts should enjoy an unfettered discretion. It is highly desirable that certain methods of assessment be established for certain situations. But it is hard to see why *any* variation in the assessment of the defendant's gain should be prevented by elevating two possible methods of assessment to two separate types of gain-based relief with differing scopes.[39]

III Exclusive Entitlements *Erga Omnes*

It is impossible here to scrutinise the whole of private law and set out all exclusive entitlements that should allow gain-based relief. Sections III and IV explain for selected rights why their violation should trigger gain-based relief. The selection is made with a view to the situations in which 'restitution for wrongs' is recognised or debated. This makes it possible to subsequently compare the exclusive-entitlement theory advocated in this book and the present law as to their scope. This section covers exclusive entitlements *erga omnes*, that is against the whole world, whereas section IV covers exclusive entitlements *inter partes*, that is against the defendant only.

---

[35] *Wrotham Park Estate Co Ltd v Parkside Homes Ltd* [1974] 1 WLR 798, 815–16 (above ch 12, V A); *Carr-Saunders v Dick McNeil Associates Ltd* [1986] 1 WLR 922, 931; *Deakins v Hookings* [1994] 1 EGLR 190, 195–96.

[36] K Barnett, 'Deterrence and Disgorging Profits for Breach of Contract' (2009) 17 *Restitution Law Review* 79, 96, suggesting that allowances for work and skill be imported into the area of 'disgorgement damages' for breach of contract.

[37] H McGregor, *McGregor on Damages*, 18th edn (London, 2009) [12–045]–[12–046].

[38] ibid [12–049], suggesting that the level of recovery might be lower where the claimant failed to restrain the defendant through an injunction when this was possible.

[39] A Burrows, 'Are "Damages on the *Wrotham Park* Basis" Compensatory, Restitutionary or Neither?' in D Saidov and R Cunnington (eds), *Contract Damages: Domestic and International Perspectives* (Oxford, 2008) 178–79.

A   Tangible and Intangible Property

The prime example of an exclusive entitlement is the ownership of (tangible or intangible) property. Subject to exceptions specifically prescribed by law, a property owner enjoys the exclusive right to use the property and can exclude everybody else from using it.[40] A landowner is thus entitled to prevent others from entering the land without authorisation, for example from exercising a right of way that does not in fact exist. If an unauthorised use through physical intrusion occurs, the owner should be entitled to claim back that use or, since the use of land cannot be returned in kind, claim the monetary value of the use, however that is calculated. Indeed, gain-based relief is recognised for cases of trespass to land.[41] However, as explained before,[42] the owner's entitlement to the trespasser's gain should be classified as an instance of autonomous unjust enrichment rather than gain-based relief for trespass as such. It should be seen as being based on the violation of the owner's exclusive right to use the land, which violation happens to constitute the tort of trespass.

A landowner may be aggrieved by disturbances other than people entering the land, such as causing physical damage to the land or interfering with the owner's enjoyment of the land through noise, smell, smoke and so on. Such disturbances can sometimes be prevented and must sometimes be tolerated. It depends on 'what is reasonable according to the ordinary usages of mankind living in … a particular society'.[43] Whether or not a disturbance is reasonable depends on a range of factors,[44] balancing the competing interests or, in economic terms, 'comparing the cost to the polluter of abating the pollution with the lower of the cost to the victim of either tolerating the pollution or eliminating it himself'.[45]

Where the disturber's conduct is unreasonable, the owner of the land affected can normally prevent the disturbance through an injunction.[46] In that case, the owner's exclusive right to the use of the land materialises. The owner can exclude the disturber from the unreasonable use of the land, and only the owner can authorise that particular use of the land. It follows that where an owner of land is disturbed by noise, smell, smoke and so on, and the owner obtained, or could have obtained, an injunction to prevent or stop the disturbance, the unauthorised use of the land infringed the owner's exclusive entitlement to the use of that land, and the owner should be entitled to claim from the disturber the monetary value of the latter's use of the land.

---

[40]   eg *Albert v Strange* (1849) 1 Mac & G 25, 42–43, 45–46; 41 ER 1171, 1178, 1179.
[41]   Above ch 12 IV C.
[42]   Above II in this chapter.
[43]   *Sedleigh-Denfield v O'Callaghan* [1940] AC 880 (HL) 903 (Lord Wright).
[44]   *Bamford v Turnley* (1862) 3 B & S 66, 79; 122 ER 27, 31 (Pollock CB).
[45]   RA Posner, *Economic Analysis of Law*, 7th edn (Austin, 2007) 63.
[46]   *Hunter v Canary Wharf Ltd* [1997] AC 655 (HL) 692 (Lord Goff).

Jones opposes the general availability of gain-based relief in cases of mass pollution.[47] He gives the example of a factory that pollutes thousands of neighbouring households with smoke and fumes because the factory owner saved the expense of an anti-pollution device. To allow gain-based recovery in this situation, says Jones, would raise intricate questions such as whether the factory owner's benefit gained at each household's expense is a proportion of the factory owner's profit, or a proportion of the sum that he saved from not installing the anti-pollution device, or the sum that he would have had to pay each landowner for the privilege of polluting his property. Jones may be right in describing these questions as difficult, but 'problems of attribution of gain are not a good reason for denying restitutionary damages to multiple plaintiffs'.[48] Furthermore, the difficulties arising in the case of mass pollution cannot justify denying gain-based relief in all instances of pollution even where only one landowner is affected.

What is true for ownership in land must also apply to other rights in land that confer an exclusive entitlement, such as the rights arising from restrictive covenants and easements. In a restrictive covenant, the owner of the servient tenement (the covenantor) undertakes, for the benefit of the dominant tenement, not to use the servient tenement in a particular way, for example not to erect buildings on it. Where, as usual, the covenantee's successors can enforce the restrictive covenant against the covenantor's successors,[49] the covenanted benefit is a property right.[50] The owner of the dominant tenement can prevent any use of the servient tenement that is in breach of the restrictive covenant. It is an exclusive entitlement, and a use of the servient tenement in breach of the restrictive covenant should therefore entitle the owner of the dominant tenement to claim back (the monetary value of) that use. The availability of gain-based relief in this situation is indeed recognised,[51] but the gain-based claim should be conceptualised as one in autonomous unjust enrichment.

Easements give the owner of the dominant tenement a right to use the servient tenement in a certain way, for example the right to pass along a way over the

---

[47] G Jones, *Goff & Jones: The Law of Restitution*, 7th edn (London, 2007) [36–008]; cited with approval in *Forsyth-Grant v Allen* [2008] EWCA Civ 505, [2008] Env LR 41 [46] (Toulson LJ).

[48] A Burrows, 'Reforming Non-Compensatory Damages' in W Swadling and G Jones (eds), *The Search for Principle: Essays in Honour of Lord Goff of Chieveley* (Oxford, 1999) 310. See also *Devenish Nutrition Ltd v Sanofi-Aventis SA (France)* [2008] EWCA Civ 1086 [92], [114] (Arden LJ); Law Commission, 'Aggravated, Exemplary and Restitutionary Damages' (Law Com No 247, 1997) [3.77]–[3.81].

[49] The benefit of a restrictive covenant runs with the dominant tenement through annexation, assignment or a scheme of development; the burden of a restrictive covenant runs with the servient tenement through registration or, where the covenant was created before 1926, notice on the successor's part: K Gray and SF Gray, *Elements of Land Law*, 5th edn (Oxford, 2009) [3.4.35]–[3.4.72].

[50] *Re Nisbet and Potts' Contract* [1905] 1 Ch 391, 397–98; *Experience Hendrix LLC v PPX Enterprises Inc* [2003] EWCA Civ 323, [2003] FSR 46 [56] (Gibson LJ); *Harbour Estates Ltd v HSBC Bank plc* [2004] EWHC 1714 (Ch), [2005] Ch 194 [34]. See also *Rhone v Stephens* [1994] 2 AC 310 (HL) 317–21.

[51] *Wrotham Park Estate Co Ltd v Parkside Homes Ltd* [1974] 1 WLR 798; *Jaggard v Sawyer* [1995] 1 WLR 269 (CA); *Gafford v Graham* (1999) 77 P & CR 73 (CA) 86.

servient tenement. Of course, the owner of the dominant tenement cannot prevent *every* use of the servient tenement. But she can prevent a use of the servient tenement that substantially[52] interferes with the easement.[53] Only the owner of the dominant tenement can permit a substantial interference with the easement. In this respect, an easement confers an exclusive entitlement upon the owner of the dominant tenement. Where an easement is infringed without authorisation, therefore, the owner of the dominant tenement should be entitled to claim the value of what the infringer has gained through the infringement. This seems to be recognised for the infringement of a right to light.[54]

Some commentators call for the availability of gain-based recovery in every instance of nuisance.[55] Under the approach advocated in this book, gain-based recovery should be available in those instances of nuisance where an exclusive entitlement of some kind is infringed. Such a claim should be classified as lying in autonomous unjust enrichment, based on the infringement of an exclusive entitlement, which infringement happens to constitute the tort of nuisance.

What is true for exclusive entitlements in land must also apply to exclusive entitlements, foremost ownership, in moveable things and intellectual property. Gain-based relief is indeed is recognised for wrongful interference with goods and for the infringement of intellectual property rights, at least where such infringement was culpable.[56] Under the approach advocated in this book, those instances of gain-based relief should be classified as lying in autonomous unjust enrichment rather than being based on the wrong as such.

An exclusive entitlement to use property in certain respects may result from its (lawful) possession. It is not possible here to survey all situations in which possession may give rise to exclusive entitlements. Suffice to say that a lease over land affords the tenant an exclusive right to use the land in certain respects.[57] Consequently, a landlord who unlawfully evicts the tenant makes unauthorised use of the tenant's exclusive entitlement and should be obliged to give up to the tenant the monetary value of that use. Damages for unlawful eviction may indeed be measured according to the increase in the property's value resulting from the eviction.[58] Under the approach advocated in this book, the tenant's claim to the

---

[52] 'Not every interference with an easement, such as a right of way, is actionable. There must be a substantial interference with the enjoyment of it': *West v Sharp* (2000) 79 P & CR 327 (CA) 332 (Mummery LJ).

[53] eg *B&Q plc v Liverpool and Lancashire Properties Ltd* (2001) 81 P & CR 246.

[54] *Tamares (Vincent Square) Ltd v Fairpoint Properties (Vincent Square) Ltd (No 2)* [2007] EWHC 212 (Ch), [2007] 1 WLR 2167; *Deakins v Hookings* [1994] 1 EGLR 190, 195–96; *Carr-Saunders v Dick McNeil Associates Ltd* [1986] 1 WLR 922, 931; above ch 12, IV E.

[55] J Edelman, *Gain-Based Damages: Contract, Tort, Equity and Intellectual Property* (Oxford, 2002) 135–36; G Virgo, *The Principles of the Law of Restitution*, 2nd edn (Oxford, 2006) 473.

[56] Above ch 12, IV B and D.

[57] A tenant can bring an action for trespass, even against the landlord, eg *Hunter v Canary Wharf Ltd* [1997] AC 655 (HL) 703 (Lord Hoffmann); *Pemberton v Southwark LBC* [2000] 1 WLR 1672 (CA) 1683 (Clarke LJ).

[58] Housing Act 1988 s 28; *Jones v Miah* (1992) 24 HLR 578 (CA) 587.

landlord's gain should be classified as lying in autonomous unjust enrichment rather than being based on the wrong as such.

B Bodily Integrity

Every human being has a right to bodily integrity,[59] that is the exclusive right to 'use' their own body and to exclude everyone else from 'using' it. It is a right exigible against the whole world and thus akin to property rights, the only difference being that the right to bodily integrity is inalienable.[60] Since the right to bodily integrity is an exclusive entitlement, its unauthorised 'use' ought to trigger gain-based relief.

This view is expressed by Friedmann, who gives the example of a person who is being shot at and grabs another person to use the latter's body as a shield.[61] Birks, who favours gain-based relief for a *deliberate* unauthorised 'use' of another person's body (but not otherwise), gives the example of A paying B to beat up C.[62] Gain-based relief in cases of battery is also supported by Street, who gives the example of a boxer who deliberately fouls in order to obtain the money that he (but not his opponent) will receive on winning, and the example of a person who 'cuts off a prince's hair without permission and sells off the locks for large sums'.[63] Another example of an unauthorised 'use' of someone's body would be a medical experiment undertaken without the test person's knowledge. The courts have yet to recognise gain-based relief in those circumstances, but this may simply be due to the rarity of such a situation occurring and coming to court.

Tettenborn opposes the availability of gain-based relief in these cases with the argument that the right to bodily integrity 'is not like a property or similar right, existing to be bought and sold: it is a right personal to the claimant, existing for his protection alone'.[64] This argument might be questioned, however, considering that it is legal and not uncommon to offer financial incentives for donating blood or participating in medical experiments. Furthermore, even if it were accepted that the right to bodily integrity is granted solely for reasons other than commercial exploitation, gain-based relief should still be available because the

---

[59] eg *Parkinson v St James and Seacroft University Hospital NHS Trust* [2001] EWCA Civ 530, [2002] QB 266 [56] (Hale LJ).

[60] R Stevens, *Torts and Rights* (Oxford, 2007) 7; EJ Weinrib, 'Restitutionary Damages as Corrective Justice' (2000) 1 *Theoretical Inquiries in Law* 1, 32.

[61] D Friedmann, 'Restitution of Benefits Obtained Through the Appropriation of Property or the Commission of a Wrong' (1980) 80 *Colum L Rev* 504, 511–12. The example is based on *Laidlaw v Sage* (1899) 158 NY 73, 52 NE 679 (NY CA), where the plaintiff claimed that the defendant had moved the plaintiff so as to shield himself from an explosion.

[62] P Birks, *An Introduction to the Law of Restitution*, revised edn (Oxford, 1989) 326. Birks' view is shared by K Mason, JW Carter and GJ Tolhurst, *Mason and Carter's Restitution Law in Australia*, 2nd edn (Chatswood, 2008) [1524].

[63] H Street, *Principles of the Law of Damages* (London, 1962) 254.

[64] A Tettenborn, *Law of Restitution in England and Ireland*, 3rd edn (London, 2002) [11–8].

defendant has in fact treated the claimant's body as a commodity and 'cannot take refuge in the argument that bodily integrity is really an inalienable pearl beyond price'.[65]

C Reputation

Human beings and private companies[66] enjoy a right to reputation,[67] that is a right not to be defamed. There are, of course, considerable exceptions. The law on defamation has developed defences such as justification (truth), fair comment, qualified privilege, absolute privilege and consent. In the absence of any defence, however, human beings and private companies can prevent themselves from being defamed, and only the person to be defamed can permit a defamatory statement. Like the right to bodily integrity, therefore, the right to reputation is exigible against the whole world and differs from property rights only in that it is inalienable.[68] A defamatory statement is thus an unauthorised use of an exclusive entitlement and ought to trigger gain-based relief.[69] This claim has yet to be recognised as such,[70] although exemplary damages have sometimes been awarded for defamation,[71] and several commentators reconceptualise those awards as involving gain-based relief.[72]

As in the case of bodily integrity, the availability of gain-based relief in instances of defamation might be opposed with the argument that the purpose of granting people a right to reputation is to enable them to protect their reputation, not to enable them to exploit their reputation by, for instance, selling a 'licence to defame'. However, again as in the case of bodily integrity, that argument cannot convince because the defendant has in fact treated the claimant's reputation as a commodity and should therefore be subject to gain-based recovery.[73]

---

[65] EJ Weinrib, 'Restitutionary Damages as Corrective Justice' (2000) 1 *Theoretical Inquiries in Law* 1, 34. See also D Friedmann, 'Restitution of Benefits Obtained Through the Appropriation of Property or the Commission of a Wrong' (1980) 80 *Colum L Rev* 504, 511.

[66] *South Hetton Coal Co Ltd v North-Eastern News Association Ltd* [1894] 1 QB 133 (CA); *McDonald's Corp v Steel (No 4)*, The Independent, 10 May 1999 (CA). Central government, local authorities and political parties enjoy no right to reputation: *Derbyshire CC v Times Newspapers Ltd* [1993] AC 534 (HL); *Goldsmith v Bhoyrul* [1998] QB 459.

[67] eg *Reynolds v Times Newspapers Ltd* [2001] 2 AC 127 (HL) 186, 206, 215.

[68] R Stevens, *Torts and Rights* (Oxford, 2007) 8.

[69] D Friedmann, 'Restitution of Benefits Obtained Through the Appropriation of Property or the Commission of a Wrong' (1980) 80 *Colum L Rev* 504, 511. See also P Birks, *An Introduction to the Law of Restitution*, revised edn (Oxford, 1989) 326 (favouring gain-based relief for defamation committed with a view to make profit); G Jones, *Goff & Jones: The Law of Restitution*, 7th edn (London, 2007) [36–006] (favouring gain-based relief for every tort); H Street, *Principles of the Law of Damages* (London, 1962) 254 (favouring gain-based relief for every tort).

[70] G Jones, ibid.

[71] *Broome v Cassell & Co* [1972] AC 1027 (HL); *Riches v News Group Newspapers Ltd* [1986] QB 256 (CA); *John v MGN Ltd* [1997] QB 586 (CA); below ch 14, IV A.

[72] Below ch 14, IV B.

[73] D Friedmann, 'Restitution of Benefits Obtained Through the Appropriation of Property or the Commission of a Wrong' (1980) 80 *Colum L Rev* 504, 511.

D Informational Rights

Under certain circumstances, a person can prevent all others from using or disclosing certain information.[74] A person who possesses previously undisclosed information, such as a business or trade secret, can prevent others from using or disclosing the information where such use or disclosure would amount to a breach of confidence. Everybody can prevent the disclosure of information on one's private matters where such disclosure would amount to a breach of confidence in its extended meaning, also called breach of privacy. A trade secret can be assigned[75] and can pass to the owner's trustee in bankruptcy.[76] There are some judicial descriptions of protected information as 'property'[77] or 'proprietary interest',[78] but this parlance has more recently been rejected by the Court of Appeal,[79] by the Supreme Court of Canada,[80] and by Lord Walker in *OBG Ltd v Allan*.[81]

Whether or not protected information may properly be described as 'property', a person who possesses information that the law protects against unauthorised use and disclosure enjoys an exclusive entitlement. That person can exclude all others from using or disclosing the information,[82] and only that person can authorise such use or disclosure. Where an unauthorised person uses protected information, by disclosing it or otherwise, the 'owner' of the information should be entitled to claim the monetary value of that use.[83] It should be irrelevant whether the claimant intended to exploit the information commercially, as the

---

[74] Above ch 12, III B.

[75] *Maxim Nordenfelt Guns & Ammunition Co v Nordenfelt* [1893] 1 Ch 630 (CA) 665 (Bowen LJ); *Mustad & Son v Dosen* [1964] 1 WLR 109 (HL) 110 (Note).

[76] *Re Keene* [1922] 2 Ch 475 (CA).

[77] *Dean v Macdowell* (1878) LR 8 Ch D 345 (CA) 354 (Cotton LJ); *Aas v Benham* [1891] 2 Ch 244 (CA) 258 (Bowen LJ); *Boardman v Phipps* [1967] 2 AC 46 (HL) 107 (Lord Hodson), 115 (Lord Guest); *Attorney-General v Guardian Newspapers Ltd* [1987] 1 WLR 1248, 1264 (Sir Nicolas Browne-Wilkinson VC).

[78] *Attorney-General v Observer Ltd, sub nom Attorney-General v Guardian Newspapers Ltd (No 2)* [1990] 1 AC 109, 140 (Scott J).

[79] *Douglas v Hello! Ltd (No 3)* [2005] EWCA Civ 595, [2006] QB 125 [126]–[127], quoting *Boardman v Phipps* [1967] 2 AC 46 (HL) 127–28 (Lord Upjohn); *Devenish Nutrition Ltd v Sanofi-Aventis SA (France)* [2008] EWCA Civ 1086 [2], [57], where Arden LJ remarked that the publication of state secrets in *Attorney-General v Blake* [2001] 1 AC 268 (HL) had been no deprivation of property; the same view is taken by F Giglio, *The Foundations of Restitution for Wrongs* (Oxford, 2007) 192.

[80] *Cadbury Schweppes Inc v FBI Foods Ltd* [1999] 1 SCR 142 (SCC) 172–73.

[81] [2007] UKHL 21, [2008] 1 AC 1 [275].

[82] 'The equitable interest of the confider in the confidential information would, in accordance with ordinary equitable principles, be enforceable against the whole world save the bona fide purchaser for value without notice of the confider's rights to confidentiality': *Attorney-General v Guardian Newspapers Ltd* [1987] 1 WLR 1248, 1264 (Sir Nicolas Browne-Wilkinson VC).

[83] D Friedmann, 'The Protection of Entitlements via the Law of Restitution—Expectancies and Privacy' (2005) 121 *LQR* 400, 417–18. See also L Clarke, 'Remedial Responses to Breach of Confidence: The Question of Damages' (2005) 24 *Civil Justice Quarterly* 316, 332–35 (gain-based relief should be confined to breaches of confidence committed by fiduciaries); N Witzleb, 'Justifying Gain-Based Remedies for Invasions of Privacy' (2009) 29 *Oxford Journal of Legal Studies* 325,

defendant has in fact treated the information as a commodity.[84] It is recognised that gain-based relief can in principle be claimed in an action for breach of confidence in both its traditional meaning and its extended meaning covering breach of privacy.[85] Under the approach advocated in this book, the gain-based claim should be classified as lying in autonomous unjust enrichment, based on the infringement of an exclusive entitlement, which infringement happens to constitute an equitable wrong (or a tort if breach privacy is regarded as a tort).

An exclusive entitlement to the use of certain information was also present in *Attorney-General v Blake (Jonathan Cape Ltd Third Party)*.[86] Section 1(1) of the Official Secrets Act 1989 makes it a criminal offence for a former or present member of the security or intelligence services to disclose, without lawful authority, any information relating to security or intelligence which he possesses by virtue of his position as a member of those services.[87] In consequence of that provision, it could be argued, the Crown has an exclusive entitlement to the use of any such information.

Even if that argument is rejected, the Crown still had an exclusive entitlement to the use of the information contained in Blake's autobiography because Blake had, in a pre-employment declaration, undertaken 'not to divulge any official information gained by me as a result of my employment, either in the press or in book form'.[88] This undertaking transferred to the Crown all entitlements to the use of the information described if the Crown did not already enjoy such entitlement under the general law. It is irrelevant to the availability of gain-based relief that the purpose of the Crown's exclusive entitlement is to maintain peace and security rather than to exploit secrets commercially. Blake actually made the information at issue a commercial asset by selling it.[89] The award of an account of profits in *Blake* is thus in line with the exclusive-entitlement theory advocated in this book. It is suggested, however, that the Crown's claim should be classified as one in autonomous unjust enrichment rather than one for breach of contract as such.

---

especially 359–60 (gain-based relief should be available for breach of confidence and for deliberate and particularly outrageous infringements of privacy).

[84] N Witzleb, ibid 356. For the same argument in the context of bodily integrity and reputation see above III B and C in this chapter.

[85] Above ch 12, III B.

[86] [2001] 1 AC 268 (HL) 283; above ch 12, V B.

[87] See also Official Secrets Act 1911 s 1(1)(c).

[88] Quoted in [2001] 1 AC 268 (HL) 277 (Lord Nicholls).

[89] The same argument was made in the context of bodily integrity and reputation; see above III B and C in this chapter.

IV   Exclusive Entitlements *Inter Partes*

Section III suggested the availability of gain-based relief for (selected) exclusive entitlement *erga omnes*, that is entitlements effective against the whole world. In that situation, the defendant is not the only person who must refrain from making an unauthorised use of the claimant's entitlement and must give up to the claimant (the monetary value of) an unauthorised use. Everybody is under the same obligation. But the reason that the infringement of an exclusive entitlement *erga omnes* leads to gain-based recovery is not the potential liability of persons other than the infringer. The reason for the infringer's liability is that, as between the right-holder and the infringer, the right holder was exclusively entitled to use the right. The right-holder's entitlement against persons other than the infringer is actually irrelevant.

A successful claim for the gain made from the unauthorised use of a right should therefore only require that, *as between the claimant and the defendant,* the claimant was exclusively entitled to use the right. Where this is the case, gain-based relief should be available even if the claimant had no exclusive entitlement to the right against anyone other than the defendant, and even if the defendant had an exclusive entitlement to the right against the whole world except the claimant. In short, the infringement of an exclusive entitlement *inter partes* should trigger gain-based relief.[90] As Lord Nicholls said in *Attorney-General v Blake (Jonathan Cape Ltd Third Party)*:

> Property rights are superior to contractual rights in that, unlike contractual rights, property rights may survive against an indefinite class of persons. However, it is not easy to see why, as between the parties to a contract, a violation of a party's contractual rights should attract a lesser degree of remedy than a violation of his property rights.[91]

While Lord Nicholls spoke of *any* 'contractual rights', the concept advocated in this book allows gain-based relief only for those contractual rights that embody an exclusive entitlement to an asset. Siems, who favours the general availability of gain-based relief for breach of contract, nonetheless rejects an equation between contractual rights and property rights with the argument that 'the parties to a contract are in general free to regulate remedies between themselves'.[92] But the parties' general ability to deviate from the default position should not affect the search for the desirable default position, and the desirable default position for infringements of exclusive entitlements *inter partes* is the availability of gain-based

---

[90]   This proposition is incompatible with the theory of efficient breach; for this theory and its rejection see below ch 16, I A and B.

[91]   [2001] 1 AC 268 (HL) 283.

[92]   M Siems, 'Disgorgement of Profits for Breach of Contract: A Comparative Analysis' [2003] *Edinburgh Law Review* 27, 49.

relief, by analogy to infringements of exclusive entitlements *erga omnes*. The following will look at selected situations for which an exclusive entitlement *inter partes* is recognised or debated.

A Contractual Right to have Property Transferred

i Land and Intangible Property

Exclusive entitlements *inter partes* arise under estate contracts such as the sale of a freehold estate. Until the conveyance of the estate to the purchaser, the vendor remains the legal owner of the estate. However, once the estate contract has become binding through an exchange of contracts, the purchaser acquires an equitable proprietary interest in the estate,[93] provided the estate contract is specifically enforceable, which is generally the case.[94] An entry of the purchaser's interest in the respective Register affords that interest effect *erga omnes*.[95] Should the vendor subsequently transfer the legal estate to a third party, the (first) purchaser can request from the third party a transfer of the estate on the terms of the contract between the purchaser and the vendor.

Without its registration,[96] the purchaser's interest is normally[97] inferior to the interest of a third party who subsequently acquires the legal estate from the vendor.[98] Thus, the vendor retains the factual power to transfer the legal estate to a third party. As between the vendor and the (first) purchaser, however, the latter is entitled to the legal estate (on the terms of the contract) as soon as the estate contract becomes enforceable. Where the vendor breaks the contract with the

---

[93] eg *Oughtred v IRC* [1960] AC 206 (HL) 240 (Lord Jenkins); *Appleton v Aspin* [1988] 1 WLR 410 (CA) 417; *Re Flint (A Bankrupt)* [1993] Ch 319, 326; *R v Tower Hamlets LBC, ex p Von Goetz* [1999] QB 1019 (CA) 1024 (Mummery LJ); *Jerome v Kelly (Inspector of Taxes)* [2004] UKHL 25, [2004] 1 WLR 1409 [32] (Lord Walker).

[94] eg *Graham v Pitkin* [1992] 1 WLR 403 (PC) 406; *McGuane v Welch* [2008] EWCA Civ 785 [42].

[95] The purchaser of a registered estate may enter a 'notice' of her interest in the Land Register: Land Registration Act 2002 s 32. That notice affords the purchaser's interest priority over interests subsequently acquired by other persons: Land Registration Act 2002 ss 28, 29(1), (2)(a)(i). The purchaser of an unregistered estate may register her interest as a Class C(iv) land charge in the Register of Land Charges: Land Charges Act 1972 s 2(4)(iv). That registration affords the purchaser's interest priority over interests subsequently acquired by other persons: Law of Property Act 1925 s 198(1).

[96] Registration of the purchaser's interest is rare in practice: K Gray and SF Gray, *Elements of Land Law*, 5th edn (Oxford, 2009) [8.1.71] fn 3.

[97] Even without its registration, the purchaser's interest in the land takes priority over the third party's interest if the third party provided no valuable consideration to the vendor: Land Registration Act 2002 ss 28, 29(1) (for registered estates); Land Charges Act 1972 s 4(6) (for unregistered estates). In the case of a registered estate, the purchaser's actual occupation of the land also affords the purchaser's interest priority over the third party's interest unless the purchaser failed to disclose her interest on inquiry or the third party did not know, and could not reasonably have known, of the purchaser's interest: Land Registration Act 2002 s 29(1), (2)(a)(ii), sch 3 para 2.

[98] For registered estates see Land Registration Act 2002 ss 28, 29(1). For unregistered estates see Land Charges Act 1972 s 4(6).

purchaser by transferring the legal estate to a third party (who pays more than the purchaser), the vendor makes unauthorised use of the purchaser's exclusive entitlement *inter partes* and should therefore be liable to give up to the purchaser the monetary value of that use.[99] That value will be the price paid by the third party to the vendor or, after setting-off what the purchaser owes the vendor, the difference between the price paid by the third party to the vendor and the price agreed between the vendor and the purchaser. The purchaser's entitlement to the price paid by the third party to the vendor seems indeed recognised. It has been held that the exchange of contracts between the vendor and the purchaser makes the vendor a qualified[100] trustee for the purchaser,[101] which entitles the purchaser to claim the proceeds of a sale of the estate to a third party.[102]

The equitable proprietary interest arising from an estate contract is said to be a result of the purchaser's general entitlement to claim specific performance of the contract.[103] This has been generalised into the principle that 'a specifically enforceable agreement to assign an interest in property creates an equitable interest in the assignee'.[104] An equitable proprietary interest has indeed been recognised to arise from certain specifically enforceable contracts such as a contract to grant a right of way,[105] a contract to create a legal mortgage,[106] and a sale of shares in a company.[107] The same should apply to a contract for the assignment of an intellectual property right, which is in general specifically enforceable.[108] Since all these contracts are treated in the same way as an estate contract with regard to the availability of specific performance and the creation

---

[99]   Gain-based relief in this situation is also supported by D Friedmann, 'Restitution of Benefits Obtained Through the Appropriation of Property or the Commission of a Wrong' (1980) 80 *Colum L Rev* 504, 516; R Nolan, 'Remedies for Breach of Contract: Specific Enforcement and Restitution' in FD Rose (ed), *Failure of Contracts: Contractual, Restitutionary and Proprietary Consequences* (Oxford, 1997) 43–44.

[100]   The trusteeship is qualified because the vendor is entitled to protect her own interest, ie the receipt of the purchase money: *Jerome v Kelly (Inspector of Taxes)* [2004] UKHL 25, [2004] 1 WLR 1409 [30]–[32] (Lord Walker). Indeed, 'the vendor has a lien on the property for the purchase money and a right to remain in possession of the property until payment is made': *Barclays Bank plc v Estates & Commercial Ltd* [1997] 1 WLR 415 (CA) 419 (Millett LJ).

[101]   eg *Lloyds Bank plc v Carrick* [1996] 4 All ER 630 (CA) 637–39; *Yaxley v Gotts* [2000] Ch 162 (CA) 179 (Robert Walker LJ). For criticisms see *Tanwar Enterprises Pty Ltd v Cauchi* [2003] HCA 57, (2003) 217 CLR 315 [53]; W Swadling, 'The Vendor-Purchaser Constructive Trust' in S Degeling and J Edelman (eds), *Equity in Commercial Law* (Sydney, 2005) 463 ff.

[102]   *Lake v Bayliss* [1974] 1 WLR 1073. See also *Daniels v Davison* (1809) 16 Ves Jun 249, 255; 33 ER 978, 981 (Lord Eldon LC); *Timko v Useful Homes Corp* (1933) 114 NJ Eq 433, 168 Atl 824 (Ct of Chancery of NJ); *Bunny Industries Ltd v FSW Enterprises Pty Ltd* [1982] Qd R 712 (QSC).

[103]   *Holroyd v Marshall* (1862) 10 HL Cas 191, 209; 11 ER 999, 1006; *Howard v Miller* [1915] AC 318 (PC) 326; *Oughtred v IRC* [1960] AC 206 (HL) 240 (Lord Jenkins); *Jerome v Kelly (Inspector of Taxes)* [2004] UKHL 25, [2004] 1 WLR 1409 [32] (Lord Walker).

[104]   *Neville v Wilson* [1997] Ch 144 (CA) 157 (Nourse LJ speaking for the court). See also *Holroyd v Marshall* (1862) 10 HL Cas 191, 209; 11 ER 999, 1006.

[105]   *May v Belleville* [1905] 2 Ch 605, 612–13.

[106]   eg *Swiss Bank Corp v Lloyds Bank Ltd* [1982] AC 584 (CA) 594–95.

[107]   *Oughtred v IRC* [1960] AC 206 (HL) 240 (Lord Jenkins).

[108]   eg *Griggs Group Ltd v Evans (No 2)* [2004] EWHC 1088 (Ch), [2005] Ch 153 (for copyright); *Collag Corp v Merck & Co Inc* [2003] FSR 16 (for patent).

of an equitable proprietary interest as soon as the contract is made, they should also be treated in the same way as an estate contract with regard to the availability of gain-based relief where the seller or grantor, in breach of the contract, transfers the property to a third party.[109]

ii Specific Chattel

In the case of the sale of a specific chattel,[110] there is first the question of when property passes to the buyer, which depends on the parties' intention.[111] Where property passes when the contract for sale is made, the buyer immediately becomes the owner of the chattel. Once the buyer has also possession of the chattel, the seller can no longer transfer property to a third party. But a seller still in possession of the chattel can pass property to a third party who receives the chattel in good faith.[112] A seller who, after the buyer has become the owner of the chattel, breaks the contract with the buyer by transferring property to a third party (who pays more than the buyer) infringes the (first) buyer's ownership and thus makes unauthorised use of an exclusive entitlement *erga omnes*. Consequently, the buyer should have a claim in autonomous unjust enrichment for the monetary value of that use, which is the price paid by the third party to the seller or, practically, the difference between the price paid by the third party to the seller and the price agreed by the seller and the buyer. Indeed, the seller's action constitutes the tort of conversion,[113] for which gain-based relief is recognised.[114]

Where a contract for the sale of a specific chattel postpones the transfer of property to a later date, for example the date of delivery or payment, the seller remains the legal owner of the chattel until that date and thus retains the factual power to pass property to a third party in the meantime. In this situation, the buyer of a specific chattel faces the same risk as the buyer of a real estate who has not protected her interest through registration. As seen before, the buyer of a real estate acquires an equitable proprietary interest in the land, which is said to stem from the buyer's general entitlement to specific performance.

Where a specific chattel is sold, the availability of specific performance cannot be described as the rule. Section 52(1) of the Sale of Goods Act 1979 simply provides that 'the court may, if it thinks fit', grant specific performance. Specific

---

[109] The availability of specific performance is regarded as a sufficient condition for gain-based relief by R Nolan, 'Remedies for Breach of Contract: Specific Enforcement and Restitution' in FD Rose (ed), *Failure of Contracts: Contractual, Restitutionary and Proprietary Consequences* (Oxford, 1997) 43–44.

[110] Specific goods are 'goods identified and agreed on at the time a contract of sale is made': Sale of Goods Act 1979 s 61(1).

[111] Sale of Goods Act 1979 s 17(1). Section 18 of that Act contains rules for ascertaining the parties' intention.

[112] Sale of Goods Act 1979 s 24; Factors Act 1889 s 8.

[113] eg *Chinery v Viall* (1860) 5 H & N 288, 157 ER 1192; *Moriarty v Various customers of BA Peters plc* [2008] EWHC 2205 (Ch) [65].

[114] Above ch 12, IV B.

performance is likely to be granted where the chattel sold is rare or unique or of special value to the buyer,[115] and is likely to be refused where the chattel sold is one item of many of the same type so that the buyer can obtain a substitute in the market.[116] This wide discretion by the court as to the grant or refusal of specific performance distinguishes the sale of a specific chattel from the sale of an estate or an intellectual property right, where a refusal of specific performance is clearly the exception. Should this difference have the consequence that the buyer of a specific chattel does not acquire an equitable proprietary interest in the chattel as soon as the contract is made, and that gain-based relief is unavailable if the seller, in breach of his contract with the buyer, transfers the ownership in the chattel to a third party?[117]

An equitable proprietary interest must indeed be denied, whatever the type of contract, once a court has actually refused to grant specific performance. Once it is clear that the purchaser will never obtain the actual property in question, it no longer makes sense to recognise an interest that expresses the expectation to receive the property at some point. But unless and until a court has refused to grant specific performance, a (provisional) equitable proprietary interest should be recognised. The reason for this is that the court decides on whether to grant specific performance on the facts at the time of that decision. Post-contractual developments may be crucial.[118] At the time of the contract, there can be no absolute certainty as to whether specific performance will later be denied or granted. Specific performance may be denied even in the case of an estate contract, and granted even where a specific chattel of common description has been sold. Since the possibility of specific performance being refused has not prevented the recognition of an equitable proprietary interest in the case of estate contracts, the possibility of specific performance being refused should not prevent the recognition of an equitable proprietary interest where a specific chattel even of common description is sold.[119]

Moreover, neither the availability of specific performance nor the existence of an equitable proprietary interest should actually be relevant to the question of whether the buyer of a specific chattel can claim the gain that the seller has made

---

[115] eg *Behnke v Bede Shipping Co Ltd* [1927] 1 KB 649, 661 (effectively unique ship); *Phillips v Lamdin* [1949] 2 KB 33, 41 (unique door).

[116] eg *Cohen v Roche* [1927] 1 KB 169, 179–181 (items of mass-produced furniture); *Société des Industries Metallurgiques SA v The Bronx Engineering Co Ltd* [1975] 1 Lloyd's Rep 465 (CA) 468–70 (machinery of a type obtainable in the market).

[117] Even where the property in the chattel has already passed to the buyer, a seller still in possession of the chattel can pass a good title to a third party who receives the chattel in good faith: Sale of Goods Act 1979 s 24; Factors Act 1889 s 8.

[118] eg *Patel v Ali* [1984] Ch 283, where the purchaser of an estate was denied specific performance because, after the exchange of contracts, one of the joint vendors became bankrupt and the other disabled.

[119] In this way possibly *Holroyd v Marshall* (1862) 10 HL Cas 191, 209–10; 11 ER 999, 1006. For the independence of a purchaser's lien from the availability of specific performance see *Hewett v Court* (1983) 149 CLR 639 (HCA).

from wrongfully transferring the ownership in the chattel to a third party.[120] All that matters is that, while a contract for the sale of a specific chattel does not necessarily include a simultaneous transfer of the ownership to the buyer, the buyer does become exclusively entitled to the chattel *as between the seller and the buyer*. If now the seller, in breach of contract, transfers ownership in the chattel to a third party, the seller makes unauthorised use of the (first) buyer's exclusive entitlement *inter partes* and should be obliged to give up to the buyer the monetary value of that use.[121] This will be the difference between the price paid by the third party and the price agreed between the seller and the buyer.

iii   Generic Goods

Where generic goods are sold, property cannot pass to the buyer until particular goods are 'ascertained',[122] that is appropriated to the contract.[123] A buyer of generic goods who has acquired property in ascertained goods is in the same position as a buyer of specific goods who has acquired property in them. A seller still in possession of the goods has the factual power to transfer property to a third party who receives the goods in good faith.[124] But a seller who does so makes unauthorised use of the buyer's entitlement *erga omnes* and is therefore unjustly enriched at the buyer's expense insofar as the price paid by the third party exceeds the price agreed between seller and buyer.

A buyer of generic goods who has not yet acquired property in ascertained goods has no entitlement *erga omnes* nor is there much room for an entitlement *inter partes*. Prior to the ascertainment of goods, there are no particular goods to which the buyer can point and say 'these are for me'. Once goods have been ascertained, but property has not passed, the buyer might be said to enjoy an entitlement *inter partes* to those goods. But this presupposes that the seller cannot revoke the ascertainment. Where the seller is factually unable to revoke the ascertainment (because, for instance, the seller has dispatched the goods and cannot recall them), the buyer may indeed be entitled to the ascertained goods *inter partes*. But the seller has then lost the factual ability to make unauthorised use of the buyer's entitlement by transferring property to a third party. Where the

---

[120]   The view that the availability of specific performance should not be decisive is also taken by D Friedmann, 'Restitution of Benefits Obtained Through the Appropriation of Property or the Commission of a Wrong' (1980) 80 *Colum L Rev* 504, 517; H McGregor, 'Restitutionary Damages' in P Birks (ed), *Wrongs and Remedies in the Twenty-First Century* (Oxford, 1996) 214.

[121]   Such obligation is favoured by JP Dawson, 'Restitution or Damages?' (1959) 20 *Ohio State Law Journal* 175, 186–87; for deliberate breaches of contract also H McGregor, ibid 214–15. For the opposite view see, eg, H Beale, 'Exceptional Measures of Damages in Contract' in P Birks (ed), ibid 243–44.

[122]   Sale of Goods Act 1979 s 16. Unless a different intention by the parties appears, property passes when goods fitting the contractual description and in a deliverable state are 'unconditionally appropriated to the contract' by one party with the other party's assent: Sale of Goods Act 1979 s 18 rule 5(1).

[123]   For the meaning of 'ascertained' goods see, eg, *Re London Wine Co (Shippers)* [1986] PCC 121.

[124]   Sale of Goods Act 1979 s 24.

seller is still factually able to revoke the ascertainment of the goods (because, for instance, the seller has separated certain goods and marked them for the buyer but has not yet dispatched them), there is no reason to deny the seller a right of revocation prior to the passing of property. As Pearson J said in *Carlos Federspiel & Co SA v Charles Twigg & Co Ltd* in the context of transfer of property:

> A mere setting apart or selection of the seller of the goods which he expects to use in performance of the contract is not enough. If that is all, he can change his mind and use those goods in performance of some other contract and use some other goods in performance of this contract.[125]

It follows that where a seller of generic goods transfers to a third party the property in particular goods fitting the description of the contract between the seller and the (first) buyer, the seller is not unjustly enriched at the buyer's expense unless those particular goods were already the buyer's property or were *irrevocably* (if that is possible) appropriated to the contract between the seller and the buyer. This approach can be illustrated by the facts of the Israeli case *Adras Building Material Ltd v Harlow & Jones GmbH*,[126] which involved a contract for the supply of (any) 7,000 tons of a certain kind of steel. It was not a sale of particular items of steel. Only some 5,000 tons of steel were delivered. The seller did acquire 7,000 tons of steel, and had them stored separately, with a view to deliver all of it to the buyer. However, the market price of steel rose soon after the contract had been made, and the seller sold some 1,700 tons out of those 7,000 tons for a higher price to third parties. The buyer, who did not buy alternative supply, sued the seller and claimed the difference between the price paid by the third parties and the price agreed between the seller and the buyer.

A minority in the Supreme Court of Israel took the view that the buyer had terminated the contract and had thus forfeited the right to claim specific performance or the seller's profit instead. Ben-Porath VP, who belonged to the minority, went on to say that she would have rejected the buyer's claim even if the contract had remained in force. In her view, the claim required that, before the seller sold the 1,700 tons of steel to third parties, the buyer had acquired a 'protected interest' in that particular steel. This, she said, was not the case because, even if the seller appropriated the steel in question to the contract with the buyer by storing it separately, the seller was free to revoke that appropriation by selling it to third parties.[127] The majority in the Supreme Court took the view that the buyer had not terminated the contract and could claim the seller's profit *whether or not the steel in question had been appropriated to the contract.*[128]

---

[125] [1957] 1 Lloyd's Rep 240, 255.
[126] [1995] RLR 235 (SC of Israel).
[127] ibid 251–54.
[128] While the other majority judges did not even discuss the issue of appropriation, Bach J (at 277) expressed the view that the steel in question had been appropriated to the contract with the buyer, but made clear that the buyer could have claimed the seller's profit even in the absence of such appropriation. Bach J said nothing on whether an appropriation can be revoked.

The case was decided under Israeli law. English law, it is submitted, ought to adopt Ben-Porath VP's approach and reject the buyer's claim in such a situation because the seller was free to revoke the appropriation (if any) of the steel to the contract with the buyer, and the buyer acquired therefore no exclusive entitlement to the steel even *inter partes*.[129]

A seller of property may make unauthorised use of the buyer's exclusive entitlement *inter partes* not only by transferring the property to a third party but also by using the property after the date at which the buyer was due to receive it. The seller may rent the property out to a third party or may use the property himself by, for instance, living in the house to be conveyed to the buyer or driving the car to be delivered to the buyer. Since the buyer should be entitled to claim the monetary value of the unauthorised use by the seller in the case of sale, the buyer should, a fortiori, also be entitled to claim that value in the case of an unauthorised use less serious than sale.[130] It seems, indeed, to be recognised that where a vendor of land, in breach of contract, delays conveyance and in the meantime rents the land out to a third party, the purchaser can claim the profit the vendor has made from the letting.[131]

B Contractual Right to be Treated as the Owner of Certain Property

The exclusive entitlement *inter partes* enjoyed by a buyer of property (in certain circumstances) is a temporary 'precursor' of the entitlement *erga omnes* to be transferred in due course. But property may be subject to an exclusive entitlement *inter partes* without an intention to change ownership. An owner of property and another person may agree that, *as between them*, the second party will have all or some of the entitlements resulting from ownership, without actually acquiring ownership. Such an agreement may feature, for instance, in the settlement of a dispute.

A good illustration is found in *Experience Hendrix LLC v PPX Enterprises Inc.*[132] PPX held the copyright in the masters not listed in the schedule, and

---

[129] The majority approach is supported by D Friedmann, 'Restitution of Profits Gained by Party in Breach of Contract' (1988) 104 *LQR* 383, 388; for deliberate breaches of contract also H McGregor, 'Restitutionary Damages' in P Birks (ed), *Wrongs and Remedies in the Twenty-First Century* (Oxford, 1996) 214–15.

[130] D Friedmann, 'Restitution of Benefits Obtained Through the Appropriation of Property or the Commission of a Wrong' (1980) 80 *Colum L Rev* 504, 519.

[131] *Tang Man Sit v Capacious Investments Ltd* [1996] AC 514 (PC).

[132] [2003] EWCA Civ 323, [2003] FSR 46; above ch 12, V A. Another example is *Lane v O'Brien Homes Ltd* [2004] EWHC 303 (QB); above ch 12, V A where the defendant contractually promised not to build more than three houses on its land without the neighbouring claimant's permission: As between the parties, the claimant was to be treated as the owner of the defendant's land insofar as it concerned the decision on whether to build more than three houses.

continued to hold the copyright after the settlement agreement. In that agreement however, PPX undertook not to grant new licences for those masters without the consent of Jimi Hendrix' estate. In other words: While PPX kept the copyright in the masters concerned, the parties agreed that, *as between them*, Jimi Hendrix' estate was to be treated as if it held the copyright insofar as it concerned the grant of new licences. By granting new licences without the consent required, PPX made unauthorised use of the exclusive entitlement *inter partes* enjoyed by Jimi Hendrix' estate and should have been obliged to disgorge the monetary value of that use. In an action for breach of contract the Court of Appeal did hold Jimi Hendrix' estate entitled to a proportion of the profit that PPX had made from the unauthorised licences. That claim, it is suggested, should be classified as one in autonomous unjust enrichment rather than for breach of contract as such.

Another example is *Surrey CC v Bredero Homes Ltd*.[133] When two local councils sold certain land to Bredero, Bredero undertook not to build more than 72 houses on the land without the councils' consent. In other words, while Bredero acquired ownership in the land, the parties agreed that, *as between them*, the two councils were to be treated as if they held ownership insofar as it concerned the right to build more than 72 houses. By building 77 houses without the councils' consent, Bredero made unauthorised use of the councils' exclusive entitlement *inter partes* and should in principle have been obliged to disgorge the monetary value of that use. The actual denial of gain-based relief in that case can still be justified on the ground that the two councils never attempted to stop the development even though they were aware of it from the beginning.[134] It is defensible to maintain that the holder of an exclusive entitlement cannot idly watch another person making unauthorised use of the entitlement and then claim the monetary value of that use.[135]

An exclusive entitlement *inter partes* may also exist where there is a dispute over who is the owner of certain property and the two contenders settle the dispute by agreeing that, irrespective of who is actually the owner, one of them will be treated as the owner at least as between them. This situation arose in *WWF-World Wide Fund for Nature v World Wrestling Federation Entertainment Inc*,[136] which concerned a dispute over the right to use the trademark 'WWF'. In 1994, the two contenders entered into a settlement agreement in which the World Wrestling Federation undertook to use the trademark 'WWF' only in the (very limited) ways permitted by the agreement. In other words, the parties agreed that, irrespective of who actually owned the trademark 'WWF', the World Wide Fund

---

[133] [1993] 1 WLR 1361 (CA); above ch 12, V A.

[134] This is the reason given by Rose LJ: [1993] 1 WLR 1361, 1371.

[135] See *Gafford v Graham* (1999) 77 P & CR 73 (CA) 80–81, where acquiescence by the owner of the dominant tenement was the reason for denying gain-based relief for certain breaches of a restrictive covenant; K Barnett, 'Deterrence and Disgorging Profits for Breach of Contract' (2009) 17 *RLR* 79, 94–95. The view that the claimant's conduct should only affect the *amount* of recovery is taken by H McGregor, *McGregor on Damages*, 18th edn (London, 2009) [12–049].

[136] [2007] EWCA Civ 286, [2008] 1 WLR 445.

for Nature was to be treated as the owner at least between the two parties (except insofar as the Federation was permitted to use the trademark). Subsequently, the Federation did use the trademark in ways not permitted by the agreement. This was an unauthorised use of the Fund's exclusive entitlement at least *inter partes*, and the Fund should therefore have been entitled to claim the monetary value of that use. In an action for breach of contract, the Court of Appeal recognised the Fund's entitlement in principle to a hypothetical-fee award and denied it only on the procedural ground that the claim for a hypothetical relaxation fee was raised too late during the proceedings. It is suggested again that this claim should be classified as one in autonomous unjust enrichment rather than for breach of contract as such.

C Contractual Right to Someone Else's 'Labour Power'?

Everybody has an exclusive right to decide whether and how to exploit the own ability to work, which may be called the 'right to one's labour power'. Unlawfully forcing somebody to do certain work therefore constitutes an unauthorised use of an exclusive entitlement *erga omnes*, and the person forced should be entitled to claim the monetary value of that use,[137] which may be calculated by reference to the profit that the person exerting the force has made from the work in question. Much more difficult is the question of whether a person can have an exclusive entitlement *inter partes* to someone else's labour power (outside fiduciary relationships, which will be considered afterwards). Suppose that an employee breaches the employment contract by working for another employer (for a higher salary). The old employer now claims from the employee the additional salary received from the new employer. This claim ought to succeed if, and only if, an employment contract confers upon the employer an exclusive entitlement *inter partes* to the employee's labour power.

Until the nineteenth century it was recognised that 'whatever an apprentice who runs away gains in another service eo nomine belongs to the master, and is earned for him'.[138] Today, an employer's claim for obtaining the profit the employee has made from breaking the employment contract has little prospect of success.[139] Should an employer be entitled to obtain that profit?[140]

A formal objection to such an entitlement is that it would effectively force the employee to stay with that employer (until the contract expires or the employee

---

[137] Similarly, P Jaffey, *The Nature and Scope of Restitution: Vitiated Transfers, Imputed Contracts and Disgorgement* (Oxford, 2000) 151.

[138] *Carsan v Watts* (1784) 3 Dougl 350, 352; 99 ER 691, 692 (Lord Mansfield). See also *Barber v Dennis* (1703) 1 Salk 68, 91 ER 63; *Hill v Allen* (1747) 1 Ves Sen 83, 27 ER 906; *Lightly v Clouston* (1808) 1 Taunt 112, 127 ER 774.

[139] *University of Nottingham v Fishel* [2000] ICR 1462, 1488–89.

[140] An affirmative answer is given by K Barnett, 'Substitutability and Disgorgement Damages in Contract' in E Bant and M Harding (eds), *Exploring Private Law* (Cambridge, 2010), forthcoming.

can lawfully terminate the contract), which would conflict with the statutory prohibition of compelling employees to do certain work through an injunction or order of specific performance.[141] This objection could be rejected on the ground that an entitlement by the employer to the profit that the employee has made from breaking the contract would not actually force the employee to work for that employer. The employee would still be factually free to work for another employer or do no work at all, albeit neither option would be financially attractive.

More substantially, gain-based recovery could be said to conflict with the policy reasons for prohibiting injunctions and specific performance against employees. To compel an employee to do certain work, it has been argued, would 'interfere unduly with his personal liberty'[142] and would 'turn contracts of service into contracts of slavery'.[143] The same effect might be ascribed to an employer's entitlement to the employee's profit from breach. While this argument may have some force, it is not insurmountable. The goal of economic and social mobility has not prevented the courts from upholding *reasonable* restrictive covenants in employment contracts, that is covenants which, to a reasonable extent, prohibit the employee from working in the employer's trade in a certain area for a certain period of time after the end of the employment.[144] Economic and social mobility could further be achieved by granting employees a right, unable to be waived, to terminate any employment contract, even for a fixed term, by giving a relatively short period of notice. If such a regime is thought to afford employers too little certainty to organise their business, the argument against gain-based recovery will appear weaker.

In deciding on whether the employer should be entitled to the employee's profit from breach, it may be appropriate to distinguish between different types of service. Gain-based recovery may be excluded in the case of ordinary services but allowed in the case of highly-skilled or unique services.[145] Where, for instance, a professional sportsperson breaks the contract with the employing club by playing for another club (for a higher salary), an entitlement of the old club to

---

[141] This prohibition is laid down in the Trade Union and Labour Relations (Consolidation) Act 1992 s 236. Conversely, nobody can normally be forced to (continue to) employ a certain person: *British Fuels Ltd v Baxendale* [1999] 2 AC 52 (HL) 77; *Wills v Mills & Co Solicitors* [2005] EWCA Civ 591 especially [29]. For Scots law see *Morrish v NTL Group Ltd* [2007] CSIH 56, 2007 SC 805 [6]. See also Employment Rights Act 1996 ss 113–17; Trade Union and Labour Relations (Consolidation) Act 1992 ss 163–66.

[142] E Peel, *Treitel on the Law of Contract* (12th edn, London, 2007) [21–035].

[143] *De Francesco v Barnum* (1890) LR 45 Ch D 430, 438 (Fry LJ). Wonnell objects that the availability of specific relief 'would economically empower employees by allowing them to extract more favorable terms from employers in exchange for *enforceable* promises to fulfil their parts of the bargain': CT Wonnell, 'The Contractual Disempowerment of Employees' (1993) 46 *Stanford Law Review* 87, 145.

[144] eg *Beckett Investment Management Group Ltd v Hall* [2007] EWCA Civ 613, [2007] ICR 1539.

[145] D Friedmann, 'Restitution of Benefits Obtained Through the Appropriation of Property or the Commission of a Wrong' (1980) 80 *Colum L Rev* 504, 520–21.

the additional salary is by no means inconceivable. Indeed, there is a widespread parlance according to which sports clubs 'buy' and 'sell' players, which reinforces an analogy to property rights.

It is not necessary to express a conclusive view. Whatever view is taken on an employer's entitlement to the employee's profit from breach, it does not affect the exclusive-entitlement theory advocated in this book. This theory is consistent with allowing gain-based relief since the employee would then be said to have made unauthorised use of the employer's exclusive entitlement *inter partes* to the employee's labour power. The theory would also be consistent with disallowing gain-based relief as it could simply be said that certain policy reasons render a person unable to grant another person an exclusive entitlement *inter partes* to the first person's labour power.

D   Right to the Loyalty of One's Fiduciary

The availability of gain-based relief for breach of fiduciary duty is usually explained on grounds of deterrence,[146] even by commentators who otherwise link gain-based relief to the unauthorised use of property or property-like rights.[147] It is suggested however, that a breach of fiduciary duty can be conceptualised as an unauthorised use of an exclusive entitlement, at least *inter partes*, enjoyed by the principal. This view shall be explained for breaches of the self-dealing rule, the fair-dealing rule and the no-profit rule.

A fiduciary who acquires property from the principal in breach of the self-dealing rule or the fair-dealing rule[148] may be said to have made unauthorised use of that property. An unauthorised use of property may thus be found, for instance, where an agent has authority to sell certain property owned by the principal and sells it to himself (a breach of the self-dealing rule) or where a solicitor is retained with respect to certain property owned by the client and purchases that very property from the client for less than its market value (a

---

[146]   eg I Samet, 'Guarding the Fiduciary's Conscience—A Justification of a Stringent Profit-stripping Rule' (2008) 28 *OJLS* 763, who invokes considerations of moral psychology.

[147]   D Friedmann, 'Restitution of Benefits Obtained Through the Appropriation of Property or the Commission of a Wrong' (1980) 80 *Colum L Rev* 504, 508–10, 551–53 (above I C in this chapter); S Worthington, 'Reconsidering Disgorgement for Wrongs' (1999) 62 *MLR* 218, 236–37 (above I H in this chapter); T Krebs, 'The Fallacy of "Restitution for Wrongs"' in A Burrows and Lord Rodger of Earlsferry (eds), *Mapping the Law: Essays in Memory of Peter Birks* (Oxford, 2006) 397 ('Regulation of conduct rather than protection of rights is at issue.').

[148]   'The self-dealing rule is (to put it very shortly) that if a trustee sells the trust property to himself, the sale is voidable by any beneficiary ex debito justitiae, however fair the transaction. The fair-dealing rule is (again putting it very shortly) that if a trustee purchases the beneficial interest of any of his beneficiaries, the transaction is not voidable ex debito justitiae, but can be set aside by the beneficiary unless the trustee can show that he has taken no advantage of his position and has made full disclosure to the beneficiary, and that the transaction is fair and honest': *Tito v Waddell (No 2)* [1977] Ch 106, 241 (Megarry VC). Approvingly quoted in *Re Thompson's Settlement* [1986] Ch 99, 110–11; *Hollis v Rolfe* [2008] EWHC 1747 (Ch) [177]–[178].

breach of the fair-dealing rule). A fiduciary who makes unauthorised use of the principal's property infringes the principal's exclusive right to use that property. Under the exclusive-entitlement theory advocated in this book, the principal can claim from the fiduciary the monetary value of the unauthorised use, which may be calculated by reference to the profit made by the fiduciary.

The no-profit rule prohibits a fiduciary from acquiring a benefit 'by reason of his fiduciary position, and by reason of the opportunity and the knowledge, or either, resulting from it'.[149] In the light of this rule it may be said that, as between the fiduciary and the principal, the principal enjoys the exclusive right to use business opportunities that the fiduciary encounters by reason of his fiduciary position. A fiduciary who uses such an opportunity for his own pocket may thus be said to have made unauthorised use of the principal's exclusive entitlement *inter partes*.[150] Again, under the exclusive-entitlement theory advocated in this book, the principal can claim from the fiduciary the monetary value of the unauthorised use, which may be calculated by reference to the profit made by the fiduciary.

Where the business opportunity in question is only open to the fiduciary in his personal capacity,[151] it might sound strange to say that the principal has an exclusive right to use that opportunity. In particular, where an agent is offered a bribe, it might sound strange to say that the principal has an exclusive right 'to be bribed'. But the exclusive-entitlement theory can still work if one separates the relationship between the principal and the fiduciary from the relationship between the principal and the third party. As between the principal and the third party, the principal has, of course, no right to use a business opportunity that the third party has offered only to the fiduciary personally. As between the principal and the fiduciary, however, the principal may well be said to have an exclusive right to use such an opportunity since the fiduciary needs the principal's consent to lawfully enter into the transaction with the third party. Where a business opportunity is only open to the fiduciary personally, the principal's exclusive right to use business opportunities encountered by the fiduciary by reason of his position boils down to an exclusive right to decide whether to allow the fiduciary to use that opportunity.

---

[149] *Regal (Hastings) Ltd v Gulliver* [1967] 2 AC 134 (HL) 154 (Lord Wright). See also *Boardman v Phipps* [1967] 2 AC 46 (HL) 103, 105, 115; Companies Act 2006 ss 175(2) and 176.

[150] Similarly H Dagan, 'Encroachments: between private and public' in D Johnston and R Zimmermann (eds), *Unjustified Enrichment: Key Issues in Comparative Perspective* (Cambridge, 2002) 361–62; EJ Weinrib, 'Restitutionary Damages as Corrective Justice' (2000) 1 *Theoretical Inquiries in Law* 1, 33–34.

[151] Examples are *Keech v Sandford* (1726) Sel Cas Ch 61, 25 ER 223; *Industrial Development Consultants Ltd v Cooley* [1972] 1 WLR 443; above ch 12, III A.

V Situations in Which 'Restitution for Wrongs' is Inappropriate

A Deceit

While the exclusive-entitlement theory advocated in this book supports the availability of gain-based relief in cases of fraud by way of bribery,[152] it rejects gain-based relief (in the absence of rescission) in cases of deceit, that is fraudulent misrepresentation that induces the other party to enter into a contract. A person making a fraudulent misrepresentation uses no asset (even in its widest sense) to which the representee is exclusively entitled. An exclusive entitlement the violation of which triggers gain-based relief cannot be seen in a 'right not to be lied to', which Robert Stevens recognises and describes as a 'right which is good against every other person'.[153] It is revealing that the 'right not to be lied to' can only be formulated in a negative way, specifying the manner of violation rather than any asset or interest enjoyed by the right-holder.

Since there should be no legal response to all everyday lies, the 'right not to be lied to' must be understood as 'right not to be lied to unlawfully'. But this is nothing other than a right not to be subjected to certain unlawful conduct. By the same token, everyone has a right not to suffer damage as a result of someone else's carelessness. If the right not to be subjected to unlawful conduct constituted an exclusive entitlement the violation of which triggers gain-based relief, gain-based relief would be available for every wrong and the notion of exclusive entitlement would be almost meaningless. In order to be meaningful, the notion of exclusive entitlement must be confined to the right to use an asset (in a wide sense), that is to use (tangible or intangible) property, to 'use' personal 'assets' such as bodily integrity, privacy or reputation, or to use business opportunities encountered by one's fiduciary.

Furthermore, in cases of deceit there is no actual need for gain-based relief in the absence of rescission, for the unjust enrichment claim following rescission and compensatory damages provide sufficient remedies for victims of deceit. First and foremost, the claimant is interested in retrieving the asset that the defendant has acquired from the claimant, or the monetary value of that asset. This poses little difficulty as the tort of deceit entitles the claimant to recover damages for the loss suffered by reason of entering into the contract, that is the loss of the asset.[154] Since the claimant's loss mirrors the defendant's gain, (compensatory) damages achieve the same effect as gain-based relief.

---

[152] Above IV D in this chapter.
[153] R Stevens, *Torts and Rights* (Oxford, 2007) 8.
[154] eg *Cobbe v Yeoman's Row Management Ltd* [2008] UKHL 55, [2008] 1 WLR 1752 [4].

Moreover, the fraudulent misrepresentation generally entitles the claimant to rescind the contract with the defendant[155] and claim back the lost asset through an action in autonomous unjust enrichment.[156] Where the defendant has transferred the asset or a right in it to a bona fide third party, the third party's title cannot be impeached through rescission.[157] But the claimant should still be entitled to claim the monetary value of the asset from the defendant.[158]

The claimant may also be interested in obtaining the further profit that the defendant has made from investing the asset acquired from the claimant. Again, the claimant may rescind the contract with the defendant to the effect that the claimant is regarded as having enjoyed equitable title in the asset throughout and may trace that asset into the proceeds of the investment.[159] If, after having discovered the misrepresentation, the claimant chooses to affirm the contract with the defendant, the claimant should no longer be able to claim the profit the defendant has made from investing the asset acquired from the claimant.[160]

B   Skimped Contractual Performance

Another situation in which the exclusive-entitlement theory advocated in this book rejects gain-based relief is where a contractual party saves money by rendering deficient, delayed or no performance. A vivid example is the Louisiana case *City of New Orleans v Firemen's Charitable Association.*[161] The claimant retained the defendant as New Orleans' fire brigade for 10 years and paid US$160,000 per year for those services. In a contract between the parties, the defendant undertook to maintain at all times a certain amount of men, horses and hose. In fact, the defendant never maintained the required amount of men, horses or hose, thus saving almost US$40,000. But this shortage caused no damage to the claimant. In particular, the defendant extinguished all fires during its tenure. The claimant's action for recovering the money paid failed.

In a situation as that present in *City of New Orleans v Firemen's Charitable Association*, the exclusive-entitlement theory advocated in this book would give the claimant no right to claim the money the defendant saved by breaching the

---

[155]   ibid.

[156]   eg *Redgrave v Hurd* (1881) LR 20 Ch D 1 (CA).

[157]   eg *Shalson v Russo* [2003] EWHC 1637 (Ch), [2005] Ch 281 [126].

[158]   B Häcker, 'Rescission and Third Party Rights' [2006] *RLR* 21; D O'Sullivan, S Elliott and R Zakrzewski, *The Law of Rescission* (Oxford, 2008) [20.07]–[20.27].

[159]   *Lonrho plc v Fayed (No 2)* [1992] 1 WLR 1, 12; *El Ajou v Dollar Land Holdings plc* [1993] 3 All ER 717, 735; *Halifax Building Society v Thomas* [1996] Ch 217 (CA) 226; *Bristol and West Building Society v Mothew* [1998] Ch 1 (CA) 22–23; *Shalson v Russo* [2003] EWHC 1637 (Ch), [2005] Ch 281 [122]–[127].

[160]   *Halifax Building Society v Thomas* [1996] Ch 217 (CA) 227, above ch 12, IV F. The opposite view is taken by C Mitchell, 'No Account of Profits for a Victim of Deceit' [1996] *Lloyd's Maritime Commercial Law Quarterly* 314, 316.

[161]   (1891) 43 La Ann 447, 9 So 486 (SC of Louisiana).

contract.[162] The defendant did not violate an exclusive entitlement enjoyed by the claimant. One might try to construe an exclusive entitlement by saying that the claimant had the exclusive right to decide whether the defendant was allowed to have less than the contractually specified amount of men, horses and hose. But such a wide interpretation of the term 'exclusive entitlement' would encompass all rights to contractual performance since the right to claim performance under a contract entails the right to relax the other party's obligation. That approach would render the notion of 'exclusive entitlement' almost meaningless and would affect its suitability as the basis for gain-based relief. As said before, the notion of 'exclusive entitlement' must be confined to the right to use an asset in a wide sense.

Furthermore, there are strong policy reasons why a party aggrieved by a breach of contract should not generally be entitled to claim the amount of money the contract-breaker saved through the breach. A contracting party is normally only interested in the outcome of the other party's efforts to perform, that is proper and timely performance, not with the amount of money necessary to achieve that outcome. In *City of New Orleans v Firemen's Charitable Association*, the claimant was not interested in the defendant spending a certain amount of money. The claimant was interested in the defendant maintaining the contractually stipulated amount of men, horses and hose, and would have been satisfied had the defendant maintained that level with the sum of money actually spent. Since the claimant was not interested in the amount of money spent, neither should the claimant's remedy.

Instead, the claimant's remedy should relate to the shortfall in the defendant's performance.[163] One remedy that does so is an award of unliquidated compensatory damages compensating the claimant for the loss suffered as a result of the shortfall. Of course, such an award cannot be made where, as in *City of New Orleans v Firemen's Charitable Association*, the claimant has suffered no loss.[164] In that situation, the shortfall in the defendant's performance can still be addressed through a clause in the contract requiring the defendant to pay a certain sum to the claimant in the event of breach. As long as the stipulated amount does not exceed the greatest loss that could have genuinely been pre-estimated at the time of the contract, the clause is enforceable as liquidated damages even if the claimant cannot prove her loss or indeed suffered no loss.[165] Thus, liquidated

---

[162] Gain-based relief is supported by D Friedmann, 'Restitution of Benefits Obtained Through the Appropriation of Property or the Commission of a Wrong' (1980) 80 *Colum L Rev* 504, 524–25.

[163] J O'Sullivan, 'Reflections on the role of restitutionary damages to protect contractual expectations' in D Johnston and R Zimmermann (eds), *Unjustified Enrichment: Key Issues in Comparative Perspective* (Cambridge, 2002) 338–42.

[164] O'Sullivan, ibid, suggests a wider notion of loss that allows a compensatory award in cases of skimped performance.

[165] *Dunlop Pneumatic Tyre Co Ltd v New Garage and Motor Co Ltd* [1915] AC 79 (HL) 86–87 (Lord Dunedin); *Philips Hong Kong Ltd v Attorney-General of Hong Kong* (1993) 61 Build LR 41, 9 Const LJ 202 (PC).

damages can overcome the problem that is sought to be resolved through gain-based relief.[166] The stipulation of a sum exceeding the highest genuine pre-estimate would be a penalty clause. Penalty clauses are currently unenforceable,[167] but there have been calls to change the law.[168]

A liquidated damages clause, or penalty clause if allowed, could have deterred the defendant in *City of New Orleans v Firemen's Charitable Association* from breaching the contract even if the stipulated sum had been less than the amount the defendant saved through the breach (US$40,000). The defendant saved this amount over a period of 10 years but the claimant could have discovered the breach much earlier. With a clause in the contract requiring the payment of a certain sum in the event of breach, the defendant would have run the risk of the breach being discovered before the defendant saved more money than the stipulated sum.

VI Exclusive-Entitlement Theory and Present Law Compared

The instances of gain-based relief under the exclusive-entitlement theory advocated in this book shall now be compared with the instances in which the courts have recognised 'restitution for wrongs'. Two questions will be investigated: can the exclusive-entitlement theory explain the outcome of all English cases recognising 'restitution for wrongs', or is the theory underinclusive; and does the exclusive-entitlement theory lead to gain-based relief in instances in which 'restitution for wrongs' is not recognised, that is, is the theory overinclusive?

The exclusive-entitlement theory is overinclusive as it does lead to gain-based relief in instances in which 'restitution for wrongs' is not recognised. Even though the previous study into exclusive entitlements examined only a selection of rights, it revealed situations in which gain-based relief is not (clearly) recognised by the courts but is called for by the exclusive-entitlement theory. These are

---

[166] H Dagan, 'Encroachments: between private and public' in D Johnston and R Zimmermann (eds), *Unjustified Enrichment: Key Issues in Comparative Perspective* (Cambridge, 2002) 357 fn 24.

[167] See especially, *Dunlop Pneumatic Tyre Co Ltd v New Garage and Motor Co Ltd* [1915] AC 79 (HL) 86–87 (Lord Dunedin); *Philips Hong Kong Ltd v Attorney-General of Hong Kong* (1993) 61 Build LR 41, 9 Const LJ 202 (PC).

[168] eg TA Downes, 'Rethinking Penalty Clauses' in P Birks (ed), *Wrongs and Remedies in the Twenty-First Century* (Oxford, 1996) 249; RA Posner, *Economic Analysis of Law*, 7th edn (Austin, 2007) 128–129; CJ Goetz and RE Scott, 'Liquidated Damages, Penalties and the Just Compensation Principle: Some Notes on an Enforcement Model and a Theory of Efficient Breach' (1977) 77 *Colum L Rev* 554; PR Kaplan, 'A Critique of the Penalty Limitation on Liquidated Damages' (1977) 50 *Southern California Law Review* 1055; GA Muir, 'Stipulations for the Payment of Agreed Sums' (1985) 10 *Sydney Law Review* 503; Scottish Law Commission, 'Report on Penalty Clauses' (Scot Law Com No 171, 1999).

instances of nuisance that violate the landowner's rights or an easement; violations of bodily integrity, privacy and reputation; and the double sale of a chattel. This overinclusivity is not problematic because, as explained when discussing the rights in question, there are cogent reasons for classifying them as exclusive entitlements, the violation of which should trigger gain-based relief.

While the exclusive-entitlement theory is overinclusive, it is not significantly underinclusive. It can explain the outcome, but not necessarily the reasoning, of virtually every English case recognising 'restitution for wrongs'. The theory can easily explain the recognition of gain-based relief for trespass to land, wrongful interference with goods and intellectual property wrongs as all these situations involve the infringement of ownership in property. The exclusive-entitlement theory can further explain the recognition of gain-based relief for breach of confidence and breach of a restrictive covenant as these situations involve the infringement of an entitlement whose exclusive nature (at least *inter partes*) cannot seriously be doubted. It is also possible to identify the infringement of an exclusive entitlement (at least *inter partes*) in the following cases involving breach of contract: *Attorney-General v Blake (Jonathan Cape Ltd Third Party)*,[169] *Experience Hendrix LLC v PPX Enterprises Inc*,[170] *Lane v O'Brien Homes Ltd*,[171] and *WWF-World Wide Fund for Nature v World Wrestling Federation Entertainment Inc*.[172] Finally, a possible, if stretched, interpretation of 'exclusive entitlement' can explain the availability of gain-based relief for fraud by way of bribery and other forms of breach of fiduciary duty.

The exclusive-entitlement theory cannot explain why an account of profits was held available in *Esso Petroleum Co Ltd v Niad Ltd*.[173] Niad did not violate an exclusive entitlement enjoyed by Esso. A mere right to relax someone else's obligation is not an exclusive entitlement the infringement of which should trigger gain-based relief.[174] However, the inability of the exclusive-entitlement theory to explain the outcome in *Esso Petroleum Co Ltd v Niad Ltd* poses no threat to the theory since the merits of that decision may be doubted in any event.[175]

Esso's main concern was to recover the money which Esso had paid to Niad as a price subsidy under the Pricewatch scheme and which Niad should have, but had not, passed on to its customers. Esso was only obliged to pay that money if Niad implemented Esso's price recommendation. Niad failed to implement the

---

[169] [2001] 1 AC 268 (HL).
[170] [2003] EWCA Civ 323, [2003] FSR 46.
[171] [2004] EWHC 303 (QB).
[172] [2007] EWCA Civ 286, [2008] 1 WLR 445.
[173] [2001] EWHC 6 (Ch), [2001] All ER (D) 324; above ch 12, V B.
[174] Above V B in this chapter.
[175] Furthermore, the significance of *Esso Petroleum Co Ltd v Niad Ltd* has been downplayed on the ground of its improper reporting: H McGregor, *McGregor on Damages*, 18th edn (London, 2009) [12–023] fn 110 ('There is no satisfactory report of the case and what there is is confusing.'), [12–043] ('ill-reported decision'; 'minimal and unsatisfactory reporting').

recommendation, hence Esso had no obligation to pay the subsidy. Since Esso's payment was made in the mistaken belief of being contractually obliged to do so, Esso had a straightforward claim in autonomous unjust enrichment for the repayment of the subsidy.[176] That claim was in fact raised by Esso, as an alternative to its claim for breach of contract, and held available.[177] Indeed, Sir Andrew Morritt VC described the claim for mistaken payment as 'the most appropriate remedy in that it matches most closely the reality of the case'.[178] Esso did not need an account of profits to get back the price subsidy.

It is true that Esso had an independent interest in Niad actually implementing Esso's price recommendation. Esso launched a radio and television campaign describing the prices charged by its fuel stations as 'amongst the lowest', and the charging of higher than recommended prices by Niad had the potential to undermine that claim and affect Esso's reputation. However, Esso had significant sanctions available: It could have excluded Niad from the Pricewatch scheme and, as a last resort, ended altogether its business relationship with Niad. If that is still thought insufficient to compel an implementation of the price recommendation, the law can be changed so as to allow parties in that situation to stipulate for a (reasonable) penalty should the fuel station breach the Pricewatch agreement.[179] That would be more effective than awarding an account of profits.[180]

To conclude, even though the availability of 'restitution for wrongs' depends on the type of wrong under the present law and on the nature of the violated interest under the exclusive-entitlement theory advocated in this book, there is an impressive overlap between the two. Virtually all English cases recognising 'restitution for wrongs' involved exclusive entitlements either *erga omnes* or *inter partes*, which suggests that the courts are unlikely to award 'restitution for wrongs' where no exclusive entitlement has been violated. The exclusive-entitlement theory advocated in this book does lead to gain-based relief in instances in which 'restitution for wrongs' is not (yet) recognised. Prime examples are the violation of the right to bodily integrity or of the right to reputation. There are cogent reasons for the availability of gain-based relief in those instances.

---

[176] eg *Kelly v Solari* (1841) 9 M & W 54, 58; 152 ER 24, 26; *Aiken v Short* (1856) 1 H & N 210, 215; 156 ER 1180, 1182; *Sempra Metals Ltd (formerly Metallgesellschaft Ltd) v IRC* [2007] UKHL 34, [2008] 1 AC 561 [22], [124], [132].

[177] [2001] EWHC 6 (Ch), [2001] All ER (D) 324 [64].

[178] ibid.

[179] See above V B in this chapter.

[180] Barnett defends the award of an account of profits in *Esso Petroleum Co Ltd v Niad Ltd* on the grounds that Niad abused Esso's trust and that there was a public interest in competitive fuel prices: K Barnett, 'Deterrence and Disgorging Profits for Breach of Contract' (2009) 17 *RLR* 79, 89.

Part 5

Exemplary Damages

14

The Present Law of Exemplary Damages

I Terminology

In actions for torts and, in some jurisdictions, other civil wrongs, the claimant is sometimes awarded a sum of money exceeding both the claimant's loss and the defendant's gain resulting from the wrong. The purpose of such an award has traditionally been described as the punishment of the defendant for committing the wrong, in order to set an example.[1] Various names have been used to reflect this purpose, including exemplary, penal, punitive, retributory or vindictive damages.[2] The term 'punitive damages' is recommended by the Law Commission for England and Wales[3] and has prevailed in all other common law jurisdictions. However, courts and commentators in England and Wales predominantly still use the term 'exemplary damages', preferred by the House of Lords in the leading cases *Rookes v Barnard*[4] and *Cassell & Co Ltd v Broome*.[5] Adopting that parlance, this Part will consistently use the term 'exemplary damages' even when referring to the law in other jurisdictions.

Before entering the study, a note on aggravated damages is due.[6] They had not been clearly separated from exemplary damages until Lord Devlin in *Rookes v Barnard* distinguished between exemplary damages, which aim to punish the defendant, and aggravated damages, which reflect the aggravation of the injury to the claimant's feelings of dignity and pride by the manner in which the defendant

---

[1] Below ch 15, I. For economic accounts of exemplary damages see below ch 15, II.

[2] See *Whitfeld v De Lauret & Co Ltd* (1920) 29 CLR 71 (HCA) 81 (Isaacs J).

[3] Law Commission, 'Aggravated, Exemplary and Restitutionary Damages' (Law Com No 247, 1997) [5.39], Appendix A, Draft Damages Bill s 1(2).

[4] [1964] AC 1129 (HL).

[5] [1972] AC 1027 (HL), where Lord Hailsham LC (at 1073) expressly rejected the adjectives 'vindictive', 'aggravated' and 'retributory' as being inaccurate.

[6] Exemplary damages must further be distinguished from 'multiple damages': below V in this chapter.

has committed the wrong, or by his motive in so doing.[7] But it creates confusion to maintain a third category of damages in addition to exemplary damages and compensatory damages for non-pecuniary loss. Indeed, if significant non-pecuniary loss were generally compensable, as argued for in Part 2 of this book, aggravated damages would be completely robbed of their habitat.[8] The concept of aggravated damages should therefore be either abandoned[9] or assimilated within the concept of compensatory damages for non-pecuniary loss.[10] The Law Commission has recommended the latter approach,[11] and the government has promised to implement this proposal 'when a suitable legislative opportunity arises'.[12]

II *Rookes v Barnard*

The present law of exemplary damages was established by the House of Lords in *Rookes v Barnard*.[13] In that case, an agreement was reached between the plaintiff's trade union and his employer that no strike should take place and that disputes should be referred to arbitration. There was also a 'closed-shop' agreement relating to the plaintiff's post. After the plaintiff had resigned his membership of the trade union, the union, acting through the defendants, told his employer that unless the plaintiff was dismissed instantly the other union members working for that employer would withdraw their own labour. In consequence, the plaintiff was dismissed. The jury found the defendants liable for the tort of intimidation and awarded the plaintiff damages of £7,500. A considerable part of that sum must have been of a punitive character.[14]

---

[7] [1964] AC 1129 (HL) 1221. See also *Khodaparast v Shad* [2000] 1 WLR 618 (CA) 632 (Otton LJ); *Vorvis v Insurance Corp of British Columbia* [1989] 1 SCR 1085 (SCC), 1098–1099; M Tilbury, 'Factors Inflating Damages Awards' in PD Finn (ed), *Essays on Damages* (Sydney, 1992) 89–99. Critically J Stone, 'Double Count and Double Talk: The End of Exemplary Damages?' (1972) 46 *Australian Law Journal* 311: exemplary and aggravated damages are largely congruent, and the former should be displaced by the latter.

[8] H Beale, 'Exceptional Measures of Damages in Contract' in P Birks (ed), *Wrongs and Remedies in the Twenty-First Century* (Oxford, 1996) 230.

[9] A Burrows, 'The Scope of Exemplary Damages' (1993) 109 *LQR* 358, 361.

[10] Lord Scott, 'Damages' [2007] *Lloyds Maritime and Commercial Law Quarterly* 465, 466. See also P Cane, 'Exceptional Measures of Damages: A Search for Principles' in P Birks (ed), *Wrongs and Remedies in the Twenty-First Century* (Oxford, 1996) 305. There is scholarly support for retaining aggravated damages as a separate category of damages for vindicatory purposes; see the discussion by N Witzleb and R Carroll, 'The role of vindication in torts damages' (2009) 17 *Tort Law Review* 16, 24–27.

[11] Law Commission, 'Aggravated, Exemplary and Restitutionary Damages' (Law Com No 247, 1997) [2.39]–[2.43], Appendix A, Draft Damages Bill s 13.

[12] Mr Lock, Parliamentary Secretary, Lord Chancellor's Department: House of Commons Debates, Hansard HC vol 337 col 502 (9 November 1999).

[13] [1964] AC 1129 (HL).

[14] ibid 1178 (Lord Devlin).

One of the questions before the House of Lords was whether the jury had been entitled to award exemplary damages. Lord Devlin, speaking for the House on that issue, started with the following statement: 'The object of exemplary damages is to punish and deter. It may well be thought that this confuses the civil and criminal functions of the law'.[15] He therefore asked 'whether it is open to the House to remove an anomaly from the law of England'.[16] After a review of all relevant cases and statutes, he concluded:

> These authorities convince me of two things. First, that your Lordships could not, without a complete disregard of precedent, and indeed of statute, now arrive at a determination that refused altogether to recognise the exemplary principle. Secondly, there are certain categories of cases in which an award of exemplary damages can serve a useful purpose in vindicating the strength of the law and thus affording a practical justification for admitting into the civil law a principle which ought logically to belong to the criminal ...

> The first category is oppressive, arbitrary or unconstitutional action by the servants of the government ...

> Cases in the second category are those in which the defendant's conduct has been calculated by him to make a profit for himself which may well exceed the compensation payable to the plaintiff ...

> To these two categories which are established as part of the common law there must of course be added any category in which exemplary damages are expressly authorised by statute.[17]

Since the case at hand could not be brought into any of the three categories, the House of Lords quashed the jury's award. Lord Devlin's statement laid down what has become referred to as the categories test. For exemplary damages to be available, the case must fall into one of his three categories. The categories will now be scrutinised.

Beforehand, it should be mentioned that the categories test established in *Rookes v Barnard* has been rejected in all other major common law jurisdictions.[18] In England and Wales, the test has not gone unchallenged either. In *Cassell & Co Ltd v Broome* the Court of Appeal launched a powerful assault, Lord Denning MR describing the categories test as 'hopelessly illogical and inconsistent'.[19] The House

---

[15] ibid 1221.
[16] ibid.
[17] ibid 1225–27.
[18] *Conway v Irish National Teachers' Organisation* [1991] 2 IR 305 (SC of Ireland) 319–20, 323–24, 326. For Australia, Canada and New Zealand see the cases cited in *Browning-Ferris Industries of Vermont, Inc v Kelco Disposal, Inc* (1989) 492 US 257 (US SC) 273, where the categories test was impliedly rejected for the US, and cited by RW Hodgin and E Veitch, 'Punitive Damages—Reassessed' (1972) 21 *International & Comparative Law Quarterly* 119, 123–26.
[19] [1971] 2 QB 354 (CA) 381. For the facts of *Broome* see below IV A in this chapter; for Lord Denning's arguments in detail see below III C and IV B in this chapter.

of Lords in *Broome*[20] conceded the illogicality of the categories test but insisted, Viscount Dilhorne dissenting, on the authoritativeness of *Rookes v Barnard*. Lord Reid defended *Rookes v Barnard*, where he had also sat on the bench, in the following way: 'We thought we had to recognise that it had become an established custom in certain classes of case to permit awards of damages which could not be justified as compensatory, and that that must remain the law'.[21] In relation to the ambit of the categories, he said:

> We were confronted with an undesirable anomaly. We could not abolish it. We had to choose between confining it strictly to classes of cases where it was firmly established, although that produced an illogical result, or permitting it to be extended so as to produce a logical result. In my view it is better in such cases to be content with an illogical result than to allow any extension.[22]

III   Abuse of Power by Civil Servants

The first of the three categories in which according to *Rookes v Barnard* exemplary damages are available comprises, in the words of Lord Devlin, 'oppressive, arbitrary or unconstitutional action by the servants of the government'.[23] This formula has been treated as if it was carved in stone[24] and is interpreted like a statutory provision. It requires of the defendant a certain conduct and status.

A   Conduct Required

According to the normal rules of language, the phrase 'oppressive, arbitrary or unconstitutional action' means oppressive *or* arbitrary *or* unconstitutional action. This provokes the question of what is meant here by 'unconstitutional'. Since the constitution requires the government to respect the law, every illegal act by a government servant could be called unconstitutional. But if 'unconstitutional' were simply a synonym for 'illegal' it would effectively render the other alternatives redundant. While Lord Devlin's phrase being a pleonasm would not raise significant problems, the availability of exemplary damages for every illegal action by the government, even where resulting from a simple mistake, might do so.

---

[20]   [1972] AC 1027 (HL).
[21]   ibid 1086.
[22]   ibid 1087.
[23]   [1964] AC 1129 (HL) 1226.
[24]   Despite the warning against doing so in *Cassell & Co Ltd v Broome* [1972] AC 1027 (HL) 1068, 1077 (Lord Hailsham LC), 1085 (Lord Reid).

The issue arose in *Holden v Chief Constable of Lancashire*,[25] where the police wrongfully arrested and detained the plaintiff for 20 minutes without mistreating him in any way. In an action for false imprisonment, the judge withdrew any consideration of exemplary damages from the jury, observing that there had been no oppressive behaviour on the part of the police. The plaintiff appealed on the ground of misdirection. Whenever police officers act without authority, he argued, they contravene Magna Carta and act 'unconstitutionally' for the purpose of Lord Devlin's first category. The Court of Appeal ordered a retrial. Purchas LJ observed in his leading judgment:

> If full effect is to be given to the word 'or' in the category 'oppressive, arbitrary or unconstitutional action' by government servants, wrongful arrest falls within the category without any of the added qualifications suggested by the judge, in which case the question whether or not to award exemplary damages should have been left to the jury with appropriate directions as to what special features of the case they might in their discretion take into account in deciding whether or not to award such damages, and, if so, how much.[26]

In other words: In every case of illegal conduct by government servants the question of exemplary damages should be left to the jury, who may (or even should?) deny such damages in the absence of aggravating circumstances. Emphasising the jury's discretion, Sir John Arnold P said in *Holden v Chief Constable of Lancashire* that 'the circumstance that a case comes within a category does not make it follow as the night the day that exemplary damages will be awarded'.[27]

Even though *Holden v Chief Constable of Lancashire* laid down that the words oppressive, arbitrary and unconstitutional must be read disjunctively,[28] it also indicated that an award of exemplary damages is inappropriate where the defendant made a simple mistake.[29] This was confirmed in *Ministry of Defence v Fletcher*,[30] where an Employment Tribunal awarded exemplary damages of £50,000 with regard to the Ministry' failure to address the claimant army officer's complaints of sexual harassment. The Employment Appeal Tribunal quashed that award, saying that while such award may have been appropriate had the Ministry

---

[25] [1987] QB 380 (CA).

[26] ibid 388.

[27] ibid 389.

[28] The same view seems to have been taken in *Attorney-General of St Christopher, Nevis and Anguilla v Reynolds* [1980] AC 637 (PC) 662, where aggravating circumstances were present.

[29] But see *Muuse v Secretary of State for the Home Department* [2009] EWHC 1886 (QB), where exemplary damages of £27,500 were awarded for the claimant's unlawful detention of 128 days which was due to mistaken identity.

[30] Appeal No UKEAT/0044/09/JOJ, 9 October 2009 (EAT).

used disciplinary procedures to victimise the claimant for pursuing complaints, it was not appropriate in a case of a mere failure to provide a proper mechanism for redress of the claimant's complaints.[31]

McGregor suggests that 'unconstitutional action will not suffice without the presence of aggravating features', exemplary damages having always required 'the presence of outrageous conduct, disclosing malice, fraud, insolence, cruelty and the like'.[32] He further draws attention to the fact that Sir Thomas Bingham MR in *AB v South West Water Services Ltd* described the defendant's arrogant and high-handed conduct *in casu* as being 'quite unlike the abuses of power which Lord Devlin had in mind'.[33] Lord Devlin's phrase, it is suggested, should be understood as 'oppressive, arbitrary or other unconstitutional action of similar gravity'.

B Status of the Defendant

Lord Devlin in *Rookes v Barnard* confined his first category to actions by 'servants of the government'.[34] As authorities he referred to three cases from the 1760s. Two cases arose out of illegal actions initiated by King George III and his ministers to stop the publication of a critical newspaper;[35] the third case concerned the unlawful flogging of a soldier.[36] In the light of these cases the term 'government' in Lord Devlin's formula could be understood as referring to the central government only. Indeed, such an interpretation would be in line with his intention to restrict the ambit of exemplary damages as far as possible under the authorities.

However, the House of Lords in *Cassell & Co Ltd v Broome* remarked *obiter* that the first category extends beyond Crown servants to the police and local and other officials.[37] In consequence, exemplary damages have been awarded in cases of unlawful police conduct.[38] Indeed, almost all post-*Rookes v Barnard* cases in which exemplary damages have been awarded by virtue of the first category involve unlawful police conduct. It has further been held that the term 'servants of the governments' includes solicitors executing an Anton Piller order as officers

---

[31] ibid [115]–[116]. The Tribunal went on to hold that if an award of exemplary damages had been appropriate, it would have reduced the amount to £7,500: ibid [117]–[118].

[32] H McGregor, *McGregor on Damages*, 18th edn (London, 2009) [11–019]. A 'flagrant and deliberate violation of some fundamental principle of the Constitution' was required in *Uren v John Fairfax & Sons Pty Ltd* (1966) 117 CLR 118 (HCA) 135 (Taylor J).

[33] [1993] QB 507 (CA) 531.

[34] [1964] AC 1129 (HL) 1226.

[35] *Huckle v Money* (1763) 2 Wils KB 205, 95 ER 768; *Wilkes v Wood* (1763) Lofft 1, 98 ER 489; below ch 17, IV A.

[36] *Benson v Frederick* (1766) 3 Burr 1845, 97 ER 1130.

[37] [1972] AC 1027 (HL) 1077–78 (Lord Hailsham LC), 1087–1088 (Lord Reid), 1120 (Lord Wilberforce), 1130 (Lord Diplock).

[38] See the cases cited by A Burrows, *Remedies for Torts and Breach of Contract*, 3rd edn (Oxford, 2004) 412.

of the court,[39] as well as the Meat Intervention Board, which is a government department established under section 6 of the European Communities Act 1972.[40] On the other hand, a nationalised body set up by statute for the purpose of supplying water to the public was regarded as a commercial entity rather than an instrument or agent of government.[41]

Even where the defendant is undoubtedly a servant of the government as just defined, it is also necessary that the act complained of was done in the exercise of a governmental function. This issue arose in *Bradford City Council v Arora*, where it was held that the selection among applicants for a senior position at a local authority college had been an exercise of a public function.[42] The need to differentiate was recognised: 'There may be cases where a junior officer of a council is carrying out some duty which cannot properly be regarded as the exercise of a public function at all'.[43] Considering that solicitors executing an Anton Piller order have been categorised as 'servants of the government', the applicability of the first category seems in truth to depend on the nature of the act in question rather than any permanent status of the defendant.

C Criticism

The limitation of the first category to public servants has been criticised even in the House of Lords on the ground that private individuals such as trade unions and international corporations can be as oppressive as the state.[44] Lord Denning MR voiced this criticism in *Broome v Cassell & Co Ltd*:

> Other people can be just as oppressive and arbitrary as the servants of the government. I recall the case of *Loudon v Ryder* [1953] 2 Q.B. 202, which was tried by Devlin J himself. The defendant was a bully who made an outrageous attack on a young woman. He broke into her flat and beat her about the head. The judge directed the jury that they could give exemplary damages. They did so. We upheld the verdict. According to *Rookes*

---

[39] *Columbia Picture Industries Inc v Robinson* [1987] Ch 38, 87. Cf *Al-Rawas v Pegasus Energy Ltd* [2008] EWHC 617 (QB), [2009] 1 All ER 346 [54] (Jack J): 'if a litigant misleads the court into granting him an order with the intention of enabling himself to steal a march in the litigation, he should be treated as falling within Lord Devlin's *second* category' (emphasis added).

[40] *R v Reading Justices, ex parte South West Meat Ltd* [1992] Crim LR 672, 673.

[41] *AB v South West Water Services Ltd* [1993] QB 507 (CA) 525, 531–32.

[42] [1991] 2 QB 507 (CA) 518–19.

[43] ibid 518 (Neill LJ). See also *Shendish Manor Ltd v Coleman* [2001] EWCA Civ 913 [62]: the making of defamatory statements by a leading local councillor is itself no abuse of power as required under the first category.

[44] *Kuddus v Chief Constable of Leicestershire* [2001] UKHL 29, [2002] 2 AC 122 [66] (Lord Nicholls); *Uren v John Fairfax & Sons Pty Ltd* (1966) 117 CLR 118 (HCA) 132–33, 137 (Taylor J); *Taylor v Beere* [1982] 1 NZLR 81 (NZCA) 92 (Richardson J); A Burrows, *Fusing Common Law and Equity: Remedies, Restitution and Reform* (Hong Kong, 2002) 15; RW Hodgin and E Veitch, 'Punitive Damages—Reassessed' (1972) 21 *ICLQ* 119, 128. In *Cassell & Co Ltd v Broome* [1972] AC 1027 (HL) 1088, Lord Reid conceded that the discrimination between public servants and private individuals could only be justified by reference to authority.

v *Barnard* [1964] A.C. 1129, we were wrong because the defendant was not a servant of the government but only a common bully. I do not think we were wrong.[45]

Lord Devlin in *Rookes v Barnard* justified the exclusion of private corporations and individuals from the ambit of his first category in the following way:

> Where one man is more powerful than another, it is inevitable that he will try to use his power to gain his ends; and if his power is much greater than the other's, he might, perhaps, be said to be using it oppressively. If he uses his power illegally, he must of course pay for his illegality in the ordinary way; but he is not to be punished simply because he is the more powerful. In the case of the government it is different, for the servants of the government are also the servants of the people and the use of their power must always be subordinate to their duty of service.[46]

True, people with extraordinarily great power must not be said to behave oppressively simply because of the great power. But why should they be treated more favourably than the powerful state where they do exert oppression? The public or private character of an oppressor should not matter,[47] particularly in the present time of decentralisation and privatisation where the boundaries between public and private sector become progressively blurred.[48] For instance, why should a teacher who has wrongfully been discriminated against for reasons of race, gender etc be able to claim exemplary damages where the employer is a state-run school but not where the employer is a private school?

Indeed, it could be argued that any discrimination between public servants and other defendants should be the other way round. While the state can punish its own servants through disciplinary measures, this way of punishment is not open in relation to private bullies. Public servants could accordingly be said to form the very group of defendants where exemplary damages are *least* needed.

IV Profit-Seeking Behaviour

The second category in which exemplary damages can be awarded is present where, in Lord Devlin's words in *Rookes v Barnard*, 'the defendant's conduct has been calculated by him to make a profit for himself which may well exceed the compensation payable to the plaintiff'.[49] This category, said Lord Devlin, is based on the maxim 'tort must not pay':

---

[45] [1971] 2 QB 354 (CA) 381. Similarly Salmon LJ (at 386) and Phillimore LJ (at 397–98).

[46] [1964] AC 1129 (HL) 1226.

[47] M Tilbury, 'Factors Inflating Damages Awards' in PD Finn (ed), *Essays on Damages* (Sydney, 1992) 103. Unconvincing, however, is the argument made by Salmon LJ in *Broome v Cassell & Co Ltd* [1971] 2 QB 354 (CA) 386, that an extraordinary legal liability on the state's part could be used as a justification for corresponding extraordinary legal rights. The state already enjoys powers that do not vest in citizens such as compulsory purchase.

[48] *Uren v John Fairfax & Sons Pty Ltd* (1966) 117 CLR 118 (HCA) 132–33 (Taylor J).

[49] [1964] AC 1129 (HL) 1226.

Where a defendant with a cynical disregard for a plaintiff's rights has calculated that the money to be made out of his wrongdoing will probably layered exceed the damages at risk, it is necessary for the law to show that it cannot be broken with impunity.[50]

A Fields of Application

Cases falling within the second category can be divided into three groups. The largest group, as Lord Denning MR explained in *Drane v Evangelou*, contains

> cases of unlawful eviction of a tenant. The landlord seeks to gain possession at the expense of the tenant—so as to keep or get a rent higher than that awarded by the rent tribunal—or to get possession from a tenant who is protected by the Rents Acts.[51]

Goff LJ added that a 'calculation by the defendant of actual money which he hoped to make out of the conduct' is not necessary.[52] Exemplary damages have thus been held available in cases involving illegal evictions of protected tenants by means of trespass to land[53] or nuisance[54] pursued by the landlord in order to re-let the property for higher rent.[55]

Another group of cases within the second category concerns defamatory statements in books or newspapers, the most prominent case being *Cassell & Co Ltd v Broome*.[56] In that case, a retired naval officer brought an action for libel against the publishers and the author of a book presented as an authentic account of a war-time disaster when a British convoy had been destroyed. The book suggested that the plaintiff had borne a share of the responsibility for the disaster. From a very early stage in the making of the book the defendants had known that the plaintiff objected to passages relating to him and that high-ranking naval experts considered the account libellous. The House of Lords upheld the jury's award of £25,000 exemplary damages. It was held[57] that, while on the one hand

---

[50] ibid 1227.

[51] [1978] 1 WLR 455 (CA) 459.

[52] ibid 462. Both Lord Denning and Goff LJ quoted this passage from *Rookes v Barnard* [1964] AC 1129 (HL) 1227 (Lord Devlin): 'This category is not confined to moneymaking in the strict sense. It extends to cases in which the defendant is seeking to gain at the expense of the plaintiff some object—perhaps some property which he covets—which either he could not obtain at all or not obtain except at a price greater than he wants to put down.'

[53] eg *Mafo v Adams* [1970] 1 QB 548 (CA) 556, 559 (exemplary damages denied on the facts); *Drane v Evangelou* [1978] 1 WLR 455 (CA) 459, 462; *Asghar v Ahmed* (1984) 17 HLR 25 (CA); *McMillan v Singh* (1984) 17 HLR 120 (CA); *Millington v Duffy* (1984) 17 HLR 232 (CA) (the claim for exemplary damages was abandoned at trial).

[54] *Guppys (Bridport) Ltd v Brookling* (1983) 14 HLR 1 (CA).

[55] A similar case is *Design Progression Ltd v Thurloe Properties Ltd* [2004] EWHC 324 (Ch), [2005] 1 WLR 1. On a tenant's application for consent to assign the lease, the landlord failed to respond within a reasonable time contrary to the Landlord and Tenant Act 1988 s 1(3). The landlord did so because he sought to recover the premises and extract a higher rent on the open market.

[56] [1972] AC 1027 (HL); above II in this chapter. Other cases include *Riches v News Group Newspapers Ltd* [1986] QB 256 (CA), where Stephenson LJ (at 269) called for an abolition of exemplary damages with regard to defamation; *John v MGN Ltd* [1997] QB 586 (CA). In the last two cases, the *amount* of exemplary damages awarded was disapproved as being excessive.

[57] [1972] AC 1027 (HL) 1079, 1088, 1094, 1101, 1130.

the fact that a tort is committed in the course of a profit-making business is not sufficient to bring the case into the second category,[58] it is on the other hand not necessary that the defendant made an arithmetical comparison between the profit and the damages.

Finally, exemplary damages have occasionally been awarded for tortious interference with business. Indeed, Lord Devlin's prime example for his second category, *Bell v Midland Railway Co*,[59] is a case of this kind. The defendant railway company wrongfully prevented trains from running to the plaintiff's wharf in order to divert trade to itself. A jury award of £1,000 which exceeded the plaintiff's pecuniary loss was upheld as a justified award of exemplary damages.

B Criticism

The second category, like the first one, has been attacked even in the House of Lords. It is unjustifiable, the critics argue, to look with less favour upon profit-seeking conduct than upon actions committed out of malice or vindictiveness.[60] As Lord Denning MR observed in *Broome v Cassell & Co Ltd*:

> Which of these two men is worse: the man who says to himself: 'I reckon I will sell enough copies of this publication to pay any damages for libel'; or the man who says: 'I will smash this professional man whatever it costs me'? If exemplary damages for libel can be awarded against the greedy seeker after profit, surely they should be able to be awarded against the wicked inventor of calumnies.[61]

A similar comparison can be drawn up for the case of wrongful eviction: Which of these two landlords is worse: the landlord who says to himself: 'I reckon I can re-let the property at a higher rent'; or the landlord who says: 'I will kick this tenant out (because I dislike him) whatever it costs me'?

---

[58] This had already been held in *Broadway Approvals Ltd v Odhams Press Ltd* [1965] 1 WLR 805 (CA) 819, 821; *Manson v Associated Newspapers Ltd* [1965] 1 WLR 1038, 1040.

[59] (1861) 10 CBNS 287, 142 ER 462. See also *Messenger Newspapers Group Ltd v National Graphical Association (1982)* [1984] IRLR 397 (CA); *Warner v Clark* (1984) 134 NLJ 763 (CA), leaving open whether aggravated or exemplary damages had been awarded; *Borders (UK) Ltd v Metropolitan Police Commissioner* [2005] EWCA Civ 197.

[60] *Kuddus v Chief Constable of Leicestershire* [2001] UKHL 29, [2002] 2 AC 122 [67] (Lord Nicholls); *Uren v John Fairfax & Sons Pty Ltd* (1966) 117 CLR 118 (HCA) 138 (Taylor J); *Taylor v Beere* [1982] 1 NZLR 81 (NZCA) 92 (Richardson J); A Burrows, *Fusing Common Law and Equity: Remedies, Restitution and Reform* (Hong Kong, 2002) 15; D Campbell, 'Exemplary damages' in D Harris, D Campbell and R Halson, *Remedies in Contract and Tort*, 2nd edn (London, 2002) 588; P Jaffey, *The Nature and Scope of Restitution: Vitiated Transfers, Imputed Contracts and Disgorgement* (Oxford, 2000) 364; PW Michalik, 'The availability of compensatory and exemplary damages in equity: A note on the *Aquaculture* decision' (1991) 21 *Victoria University of Wellington Law Review* 391, 410; M Tilbury, 'Factors Inflating Damages Awards' in PD Finn (ed), *Essays on Damages* (Sydney, 1992) 103–104. In *Cassell & Co Ltd v Broome* [1972] AC 1027 (HL) 1088, Lord Reid conceded that only precedence could explain the distinction between greed and malice.

[61] [1971] 2 QB 354 (CA) 381.

As these examples illustrate, it is indefensible to withhold exemplary damages from the case of spiteful behaviour while allowing them in the case of profit-seeking behaviour. Indeed, any discrimination between greed and malice should be the other way round. More favour should be shown towards defendants who have been guided not by spite against the claimant but by the rational motive of making profit.

In an attempt to defend Lord Devlin's second category, it has been argued that this category aims to strip the defendant of the ill-gotten gain rather than to punish him.[62] This would indeed explain the focus on greed as opposed to malice. However, awards of exemplary damages in the second category have rarely been assessed by reference to the value of the defendant's gain and therefore can hardly be reconceptualised as being gain-based.[63] Where the amount of exemplary damages awarded exceeds the value of the defendant's gain,[64] a punitive element is indisputably present. Conversely, where the value of the defendant's gain exceeds the amount of exemplary damages awarded, the aim of stripping the defendant of the entire ill-gotten gain is partially missed.

V Statutory Authorisation

Legislation may authorise an award of exemplary damages. Interestingly, there is no statute of practical significance that clearly does so.

Lord Devlin in *Rookes v Barnard* gave only one example for his third category: section 13(2) of the Reserve and Auxiliary Forces (Protection of Civil Interests) Act 1951.[65] This Act makes the enforcement of judgments against members of the armed forces dependent on certain conditions. Section 13(2) provides that in actions that lie by virtue of the non-fulfilment of these conditions 'the court may take account of the conduct of the defendant with a view, if the court thinks fit, to awarding exemplary damages'. Even this seemingly clear authorisation of exemplary damages has been contested. Lord Kilbrandon in *Cassell & Co Ltd v Broome* interpreted 'exemplary' in section 13(2) as meaning 'aggravated'.[66] Pursuant to section 13(6), he argued, the provision applies to Scotland where

---

[62] *McCarey v Associated Newspapers Ltd (No 2)* [1965] 2 QB 86 (CA) 107 (Diplock LJ); *Cassell & Co Ltd v Broome* [1972] AC 1027 (HL) 1129 (Lord Diplock); H McGregor, *McGregor on Damages*, 18th edn (London, 2009) [11–027]; EJ Weinrib, 'Punishment and Disgorgement as Contract Remedies' (2003) 78 *Chicago-Kent Law Review* 55, 91.

[63] M Tilbury, 'Factors Inflating Damages Awards' in PD Finn (ed), *Essays on Damages* (Sydney, 1992) 104. An exception is *Borders (UK) Ltd v Metropolitan Police Commissioner* [2005] EWCA Civ 197. For the superiority of gain-based relief see below ch 17, IV A.

[64] As in *McMillan v Singh* (1984) 17 HLR 120 (CA): profit of £60–£70, exemplary damages of £250.

[65] [1964] AC 1129 (HL) 1225. He also mentioned the Law Reform (Miscellaneous Provisions) Act 1934 s 1(2)(a), pursuant to which an exemplary damages claim does not survive the victim's death.

[66] [1972] AC 1027 (HL) 1133.

exemplary damages are not recognised. This argument is not unimpeachable. Section 13(2) addresses a very specific situation. The legislator might have taken the view, if the issue was considered at all, that the 'intrusion' of exemplary damages into Scotland effected by this provision is negligible.

Another statutory provision discussed in this context is section 97(2) of the Copyright, Designs and Patents Act 1988. Section 96(2) of that Act confirms the availability of damages and other remedies in actions for copyright infringement.[67] Section 97(2) empowers the court to 'award such additional damages as the justice of the case may require', considering in particular the flagrancy of the infringement and any benefit accruing to the defendant by reason of it.[68] Does section 97(2) authorise an award of purely exemplary damages? An affirmative answer was given with regard to the predecessor of section 97(2)[69] by the Court of Appeal[70] prior to *Rookes v Barnard*. The question has been expressly left open in the House of Lords on several occasions,[71] except that Lord Kilbrandon in *Cassell & Co Ltd v Broome* committed to the view that what is now section 97(2) does not authorise an award of exemplary damages.[72] His view has found wide support among courts below the House of Lords[73] and among commentators.[74] Although the issue is still controversial,[75] section 97(2) probably cannot be placed in Lord Devlin's third category.[76]

Finally, a tenant who wrongfully holds over after having been given notice to leave is liable to pay twice the annual value of the land for the time of the

---

[67]   Above ch 12, IV D.

[68]   Sections 191J(2) and 229(3) provide the same for performers' property rights and UK unregistered design respectively.

[69]   Copyright Act 1956 s 17(3), which said essentially the same as s 97(2) of the 1988 Act.

[70]   *Williams v Settle* [1960] 1 WLR 1072 (CA) 1082, 1086, 1087–1088.

[71]   *Rookes v Barnard* [1964] AC 1129 (HL) 1225; *Cassell & Co Ltd v Broome* [1972] AC 1027 (HL) 1080 (Lord Hailsham LC). See also *Redrow Homes Ltd v Bett Brothers plc* 1998 SC (HL) 64, 69 (Lord Jauncey), 71 (Lord Clyde), with Lord Clyde saying (at 71) that additional damages under s 97(2) are 'more probably' aggravated damages.

[72]   [1972] AC 1027 (HL) 1134.

[73]   *Beloff v Pressdram Ltd* [1973] 1 All ER 241, 265–67; *Rank Film Distributors Ltd v Video Information Centre* [1982] AC 380, 390–92 (Whitford J); 395 (CA) 425 (Templeman LJ); *Redrow Homes Ltd v Bett Brothers plc* 1997 SC 142 (CSIH); *Michael O'Mara Books Ltd v Express Newspapers plc* [1999] FSR 49, 57 (Neuberger J: 'a separate category of damages which may have some features which are similar to those of exemplary or aggravated damages'); *Ludlow Music Inc v Williams* [2002] EWHC 638 (Ch), [2002] FSR 57, [54]–[55]; *Nottinghamshire Healthcare NHS Trust v News Group Newspapers Ltd* [2002] EWHC 409 (Ch), [2002] RPC 49 [48]–[51].

[74]   DI Bainbridge, *Intellectual Property*, 6th edn (Harlow, 2007), 175; K Garnett, G Davies and G Harbottle (eds), *Copinger & Skone James on Copyright*, 15th edn (London, 2005) [22–171]; H Laddie, P Prescott, M Vitoria, A Speck and L Lane, *The Modern Law of Copyright and Designs*, 3rd edn (London, 2000) [39.42]–[39.43]; H McGregor, *McGregor on Damages*, 18th edn (London, 2009) [11–032].

[75]   In favour of exemplary damages: *Home Office v Central Broadcasting Ltd* [1993] EMLR 253 (CA) 266; C Michalos, 'Copyright and Punishment: The Nature of Additional Damages' (2000) 22 *European Intellectual Property Review* 470, 471 ff.

[76]   Exemplary damages may in any event be awarded for copyright infringement where the case falls into one of the common law categories: K Garnett, G Davies and G Harbottle (eds), *Copinger & Skone James on Copyright*, 15th edn (London, 2005) [22–164].

wrongful occupation,[77] and an employer who fails to pay the minimum wage can be required to pay to the state a 'financial penalty' of twice the minimum wage for each employee and each day of non-compliance.[78] The amount that the defendant in those situations must pay in excess of the claimant's loss may be regarded as an award of exemplary damages provided for by statute.[79] It has been suggested, however, that these 'multiple damages' should be classified as a category of their own since they are awarded 'to coerce the defendant rather than to express disapproval of his conduct'.[80]

VI   The 'Cause of Action' Test

Is the availability of exemplary damages at common law restricted not only to the two categories set out in *Rookes v Barnard* [81] but also to those torts for which they had been awarded prior to 1964 (the year in which that case was decided)? In other words, is the categories test supplemented by a 'cause of action' test?

An affirmative answer was given by the Court of Appeal in *AB v South West Water Services Ltd*.[82] There, the accidental contamination of a drinking water system led to a group action against the water authority for public nuisance, negligence and breach of statutory duty. In addition to compensation for their injuries, the plaintiffs claimed exemplary damages, alleging an arrogant and high-handed manner in which the water authority had handled the customers' complaints. The Court of Appeal struck out the claim for exemplary damages on the ground that the case failed not only the categories test but also the 'cause of action' test as exemplary damages had not been awarded prior to 1964 in any of the torts alleged.[83] The Court conceded that the 'cause of action' test could not be found in *Rookes v Barnard* but relied on dicta in *Cassell & Co Ltd v Broome*.[84]

The opposite view was subsequently taken by the House of Lords in *Kuddus v Chief Constable of Leicestershire*,[85] where the plaintiff reported a theft in his flat to the police. A police constable assured him that the matter would be investigated. Later the constable forged the plaintiff's signature on a statement purporting to be a withdrawal of the complaint, and the investigation ceased. The plaintiff sued

---

[77]   Landlord and Tenant Act 1730 s 1; Distress for Rent Act 1737 s 18.
[78]   National Minimum Wage Act 1998 s 21.
[79]   H McGregor, *McGregor on Damages*, 18th edn (London, 2009) [11–030].
[80]   E Peel, *Treitel on the Law of Contract*, 12th edn (London, 2007) [20–016].
[81]   [1964] AC 1129 (HL); above II in this chapter.
[82]   [1993] QB 507 (CA). See also *Catnic Components Ltd v Hill & Smith Ltd* [1983] FSR 512, 540–41; *Metall und Rohstoff AG v ACLI Metals (London) Ltd* [1984] 1 Lloyd's Rep 598 (CA) 612. The 'cause of action' test is endorsed by A Burrows, 'The Scope of Exemplary Damages' (1993) 109 *LQR* 358, 361.
[83]   [1993] QB 507 (CA) 519–21, 529–30.
[84]   [1972] AC 1027 (HL). For the facts of *Broome* see above IV A in this chapter.
[85]   [2001] UKHL 29, [2002] 2 AC 122.

for misfeasance in a public office, a tort 'which had been almost forgotten in 1964'.[86] His claim for exemplary damages was struck out on the ground that it failed the cause of action test for want of pre-1964 awards in that tort. The House of Lords allowed the claim to proceed to trial. While their Lordships disagreed as to whether the cause of action test had been expressed in *Cassell & Co Ltd v Broome*,[87] they unanimously rejected an application of the test today.[88] But only Lord Slynn and Lord Scott rejected the test on principle, holding it irrational to make the availability of exemplary damages dependent on the accidents of litigation and law reporting prior to 1964, and to require a tedious trawl through ancient authorities.[89] Lord Mackay even defended the test on principle as a 'perfectly natural and reasonable' way of limiting the anomaly of exemplary damages.[90]

On the basis, accepted by the House of Lords in both *Rookes v Barnard* and *Cassell & Co Ltd v Broome*, that exemplary damages are an anomaly but can only be abolished by the legislator, the decision on the 'cause of action' test is a choice between *Scylla* and *Charybdis*. The Court of Appeal in *AB* surrendered to the *Scylla* of chaining the law to historical accidents. The House of Lords in *Kuddus* surrendered to the *Charybdis* of allowing an anomaly to conquer new territory. Either course is moribund, which demonstrates the need for reform.

VII   Exemplary Damages in Contract

Outside tort, the law of England and Wales is hostile to exemplary damages. They have been held unavailable particularly in contract actions,[91] save for the now abolished[92] action for breach of promise of marriage.[93] Lord Atkinson in *Addis v*

---

[86]   WVH Rogers, *Winfield and Jolowicz on Tort*, 17th edn (London, 2006) [22–11].

[87]   Lord Nicholls ([2001] UKHL 29, [2002] 2 AC 122 [57]–[60]) and Lord Scott (at [113]–[116]) thought that it had whereas Lord Slynn (at [13]–[21]), Lord Mackay (at [43]–[44]) and Lord Hutton (at [83]–[89]) thought otherwise.

[88]   [2001] UKHL 29, [2002] 2 AC 122 [22], [44]–[45], [68], [89], [122]. Lord Scott (at [122]), however, excluded exemplary damages from negligence, nuisance, strict liability and breach of statutory duty.

[89]   [2001] UKHL 29, [2002] 2 AC 122 [22]–[23] (Lord Slynn), [117] (Lord Scott). See also Law Commission, 'Aggravated, Exemplary and Restitutionary Damages' (Law Com No 247, 1997) [5.49]; D Campbell, 'Exemplary damages' in D Harris, D Campbell and R Halson, *Remedies in Contract and Tort*, 2nd edn (London, 2002) 589–90; M Tilbury, 'Factors Inflating Damages Awards' in PD Finn (ed), *Essays on Damages* (Sydney, 1992) 105–106; WVH Rogers, *Winfield and Jolowicz on Tort*, 17th edn (London, 2006) [22–11].

[90]   [2001] UKHL 29, [2002] 2 AC 122 [34].

[91]   *Butterworth v Butterworth* [1920] P 126, 136; *Herbert Clayton & Jack Waller Ltd v Oliver* [1930] AC 209 (HL) 220 (Lord Buckmaster); *Perera v Vandiyar* [1953] 1 WLR 672 (CA) 676–78; *Kenny v Preen* [1963] 1 QB 499 (CA) 513; *Guppys (Bridport) Ltd v Brookling* (1983) 14 HLR 1 (CA) 26–27.

[92]   Law Reform (Miscellaneous Provisions) Act 1970 s 1.

[93]   *Addis v Gramophone Co Ltd* [1909] AC 488 (HL) 495, 498; *Butterworth v Butterworth* [1920] 126, 136.

Gramophone Co Ltd denied compensating the harsh and humiliating manner of an employee's dismissal on the ground that such an award would inappropriately contain a punitive element.[94] Furthermore, Lord Hailsham LC in *Cassell & Co Ltd v Broome* thought that the reason for the lack of pre-1964 awards of exemplary damages in deceit 'may lie in the close connection that the action has always had with breach of contract'.[95] Burrows suggests, however, that three recent developments may give rise to a reconsideration of the law.[96] These are the recognition by the House of Lords that an account of profits may exceptionally be awarded for breach of contract,[97] the abolition of the 'cause of action' test,[98] and the recognition by the Supreme Court of Canada that exemplary damages may be awarded for breaches of contract that depart markedly from ordinary standards of decency and constitute an independent actionable wrong.[99]

VIII   Exemplary Damages in Equity

Can punitive awards be made in equity's inherent or exclusive jurisdiction?[100] For convenience, such awards will be called exemplary damages even though this is terminologically incorrect. Equitable exemplary damages have been recognised in Canada, Hong Kong, New Zealand and the United States,[101] but have been denied in Australia.[102] In England and Wales, equitable exemplary damages have never been awarded[103] and were held unavailable by Eady J in *Mosley v News Group Newspapers Ltd*.[104]

---

[94] [1909] AC 488 (HL) 494–96; above ch 7, II.

[95] [1972] AC 1027 (HL) 1076.

[96] A Burrows, *Remedies for Torts and Breach of Contract*, 3rd edn (Oxford, 2004) 409–10.

[97] *Attorney-General v Blake (Jonathan Cape Ltd Third Party)* [2001] 1 AC 268 (HL); above ch 12, V B.

[98] Above VI in this chapter.

[99] The breakthrough came in *Whiten v Pilot Insurance Co* [2002] SCC 18, [2002] 1 SCR 595; confirmed in *Fidler v Sun Life Assurance Co of Canada* [2006] SCC 30, [2006] 2 SCR 3 [62]–[63]; *Honda Canada Inc v Keays* [2008] SCC 39, [2008] 2 SCR 362 [62]. A forerunner was *Vorvis v Insurance Corp of British Columbia* [1989] 1 SCR 1085 (SCC).

[100] The power to award exemplary damages in equity's concurrent or auxiliary jurisdiction (to award equitable damages for common law wrongs) is suggested by ICF Spry, *The Principles of Equitable Remedies: Specific Performance, Injunctions, Rectification and Equitable Damages*, 8th edn (Sydney, 2010) 636.

[101] *China Light & Power Co Ltd v Ford* [1996] 1 HKLR 57 (CA of Hong Kong), and the cases cited in *Harris v Digital Pulse Pty Ltd* [2003] NSWCA 10, (2003) 197 ALR 626, [357]–[393] (Heydon JA).

[102] *Harris v Digital Pulse Pty Ltd* [2003] NSWCA 10, (2003) 197 ALR 626; below ch 16, II. See also *Bailey v Namol Pty Ltd* (1994) 53 FCR 102 (FCA) 112–13.

[103] D Hayton, P Matthews and C Mitchell, *Underhill and Hayton: Law Relating to Trusts and Trustees*, 17th edn (London, 2007) [89.75].

[104] [2008] EWHC 1777 (QB).

That case involved the new action for 'breach of privacy' which has developed out of the equitable action for breach of confidence.[105] Eady J held exemplary damages unavailable on the ground that they are unavailable in equity and that breach of privacy must still be classified as an equitable wrong rather than a tort.[106] However, he also described exemplary damages as an anomaly that should not be extended to the new action for breach of privacy.[107] Eady J, it seems, would still have held exemplary damages unavailable in actions for breach of privacy even if he had classified that wrong as a tort. His decision may thus not be strong authority for the unavailability of exemplary damages in equity. Nor are the statements in two old cases that equity has no penal jurisdiction,[108] for neither statement concerned exemplary damages.

It should also be noted that in the previous privacy case *Douglas v Hello! Ltd (No 3)* Lindsay J had based his denial of exemplary damages purely on the facts, being 'content to assume, without deciding, that exemplary damages (or equity's equivalent) are available in respect of breach of confidence'.[109] Moreover, equitable exemplary damages were recognised *obiter* by Brett LJ in *Smith v Day*,[110] where an injunction against the defendant was granted and the plaintiff's action then dismissed by the Court of Appeal. Brett LJ said:

> If the injunction had been obtained fraudulently or maliciously, the Court, I think, would act by analogy to the rule in the case of fraudulent or malicious breach of contract, and not confine itself to proximate damages, but give exemplary damages.[111]

The force of this statement is impaired by its wrong premise that exemplary damages are available in contract. In conclusion, *Mosley v News Group Newspapers Ltd* contains not only the most recent but also the most authoritative statement on the matter. It follows that an award of equitable exemplary damages in England and Wales is unlikely but cannot be completely ruled out.

---

[105]   Above ch 8, II.
[106]   [2008] EWHC 1777 (QB) [181]–[190].
[107]   ibid [194], [196].
[108]   *Vyse v Foster* (1872) LR 8 Ch App 309 (CA) 333 (James LJ: 'This Court is not a Court of penal jurisdiction. It compels restitution of property unconscientiously withheld; it gives full compensation for any loss or damage through failure of some equitable duty; but it has no power of punishing any one.'); *Re Brogden* (1888) LR 38 Ch D 546, 557 (North J: 'It is clear that the Court will not punish a trustee pecuniarily for his breach of trust except so far as loss has resulted therefrom to the trust estate.').
[109]   [2003] EWHC 786 (Ch), [2003] 3 All ER 996 [273].
[110]   (1882) LR 21 Ch D 421, 428.
[111]   (1882) LR 21 Ch D 421, 428.

IX Need for Reform

The categories set out in *Rookes v Barnard* cannot be justified on principle. Reform is needed. The Law Commission has recommended that exemplary damages should remain unavailable in contract but should be available for any tort or equitable wrong where the defendant's conduct shows a deliberate and outrageous disregard of the claimant's rights. It should further be required, says the Commission, that the defendant's conduct deserves punishment and that the other remedies available are inadequate to effect punishment.[112] However, 'the Government have decided not to take forward the Law Commission's proposals for legislation on exemplary damages. It may be that some further judicial development of the law in this area might help clarify the issues'.[113]

Chapter 17 will investigate whether exemplary damages should be abolished. Chapter 16 will examine whether exemplary damages, *if* they are retained, can justifiably be banned from contract and equity. Since the way of reform depends on the objective of exemplary damages, this issue will be explored next.

---

[112] Law Commission, 'Aggravated, Exemplary and Restitutionary Damages' (Law Com No 247, 1997) [5.1] ff. Appendix A of the Report contains a draft bill; below ch 17, II A.

[113] Mr Lock, Parliamentary Secretary, Lord Chancellor's Department: House of Commons Debates, Hansard HC vol 337, col 502 (9 November 1999). Lord Scott in *Kuddus v Chief Constable of Leicestershire* [2001] UKHL 29, [2002] 2 AC 122 [24], said in response: 'I do not think that the Government's view ... should inspire your Lordships to the view that the whole matter should be reopened and the Law Commission's Report revisited. It is no more than a comment that issues might become clearer as decisions on particular facts emerge.'

15

Objective of Exemplary Damages

I Penalising Reprehensible Behaviour

In *Wilkes v Wood*, which is one of the cases that introduced exemplary damages to the legal scene, Pratt LCJ said that exemplary damages are designed 'as a punishment to the guilty, to deter from any such proceeding for the future, and as a proof of the detestation of the jury to the action itself'.[1] This *trias* of objectives of exemplary damages—punishment, deterrence and detestation—was reaffirmed by Lord Devlin in *Rookes v Barnard*,[2] and still rates highly with courts[3] and commentators[4] throughout the common law world. A purely semantic change has been suggested by the Supreme Court of Canada. Regarding Pratt LCJ's phrase as pleonastic since punishment includes both retribution and denunciation, the Court prefers the phrase 'retribution, deterrence and denunciation'.[5] If these are the objectives of exemplary damages, they cannot be

---

[1] (1763) Lofft 1, 18–19; 98 ER 489, 498–99. See also *Davis v Wal-Mart Stores, Inc* (2001) 93 Ohio St.3d 488 (SC of Ohio) 493 (Sweeney J): 'The purpose of punitive damages is not to compensate a plaintiff but to punish the guilty, deter future misconduct, and to demonstrate society's disapproval'. Approvingly quoted in *Dardinger v Anthem Blue Cross & Blue Shield* (2002) 98 Ohio St.3d 77 (SC of Ohio) 104 (Pfeifer J).

[2] [1964] AC 1129 (HL) 1228: A jury may award exemplary damages if the compensatory sum 'is inadequate to punish [the defendant] for his outrageous conduct, to mark their disapproval of such conduct and to deter him from repeating it'. Approvingly quoted in *Cassell & Co Ltd v Broome* [1972] AC 1027 (HL) 1059 (Lord Hailsham LC), 1103 (Viscount Dilhorne); *A v Bottrill* [2002] UKPC 44, [2003] 1 AC 449 [21] (Lord Nicholls).

[3] *Cooper Industries, Inc v Leatherman Tool Group, Inc* (2001) 532 US 424 (US SC) 432 (Stevens J: 'punish the defendant', 'deter future wrongdoing', 'moral condemnation'); *State Farm Mutual Automobile Insurance Co v Campbell* (2002) 538 US 408 (US SC) 416 (Kennedy J: 'deterrence and retribution').

[4] M Galanter and D Luban, 'Poetic Justice: Punitive Damages and Legal Pluralism' (1993) 42 *American University Law Review* 1393, 1428 ff; AJ Sebok, 'What Did Punitive Damages Do? Why Misunderstanding the History of Punitive Damages Matters Today' (2003) 78 *Chicago-Kent Law Review* 163, 175, 205–206. The view that deterrence and retribution are incompatible is taken by A Duggan, 'Exemplary Damages in Equity: A Law and Economics Perspective' (2006) 26 *Oxford Journal of Legal Studies* 303, 319–21.

[5] *Whiten v Pilot Insurance Co* [2002] SCC 18, [2002] 1 SCR 595 [43] (Binnie J on behalf of the majority). Confirmed in *Fidler v Sun Life Assurance Co of Canada* [2006] SCC 30, [2006] 2 SCR 3 [61].

available for every civil wrong but only for socially reprehensible behaviour. Adjectives and phrases used to describe such behaviour include 'malicious, vindictive, high-handed, wanton, wilful, arrogant, cynical, oppressive, and contumelious disregard of the plaintiff's rights'.[6]

II Fostering Efficient Deterrence

While the traditional concept of exemplary damages regards deterrence more or less as a 'by-product' of punishment,[7] American law-and-economics scholars account for exemplary damages primarily on the basis of efficient deterrence. Punishment being no longer an aim of exemplary damages, they are renamed as augmented,[8] extracompensatory,[9] overcompensatory,[10] societal,[11] supercompensatory[12] or supracompensatory[13] damages. For convenience, the following discussion of the main economic theories sticks to the adjective exemplary.

A Correction for Undercompensation

Exemplary damages have been described[14] as a rough-hewn compensation for loss that is not, or not fully, covered by compensatory damages, such as non-

---

[6] *A v Bottrill* [2002] UKPC 44, [2003] 1 AC 449 [25] (Lord Nicholls). See also NJ McBride, 'Punitive Damages' in P Birks (ed), *Wrongs and Remedies in the Twenty-First Century* (Oxford, 1996) 184–87.

[7] In *A v Bottrill* [2002] UKPC 44, [2003] 1 AC 449 [29], Lord Nicholls said about exemplary damages: 'Their primary function is to punish. They also serve as an emphatic vindication of the plaintiff's rights and as a deterrent.'

[8] TC Galligan, 'Augmented Awards: The Efficient Evolution of Punitive Damages' (1990) 51 *Louisiana Law Review* 3 passim.

[9] B Perlstein, 'Crossing the Contract–Tort Boundary: An Economic Argument for the Imposition of Extracompensatory Damages for Opportunistic Breach of Contract' (1992) 58 *Brooklyn Law Review* 877 passim.

[10] R Craswell, 'Contract Remedies, Renegotiation, and the Theory of Efficient Breach' (1988) 61 *Southern California Law Review* 629, 638 passim.

[11] CM Sharkey, 'Punitive Damages as Societal Damages' (2003) 113 *Yale Law Journal* 347 passim.

[12] DA Farber, 'Reassessing the Economic Efficiency of Compensatory Damages for Breach of Contract' (1980) 66 *Virginia Law Review* 1443, 1445 passim.

[13] JS Johnston, 'Punitive Liability: A New Paradigm of Efficiency in Tort Law' (1987) 87 *Columbia Law Review* 1385, 1395 passim; JA Sebert, 'Punitive and Nonpecuniary Damages in Actions Based Upon Contract: Toward Achieving the Objective of Full Compensation' (1986) 33 *University of California at Los Angeles Law Review* 1565, 1570 passim.

[14] TC Galligan, 'Augmented Awards: The Efficient Evolution of Punitive Damages' (1990) 51 *La L Rev* 3, 40–58; DG Owen, 'A Punitive Damages Overview: Functions, Problems and Reform' (1994) 39 *Villanova Law Review* 363, 378–79. In the view of the Michigan courts, exemplary damages aim at compensation, and the jury must not be led to believe that they may punish the defendant: *Stillson v Gibbs* (1884) 53 Mich 280 (SC of Michigan) 283–84; *Wilson v Bowen* (1887) 64 Mich 133 (SC of Michigan) 141–42; *Ten Hopen v Walker* (1893) 96 Mich 236 (SC of Michigan) 240; *Oppenhuizen v Wennersten* (1966) 2 Mich App 288 (CA of Michigan) 297–98.

pecuniary loss,[15] litigation costs[16] and loss that is too remote.[17] Under this theory, exemplary damages are no longer linked to outrageous behaviour since the exclusion of certain loss from compensation rarely depends on the defendant's culpability. In particular, exemplary damages are no longer excluded from contract.[18] Indeed, since contract is still less generous to the claimant than tort, especially with regard to remoteness of damage[19] and non-pecuniary loss,[20] the compensatory theory points to a greater need for exemplary damages in contract than in tort. However, the theory fails.

A principle that restricts compensatory damages is either justified or unjustified. Restrictions that are justified ought not to be circumvented by an award of exemplary damages. If, for instance, difficulties of assessing distress were a valid reason for excluding distress from the ambit of compensatory damages,[21] it would be wrong to compensate distress in the guise of exemplary damages, for the difficulties of assessment are not the least bit lessened because the loss is considered under a different head of damages.[22]

Restrictions that are *not* justified should simply be removed and not be counter-balanced by exemplary damages.[23] Sebert takes the opposite view with regard to US contract law. He argues that the alteration of some of the offending

[15] See especially *Stillson v Gibbs* (1884) 53 Mich 280 (SC of Michigan) 284; *Ten Hopen v Walker* (1893) 96 Mich 236 (SC of Michigan) 240; *Oppenhuizen v Wennersten* (1966) 2 Mich App 288 (CA of Michigan) 297–98; *Ray v City of Detroit* (1976) 67 Mich App 702 (CA of Michigan) 704. See also below ch 16, I F.

[16] See especially DG Owen, 'A Punitive Damages Overview: Functions, Problems and Reform' (1994) 39 *Vill LRev* 363, 378–79. In Connecticut, the amount of punitive damages is limited to the plaintiff's litigation expenses less taxable costs. This rule 'fulfills the salutary purpose of fully compensating a victim for the harm inflicted on him': *Waterbury Petroleum Products, Inc v Canaan Oil and Fuel Co, Inc* (1984) 193 Conn 208 (SC of Connecticut) 238 (Healey J).

[17] See especially TC Galligan, 'Augmented Awards: The Efficient Evolution of Punitive Damages' (1990) 51 *La L Rev* 3, 41–53.

[18] FJ Cavico, 'Punitive Damages for Breach of Contract—A Principled Approach' (1990) *St Mary's Law Journal* 357, 373–75, 440–42; L Curtis, 'Damage Measurements for Bad Faith Breach of Contract: An Economic Analysis' (1986) 39 *Stanford Law Review* 161, 168–70; JA Sebert, 'Punitive and Nonpecuniary Damages in Actions Based Upon Contract: Toward Achieving the Objective of Full Compensation' (1986) 33 *UCLA LR* 1565, 1647–52, 1656–68. See also R Craswell, 'Contract Remedies, Renegotiation, and the Theory of Efficient Breach' (1988) 61 *S Cal L Rev* 629, 662–63.

[19] Above ch 4, I. This book suggests that contract be aligned with tort: above ch 4, IV.

[20] Above chs 6 and 7. This book suggests that contract be aligned with tort: above ch 7, VIII and IX.

[21] Assessment difficulties should not generally lead to a denial of damages: above ch 7, VIII E.

[22] P Cane, 'Exceptional Measures of Damages: A Search for Principles' in P Birks (ed), *Wrongs and Remedies in the Twenty-First Century* (Oxford, 1996) 305; DD Ellis, 'Fairness and Efficiency in the Law of Punitive Damages' (1982) 56 *S Cal L Rev* 1, 31; A Mitchell Polinsky and S Shavell, 'Punitive Damages: An Economic Analysis' (1998) 111 *Harv L Rev* 869, 940.

[23] A Burrows, 'Reforming Exemplary Damages: Expansion or Abolition?' in P Birks (ed), ibid 156; MJ Barrett, '"Contort": Tortious Breach of the Implied Covenant of Good Faith and Fair Dealing in Noninsurance, Commercial Contracts—Its Existence and Desirability' (1985) 60 *Notre Dame Law Review* 510, 527–28; RL Birmingham, 'Breach of Contract, Damage Measures, and Economic Efficiency' (1970) 24 *Rutgers Law Review* 273, 285; S Chutorian, 'Tort Remedies for Breach of Contract: The Expansion of Tortious Breach of the Implied Covenant of Good Faith and Fair Dealing into the Commercial Realm' (1986) 86 *Colum L Rev* 377, 402–405; A Mitchell Polinsky and S Shavell,

rules such as the general uncompensability of non-pecuniary loss and of pre-judgment interest 'could be quite complex and difficult'.[24] This may be true. But only a compensatory remedy secures an accurate measure of the loss,[25] and exemplary damages can only help out where they are actually awarded, which will always be rare.[26] The vast majority of cases would still be affected by the shortcomings in compensatory awards. It is therefore much better to go the distance and revise the offending rules than to be content with the makeshift solution of exemplary damages.

B Correction for Underenforcement

Most prominent is the following economic account of exemplary damages.[27] Not every wrong actually encounters a remedial response. The victim may not detect the wrong or may detect it only after her claim has become time-barred. The victim may not know who is the wrongdoer or may be unable to prove the wrong. Or the victim may shy away from litigation given its costs and hazards. This underenforcement encourages inefficient behaviour, for wrongdoers fail to internalise the full cost of their actions to society even if all harm is legally compensable. As a remedy, the compensatory damages awarded to the victims who do sue ought to be multiplied by the inverse of the probability of suit.

Cooter and Ulen provide the following simple illustration.[28] A manufacturer of a fuel additive for car engines can set quality control at a high or a low level. High-level control costs $9,000 per year and guarantees that the fuel additive is pure and never causes harm. Low-level control is costless but results in some batches of the fuel additives being flawed with expected damage to cars amounting to $10,000 per year. Since the spending of $9,000 on quality control can save expected damage of $10,000, efficiency requires the manufacturer to set control

---

ibid 939–40; EA Scallen, 'Sailing the Uncharted Seas of Bad Faith: Seaman's Direct Buying Service, Inc. v. Standard Oil Co.' (1985) 69 *Minnesota Law Review* 1161, 1189–96.

[24] JA Sebert, 'Punitive and Nonpecuniary Damages in Actions Based Upon Contract: Toward Achieving the Objective of Full Compensation' (1986) 33 *UCLA LR* 1565, 1664.

[25] A Mitchell Polinsky and S Shavell, 'Punitive Damages: An Economic Analysis' (1998) 111 *Harv L Rev* 869, 940.

[26] ibid 940–41.

[27] ibid 887 ff; R Cooter and T Ulen, *Law and Economics*, 5th edn (Boston, 2008) 396–97; S Shavell, *Economic Analysis of Accident Law* (Cambridge/Mass, 2003) ch 4, [9.3]. Similarly TA Diamond, 'The Tort of Bad Faith Breach of Contract: When, If At All, Should It Be Extended Beyond Insurance Transactions?' (1981) 64 *Marqette Law Review* 425, 439–46; DA Farber, 'Reassessing the Economic Efficiency of Compensatory Damages for Breach of Contract' (1980) 66 *Va L Rev* 1443, 1459 ff; J Glover, *Commercial Equity: Fiduciary Relationships* (Sydney, 1995) [6.129]; CM Sharkey, 'Punitive Damages as Societal Damages' (2003) 113 *Yale LJ* 347, 389 ff; *Cassell & Co Ltd v Broome* [1972] AC 1027 (HL) 1130 (Lord Diplock): 'But to restrict the damages recoverable to the actual gain made by the defendant if it exceeded the loss caused to the plaintiff, would leave a defendant contemplating an unlawful act with the certainty that he had nothing to lose to balance against the chance that the plaintiff might never sue him or, if he did, might fail in the hazards of litigation.'

[28] R Cooter and T Ulen, ibid 396.

at the high level. And the manufacturer will do so if he expects being sued by every single consumer harmed. But if only every second consumer harmed brings a suit, the manufacturer's expected liability in the case of low-level quality control is $5,000 and he will not spend $9,000 to escape liability. This is inefficient as the total damage caused is still $10,000. Doubling the compensatory amount restores the manufacturer's expected liability to $10,000 and encourages him to spend $9,000 on quality control.

Under this theory, exemplary damages may be awarded for all types of wrongs given that there is an omnipresent possibility of escaping liability.[29] They may in particular be awarded for breach of contract,[30] as contract-breakers sometimes escape liability, if less frequently than tortfeasors.[31] More significantly, exemplary damages are no longer confined to cases of egregious behaviour.[32] On the contrary, the more egregious the behaviour is, the less will usually be the defendant's chance of escaping liability and thus the need for exemplary damages. The virtual certainty of suit forbids exemplary damages, for instance, in a scenario like the Exxon Valdez oil spill disaster[33] (where US$5 billion punitive damages were awarded), and in the case of a plane crash caused by horrendous negligence on the part of the airline.[34] Conversely, the distinct possibility that bungling doctors escape liability may compel large exemplary damages awards in the case of even minor medical malpractice.[35] From a moral view, such results are very hard to swallow, for 'citizens and legislators may rightly insist that they are willing to tolerate some loss in economic efficiency in order to deter what they consider morally offensive conduct, albeit cost-beneficial morally offensive conduct'.[36]

Furthermore, the concept of multiplying compensatory awards by the inverse of the probability of suit cannot work in practice. How is the court or legislator to

---

[29] In the view of A Duggan, 'Exemplary Damages in Equity: A Law and Economics Perspective' (2006) 26 *OJLS* 303, 311–13, breach of fiduciary duty should not routinely attract exemplary damages since equity has other ways of addressing underenforcement, eg gain-based remedies and strict liability.

[30] DA Farber, 'Reassessing the Economic Efficiency of Compensatory Damages for Breach of Contract' (1980) 66 *Va L Rev* 1443, 1459 ff; B Perlstein, 'Crossing the Contract–Tort Boundary: An Economic Argument for the Imposition of Extracompensatory Damages for Opportunistic Breach of Contract' (1992) 58 *Brook L Rev* 877, 885. See also R Craswell, 'Contract Remedies, Renegotiation, and the Theory of Efficient Breach' (1988) 61 *Southern California Law Review* 629, 664–65, and the authors cited there in fn 74.

[31] Sporadic exemplary damages awards in contract are expected by A Mitchell Polinsky and S Shavell, 'Punitive Damages: An Economic Analysis' (1998) 111 *Harvard Law Review* 869, 891, 936–39.

[32] ibid 890–91; TB Colby, 'Beyond the Multiple Punishment Problem: Punitive Damages as Punishment for Individual, Private Wrongs' (2003) 87 *Minn L Rev* 583, 611–12.

[33] A Mitchell Polinsky and S Shavell, 'Punitive Damages: An Economic Analysis' (1998) 111 *Harv L Rev* 869, 891, 904.

[34] M Galanter and D Luban, 'Poetic Justice: Punitive Damages and Legal Pluralism' (1993) 42 *Am U L Rev* 1393, 1449–50.

[35] ibid 1450.

[36] ibid. Approvingly quoted in *Cooper Industries, Inc v Leatherman Tool Group, Inc* (2001) 532 US 424 (US SC) 439–40 (Stevens J).

know the probability of suit for certain conduct? Obtaining all the data required will often be prohibitively expensive or even infeasible. Mitchell Polinsky and Shavell are more optimistic and assert that the probability of suit 'might be relatively easily calculated'.[37] But their assertion is refuted by their own illustration:

> [S]uppose a firm dumps toxic waste at night along an infrequently used road, but is caught as a result of the report of a driver who happened to notice the firm's activities. In such a case, pressure-sensitive recording devices laid across the road could be used to determine the volume of traffic on the road at night, and the resulting data could be employed to calculate the odds that someone would drive by during a particular interval of time. The reciprocal of this probability could then be used as the total damages multiplier.[38]

The authors are bold in suggesting that the laying of recording devices across a public road is an easy way to determine the multiplier. In addition, the incident where the firm was caught was probably not the only illegal disposal by that firm. In order to determine the probability of detection one needs to know the time of day that other illegal disposals took place, information that the firm will hardly volunteer. Moreover, as the authors themselves concede,[39] the probability of suit depends not only on the chance of a driver passing by but also on the chance of the driver actually reporting the activity. This can only be determined through interviewing a significant number of people using that road at the relevant time. Consequently, the illustration proves just the contrary of what it is meant to prove. Even the simple scenario of dumping waste along a road shows how difficult, if not infeasible, it would be to determine the probability of suit and the factor by which the compensatory amount is to be multiplied.[40]

C Correction for Court Errors

Johnston integrates exemplary damages into a regime that aims to combat the deterrence-distorting effect of court errors in determining negligence.[41] He starts by observing that careful defendants are sometimes found liable whilst careless defendants are sometimes found not liable.[42] This uncertainty may lead to

---

[37] A Mitchell Polinsky and S Shavell, 'Punitive Damages: An Economic Analysis' (1998) 111 *Harv L Rev* 869, 891.

[38] ibid 891–92; citation omitted.

[39] ibid 892 fn 58.

[40] Mitchell Polinsky and Shavell (ibid 892) argue that even if jurors make significant errors in determining the multiplier, optimal deterrence will still be achieved as potential injurers will expect the assessment of juries to be approximately correct on average. Since this argument presupposes a widespread use of juries in civil cases, it has little significance for England and Wales.

[41] JS Johnston, 'Punitive Liability: A New Paradigm of Efficiency in Tort Law' (1987) 87 *Colum L Rev* 1385, 1389 ff; similarly DG Owen, 'Civil Punishment and the Public Good' (1982) 56 *S Cal L Rev* 103, 119.

[42] JS Johnston, ibid 1389–90, 1392.

inefficiency in either of two ways.[43] On the one hand, the knowledge that taking an optimal level of care cannot guarantee escaping liability may induce defendants to be overcautious and to increase care beyond the socially beneficial level (overdeterrence). On the other hand, the knowledge that the failure to take an optimal level of care does not necessarily result in liability being imposed may lead defendants to take suboptimal care (underdeterrence). Neither effect can be ruled out as a matter of intuition or statistics.

In order to eliminate both effects, Johnston suggests two simultaneous measures. One is the imposition of exemplary damages high enough to deter.[44] The other is a change in the test for establishing negligence. Instead of the current test which requires that a preponderance of evidence shows a failure to take reasonable care, defendants should be found liable only if there is 'gross negligence by clear and convincing evidence'.[45]

Johnston claims that, although courts will still make errors, the proposed regime eliminates both overdeterrence and underdeterrence.[46] Nobody will take supraoptimal care (overdeterrence), as everybody can be sure that if optimal care is taken, the court will not make such a gross error as to find gross negligence by clear and convincing evidence. On the other hand, the notional exclusion of slight negligence from the ambit of liability will create no incentive to take suboptimal care (underdeterrence), as there exists the possibility that a court will erroneously qualify slight negligence as gross negligence and will then impose exemplary damages. The inherent possibility of exemplary damages being awarded in a case of slight negligence shows that Johnston's regime is solely concerned with optimal deterrence and not with retribution.[47]

An account similar to Johnston's is offered by Posner.[48] According to him, exemplary damages make up for court errors not in deciding on the question of liability, but in assessing the damages. Courts make errors in assessing the claimant's loss. An erroneous underestimation fails to deter effectively. One means of ensuring that the claimant's true loss is always compensated is to add a 'dollop' of exemplary damages to the estimate of the claimant's loss. Since the claimant will now often get more than his actual loss which might lead to overdeterrence, Posner confines the ambit of exemplary damages to intentional torts, which are inefficient.

---

[43] ibid 1394–395.

[44] ibid 1397.

[45] ibid 1396. Many US states have indeed introduced a 'clear and convincing evidence' standard for the collection of any punitive damages or of punitive damages in excess of a statutory cap: see the statutes and cases listed in *Transportation Insurance Co v Moriel* (1994) 879 S.W.2d 10 (SC of Texas) 31.

[46] JS Johnston, 'Punitive Liability: A New Paradigm of Efficiency in Tort Law' (1987) 87 *Colum L Rev* 1385, 1397–98.

[47] As Johnston himself emphasises: ibid 1429–32.

[48] RA Posner, *Economic Analysis of Law*, 7th edn (Austin, 2007) 206.

It is true that courts, even professional judges, make mistakes from time to time. But the mistake can go either way. Absent evidence to the contrary, it must be assumed that the probability of either aberration is equal.[49] In other words, an error favouring the claimant is as likely as an error favouring the defendant. Neither Johnston nor Posner suggests otherwise. If a court error can go either way with equal chance, a potential defendant will assume the average outcome of the potential trial, which is a correct finding. Deterrence is optimal.[50]

D   Offsetting Illicit Benefits and Exceptional Costs

Exemplary damages have been said to offset illicit benefits gained from a wrong and exceptional costs saved by committing a wrong.[51] Illustrations of an illicit benefit include 'the pleasure of defaming your enemy or breaking his nose'[52] or breaking his windows,[53] and the satisfaction stemming from injuring one's adulterous partner.[54] Because of the satisfaction or pleasure gained, the argument goes, purely compensatory damages would not sufficiently deter. Exceptional costs have been identified, for instance, where compliance with traffic laws would be extremely bothersome for the driver[55] or would result in the driver missing his daughter's wedding.[56] Inducing such a driver to comply with traffic laws is said to require a level of damages exceeding losses.

One problem of this theory is that it cannot explain which benefits are illicit and which costs are exceptional.[57] Furthermore, illicit benefits and exceptional costs are of a non-pecuniary nature. Why, then, should a damages award be the best response? It seems more appropriate if the response also contains a non-pecuniary element. A criminal conviction even in the form of a fine achieves this aim because it carries a stigma not shared by an award of exemplary damages.

---

[49]   DD Haddock, FS McChesney and M Spiegel, 'An Ordinary Economic Rationale for Extraordinary Legal Sanctions' (1990) 78 *California Law Review* 1, 11.

[50]   ibid.

[51]   RD Cooter, 'Economic Analysis of Punitive Damages' (1982) 56 *S Cal L Rev* 79, 86–89; DD Ellis, 'Fairness and Efficiency in the Law of Punitive Damages' (1982) 56 *S Cal L Rev* 1, 31–32; DG Owen, 'Civil Punishment and the Public Good' (1982) 56 *S Cal L Rev* 103, 112–14. The theory is also presented, but not endorsed, by S Shavell, *Economic Analysis of Accident Law* (Cambridge, Mass, 2003) ch 4, [9.4].

[52]   RD Cooter, ibid 89.

[53]   S Shavell, *Economic Analysis of Accident Law* (Cambridge, Mass, 2003) ch 4, [9.4].

[54]   DD Ellis, 'Fairness and Efficiency in the Law of Punitive Damages' (1982) 56 *S Cal L Rev* 1, 32.

[55]   ibid fn 90.

[56]   RD Cooter, 'Economic Analysis of Punitive Damages' (1982) 56 *S Cal L Rev* 79, 86–89.

[57]   DD Haddock, FS McChesney and M Spiegel, 'An Ordinary Economic Rationale for Extraordinary Legal Sanctions' (1990) 78 *CLR* 1, 12; S Shavell, *Economic Analysis of Accident Law* (Cambridge, Mass, 2003) ch 4, [9.4] fn 89. In the view of DG Owen, 'Civil Punishment and the Public Good' (1982) 56 *S Cal L Rev* 103, 112–14, the category 'appears to cover at least most cases of flagrant misbehavior'.

E   Encouraging Negotiations about the Use of Rights

Exemplary damages have been said to encourage negotiations about the use of rights where communication between the prospective user and the owner of the right prior to the use is possible.[58] The notorious example is copyright. A person who intends to use someone else's copyright has the choice between negotiations about a licence on the one hand and illegal infringement and litigation on the other. Prior negotiations are normally more efficient and are encouraged if illegal infringement attracts exemplary damages.

This theory may work where intellectual property rights are infringed but it cannot account for exemplary damages across the board. By definition, the theory is limited to circumstances in which communication between the wrong-doer and the victim prior to the wrong is possible. More importantly, the theory can only work in a business context where negotiations about a licence are conceivable. But these have not been the usual facts of the cases in which exemplary damages have been awarded. Police officers, for instance, would not pay for the right to mistreat citizens and citizens would not allow mistreatment for cash.

F   Conclusion

None of the economic models offered by American law-and-economics scholars can comprehensively account for exemplary damages. That is not to say that all these models are completely ill-founded. Sometimes exemplary damages do compensate loss otherwise neglected, or counterbalance the chance of escaping liability and so on. But none of the models possesses sufficient robustness in both its theoretical concept and its practical applicability to form a solid basis for explaining exemplary damages across the board. It speaks volumes that the US courts in general show no inclination to subscribe to any of the models.[59] Even less likely is a judicial adoption in England and Wales. We are therefore left with the traditional punitive concept under which exemplary damages aim at retribution, deterrence and denunciation. This concept forms the basis of the following study.

---

[58]   S Shavell, ibid [9.5]. See also DD Haddock, FS McChesney and M Spiegel, ibid 13–24.
[59]   'After all, deterrence is not the only purpose served by punitive damages … Moreover, it is not at all obvious that even the *deterrent* function of punitive damages can be served *only* by economically "optimal deterrence"': *Cooper Industries, Inc v Leatherman Tool Group, Inc* (2001) 532 US 424 (US SC) 439 (Stevens J).

16

Defensibility of Confining Exemplary Damages to Tort

I Defensibility of Banning Exemplary Damages from Contract

A Theory of Efficient Breach

Is it defensible to ban exemplary damages from contract while allowing them in tort? By far the most popular defence of such a ban is the argument that the availability of exemplary damages in contract would deter efficient breaches of contract. The basis for this argument is the theory of efficient breach. This theory holds that a breach of contract is efficient if the contract-breaker is better off by breaching the contract and compensating the aggrieved party for all her loss than by performing. Efficient breaches, it is said, should be allowed and indeed encouraged by the law. Posner, a principal advocate of this theory, gives the following illustration:

> Suppose I sign a contract to deliver 100,000 custom-ground widgets at 10¢ apiece to A for use in his boiler factory. After I have delivered 10,000, B comes to me, explains that he desperately needs 25,000 custom-ground widgets at once since otherwise he will be forced to close his pianola factory at great cost, and offers me 15¢ apiece for them. I sell him the widgets and as a result do not complete timely delivery to A, causing him to lose $1,000 in profits. Having obtained an additional profit of $1,250 on the sale to B, I am better off even after reimbursing A for his loss, and B is also better off.[1]

---

[1] RA Posner, *Economic Analysis of Law*, 7th edn (Austin, 2007) 120. See also D Campbell, 'Introduction: the function and structure of remedies for failure to perform a contractual obligation' in D Harris, D Campbell and R Halson, *Remedies in Contract and Tort*, 2nd edn (London, 2002) 11–21; RL Birmingham, 'Breach of Contract, Damage Measures, and Economic Efficiency' (1970) 24 *Rutgers Law Review* 273, 284–85; DW Barnes, 'The Anatomy of Contract Damages and Efficient Breach Theory' (1998) 6 *Southern California Interdisciplinary Law Journal* 397 ff; TA Diamond, 'The Tort of Bad Faith Breach of Contract: When, If At All, Should It Be Extended Beyond Insurance Transactions?' (1981) 64 *Marquette Law Review* 425, 433–38; *Bank of America Canada v Mutual Trust Co* [2002] SCC 43, [2002] 2 SCR 601 [31]; Introductory note to ch 16 of the US *Restatement (Second) of Contracts*.

On this view, exemplary damages impair efficiency. In the words of Posner:

> Even if the breach is deliberate, it is not necessarily blameworthy. The promisor may simply have discovered that his performance is worth more to someone else. If so, efficiency is promoted by allowing him to break his promise, provided he makes good the promisee's actual losses. If he is forced to pay more than that, an efficient breach may be deterred, and the law doesn't want to bring about such a result.[2]

B Objections to the Theory of Efficient Breach

Appealing though it may seem at first sight, the theory of efficient breach faces convincing objections. While its opponents concede that goods should end up in the hands of the person who values them most, that is who offers the highest price for them, they point out that this outcome can be achieved without breach through renegotiation.[3] If the seller in Posner's pianola illustration[4] were deterred from breach by the threat of exemplary damages, this would not mean that B who offers the highest price for the widgets cannot get them. The seller could negotiate with A about a release from his obligation or B could negotiate with A about an assignment of A's contractual claim.

While conceding the possibility of renegotiation, the advocates of the theory of efficient breach argue that a breach saves the transaction cost of negotiation.[5] The opponents, in turn, point to the cost of litigating or negotiating the damages payable for the breach.[6] The debate about the efficiency of breach has thus become a debate about the amount of the respective transaction cost.

Many advocates of the theory trace back the notion of a real choice between performing and paying damages to Oliver Wendell Holmes' statement 'The duty to keep a contract at common law means a prediction that you must pay damages if you do not keep it,—and nothing else': OW Holmes, 'The Path of the Law' (1897) 10 *Harvard Law Review* 457, 462; similarly OW Holmes, *The Common Law* (London, 1882) 301. But this might be a misinterpretation of Holmes' statement: JM Perillo, 'Misreading Oliver Wendell Holmes on Efficient Breach and Tortious Interference' (2000) 68 *Fordham Law Review* 1085–91.

[2] *Patton v Mid-Continent Systems, Inc* (1988) 841 F.2d 742 (US CA for 7th Circuit) 750 (Posner J). See also D Campbell, 'Exemplary damages' in D Harris, D Campbell and R Halson, *Remedies in Contract and Tort*, 2nd edn (London, 2002) 594, 604; SM Waddams, *The Law of Damages*, 3rd edn (Toronto, 1997), [11.250]; Law Commission, 'Aggravated, Exemplary and Restitutionary Damages' (Law Com No 247, 1997) [5.72].

[3] WS Dodge, 'The Case for Punitive Damages in Contracts' (1999) 48 *Duke Law Journal* 629, 665 ff; MA Eisenberg, 'The Principle of Hadley v Baxendale' (1992) 80 *California Law Review* 563, 585; DA Farber, 'Reassessing the Economic Efficiency of Compensatory Damages for Breach of Contract' (1980) 66 *Virginia Law Review* 1443, 1449 ff; D Laycock, *The Death of the Irreparable Injury Rule* (New York, 1991) 247–48; IR Macneil, 'Efficient Breach of Contract: Circles in the Sky' (1982) 68 *Va L Rev* 947, 951–52; LD Smith, 'Disgorgement of the Profits of Breach of Contract: Property, Contract and "Efficient Breach"' (1995) 24 *Canadian Business Law Journal* 121, 134.

[4] Above I A in this chapter.

[5] RA Posner, *Economic Analysis of Law*, 7th edn (Austin, 2007) 120.

[6] FJ Cavico, 'Punitive Damages for Breach of Contract—A Principled Approach' (1990) *St Mary's Law Journal* 357, 374; WS Dodge, 'The Case for Punitive Damages in Contracts' (1999) 48 *Duke L J* 629, 665–66, 673–75; J Edelman, *Gain-Based Damages: Contract, Tort, Equity and Intellectual Property* (Oxford, 2002) 164; MA Eisenberg, 'The Principle of Hadley v Baxendale' (1992) 80 *CLR* 563, 586; DA

Posner asserts that litigation is cheaper than renegotiation since the latter would take place in a bilateral-monopoly situation.[7] The opponents point out that litigation too, features a bilateral monopoly.[8] Litigation, they say, may not be cheaper than renegotiation[9] and may even be more expensive as it involves the additional cost of hiring lawyers, of engaging in discovery and of trying and appealing cases.[10]

Another economic argument against the theory of efficient breach is that this theory neglects the cost which breaches of contract impose upon society.[11] By allowing promisors to desist from performance whenever this is more profitable than to perform the law weakens the general trust in contractual promises.[12] In consequence, people may be more reluctant to enter into contracts or may take more precautions against the effects of breach, both of which generate cost.[13]

The theory of efficient breach further encounters the following objections from a non-economic perspective. First, the theory makes unrealistic assumptions, in particular that people are motivated by economic considerations alone and not by emotions, and that the aggrieved party's loss is fully compensated.[14] Secondly, economic efficiency is only one of the goals pursued by law. Others include the protection of reliance and expectancies and the preservation of peace and tranquillity.[15] Thirdly, the notion that the law permits deliberate breaches of

---

Farber, 'Reassessing the Economic Efficiency of Compensatory Damages for Breach of Contract' (1980) 66 *Va L Rev* 1443, 1450–51; D Friedmann, 'The Efficient Breach Fallacy' (1989) 18 *Journal of Legal Studies* 1, 6–7.

[7] RA Posner, *Economic Analysis of Law*, 7th edn (Austin, 2007) 120.

[8] WS Dodge, 'The Case for Punitive Damages in Contracts' (1999) 48 *Duke L J* 629, 665 ff; J Edelman, *Gain-Based Damages: Contract, Tort, Equity and Intellectual Property* (Oxford, 2002) 164; LD Smith, 'Disgorgement of the Profits of Breach of Contract: Property, Contract and "Efficient Breach"' (1995) 24 *CBLJ* 121, 134.

[9] LD Smith, ibid 134–35. See also *Adras Building Material Ltd v Harlow & Jones GmbH* (1995) 3 RLR 235 (SC of Israel) 272 (Barak J); above ch 13, IV A iii.

[10] WS Dodge, 'The Case for Punitive Damages in Contracts' (1999) 48 *Duke L J* 629, 673–75; IR Macneil, 'Efficient Breach of Contract: Circles in the Sky' (1982) 68 *Va L Rev* 947, 968–69. See also MA Eisenberg, 'The Principle of Hadley v Baxendale' (1992) 80 *CLR* 563, 586–87; DA Farber, 'Reassessing the Economic Efficiency of Compensatory Damages for Breach of Contract' (1980) 66 *Va L Rev* 1443, 1453–55; D Friedmann, 'The Efficient Breach Fallacy' (1989) 18 *JLS* 1, 6–7.

[11] FJ Cavico, 'Punitive Damages for Breach of Contract—A Principled Approach' (1990) *St Mary's LJ* 357, 375; D Friedmann, ibid 7; A Phang and PW Lee, 'Restitutionary and Exemplary Damages Revisited' (2003) 19 *Journal of Contract Law* 1, 16.

[12] D Friedmann, ibid; JM Perillo, 'Misreading Oliver Wendell Holmes on Efficient Breach and Tortious Interference' (2000) 68 *Fordham Law Review* 1085, 1099; M Siems, 'Disgorgement of Profits for Breach of Contract: A Comparative Analysis' [2003] *Edinburgh Law Review* 27, 52.

[13] D Friedmann, ibid; M Siems, ibid.

[14] FJ Cavico, 'Punitive Damages for Breach of Contract—A Principled Approach' (1990) *St Mary's L J* 357, 372–73; JM Perillo, 'Misreading Oliver Wendell Holmes on Efficient Breach and Tortious Interference' (2000) 68 *Fordham L Rev* 1085, 1099; CS Warkol, 'Resolving the Paradox Between Legal Theory and Legal Fact: The Judicial Rejection of the Theory of Efficient Breach' (1998) 20 *Cardozo Law Review* 321, 343–45, 348–51; *Adras Building Material Ltd v Harlow & Jones GmbH* (1995) 3 RLR 235 (SC of Israel) 241 (S Levin J).

[15] JM Perillo, ibid 1092–93; *Adras Building Material Ltd v Harlow & Jones GmbH* (1995) 3 RLR 235 (SC of Israel) 272 (Barak J). See also D Laycock, *The Death of the Irreparable Injury Rule* (New York, 1991) 253–59; CS Warkol, ibid 345–46.

contract where they are efficient severely conflicts with the fact that inducing breach of contract is a tort[16] for which Canadian and US courts have awarded exemplary damages.[17] Finally, it is unjustified to treat contractual rights so differently from property rights which must be purchased and cannot simply be expropriated. There is no 'efficient conversion' or 'efficient theft'.[18]

C   Relevance of the Theory of Efficient Breach

The theory of efficient breach encounters convincing objections. But even if the theory is accepted, it cannot justify a complete ban of exemplary damages from contract. First, the theory protects only efficient breaches and is thus perfectly consistent with the deterrence of inefficient, opportunistic breaches such as the refusal to perform after the other party has already performed.[19] Indeed, efficiency *requires* that opportunistic breaches be deterred. Even those who seek to encourage efficient breaches agree that opportunistic breaches should attract extra-compensatory remedies[20] such as exemplary damages[21] or gain-based relief.[22]

Secondly, where a contract-breaker resorts to fraud or force, the breach may deserve punishment even if the outcome is efficient.[23] Suppose that a landlord cuts off the supply of gas, water or electricity in the cold season to get rid of his protected tenant who is about 80 years old[24] or has a two-year-old child.[25] Finally, breaches considered efficient by the theory of efficient breach and not committed

---

[16]   D Friedmann, 'The Efficient Breach Fallacy' (1989) 18 *JLS* 1, 20–21; NJ McBride, 'Punitive Damages' in P Birks (ed), *Wrongs and Remedies in the Twenty-First Century* (Oxford, 1996) 192; FS McChesney, 'Tortious Interference With Contract Versus "Efficient" Breach: Theory and Empirical Evidence' (1999) 28 *JLS* 131, 132 ff; JM Perillo, ibid 1100; *Adras Building Material Ltd v Harlow & Jones GmbH* (1995) 3 RLR 235 (SC of Israel) 272 (Barak J).

[17]   NJ McBride, 'A Case for Awarding Punitive Damages in Response to Deliberate Breaches of Contract' (1995) 24 *Anglo-American Law Review* 369, 384–386, referring, inter alia, to *HL Weiss Forwarding Ltd v Omnus* [1976] 1 SCR 776 (SCC).

[18]   J Edelman, *Gain-Based Damages: Contract, Tort, Equity and Intellectual Property* (Oxford, 2002) 164; IR Macneil, 'Efficient Breach of Contract: Circles in the Sky' (1982) 68 *Va L Rev* 947, 963–64; LD Smith, 'Disgorgement of the Profits of Breach of Contract: Property, Contract and "Efficient Breach"' (1995) 24 *CBLJ* 121, 135. See also D Friedmann, 'The Efficient Breach Fallacy' (1989) 18 *JLS* 1, 4–6; CS Warkol, 'Resolving the Paradox Between Legal Theory and Legal Fact: The Judicial Rejection of the Theory of Efficient Breach' (1998) 20 *Cardozo L Rev* 321, 346.

[19]   GM Cohen, 'The Fault Lines in Contract Damages' (1994) 80 *Va L Rev* 1225, 1312 fn 340.

[20]   B Perlstein, 'Crossing the Contract–Tort Boundary: An Economic Argument for the Imposition of Extracompensatory Damages for Opportunistic Breach of Contract' (1992) 58 *Brooklyn Law Review* 877, 881–90.

[21]   D Campbell, 'Exemplary damages' in D Harris, D Campbell and R Halson, *Remedies in Contract and Tort*, 2nd edn (London, 2002) 594, 604–608.

[22]   RA Posner, *Economic Analysis of Law*, 7th edn (Austin, 2007) 119.

[23]   D Markovits, 'Contract and Collaboration' (2004) 113 *Yale Law Journal* 1417, 1510.

[24]   This happened in *Guppys (Bridport) Ltd v Brookling* (1983) 14 HLR 1 (CA), where exemplary damages were awarded for nuisance.

[25]   This happened in *Perera v Vandiyar* [1953] 1 WLR 672 (CA), where an award of exemplary damages was quashed on the ground that no tort had been committed.

through illegal means will rarely be egregious enough to warrant exemplary damages.[26] The ambit of exemplary damages in contract could even be expressly confined to inefficient[27] or opportunistic[28] breaches.[29]

D Inducement of Breach

It has been suggested that the prospect of obtaining exemplary damages in the event of breach would entice contracting parties to induce the other party to breach. In particular, they could refuse the cooperation necessary for the other party's performance.[30] But an inducement of breach would surely influence the decision on both the propriety and the amount of an exemplary award[31] just as the provocation of a tort by the victim 'is relevant to the question of whether or not exemplary damages should be awarded, and, if so, how much'.[32] An inducement of breach would not be 'rewarded' with exemplary damages.

E Cost of Contracting

It has further been suggested that an introduction of exemplary damages into contract would increase the price of goods and services, as suppliers would reflect

---

[26] The requirement of a malicious or oppressive breach is suggested by FJ Cavico, 'Punitive Damages for Breach of Contract—A Principled Approach' (1990) *St Mary's L J* 357, 444–51.

[27] TA Diamond, 'The Tort of Bad Faith Breach of Contract: When, If At All, Should It Be Extended Beyond Insurance Transactions?' (1981) 64 *Marq L Rev* 425, 443–46. The opposite view is taken by JA Sebert, 'Punitive and Nonpecuniary Damages in Actions Based Upon Contract: Toward Achieving the Objective of Full Compensation' (1986) 33 *UCLA Law Review* 1565, 1659–60, who asserts an undercompensation of victims in the cases exempted from exemplary damages. But undercompensation should not be counter-balanced by exemplary damages: above ch 15, II A.

[28] B Perlstein, 'Crossing the Contract–Tort Boundary: An Economic Argument for the Imposition of Extracompensatory Damages for Opportunistic Breach of Contract' (1992) 58 *Brook L Rev* 877, 881–90, who takes the view that even an efficient breach can be opportunistic if the contract-breaker engages in manipulative behaviour.

[29] It is argued that efficient breaches could still be deterred out of fear that a court misjudges the issue of efficiency: R Craswell, 'Contract Remedies, Renegotiation, and the Theory of Efficient Breach' (1988) 61 *Southern California Law Review* 629, 667. To dispel this problem, the claimant could be required to establish the inefficiency of the breach: TA Diamond, 'The Tort of Bad Faith Breach of Contract: When, If At All, Should It Be Extended Beyond Insurance Transactions?' (1981) 64 *Marq L Rev* 425, 447–49 (who further suggests making determinant the contract-breaker's reasonable belief in efficiency at the time of the breach); B Perlstein, ibid 889.

[30] GM Cohen, 'The Fault Lines in Contract Damages' (1994) 80 *Va L Rev* 1225, 1314; D Markovits, 'Contract and Collaboration' (2004) 113 *Yale LJ* 1417, 1509.

[31] Conceded by GM Cohen, ibid 1315.

[32] *Lane v Holloway* [1968] 1 QB 379 (CA) 391 (Salmon LJ). Accordingly, exemplary (as well as aggravated) damages were denied in *O'Connor v Hewitson* [1979] Crim LR 46 (CA), where the minor assault committed by a police officer on a detainee had been provoked by the latter. Note that an unlawful eviction cannot be said to have been provoked by the tenant's failure to pay the rent: *McMillan v Singh* (1984) 17 HLR 120 (CA).

the risk of having to pay exemplary damages in their prices.[33] But such effect is not certain. Suppliers may exclude their liability for exemplary damages through a clause in the contract. If they can be sure that the courts will enforce this clause, they have no reason to charge a higher price.[34] In addition, the price-increasing effect of higher liability may be offset by the price-decreasing effect of people being more willing to enter into contracts because of their strengthened trust in contractual promises.[35]

F   Crucial Differences between Contract and Tort

There have been attempts to identify crucial differences between a tort and a breach of contract that justify a different attitude toward exemplary damages.[36] Loss caused by a breach of contract, says the Law Commission, is primarily of a pecuniary nature whereas the torts for which exemplary damages are most commonly awarded, and are likely to continue to be most commonly awarded, usually give rise to non-pecuniary loss.[37] This assertion may be correct. But why is it relevant to the availability of exemplary damages? True, in the early days of exemplary damages awards the courts both in England and Wales and in the United States vacillated between an explanation on the ground of compensation for wounded dignity, injured feelings and so on, on the one hand and punishment and deterrence on the other.[38] But the punitive theory has long prevailed.[39] Lord Devlin in *Rookes v Barnard* separated aggravated compensatory damages

---

[33]   GM Cohen, 'The Fault Lines in Contract Damages' (1994) 80 *Va L Rev* 1225, 1314; R Craswell, 'Contract Remedies, Renegotiation, and the Theory of Efficient Breach' (1988) 61 *S Cal L Rev* 629, 642.

[34]   Conceded by GM Cohen, ibid.

[35]   See the similar discussion in the context of non-pecuniary loss above ch 7, VIII F.

[36]   In addition to the arguments discussed here see also the arguments discussed by NJ McBride, 'A Case for Awarding Punitive Damages in Response to Deliberate Breaches of Contract' (1995) 24 *Anglo-Am LR* 369, 379–84.

[37]   Law Commission, 'Aggravated, Exemplary and Restitutionary Damages' (Law Com No 247, 1997) [5.72].

[38]   Demonstrated by TB Colby, 'Beyond the Multiple Punishment Problem: Punitive Damages as Punishment for Individual, Private Wrongs' (2003) 87 *Minnesota Law Review* 583, 614–19; DD Ellis, 'Fairness and Efficiency in the Law of Punitive Damages' (1982) 56 *S Cal L Rev* 1, 14–16. See also AJ Sebok, 'What Did Punitive Damages Do? Why Misunderstanding the History of Punitive Damages Matters Today' (2003) 78 *Chicago-Kent Law Review* 163, 190–94.

[39]   'Until well into the 19th century, punitive damages frequently operated to compensate for intangible injuries, compensation which was not otherwise available under the narrow conception of compensatory damages prevalent at the time ... As the types of compensatory damages available to plaintiffs have broadened ... the theory behind punitive damages has shifted toward a more purely punitive (and therefore less factual) understanding' *Cooper Industries, Inc v Leatherman Tool Group, Inc* (2001) 532 US 424 (US SC) 437 fn 11 (Stevens J). The compensatory theory still finds support in the US, see above ch 15, II A.

from exemplary damages.[40] The Law Commission cannot be taken to suggest that the compensation of non-pecuniary loss is the primary objective of exemplary damages.

Perhaps the Law Commission means to say that exemplary damages, even though not directly aiming at compensating non-pecuniary loss, do as a welcome side effect counter-balance a tendency toward undercompensating non-pecuniary loss. But if undercompensation is thought a problem, the remedy should be an increase in *compensatory* awards for non-pecuniary loss.[41] Or perhaps the Law Commission means to say that the magnitude of the non-pecuniary loss caused indicates how severely the claimant has been affected by the wrong and accordingly how much the defendant's conduct deserves punishment. But such an argument could still not explain why exemplary damages should be banned per se from contract. Some breaches of contract do cause significant non-pecuniary loss. It seems preferable, as in tort, to leave it to the courts to judge each case on its merits.[42]

Corbin faces the same objection to his argument that breaches of contract

> do not in general cause as much resentment or other mental and physical discomfort as do the wrongs called torts and crimes. Therefore, the remedies to prevent them and to prevent disorder and breach of the peace by satisfying the injured parties, are not so severe upon the wrongdoer.[43]

True, breaches of contract are usually less severe than torts and crimes. But some breaches *are* equally severe, for instance the cutting off of gas, water or electricity supply to a flat in the cold season in order to force a tenant out of his home.[44] Even a significantly lower frequency of outrageous behaviour in contract than in tort cannot explain why exemplary damages are to be banned per se from contract.

The Law Commission shares the view that the notion of state punishment is more readily applicable to tort than to contract for the reason that a contract is a private arrangement in which parties negotiate rights and duties while tortious duties are imposed by law.[45] True, people can freely choose their contract-partner and negotiate the contents of contracts. But once a contract has been formed, the parties are bound by it. The law imposes the rule *pacta sunt servanda* just as it imposes tortious duties. It is by no means inconceivable for the law to foster compliance with that rule by a threat of exemplary damages.

---

[40]   [1964] AC 1129 (HL) 1229–30; above ch 14, I.

[41]   See also above ch 15, II A.

[42]   The fact that a breach of contract may exceptionally merit punishment is also emphasised by A Burrows, *Remedies for Torts and Breach of Contract*, 3rd edn (Oxford, 2004) 429.

[43]   AL Corbin, *Corbin on Contracts: A Comprehensive Treatise on the Working Rules of Contract Law*, Vol 5 (St Paul, 1964) 438.

[44]   This happened in *Perera v Vandiyar* [1953] 1 WLR 672 (CA); *Guppys (Bridport) Ltd v Brookling* (1983) 14 HLR 1 (CA).

[45]   Law Commission, 'Aggravated, Exemplary and Restitutionary Damages' (Law Com No 247, 1997) [5.72].

Finally, the Law Commission argues that since the need for certainty is perceived to be greater in contract than in tort, there is less scope in contract for the discretion the courts must have in determining the availability and quantum of exemplary damages.[46] But even if exemplary damages were introduced into contract, their ambit would be confined to egregious behaviour. Businesses could be certain that as long as they seek to fulfil their contractual obligations in good faith they cannot become liable to pay exemplary damages where they do happen to break a contract.[47]

G   Conclusion

If exemplary damages were to be put on a principled basis and made available for all egregious wrongs, it could not be justified to exclude egregious breaches of contract from their ambit. The introduction of exemplary damages into contract would necessitate enforcing (reasonable) penalty clauses in contracts, for it would be inconsistent to grant a state-supplied right to sue for exemplary damages while denying a contract-supplied right to sue for a penalty.[48] Whether exemplary damages should in fact be retained as a matter of principle will be considered in chapter 17 below.

II   Defensibility of Banning Exemplary Damages from Equity

Is it defensible to ban exemplary damages from equity while allowing them in tort? By far the most detailed debate on that issue involving a comprehensive review of cases, academic writing and law commission reports throughout the Commonwealth, was that undertaken in the New South Wales case *Harris v Digital Pulse Pty Ltd*.[49] The facts were simple enough. Two employees of Digital, who were contractually prohibited from competing with Digital during their employment, secretly established their own business while still employed by Digital, and secured contracts with existing or potential clients of Digital. They were found liable for breach of contract, breach of their fiduciary duty of loyalty, and misuse of confidential information. Exercising equitable jurisdiction Palmer J awarded, over and above compensation and account of profits (between which

---

[46]   ibid. On similar grounds the Law Commission opposes an apportionment of liability by virtue of contributory negligence in cases of strict contractual liability: above ch 10, VII C.

[47]   NJ McBride, 'A Case for Awarding Punitive Damages in Response to Deliberate Breaches of Contract' (1995) 24 *Anglo-Am LR* 369, 382.

[48]   A Duggan, 'Exemplary Damages in Equity: A Law and Economics Perspective' (2006) 26 *Oxford Journal of Legal Studies* 303, 325.

[49]   [2002] NSWSC 33, (2002), 166 FLR 421 (Palmer J); [2003] NSWCA 10, (2003) 197 ALR 626.

Digital had to choose), exemplary damages of Aus$10,000 against each employee. The latter award, which was the only award of equitable exemplary damages ever made in Australia, was quashed by a majority (Spigelman CJ and Heydon JA; Mason P dissenting) in the New South Wales Court of Appeal.

Reflecting the general discussion on the availability of exemplary damages in equity, the debate in *Harris v Digital Pulse Pty Ltd* between Palmer J and Mason P (the 'pro-side') on the one hand and Spigelman CJ and Heydon JA (the 'contra-side') on the other centred on two questions: is punishment a traditional objective of equitable principles and remedies? If not, should exemplary damages now become available in equity?

A   Is Punishment a Traditional Objective of Equity?

In an attempt to show that punishment is a traditional objective of equitable principles and remedies, the pro-side in *Harris v Digital Pulse Pty Ltd* pointed out that where an account of profit is ordered, dishonesty on the part of a defaulting fiduciary leads to an award of higher interest and to a reduction or even complete denial of allowances for the fiduciary's work and skill.[50] The contra-side denied that these rules are of a punitive nature. Spigelman CJ said that the conduct of the fiduciary merely influences the choice among alternative methods of computing the profit made. This choice involves a balancing exercise of justice *inter partes* but engages no public interest.[51] Heydon JA said that the award of higher interests in the case of dishonesty is simply meant to ensure that the fiduciary retains no profit.[52] With regard to the allowances, Heydon JA pointed out that the defendant bears the onus of establishing the inequity of having to disgorge the entire profit, 'and hence the position is not so much that an account of the entire profits is a punishment, but rather that an absence of grave misconduct is a passport to an indulgence in favour of the defendant'.[53]

---

[50]   [2002] NSWSC 33, (2002) 166 FLR 421 [165], [171]; [2003] NSWCA 10, (2003) 197 ALR 626 [164] (Mason P). Palmer J further pointed out (at [164], [171]) that in the 16th and 17th centuries chancery judges punished wrongs such as forgery and perjury with imprisonment, fines, the pillory and irons; see also PW Michalik, 'The availability of compensatory and exemplary damages in equity: A note on the *Aquaculture* decision' (1991) 21 *Victoria University of Wellington Law Review* 391, 412. The New South Wales Court of Appeal unanimously objected that the exercise of criminal jurisdiction says nothing about the civil jurisdiction to award exemplary damages: (2003) 197 ALR 626 (NSWCA) [46], [115], 423]–[433]; likewise RP Meagher, JD Heydon and MJ Leeming, *Meagher, Gummow and Lehane's Equity: Doctrines and Remedies*, 4th edn (Sydney, 2002) [2–310].

[51]   [2003] NSWCA 10, (2003) 197 ALR 626 [49]–[51].

[52]   ibid [303]. See also *Westdeutsche Landesbank Girozentrale v Islington LBC* [1996] AC 669 (HL) 691, 695 (Lord Goff). An intention of the court to punish the defendant is made out for some cases by AJ Oakley, *Parker and Mellows: The Modern Law of Trusts*, 9th edn (London, 2008) [22–035].

[53]   [2003] NSWCA 10, (2003) 197 ALR 626, [335].

More generally, the pro-side asserted that the strict rules of equity, in particular the obligation to disgorge profit, are deterrent and punitive in character.[54] Heydon JA conceded a deterrent purpose in the sense of combating any temptation on the fiduciary's part to act against the principal but insisted that equitable remedies 'are not penal or punitive in the sense of exacting any money sanction greater than that which is needed either to give full compensation for loss or full disgorgement of gain'.[55] The contra-side further rejected Michalik's argument that equity's aim of restoring good conscience between the parties may sometimes require a punishment of the defendant.[56] No equity judge has ever considered exemplary damages[57] or indeed any purely punitive remedy[58] as a means of purging the defendant's conscience. The contra-side, it is submitted, persuasively demonstrated that the infliction of punishment is traditionally foreign to equity and would be a novel step.[59]

B Should Exemplary Damages be Available in Equity?

With regard to the question of whether equity should take the novel step of awarding exemplary damages,[60] the contra-side in *Harris v Digital Pulse Pty Ltd* objected that this would subscribe to the fallacy of a fusion of common law and equity.[61] Mason P convincingly replied that to allow exemplary damages would represent a legitimate development of equity's inherent or exclusive jurisdiction without any fusion with the common law.[62] Mason P was also convincing in

---

[54] [2002] NSWSC 33, (2002) 166 FLR 421 [167]; [2003] NSWCA 10, (2003) 197 ALR 626 [161]–[173] (Mason P). See also Law Commission, 'Aggravated, Exemplary and Restitutionary Damages' (Law Com No 247, 1997) [5.55]; WMC Gummow, 'Compensation for Breach of Fiduciary Duty' in TG Youdan (ed), *Equity, Fiduciaries and Trusts* (Toronto, 1989) 79.

[55] [2003] NSWCA 10, (2003) 197 ALR 626 [407].

[56] PW Michalik, 'The availability of compensatory and exemplary damages in equity: A note on the *Aquaculture* decision' (1991) 21 *VUWLR* 391, 412–413. Concurring D Jensen, 'Punitive Damages for Breach of Fiduciary Obligation' (1996) 19 *University of Queensland Law Journal* 125, 130.

[57] [2003] NSWCA 10, (2003) 197 ALR 626 [460] (Heydon JA).

[58] ibid [54] (Spigelman CJ).

[59] The step is too novel, said Heydon JA, to be taken by an intermediate appellate court: ibid, [352], [403], [435]–[458]. For the opposite view see Mason P, ibid [217]–[223]; A Burrows, 'Remedial Coherence and Punitive Damages in Equity' in S Degeling and J Edelman (eds), *Equity in Commercial Law* (Sydney, 2005) 398.

[60] Affirmatively J Glover, *Commercial Equity: Fiduciary Relationships* (Sydney, 1995) [6.129]–[6.130]; C Rickett, 'Compensating for Loss in Equity—Choosing the Right Horse for Each Course' in P Birks and F Rose (eds), *Restitution and Equity, Vol 1: Resulting Trusts and Equitable Compensation* (London, 2000) 183.

[61] [2003] NSWCA 10, (2003) 197 ALR 626 [6]–[20] (Spigelman CJ), [353]–[391] (Heydon JA). The idea of a fusion was indeed invoked as the basis of awarding exemplary damages in equity by the majority in *Aquaculture Corp v New Zealand Green Mussel Co Ltd* [1990] 3 NZLR 299 (NZCA) 30–302.

[62] [2003] NSWCA 10, (2003) 197 ALR 626 [139]–[152]. See also *White v Ruditys* (1983) 117 Wis.2d 130 (CA of Wiskonsin) 141 (Wedemeyer PJ): 'We do not, however, conclude that the power to award punitive damages [in equity] is the result of the merger of courts of law and courts of equity. We determine that the power to award punitive damages is derived from the flexibility a court of

rejecting Aitken's argument that compensation 'lies at the heart of the equitable intervention':[63] equity often goes beyond compensation by granting an account of profits, injunction, rescission, specific performance and so on.[64]

The crucial argument by the pro-side was that the availability of exemplary damages must be co-extensive with their rationale. Since their rationale is the punishment of outrageous behaviour, they must be available for outrageous equitable wrongs.[65] Palmer J asked:

> Can it seriously be suggested that if my solicitor grossly deceives me in the course of his professional dealing with me and decamps with my life's savings, the law regards my sense of outrage as demonstrably greater if I sue him in a common law court for deceit than if I sue him in an equity court for breach of fiduciary duty?[66]

Heydon JA replied that deceit and breach of fiduciary duty show differences not only in their attitude towards exemplary damages but also in other aspects: Deceit involves a higher burden of proof, a more onerous test for breach, causation and remoteness, it is not covered by the solicitor's insurance and carries for the solicitor the real risk of being struck off the roll.[67] Leaving aside that some of these differences are questionable themselves,[68] the differences exist because a breach of fiduciary duty may be committed through conduct not amounting to deceit. They cannot explain the different attitude towards exemplary damages where a breach of fiduciary duty does amount to deceit.

The contra-side further opposed an analogy to tort on the ground that 'the roots of tort and crime' are 'greatly intermingled'.[69] Traditionally, said Spigelman CJ, many torts constituted crimes and thus raised issues of public interest, which made considerations of punishment and deterrence entirely appropriate.[70] The pro-side rightly replied that public interests can be affected by equitable wrongs

---

equity has in fashioning its relief.' Palmer J, taking the view that equity has always had jurisdiction to punish, saw no need to invoke the idea of fusion either: [2002] NSWSC 33, (2002) 166 FLR 421 [171].

[63] L Aitken, 'Developments in Equitable Compensation: Opportunity or Danger?' (1993) 67 *Australian Law Journal* 596, 600.

[64] [2003] NSWCA 10, (2003) 197 ALR 626 [120], [126]–[128].

[65] [2002] NSWSC 33, (2002) 166 FLR 421 [156], [170]; (2003) 197 ALR 626, [195] (Mason P). See also Law Commission, 'Aggravated, Exemplary and Restitutionary Damages' (Law Com No 247, 1997) [5.55]; A Burrows, *Remedies for Torts and Breach of Contract*, 3rd edn (Oxford, 2004) 626–27; SB Elliott and C Mitchell, 'Remedies for Dishonest Assistance' (2004) 67 *Modern Law Review* 16, 38 (for tort-style equitable wrongs); NJ McBride, 'Punitive Damages' in P Birks (ed), *Wrongs and Remedies in the Twenty-First Century* (Oxford, 1996) 181–83; PW Michalik, 'The availability of compensatory and exemplary damages in equity: A note on the *Aquaculture* decision' (1991) 21 *VUWLR* 391, 413; SM Waddams, *The Law of Damages*, 3rd edn (Toronto, 1997) [11.240].

[66] [2002] NSWSC 33, (2002) 166 FLR 421 [156].

[67] [2003] NSWCA 10, (2003) 197 ALR 626 [398]. See also RP Meagher, JD Heydon and MJ Leeming, *Meagher, Gummow and Lehane's Equity: Doctrines and Remedies*, 4th edn (Australia, 2002) [2–310].

[68] For causation and remoteness of damage see above ch 2, VII and ch 5, III.

[69] [2003] NSWCA 10, (2003) 197 ALR 626 [34] (Spigelman CJ), [399] (Heydon JA), both quoting *Uren v John Fairfax & Sons Pty Ltd* (1966) 117 CLR 118 (HCA) 149 (Windeyer J).

[70] [2003] NSWCA 10, (2003) 197 ALR 626 [33]. See also V Vann, *Equitable Compensation in Australia: Principles and Problems* (Saarbrücken, 2009) 351–52.

too.[71] Indeed, public interests were affected in the instant case. Palmer J rightly observed that 'the character of the defendants' dishonest conduct strikes at the heart of commercial integrity, upon which the business community, and ultimately the community as a whole, depends'.[72]

Heydon JA pointed out that common law crimes usually involve issues of motivation, intention to injure and malign purposes such as dishonesty, all of which are relevant to the grant of exemplary damages. Equitable duties, he said, do not normally turn on those mental states.[73] The last statement is true but applies equally to many torts.[74] Trespass to land, for instance, does not require any malicious intention or indeed any intention to trespass.[75] Here the mental state required for an award of exemplary damages must be established specifically for the purpose of such an award.[76]

Spigelman CJ argued that in a situation like the one at hand, where the essential basis of the fiduciary duties is a contractual relationship, an analogy should be drawn, if at all, not to tort but to contract where exemplary damages are unavailable.[77] Similarly, Heydon JA argued that even if it were considered anomalous that in a case of concurrent liability in tort and equity exemplary damages are available in relation to the former cause of action but not the latter, an introduction of exemplary damages into equity would create a new anomaly in the case of concurrent liability in contract and equity.[78]

Mason P rejected an analogy to contract on the ground that fiduciary obligations are not simply negotiated but are imposed by law in the case of a certain relationship or conduct. Accordingly, there is no principle of efficient breach underpinning remedies for breach of fiduciary duty.[79] It is not necessary here to examine that argument. In the light of the earlier suggestion that the unavailability of exemplary damages in contract is itself indefensible if exemplary damages are retained in tort,[80] an analogy to contract would *favour* exemplary damages in equity. As Burrows observes: 'once it is accepted that punitive

---

[71] ibid [131] (Mason P), giving the example of an injunction to restrain the flouting of urban planning law.

[72] [2002] NSWSC 33, (2002) 166 FLR 421 [134].

[73] [2003] NSWCA 10, (2003) 197 ALR 626, [399].

[74] P Cane, '*Mens Rea* in Tort Law' (2000) 20 *OJLS* 533, 539–41, 545–48, 552–55.

[75] It is no defence that the defendant believed he was on his own land: *Conway v George Wimpey & Co Ltd* [1951] 2 KB 266 (CA) 273.

[76] Which was done in *Merest v Harvey* (1814) 5 Taunt 442, 128 ER 761; *Lavender v Betts* [1942] 2 All ER 72.

[77] [2003] NSWCA 10, (2003) 197 ALR 626, [36]–[44].

[78] ibid [397].

[79] ibid [184]. The argument is supported by A Burrows, 'Remedial Coherence and Punitive Damages in Equity' in S Degeling and J Edelman (eds), *Equity in Commercial Law* (Sydney, 2005) 399–400.

[80] Above I in this chapter.

damages should be available for all common law wrongs, there appears to be no rational counter-argument left for denying punitive damages for equitable wrongs'.[81]

Spigelman CJ further argued that the power to award exemplary damages in equity would be incompatible with the principles on penalty clauses in contracts.[82] Imagine, he said, that the two employees had promised in their employment contract to pay $10,000 over and above damages or account of profits in the event of a breach of duty such as occurred. According to established common law doctrine the promise would be struck down *ab initio* as a penalty. Nothing suggests that equity would intervene to override the application of the common law doctrine on the basis of egregious behaviour on the part of the employee. Mason P convincingly replied that the unenforceability of the penalty clause would not prevent an award of exemplary damages in tort where the employees' conduct amounted to a tort attracting exemplary damages.[83]

Finally, Heydon JA saw a conflict with the criminal law.[84] The equitable wrong in question, he said, is either a criminal offence or it is not. If it is not, the objections to the creation of new crimes by the courts apply equally to the introduction of exemplary damages into equity. If the equitable wrong is a crime, the question arises how the criminal sanction and exemplary damages would influence each other. Could one sanction be imposed after the other has already been imposed? Would the amount of exemplary damages be limited by the maximum criminal fine imposable? Heydon JA's concerns are valid but they apply equally to an award of exemplary damages in tort. It is no argument for banning exemplary damages specifically from equity while retaining them in tort.

The contra-side, it is submitted, could not defeat the strong pro-argument that the availability of exemplary damages must be co-extensive with its rationale. Consequently, if exemplary damages were to be put on a principled basis and made available for every egregious wrong, their ambit should include egregious equitable wrongs. Since their ambit should also include egregious breaches of contract,[85] the retention of exemplary damages on a principled basis should lead to a regime uniform in contract, tort and equity. Whether exemplary damages should in fact be retained will be considered in the following chapter.

---

[81] A Burrows, 'Remedial Coherence and Punitive Damages in Equity' in S Degeling and J Edelman (eds), *Equity in Commercial Law* (Sydney, 2005) 401–402. See also A Duggan, 'Exemplary Damages in Equity: A Law and Economics Perspective' (2006) 26 *OJLS* 303, 324.

[82] [2003] NSWCA 10, (2003) 197 ALR 626 [57]–[61]. Heydon JA (at [338]) based a similar argument on the *equitable* rule against penalty clauses. For the present unenforceability of penalty clauses and calls for reform see above ch 13, V B.

[83] [2003] NSWCA 10, (2003) 197 ALR 626 [187].

[84] ibid [352].

[85] See above I in this chapter.

17

The Abolition or Retention of
Exemplary Damages

I The Division between Civil Law and Criminal Law

Can there be a place for a civil remedy aiming at retribution, deterrence and denunciation[1] when punishment is the raison d'être of the criminal law? The debate on this key issue[2] featured prominently in *Cassell & Co Ltd v Broome* where Lord Reid regarded exemplary damages as 'highly anomalous':

> It is confusing the function of the civil law which is to compensate with the function of the criminal law which is to inflict deterrent and punitive penalties. Some objection has been taken to the use of the word 'fine' to denote the amount by which punitive or exemplary damages exceed anything justly due to the plaintiff. In my view the word 'fine' is an entirely accurate description of the part of any award which goes beyond anything justly due to the plaintiff and is purely punitive.[3]

Lord Wilberforce objected:

> It cannot lightly be taken for granted, even as a matter of theory, that the purpose of the law of tort is compensation, still less that it ought to be, an issue of large social import, or that there is something inappropriate or illogical or anomalous (a question-begging word) in including a punitive element in civil damages, or, conversely, that the criminal law, rather than the civil law, is in these cases the better instrument for conveying social disapproval, or for redressing a wrong to the social fabric, or that damages in any case

---

[1] These being the objectives of exemplary damages: above ch 15.

[2] Law Commission, 'Aggravated, Exemplary and Restitutionary Damages' (Law Com No 247, 1997) [5.16]; A Burrows, 'Reforming Exemplary Damages: Expansion or Abolition?' in P Birks (ed), *Wrongs and Remedies in the Twenty-First Century* (Oxford, 1996) 158.

[3] [1972] AC 1027 (HL) 1086. More forcefully *Fay v Parker* (1872) 53 NH 342 (SC of New Hampshire) 382 (Foster J): 'How could the idea of punishment be deliberately and designedly installed as a doctrine of civil remedies? Is not punishment out of place, irregular, anomalous, exceptional, unjust, unscientific, not to say absurd and ridiculous, when classed among civil remedies? What kind of a civil remedy for the plaintiff is the punishment of the defendant? The idea is wrong. It is a monstrous heresy. It is an unsightly and an unhealthy excrescence, deforming the symmetry of the body of the law.'

can be broken down into the two separate elements. As a matter of practice English law has not committed itself to any of these theories: it may have been wiser than it knew.[4]

The arguments for and against will now be examined in more detail.

A Attack on Exemplary Damages

Exemplary damages are opposed with the following first-level argument.[5] Since punishment is the sole objective of the criminal law, there can be no place for punitive remedies in civil cases. Wherever punishment is warranted, it ought to be imposed through the criminal law. Exemplary damages are thus a fine in the disguise of a civil remedy. This sanction has somehow found its way into the civil law but ought now to be abolished in order to establish a clear distinction between civil and criminal sanctions.

The view that exemplary damages are in truth a fine generates a plethora of second-level arguments.[6] Most notorious are the following. Imposing a fine in civil proceedings undermines the safeguards afforded to defendants in criminal proceedings. While the conviction for a crime requires proof beyond reasonable doubt, civil cases are decided on a balance of probabilities. The rules as to the admissibility of evidence are less restrictive in civil proceedings. Exemplary damages may exceed the statutory maximum fine for the same or similar conduct. Where juries are still involved in civil cases (most prominently in defamation cases), they determine not only the 'guilt' of the defendant but also the appropriate 'punishment', which is unheard of in criminal cases (in England and Wales).

Exemplary damages also undermine the prohibition of double punishment in respect of the same conduct, the narrow approach of the criminal law to vicarious liability, and the general prohibition of insurance against liability to pay a criminal fine.[7] Furthermore, where punishment takes the form of a fine, it ought to be payable to the state and not to the individual victim. Exemplary damages are therefore an undeserved windfall in the hands of the victim.

---

[4] [1972] AC 1027 (HL) 1114.

[5] H McGregor, *McGregor on Damages*, 18th edn (London, 2009) [11–001], [11–006]. See also Lord Scott, 'Damages' [2007] *Lloyd's Maritime and Commercial Law Quarterly* 465, 469.

[6] The arguments are presented but not necessarily endorsed by the Law Commission, 'Aggravated, Exemplary and Restitutionary Damages' (Law Com No 247, 1997) [5.21]; H Street, *Principles of the Law of Damages* (London, 1962) 34–35; S Deakin, A Johnston and B Markesinis, *Markesinis and Deakin's Tort Law*, 6th edn (Oxford, 2008) 949–50; A Burrows, 'Reforming Exemplary Damages: Expansion or Abolition?' in P Birks (ed), *Wrongs and Remedies in the Twenty-First Century* (Oxford, 1996) 160–63.

[7] 'It is clearly contrary to public policy to insure against the commission of an act, knowing what act is being committed, which is a crime': *Haseldine v Hosken* [1933] 1 KB 822 (CA) 833 (Scrutton LJ). Approvingly quoted in *Lancashire CC v Municipal Mutual Insurance Ltd* [1997] QB 897 (CA) 907 (Simon Brown LJ).

In *Mosley v News Group Newspapers Ltd* Eady J used the arguments mentioned as policy reasons for holding exemplary damages unavailable in actions for breach of privacy (but not unavailable in all civil actions):

> It is trite knowledge that punitive damages are anomalous in civil litigation in a number of respects. First, they bring the notion of punishment into civil litigation when damages are usually supposed to be about compensation. Secondly, the defendant's means can be taken into account because these damages are in some ways analogous to a fine ... Thirdly, despite that, every such sum awarded goes not to the state itself, as is the case with a fine, but to the claimant in the litigation. It represents to that extent a windfall. Fourthly, in the context of those civil claims where a jury is still available, it is the jury rather than the judge which determines the amount of the appropriate penalty.[8]

B Defence of Exemplary Damages

The attack on exemplary damages on the ground that they conflict with the principles of the criminal law is met with two different lines of defence. One line of defence is the suggestion that the award of exemplary damages be made subject to all the safeguards afforded to defendants in criminal cases.[9] Under this approach, exemplary damages could be awarded only if the court believes in the defendant's guilt beyond reasonable doubt.[10] Their amount would have to be determined by a judge rather than a jury and so on.

This defence must fail, for it would be difficult, if not infeasible, to implement the measures suggested. A bifurcation of the trial separating a first stage dealing with the compensatory damages claim and a second stage dealing with the exemplary damages claim is of course possible as the practice in some jurisdictions in the United States shows.[11] But to apply different procedural rules in the two stages would pose insurmountable difficulties.[12] Having considered, in the first stage, all evidence admissible in civil proceedings and found the defendant liable, the judge would then, in the second stage, have to make a fresh decision on liability and also decide on the requirements for awarding exemplary damages. In making those decisions the judge would have to 'forget' all evidence inadmissible

---

[8] [2008] EWHC 1777 (QB) [194].

[9] NJ McBride, 'Punitive Damages' in P Birks (ed), *Wrongs and Remedies in the Twenty-First Century* (Oxford, 1996) 199; ME Wheeler, 'The Constitutional Case for Reforming Punitive Damages Procedures' (1983) 69 *Virginia Law Review* 269, 322–51. See also S Deakin, A Johnston and B Markesinis, *Markesinis and Deakin's Tort Law*, 6th edn (Oxford, 2008) 949: the second-level objections mentioned above, I A in this chapter are 'serious, but not necessarily insurmountable'.

[10] As indeed is required in Colorado: Colorado Revised Statutes § 13–25–127(2).

[11] See the statutes and cases listed in *Transportation Insurance Co v Moriel* (1994) 879 S.W.2d 10 (SC of Texas) 30 fn 28. But note that most of these states postpone only the decision on the *amount* of exemplary damages.

[12] The difficulties which would arise if compensatory damages and exemplary damages were subject to different concepts of vicarious liability or to a different standard of proof are recognised by the Law Commission, 'Aggravated, Exemplary and Restitutionary Damages' (Law Com No 247, 1997) [5.225], [5.233].

in criminal proceedings and apply a stricter standard of proof than in the first stage. This would be a tremendous psychological challenge. Instead of 'mimicking' a criminal trial within civil proceedings, the law should go the whole hog and leave the awarding of fines to criminal proceedings proper.

The second and main line of defence is to deny the criminal character of exemplary damages altogether.[13] Several arguments are offered. First, while an exemplary damages award is sought and enforced by the individual victim, criminal punishment is sought and enforced by the state.[14] Even where the victim brings a private prosecution she will be regarded as acting on behalf of the state.[15] Secondly, exemplary damages do not involve threats to personal liberty.[16] Finally, an award of exemplary damages does not stigmatise the wrongdoer in the same way as a criminal conviction which affects employment prospects and a person's status in general.[17] Denying the criminal character of exemplary damages pulls the rug out from under the second-level objections mentioned before.[18] The differences between civil and criminal proceedings as to the standard of proof, the admissibility of evidence, the role of judge and jury and so on are perfectly acceptable if they concern different types of punishment.

C Conclusion

The debate on whether the availability of exemplary damages undermines the safeguards afforded to defendants in criminal proceedings reflects different views on the functions of the civil and the criminal branch of the law. If one sees room for civil punishment alongside criminal punishment, exemplary damages are acceptable. If not, they must be abolished. It is difficult to resolve the controversy as it is deeply rooted in different 'beliefs'. This book therefore adopts the Law Commission's approach of leaving the relation between civil and criminal proceedings open and deciding the fate of exemplary damages on policy grounds.[19]

---

[13] ibid [5.22]–[5.25]. In general also M Galanter and D Luban, 'Poetic Justice: Punitive Damages and Legal Pluralism' (1993) 42 *American University Law Review* 1393, 1457–60.

[14] Law Commission, ibid [5.23]; M Galanter and D Luban, ibid 1457. See also *W v W* [1999] 2 NZLR 1 (PC) 6–7.

[15] Law Commission, ibid.

[16] M Galanter and D Luban, 'Poetic Justice: Punitive Damages and Legal Pluralism' (1993) 42 *Am U L Rev* 1393, 1458, 1460.

[17] ibid; Law Commission, 'Aggravated, Exemplary and Restitutionary Damages' (Law Com No 247, 1997) [5.23].

[18] Above I A in this chapter.

[19] Law Commission, 'Aggravated, Exemplary and Restitutionary Damages' (Law Com No 247, 1997) [5.26].

II Policy Arguments Against Exemplary Damages

A Uncertainty as to Availability and Amount

A prominent argument supporting the abolition of exemplary damages is the inevitable[20] uncertainty as to both their availability and their assessment.[21] Any principled definition of their ambit is considered too vague, and the necessary discretion of the courts in determining the amount is considered too wide. But the uncertainty feared can be prevented by prescribing the guiding principles in legislation and refining those principles through case law.

Sufficient certainty is achieved, for instance, by the Law Commission's draft bill. It provides that exemplary damages may be awarded only where the defendant's conduct shows a deliberate and outrageous disregard of the claimant's rights. It is further required that the conduct deserves punishment and that the other remedies available are inadequate to effect punishment.[22] Admittedly, these draft provisions are still broad and open to different interpretations. But the law features equally vague concepts, for instance the concept of duty of care. If the proposed bill were to be implemented, its provisions would over time be refined by case law. Consistent decisions would be facilitated by the Law Commission's proposal that both the availability and the assessment of exemplary damages be always decided by the judge and never by the jury.[23]

With regard to the quantum of exemplary damages, the Law Commission's draft bill provides that the amount must not exceed the minimum needed to punish the defendant and that it must be proportionate to the gravity of the defendant's conduct.[24] This is supplemented by a list of factors to be considered such as the defendant's state of mind and the extent of the harm caused.[25] Again, this proposal still leaves significant discretion with the courts. But, given that the amount is always determined by a judge and never by a jury, the courts can be expected to consider previous awards in order to be consistent. Consistency can further be promoted, as the Law Commission points out,[26] through guideline judgments by the Court of Appeal (which are already used in the field of criminal

---

[20] 'A degree of uncertainty is inevitable, with a standard such as outrageous conduct': *A v Bottrill* [2002] UKPC 44, [2003] 1 AC 449 [34] (Lord Nicholls).

[21] For this argument and its rejection see Law Commission, 'Aggravated, Exemplary and Restitutionary Damages' (Law Com No 247, 1997) [5.31]–[5.32]; DG Owen, 'A Punitive Damages Overview: Functions, Problems and Reform' (1994) 39 *Villanova Law Review* 363, 384–85.

[22] Law Commission, ibid [5.44]–[5.48], Appendix A, Draft Damages Bill s 3(6), (7). See also above ch 14, IX.

[23] Law Commission, ibid Appendix A, Draft Damages Bill s 2.

[24] ibid [5.44]–[5.48], Appendix A, Draft Damages Bill s 5(1).

[25] ibid Appendix A, Draft Damages Bill s 5(2).

[26] ibid [5.32].

sentencing) and through the development of a tariff system akin to the one used for non-pecuniary loss resulting from personal injury.[27]

B   Ineffectiveness of Predictable Awards

Just from the opposite direction comes the argument that if the amount of exemplary damages *is* predictable, they will not deter effectively. Defendants will then be able to engage in cost-benefit calculations and will commit wrongs where the expected benefits exceed the damages payable (including exemplary damages).[28] But such calculating conduct can effectively be deterred by either granting a gain-based remedy in addition to exemplary damages or by linking the exemplary award to the amount of the benefit made or expected. Both ways are open under the legislation proposed by the Law Commission.[29]

C   Incentive for Bogus Claims

Exemplary damages might be opposed with the argument that the prospect of receiving a (considerable) sum in addition to compensation for the loss suffered entices people to bring ill-founded claims.[30] Such a fear would, however, be ill-founded. Since the claimant bears the onus of proof, the prospect of receiving exemplary damages will tempt people to take upon themselves the costs and hazards of litigation only where they believe they can establish both the wrong and the requirements for an award of exemplary damages. Such a suit is legitimate even if it fails eventually.

III   Policy Arguments in Favour of Exemplary Damages

A   Appeasing the Victim

Exemplary damages have been described as a form of 'private retribution'[31] which serves 'to assuage any urge for revenge felt by victims and to discourage

---

[27]   See Judicial Studies Board, *Guidelines for the Assessment of General Damages in Personal Injury Cases*, 9th edn (Oxford, 2008).

[28]   For this argument and its rejection see Law Commission, 'Aggravated, Exemplary and Restitutionary Damages' (Law Com No 247, 1997) [5.36].

[29]   ibid [5.36], Appendix A, Draft Damages Bill ss 5(2)(d), 12.

[30]   For this argument and its rejection see ibid [5.30]; DG Owen, 'A Punitive Damages Overview: Functions, Problems and Reform' (1994) 39 *Vill L Rev* 363, 396–97.

[31]   AJ Sebok, 'Punitive Damages: From Myth to Theory' (2007) 92 *Iowa Law Review* 957.

any temptation to engage in self-help likely to endanger the peace'.[32] Indeed, until the early nineteenth century the courts explained large damages awards for insulting behaviour on the ground that they aimed to prevent duelling.[33] However, even though the preservation of peace may have been an important purpose of exemplary damages when they emerged, changes in society over the past centuries have profoundly reduced the peacekeeping function of exemplary damages.[34] Robinette points to three significant developments:

> First, as a society, we have come to rely on criminal law as the principal legal means to control antisocial behaviour. Second, the increasing number of cases against corporations, as opposed to individuals, reduces the likelihood of violent retaliation. Finally, the most intangible, but perhaps most significant, factor is the extent to which society has become accustomed to solving its problems through non-violent means.[35]

B Possibility of Vicarious Liability

Where an employee in the course of his employment commits a tort against a third party, the employer is vicariously liable.[36] Whenever exemplary damages were awarded in a vicarious liability case it was tacitly assumed that the employer must pay the exemplary damages too.[37] In most of the cases for police misconduct,[38] for instance, exemplary damages were awarded not against the individual police officer but against the chief constable.[39] But, apart from a few dicta,[40] the

---

[32] *Lamb v Cotogno* (1987) 164 CLR 1 (HCA) 9 (Mason CJ, Brennan J, Deane J, Dawson J and Gaudron J). See also *Gray v Motor Accident Commission* [1998] HCA 70, (1998) 196 CLR 1 (HCA) [32], [126]–[127]; *Harris v Digital Pulse Pty Ltd* [2002] NSWSC 33, (2002) 166 FLR 421 [113]–[114]; [2003] NSWCA 10, (2003) 197 ALR 626 [55]–[56] (Spigelman CJ); *W v W* [1999] 2 NZLR 1 (PC) 7 (Lord Hoffmann: 'therapeutic value'); *Alcorn v Mitchell* (1872) 63 Ill 553 (SC of Illinois) 554; and the cases cited by CJ Robinette, 'Peace: A Public Purpose for Punitive Damages?' (2008) 2 *Charlston Law Review* 327, 339 fns 67–69.

[33] *Grey v Grant* (1764) 2 Wils KB 252, 253; 95 ER 794, 795; *Merest v Harvey* (1814) 5 Taunt 442, 444; 128 ER 761; DD Ellis, 'Fairness and Efficiency in the Law of Punitive Damages' (1982) 56 *Southern California Law Review* 1, 17–18.

[34] The justification of exemplary damages as a means of peacekeeping has been called 'old-fashioned' by M Tilbury, 'Factors Inflating Damages Awards' in PD Finn (ed), *Essays on Damages* (Sydney, 1992) 103.

[35] CJ Robinette, 'Peace: A Public Purpose for Punitive Damages?' (2008) 2 *Char LR* 327, 340. The heightened role of the criminal law has also been stressed by DD Ellis, 'Fairness and Efficiency in the Law of Punitive Damages' (1982) 56 *S Cal L Rev* 1, 29; OW Holmes, *The Common Law* (London, 1882) 39–42.

[36] eg *Lister v Hesley Hall Ltd* [2001] UKHL 22, [2002] 1 AC 215; *Majrowski v Guy's and St Thomas's NHS Trust* [2006] UKHL 34, [2007] 1 AC 224.

[37] eg *Racz v Home Office* [1994] 2 AC 45 (HL).

[38] See the cases cited by A Burrows, *Remedies for Torts and Breach of Contract*, 3rd edn (Oxford, 2004) 412, and above ch 14, III B.

[39] The chief constable's vicarious liability is now laid down in the Police Act 1996 s 88(1).

[40] *Thompson v Metropolitan Police Commissioner* [1998] QB 498 (CA) 512–13 (Lord Woolf MR); *Kuddus v Chief Constable of Leicestershire* [2001] UKHL 29, [2002] 2 AC 122 [79], [94] (Lord Hutton), [123]–[139] (Lord Scott).

courts have never really discussed the issue[41] since defendants have never argued that vicarious liability excludes liability to pay exemplary damages.[42] The Law Commission has recommended no change to the law in that respect.[43]

In *Kuddus v Chief Constable of Leicestershire* Lord Hutton saw an advantage of exemplary damages over criminal punishment in that tort allows vicarious liability to a much wider extent than the criminal law.[44] With regard to misconduct by police officers or soldiers he advanced the following argument. An award of exemplary damages against the officers in command is an effective deterrent because it brings home to them that discipline must be maintained at all times. In addition, it is sometimes impossible to identify the individual wrongdoer so that criminal proceedings cannot be brought against him whereas exemplary damages may be awarded against the chief constable or the Minister of Defence on the basis of vicarious liability.

One might be tempted to defeat Lord Hutton's argument with the suggestion that the criminal law adopt the tortious concept of vicarious liability. This suggestion would be unrealistic however. 'The criminal law contains nothing like the general doctrine of vicarious liability that we know from tort',[45] and even though the criminal law does recognise vicarious liability in certain limited situations,[46] it is unlikely to adopt a general concept of vicarious liability comparable to the tortious one. It is not an appealing concept that a person should be subject to criminal sanctions including imprisonment for a crime committed by another person.

Lord Hutton's argument fails nonetheless. First, the deterrent effect he ascribes to vicarious liability to pay exemplary damages is not that apparent, particularly not in the situations he referred to. Damages awarded on the basis of vicarious liability against a police force or the Ministry of Defence will be paid out of tax funds and not by the chief constable or the minister personally. Therefore, the assertion that exemplary awards against the state can have a deterrent effect seems to be unrealistic and was even called 'fanciful' by Lord Scott in *Kuddus*.[47] Of course, frequent or high awards of exemplary damages will be accompanied by an intensive media attention which may exert enormous pressure on a member of government or a chief constable. But the media attention will result from the severity of the conduct in question rather than from the exemplary award as such.

---

[41] Noted in *Kuddus v Chief Constable of Leicestershire* [2001] UKHL 29, [2002] 2 AC 122 [126] (Lord Scott).

[42] Noted by the Law Commission, 'Aggravated, Exemplary and Restitutionary Damages' (Law Com No 247, 1997) [5.209].

[43] ibid [5.212]–[5.224].

[44] [2001] UKHL 29, [2002] 2 AC 122 [79]; above ch 14, VI.

[45] AP Simester and GR Sullivan, *Criminal Law: Theory and Doctrine*, 3rd edn (Oxford, 2007) 247.

[46] See ibid 248–55.

[47] [2001] UKHL 29, [2002] 2 AC 122 [108]. See also DD Ellis, 'Fairness and Efficiency in the Law of Punitive Damages' (1982) 56 *S Cal L Rev* 1, 65–66.

Secondly, the concept of vicarious liability to pay exemplary damages may itself be challenged. The concept is clearly intolerable if exemplary damages are regarded as a criminal fine in the guise of a civil remedy,[48] for on this basis the application of the wider tortious concept of vicarious liability circumvents the restrictions upon vicarious liability in the criminal law. But even if an award of exemplary damages is regarded as being different in nature from criminal punishment, it still forms a kind of punishment. Punishing employers for wrongs committed by their employees seems defensible only where the wrong was in some way facilitated by lack of proper supervision.[49] But it cannot be said that all instances of misconduct on the part of police officers or soldiers, to take Lord Hutton's example, result from lack of supervision. As Lord Woolf MR said in *Thompson v Metropolitan Police Commissioner*:

> The fact that the defendant is a chief officer of police also means that here exemplary damages should have a lesser role to play. Even if the use of civil proceedings to punish a defendant can in some circumstances be justified it is more difficult to justify the award where the defendant and the person responsible for meeting any award is not the wrongdoer but his 'employer.' While it is possible that a chief constable could bear a responsibility for what has happened, due to his failure to exercise proper control, the instances where this is alleged to have occurred should not be frequent.[50]

If the ambit of exemplary damages were to be widened, the concept of vicarious liability to pay exemplary damages would primarily affect private companies rather than the state. In the case of private companies too, the concept of punishing the employer for wrongs committed by its employees rests on shaky ground. Mitchell Polinsky and Shavell offer the following arguments why.[51] First, it may be difficult to identify the employees responsible for the wrong. Secondly, where the culpable employees *are* identifiable, they will already face internal sanctions because of the company's liability to pay compensation. An additional award of exemplary damages against the firm may not significantly increase these sanctions. Thirdly, since decisions in companies are often made by many individuals, it may be that no one individual has the full knowledge of the risk created and thus of the culpability of the joint actions.[52] Finally, an award of exemplary damages against a company may penalise its shareholders and,

---

[48] For the debate on that issue see above I in this chapter.

[49] The opposite view is taken by RW Hodgin and E Veitch, 'Punitive Damages—Reassessed' (1972) 21 *International Commercial Law Quarterly* 119, 128–29.

[50] [1998] QB 498 (CA) 512–13. Similarly *Kuddus v Chief Constable of Leicestershire* [2001] UKHL 29, [2002] 2 AC 122 [128]–[137] (Lord Scott).

[51] A Mitchell Polinsky and S Shavell, 'Punitive Damages: An Economic Analysis' (1998) 111 *Harvard Law Review* 869, 950–52. Similarly DD Ellis, 'Fairness and Efficiency in the Law of Punitive Damages' (1982) 56 *S Cal L Rev* 1, 66–71.

[52] 'One person may decide to put a toxic liquid in a storage tank, believing that the tank can never leak, and another person may leave the tank in a state in which a leak can occur, thinking that the liquid in the tank is not toxic, so that a leak would not cause harm': A Mitchell Polinsky and S Shavell, ibid 951.

through increased product prices, its customers. Passive shareholders and customers can seldom be blamed for misconduct by the company's employees.

IV Need for Exemplary Damages

A The Long-Standing Practice of Exemplary Awards

Is there a need for exemplary damages? A need seems to be evidenced by the
practice of awarding exemplary damages for almost 250 years.[53] This practice will
now be scrutinised. In *Rookes v Barnard* Lord Devlin identified two categories in
which exemplary damages had previously been awarded (the third category of
express authorisation by statute having little practical importance): abuse of
power by public servants and profit-seeking behaviour.[54] The award of exemplary
damages in these categories seems to have been a reaction to defects in other
areas of law. Remedying those defects would remove the need for exemplary
damages 'helping out'.

The award of exemplary damages in the first category has obviously been a
response to shortcomings in the criminal system, for the committing of a serious
wrong by a public servant ought to be a crime and be prosecuted as such. Indeed,
the failure to prosecute government servants triggered the first ever awards of
exemplary damages.[55] King George III and his ministers sought to stop the
publication of the critical weekly paper *The North Briton*. On the basis of an
illegal warrant granted by the secretary of state, king's messengers raided the
homes of the editor and the printer of the paper and imprisoned the latter for six
hours. Considering who initiated the actions, there was of course no criminal
prosecution against the messengers. But the government could not escape civil
suits in which the juries marked their disapproval of the government's actions by
awarding exemplary damages.

Today, exemplary damages cannot be justified as a means of making good
deficiencies in the criminal law. As Cane observes, 'if the criminal law is deficient,
it would be better to work for its reform than for the wider availability of civil
fines'.[56] Proponents of exemplary damages assert that the criminal law and

---

[53] 'To abolish exemplary damages would be to fly in the face of the traditions of the common law,
for common law judges have long found exemplary damages to be useful': Law Commission,
'Aggravated, Exemplary and Restitutionary Damages' (Law Com No 247, 1997) [5.27]. Similarly NJ
McBride, 'Punitive Damages' in P Birks (ed), *Wrongs and Remedies in the Twenty-First Century*
(Oxford, 1996) 176–77.

[54] [1964] AC 1129 (HL) 1225–27; above ch 14, II.

[55] *Huckle v Money* (1763) 2 Wils KB 205, 95 ER 768; *Wilkes v Wood* (1763) Lofft 1, 98 ER 489.

[56] P Cane, 'Exceptional Measures of Damages: A Search for Principles' in P Birks (ed), *Wrongs and
Remedies in the Twenty-First Century* (Oxford, 1996) 309.

criminal-justice system will always be imperfect.[57] If this is true, it must be equally true for the civil-justice system and the law of exemplary damages. Why, then, should shortcomings of the criminal regime be filled by an equally imperfect regime of exemplary damages, instead of making the criminal law as good as possible and accepting the imperfections that inevitably remain?

The award of exemplary damages in the category of profit-seeking behaviour may be due to the fact that the law of 'restitution for wrongs', discussed in chapter 12, has developed in a piecemeal fashion. It is suggested in chapter 13 that gain-based relief should be available whenever an asset exclusively reserved for one person is used by another person without authorisation. This definition includes the two main situations in which exemplary damages have been awarded in the second category: the unlawful eviction of protected tenants and defamation.[58] While gain-based relief in cases of defamation is not (yet) recognised, damages for unlawful eviction may now be measured according to the increase in the property's value resulting from the eviction.[59] A full implementation of this book's suggestions on gain-based relief may remove the need, if any, of exemplary damages in the second category.

Whichever view is taken on the proper scope of 'restitution for wrongs', Lord Devlin's second category is redundant. Where it is thought inappropriate to strip the defendant of the profit made from the wrong, one must deny not only a gain-based remedy but also an award of exemplary damages that aims to strip the defendant of the profit. Conversely, where it is thought appropriate to strip the defendant of the profit, this should be achieved through a 'tailored' gain-based remedy rather than the 'blunt instrument'[60] of exemplary damages under Lord Devlin's second category.[61] Where persons contemplating whether or not to engage in illegal profit-seeking activities face the prospect of losing all profit through a gain-based remedy, they will in most cases abstain from committing

---

[57] Law Commission, 'Aggravated, Exemplary and Restitutionary Damages' (Law Com No 247, 1997) [5.27]; RW Hodgin and E Veitch, 'Punitive Damages—Reassessed' (1972) 21 *ICLQ* 119, 131; NJ McBride, 'Punitive Damages' in P Birks (ed), ibid 192–93; PW Michalik, 'The availability of compensatory and exemplary damages in equity: A note on the *Aquaculture* decision' (1991) 21 *Victoria University of Wellington Law Review* 391, 410.

[58] For awards of exemplary damages in those situations see above ch 14, IV A; for gain-based relief in those situations see above ch 13, III A and C.

[59] Housing Act 1988 s 28; *Jones v Miah* (1992) 24 HLR 578 (CA) 587.

[60] M Tilbury, 'Factors Inflating Damages Awards' in PD Finn (ed), *Essays on Damages* (Sydney, 1992) 104.

[61] J Berryman, 'The Case for Restitutionary Damages over Punitive Damages: Teaching the Wrongdoer that Tort Does Not Pay' (1994) 73 *Canadian Bar Review* 320, 345; P Cane, 'Exceptional Measures of Damages: A Search for Principles' in P Birks (ed), *Wrongs and Remedies in the Twenty-First Century* (Oxford, 1996) 305; H McGregor, *McGregor on Damages*, 18th edn (London, 2009) [11–029], who calls exemplary damages 'a somewhat makeshift and arbitrary method' and a 'rather clumsy device'; J Stone, 'Double Count and Double Talk: The End of Exemplary Damages?' (1972) 46 *Australian Law Journal* 311, 325–26.

the wrong.[62] Some may still act, relying on the chance of not being detected and pursued.[63] But those wrongdoers may not be deterred by exemplary damages either.

The Law Commission insists on the need for exemplary damages with the argument that a gain-based remedy clutches at thin air where the defendant, although intending to make a profit, failed to do so.[64] Of course, a gain-based remedy is unavailable where there is no gain to be given up. But, again, where potential wrongdoers know that if they do make a profit they will have to disgorge it, most of them will not commit the wrong in the first place. Where further deterrence is needed, the wrong concerned ought to be made a crime.

B   The Law Commission's Ten Examples

The Law Commission attempts to demonstrate a need for exemplary damages by giving 10 practical examples,[65] which will now be scrutinised. Each example will be sketched (the Commission provides more vivid illustrations), and it will be asked whether or not exemplary damages are in fact needed. It should be noted that in the view of the Law Commission exemplary damages are currently available in the first four examples but not in the others.

In the first example, police officers arrest and detain a man without grounds. They use excessive force, fabricate evidence and bring a prosecution that fails. Misconduct by police officers is a notorious example for the need of exemplary damages. An obvious objection is that since serious misconduct constitutes a criminal offence, the availability of criminal prosecution and disciplinary measures should sufficiently deter. In the past, however, these measures did not always prove effective. This may have changed since the establishment of the Independent Police Complaints Commission,[66] which may supervise the police investigation into a case and may carry out investigations into serious incidents or allegations of police misconduct. The need for exemplary damages, if any, should accordingly vanish.

In the second example, a newspaper publishes a sensationalist story, knowing it to be false, about a teacher who had a sexual relationship with an under-age pupil who became pregnant. The newspaper does so in order to boost its circulation. In

---

[62]   PW Michalik, 'The availability of compensatory and exemplary damages in equity: A note on the *Aquaculture* decision' (1991) 21 *VUWLR* 391, 411; J Stone, ibid.

[63]   As pointed out in *Cassell & Co Ltd v Broome* [1972] AC 1027 (HL) 1130 (Lord Diplock); J Glover, *Commercial Equity: Fiduciary Relationships* (Sydney, 1995) [6.129]; D Jensen, 'Punitive Damages for Breach of Fiduciary Obligation' (1996) 19 *University of Queensland Law Journal* 125, 132–33.

[64]   Law Commission, 'Aggravated, Exemplary and Restitutionary Damages' (Law Com No 247, 1997) [5.27]. See also A Phang and PW Lee, 'Restitutionary and Exemplary Damages Revisited' (2003) 19 *Journal of Contract Law* 1, 36.

[65]   Law Commission, 'Aggravated, Exemplary and Restitutionary Damages' (Law Com No 247, 1997) [1.24].

[66]   By virtue of the Police Reform Act 2002 s 9.

his action for defamation, the teacher is unable to establish that his story led to a measurable increase in the newspaper's profit. This book suggests that gain-based relief should be available in cases of defamation. In general, the teacher would have to prove that the newspaper has gained from the story, but the court could be allowed to make a generous estimation of that profit just as the court may estimate a claimant's loss. A victim of libel could also be given the right to get a retraction of the story published by the newspaper at the same place and with the same layout as the original false story. Libel is further a criminal offence[67] punishable by imprisonment of two years if the libel was known to be false[68] (as in this example) and one year in other cases.[69] Prosecution of libel is rare and has been described as 'an option only to be resorted to in comparatively exceptional circumstances'.[70] But this could be changed at least where the libel is known to be false. Exemplary damages are not needed.

In the third example, a medical practitioner carries out large-scale, intrusive and unnecessary surgery on a private patient in order to obtain a higher fee. In tort law, the doctor's fraud vitiates the patient's consent and renders the doctor liable in battery.[71] In criminal law, the patient's consent is valid[72] and the doctor cannot be charged with assault occasioning actual bodily harm but can probably be charged with deception. Furthermore, the General Medical Council can withdraw the doctor's licence to practise on the ground of unfitness. All these sanctions appear to be sufficiently deterrent.[73]

In the fourth example,[74] a photographer takes photos at a wedding. When later the murder of the groom's father attracts wide publicity, the photographer sells copies of the wedding photos to the national press, thereby infringing the groom's copyright. Here, the photographer and, if the *mens rea* is present, also the people publishing the photos in the press have committed a criminal offence pursuant to section 107(1) of the Copyright, Designs and Patents Act 1988. If need be, the criminal sanctions could be tightened. Exemplary damages are not needed.

---

[67] See eg, *Gleaves v Insall* [1999] EMLR 779 (DC).

[68] Libel Act 1843 s 4.

[69] Libel Act 1843 s 5.

[70] *Gleaves v Insall* [1999] EMLR 779 (DC) 783 (Kennedy LJ).

[71] *Chatterton v Gerson* [1981] QB 432, 443; *Sidaway v Board of Governors of the Bethlem Royal Hospital and the Maudsley Hospital* [1984] QB 493 (CA) 511 (Sir John Donaldson MR); *Freeman v Home Office (No 2)* [1984] QB 524 (QBD) 537; [1984] QB 543 (CA) 556 (Sir John Donaldson MR); *Re T (Adult: Refusal of Treatment)* [1993] Fam 95 (CA) 115 (Lord Donaldson MR); *Appleton v Garrett* (1995) 34 BMLR 23, 26.

[72] *R v Richardson (Diane)* [1999] QB 444 (CA) 450.

[73] The deterrent effect of compensatory damages is stressed by J Stone, 'Double Count and Double Talk: The End of Exemplary Damages?' (1972) 46 *ALJ* 311, 323–26.

[74] Based on the facts of *Williams v Settle* [1960] 1 WLR 1072 (CA), where exemplary damages of £1,000 were awarded against the photographer by virtue of what is now the Copyright, Designs and Patents Act 1988 s 97(2). It has since become very doubtful, however, whether s 97(2) really authorises exemplary damages: above ch 14, V.

In the fifth example, an employee is subjected to an enduring campaign of racial harassment by fellow employees ranging from taunting to violence. She complains to her employer to no avail. Victims of racial harassment may claim compensation for their loss, pecuniary and otherwise, under the anti-discrimination and the anti-harassment legislation.[75] Employers are vicariously liable for harassment committed by their employees in the course of the employment.[76] In a case fitting the fifth example, the victim was awarded £20,000 for injured feelings and £7,500 aggravated damages against his employer.[77] Harassment also constitutes a criminal offence.[78] Racial motivation increases the maximum penalties for harassment and violent offences[79] and forms an aggravating factor in sentencing for all offences.[80] There is now a wide range of sanctions for racial harassment which need not be supplemented by exemplary damages.

In the sixth example, a private store detective accuses a shopper of shoplifting without basis, forces her to undergo an intrusive bodily search and fabricates evidence. The shop initiates a private prosecution against the shopper, which fails. Since the shop is vicariously liable for the torts (assault, false imprisonment) committed by the detective, the latter faces dismissal which should sufficiently deter.

In the seventh example, an employer decides to save the money for installing proper health and safety measures, as a result of which some employees suffer respiratory problems. Health and safety on business premises is supervised by the authorities who can respond to shortcomings by a variety of tools, ranging from issuing a warning, issuing and publishing an improvement or prohibition notice, withdrawal of approval, variation of licence, and formal caution, to criminal prosecution. This regime seems to be effective. Should it not be, it would be better to tighten up the tools of the health and safety authorities than to award exemplary damages.

In the eighth example, an ex-employee of a software company sets up a rival business, using information that he obtained in confidence during his former employment. This is a breach of confidence remediable through an account of profits, damages or an injunction.[81] Serious breaches could be made a crime. Indeed, the Law Commission itself has, in a consultation paper, provisionally

---

[75] Race Relations Act 1976 s 57; Protection from Harassment Act 1997 s 3.

[76] *Majrowski v Guy's and St Thomas's NHS Trust* [2006] UKHL 34, [2007] 1 AC 224.

[77] *HM Prison Service v Johnson* [1997] ICR 275 (EAT).

[78] Protection from Harassment Act 1997 s 2. For harassment outside a dwelling also the Public Order Act 1986 ss 4A, 5.

[79] Crime and Disorder Act 1998 ss 29–32.

[80] Criminal Justice Act 2003 s 145.

[81] *Ocular Sciences Ltd v Aspect Vision Care Ltd* [1997] RPC 289, 394–416; *Attorney-General v Blake (Jonathan Cape Ltd Third Party)* [2001] 1 AC 268 (HL) 278 ff. For an account of profits see above ch 12, III B.

concluded that there is 'a strong case for criminalisation'.[82] Furthermore, the former employer could have stipulated for a clause in the employment contract prohibiting the employee from working in the same industry for a certain period after the end of the employment. Such a restrictive covenant is valid if it is reasonable,[83] particularly with regard to its duration, its geographical scope, and the type of the activities prohibited.[84] Employers cannot currently enforce a contractual clause requiring employees to pay a penalty should they breach the contract.[85] But there have been calls for making reasonable penalty clauses enforceable.[86] Allowing parties to agree in advance on the availability and amount of a penalty in the case of breach is preferable to an unpredictable award of exemplary damages.

In the ninth example,[87] a source of drinking water is contaminated. The water authority deliberately misinforms its customers, as a result of which some of them become ill. After the privatisation of the water industry, the quality of drinking water in England and Wales is now monitored by the Drinking Water Inspectorate which carries out regular tests and investigates contamination incidents. Water companies that fail to maintain the standard required may be prosecuted. Should the current monitoring regime be insufficiently rigorous, it could be tightened. Increasing the controls of water quality and thus keeping the water companies on a short leash may be more effective than a threat of exemplary damages.

In the tenth and final example, a solicitor dishonestly assists a company director in laundering company funds. To bar the argument that criminal punishment is available here, the description of the example goes on to state that the solicitor acts in a way that renders it impossible in practice to establish that a criminal offence has been committed. However, since the solicitor could not be sure of escaping criminal prosecution when he contemplated whether or not to engage in the illegal activities, the criminal law does have some deterrent effect. More importantly, the example assumes—since the issue of exemplary damages would not arise otherwise—that the director's breach of fiduciary duty and the solicitor's assisting in the breach can be proven. This means that professional misconduct on the part of the solicitor is established. The Solicitors Disciplinary Tribunal can respond to such conduct through a variety of sanctions ranging from reprimand, fine, and suspension, to striking the solicitor off the Roll. These sanctions are certainly more deterrent than exemplary damages.[88]

---

[82] Law Commission, 'Legislating the Criminal Code: Misuse of Trade Secrets' (Law Com Consultation Paper No 150, 1997) [1.28].

[83] *Nordenfelt v The Maxim Nordenfelt Guns and Ammunition Co Ltd* [1894] AC 535 (HL).

[84] *Scully UK Ltd v Lee* [1998] IRLR 259 (CA) 261–64 (Aldous LJ).

[85] *Murray v Leisureplay plc* [2005] EWCA Civ 963, [2005] IRLR 946.

[86] Above ch 13, V B.

[87] Based on the facts of *AB v South West Water Services Ltd* [1993] QB 507 (CA); above ch 14, VI.

[88] A deterrent effect of exemplary awards in equity is also doubted by V Vann, *Equitable Compensation in Australia: Principles and Problems* (Saarbrücken, 2009) 358–59.

In conclusion, the 10 examples demonstrate just the contrary of what they are meant to demonstrate. Exemplary damages are *not* needed.

C Comparative View

If exemplary damages were needed in England and Wales, one would expect to find them in all other countries with a similar state of economy and society, particularly in Scotland and Continental Europe. Yet exemplary damages are unique to systems of law derived from the law of England and Wales or closely associated with it.[89] They are unheard of in most civil law jurisdictions and in Scotland.[90] If Scotland can manage without exemplary damages, they are hardly needed in the rest of the United Kingdom.

V Conclusion

The key question of whether punishment imposed by the state is reserved for the criminal law, is almost an issue of faith and shall remain undecided. Policy arguments ought to clinch matters. But no compelling policy argument appears on either side. Considering that the parallel availability of both civil and criminal punishment does generate conflicts on a practical level,[91] and that courts throughout the common law world have acknowledged the unusual nature of civil punishment,[92] exemplary damages should be abolished unless there exists an undeniable need for them. Such a need cannot be found. In a 'close finish', the case for the abolition of exemplary damages prevails over the case for their retention.

[89] M Tilbury, 'Factors Inflating Damages Awards' in PD Finn (ed), *Essays on Damages* (Sydney, 1992) 100; GH Treitel, *Remedies for Breach of Contract: A Comparative Account* (Oxford, 1988) [78].

[90] A Burrows, 'Reforming Exemplary Damages: Expansion or Abolition?' in P Birks (ed), *Wrongs and Remedies in the Twenty-First Century* (Oxford, 1996) 157.

[91] While the 'no double punishment' rule seems to exclude exemplary damages where the defendant has already been convicted and punished in the criminal system for the conduct in question (*Archer v Brown* [1985] QB 401, 423), it is unclear whether an *acquittal* in criminal proceedings bars a subsequent claim for exemplary damages for the same conduct. An affirmative answer was given in *W v W* [1999] 2 NZLR 1 (PC). The correlation between a criminal conviction on an exemplary damages award for the same conduct is discussed by RW Hodgin and E Veitch, 'Punitive Damages—Reassessed' (1972) 21 *ICLQ* 119, 131.

[92] As noted in *A v Bottrill* [2002] UKPC 44, [2003] 1 AC 449 [41].

18

Conclusion

This book has challenged certain differences between contract, tort and equity with regard to the measure of damages, and has suggested a harmonisation of the relevant principles within the law of obligations. This suggestion is consistent with, but not dependent on, the idea of a fusion of common law and equity. A harmonisation of the measure of damages is generally desirable because the present differences between contract, tort and equity are awkward in cases of concurrent liability, and because a harmonisation lessens the significance of controversies on whether certain wrongs should be classified as contractual, tortious or equitable in nature. Focussing on the law of England and Wales, five aspects of the measure of damages have been discussed: remoteness of damage, non-pecuniary loss, contributory negligence, gain-based relief and exemplary damages. The main arguments were as follows.

Remoteness of damage is determined in negligence (and several other torts) and contract by considering the reasonable foreseeability of the loss in question. Liability is narrower in contract where a higher degree of foresight is required ('not unlikely' or 'serious possibility' as opposed to 'possible unless it can be brushed aside as far fetched' in tort) and where foreseeability is judged not at the time of the wrong (the breach) but at the time of the contract. The additional hurdles in contract are said to foster efficiency because they give contracting parties an incentive to inform each other about the prospect of unusually high loss in the event of breach, which allows an optimisation of precautions against breach. This argument is dubious. Opponents assert that the present remoteness test is neither necessary nor sufficient to achieve efficiency. It is not necessary because the promisor can control the extent of his expected liability by offering a menu with different liability-price-packages. It is not sufficient because a revelation of unusual circumstances may still be prevented by the cost involved or the prospect of being exploited by a stronger contract-partner. Since a harmonisation of the measure of damages within the common law is desirable, the remoteness test in contract should be aligned with the one in negligence.

A difference to the remoteness test in negligence is also undesirable for equity save for a trustee's obligation to make good unauthorised disbursement, which is more akin to the specific performance of a contract and thus not subject to remoteness doctrine. Contract and equity should therefore adopt the remoteness test applied in negligence. Throughout the law of obligations, the foreseeability test is, or should be, subject to the overriding criterion that loss cannot be compensated unless it falls within the scope of the duty breached. Remoteness of damage should therefore be determined, in contract, tort and equity, by the following principles. Loss is too remote if it falls outside the scope of the duty breached. Absent special considerations relating to the particular duty in question, loss is recoverable if a reasonable person in the position of the wrongdoer could, at the time of the wrong, have foreseen the type of loss as possible unless it could have been brushed aside as far fetched.

Non-pecuniary loss is compensable in contract and tort to the same extent where it results from personal injury or physical inconvenience. But the 'litmus test' for the attitude towards non-pecuniary loss in general is the treatment of non-physical distress (also called injured feelings) and mere loss of reputation. While contract allows compensation for these forms of loss only where their prevention was a major object of the contract breached, tort shows a much more generous attitude, although it has yet to be recognised that distress is generally recoverable in negligence (provided that the defendant's conduct is actionable) and that recovery for loss of reputation is not confined to the tort of defamation.

The restrictive attitude of contract has been defended on several grounds but it essentially comes down to the fear of a floodgate of litigation. This fear is unfounded, for the flood can be stemmed through a strict application of the *de minimis* principle and of the doctrines of remoteness and mitigation. It follows that contract should be aligned with tort. Equity should follow suit as there is no reason for equity to be more restrictive than the common law. Indeed, the compensability of non-pecuniary loss is already recognised for breach of confidence including 'breach of privacy'. Subject to the usual limitations of liability such as remoteness of damage, non-pecuniary loss that is not *de minimis* should be generally compensable throughout the law of obligations.

Contributory negligence denotes the claimant's contribution to the occurrence of the wrong or the ensuing loss through unreasonable conduct prior to (the claimant becoming aware of) the wrong. Apart from the Law Reform (Contributory Negligence) Act 1945, contributory negligence is in general a complete defence to many torts while not affecting liability in contract or equity. The 1945 Act replaced the tortious defence with an apportionment of liability according to each party's share in the responsibility for the loss. The concept that a claimant guilty of contributory negligence should bear a part of her loss is of immediate appeal. It is fair and just, and it fosters efficiency by giving the claimant an incentive to take cost-efficient precautions.

Stretching its wording to the limit, the 1945 Act may be applied to all torts and to those breaches of contract where the contract-breaker has been at fault or is concurrently liable in tort. The courts already apply the Act to contractual liability where a duty of care co-extensive in contract and tort has been breached. But there is no justification for withholding apportionment from other instances of contractual liability. In particular, the risk of uncertainty seems to have been exaggerated. Nor is it justified to withhold apportionment from equity. There should be a general principle throughout the law of obligations that the compensation awardable for a wrong may be reduced according to each party's share in the responsibility for the damage.

The three issues mentioned concern the compensation of loss suffered by victims of wrongs. This book has also asked when wrongdoers are, and should be, ordered to give up the profit made from the wrong, and when exemplary (or punitive) damages are, and should be, available.

Gain-based relief in the form of an account of profits is available in actions for breach of fiduciary duty, (deliberate) breach of confidence (in its core meaning) and probably also breach of confidence in its extended meaning ('breach of privacy'). Various types of gain-based awards have been made in cases of 'proprietary torts', that is wrongful interference with goods, trespass to land, and intellectual property wrongs. Most important is the 'user principle': Where property is temporarily misappropriated, damages can be assessed by reference to a reasonable licence fee, even where the parties would not in fact have negotiated a licence agreement had they met beforehand. The nature of hypothetical-fee awards is controversial, but such awards are best characterised as being gain-based. Gain-based relief is unavailable in actions for deceit (unless the contract is rescinded), defamation, trespass to the person, or nuisance other than infringement of easements. With regard to breach of contract, hypothetical-fee awards have been made in cases involving breach of a restrictive covenant and some other cases, and the exceptional availability of an account of profits has also been recognised.

There are many different theories as to the proper scope of 'restitution for wrongs'. Under a widespread view, gain-based awards in actions for civil wrongs can be justified by the maxim 'wrongdoers must not profit from their wrongs', and 'wrong' in this context is effectively defined as conduct triggering a compensatory remedy. But it cannot be explained why the requirements for being liable to pay compensation should be either sufficient (even if a certain degree of culpability is additionally required) or necessary for ordering a wrongdoer to give up the profit that was made from the wrong and is still left after paying compensation. Gain-based relief can only be justified where there is a link between the claimant and the defendant's gain.

This link is the fact that the defendant made the gain by exploiting, without authorisation, an asset exclusively reserved for the claimant. Such an exclusive entitlement can be either *erga omnes* (for instance tangible and intangible property, right to bodily integrity, right to reputation and informational rights) or *inter partes* (for instance the contractual right to have property transferred and the right to the loyalty of one's fiduciary). What many call 'restitution for wrongs' should thus be available if, and only if, an exclusive entitlement has been infringed, whether or not the defendant's conduct triggers a compensatory remedy. The claim for the defendant's gain should be characterised as a claim in autonomous unjust enrichment rather than a claim for a wrong as such.

Exemplary (or punitive) damages are currently confined to three categories of tortious behaviour: abuse of power by public servants, profit-seeking behaviour and cases where exemplary damages are authorised by statute. While the last category is negligible, the first two cannot be justified on principle. Private persons such as large companies or trade unions can be as oppressive as public servants, and between greedy and malicious conduct it is difficult to choose the more reprehensible. Reform is needed. Any reform must be in line with the objectives that exemplary damages pursue. These have traditionally been retribution, deterrence and denunciation. There have been attempts to explain exemplary damages primarily on the basis of efficient deterrence, defining their purpose as, for instance, the correction for undercompensation or underenforcement. But none of the economic models offers a comprehensive and robust account of exemplary damages. The traditional, punitive concept still leads the way.

If exemplary damages are retained, can they defensibly be confined to tort and excluded per se, without considering the merits of the individual case, from contract and equity? The main pro-ban argument in relation to contract is the protection of efficient breaches. But this argument cannot explain the exclusion of exemplary damages from all breaches of contract regardless of their efficiency. It also faces substantial objections, in particular the reference to the cost of litigation and the social cost of a weakened confidence in contractual promises. In relation to equity, a ban of exemplary damages cannot be defended on other than purely historical grounds. Accordingly, if exemplary damages were to be put on a principled basis, their ambit should extend beyond tort to contract and equity. They would then be uniformly available in all cases of egregious conduct.

But should exemplary damages be retained or should they be abolished? The key question of whether punishment imposed by the state is reserved for the criminal law is almost an issue of belief and has been left open. Nor are there compelling policy arguments either way. Since a practical conflict between civil and criminal punishment is undeniable, exemplary damages should be abolished unless they are definitely needed. Such a need cannot be shown given that Continental Europe and indeed Scotland manage perfectly without them. Exemplary damages should therefore be unavailable throughout the law of obligations.

The categories of damages available in response to a wrong should therefore include neither exemplary (punitive) damages, which should be abolished, nor gain-based damages because all instances of gain-based relief ought to be conceptualised as instances of autonomous unjust enrichment and never as a response to a wrong as such. If nominal damages were replaced with a judicial declaration that a wrong has been committed, and if, as the Law Commission has suggested, aggravated damages were reconceptualised as compensation for non-pecuniary loss, the only significant type of damages left would be compensatory damages. Both (common law) damages and equitable compensation could then be simply called compensation.

While the abolition of exemplary damages would be a change of paradigm, the other changes in the measure of damages suggested in this book are by no means revolutionary. With regard to remoteness of damage, the present differences between contract, tort and equity are not as huge as they may seem. With regard to non-pecuniary loss, a lifting of the general bar which exists for breach of contract and may exist for equitable wrongs other than breach of confidence (or 'breach of privacy') would not lead to a flood of awards, at least not under a rigid *de minimis* rule. With regard to contributory negligence, an extension of the apportionment regime to equitable wrongs and all types of breach of contract should not significantly increase the number of cases dealing with unreasonable behaviour on the claimant's part, not least because the general availability of apportionment would obviate the need to consider unreasonable claimant behaviour under the guise of causation, remoteness or mitigation. With regard to gain-based relief, an adoption of the exclusive-entitlement theory advocated in this book would not require the courts to reject gain-based relief in circumstances in which it is already recognised. However, it would require the courts to recognise gain-based relief in cases of defamation and trespass to the person.

Who should effect the proposed changes in the measure of damages—the courts or the legislator? It depends on the aspect of measure. Legislation seems required for an abolition of exemplary damages or, alternatively, for their introduction into contract and equity. The House of Lords has considered exemplary damages on several occasions and seems unable to reform them either way. It is unfortunate and indeed difficult to understand that the government has recently shelved the reform of exemplary damages on the ground that it awaits further judicial clarification of the law.

Legislation is further required for making an apportionment of liability on the ground of contributory negligence available throughout the law of obligations. The Law Reform (Contributory Negligence) Act 1945 cannot, even under the most stretched interpretation, be generally applied to contract or equity. Since the common law is effectively, if incorrectly, regarded as 'frozen' in its 1945 state, the development of a general apportionment regime at common law cannot be expected. The 1945 Act should be replaced by legislation which allows apportionment throughout the law of obligations and also clarifies the issues controversial under the 1945 Act.

Legislation is neither necessary nor desirable for remoteness of damage, non-pecuniary loss and gain-based relief. It is not necessary because those three aspects of the measure of damages have seen considerable changes over the past 150 years without legislative intervention and have thus proven to be open to judicial development. Legislation is not even desirable because prescribing a uniform regime by statute would not only harmonise the principles but may also 'freeze' them. The harmonised principles should remain open to further (uniform) development.

Bibliography

Aitken, L, 'Developments in Equitable Compensation: Opportunity or Danger?' (1993) 67 *Australian Law Journal* 596

Andrews, NH, 'No Apportionment for Contributory Negligence in Contract' [1986] *Cambridge Law Journal* 8

Ayres, I, and Gertner, R, 'Filling Gaps in Incomplete Contracts: An Economic Theory of Default Rules' (1989) 99 *Yale Law Journal* 87

—'Strategic Contractual Inefficiency and the Optimal Choice of Legal Rules' (1992) 101 *Yale Law Journal* 729

Bainbridge, DI, *Intellectual Property*, 6th edn (Harlow, Pearson Longman, 2007)

Baker, JH, *An Introduction to English Legal History*, 4th edn (London, Butterworths, 2002)

Bant, E, and Harding, M (eds), *Exploring Private Law* (Cambridge, Cambridge University Press, 2010), forthcoming

Barnes, DW, 'The Anatomy of Contract Damages and Efficient Breach Theory' (1998) 6 *Southern California Interdisciplinary Law Journal* 397

Barnett, K, 'Deterrence and Disgorging Profits for Breach of Contract' (2009) 17 *Restitution Law Review* 79

Barrett, MJ, '"Contort": Tortious Breach of the Implied Covenant of Good Faith and Fair Dealing in Noninsurance, Commercial Contracts—Its Existence and Desirability' (1985) 60 *Notre Dame Law Review* 510

Beale, HG (gen ed), *Chitty on Contracts, Vol 1: General Principles*, 30th edn (London, Sweet & Maxwell, 2008)

Beatson, J, *Anson's Law of Contract*, 28th edn (Oxford, Oxford University Press, 2002)

—*The Use and Abuse of Unjust Enrichment: Essays on the Law of Restitution* (Oxford, Clarendon Press, 1991)

Bebchuk, LA, and Shavell, S, 'Information and the Scope of Liability for Breach of Contract: The Rule of *Hadley v Baxendale*' (1991) 7 *Journal of Law, Economics and Organization* 284

Bently, L, and Sherman, B, *Intellectual Property Law*, 3rd edn (Oxford, Oxford University Press, 2009)

Berg, A, 'Bribery—transaction validity and other civil law implications' [2001] *Lloyd's Maritime and Commercial Law Quarterly* 27

Berryman, J, 'Equitable Compensation for Breach by Fact-Based Fiduciaries: Tentative Thoughts on Clarifying Remedial Goals' (1999) 37 *Alberta Law Review* 95

—'The Case for Restitutionary Damages over Punitive Damages: Teaching the Wrongdoer that Tort Does Not Pay' (1994) 73 *Canadian Bar Review* 320

Birks, P, *An Introduction to the Law of Restitution*, revised edn (Oxford, Clarendon Press, 1989)

—'Equity in the Modern Law: An Exercise in Taxonomy' (1996) 26 *University of Western Australia Law Review* 1

Birks, P (ed), *Privacy and Loyalty* (Oxford, Clarendon Press, 1997)

—*The Classification of Obligations* (Oxford, Clarendon Press, 1997)

—*Wrongs and Remedies in the Twenty-First Century* (Oxford, Clarendon Press, 1996)

Birks, P, and Pretto, A (eds), *Breach of Trust* (Oxford, Hart Publishing, 2002)

Birks, P, and Rose, F (eds), *Restitution and Equity, Vol 1: Resulting Trusts and Equitable Compensation* (London, Mansfield Press, 2000)

Birmingham, RL, 'Breach of Contract, Damage Measures, and Economic Efficiency' (1970) 24 *Rutgers Law Review* 273

Bridge, MG, 'Contractual Damages for Intangible Loss: A Comparative Analysis' (1984) 62 *Canadian Bar Review* 323

—*The International Sale of Goods: Law and Practice*, 2nd edn (Oxford, Oxford University Press, 2007)

Burrows, A, 'Contributory Negligence in Contract: Ammunition for the Law Commission' (1993) 109 *Law Quarterly Review* 175

—*Fusing Common Law and Equity: Remedies, Restitution and Reform* (Hong Kong, Sweet & Maxwell, 2002)

—'Mental distress damages in contract—a decade of change' [1984] *Lloyd's Maritime and Commercial Law Quarterly* 119

—*Remedies for Torts and Breach of Contract*, 3rd edn (Oxford, Oxford University Press, 2004)

—*The Law of Restitution*, 2nd edn (London, Butterworths, 2002)

—'The Scope of Exemplary Damages' (1993) 109 *Law Quarterly Review* 358

—*Understanding the Law of Obligations: Essays on Contract, Tort and Restitution* (Oxford, Hart Publishing, 1998)

—'We Do This At Common Law But That In Equity' (2002) 22 *Oxford Journal of Legal Studies* 1

Burrows, A (ed), *English Private Law*, 2nd edn (Oxford, Oxford University Press, 2007)

Burrows, A, and Peel, E (eds), *Commercial Remedies: Current Issues and Problems* (Oxford, Oxford University Press, 2003)

Burrows, A, and Lord Rodger of Earlsferry (eds), *Mapping the Law: Essays in Memory of Peter Birks* (Oxford, Oxford University Press, 2006)

Cane, P, '*Mens Rea* in Tort Law' (2000) 20 *Oxford Journal of Legal Studies* 533

—*Tort Law and Economic Interests*, 2nd edn (Oxford, Clarendon Press, 1996)

Carter, JW, Peden, E, and Tolhurst, GJ, *Contract Law in Australia*, 5th edn (Chatswood, LexisNexis Butterworths, 2007)

Cartwright, J, 'Remoteness of Damage in Contract and Tort: A Reconsideration' [1996] *Cambridge Law Journal* 488

Carty, H, 'Contract Theory and Employment Reality' (1986) 49 *Modern Law Review* 240

Cavico, FJ, 'Punitive Damages for Breach of Contract—A Principled Approach' (1990) *St Mary's Law Journal* 357

Chambers, R, Mitchell, C, and Penner, J (eds), *Philosophical Foundations of the Law of Unjust Enrichment* (Oxford, Oxford University Press, 2009)

Chandler, PA, 'Contributory Negligence and Contract: Some Underlying Disparities' (1989) 40 *Northern Ireland Legal Quarterly* 152

Bibliography

Chapman, S, 'Apportionment of Liability Between Tortfeasors' (1948) 64 *Law Quarterly Review* 26

Chutorian, S, 'Tort Remedies for Breach of Contract: The Expansion of Tortious Breach of the Implied Covenant of Good Faith and Fair Dealing into the Commercial Realm' (1986) 86 *Columbia Law Review* 377

Clarke, L, 'Remedial Responses to Breach of Confidence: The Question of Damages' (2005) 24 *Civil Justice Quarterly* 316

Cohen, GM, 'The Fault Lines in Contract Damages' (1994) 80 *Virginia Law Review* 1225

Cohen, N, and McKendrick, E (eds), *Comparative Remedies for Breach of Contract* (Oxford, Hart Publishing, 2005)

Colby, TB, 'Beyond the Multiple Punishment Problem: Punitive Damages as Punishment for Individual, Private Wrongs' (2003) 87 *Minnesota Law Review* 583

Conaglen, M, 'Strict Fiduciary Loyalty and Accounts of Profits' [2006] *Cambridge Law Journal* 278

Cooke, J, and Oughton, D, *The Common Law of Obligations*, 3rd edn (London, Butterworths, 2000)

Cooke, R, 'Remoteness of Damages and Judicial Discretion' [1978] *Cambridge Law Journal* 288

Coote, B, 'Contributory Negligence Reform and the Right to Rely on a Contract' [1992] *New Zealand Recent Law Review* 313

—'Damages, *The Liesbosch*, and Impecuniosity' [2001] *Cambridge Law Journal* 511

Cooter, RD, 'Economic Analysis of Punitive Damages' (1982) 56 *Southern California Law Review* 79

Cooter, R, and Ulen, T, *Law and Economics*, 5th edn (Boston, Pearson Addison Wesley, 2008)

Corbin, AL, *Corbin on Contracts: A Comprehensive Treatise on the Working Rules of Contract Law*, Vol 5 (St Paul, West Publishing Co, 1964)

Cornish, W and Llewelyn, D, *Intellectual Property: Patents, Copyright, Trademarks and Allied Rights*, 6th edn (London, Sweet & Maxwell, 2007)

Cornish, WR, Nolan, R, O'Sullivan, J, and Virgo, G (eds), *Restitution: Past, Present and Future* (Oxford, Hart Publishing, 1998)

Craswell, R, 'Contract Remedies, Renegotiation, and the Theory of Efficient Breach' (1988) 61 *Southern California Law Review* 629

Cunnington, R, 'The Assessment of Gain-Based Damages for Breach of Contract' (2008) 71 *Modern Law Review* 559

Curtis, L, 'Damage Measurements for Bad Faith Breach of Contract: An Economic Analysis' (1986) 39 *Stanford Law Review* 161

Danzig, R, 'Hadley v. Baxendale: A Study in the Industrialization of the Law' (1975) 4 *Journal of Legal Studies* 249

Davidson, IE, 'The Equitable Remedy of Compensation' (1982) 13 *Melbourne University Law Review* 349

Davis, G, and Knowler, J, 'Astley v Austrust Ltd' (1999) 23 *Melbourne University Law Review* 795

Dawson, F, 'General Damages in Contract for Non-pecuniary Loss' (1983) 10 *New Zealand Universities Law Review* 232

Dawson, JP, 'Restitution or Damages?' (1959) 20 *Ohio State Law Journal* 175

Deakin, S, Johnston, A, and Markesinis, B, *Markesinis and Deakin's Tort Law*, 6th edn (Oxford, Clarendon Press, 2008)

Bibliography

Degeling, S, and Edelman, J (eds), *Equity in Commercial Law* (Sydney, Lawbook Co, 2005)

Descheemaeker, E, 'Protecting Reputation: Defamation and Negligence' (2009) 29 *Oxford Journal of Legal Studies* 603

Diamond, TA, 'The Tort of Bad Faith Breach of Contract: When, If At All, Should It Be Extended Beyond Insurance Transactions?' (1981) 64 *Marquette Law Review* 425

Dias, RWM, 'Remoteness of Liability and Legal Policy' [1962] *Cambridge Law Journal* 178

Dodge, WS, 'The Case for Punitive Damages in Contracts' (1999) 48 *Duke Law Journal* 629

Dugdale, AM, and Jones, MA, *Clerk & Lindsell on Torts*, 19th edn (London, Sweet & Maxwell, 2006)

Duggan, A, 'Exemplary Damages in Equity: A Law and Economics Perspective' (2006) 26 *Oxford Journal of Legal Studies* 303

Edelman, J, *Gain-Based Damages: Contract, Tort, Equity and Intellectual Property* (Oxford, Hart Publishing, 2002)

Eisenberg, MA, 'The Principle of Hadley v Baxendale' (1992) 80 *California Law Review* 563

Elliott, SB, 'Remoteness Criteria in Equity' (2002) 65 *Modern Law Review* 588

Elliott, S, and Edelman, J, '*Target Holdings* Considered in Australia' (2003) 119 *Law Quarterly Review* 545

Elliott, SB, and Mitchell, C, 'Remedies for Dishonest Assistance' (2004) 67 *Modern Law Review* 16

Ellis, DD, 'Fairness and Efficiency in the Law of Punitive Damages' (1982) 56 *Southern California Law Review* 1

Enonchong, N, 'Breach of Contract and Damages for Mental Distress' (1996) 16 *Oxford Journal of Legal Studies* 617

Epstein, RA, 'Beyond Foreseeability: Consequential Damages in the Law of Contract' (1989) 18 *Journal of Legal Studies* 105

Farber, DA, 'Reassessing the Economic Efficiency of Compensatory Damages for Breach of Contract' (1980) 66 *Virginia Law Review* 1443

Ferrari, F, 'Comparative Ruminations on the Foreseeability of Damages in Contract Law' (1993) 53 *Louisiana Law Review* 1257

Finn, PD (ed), *Essays on Damages* (Sydney, Law Book Co, 1992)

FitzPatrick, TM, 'Contributory Negligence and Contract—A Critical Reassessment' (2001) 30 *Common Law World Review* 255 and 412

Fleming, JG, *The Law of Torts*, 9th edn (Sydney, Law Book Co, 1998)

—'The Passing of Polemis' (1961) 39 *Canadian Bar Review* 489

Fox, DM, 'Remedies for Interference with a Prescriptive Right to Light' [2007] *Cambridge Law Journal* 267

Friedmann, D, 'Restitution of Profits Gained by Party in Breach of Contract' (1988) 104 *Law Quarterly Review* 383

—'Restitution of Benefits Obtained Through the Appropriation of Property or the Commission of a Wrong' (1980) 80 *Columbia Law Review* 504

—'The Efficient Breach Fallacy' (1989) 18 *Journal of Legal Studies* 1

—'The Performance Interest in Contract Damages' (1995) *Law Quarterly Review* 628

—'The Protection of Entitlements via the Law of Restitution—Expectancies and Privacy' (2005) 121 *Law Quarterly Review* 400

Fuller, LL, and Perdue, WR, 'The Reliance Interest in Contract Damages: 1' (1936) 46 *Yale Law Journal* 52

Furmston, M (ed), *The Law of Contract*, 2nd edn (London, Butterworths, 2003)

Galanter, M, and Luban, D, 'Poetic Justice: Punitive Damages and Legal Pluralism' (1993) 42 *American University Law Review* 1393

Galligan, TC, 'Augmented Awards: The Efficient Evolution of Punitive Damages' (1990) 51 *Louisiana Law Review* 3

Garnett, K, Davies, G, and Harbottle, G (eds), *Copinger & Skone James on Copyright*, 15th edn (London, Sweet & Maxwell, 2005)

Giglio, F, *The Foundations of Restitution for Wrongs* (Oxford, Hart Publishing, 2007)

Glover, J, *Commercial Equity: Fiduciary Relationships* (Sydney, Butterworths, 1995)

Goetz, CJ, and Scott, RE, 'Liquidated Damages, Penalties and the Just Compensation Principle: Some Notes on an Enforcement Model and a Theory of Efficient Breach' (1977) 77 *Columbia Law Review* 554

Goodhart, AL, *Essays in Jurisprudence and the Common Law* (Cambridge, Cambridge University Press, 1937)

Gray, K, and Gray, SF, *Elements of Land Law*, 5th edn (Oxford, Oxford University Press, 2009)

Greig, DW, and Davis, JLR, *The Law of Contract* (Sydney, Law Book Co, 1987)

Guest, AG (gen ed), *Benjamin's Sale of Goods*, 7th edn (London, Sweet & Maxwell, 2006)

Häcker, B, 'Rescission and Third Party Rights' [2006] *Restitution Law Review* 21

Haddock, DD, McChesney, FS, and Spiegel, M, 'An Ordinary Economic Rationale for Extraordinary Legal Sanctions' (1990) 78 *California Law Review* 1

Handford, PR, *Mullany and Handford's Tort Liability for Psychiatric Damage*, 2nd edn (Sydney, Lawbook Co, 2006)

Harder, S, 'Is a Defaulting Fiduciary Exculpated by the Principal's Hypothetical Consent?' (2008) 8 *Oxford University Commonwealth Law Journal* 25

Harris, D, Campbell, D, and Halson, R, *Remedies in Contract and Tort*, 2nd edn (London, Butterworths, 2002)

Harris, D, Ogus, A, and Phillips, J, 'Contract Remedies and the Consumer Surplus' (1979) 95 *Law Quarterly Review* 581

Hart, HLA, and Honoré, T, *Causation in the Law*, 2nd edn (Oxford, Clarendon Press, 1985)

Hayton, D, Matthews, P, and Mitchell, C, *Underhill and Hayton: Law Relating to Trusts and Trustees*, 17th edn (London, LexisNexis Butterworths, 2007)

Hervey, T, '"Responsibility" Under the Civil Liability (Contribution) Act 1978' (1979) 129 *New Law Journal* 509

Heydon, JD, 'Causal Relationships Between a Fiduciary's Default and the Principal's Loss' (1994) 110 *Law Quarterly Review* 328

Ho, L, 'Attributing losses to a breach of fiduciary duty' (1998) 12 *Trust Law International* 66

Hodgin, RW, and Veitch, E, 'Punitive Damages—Reassessed' (1972) 21 *International & Comparative Law Quarterly* 119

Holmes, OW, *The Common Law* (London, Macmillan, 1882)

—'The Path of the Law' (1897) 10 *Harvard Law Review* 457

Hudson, AH, 'Contributory negligence as a defence to battery' (1984) 4 *Legal Studies* 332

Ibbetson, D, *A Historical Introduction to the Law of Obligations* (Oxford, Oxford University Press, 1999)

Jackman, IM, 'Restitution for Wrongs' [1989] *Cambridge Law Journal* 302

Jackson, BS, 'Injured Feelings Resulting from Breach of Contract' (1977) 26 *International & Comparative Law Quarterly* 502

Jaffey, P, *The Nature and Scope of Restitution: Vitiated Transfers, Imputed Contracts and Disgorgement* (Oxford, Hart Publishing, 2000)

Jensen, D, 'Punitive Damages for Breach of Fiduciary Obligation' (1996) 19 *University of Queensland Law Journal* 125

Jones, G, *Goff & Jones: The Law of Restitution*, 7th edn (London, Sweet & Maxwell, 2007)

Johnson, H, 'Distressed Customers' (1993) 12 *International Banking and Financial Law* 51

Johnston, D, and Zimmermann, R (eds), *Unjustified Enrichment: Key Issues in Comparative Perspective* (Cambridge, Cambridge University Press, 2002)

Johnston, JS, 'Punitive Liability: A New Paradigm of Efficiency in Tort Law' (1987) 87 *Columbia Law Review* 1385

—'Strategic Bargaining and the Economic Theory of Contract Default Rules' (1990) 100 *Yale Law Journal* 615

Jones, G, 'Restitution of Benefits Obtained in Breach of Another's Confidence' (1970) 86 *Law Quarterly Review* 463

Jones, MA, and Morris, AE, 'The distressing effects of professional incompetence' (2004) 20 *Professional Negligence* 118

Judicial Studies Board, *Guidelines for the Assessment of General Damages in Personal Injury Cases*, 9th edn (Oxford, Oxford University Press, 2008)

Kaplan, PR, 'A Critique of the Penalty Limitation on Liquidated Damages' (1977) 50 *Southern California Law Review* 1055

Keeton, WP (gen ed), *Prosser and Keeton on the Law of Torts*, 5th edn (St Paul, West Publishing Co, 1984)

Kidner, R, 'Remoteness of damage: the duty-interest theory and the re-interpretation of the Wagon Mound' (1989) 9 *Legal Studies* 1

Kramer, A, 'Proximity as principles: Directness, community norms and the tort of negligence' (2003) 11 *Tort Law Review* 70

—'The New Test of Remoteness in Contract' (2009) 125 *Law Quarterly Review* 408

Laddie, H, Prescott, P, Vitoria, M, Speck, A, and Lane, L, *The Modern Law of Copyright and Designs*, 3rd edn (London, Butterworths, 2000)

Lando, O, and Beale, H (eds), *Principles of European Contract Law, Parts I and II, Combined and Revised* (The Hague, Kluwer Law International, 2000)

Law Commission, 'Aggravated, Exemplary and Restitutionary Damages' (Law Com No 247, 1997)

Law Commission, 'Contributory Negligence as a Defence in Contract' (Law Com No 219, 1993)

Law Commission, 'Legislating the Criminal Code: Misuse of Trade Secrets' (Law Com Consultation Paper No 150, 1997)

Laycock, D, *The Death of the Irreparable Injury Rule* (New York, Oxford University Press, 1991)

Linden, AM, 'Down With Foreseeability! Of Thin Skulls and Rescuers' (1969) 47 *Canadian Bar Review* 545

Macdonald, E, 'Contractual Damages for Mental Distress' (1994) 7 *Journal of Contract Law* 134

Macneil, IR, 'Efficient Breach of Contract: Circles in the Sky' (1982) 68 *Virginia Law Review* 947

Markovits, D, 'Contract and Collaboration' (2004) 113 *Yale Law Journal* 1417

Mason, K, Carter, JW, and Tolhurst, GJ, *Mason and Carter's Restitution Law in Australia*, 2nd edn (Chatswood, LexisNexis Butterworths, 2008)

McBride, NJ, 'A Case for Awarding Punitive Damages in Response to Deliberate Breaches of Contract' (1995) 24 Anglo-American Law Review 369

McChesney, FS, 'Tortious Interference With Contract Versus "Efficient" Breach: Theory and Empirical Evidence' (1999) 28 Journal of Legal Studies 131

McGregor, H, *McGregor on Damages*, 18th edn (London, Sweet & Maxwell, 2009)

McInnes, M, 'Contractual Damages for Mental Distress—Again' (2009) 125 *Law Quarterly Review* 16

—'Gain, Loss and the User Principle' (2006) 14 *Restitution Law Review* 76

McKendrick, E, 'Breach of Contract and the Meaning of Loss' (1999) 52 *Current Legal Problems* 37

McLauchlan, D, 'Remoteness Re-Invented?' (2009) 9 *Oxford University Commonwealth Law Journal* 109

Meagher, RP, Heydon, JD, and Leeming, MJ, *Meagher, Gummow and Lehane's Equity: Doctrines and Remedies*, 4th edn (Sydney, Butterworths, 2002)

Michalik, PW, 'The availability of compensatory and exemplary damages in equity: A note on the *Aquaculture* decision' (1991) 21 *Victoria University of Wellington Law Review* 391

Michalos, C, 'Copyright and Punishment: The Nature of Additional Damages' (2000) 22 *European Intellectual Property Review* 470

Millett, PJ, 'Equity's Place in the Law of Commerce' (1998) 114 *Law Quarterly Review* 214

Mitchell, C, 'No Account of Profits for a Victim of Deceit' [1996] *Lloyd's Maritime and Commercial Law Quarterly* 314

Mitchell Polinsky, A, and Shavell, S, 'Punitive Damages: An Economic Analysis' (1998) 111 *Harvard Law Review* 869

Muir, GA, 'Stipulations for the Payment of Agreed Sums' (1985) 10 *Sydney Law Review* 503

Murphey, AG, 'Consequential Damages in Contracts for the International Sale of Goods and the Legacy of Hadley' (1989) 23 *George Washington Journal of International Law and Economics* 415

Murphy, J, *Street on Torts*, 12th edn (Oxford, Oxford University Press, 2007)

Newman, PL, 'The Law Reform Act 1945 and Breaches of Contract' (1990) 53 *Modern Law Review* 201

Oakley, AJ, *Parker and Mellows: The Modern Law of Trusts*, 9th edn (London, Sweet & Maxwell, 2008)

Oakley, AJ (ed), *Trends in Contemporary Trust Law* (Oxford, Clarendon Press, 1996)

Ogus, AI, 'Damages for Lost Amenities: For a Foot, a Feeling or a Function?' (1972) 35 *Modern Law Review* 1

—*The Law of Damages* (London, Butterworths, 1973)

Oliphant, K (gen ed), *The Law of Tort*, 2nd edn (London, LexisNexis Butterworths, 2007)

Oppenheim, R, 'The "Mosaic" of Tort Law: The Duty of Care Question' [2003] *Journal of Personal Injury Law* 151

O'Sullivan, D, Elliott, S, and Zakrzewski, R, *The Law of Rescission* (Oxford, Oxford University Press, 2008)

Owen, DG, 'A Punitive Damages Overview: Functions, Problems and Reform' (1994) 39 *Villanova Law Review* 363

—'Civil Punishment and the Public Good' (1982) 56 *Southern California Law Review* 103

Palmer, NE, and Davies, PJ, 'Contributory Negligence and Breach of Contract—English and Australasian Attitudes Compared' (1980) 29 *International & Comparative Law Quarterly* 415

Paterson, J, Robertson, A, and Duke, A, *Principles of Contract Law*, 3rd edn (Sydney, Lawbook Co, 2009)

Payne, D, 'Foresight and Remoteness of Damage in Negligence' (1962) 25 *Modern Law Review* 1

Pearce, D, and Halson, R, 'Damages for Breach of Contract: Compensation, Restitution and Vindication' (2008) 28 *Oxford Journal of Legal Studies* 73

Peel, E, *Treitel on the Law of Contract*, 12th edn (London, Sweet & Maxwell, 2007)

Perillo, JM, 'Misreading Oliver Wendell Holmes on Efficient Breach and Tortious Interference' (2000) 68 *Fordham Law Review* 1085

Perlstein, B, 'Crossing the Contract–Tort Boundary: An Economic Argument for the Imposition of Extracompensatory Damages for Opportunistic Breach of Contract' (1992) 58 *Brooklyn Law Review* 877

Phang, A, 'The Crumbling Edifice? The Award of Contractual Damages for Mental Distress' [2003] *Journal of Business Law* 341

Phang, A, and Lee, PW, 'Restitutionary and Exemplary Damages Revisited' (2003) 19 *Journal of Contract Law* 1

Plibersek, R, 'Assessment of Damages for Breach of Confidence in England and Australia' (1991) 13 *European Intellectual Property Review* 283

Porat, A, 'Contributory Negligence in Contract Law: Toward a Principled Approach' (1994) 28 *University of British Columbia Law Review* 141

Posner, RA, *Economic Analysis of Law*, 7th edn (Austin, Aspen: Wolters Kluwer Law & Business, 2007)

Postema, GJ (ed), *Philosophy and the Law of Torts* (Cambridge, Cambridge University Press, 2001)

Prosser, WL, 'Palsgraf Revisited' (1953) 52 *Michigan Law Review* 1

Quillen, GD, 'Contract Damages and Cross-subsidization' (1988) 61 *Southern California Law Review* 1125

Ramsay, I, Note (1977) 55 *Canadian Bar Review* 169

Reiter, BJ, and Swan, J (eds), *Studies in Contract Law* (Toronto, Butterworths, 1980)

Rickett, CEF (ed), *Justifying Private Law Remedies* (Oxford, Hart Publishing, 2008)

Rickett, C, and Gardner, T, 'Compensating for loss in equity: The evolution of a remedy' (1994) 24 *Victoria University of Wellington Law Review* 19

Robertson, A, 'The basis of the remoteness rule in contract' (2008) 28 *Legal Studies* 172

Robertson, A (ed), *The Law of Obligations: Connections and Boundaries* (London, UCL Press, 2004)

Robinette, CJ, 'Peace: A Public Purpose for Punitive Damages?' (2008) 2 *Charleston Law Review* 327

Rogers, WVH, *Winfield and Jolowicz on Tort*, 17th edn (London, Sweet & Maxwell, 2006)

Rose, FD (ed), *Failure of Contracts: Contractual, Restitutionary and Proprietary Consequences* (Oxford, Hart Publishing, 1997)

Rotherham, C, 'The Conceptual Structure of Restitution for Wrongs' [2007] *Cambridge Law Journal* 172

—'"*Wrotham Park* damages" and accounts of profits: compensation or restitution?' [2008] *Lloyd's Maritime and Commercial Law Quarterly* 25

Rowe, PJ, 'The Demise of the Thin Skull Rule?' (1977) 40 *Modern Law Review* 377

Saidov, D, and Cunnington, R (eds), *Contract Damages: Domestic and International Perspectives* (Oxford, Hart Publishing, 2008)

Samet, I, 'Guarding the Fiduciary's Conscience—A Justification of a Stringent Profit-stripping Rule' (2008) 28 *Oxford Journal of Legal Studies* 763

Samuel, G, *Law of Obligations and Legal Remedies*, 2nd edn (London, Cavendish, 2001)

Scallen, EA, 'Sailing the Uncharted Seas of Bad Faith: Seaman's Direct Buying Service, Inc. v. Standard Oil Co.' (1985) 69 *Minnesota Law Review* 1161

Scott of Foscote, Lord, 'Damages' [2007] *Lloyd's Maritime and Commercial Law Quarterly* 465

Scottish Law Commission, 'Report on Penalty Clauses' (Scot Law Com No 171, 1999)

——'Report on Remedies for Breach of Contract' (Scot Law Com No 174, 1999)

Seavey, WA, 'Mr. Justice Cardozo and the Law of Torts' (1939) 39 *Columbia Law Review* 20

Sebert, JA, 'Punitive and Nonpecuniary Damages in Actions Based Upon Contract: Toward Achieving the Objective of Full Compensation' (1986) 33 *UCLA Law Review* 1565

Sebok, AJ, 'Punitive Damages: From Myth to Theory' (2007) 92 *Iowa Law Review* 957

——'What Did Punitive Damages Do? Why Misunderstanding the History of Punitive Damages Matters Today' (2003) 78 *Chicago-Kent Law Review* 163

Sharkey, CM, 'Punitive Damages as Societal Damages' (2003) 113 *Yale Law Journal* 347

Sharpe, RJ, and Waddams, SM, 'Damages for lost opportunity to bargain' (1982) 2 *Oxford Journal of Legal Studies* 290

Shavell, S, *Economic Analysis of Accident Law* (Cambridge, Massachusetts, National Bureau of Economic Research, 2003)

Siems, M, 'Disgorgement of Profits for Breach of Contract: A Comparative Analysis' [2003] *Edinburgh Law Review* 27

Simester, AP, and Sullivan, GR, *Criminal Law: Theory and Doctrine*, 3rd edn (Oxford, Hart Publishing, 2007)

Smith, C, 'Recognising a Valuable Lost Opportunity to Bargain when a Contract is Breached' (2005) 21 *Journal of Contract Law* 250

Smith, JC, *Liability in Negligence* (London, Sweet & Maxwell, 1984)

Smith, LD, 'Disgorgement of the Profits of Breach of Contract: Property, Contract and "Efficient Breach"' (1995) 24 *Canadian Business Law Journal* 121

——'The Province of the Law of Restitution' (1992) 71 *Canadian Bar Review* 672

Soh, KB, 'Anguish, Foreseeability and Policy' (1989) 105 *Law Quarterly Review* 43

Spry, ICF, *The Principles of Equitable Remedies: Specific Performance, Injunctions, Rectification and Equitable Damages*, 8th edn (Sydney, Lawbook Co, 2010)

Stapleton, J, 'Legal Cause: Cause-In-Fact and the Scope of Liability for Consequences' (2001) 54 *Vanderbilt Law Review* 941

——'Negligent Valuers and Falls in the Property Market' (1997) 113 *Law Quarterly Review* 1

——'Risk-Taking by Commercial Lenders' (1999) 115 *Law Quarterly Review* 527

——'The Normal Expectancies Measure in Tort Damages' (1997) 113 *Law Quarterly Review* 257

Stevens, R, *Torts and Rights* (Oxford, Oxford University Press, 2007)

Stone, J, 'Double Count and Double Talk: The End of Exemplary Damages?' (1972) 46 *Australian Law Journal* 311

Street, H, *Principles of the Law of Damages* (London, Sweet & Maxwell, 1962)

Swadling, W, and Jones, G (eds), *The Search for Principle: Essays in Honour of Lord Goff of Chieveley* (Oxford, Oxford University Press, 1999)

Swanton, J, 'Contributory Negligence as a Defence to Actions for Breach of Contract' (1981) 55 *Australian Law Journal* 278

—'Contributory Negligence is Not a Defence to Actions for Breach of Contract in Australian Law—Astley v Austrust Ltd' (1999) 14 *Journal of Contract Law* 251

Swanton, J, and McDonald, B, 'Measuring contractual damages for defective building work' (1996) 70 *Australian Law Journal* 444

Taylor, AS, 'Contributory Negligence—A Defence to Breach of Contract?' (1986) 49 *Modern Law Review* 102

Tettenborn, A, 'Gain, loss and damages for breach of contract: what's in an acronym?' (2006) 14 *Restitution Law Review* 112

—'Hadley v Baxendale Foreseeability: a Principle Beyond Its Sell-by Date?' (2007) 23 *Journal of Contract Law* 120

—*Law of Restitution in England and Ireland*, 3rd edn (London, Cavendish, 2002)

Tilbury, MJ, *Civil Remedies, Vol 1: Principles of Civil Remedies* (Sydney, Butterworths, 1990)

Tilbury, M, and Carter, JW, 'Converging Liabilities and Security of Contract: Contributory Negligence in Australian Law' (2000) 16 *Journal of Contract Law* 78

Tomain, JP, 'Contract Compensation in Nonmarket Transactions' (1985) 46 *University of Pittsburgh Law Review* 867

Treitel, GH, *Remedies for Breach of Contract: A Comparative Account* (Oxford, Clarendon Press, 1988)

—*The Law of Contract*, 11th edn (London, Sweet & Maxwell, 2003)

Vann, V, 'Causation and Breach of Fiduciary Duty' [2006] *Singapore Journal of Legal Studies* 86

—*Equitable Compensation in Australia: Principles and Problems* (Saarbrücken, VDM Verlag Dr Müller, 2009)

Veitch, E, 'Sentimental Damages in Contract' (1977) 16 *University of Western Ontario Law Review* 227

Virgo, G, *The Principles of the Law of Restitution*, 2nd edn (Oxford, Oxford University Press, 2006)

Waddams, SM, *The Law of Damages*, 3rd edn (Toronto, Canada Law Book, 1997)

Warkol, CS, 'Resolving the Paradox Between Legal Theory and Legal Fact: The Judicial Rejection of the Theory of Efficient Breach' (1998) 20 *Cardozo Law Review* 321

Washington, GT, 'Damages in Contract at Common Law, II, The Period Transitional to the Modern Law' (1932) 48 *Law Quarterly Review* 90

Waters, DWM (ed), *Equity, Fiduciaries and Trusts 1993* (Toronto, Carswell, 1993)

Weaver, M, 'The Fragile Glassware Rule or How to Take a Risk' (1970) 33 *Modern Law Review* 446

Webb, C, 'What is Unjust Enrichment?' (2009) 29 *Oxford Journal of Legal Studies* 215

Weinrib, EJ, 'Punishment and Disgorgement as Contract Remedies' (2003) 78 *Chicago-Kent Law Review* 55

—'Restitutionary Damages as Corrective Justice' (2000) 1 *Theoretical Inquiries in Law* 1

—*The Idea of Private Law* (Cambridge, Massachusetts, Harvard University Press, 1995)

Weir, JA, 'Compensability of Unforeseeable Damage Resulting Directly from Negligent Acts' (1961) 35 *Tulane Law Review* 619

Wheeler, ME, 'The Constitutional Case for Reforming Punitive Damages Procedures' (1983) 69 *Virginia Law Review* 269

Whincup, M, 'Remoteness reconsidered' (1992) 142 *New Law Journal* 389, 433

Wightman, J, 'Negligent Valuations and a Drop in the Property Market: the Limits of the Expectation Loss Principle' (1998) 61 *Modern Law Review* 68

Williams, GL, *Joint Torts and Contributory Negligence: A Study of Concurrent Fault in Great Britain, Ireland and the Common-Law Dominions* (London, Stevens, 1951)

——'The Risk Principle' (1961) 77 *Law Quarterly Review* 179

——'The Two Negligent Servants' (1954) 17 *Modern Law Review* 66

Witzleb, N, 'Justifying Gain-Based Remedies for Invasions of Privacy' (2009) 29 *Oxford Journal of Legal Studies* 325

——'Monetary remedies for breach of confidence in privacy cases' (2007) 27 *Legal Studies* 430

Witzleb, N, and Carroll, R, 'The role of vindication in torts damages' (2009) 17 *Tort Law Review* 16

Wolcher, LE, 'Price Discrimination and Inefficient Risk Allocation Under the Rule of *Hadley v Baxendale*' (1989) 12 *Research in Law and Economics* 9

Wonnell, CT, 'The Contractual Disempowerment of Employees' (1993) 46 *Stanford Law Review* 87

Worthington, S, 'Reconsidering Disgorgement for Wrongs' (1999) 62 *Modern Law Review* 218

——'Review of *Hochelaga Lectures. Fusing Common Law and Equity: Remedies, Restitution and Reform* by Andrew Burrows' (2003) 119 *Law Quarterly Review* 519

Yates, D, 'Damages for Non-pecuniary Loss' (1973) 36 *Modern Law Review* 535

Youdan, TG (ed), *Equity, Fiduciaries and Trusts* (Toronto, Carswell, 1989)

Index